D0795592

**Third Edition**

# CANADIAN CRIMINOLOGY

## John Winterdyk

OXFORD
UNIVERSITY PRESS

# OXFORD
UNIVERSITY PRESS

Oxford University Press is a department of the University of Oxford.
It furthers the University's objective of excellence in research, scholarship,
and education by publishing worldwide. Oxford is a registered trade mark of
Oxford University Press in the UK and in certain other countries.

Published in Canada by Oxford University Press
8 Sampson Mews, Suite 204, Don Mills, Ontario  M3C 0H5 Canada

www.oupcanada.com

Copyright © Oxford University Press Canada 2016

The moral rights of the author have been asserted

Database right Oxford University Press (maker)

First Edition: Copyright © 2000 Pearson Education Canada, a division of Pearson Canada Inc. Toronto, Ontario
Second Edition: Copyright © 2006 Pearson Education Canada, a division of Pearson Canada Inc. Toronto, Ontario

All rights reserved. No part of this publication may be reproduced, stored in a retrieval system, or transmitted,
in any form or by any means, without the prior permission in writing of Oxford University Press, or as expressly
permitted by law, by licence, or under terms agreed with the appropriate reprographics rights organization.
Enquiries concerning reproduction outside the scope of the above should be sent to the Permissions Department
at the address above or through the following url: www.oupcanada.com/permission/permission_request.php

Every effort has been made to determine and contact copyright holders.
In the case of any omissions, the publisher will be pleased to make
suitable acknowledgement in future editions.

**Library and Archives Canada Cataloguing in Publication**

Winterdyk, John, author
Canadian criminology / John A. Winterdyk. – Third edition.

Includes bibliographical references and index.
ISBN 978-0-19-900146-0 (paperback)

1. Criminology–Textbooks.  2. Crime–Canada–Textbooks.
I. Title.

HV6025.W56 2016                 364                 C2015-906398-1

Cover image: Tommy Flynn/Getty
Part I: Fred Van Diem/Shutterstock.com;
Part II:  THE CANADIAN PRESS IMAGES/Mario Beauregard;
Part III: Nic Neufeld/Shutterstock.com; Part IV: iStock.com/Jen Grantham

Oxford University Press is committed to our environment.
Wherever possible, our books are printed on paper
which comes from responsible sources.

Printed and bound in Canada

2 3 4 — 19 18 17

# Contents at a Glance

# Contents

# Figures and Tables

## Figures

# Preface

Despite a downward trend in crime rates both nationally and internationally, there is still a discernable urgency around crime today. One cannot go online, turn on the news, or pick up a newspaper without encountering sensational coverage of criminal events occurring close to home or around the world.

If the prevalence of crime stories is an accurate indication of public interest, then the subject of crime and criminality is a "hot" topic. Indeed, it is not just the news media that are delivering crime to an eager audience. Recent decades have seen a lemming-like trend in the creation of crime shows, ranging from procedural crime dramas and studies of the criminal justice system to reality cop shows and documentaries. As I write this (in February 2016), there is considerable buzz around a Netflix documentary, *Making a Murderer*, that revolves around a murder case that happened over 10 years ago. Others have been quick to capitalize on the show's success, including pop psychologist Dr Phil, who recently dedicated an entire episode of his show to the documentary's central character, Steven Avery. Crime has become a commodity that has captured the fascination of the general public.

All of this public interest reflects a widely held desire to better understand crime, its causes, and its actors. Of late, we've seen this interest extend to academia. Today, most criminology and criminal justice programs at Canadian colleges and universities do not have enough placements to accommodate the demand from qualified students. This has contributed to a proliferation of online courses in recent years, as well as an increase in the number of graduate programs across Canada and internationally. An interest in crime and criminal justice is likely what led you to select the course you're now taking. If so, I hope this textbook will not only satisfy some of your curiosity but also inspire you to want to learn more. There are many avenues of research open to aspiring criminologists.

Criminology is the dynamic study of crime and how to prevent or control crime. As we will see time and again throughout this textbook, there is no simple or single answer to questions such as why people commit crime or how we can prevent it.

Historically, most introductory textbooks on criminology in Canada have embraced either a sociological or a psychological approach. In an effort to acknowledge the complexity of human behaviour and the diversity of factors that influence crime rates, this textbook embraces an *integrative* and *interdisciplinary* approach to the topic, drawing on a wide range of complementary theories as well as insights from disciplines beyond sociology and psychology, including biology, economics, and political science.

In an effort to make the text more student-friendly, the chapters have been designed to provide key information without too much distracting secondary material. Each chapter does, however, contain certain pedagogical features meant to help readers better assimilate the central themes and ideas. These include learning objective, presented at the start of each chapter; a selection of sidebars and feature boxes that enliven the main text with information about fascinating figures, cases, and research; and several end-of-chapter features designed to help students review the material, including a bullet-point summary of the chapter, a set of discussion questions that can be tackled individually or in groups, and links to relevant online resources.

**Part I** comprises four chapters that together provide the foundation for the study of crime. **Chapter 1** introduces the reader to the meaning of crime, deviance, and criminology. It also traces the evolving history of criminology and provides the basis for understanding the value of an interdisciplinary and integrated approach. **Chapter 2** examines the role of the public and the media. Both play an integral role in forging perceptions of crime, determining the issues criminologists examine, and directing criminal justice policy. The chapter argues that criminology needs to understand the role of the public and the media when studying crime.

Criminological theory and criminal justice policy are influenced by cultural values and politics. These elements can be tempered when objective criminological data are used to support policies and educate the public. **Chapter 3** reviews the various methods of collecting and analyzing information about crime and criminals, and concludes with some cautionary observations on criminological data. **Chapter 4**, which is co-authored, examines issues related to victims and victimology, a topic that, since the early 1990s, has become increasingly mainstream in Canadian criminology. It rightfully deserves a chapter of its own, strategically placed towards the start of the textbook.

In **Part II**, the attention shifts to the range of theories used to explain crime. These theories represent the various epistemological perspectives used to engage in criminological inquiry. Textbooks differ in their orientation and method of coverage, but they generally reflect competing disciplinary approaches rather than offering an interdisciplinary, integrated approach. Chapter 5 covers the three major schools of criminological thought and offers an overview of some of the discipline's Canadian and international pioneers. The presentation of material is considered a relatively unique feature of this book as it not found in any detail in other Canadian introductory criminology textbooks. The final section of the chapter provides the rationale for an integrated approach to the study of criminology and a call for criminologists to shift their focus to crime prevention and interdisciplinary models.

The remaining chapters in the part reflect this interdisciplinary approach. The major criminological theories are divided into the three primary multidisciplinary areas: biology (**Chapter 6**), psychology (**Chapter 7**), and sociology (**Chapter 8**, co-authored with Nick Jones). While providing coverage of the main theories stemming from each discipline, the three chapters examine some newer integrated, multifactor, and interdisciplinary approaches. Recognizing that many criminology and criminal justice programs include a course on theory, the intention here is to provide an overview and not a comprehensive summary of all theories.

**Part III** is divided into five chapters. **Chapter 9** provides an overview of the violent crimes that are most recorded by the police—and that typically draw the most attention from the media and the public. In addition, there is a brief overview of some emerging forms of violence, such as hate crime, honour killing, and terrorism, a topic we revisit with greater attention in Chapter 13. **Chapter 10** consists of an overview of crimes against property. In particular, the chapter focuses on conventional crimes such as fraud, theft, motor-vehicle crime, and arson. In **Chapter 11**, the third co-authored chapter, the focus shifts to non-conventional crime, including organized crime, corporate crime, and cybercrime, a topic given extensive treatment again in Chapter 13. In addition to reviewing current trends, the chapter surveys some of the explanations that criminologists have offered to account for these types of crime. **Chapter 12** addresses what are often referred to as crimes against public order, such as gambling, prostitution, and substance abuse. Although these crimes often involve organized crime groups, they are treated separately because of their status as victimless or consensual crimes. To some, they are crimes of morality involving willing participants; as such, they do not belong in the domain of state control. To others, they make victims of their participants and have a direct impact on public safety and well-being; they deserve our censure.

**Chapter 13** is devoted to certain transnational crimes that have come to prominence in recent decades. Some of these are not new: human trafficking, for instance, is one of the oldest known crimes. Others, like cybercrime, are essentially old crimes (fraud and theft, in this case) carried out by new means. Terrorism, likewise, is an old form of violence that has gained strength from new ways of reaching targets, audiences, and potential recruits. What these emerging crimes have in common is that they make use of the technological advances and globalizing processes that define our modern age.

Lastly, **Chapter 14**, the only chapter of **Part IV**, looks into the proverbial crystal ball in an effort to identify the issues that future criminologists will grapple with. It highlights the growing importance of comparative research, crime prevention, and the knowledge explosion in criminology. The chapter concludes with an overview of restorative justice: one of the dominant emerging trends in criminology and one that reflects an integrated and interdisciplinary approach to social order.

At the end of the book is a **Glossary**, providing, in many cases, expanded explanations of the key terms that are glossed briefly in the margins of the book's chapters. These definitions, collected at the back of the book, serve as a study tool for students preparing for exams and provide a solid footing for anyone striving to gain a better understanding of criminology overall.

To help students and instructors get the most out of this textbook, there are several resources available on the companion website for the book, hosted by Oxford University Press. These include an **instructor's manual**, **PowerPoint slides**, and a **test generator file** for instructors, and a **study guide** for students. The files are available at www.oupcanada.com/Criminology (a password is required to access the instructor resources).

Although I have tried to do justice to the evolving nature of criminology by adopting an interdisciplinary and integrated approach, I must call on students and instructors to fill some gaps from time to time. I see this textbook—like criminology itself—as a work in progress. Should you find this book interesting and intellectually stimulating, then my efforts have not been in vain. Nevertheless, rest assured the journey is not complete and that constructive feedback is always welcome.

## Acknowledgements

Although I remain solely responsible for the content of this textbook, it reflects the collective input and support of numerous people, only a handful of whom are named in the paragraphs that follow. Whether named or not, my heartfelt thanks goes out to them all.

Whenever I undertake an effort such as the writing of this book, I am reminded not only of how important friendships and loved ones are but of how important it is for us to recognize and appreciate that we are part of a larger community.

My grandfather, Dirk Winterdyk, has been the most influential academic force in my life. In addition to embodying all the quintessential traits of a wonderful grandfather, he was an educator extraordinaire, and his dedication and unending thirst for learning have remained a powerful influence on me even as I became a grandfather for the first time during the final stages of completing this book.

I would like to acknowledge the assistance of three young and promising former students with whom I have had the pleasure to work. Jesse Cale, Nick Jones, and Mike Beke provided invaluable assistance in the preparation of chapters 4, 8, and 11, respectively, and it is a joy and honour to be able to acknowledge them as co-authors for these three chapters and to be able to witness the blossoming of their respective careers.

Throughout my academic years, I have been fortunate to study and learn from several esteemed leaders in the academic community. These include Ronald Roesch, Ray Corrado, Paul Maxim, Paul and Patricia Brantingham, Hans-Jorg Albrecht, and many others. Of my colleagues at Mount Royal University, where I have worked since 1988, I would like to recognize Professor Doug King, who has provided me with invaluable intellectual discourse, feedback, and support over the years.

To Rose: the patience, tolerance, and support I demanded of you at times bordered on impracticable! You are the true pillar of strength in our relationship, and I thank you for being you! To Michael and Alex, our now young adult sons, thank you for enduring the journey; I am thrilled and honoured to be able to watch you grow into wonderful young men as you now embark on your respective journeys.

I would like to thank the team at Oxford University Press, and particularly David Stover, who encouraged me to revise and update this textbook. I would like to extend a special thank-you to Amy Gordon, my developmental editor, who diligently helped nurse and nudge this edition into completion. Her wonderful sense of humour, boundless kindness, and enduring patience helped make the tough days much easier. Copy editors Sally Livingston and Eric Sinkins helped bring the manuscript to the goal line; although the final product is my responsibility, they are, in many respects, the unsung heroes who helped to ensure that you, the reader, will find the book not only interesting and informative but highly accessible.

Finally, I would like to thank Sam Alvaro, J. Bryan Kinney, and the anonymous reviewers who spent many hours reading the manuscript in rough form and offering constructive criticisms and insightful suggestions for the new edition.

John Winterdyk, Professor of Criminology and Criminal Justice
Department of Economics, Justice and Policy Studies
Mount Royal University
Calgary, Alberta T3E 6K6
e-mail: jwinterdyk@mtroyal.ca

# Guided Tour of the New Edition

In preparing this new edition of *Canadian Criminology*, we have been guided by the goal of producing the most balanced, engaging, and accessible introduction to criminology available to Canadian students. With updated data and illustrations, and complemented by a full suite of online ancillary materials, we are confident that *Canadian Criminology* will become an indispensable resource for students and instructors alike.

## Brand-New Chapter on Emerging Crime Trends

The new Chapter 13 covers terrorism, human trafficking, intellectual property crime, counterfeiting, cybercrime, and cyberterrorism, while engaging students in the ongoing policy and legislative debates that will shape crime and criminology in Canada's future.

**Chapter 13**

Emerging Crime Trends: Transnational Crime, Terrorism, Human Trafficking, and Cybercrime

CP PHOTO/ Ian Barrett

Our lives are not our own. From womb to tomb we are bound to others, past and present, and by each crime and every kindness we birth our future.
DAVID MITCHELL, *CLOUD ATLAS*

Banking security is everyone's responsibility—the banks' and customers' alike—and we hope that some of the information we have provided, in some small measure, helps towards saving other people from experiencing such a cruel, harrowing, and near life-wrecking ordeal.
ANONYMOUS VICTIM OF "VISHING" FRAUD, CITED IN DREW (2014)

Chapter 13 | Emerging Crime Trends: Transnational Crime, Terrorism, Human Trafficking, and Cybercrime

**BOX 13.10  REALITY CHECK**

**Internet Scams: Fool Me Once . . .**

In August 2013, four Canadians and several American accomplices were charged with fraud involving a penny stock scam. The accused allegedly bought fledgling start-up companies and inflated their value artificially through fictitious e-mails, news releases, and social media messages so that they could sell off penny stocks issued by the companies. The fraudsters relied on call centres in Canada, Thailand, and Britain, and bilked investors in 35 countries out of more than $140 million over a relatively short period of time. They then cheated their victims a *second* time by posing as US Internal Revenue Service agents to help investors reclaim their losses in exchange for a small fee.

When interviewed, a Canadian legal expert pointed out that such scams are becoming increasingly sophisticated and hence more difficult to detect and prosecute. It took the co-operation of several police forces and banks from around the world to discover the breadth of this particular criminal operation ("4 Canadians charged," 2013).

What aspects of cybercrime make a scheme like the one described here possible to carry out? Consider some of the premises of space transition theory described in Box 13.9.

been developed jointly by the United States and Israel (Finkle, 2013), was designed to steal confidential information and damage equipment at the Iranian nuclear facility. Clifford (2011), in his review of the incident, suggests this might have been the very first incident of cyberwarfare.

**Different Forms of Cybercrime**

*Theft and Illegal Use of Information*

In the course of shopping, banking, selling, and dating online, we put an enormous amount of information about ourselves on the Internet. The transmission of this information, even through apparently secure channels, makes us vulnerable to the crime of identity theft, in which an individual's identity information—from user name and password to signature, fingerprint, or DNA profile—is taken or held without consent by another person for fraudulent purposes, such as purchasing goods or obtaining funds using the individual's banking details.

Identity theft is a fairly recent crime, prohibited by a law that has been in place only since January 2010, when Bill S-4 came into effect. Identity theft may give rise to identity fraud, which is the act of *using* stolen identity information—or impersonating someone by other means—in order to gain something, to avoid arrest, or to harm the reputation of the person whose identity is used. Cases of identity fraud significantly outnumber cases of identity theft in Canada (see Figure 13.7).

Traditional methods of identity theft could be quite unsophisticated: think, for example, of stealing someone's mail or going through someone's garbage to gather their personal information. By contrast, computer-mediated identity theft can be very sophisticated. It might involve an official-looking e-mail sent purportedly by your bank and advising you that your account has been compromised. In this scam, the recipient is instructed that the problem will be fixed once the recipient provides "the bank" with personal information via an e-mail address or phone number specified in the e-mail. Another scam involves an e-mail supposedly from the Canada Revenue Agency advising the recipient of a pending refund that will be deposited into the recipient's bank account once the appropriate banking information has been provided. These "phishing" scams don't rely on hacking; they depend on the fact that individuals

**identity theft**
The act of obtaining or possessing another person's name and personal identity information without consent in order to commit fraud or another offence.

**identity fraud**
The fraudulent impersonation of a person, living or dead, to gain some advantage, to avoid identification, or to harm the reputation of the person whose identity is used.

## New Visual Approach

Carefully chosen photos and captions have been added to every chapter in order to engage visual learners and encourage critical thinking in every student.

---

**BOX 6.6     FACTS AND FIGURES   SUBSTANCE ABUSE AND CRIME**

A growing body of literature shows a link between substance abuse and criminal behaviour. Consider, for example, the following points, compiled from the website of the Canadian Centre on Substance Abuse (CCSA—www.ccsa.ca/eng/Pages/default.aspx):

- Impaired driving is the most prominent factor contributing to serious road crashes.
- Based on data from 2006, the CCSA estimated the total societal cost of substance abuse to be $39.8 billion, or $1,267 for every Canadian.
- Alcohol causes over $14 billion annually in economic harm—yet anyone over the age of 18 can legally buy and consume it.
- Canada's youth (18–24 years of age) have the highest self-reported rate of marijuana use among all Canadians surveyed. It is estimated that marijuana use accounts for $8.2 billion of the $40 billion spent on illicit drugs.

Among the key findings of a CCSA report on substance abuse in Canadian prisons (Weekes, Thomas, & Graves, 2004) are the following:

- More than 70 per cent of federal inmates have engaged in "problematic use of alcohol or drugs" while in prison.
- Fetal alcohol spectrum disorder (see Box 6.7) has emerged as a potentially serious problem among inmates, especially Aboriginal inmates. Several institutions now have special units and/or programs for offenders suffering from FASD.
- The three drugs most commonly used by inmates are marijuana, alcohol, and cocaine.

What do you think of the recent legalization of the use and sale of marijuana in Colorado and Washington?

Pro-marijuana demonstrators rally in Toronto during a 4/20 event. What are some of the barriers to legalizing marijuana in Canada? What are some of the reasons for keeping marijuana criminalized?

---

levies. While the anti-tobacco measures have received public support, the higher prices now charged for legal cigarettes have stimulated the market for cheaper, illegal products.

In 2000, Ovide Mercredi, former National Chief of the Assembly of First Nations, prepared a report in which he called for initiatives that promote a path of healing and positive contribution in the community for gang members, based on a model of restorative justice (see Chapter 14). However, the best solution to fighting Aboriginal crime organizations may lie in ending the persistent marginalization of Canada's Aboriginal people and providing them opportunities to attain a socioeconomic standard and lifestyle that are more appealing than what can be gained from gang membership. Many of these ideas are captured in the report of the Truth and Reconciliation Commission, released in December 2015.

*Cartels*

**cartel**
An association of manufacturers or suppliers who have entered into an informal agreement to fix prices, to limit supply, and minimize competition by various means, some of which may be illegal and may involve violence.

A cartel is an informal association of independent commercial enterprises designed to limit competition. The term was coined in the late 1800s by the Austrian economist Friedrich Kleinwächter, who used it to refer to "the alliance of enterprises." Since then, the term has taken on a more sinister meaning that encompasses the illegal business practices and sometimes violent criminal behaviour that are associated with cartels. In a special report in *Criminal Justice International* (1994) the cartels were described as a new breed of international organized crime

Mexican drug lord Joaquín Archivaldo Guzmán Loera, shown during his arrest in February 2014, rose to power as the head of the Sinaloa Cartel during the 1980s. In 1993, Guzmán (or "El Chapo," as he is known) was arrested and sentenced to 20 years for murder and drug trafficking. In 2001, he escaped a maximum-security prison after bribing his guards. Despite multi-million dollar rewards offered by the Mexican and US governments for information leading to his arrest, he evaded capture for 13 years. In July 2015—just 16 months after this photo was taken—El Chapo again escaped from a maximum-security prison, this time through an underground tunnel. He remained at large until January 2016, when he was captured shortly after a secret meeting with Hollywood actor Sean Penn, who had interviewed the drug lord for an article in *Rolling Stone* magazine.

---

## New Overview of the Canadian Criminal Justice System

An introduction to the criminal justice system in Chapter 1 ensures that students have a solid grasp of how the CCJS works before diving into theory.

---

**Table 1.1   Authority Structure of the Canadian Criminal Justice System**

|  | Federal Jurisdiction | Provincial/Territorial Jurisdiction |
|---|---|---|
| Courts | Department of Justice | Ministry of the Attorney General |
| Police/corrections | Department of Public Safety | Ministry of Public Safety |

**Functions of the CJS**

The main functions of the criminal justice system are as follows:

- to investigate criminal offences as defined in the Canadian Criminal Code (CCC); this is primarily the responsibility of the police
- to lay charges as defined under the CCC; this function is usually administered by the police
- to prosecute the accused in court, in accordance with the law; this role is performed by the prosecution, or "the Crown"
- to determine guilt or innocence, either by a judge or (for more serious crimes) a judge and jury
- to sentence those found guilty, within the upper and lower limits prescribed by the CCC
- to administer the sentence; this falls within the scope of the correctional branch of the CJS

Figure 1.2 illustrates how the CJS works. For a brief historical overview of the CJS in Canada, see Chapter 5.

**Historical Overview**

For most of human history, the study of crime (along with all other aspects of human behaviour) was the domain of philosophy, law, and theology. Socrates, for example, was known to have commented on the plight of young people; he argued that they were disrespectful

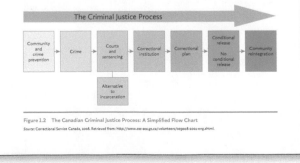

**Figure 1.2   The Canadian Criminal Justice Process: A Simplified Flow Chart**
Source: Correctional Service Canada, 2008. Retrieved from: http://www.csc-scc.gc.ca/volunteers/003008-2001-eng.shtml.

# New Theoretical Coverage of Psychological and Sociological Explanations of Crime

Updates to Chapters 7 and 8 have deliver the most contemporary perspectives on crime and criminality in psychology and sociology.

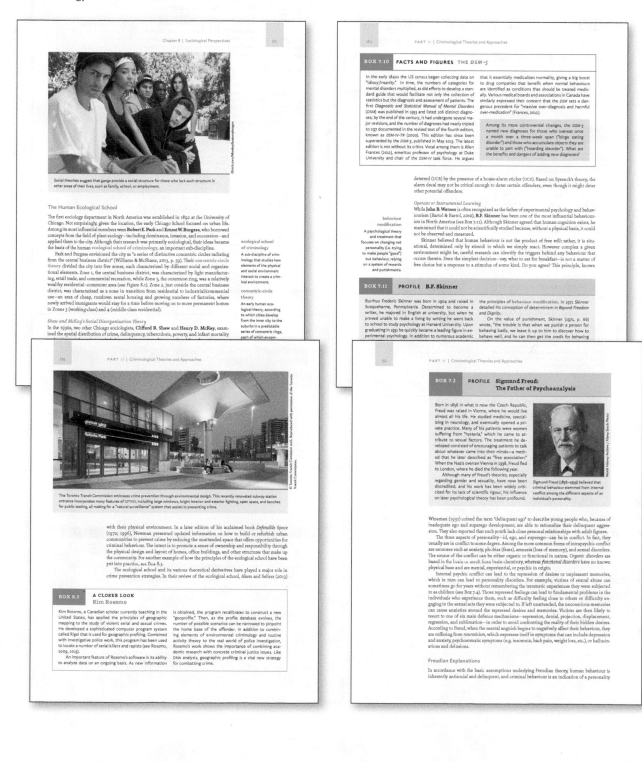

## Updated and Visually Engaging Boxes

*Canadian Criminology* includes five recurring boxed features scattered throughout every chapter to highlight issues, cases, and people at the centre of criminological investigation and research.

▶ **Facts and Figures boxes** offer brief facts about the topic under consideration or supplement the author's narrative with relevant statistics

▲

**A Closer Look boxes** provide case studies about a particular crime, report, or incident.

▶ **Reality Check boxes** challenge general assumptions or "common knowledge" about crime and criminology.

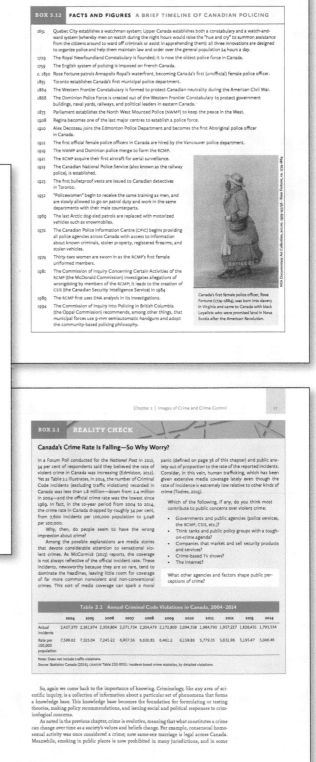

---

**BOX 8.8 WHAT DO YOU THINK?**

**Do You Agree with Canada's New Prostitution Laws?**

In 2014 the federal government passed Bill C-36 (the Protection of Communities and Exploited Persons Act), which creates new offences for clients and pimps engaged in prostitution but does not criminalize the prostitutes themselves. The government created this legislation in response to a Supreme Court ruling that had struck down the old anti-prostitution laws on the grounds that they unduly increased the physical risk to prostitutes and therefore violated the charter right to security of the person. As John Lowman, one of Canada's top experts on prostitution, noted in an interview: "We're trying to fix complex social issues with a very ham-fisted approach."

> How do you think a conflict theorist would explain the causes of prostitution? What about a proponent of labelling theory? What solutions might each one propose? How do you think we as a society should handle prostitution?

**Peacemaking Theory**

Former conflict theorists **Harold E. Pepinsky** and **Richard Quinney** have been strong advocates of this relatively new (early 1990s) school of thought in North America (Cullen, Wright, & Blevins, 2011). Dissatisfied with the traditional conflict perspective, both Quinney and Pepinsky searched for a "radical humanistic understanding of social existence and human experience" (Friedrichs, 1991, p. 102). They recognized that even though most people prefer peace to violence, sometimes violence seems unavoidable. But is it necessary? Or natural?

Quinney and Pepinsky argue that the traditional criminal–non-criminal dualism, pitting "us" versus "them," has done little to alleviate the crime problem. No matter how we define crime and punishment, we cannot punish acts, only the actors (Pepinsky, 2000). As the esteemed Norwegian criminologist Nils Christie observed, "you're more likely to see that a person's soul is not embodied in any single act, and that you cannot punish an act without contaminating a complex actor" (cited in Pepinsky, 1991, p. 107). Hence, there can be no justification for using punishment to resolve disputes, and people should not be labelled or "pigeonholed" based on acts they have committed. Peacemaking theory, like all conflict-based theories, posits that fundamental changes in the structure of society are required if crime is to be reduced.

Pepinsky and Quinney, among other advocates of peacemaking theory, point out that the criminal justice system is based on the "warlike" principle of vengeance (see Braswell, Fuller, & Lozoff, 2001). They see punishment as no less violent than crime. However, Pepinsky adds that non-retaliation alone is not enough. He argues that we all need to be participants in the democratic process, which involves the social process by which empathy prevails over the use of violence (i.e. punitivity).

Judging from the main anthologies on the subject, the peacemaking model has not been widely embraced (see Cullen, Wright, & Blevins, 2011). But perhaps it is making itself felt in more practical ways—for example, in the support that the concept of restorative justice has attracted in recent years (see Chapter 14).

**peacemaking theory** A humanistic approach to crime control that emphasizes reconciliation through mediation and dispute settlement, rather than punishment and retribution.

**Feminist Perspectives**

Even though Lombroso himself wrote a book on female criminality more than a century ago, female offenders were largely ignored in criminology until the late 1960s. Typically, criminologists studying crime among women and girls focused only on crimes such as prostitution and

◄ **What Do You Think boxes** outline a particular crime, study, or incident, and ask students critical thinking questions.

---

▶ **Profile boxes** highlight key thinkers, theorists, and scholars who have made important contributions to criminological research, past and present.

**BOX 5.2 PROFILE Jeremy Bentham**

A leading proponent of the doctrine of utilitarianism, Jeremy Bentham was a central figure in a reform movement that helped mitigate the severity of punishments for offenders; abolish usury laws; and remove the "exclusionary laws of evidence" (Geiss, 1973, p. 66), so that evidence could not be introduced if it violated a defendant's constitutional rights. He was instrumental in introducing principles of crime prevention into the judicial process (ibid.).

In 1799, Bentham embodied his ideas on penal reform in a prison design that he called the *Panopticon*, a literally "all-seeing" facility. The intent behind the octagonal design was to enable a guard to keep an eye on all cells from a central control area, while making prisoners constantly aware that they might be under observation: this, he believed, would allow for constructive supervision and reform. Although no such institution was ever built, some early American prisons were modelled after Bentham's design, and some Canadian institutions for young offenders (e.g. Huron County Gaol (jail) in Goderich, Ontario, open 1839–1972) have incorporated a modified version.

© FALKENSTEINFOTO / Alamy Stock Photo

Elevation, section and plan of Jeremy Bentham's Panopticon penitentiary, drawn by Willey Reveley, 1791. From The works of Jeremy Bentham vol. IV, 1843

Mary Evans / Peter Higginbotham Collection

Bentham designed the Panopticon (*left*) with the idea that if inmates felt they were being watched at all times, they would be less likely to act out. Among the prisons modelled after it is the one in Joliet, Illinois (*right*).

2. *attachment costs* (an arrest can result in harm to personal circumstances)
3. *stigma* (an arrest can damage one's personal and/or public image)

Overall, however, Akers and Sellers (2013) conclude that the correlations found "between the perceptions of risk and subsequent offenses are too weak to validate deterrence theory." Even when a modified version of deterrence theory came into fashion (Cornish and Clarke's rational choice theory: see Chapter 8), its supporters were unable to clearly define what is meant by the "reasoning criminal" (Akers & Sellers, 2013). The classical doctrine also seems questionable when it comes to the reform and rehabilitation of criminals. Rates of *recidivism*

## All-New Suite of Online Resources

*Canadian Criminology* is part of a comprehensive package of learning and teaching tools that includes ancillary resources for both instructors and students.

### For Instructors

A comprehensive **Instructor's Manual** provides extensive pedagogical tools and suggestions for every chapter, including suggested lecture topics, recommended resources, discussion or debate ideas, and class assignments or activities.

Classroom-ready **PowerPoint Slides** summarize key points from each chapter and incorporate graphics from the book for ease of presentation.

An extensive **Test Generator** enables instructors to sort, edit, import, and distribute hundreds of questions in multiple-choice, true/false, and short answer formats.

### For Students

The **Student Study Guide** includes chapter overviews, key terms and key figures from each chapter, and review questions (with answer key) in multiple-choice, true/false, and short answer format in order to aid in studying for tests and assignments, and to allow students to self-quiz in preparation for exams.

COMPANION WEBSITE

John Winterdyk

*Canadian Criminology, Third Edition*

ISBN 13: 9780199001460

Inspection copy request

Ordering information

Contact & Comments

**About the Book**

Taking an interdisciplinary approach, the third edition of Canadian Criminology draws on a wealth of contemporary research, powerful examples and case studies, and the very latest Canadian statistics to provide a comprehensive introduction to criminology and the state of crime in Canada today. Designed to encourage students to think critically about the way we view and tackle crime, the text balances the theoretical underpinnings of the discipline with coverage of its real-world applications in order to bring criminology to life for readers new to the field.

**Sample Material**

Get Adobe PDF reader [ US | UK ]

Instructor Resources

You need a password to access these resources. Please contact your local Sales and Editorial Representative for more information.

Student Resources

www.oupcanada.com/Criminology

# PART I

## Introduction to the Study of Crime

# Chapter 1

## Criminology: Its Nature and Structure

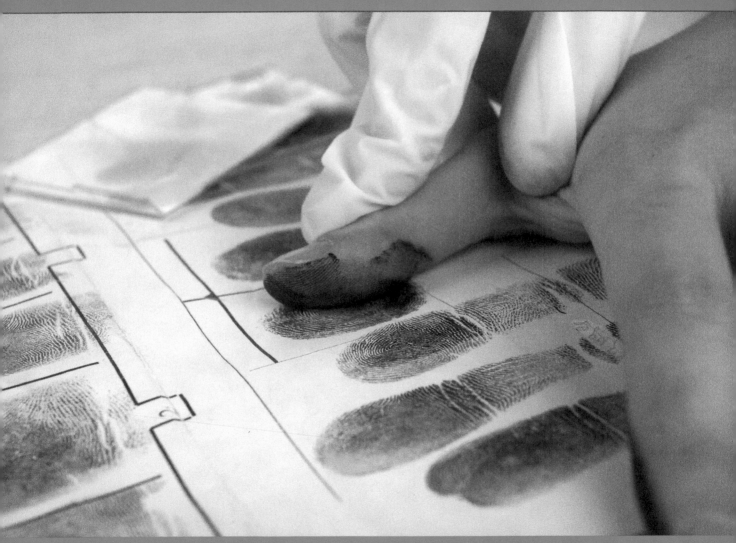

Africa Studio/Shutterstock.com

When there is crime in society there is no justice.
PLATO

[C]rime . . . must no longer be conceived as an evil that cannot be too much suppressed. . . .
crime is not pathological at all . . . and its true function [purpose] must be sought elsewhere.
ÉMILE DURKHEIM (1895)

## Learning Outcomes

After reading this chapter, you should be able to

- Understand the complexity of both crime and criminology, particularly in the Canadian context;
- Recognize the main elements of the criminal justice system;
- Differentiate between crime and deviance;
- Understand the role of criminologists, their methods of inquiry, and the elements that make up the discipline of criminology;
- Appreciate the impact of the social sciences on the development of criminology; and
- Recognize the importance of an interdisciplinary approach.

## Introduction

The quotations that open this chapter reflect diametrically opposed perspectives: whereas Plato sought to eradicate crime altogether, Durkheim argued that crime serves an essential function or purpose in society. Welcome to the controversial subject of crime and, more generally, the discipline of criminology.

Before we begin, take a few minutes to think about the following questions.

- What does the word *crime* mean?
- What are the most serious crimes?
- Who is a criminal?
- Is crime increasing in Canada?
- What do criminologists do?
- Why are police budgets increasing at a time when crime rates have been declining for decades?
- Why do crime rates vary with age, gender, and ethnic/racial group?
- Why do some individuals seem more prone to criminal behaviour than others?
- Why do certain types of crimes tend to be committed by certain individuals and not others?
- Why does the crime rate vary within Canada and internationally?
- Should capital punishment (the death penalty) be reinstated? Why?
- Is it better to focus on punishing crime, or preventing it?

These questions are intended to get you thinking about your own perceptions of crime and criminality, and those of society generally. The answers are arguably the cornerstones of criminology.

In this chapter, we will begin by examining the fundamental principles of crime, criminality, and deviance. Following a brief introduction to Canada's criminal justice system, an overview of the historical roots of criminology will help to explain how and why criminology has become increasingly interdisciplinary. The chapter will conclude with a look at some of the practical issues that criminologists must consider.

## What Is Crime?

*Crime* (from Latin *crimen*, "accusation") is a generic term now used to refer to a wide range of acts that have been defined—socially, culturally, and/or legally—as "wrong" or "anti-social" (Siegel, 2010). But this was not always the case. Originally, crime was a private matter: those who had been wronged would seek retribution themselves. In time, crime came to be seen as a social phenomenon, and the informal, personal pursuit of justice was replaced by formal criminal justice systems.

There is no universal definition of crime. However, all legal definitions share one characteristic: a crime is a violation of a criminal law. In other words, without a law forbidding a particular act, there is no crime. Crime is also a *normative* concept—that is, one based on moral values. Therefore, how we define crime will determine how we study it. For the purposes of this book, crime is a socially constructed concept used to categorize certain behaviours as requiring formal control and some form of social intervention.

In Canada, crimes are defined in federal legislation and codified in the Criminal Code, as well as in peripheral legislation such as the Youth Criminal Justice Act and the Controlled Drugs and Substances Act. Legally, a crime is simply an act punishable by law. However, it can also be argued that a crime is a type of social harm that—depending on the norms and values of society—may or may not be explicitly defined as a crime. For example, before the terrorist attacks of 11 September 2001, the Canadian Criminal Code made no specific reference to terrorism. Even though terrorism was widely recognized as a social harm, it was not added to the Criminal Code until December 2001, when the Anti-Terrorism Act was passed by the Liberal government.

## Crime versus Offence

In the media, the terms *crime* and *offence* are sometimes used interchangeably. Is there a difference? The Scots and the French still distinguish between crimes—breaches of the law—and offences—violations of morality. A similar distinction is made in the United States, where less serious offences (e.g. public drunkenness) are called *misdemeanours* and more serious crimes (e.g. assault and murder) are called *felonies*. Until 1967, England made the same distinction; however, that country now classifies criminal offences as *arrestable* and *non-arrestable*: the former are crimes for which a person can be arrested without a warrant, while the latter are offences that do require a warrant.

In Canada, serious crimes such as robbery, assault, and homicide are called indictable offences, while less serious ones, such as certain property offences, are summary offences. In short, *crime* is a general term that refers to any infraction of the law, while *offence* (summary or indictable) refers to a specific infraction.

The list of activities defined as crimes in Canada is long and varied (see Box 1.1). One method of classification divides them into *conventional* and *non-conventional* categories (although other classifications exist). Conventional crimes are those committed by individuals or small groups in which some degree of direct (e.g. personal) or indirect (e.g. property)

**crime**
A socially constructed concept defining certain behaviours as requiring formal control and social intervention.

**indictable offence**
A serious offence such as assault, theft over $5000, robbery (with or without a firearm), or murder.

**summary offence**
A less serious offence, such as theft under $5000, impersonating a police officer, or taking a motor vehicle without consent.

**conventional crime**
Illegal activity committed by individuals or small groups, involving some degree of direct or indirect contact, e.g. robbery, vehicle theft, and break-and-enter.

**BOX 1.1    FACTS AND FIGURES THE PROLIFERATION OF LAWS**

In the 1953–4 *Canadian Criminal Code* (CCC) the volume had 104 pages and 46 sections. The 2015 edition of the CCC had 2490 pages and 848 sections, along with some 54 legal forms. These numbers reflect the dramatic proliferation of criminal laws in Canada over the last 60-odd years.

Has crime really increased so dramatically since 1953? Or does the growth of this volume reflect changes in the way certain acts and behaviours are viewed by society, the courts, and our legislators?

| BOX 1.2 | **A CLOSER LOOK**<br>Cybercrime |

The following news flashes speak to the spread of illegal Internet use.

- 9 November 2012: A report by the Public Safety Department expresses concern that Canada is "becoming a digital launching pad for—not just a target of—malicious cyber-activities." The report notes that historically, most cybercrime schemes have originated in places like Eastern Europe, East Asia, and Africa, but that there has been a recent shift to more developed countries like Canada (Bronskill, 2012).
- 3 January 2013: CBC News (online) reports on a new scam that uses a fake RCMP pop-up message that accuses computer users of cybercrime. Clicking the message releases a virus that locks the computer and "demands a $100 fine for alleged crimes of copyright infringement, pornography, or even terrorism" (CBC News, 2013).

Why do you think Canada has become a "host" for cybercrime? Do you know the top ten steps you can

"Heartbleed" is the name given to a security flaw or bug that was discovered by a security company in April 2014 and that left many computer systems vulnerable to cyber-criminals. The company, Codenomicon, created the logo to help in promoting public awareness.

take to minimize your risk of becoming a victim of such exploitation? (see www.rcmp-grc.gc.ca/tops-opst/tc-ct/cyber-tips-conseils-eng.htm).

contact occurs. Crimes of this type, which include street crimes such as robbery, motor-vehicle theft, and break-and-enter, are also the offences that most frequently come to the attention of both the criminal justice system and the media. We will look at the most common conventional crimes and some emerging variations on them (e.g. stalking, home invasion, and hate crime) in chapters 9 and 10.

Non-conventional crimes are not necessarily pursued by the criminal justice system, yet their impact—social, financial, and personal—may be far more serious than that of many conventional crimes. For example, cybercrime (see Box 1.2) has been described as a type of theft, but its impact can be devastating, and more far-reaching, than that of "simple" theft. Other examples of the non-conventional type include organized crime, offences against public order (i.e. vice crimes such as prostitution or drug trafficking), terrorism, transnational crime, and white-collar crime. In addition, as with conventional crimes, there are some forms of non-conventional crime that the criminal justice system is only now recognizing, or that have emerged in response to particular social, economic, or political situations (e.g. the trade in human organs, or the dissemination of child pornography on the Internet). We will examine some of these crimes in Chapter 13.

**non-conventional crime**
Illegal activity that may not be associated with crime and that may not be pursued by the criminal justice system, e.g. organized crime, political crime, and cybercrime.

### Deviance

Another word that needs clarification is deviance, a sociological term referring to behaviour that violates a social norm but that is not necessarily prohibited by law. While *deviance* is occasionally used interchangeably with *crime*, there is a significant difference in meaning.

**deviance**
Behaviour that violates a social norm but is not necessarily prohibited by law, e.g. butting in line at a supermarket or cutting off another driver.

Deviant behaviour encompasses a wide spectrum of conduct that may be considered offensive to some degree. Deviant activities may or may not be against the law, but they clearly depart from social norms. For example, face tattooing, while not illegal, is widely considered deviant. On the other hand, recreational marijuana use, which *is* illegal in Canada, is not universally regarded as deviant: according to a 2013 Forum Research poll, 70 per cent of Canadians supported either legalizing or decriminalizing marijuana use (Grenier, 2013). The lines between criminal and non-criminal, deviant and non-deviant behaviour are often fine, and they vary with time and place. In other words, the concept of crime is not absolute, but relative. Crime is also evolutive, developing new forms and meanings over time. Illegally downloading music from the Internet and burning copies of DVDs are modern-day versions of theft that illustrate how "new" crimes can emerge in response to changes in technology and/or opportunities.

The idea that crime is relative is fundamentally incompatible with the notion that certain people are "born criminals"—predisposed to crime through heredity (an idea with major theoretical implications, as we will see in Part II). It reflects the historical fact that activities deemed criminal in one particular community, or at one particular time, are often accepted in another community or at another time. Examples in Canadian history include alcohol consumption, gay sex, and abortion. So is criminal behaviour qualitatively different from non-criminal behaviour? Where and how do we draw the lines? These questions represent major challenges to criminologists.

**decriminalization**
The reduction or removal of criminal penalties attached to an act but without legalizing it.

**relative**
When applied to crime, the idea that what is defined as crime can vary with time and location.

**evolutive**
When applied to crime, the idea that the characteristics of crime can change, taking different forms over time.

Fans celebrate the 2014 Olympic gold-medal win by the Canadian women's team in Sochi with a bottle of wine. Both Canada and Russia prohibited alcohol consumption in the early decades of the twentieth century.

Iurii Osadchi/Shutterstock.com

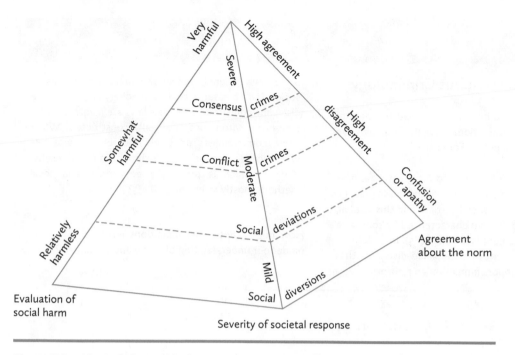

**Figure 1.1   Hagan's Pyramid: Consensus versus Conflict**

*Source*: J. Hagan, *The Disreputable Pleasures*, 3rd ed. (Toronto: McGraw-Hill Ryerson Ltd 1991: p. 13).

## The Crime and Deviance Hierarchy

Former University of Toronto criminology professor John Hagan developed a schematic diagram to illustrate the difference between crime and deviance (see Figure 1.1). According to his conception, the difference between crime and simple deviance is sometimes subtle.

At the bottom of the pyramid are *social diversions*: minor forms of deviance, such as unconventional dress or the use of offensive language, that are generally considered relatively harmless and that are not subject to regulation. The next level, *social deviations*, consists of behaviours that are considered disreputable in certain social settings and are therefore regulated: for example, the use of offensive language to a police officer or in court. At the top of the pyramid are behaviours that are generally considered very harmful and deserving of sanction. These are referred to as consensus crimes. Examples of consensus crimes in Canada include homicide, sexual assault, and treason. Even within the category of consensus crimes lies some dispute about whether certain actions or behaviours should, in fact, be considered crimes in every case or situation (Gaughan, 2009).

By contrast, conflict crimes are not necessarily thought of as crimes by the public, even though they are legally defined as such. Currently in Canada, these include the possession of non-medical marijuana in small quantities, procuring the services of a prostitute, driving without a seatbelt, or smoking in a public place.

In short, our perceptions of deviance and criminality vary over time and place. As Sacco and Kennedy point out, "the essence of deviance is to be found not in the behaviour defined as deviance, but in the social processes that define deviance" (1988, p. 7). In other words, what is important is not the behaviour defined as deviant but the social forces that shape the definition.

**consensus crimes**
Activities that are generally considered very harmful; therefore there is strong support for sanctioning and controlling them.

**conflict crimes**
Activities that are not universally considered crimes, although they are legally defined as such, e.g. possessing non-medical marijuana, procuring the services of a prostitute.

BOX 1.3    REALITY CHECK

## Two Misconceptions about Criminology

As an "applied" science, criminology has had to contend with some misconceptions about how its findings have been applied to practical policy. For example:

1. Criminologists have often argued for greater fairness in law and punishment, in the use of the death penalty, and in other issues of social justice. For this reason, criminology has often been characterized by some as a humanitarian movement (see Chapter 5). In fact, however, it is primarily an evidence-based discipline that relies on data to support humanitarian reform.

2. Since laws generally reflect the values and norms of society, some assume that criminology is a *normative* discipline concerned with how laws are involved in the way our environment is socially constructed. While some criminologists do study the relationships between values and their entrenchment in social norms, their approach is principally descriptive and their methods mostly scientific.

How might these misconceptions either assist or hinder our understanding of crime and its control?

## What Is Criminology?

*The objective of criminology is the development of a body of general and verified principles and of other types of knowledge regarding ... law, crime, and treatment.* (Sutherland & Cressey, 1960, p. 3)

**criminology**
An interdisciplinary science that studies criminal behaviour, crime causation, crime prevention, and the punishment and rehabilitation of offenders.

**criminologist**
A behavioural scientist who specializes in the identification, classification, and description of criminal behaviour.

**interdisciplinary approach**
In criminology, the integration of knowledge from a variety of disciplines to formulate theories of criminal behaviour.

Criminology can be broadly defined as the scientific study of criminal behaviour, crime causation, crime prevention, and the punishment and rehabilitation of offenders. To the extent that its findings are used to guide public policy, it is an applied science (see Box 1.3). A criminologist today is essentially a behavioural scientist who may draw on many disciplines, including law and ethics, psychology and sociology, anthropology and biology, economics and political science. Although this interdisciplinary approach is not yet universal in criminology, it is increasingly accepted (see e.g. the homepage for the School of Criminology at Simon Fraser University, which defines criminology as "the interdisciplinary study of crime": www.sfu.ca/fass/departments--schools-and-programs/criminology-learn-more.html).

## The Criminal Justice System in Canada

The English criminologist **Leon Radzinowicz** was an early advocate of an interdisciplinary approach to the study of criminology—one that would include criminal justice and criminal law (Jeffery, 1990). Although in Canada criminology and criminal justice are still generally taught as separate subjects, no criminology text can be complete without a basic introduction to the criminal justice system (CJS), which Jeffery defines as "the agencies of social control which define and react to those behaviours falling within the purview of the criminal law" (1990, p. 3).

The Canadian CJS consists of three agencies:

- the police
- the courts
- the correctional/prison system

All three of these agencies operate under the authority of the federal and provincial/territorial governments (see Table 1.1).

| Table 1.1 | Authority Structure of the Canadian Criminal Justice System | |
| --- | --- | --- |
| | **Federal Jurisdiction** | **Provincial/Territorial Jurisdiction** |
| Courts | Department of Justice | Ministry of the Attorney General |
| Police/corrections | Department of Public Safety | Ministry of Public Safety |

## Functions of the CJS

The main functions of the criminal justice system are as follows:

- to investigate criminal offences as defined in the Canadian Criminal Code (CCC); this is primarily the responsibility of the police
- to lay charges as defined under the CCC; this function is usually administered by the police
- to prosecute the accused in court, in accordance with the law; this role is performed by the prosecution, or "the Crown"
- to determine guilt or innocence, either by a judge or (for more serious crimes) a judge and jury
- to sentence those found guilty, within the upper and lower limits prescribed by the CCC
- to administer the sentence; this falls within the scope of the correctional branch of the CJS

Figure 1.2 illustrates how the CJS works. For a brief historical overview of the CJS in Canada, see Chapter 5.

## Historical Overview

For most of human history, the study of crime (along with all other aspects of human behaviour) was the domain of philosophy, law, and theology. Socrates, for example, was known to have commented on the plight of young people; he argued that they were disrespectful

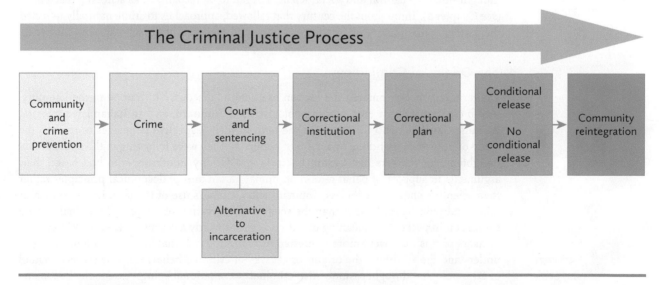

**Figure 1.2 The Canadian Criminal Justice Process: A Simplified Flow Chart**

*Source*: Correctional Service Canada, 2008. Retrieved from: http://www.csc-scc.gc.ca/volunteers/003008-2001-eng.shtml.

BOX 1.4 **FACTS AND FIGURES** THE COST OF OPERATING THE CJS

After adjusting for inflation, the per capita cost of the CJS has risen dramatically, from $4.38 per Canadian in 1961 to $388 per Canadian in 2011–12. Total government spending on police, courts, legal aid, and corrections increased from $17 billion in 2002–3 to $20.3 billion in 2011–12, even though crime rates have been dropping since the mid-1990s (see Figure 1.3 and chapters 9 and 10). The cost of the correctional system alone is immense. In 2010–11 Canada spent on average almost ten times as much to incarcerate a prisoner for a year as it did to educate a K–12 student: $114,364 to $12,557 (Public Safety Canada, 2014a; Woo, 2014).

Despite the significant sums of money spent on law and order, a 2014 report found that many Canadians today lack confidence in the CJS (Doob, 2014).

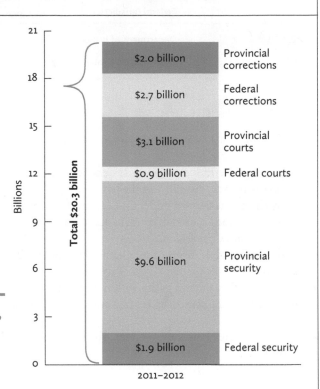

**Figure 1.3    Criminal Justice Expenditure, Canada, 2011–2012**

*Source*: Office of the Parliamentary Budget Officer, 2013. Supplementary Data http://www.pbo-dpb.gc.ca/en/supp_data.

and in need of punishment. However, it was not until the eighteenth century—a period referred to as the Enlightenment, or Age of Reason, because it was marked by the rise of secular thought—that the natural and social sciences began to be recognized as scholarly disciplines (see Chapter 2). Throughout the century that followed, approaches to crime naturally reflected the particular disciplinary orientations, or frames of reference, of the scholars who studied it.

## The Origins of Criminology

The term *criminology* entered the lexicon of scientific discourse in Europe in the late nineteenth century. It was a French anthropologist, **Paul Topinard**, and an Italian law professor, **Raffaele Garofalo**, who in 1879 used the term in their respective languages to refer to the study of punishment and the treatment of criminals. They were following in the path of early Enlightenment thinkers like **Cesare Beccaria** and **Jeremy Bentham**, who had based their arguments in support of penal reform on humanitarian and philosophical principles rather than scientific ones. Nevertheless, Topinard and Garofalo's use of the term in the context of crime and punishment, rather than the scientific observation of crime and criminals, had a significant impact on the meaning of criminology for nearly a century thereafter. Writers and thinkers of this time were more interested in reforming criminal law than in attempting to understand the etiology—the origins or causes—of criminal behaviour. This classical school of criminological thought assumed that criminals were rational beings, essentially hedonistic and acting of free will, and that the certainty of punishment would serve as the most effective deterrent to their criminal behaviour.

**etiology**
The study of the origins or causes of a phenomenon.

With the shift in orientation from legal reform to scientific research, criminology began to gain wider acceptance as a subject of study. The first to give the subject a credible platform in North America was John Henry Wigmore of Northwestern University in Chicago, who in 1909 organized a conference on the subject. Out of the conference proceedings emerged the *Journal of Criminal Law and Criminology*, in which scholars could publish their research. Significant breakthroughs occurred in 1918, when the sociologist **Maurice Parmelee** published the first criminology textbook, and in 1924, with the publication of Edwin H. Sutherland's *Principles of Criminology*, which reinforced the influence of sociologically oriented positivism (Gibbons, 1979). Many sociology-based criminology textbooks followed, and between 1930 and 1950 an alliance was forged between criminology and sociology departments in North America. Many of the most prominent and enduring sociological theories of crime emerged during this era (see Part II).

One of the pioneers of Canadian criminology, André Normandeau, recently summarized the growth of the discipline in this country. He identified Denis Szabo, who launched the criminology program at the University of Montreal in 1960, as the "founding father of Canadian criminology" (Normandeau, 2012). Other central figures in the discipline's history include John Edwards, who established the Centre for Criminology at the University of Toronto in 1960; Tadeusz Grygier, who started the criminology and correctional administration program at the University of Ottawa in 1967; and Ezzat Fattah, who established Simon Fraser University's criminology program in 1975 (see Chapter 5 in this textbook). Today there are few universities across the country that do not have a criminology or criminal justice program, and many colleges offer two-year diplomas in areas such as law enforcement, corrections, and child and youth care.

In summary, the discipline of criminology has evolved in both meaning and scope, and it continues to be a dynamic area of study. Criminologists are no longer concerned only with penology or the sociology of law, and it is increasingly recognized that their field of study is by nature interdisciplinary.

**penology**
The study of how crime is punished.

## Sub-areas of Criminology

Figure 1.4 shows the core sub-areas that make up the discipline of criminology today. We will examine each of these areas in turn.

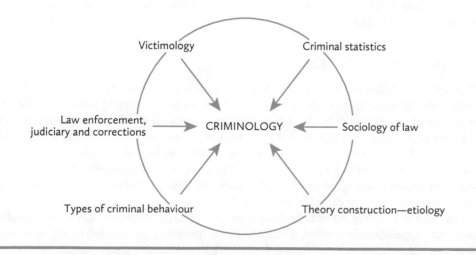

**Figure 1.4   The Core Sub-areas of Criminology**

## 1. Criminal Statistics

Researchers rely on crime data to understand and predict criminal behaviour, and to assess the impact of crime prevention or intervention programs. For example, consider the problem of human trafficking in Canada. How widespread is it? For what forms of exploitation are people most often trafficked in Canada—the sex trade, illegal forced labour, domestic servitude, or something else? Where do most of the victims of the different types of trafficking come from? What impact, if any, can the National Action Plan to Combat Human Trafficking (2014) be expected to have? Obtaining reliable answers to questions like these requires the collection of scientific evidence from a variety of sources.

Scientific evidence is data that can be repeatedly observed and measured to test theories for their validity and reliability. If we were to rely only on anecdotal information, we would risk making decisions that could be counterproductive. For this reason, before creating its Action Plan, the federal government had the RCMP conduct a human trafficking threat assessment to determine the profile and extent of vulnerable populations in Canada. The goal was to focus the plan and ensure that the new policy was based on solid evidence.

We will review some of the most common data-gathering techniques in Chapter 3. In chapters 9–13, we will examine how data can be used to describe the patterns and characteristics of crime.

## 2. Sociology of Law

The sociology of law is concerned with the origins of law and legal thought. Specialists in this area examine how various economic, political, and social forces have influenced the formalization of social control and social order. The sociology of law is also concerned with exploring the central themes of social order, social conflict, and power relations as they pertain to law. This sub-area is closely aligned with the school of thought known as *critical criminology* (see Chapter 8).

A prominent American proponent of this perspective is Richard Quinney (1977), who has argued that the law is defined by those people in power; agents of the law (such as legislators, police, prosecutors, and judges), who have vested interests in protecting and maintaining their power and authority. In their edited book on critical criminology, Doyle and Moore (2011) present an anthology of Canadian essays in this area, covering topics that range from the future of critical criminology in Canada to the role of criminologists in politics and criminal justice policy in Canada.

## 3. Theory Construction: Etiology

This area of study has expanded greatly since the mid-twentieth century. It is concerned with understanding the causes of crime, its rates and trends, and predicting behaviour, whether of groups or individuals. Why did Robert "Willie" Pickton kill more than 30 women on his pig farm near Vancouver? How is it that, in 2014, a 22-year-old university graduate named Matthew de Grood went to a house party and fatally stabbed five other students, committing the worst mass murder in Calgary's history? Were these offenders suffering from some biological or neuropsychological problem? Was their behaviour somehow learned? Were there other social, economic, or causal factors at play?

In order to answer questions like these in an objective and "value-free" manner, criminologists rely on the scientific method, which consists of observing criminal behaviour, collecting data on it, formulating hypotheses, and then testing their ability to predict similar behaviour.

At the same time, all theories reflect the ideological or political climate of the day. In the 1960s, for example, Cloward and Ohlin's theory of differential opportunity (see Chapter 8) was inspired in part by the political belief that the root of most crime was lack of opportunity. In the United States, the Kennedy and Johnson administrations launched all-out campaigns against the slums that were believed to be the root of crime. The $12 million initiative referred to as the "war on poverty" involved a program called Mobilization for Youth, based in the slum areas of New York City. Unfortunately, as a result of poor management and practical and conceptual limitations, the program was unable to bring about any structural social change.

Because the study of criminology is interdisciplinary, there are a variety of criminological theories and theoretical orientations. Researchers have developed several approaches for classifying these variations; different criminology textbooks approach these classifications differently, according to the ideological and/or methodological orientations of their authors. Unfortunately, this inconsistency has done little to help students understand crime and criminality. This textbook will group theories according to their disciplinary orientations (chapters 6–9), in order to demonstrate the necessity of an interdisciplinary orientation.

## 4. Types of Criminal Behaviour

The use of criminal typologies is a way of trying to understand and organize criminal behaviour. It is an approach that can be traced back to the early twentieth-century work of **Cesare Lombroso**, who identified such typologies as "the born criminal," "criminals by passion," "criminaloids," and others (see Chapter 5). Today, official police data (see the discussion of Uniform Crime Reporting in Chapter 3) record and classify crimes according to specific types as defined by law.

With advances in theory and research methodologies, many criminologists believe that different types of crime have different causal explanations. In fact, disciplines like sociology and psychology have developed criminal typologies based on their respective disciplinary perspectives. For example, drawing on a social-psychology perspective, Mark Totten's recent *Gang Life* (2014) offers an insightful overview of the diversity of gang life and activity in Canada using first-person accounts. In the 1970s, Don Gibbons (1979) was among the first to develop criminal typologies for both juvenile and adult offenders. Totten's typologies are largely person-centred typologies, while Gibbon's typologies were mostly crime-centred.

Criminologists interested in criminal typologies often attempt to explain how and why different types of criminals commit different types of crimes. This area of inquiry is concerned with understanding the causes and motivations underlying, for example, violent crime, corporate crime, serial murder, property offences, or soccer hooliganism. We will look at some of these subjects in Part III of this book.

## 5. Law Enforcement, Judiciary, and Corrections

As described above, the criminal justice system consists of three formal elements: police, courts, and corrections. How these elements, individually and collectively, fulfill their tasks—detecting crime, dealing with criminals, and protecting society—has been the subject of much research (see e.g. Goff, 2014). For this reason, many criminology programs offer separate courses on each element that allow students to examine each in detail. In this textbook, we will not be examining these elements in any specific chapter; only those issues pertinent to the understanding of crime and criminals will be covered.

## 6. Victimology

Since the early 1970s, the relationships between criminals and their victims have attracted both public and academic interest. The origins of victimology can be traced to early work of Lombroso and Garofalo, who recognized the importance of the victim's relationship to the crime he or she suffered and to the offending individual. One pioneer of victimology, Hans von Hentig (1948, p. 383), posited that many victims contribute to their own victimization through their lifestyle, mannerisms, or other forms of behaviour and expression; hence, he concluded, the relationship between the offender and the victim is "much more intricate than the rough distinction of criminal law." A classic example used by von Hentig is an individual who goes to seedy bars alone, dressed in a way that does not fit the surroundings, and so may invite trouble, albeit unwittingly. Based on Fattah's (1991, p. 101) typologies, such a person could be described as a deserving target because of his or her "reckless behaviour."

Victimology can also include the scientific study of the relationship between the victim and the criminal justice system. Doerner and Lab (2015), among others, point out how victims can be further victimized by the system itself if it allows insensitive questioning by police, harsh cross-examination in the courts, or the withholding of evidence until a case is resolved. The state, too, can be viewed as an offender if it fails to provide sufficient protection for the victim, or to restrain or deter the criminal, because of some fault in the social control network.

Finally, the system can also make victims of innocent people who are wrongfully convicted of crime. One of the most powerful tools in the effort to protect the rights of the innocent has been the DNA test. Introduced in 1988, DNA testing came to Canada in 1989, and the first case in which it was successfully used to free a wrongfully convicted person was that of Guy Paul Morin, who had been charged with the brutal sex slaying of a young girl in 1985 and was finally proven innocent in 1995. Another noteworthy victim of wrongful conviction was David Milgaard, who spent 23 years behind bars for a murder he did not commit. He was finally released from prison in 1992 and his name cleared in 1997, when the Supreme Court of Canada admitted that, based on the evidence, there had been a miscarriage of justice. In that case, DNA was also used to convict the offender who had actually committed the 1969 murder for which Milgaard had been jailed. Thanks to the DNA evidence, Larry Fisher was arrested in 1997 and convicted in 1999—30 years after the murder. Unfortunately, since DNA evidence is not available in every case, wrongful conviction remains a serious problem (see Box 1.5). We will explore the topic of victimology further in Chapter 4.

Specialists in the various sub-areas of criminology may pursue the same questions (such as how to control criminality), but they generally come out with different answers. This lack of consensus leads to confusion and makes it difficult to design sound policy.

| BOX 1.5 | **A CLOSER LOOK**<br>Wrongful Conviction |
|---|---|

One issue that plagues the CJS has been its inability to ensure due process and reach a just decision as to the guilt or innocence of an accused person based on legal protocols. In one of the first books to discuss the risk of predicting violent behaviour, John Monahan (1981) wrote about the issue of false positives (incorrect predictions of behaviour) among psychiatric predictions of the future dangerousness of offenders. Monahan observed that if psychiatrists can be wrong 56–80 per cent of the time, how often are innocent people falsely convicted when judges and juries make decisions based on incorrect interpretations of the evidence?

Consider the case of Rubin "Hurricane" Carter (1937–2014), the American boxer who was wrongfully convicted of murder and who spent 19 years in prison before his conviction was overturned in 1985 on the grounds that it had been "predicated upon an appeal to racism" (Gray, 2014). His story inspired the 1975 Bob Dylan song "Hurricane" and the 1999 movie *The Hurricane*. In 1993, he moved to Canada and became a champion of the wrongfully convicted.

What price is society willing to pay for a sense of security? How can criminology help to reduce the risk of wrongful conviction?

In the next two sections, we will review the primary disciplinary perspectives that make up the study of crime and criminality. Then we will look at the importance of linking criminological findings with policy.

## Disciplinary Perspectives

So how do criminologists view crime? Because of the complexity of crime and its pervasive influence on all levels of society—economic, political, environmental, and even spiritual—virtually every major discipline has contributed something to the study of crime. Regardless of their disciplinary bias or theoretical orientation, criminologists are primarily interested in understanding why crimes are committed by certain individuals and not by others. Nevertheless, the range of topics in criminological research is very broad, as Figure 1.5 suggests.

The following are six of the more important criminological perspectives that you are likely to encounter as a student. The perspectives are presented in alphabetic order.

### 1. Biology

Is it possible that certain human traits are biological, or "hard-wired"? Or that certain crimes are a function of chemical, genetic, and/or neurological aberrations? The idea that biological

**CRIMINOLOGY RESEARCH TOPICS**

- CONVENTIONAL CRIME
- NON-CONVENTIONAL CRIME
- GENDER, CRIME, AND JUSTICE
- YOUTH AT RISK
- BATTERED WOMAN SYNDROME
- CHILD ABDUCTION
- DOMESTIC VIOLENCE
- VICTIMS
- PRISON LIFE AND ITS EFFECTS
- GANGS
- IDENTITY THEFT
- HATE CRIME
- HUMAN TRAFFICKING AND SMUGGLING
- CRIME PREVENTION
- THEORIES OF CRIME AND CRIMINALITY
- CYBERCRIME

**Figure 1.5   Sample List of Criminology Research Topics**

*Source:* Adapted from http://crime-study.blogspot.ca/2010/03/introduction-to-criminology-problems.html

factors might play a role in criminal behaviour was initially met with a fair degree of skepticism. However, the acclaimed work of J.Q. Wilson and R. Herrnstein, *Crime and Human Nature* (1985), sparked new interest in this area of research. Since then, the biological/genetic perspective has attracted a respectable following (see Owen, 2014). We will examine some biological interpretations of criminal behaviour in Chapter 6.

## 2. Economics

Over the years, many studies have demonstrated links between unemployment, economic recession, capitalism, and crime. Is crime a function of competition for limited resources and/or social status and power? Do people who "have everything" commit as many crimes as those who do not?

Karl Marx is the thinker most often associated with the notion that economic factors lie at the root of all social phenomena, including crime. However, while economics has often been used as an explanatory variable (or as part of a grander theoretical model), few researchers since the Dutch criminologist Willem Adriaan Bonger, author of the classic *Criminality and Economic Conditions* (1905), have seen economic factors as the primary predictors of crime. Likewise, the economic perspective has never been as widely embraced by Canadian criminologists as have some other perspectives. Nevertheless, there have been a number of interesting works that can be loosely aligned with this view (see, generally, DeKeseredy & Perry, 2006; Doyle & Moore, 2011), and we will draw attention to them where appropriate throughout this book.

## 3. Geography and the Environment

If you're a fan of crime shows or horror movies, you will know that certain settings tend to show up again and again: a foggy night down by the waterfront, an unlit alleyway in a run-down area of town. Is it possible that crimes are a by-product of physical and environmental dynamics? Criminologists seeking to predict crime have developed sophisticated models and theories based on a wide range of environmental factors, from barometric pressure and even phases of the moon, to the physical appearance and layout of a business, residence, social area, or community.

What is unique about this line of inquiry is that its findings can often be used proactively to prevent crime. Installing an alarm system in your home or making sure that your lawn is cut and your mail picked up while you are away are examples of simple crime prevention techniques using elementary environmental modifications.

## 4. Political Science

Political decisions regarding criminal justice have a direct impact on the community at large. As a student of criminology, you might be interested in exploring why it took more than 20 years of debate before the Young Offenders Act was passed in 1984 (see Green, 2013). You might also ask what the politicians who passed the legislation were trying to accomplish, and in whose interests they were acting—especially given the act's public reception and the fact that in 2003 it was replaced with the Youth Criminal Justice Act (see e.g. Caputo & Vallee, 2010).

Alternatively, you might ask why political decisions do not always appear to reflect the interests of society. For example, why is it that marijuana is still illegal, when a Forum Research poll conducted in 2014 suggests that 70 per cent of Canadians support legalization or decriminalization? Throughout this book, but particularly in Chapter 14, we will see how political science has contributed to criminology.

## 5. Psychology

Psychology is the study of the mind and behaviour. In their textbook *Criminal Behavior: A Psychological Approach*, Bartol and Bartol (2012) explain that criminology from a psychological perspective focuses on how individual criminal behaviour is acquired, evoked, and maintained. Therefore, criminologists with an interest in psychology look at differences in personality and mental characteristics between criminals and others. For example, some researchers have focused on mental abilities such as IQ (see Box 1.6).

Although psychology is a popular area of study, it is less well established in criminology than the sociological perspective (below). However, two notable Canadian contributors to the field, Andrews and Bonta (2010), make a strong argument for psychological perspectives in criminology, arguing that until recently sociologists have tended to ignore individual elements in explaining criminal behaviour. However, they point out that "the most important contributions in the last 20 years have been made by sociologists who conducted studies of the social psychology variety" (p. 64). We will examine some psychological interpretations of crime in Chapter 7.

## 6. Sociology

The sociological perspective is the dominant criminological perspective in North America. Sociology is the science of interaction among people; it studies the effects of that interaction on human behaviour, as well as the forces (such as values, norms, mores, and laws) that underlie regularities in human behaviour. In essence, sociologists are interested in culture and social structure. As we noted earlier in this chapter, crime is a social phenomenon.

As we will see in Chapter 7, sociology views crime and criminal behaviour from a variety of perspectives, from social structure to social process to social organization.

Finally, it is interesting that while North American criminologists tend to align themselves with one or more of the social science perspectives described above, Europeans have generally approached crime from a legal standpoint, focusing on the means of controlling it. In fact, most European criminologists have trained first as lawyers and only later taken an interest in social science (see Winterdyk & Cao, 2004).

---

**BOX 1.6**

**A CLOSER LOOK**
**Crime and Intelligence**

Harvard psychologist Howard Gardner (1983) proposed that intelligence cannot be measured through intelligence quotient (IQ) tests. He was among the first to propose that humans have multiple intelligences—linguistic, logical/mathematical, musical, spatial, bodily kinesthetic (the intelligence possessed by athletes, actors, and dancers), interpersonal, intrapersonal, and even naturalistic (the ability to understand flora and fauna). Thus, he argues that we need to broaden our understanding of intelligence (Gilman, 2012).

Early criminological researchers such as Lombroso thought that criminals were atavistic—of primitive or subhuman features characteristics by various physical characteristics and below-average intelligence. However, contemporary research and theory suggest that in order to be successful, a criminal must be not only intelligent enough to devise a plan that includes a strategy for avoiding apprehension but also creative enough to improvise if things don't go according to plan.

What implications might the study of crime and multiple intelligence have for understanding of criminal behaviour and our responses to it?

## Interdisciplinary Criminology

In the past, most Canadian criminologists received their training in other disciplinary fields, usually sociology or psychology, and to a lesser extent political science. Since the 1960s, however, criminology, criminal justice, and human justice programs have sprung up across the country, and today nearly a dozen schools offer graduate-level programs, most of which take an interdisciplinary approach (see Figure 1.6 and Box 1.7). As a consequence, the discipline is likely to continue evolving in an integrated and interdisciplinary direction.

As we have seen, the roots of criminology lie in two schools of thought: classical and positivist. As a consequence, criminologists recognize that criminal behaviour is the product of both free will and deterministic forces. As Barak (1998), among others, has noted, human behaviour is not an either–or phenomenon, and it is arguably impossible for criminologists to clearly delineate behaviour arising from free will and behaviour produced by deterministic forces. Hence, as the esteemed C.R. Jeffery argued in the journal *Criminology* in 1978, criminology should be seen as an *interdisciplinary* science, drawing on many research disciplines in its search for explanations of criminal behaviour. Jeffery recalled that as a student he was baffled by the failure of his mentors (among them Edwin Sutherland) to see that human behaviour was far too complex to be reduced to a single explanation. But he then "heard about a strange man, . . . B.F. Skinner," who helped to galvanize his search for a different perspective from which to study crime and criminality—an interdisciplinary perspective (Jeffery, 1978, p. 147). Although controversial at the time, this perspective has arguably become the mainstream (see e.g. Binder, 1979; Gibbs, 2006; Walsh & Ellis, 2007; Walsh & Hemmens, 2013). It is also the perspective embraced in this book, although this does not mean that it is the definitive perspective. No perspective should be accepted without careful reflection on its implications for our understanding of critical real-world issues (see Box 1.7).

An interdisciplinary approach attempts to take all perspectives into account, integrating the competing notions of crime as a product of free will and as a product of various external and internal factors. Consider the case of Russell Williams, the decorated military pilot and former colonel who become a serial sex offender and was eventually convicted of murdering two Ontario women in 2009–10. Those who support the free-will model might say that he freely chose to commit those crimes, having calculated that no one would suspect a decorated soldier of such behaviour, making the risk of apprehension be very low. By contrast, those who support the positivist model might say that Williams was predisposed to offend by factors

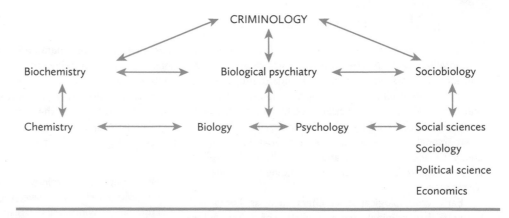

**Figure 1.6    Interdisciplinary Criminology**

*Source*: Adapted from C.R. Jeffrey, *Criminology: An Interdisciplinary Approach* (Englewood Cliffs, NJ: Prentice-Hall 1990).

| BOX 1.7 | WHAT DO YOU THINK? |
|---|---|

## How Would You Answer These Criminological Questions?

Criminologists routinely face situations where they must decide which ideological or disciplinary approach is the best one to apply to certain questions and issues. Often, the questions that criminologists confront need to be looked at from more than one viewpoint. Consider the following questions.

1. Despite popular perceptions to the contrary, official statistics suggest crime has been decreasing in Canada. How can we explain the trend?
2. What factors—age, gender, ethnicity, psychological traits, upbringing, etc.—play the greatest role in determining crime patterns?
3. Are certain social and/or ethnic groups overrepresented in the Canadian justice system? If so, why? What would it take to correct this situation?
4. Should pornography be censored? Should lap dancing be banned? Should prostitution be legalized? What are the arguments for and against?
5. Should marijuana be treated differently from alcohol and cigarettes? Why or why not?
6. Is punishment of offenders the best way to improve public safety?
7. Should prisoners be allowed conjugal visits?
8. Should solitary confinement be banned?

Note that there are no right or wrong answers to these questions. The exercise is intended to illustrate the complexity of criminological issues and the difficulty of reaching conclusive answers, and hence the need for flexibility in thinking about them.

such as the pressure of his status and responsibilities, family stress, and/or a troubled childhood. An interdisciplinary approach would suggest that Williams committed his crimes based on a combination of rational and irrational factors. Once tempted, he may have lost his ability to maintain any perspective. An integrated and interdisciplinary approach may be applied generally to all crimes) or specifically to a particular crime, and it may rely on some perspectives more than others to understand a situation.

## Putting Theory into Practice

### The Gap between Theory and Practice

*In theory, theory and practice are the same. In practice, they are not.* (attributed to Albert Einstein)

Crime receives considerable media coverage, and public anxiety over crime is higher than ever before (see e.g. Brennan, 2013). One of the consequences of this fear is that more homeowners are investing in home security devices. In theory, ensuring that our residences are protected with secure locks and a reliable alarm system should not only reduce the risk of break-and-enters but also increase our sense of personal safety. Yet, as we will see in more detail next chapter, break-and-enters remain one of the most common crimes in Canada. This suggests there is a gap between what we know about this kind of crime and our responses to it (Edmiston, 2012).

The gap between theory and practice is a recurring theme in criminology. In this vein, consider Bill C-10, the federal government's "tough on crime" legislation, also known as the Safe Streets and Communities Act. Among the measures it introduced were mandatory-minimum sentences—which limit the ability of judges to be lenient when sentencing convicted offenders—and the expansion of Canada's prison system. And yet, the act was passed in 2012, when Canada's crime rate was at its lowest point since 1973. The legislation was widely criticized by the public and by academics, who viewed many of the act's measures as unnecessarily strict. Once again, there appears to be a gap between what we know about crime and how we respond to it—in other words, between theory and practice.

**crime rate**

The number of criminal offences in a category, recorded in a fixed ratio, such as per 100,000 people.

© Richard Levine / Alamy Stock Photo

A collage of front pages of various newspapers from Canada, the United States, and the UK, following the Ottawa shootings of October 2014. Extensive media coverage encourages fear of crime.

As practitioners of an "applied" social science, criminologists use their data and theoretical perspectives to formulate workable solutions to existing problems. Their successes have been disappointingly few. This is partly because they are often contending with competing approaches to, and interpretations of, the same issue. Hackler (2006) offers another interesting explanation: he suggests that if criminologists would be less *inconsistent* in their ideology and more *consistent* in their use of science, criminology would undoubtedly create a more reliable knowledge base. Criminologists, he argues, would be more productive if they better understood and used scientific procedures.

If Hackler is correct, then criminologists must accept part of the blame for the gap between theory and practice. Even so, it is worth noting that criminologists' research and recommendations have much to offer. For example, without scientific proof of its effectiveness, the victim–offender reconciliation program might never have been introduced in Canada. Indeed, governments must rely on the theoretical guidance of criminologists when making policy decisions. Throughout this book, we will review several examples of how theory, coupled with strong research, has been used to develop sound public policy.

## Ethical Issues in Criminology

A final point to emphasize here—and revisit throughout this book—is the ethical responsibility that criminologists must accept when they engage in criminological inquiry. After all, their findings and recommendations can have serious political and social consequences. For instance, Sanguins recently suggested that Canada's "tough on crime" discourse and policies in spite of falling crime rates are being "perpetuated through selective valuation of 'evidence'" (Sanguins, 2014, p. 54). So, in addition to ethical issues associated with the manner in which criminologists conduct their research (see Chapter 2), criminologists must be sensitive to the implications of their findings on policy creation. Their recommendations on such policy questions as whether victims of human trafficking should be returned to their homelands, whether chemical castration should be used to treat sex offenders, and whether prostitution should be legalized can have profound effects on many lives. The ethical concerns only multiply when the research will result in recommendations intended to influence public policy, since criminologists' recommendations can have a profound effect on many people's lives.

Darren Calabrese/The Canadian Press

Carrying her signature riding crop, retired dominatrix Terri-Jean Bedford (*right*) and former prostitute Valerie Scott (*left*), two of the three applicants who eventually brought Canada's prostitution laws to the Supreme Court, make their way to the Ontario Superior Court in October 2009. Do you think people should have the same rights to security and safety regardless of their occupation? When might a policy of any kind represent an infringement of basic civil liberties and/or a violation of moral standards? How should criminologists approach such issues?

In short, criminology is a dynamic discipline that can be very rewarding, but criminologists cannot forget the social responsibility that comes with working in an applied discipline whose findings and recommendations inform public policy. As we will see in Chapter 2, criminologists can arm themselves against charges of bias and ethical breaches by grounding their research in sound theories and well-founded methodologies.

## Summary

- Criminology is a comparatively young, increasingly interdisciplinary science dedicated to the systematic and objective study of criminal behaviour.
- The criminal justice system is the formal control agency that is responsible for dealing with those individuals who come into conflict with the law.
- Although sociological thought has played a major role in North American criminology, no single discipline alone can explain all aspects of crime. As the noted American sociologist Thomas Kuhn (1970), among others, has noted, the paradigms that individual criminologists use will naturally influence the types of information they seek, the strategies they use, and the interpretations they arrive at.

- As an applied science, criminology uses theory and research methods to explain the causes of criminal behaviour, often to help guide policy-making in the criminal justice system. Consequently, criminologists often face ethical issues when conducting research.
- Criminology is akin to a living organism: dynamic, evolving, and challenging. Embracing an interdisciplinary approach to the study of criminal behaviour, it offers opportunities in a large number of professions and related areas of employment and study.

## Discussion Questions

1. Why is it important to study criminology in the Canadian context?
2. Why is it important to understand criminology's historical roots?
3. What are the major sub-areas of criminology?
4. Provide examples of the ethical issues faced by criminologists and how they can be resolved.
5. The use of marijuana is one example of the relative nature of crime/deviance. What are some other examples? Explain how attitudes toward these behaviours have changed (or are changing) and explore why this might be the case.

## Key Concepts

conflict crime
consensus crime
conventional crime
crime
criminologist
criminology
decriminalization
deviance

etiology
evolutive, crime as
indictable offence
interdisciplinary approach
non-conventional crime
relative, crime as
summary offence

## Key Names

Cesare Beccaria (1738–1794)
Jeremy Bentham (1748–1832)
Raffaele Garofalo (1851–1934)
Cesare Lombroso (1835–1909)

Maurice Parmelee (1882–1969)
Sir Leon Radzinowicz (1906–1999)
Paul Topinard (1830–1911)

## Weblinks

Most Canadian post-secondary criminology/criminal justice departments have their own resource pages. The following are particularly good.

**St Mary's University: Sociology and Criminology,**
St Mary's University has one of the fastest-growing criminology programs in the Maritimes; its library's website contains excellent good links to criminology associations and publications.
www.smu.ca/academics/departments/soc-crim-criminology-links.html

**The University of Winnipeg: Criminal Justice/Criminology Links,**
The University of Winnipeg offers links not only to corrections and criminal justice sites but also to sites on research methods.
www.uwinnipeg.ca/criminal-justice/student-information/cj-links.html

**University of Toronto Mississauga: Careers by Major—Criminology and Socio-Legal Studies**
The University of Toronto offers career information for graduates of its criminology and socio-legal studies program.
www.utm.utoronto.ca/careers/careers-by-major-criminology-and-socio-legal-studies

**University of Ottawa Department of Criminology: Associations, Organizations, and Partners**
The University of Ottawa's criminology department offers useful links to correction, social, and police services organizations.
http://socialsciences.uottawa.ca/crm/associations-organizations-partners

# Chapter 2

## Images of Crime and Crime Control

Zoran Karapancev / Shutterstock.com

Accounts of life in the urban centres of the late 1800s and early 1900s
are hair-raising. Crime was a real threat, but then as now the picture of the
crime problem painted by official statistics was seriously distorted. . . .
H. PEPINSKY & P. JESILOW (1984, p. 22)

## Learning Outcomes

After reading this chapter, you should be able to

- Recognize and identify the five basic ways in which we acquire knowledge and understanding;
- Know what influences our frames of reference;
- Distinguish between rationalism and empiricism, and understand how they affect our conceptions of crime and criminality; and
- Appreciate the social responsibility attached to disclosing research findings.

Having read Chapter 1, you know that criminology is a complex subject that has been influenced by different ideologies and disciplinary perspectives. Even criminologists disagree over what they should be studying and how they should be studying it—sociologically, psychologically, politically, and so on. We will examine some of these diverging views in Part II of this book. In this chapter, we will look at the way the public perceives crime, and the role the mass media play in shaping these perceptions.

Many observers have noted that the mass media play a significant role in creating the public's perceptions of crime. As a consequence, most people are information-rich and knowledge-poor when it comes to crime. As Roberts and Hough (2005) and Rosenzweig (2013), among others, point out, most people are not well informed about either the actual extent of crime or how the criminal justice system works. Even so, according to Flanagan (1996), "public opinion polls about crime and justice can act as a social barometer providing important data to policy-makers regarding what the public is willing, or is not willing, to accept when it comes to proposed legislation and/or intervention programming" (as cited in Sims & Johnston, 2004, p. 270). In other words, policy-makers take their cue from a public that is sometimes misinformed or simply naive, and for this reason, as critics like Ballard (1998) and Cavender (2004) have argued, media coverage of crimes can play a more important role in the legislative processes than it should. While the average person has some general ideas about crime, some researchers have observed that these ideas tend to have an information-rich/knowledge-poor foundation. How do we form opinions about the world of crime around us? To what extent is our fear of crime justified? Do the media distort or overrepresent certain crime stories? Are official sources of crime data reliable?

The objective of this chapter is to examine how people come to form their perceptions of crime and criminality. After some initial discussion, we will examine the four main ways in which people come to perceive their reality.

## Public Perceptions of Crime

> *Ignorance is preferable to error; and he is less remote from the truth who believes nothing, than he who believes what is wrong.* (Thomas Jefferson, *Notes on the State of Virginia*, 1781–3)

How we form our opinions of reality has been the subject of numerous philosophical debates and social science studies. The perspective, or frame of reference, we choose is influenced by the way we have been socialized, by our individual psychological makeup, and even by such biological factors as diet and environmental conditions. The pioneering Canadian criminologist Gwynn Nettler (1984, pp. 17–19) observed that how we view something does not necessarily reflect what we know about it: for example, you might believe that capital punishment is an effective deterrent to murder, even if you know that your view is not supported by research findings. Furthermore, how much knowledge you have to make an informed decision about a particular issue depends not just on the *amount* of information you consume but on the *nature* of that information and where it comes from. Since the media have a code of conduct that requires journalists to report the news accurately, you may believe that media reports are reliable sources of information on crime. However, if you are aware that the news media tend to focus their coverage on "what is out of place: deviant, equivocal, and unpredictable" (Ericson, Baranek, & Chan, 1991, p. 4), you may take a more cautious view of their reliability. A number of studies have shown that as many as three-quarters of Canadians polled overestimate the incidence of crime involving violence (see O'Connell & Whelan, 1996; Roberts et al., 2003; Jackson & Gray, 2010; Edmiston, 2012). This suggests that most of us are not as well informed as we might think. How then does the public acquire its knowledge about crime?

## General Methods of Knowing

What are the differences between knowledge, belief, and truth? Based on actual crime statistics, you might know that Canada's crime rate has been declining since around the mid-1990s (see Box 2.1). However, based on personal experience and/or other methods of knowing, you might not believe everything you read. So what is the reality?

The French thinker and "father" of modern philosophy **René Descartes** laid the foundation of rationalism, according to which some kinds of knowledge are innate while others can be acquired through reasoning, independent of experience. By contrast, proponents of empiricism, such as **John Locke** and **David Hume**, argued that knowledge is acquired only through experience. Locke used the analogy of the *tabula rasa*, or "blank slate": the mind begins as a blank sheet on which life experiences write our reality (Wolff, 1971).

The line between fact and fiction becomes even more uncertain when we consider the work of German philosopher **Immanuel Kant**. In his *Critique of Pure Reason* (1781) Kant argued that we never have knowledge of reality: rather, our mind forms appearances of reality, and our ways of acquiring knowledge are simply the mental filters through which the mind processes and constructs our reality. Thus, it is possible for two researchers looking at the same phenomenon but working within two different *paradigms* (i.e. frameworks, or sets of underlying assumptions) to produce considerably different accounts. The situation is not unlike a trial at which the Crown and defence teams each bring in their own experts to testify. Each team believes its experts' knowledge to be superior to and more credible than the other's. Yet all the experts are speaking on the same subject. So who is telling the "truth"? Since they are testifying under oath, we must assume that they all are.

It is beyond the scope of this chapter to debate the strengths and weaknesses of the philosophical positions outlined above. Still, they serve as reminders that what we believe to be concrete facts may be only perceptions or illusions, and that there may be a greater reality that we have not yet seen. If there can be no single objective truth—only multiple theories reflecting the different beliefs that scientists hold—then reality can be described as consisting of multiple paradigms. However, scientific paradigms are subject to constant scrutiny, and when the prevailing model is overwhelmed by new findings, the discipline experiences what Thomas Kuhn (1970) called a paradigm shift. In the case of criminology, our understanding was once dominated by the legal and sociological perspectives. As we have gained more empirical knowledge about crime and criminality, however, we have seen a shift toward a more interdisciplinary approach that embraces additional perspectives from psychology, biology, and political science (Barak, 2009; Walsh & Ellis, 2007).

**rationalism**
The principle that some kinds of knowledge are innate and others can be acquired through reasoning, independent of experience.

**empiricism**
The principle that knowledge is acquired only through experience.

**paradigm shift**
A fundamental change in the prevailing model or theoretical orientation.

## BOX 2.1 — REALITY CHECK

### Canada's Crime Rate Is Falling—So Why Worry?

In a Forum Poll conducted for the *National Post* in 2012, 54 per cent of respondents said they believed the rate of violent crime in Canada was increasing (Edmiston, 2012). Yet as Table 2.1 illustrates, in 2014, the number of Criminal Code incidents (excluding traffic violations) recorded in Canada was less than 1.8 million—down from 2.4 million in 2004—and the official crime rate was the lowest since 1969. In fact, in the 10-year period from 2004 to 2014, the crime rate in Canada dropped by roughly 34 per cent, from 7,600 incidents per 100,000 population to 5,046 per 100,000.

Why, then, do people seem to have the wrong impression about crime?

Among the possible explanations are media stories that devote considerable attention to sensational violent crimes. As McCormick (2013) reports, the coverage is not always reflective of the official incident rate. These incidents, newsworthy because they are so rare, tend to dominate the headlines, leaving little room for coverage of far more common nonviolent and non-conventional crimes. This sort of media coverage can spark a moral panic (defined on page 36 of this chapter) and public anxiety out of proportion to the rate of the reported incidents. Consider, in this vein, human trafficking, which has been given extensive media coverage lately even though the rate of incidence is extremely low relative to other kinds of crime (Todres, 2015).

Which of the following, if any, do you think most contribute to public concerns over violent crime:

- Governments and public agencies (police services, the RCMP, CSIS, etc.)?
- Think tanks and public policy groups with a tough-on-crime agenda?
- Companies that market and sell security products and services?
- Crime-based TV shows?
- The Internet?

What other agencies and factors shape public perceptions of crime?

| Table 2.1 Annual Criminal Code Violations in Canada, 2004–2014 | | | | | | | | | | |
|---|---|---|---|---|---|---|---|---|---|---|
| | 2004 | 2005 | 2006 | 2007 | 2008 | 2009 | 2010 | 2011 | 2012 | 2013 | 2014 |
| Actual incidents | 2,427,370 | 2,361,974 | 2,359,804 | 2,271,754 | 2,204,479 | 2,172,809 | 2,094,338 | 1,984,790 | 1,957,227 | 1,826,431 | 1,793,534 |
| Rate per 100,000 population | 7,599.62 | 7,325.04 | 7,245.22 | 6,907.56 | 6,630.85 | 6,461.2 | 6,158.86 | 5,779.35 | 5,631.96 | 5,195.47 | 5,046.46 |

Note: Does not include traffic violations.
*Source:* Statistics Canada (2014), CANSIM Table 252-0051: Incident-based crime statistics, by detailed violations.

So, again we come back to the importance of knowing. Criminology, like any area of scientific inquiry, is a collection of information about a particular set of phenomena that forms a knowledge base. This knowledge base becomes the foundation for formulating or testing theories, making policy recommendations, and issuing social and political responses to criminological concerns.

As noted in the previous chapter, crime is evolutive, meaning that what constitutes a crime can change over time as a society's values and beliefs change. For example, consensual homosexual activity was once considered a crime; now same-sex marriage is legal across Canada. Meanwhile, smoking in public places is now prohibited in many jurisdictions, and in some places it is illegal to ride a bicycle without wearing a helmet. In short, what is considered a crime depends on the time and place.

Consider the following example. On Sundays in Indonesia, it is illegal to express affection in public; doing so can result in a prison sentence. But if you were to visit the beautiful open squares of Rome on a warm Sunday, you would likely see many couples displaying their affection in public. Similarly, in Canada such expressions are not sanctionable unless they violate public conduct regulations. We can draw two conclusions from this. First, our knowledge of crime is limited by our knowledge of social and cultural values around the world. Second, the concept of crime is relative to time, place, culture, and values. In other words, there are no absolutes about our knowledge of what constitutes a crime.

The consumption of certain substances is another example. Today alcoholism is widely considered a disease, but at the turn of the twentieth century it was seen as a moral failing (Schlaadt, 1992). In Canada, the 1878 Dominion Temperance Act gave local jurisdictions the right to vote "dry" (Hatch, 1995), and during the First World War, alcohol was banned across Canada as part of the war effort. Most provinces repealed their prohibition laws in the 1920s, however, and by the 1960s, ads promoting alcohol consumption as a central part of any social occasion were standard. Meanwhile, during the period when alcohol consumption was discouraged, it was legal to consume drugs such as marijuana. In fact, Coca-Cola originally contained ingredients derived from both kola nuts (hence "cola") and cocaine ("coca"). Kola nuts (and cocaine) are currently on the International Olympic Committee's list of banned substances because of their stimulant effects, and Coca-Cola today is free of cocaine from coca and caffeine from kola nuts. The popular soft drink does, however, contain substantial amounts of sugar and caffeine, both of which are legal despite their addictive properties (Fishbein & Pease, 1996).

In summary, our perceptions of crime involve a complex interplay of the facts available to us and the choices we make as to which of them, if any, we will believe and how strongly,

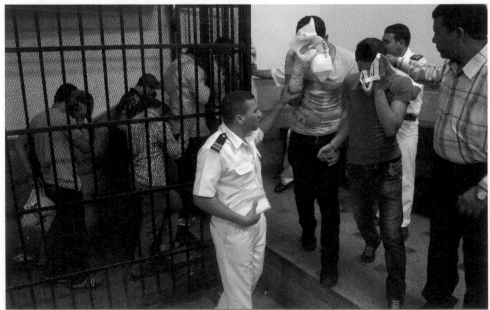

AP Photo/Hassan Ammar

Law is contextual to time, place, culture, and values. For example, in this photo, eight men leave the defendants' cage in a courtroom in Cairo, Egypt, having been convicted of "inciting debauchery" after they appeared in a video of an alleged same-sex wedding party.

based on our experience, values, and norms. We have also seen that what may appear factually accurate in one place and time may later be disproved. The weight we give to these competing perspectives helps determine whether and why we might choose to respond to some crimes and not to others.

## Acquiring Knowledge on Crime

With the line between fact and fiction already obscure and subject to change, the problem of gaining understanding is further complicated by the fact that we are exposed to an endless flow of information on a seemingly endless variety of subjects. How can we make sense of it all? In general, there are five basic means by which we acquire information and gain understanding. Unfortunately, each of them has flaws that makes it unreliable if used on its own.

### 1. Logical Reasoning

We often form conclusions based on what we believe to be logical speculation. For example, we might reason that too much free time leads to boredom, then speculate that deviant activity alleviates boredom, and on those grounds conclude that idleness leads to crime. However, our reasoning may be undermined by such factors as limited knowledge, our personal biases, and our capacity to ignore contradictions in our thinking.

### 2. Authority

When an authority (such as a parent, a teacher, or an "expert") says that something is so, we often accept it as fact. Using an expert to affirm our belief lends credibility to it. Yet research shows that, just as we tend to seek out friends with whom we feel a "connection," so we tend to seek out those experts with whom we can identify and whose views already align with our own.

### 3. Consensus

We often rely on the wisdom of our peer group. However, the people who make up that group are likely to be people who have come together because they share a common view. Even those group members who do not share the common view may be unwilling to challenge other group members. A number of years ago, Kidder and Judd (1986, p. 15) observed that "groups of people can be notoriously poor as independent judges," because they tend to want to reach consensus rather than appearing conflictual or combative. For an illustration of this dynamic, see the movie *12 Angry Men* (1957, or the 1997 made-for-TV remake).

### 4. Observation

Suppose you have heard from your peers that a certain instructor is very demanding. Not wanting to rely on their opinion, you decide to sit in on a class to see for yourself. Although in this case you are not relying entirely on the opinion of your peers, it will already have influenced your view, and since your observation may be limited to a single class, your assessment is still unlikely to be objective.

### 5. Past Experience

This is the most common source of support for our hypotheses. We draw on prior instances or events that confirm our assumptions and then attempt to modify incongruent elements. For

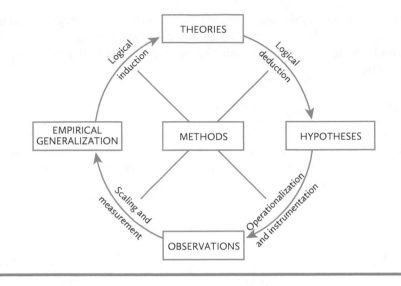

**Figure 2.1    The Research Cycle**

*Source*: Reprinted with permission from Walter L. Wallace, *Sociological Theory: An Introduction* (New York: Aldine de Gruyter). Copyright 1969, Walter L. Wallace. In Miller & Whitehead, 1996:15.

example, if you were a victim of a robbery while walking alone late at night in a brightly lit area of town, you might not feel safe even though research suggests that such risk is low if the area is well lit. Studies have shown that information that is consistent with our expectations is more easily remembered than information that is not. Thus it is generally "unlikely that hypotheses will be disconfirmed by recollected observations" (Kidder & Judd, 1986, p. 17).

These "naive" methods of acquiring information can result in misconceptions because they are not objective or systematic in their approach—in other words, they are not *scientific*. By contrast, scientific inquiry relies on the collection of measurable data from representative samples and rigorous testing of hypotheses using prescribed research methods. Figure 2.1 provides a model of the scientific method of inquiry. The model is circular to indicate that knowledge is a process of continually retesting and refining our understanding of the phenomenon in question. Theories are repeatedly tested under different conditions to see whether they stand up to objective evaluation over time. Theories that do stand-up tend to become the dominant perspectives among researchers.

We will look closely at the tools of scientific inquiry in Chapter 3. Over the remainder of this chapter, we will examine public perceptions of crime in more detail.

## Factors That Shape Public Perceptions of Crime

In Box 2.1 you were asked to think about some of the factors that influence the way the public views crime. This section examines four major influences on public attitudes regarding criminal activity and behaviour:

1.  personal knowledge
2.  the mass media
3.  official state knowledge
4.  theoretical knowledge

We will look at each of these in turn, beginning with personal knowledge.

| BOX 2.2 | WHAT DO YOU THINK? |
| --- | --- |

## Which Are Canada's Safest Cities?

Take a moment to rank the following eight Canadian census metropolitan areas (CMAs) from safest (1) to least safe (8), based only on what you know or believe of each city.

_____ Calgary, Alberta
_____ Edmonton, Alberta
_____ Halifax, Nova Scotia
_____ Quebec City, Quebec
_____ Regina, Saskatchewan
_____ St John's, Newfoundland and Labrador
_____ Thunder Bay, Ontario
_____ Toronto, Ontario

If you said you'd feel safest in Quebec City, you're right—at least, according to Statistics Canada's violent crime severity index (Boyce, Cotter, & Perreault, 2013, p. 30). The crime severity index, or CSI, differs from the traditional crime rate by accounting for the seriousness, as well as the volume, of crime. Quebec City is one of three cities in this list with violent CSI scores below the national average. The others are Calgary and Toronto.

The least safe of these cities, based on violent CSI scores, is Thunder Bay, followed by Regina and Edmonton.

Halifax and St John's round out the top five, all with CSI scores above the national average.

Here are the eight cities, from safest to least safe, with their violent CSI scores.

| | | |
| --- | --- | --- |
| 1 | Quebec City | **48.3** |
| 2 | Calgary | **62.0** |
| 3 | Toronto | **68.2** |
| | *CANADA* | ***73.7*** |
| 4 | Halifax | **84.8** |
| 5 | St John's | **79.5** |
| 6 | Edmonton | **89.7** |
| 7 | Regina | **105.8** |
| 8 | Thunder Bay | **110.9** |

For the full list, see Boyce, Cotter, & Perreault (2014).

Which of the five methods outlined on pages 29 to 30—logical reasoning, authority, consensus, observation, past experience—did you use to rank the cities initially? Were they reliable, based on your success in assessing the safety of the eight cities?

How reliable do you think a statistic like the crime severity index is in assessing the overall safety of a city? To accurately judge the safety of a city, what other kinds of information would you want to have?

## 1. Personal Knowledge

The public has been described as the hidden element of the criminal justice system (Griffiths & Verdun-Jones, 1994). In many cases, through public opinion polls, media stories, and activist groups, the public has a voice in decisions about the administration of criminal justice. And since the administration of justice is seen as a crucial role of government, the government in power has a vested interest in responding to the public's will. As a result, public perception can have a dramatic impact on the criminal justice system.

A case in point involved a 13-year-old Calgary student, Ryan Garrioch, who was killed in his schoolyard by another youth. Public anger over the incident led to a change in the Young Offenders Act (YOA), with the penalty for young offenders convicted of murder increased from 7 to 10 years. In 1999, the government tabled a bill to replace the YOA with new legislation, the Youth Criminal Justice Act (YCJA), which came into force in 2003. The revised act promoted various social values—greater accountability and personal responsibility for crimes, and increased emphasis on offender rehabilitation and reintegration into society—in an attempt to stem public criticism and restore confidence in the criminal justice system. Declining public confidence in the CJS prompted a review of Canada's justice system and its sentencing practices, led by MP David Daubney. *Taking Responsibility: Report of the Standing Committee on Justice and Solicitor General on Its Review of Sentencing, Conditional Release and Related Aspects of Corrections* (1988), otherwise known as the Daubney Report, was one of the first of now many Canadian studies to take into account the impressions expressed by the public in the media.

Despite the public's undeniable interest in crime, Sanders and Roberts (2004) have found that most Canadians have limited knowledge of actual crime rates, tend to overestimate the incidence of violent crime, and are ill informed about other key aspects of criminal justice functions. This might explain why the public continues to express a low level of satisfaction with the CJS, even as improvements are being made. In 2014, an internal Justice Department report revealed that a majority of Canadians have little confidence in either the courts (too slow in delivering justice and too lenient in sentencing) or the prison system (not doing a good job of rehabilitating offenders). Similar surveys in Australia, New Zealand, and the United States have consistently shown that the public has an inaccurate and negative view of crime trends in their respective countries (Paulin, Searle, & Knaggs, 2003).

Public perception of the risk of being victimized by crime varies according to age, gender, occupation, lifestyle, and a variety of personal attributes (Karmen, 1996; Perreault & Brennan, 2010). Although most Canadians feel relatively safe from crime, women, according to Brennan (2011), tend to feel less safe when alone at night, and seniors are more fearful of being victimized than those in younger age groups. Because of their fear, some people use sophisticated car and house alarms or carry protective devices such as pepper spray and personal alarms. Although residential burglaries have continued to decline since the mid-1990s (see Chapter 9), a break-in still occurs every 90 seconds in Canada (King, 2011). Gannon and Taylor-Butts (2006) point out that the decline in break-ins in Canada can be explained in part by an increase in the use of home security devices and services, suggesting that this response to the perceived risk of being victimized has been somewhat successful in mitigating personal risk.

Since the 1980s, there have been several large-scale Canadian studies of victimization. Brillon (1987), Fattah and Sacco (1989), and Ogrodnick (2007, 2008) examined victimization among the elderly. These studies have shown, among other findings, that actual victimization of seniors and older Canadians was low, but that seniors' fear levels were raised by feelings of fragility and vulnerability reflecting factors such as declining health, reduced income, and lack of information about actual risks. (A fuller account of this research will be given in Chapter 4.)

Prior to Brillon's study, very little research had been conducted on the victimization of the elderly. More recently, studies of elder abuse and other forms of elder victimization have been growing, giving crime researchers a greater body of data on crime as it affects older citizens. We now know, for example, that the elderly are more likely to be victimized at, or near, their homes than are other age groups. At the same time, although many older people believe they are likely to become victims of crime, Ogrodnick (2007) observed that seniors are significantly less likely to encounter violent crime than are younger age groups (see also Figure 2.2). While people aged 65 and older made up roughly 16 per cent of the Canadian population in 2013, they were victims of just 3 per cent of all violent crimes. About half of these involved minor assaults (Ogrodnick, 2007).

Even though we should not view the problem lightly, Canadian critical criminologist Brian MacLean (1986) argued that, from the perspective of the state, growing awareness of victimization may well represent an excuse for net widening: extending the "net" of social control. He notes, for example, that spending on criminal justice tends to increase at a faster pace than other state expenditures. Based on a 2012 Parliamentary Budget Office report, the trend does not appear to have abated, as the per capita spending on the CJS rose from approximately $400 per capita in 2002 to $480 in 2012 (in 2002 dollars).

There are two sides to social reality: the reality perceived by the public, and the one perceived by criminology researchers and criminal justice officials. The challenge for criminologists is to try to determine which reality is more plausible and how to balance the two perspectives. This is why virtually all criminologists ground their research in theoretical principles and empirical data.

**net widening**
The process by which the state expands its control over behaviour through changes to sentencing laws and administrative policies.

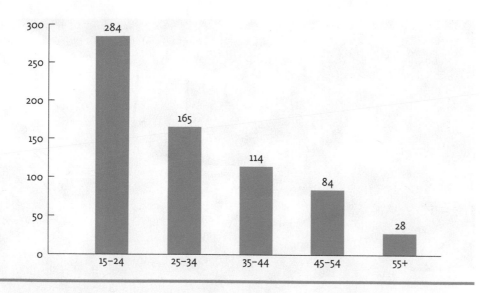

**Figure 2.2    Self-Reported Rate of Violent Victimization by Age Group, Canada 2009**

*Source*: Data from Statistics Canada, General Social Survey, 2009.  Self-reported violent victimization and theft of personal property by selected demographic characteristics, 2009

## 2. The Mass Media

> *All I know is just what I read in the papers, and that's an alibi for my ignorance.* (Will Rogers, 1879–1973)

Much of what people come to think about current events comes not from direct experience but from media reports. And there are plenty to choose from. Many radio stations broadcast news at least once every hour. On television, there are several all-news stations, including CNN, CTV, and CBC News Network, plus scores of crime-based dramas, movies, and documentaries. On the Internet, blogs and social networks such as About.me, Facebook, and Twitter make news from around the world accessible 24 hours a day.

In many respects, these media reports, with the exception of those broadcast via social media, reflect our conventional methods of knowing. Television news sources represent authority (in the form of the trusted news anchor), consensus (all outlets tend to cover the same stories from a similar point of view), and observation (the stories are presented with video footage, graphics, or other visuals). At the same time, repetition can make the news seem to be just "more of the same," and the agents responsible for delivering the news—whether on TV, on radio, on the Web, or in print—are constantly challenged to provide more sensational coverage in their competition for viewers' attention.

The effects of news reporting on public perceptions of crime has been a point of interest and concern for criminologists and the public alike for many years. For example, a series of Canadian studies conducted by Ericson, Baranek, and Chan (1987, 1991) found that public perceptions of crime could be shaped by the format of the news coverage, specifically whether it was in print or on television.

The media's presentation of crime and violence may do more than affect public perceptions. Over the years, many institutions, including the Canadian government, have expressed concern about the perceived effects of television and movies on *behaviour*. Social researchers have responded with literally hundreds of studies on the effects of TV violence on children

The dauntless police officer, the hooded delinquent, the intrepid reporter, and even the yellow caution tape are all elements we have come to expect in the media's presentation of crime. What other elements are commonly found in news reports? How do they shape our perceptions of crime?

and adolescents, and certain facts are fairly consistent. For example, according to one study, children and young people may

- become immune or desensitized to the horror of violence;
- gradually accept violence as a way to resolve problems;
- imitate the violence they observe on TV; and
- identify with certain characters, victims, and/or victimizers (American Academy of Child and Adolescent Psychiatry, 2011).

The study points out that practical factors such as lower amounts of viewing time and greater amounts of parental supervision can mitigate the influence of TV violence. Another study is worth noting here: Huesmann and a team of colleagues (2003) conducted a 15-year longitudinal study that found that violent TV viewing by children aged 6–9 caused them to identify with aggressive TV characters. Not only that, but there was a strong correlation between violent TV viewing in childhood and aggression later in life. The study suggests that childhood TV viewing habits can predict violent behaviour in adulthood.

Among the first to demonstrate a link between watching and performing violence was the influential Alberta-born social psychologist Albert Bandura. In a series of then unique experiments, Bandura (1979) found that violent behaviour is learned through symbolic modelling. Drawing on the principles of social learning theory (discussed in Chapter 7), Bandura observed that children readily imitated behaviour they observed on television and in controlled video presentations. This process is known as *vicarious reinforcement*. The theory asserts that our social environment contributes to the learning process. According to this line of reasoning, therefore, it is possible to learn not only from those around us, but also from what we gather from the vast array of multimedia sources to which we have access.

Thinkstock/Digital Vision/Getty

---

**BOX 2.3     FACTS AND FIGURES** GOVERNMENT STUDIES ON MEDIA VIOLENCE, 1975–2000

---

Concerns about the effects of television violence on young people are almost as old as television itself. In June 1952, long before TV sets became a fixture in most Canadian homes, the US House Interstate and Foreign Commerce Subcommittee held a congressional hearing on the impact of violence in radio and television on American children (Alter, 1997). The following are some of the milestones in Canadian government research and action on the topic during the late twentieth century, when public concerns about violent TV were particularly high.

- 1977: The Ontario Royal Commission on Violence in the Communications Industry releases a report showing a connection between violence in the media and the incidence of violent crimes in society.
- October 1980: The Standing Senate Committee on Health, Welfare and Science, having studied early childhood experiences as causes of criminal behaviour, recommends that the Canadian Radio-television and Telecommunications Commission (CRTC) and the CBC take steps to ensure a high standard in children's programming.

- May 1992: The CRTC releases two violence studies—*Scientific Knowledge about Television Violence* and *Summary and Analysis of Various Studies on Violence and Television*—initiated following the December 1989 shooting of 14 women at Montreal's École Polytechnique.
- June 1993: The House of Commons Standing Committee on Communications and Culture releases its report *Television Violence: Fraying Our Social Fabric*, which concludes that the problem should be addressed by all stakeholders—parents, government, and industry—on a voluntary basis and with minimal legislative intervention.
- June 1997: The CRTC approves a new classification system for violence in television programming and commits to making V-chip technology available to Canadian consumers and to introducing onscreen displays of program-rating icons to help parents regulate their children's television viewing habits.

Source: Alter, 1997.

---

The research is not as one-sided as these studies would indicate. There are, in fact, studies that show violent media images have no effect on behaviour. The lack of congruence in the literature reflects not only the different intellectual backgrounds of the authors but also practical and methodological limitations of their studies. These include limited ability to control for elements such as the individual characteristics of the viewers/readers studied.

The media's coverage of crime is shaped in part by the fact that people are more inclined to pay attention to stories that fit their frame of reference. Thus, the media have a stake in reinforcing ideas that are familiar to the public, even if they are not accurate. Since most people have limited experience with crime, this means that the media tend to perpetuate public misconceptions (see, generally, Roeder, Eisen, & Bowling, 2015).

*Crime: A Growing Concern*

Since the 1960s, there has been a dramatic growth in media coverage of crime (Surette, 2015). Is this due to an increase in crime, or does it simply reflect the fact that sensational crime stories sell? What type of crime stories do you typically hear or read about? Is the coverage representative of the picture offered by official sources? If not, what concerns or issues might that raise regarding our understanding of crime?

A report prepared at Columbia University's School of Journalism in New York points out that despite declining levels of violent crime since the mid-1990s, the media's reporting "is not reflective of the actual crime rates" (Tiegreen & Newman, 2009). Although there is no comparably recent Canadian research on the topic, similar results were reported in the late 1990s by the conservative think tank the Fraser Institute (Fraser Forum, 1996).

**moral panic**
Widespread exaggerated
public concern over
issues associated
with morality
(e.g. prostitution,
pornography).

Moral panic is a sociological term used to describe the widespread, exaggerated concern that can take hold of the public over issues associated with morality, such as prostitution, pornography, or gambling. News media have sometimes been accused of causing moral panic by publishing sensationalistic accounts of such issues. For example, in a 2013 *National Post* article, the author points out that although former Toronto Mayor Rob Ford was beset by a range of issues, including alcohol abuse, obesity, and reckless behaviour, it was his admitted use of crack cocaine that appeared to cause the greatest sense of scandal among the city's residents (Brean, 2013).

Another Canadian case that attracted intense media coverage was the 2013 killing of Jun Lin by Luka Magnotta. After murdering the Chinese student and then dismembering his body, Magnotta mailed parts of the body to several elementary schools and federal political party offices. Prior to the killing, Magnotta had already attracted media attention when he claimed to have dated Karla Holmolka, the former partner of serial killer and rapist Paul Bernardo.

From a criminological standpoint, it may be interesting to explore the relationship between the frequency with which people are exposed to news media and their perceptions of crime. David Grossman and Gloria DeGaetano (1999), for example, argue that as a society we have become desensitized to violence through media exposure. Likewise, Steven Chermak (1995) suggests that our reading of crime news has become little more than a "ritual moral exercise" that is not dissimilar to other routines we engage in, such as exercising or having our morning coffee. Yet only a few decades ago, an Ontario-based study reported that there was a significant relationship "between media use and perceptions of crime seriousness" (Geboyts, Roberts, & DasGupta, 1988, p. 3). In other words, the more people watched television news, for example, the more likely they were to perceive crime as serious (see also Tiegreen & Newman, 2009). The researchers also found that women and those respondents who had not been victimized within the previous year expressed greater fear than did men and recent victims. Geboyts et al. reaffirmed the findings of earlier Canadian studies by Akman and Normandeau (1967), Sacco (1982), and, more generally, the views expressed by the former Canadian Coalition Against Violent Entertainment (1991–7) and the Coalition for Responsible Television (1995–9). What was not taken into account were any possible social, economic, or demographic variables other than gender.

In 1991, Martinez presented a report to the CRTC based on analysis of hundreds of studies linking radio and television violence to individual aggression and violent crime. In particular, the report noted that children were especially affected by media violence (Martinez, as cited in Barbara, 1995). In a follow-up study done 30 years after their initial study, Huesmann et al. (2003) found that people who had watched violent television in their youth had become less sensitive to the pain and suffering of others, more fearful of the world around them, and more likely to behave in aggressive or harmful ways toward others. A meta-analysis conducted by Anderson and Bushman (2001) came to a similar conclusion. However, their report points out that adults can also be affected by media violence because it tends to erode their ability to socialize and stunt their moral development.

At the same time, the amount of time Canadians spend watching television or online media content has only increased. During the late 1970s and early 1980s, when research into the connection between violent TV viewing and aggressive behaviour was taking off, the amount of violent content on television increased by more than 30 per cent, according to the former Canadian Coalition Against Violent Entertainment and the Coalition for Responsible Television (CRTC, 1996). More recently, Caron and his colleagues at the University of Montreal's Centre for Youth and Media Studies (2010) reported that Canadians viewed nearly 23 hours of television per week; that almost half (48 per cent) of young people aged 8–15 had their own TV sets; and that preschoolers (aged 2–6) watched an estimated 19 hours per week—about the same amount as those aged 7–12. The report also points out that there appears to be a strong correlation between the amount of TV viewing and aggressive behaviour. Television viewing has declined since the late 1990s, only to be replaced by the consumption of media content online via tablets and smartphones. Video games are also a concern: in 2007, David Walsh of the American National Institute on Media and the Family reported that youth between the ages of 7 and 17 play video games for an average of eight hours per week. And while many games can help to develop practical problem-solving skills, a growing number of games have less social merit, appealing mainly to young people's tendency for vicarious thrill-seeking.

Since we now live in a world filled with portable and readily accessible multimedia sources, including iPads and smartphones with streaming and gaming options, the viewing habits of young people and adults, and the relationship between media and violence, will remain fertile fields for research for many years to come.

---

**BOX 2.4**　　　**WHAT DO YOU THINK?**

## Do Violent Video Games Encourage or Discourage Violent Behaviour?

While the link between television violence and violent behaviour remains a concern for many, perhaps of greater relevance today is the potential impact of violent video games on young people. In 2013, Bajovic and a team of researchers from Brock University studied the effects of playing violent video games on 109 Grade 8 students from seven public schools in Canada who played for a minimum of three hours a day. Using the Sociomoral Reflection Measure, the researchers found that extensive viewing/playing of violent video games had a statistically significant negative impact on the participants' moral reasoning or moral judgement skills (see also Anderson & Dill, 2000, for similar findings). This research combats a popularly held view that violent video games serve as an outlet for aggressive tendencies and thus diminish violent behaviour.

How much gaming do you do? How much of your gaming would you consider to be violent? Do you feel that it has had any negative impact on you? Is it possible it has had a positive impact? Explain.

Do you think that exposure to violent images through video games desensitizes children and teenagers to violence? Do you think it can affect future behaviour?

© David Grossman / Alamy Stock Photo

*Antisocial Behaviour and Multimedia Viewing*

It cannot be denied that many television programs and video games contain violence in one form or another, whether physical, verbal, or (occasionally) symbolic. Moreover, it is natural to believe that violent media content has some influence on our perceptions and performance of violence. As former CRTC chair Keith Spicer remarked, "common sense tells us that this must be true. . . . Why else do advertisers spend millions on television commercials if there is no impact on our behaviour?" (as quoted in Murphy, 1995, p. 109). Yet even though there have now been hundreds of studies published worldwide on violent entertainment (Kaplan, 2012), the findings of this research have been neither conclusive nor wholly consistent. Collectively, at least, the evidence points to a relationship between the viewing of violence and subsequent maladaptive behaviour. Even if there is no direct link, some experts suggest that the cumulative effect of such exposure can be harmful to future behaviour. And although television viewing has declined since 1995 (TV Basics, 2014), Canadians are spending more time participating in interactive activities on the Internet. As a result, TV networks such as the CBC are turning to Facebook, Reddit, and Twitter to make watching TV more interactive (Oliveira, 2013). What impact multimedia sources will have on behaviour remains to be seen. However, there is a growing concern about the availability of child pornography online and the proliferation of material that is difficult to censor.

Understanding how the public forms its perceptions of criminological issues is important, as those perceptions can have an impact on criminal justice policy and practices. In 2012, for example, the Calgary Police Association placed an ad in a local paper with the caption, "We have just one police officer for every 674 Calgarians." It seems clear the police were trying to gain public support in their fight for increased funding by appealing to the public perception that crime is increasing with amid cutbacks to police resources. The ad began by citing lower police-to-resident ratios in most other major Canadian cities. And while it acknowledged the high levels of satisfaction that Calgarians expressed toward the police, it offered the ominous warning that unless things changed, "sooner or later, something's got to give." Interestingly, the ad neglected to mention that there was no research supporting the premise that increases in the number of police officers reduce crime, decrease wait times, or improve overall service.

The police have also worked with the public through initiatives such as Crime Stoppers. However, while most Crime Stoppers programs have had considerable success (see Box 2.5), TV programs such as *America's Most Wanted* and *American Justice* may serve to create inaccurate perceptions of crime seriousness and increase public fear levels, while promoting the sale of unnecessary security devices. For criminologists trying to understand the roots of public perceptions of crime, these shows have both theoretical and ethical implications, and raise further questions about the role of the media as social and political instruments in the fight against crime.

### Table 2.2   Number of Residents per Police Officer in Canadian CMAs, 2012

| Census Metropolitan Area | Number of residents per police officer |
|---|---|
| Winnipeg, MB | 505.05 |
| Thunder Bay, ON | 526.32 |
| Regina, SK | 526.32 |
| Saint John, NB | 529.10 |
| Saskatoon, SK | 558.66 |
| St John's, NL | 561.80 |
| Montreal, QC | 561.80 |
| Windsor, ON | 561.80 |
| Brantford, ON | 571.43 |
| Toronto, ON | 578.03 |
| Halifax, NS | 584.80 |
| St Catharines–Niagara, ON | 606.06 |
| Calgary, AB | 609.76 |
| Vancouver, BC | 613.50 |
| Edmonton, AB | 621.12 |
| Greater Sudbury, ON | 621.12 |
| Barrie, ON | 641.03 |
| London, ON | 649.35 |
| Guelph, ON | 649.35 |
| Peterborough, ON | 649.35 |
| Hamilton, ON | 653.59 |
| Victoria, BC | 657.89 |
| Kitchener-Cambridge-Waterloo, ON | 662.25 |
| Ottawa , ON | 675.68 |
| Abbotsford-Mission, BC | 680.27 |
| Kingston, ON | 689.66 |
| Gatineau, QC | 714.29 |
| Sherbrooke, QC | 763.36 |
| Quebec, QC | 763.36 |
| Trois-Rivières, QC | 793.65 |
| Saguenay, QC | 813.00 |
| Kelowna, QC | 884.96 |
| Moncton, NB | 952.38 |

*Source:* Adapted from Statistics Canada, 2013a. Calculated from http://www.statcan.gc.ca/pub/85-225-x/2012000/t003-eng.htm.

---

| BOX 2.5 | **A CLOSER LOOK**<br>**Crime Stoppers: A Community Effort** |

In July 1976, in Albuquerque, New Mexico, a university student was killed during a gas station robbery. After nearly two months of investigation, police were unable to come up with any leads. Then detective Greg MacAleese obtained permission to re-enact the crime on a local television station. A reward was offered to anyone who could provide information leading to an arrest. Within 72 hours of the broadcast the police had enough leads to arrest the two men responsible for the killing. This was the beginning of Crime Stoppers.

Today there are more than 950 Crime Stoppers programs worldwide. On its website, Crime Stoppers International notes that since it was first founded, it has helped police recover more than $10 billion in drugs and property while clearing more than 1 million cases—equivalent to solving a crime every 14 minutes, somewhere in the world. Most major cities in Canada have a Crime Stoppers tip line and use television, radio, newspaper bulletins to seek public assistance with unsolved cases and wanted persons. Increasingly, Crime Stoppers is now also using online platforms such as YouTube, Twitter, and Facebook to disseminate its appeals. In Canada, rewards of up to $2,000 are offered to anyone providing information leading to an arrest. All informants can remain anonymous if they wish. Funds for the project are supported by donations of money, goods, or services from the community.

In Canada, Crime Stoppers currently serves over 4,000 communities through its 107 programs, operated mostly by citizen volunteers working closely with local police departments. The fact that Crime Stoppers operates in every Canadian province and territory points to the public's willingness to assist in combatting crime and improving public safety; it is also proof of the willingness of law enforcement agencies to work closely with the public.

Crimestoppers/ DDB, Toronto, Canada

How effective do you find this advertisement for Crime Stoppers? Would it make you more willing to report a crime? Why or why not?

What limitations or challenges might Crime Stoppers face? For example, do you think it works equally for all types of offences? What factors might affect the program's effectiveness?

---

### Crime and the Media: Theoretical Explanations

Basing his argument on the principles of **conflict theory** (see Chapter 8), Richard Quinney (1970) argued that the media are agents of a capitalistic society that interpret social reality in terms of interpersonal violence and property crimes. He further argued that the media were responsible for conveying an image of rapidly increasing crime rates. His arguments have been supported by the **left-realist** perspective in the writings of Jock Young (1986, 2002) and others. It can be said that collectively, the media play a significant role in society in crime control policy "because they have the power to decide what issues are worthy of public consumption" (Chermak, 1995, p. 167). Do the media really have this much influence? In his study of Satanism in Canada, Lippert (1990) suggested that what was widely perceived to problem in the late 1980s might have been nothing more than a media-fed illusion (see also

**conflict theory**

A theoretical perspective that views crime as a natural product of a society that promotes competition and, hence, social and economic disparity.

**left-realism**

A theoretical perspective that aims to better understand the implications of crime control policies rather than the causes of crime.

the discussion of satanic ritual abuse in Chapter 7). If the media are so influential, where do we draw the boundaries of freedom of speech? Should the media be subject to government censorship? Should they monitor themselves? Where does individual responsibility for interpreting media messages come into play?

It was to help parents screen out sex and violence on television that V-chip technology was invented in the early 1990s (credit is generally given to Simon Fraser University engineering professor Tim Collings). In 1996, American president Bill Clinton signed a law requiring all new television sets to have a V-chip by 1998; the Canadian Radio-television and Telecommunications Commission began to require the use of V-chip program-blocking technology in 2000; today, most televisions, analog and digital, include it. However, a 2007 American study found that less than 20 per cent of families knew they had a V-chip and even fewer used it (Federal Communications Commission, 2007). This raises questions about the soundness of the research that went into the government decision to require the V-chip, since few households appear to have taken advantage of the technology.

In defence of the media, few if any studies have ever proven that media exposure to violence "causes" violent behaviour. The difficulties in studying the impact of the media include understanding how people respond to different channels of information (radio versus newsprint versus television versus the Internet), which ones they prefer, how their personal experiences have influenced their views, and what their state of emotional and physiological arousal is at the time of receiving the media information (see e.g. Cho, Reimer, & McComas, 2015). The challenge of forming an objective assessment of the media's influence on public perceptions of crime is analogous to the difficulty of selecting a jury for a case that has been widely publicized in the media: when almost everyone has heard something about a case, it can be difficult to find twelve people who will be truly objective.

## 3. Official State Knowledge

Within the criminal justice system, there are three primary sources of official data:

- the police
- the judicial system
- the corrections system

As we will see in Chapter 3, these three bodies are required by law to produce information, typically in the form of statistics, that is used largely to measure their performance. The collection and dissemination of this information is thus a form of public accountability. Much of the statistical and general information used by the media and criminologists comes from these primary sources. For example, the federal justice department regularly issues press releases covering a wide range of subjects and information requests. In addition, the Canadian Centre for Justice Statistics (CCJS) annually publishes information service bulletins under the title Juristat. These publications summarize information on a broad range of topics, including criminal justice expenditures, violent offences among young offenders, and issues related to law enforcement, sentencing, and correctional practices, to name just a few. Unfortunately, all these sources have inherent limitations.

### Limitations of Official Data

Whatever the phenomenon in question, measurement is always subject to limitations. These limitations affect both the reliability of the data (i.e. does the instrument measure the phenomenon consistently each time?) and its validity (i.e. does the instrument measure what and only what it is supposed to measure?). A crucial factor in any survey project is sampling.

**Juristat**
A regular publication of the Canadian Centre for Justice Statistics, considered the most authoritative source of criminal justice statistics in Canada.

**reliability**
The likelihood that an observed relationship between two or more variables can or will be observed in a consistent manner.

**validity**
The likelihood that the relationships observed and measured are real.

**sampling**
The process of selecting a group of research subjects that is representative of the entire population under investigation.

**Random error** refers to unintentional or unexpected mistakes made during the data collection process. For example, all municipalities are required to report counts of the same criminal offences to Statistics Canada. However, differences in administration, variable enforcement practices, and even human error can inadvertently affect the way criminal offences are counted and reported. One way to minimize the significance of random error is to use a sample large enough that any random errors have little impact on the overall results.

**Systematic error** refers to predictable errors made during the data collection process. For example, when recording crime data, municipalities need to be sensitive to details such as the fact that property crimes are less likely to be reported than are more serious violent crimes. Thus, researchers know that the margin of error for officially recorded property crimes is greater than that for serious violent offences. Researchers studying the incidence of crime in a particular area must be aware of such differences in reporting so they can interpret their findings accordingly.

Measuring crime data at different times can also lead to interpretative errors. For example, consider the history of cannabis in Canada. For centuries, hemp fibre, which comes from the stalk of the plant, was used to make rope and sails, and farmers in Canada were encouraged, first by the French regime and later by the British, to grow cannabis as an economical and durable building material. During the nineteenth century, a different strain of cannabis was developed for medicinal use, and it is the variety of the plant that also came to be used as a recreational drug. By the 1920s, the Canadian social reformer Emily Murphy was condemning marijuana comparable to narcotics such as opium in terms of the dangers is posed for society. Her campaign may have helped to persuade the federal government to criminalize all cannabis, including hemp, in the Opium and Narcotic Drug Act of 1923. The current maximum penalties for cannabis trafficking are 5 years less a day for quantities up to 3 kilograms, and life for larger quantities. In short, the political and legal contexts surrounding cannabis possession in Canada have varied significantly over time; thus to understand the meaning of data on the subject, it is essential to know the context in which the data were collected.

Similar examples can be found for prostitution (Lowman, 1995), murder (Boyd, 1991; Sinha, 2013), and crimes against women (Boritch, 1997; Sinha, 2013), and for official crime data more generally. In fact, whenever you examine crime statistics that span a significant period of time, you are likely to find that data have not been reported and recorded in the same manner from year to year. The variations may be the result of administrative changes, changes in the law, or some other intervening variable that is not necessarily evident. Overlooking such differences in the data can lead to serious errors in interpretation.

Another factor that can affect the interpretation of crime data is the so-called **crime funnel**: the fact that the number of cases processed decreases at successive levels of the criminal justice system. At the broad top of the funnel are the police, who for most offenders represent the point of contact with the system. Whether the offence proceeds to the next stage of the system, the courts, depends on whether or not the police lay a charge. Then, depending on the decision of the courts the case may or may not proceed beyond the court to corrections. Figure 2.3 shows how statistics on sexual assault can change, depending on which level of the "funnel" the numbers come from.

The reliability of crime data collected by municipalities can thus be affected by inconsistent reporting practices, technical and human errors, and even bias and political manipulation. These "information contaminants" carry potential risks for interpreting data at different levels of the system. Fortunately, steps can be taken to identify potential pitfalls. Researchers need to be familiar with the characteristics of their crime statistics in order to make sound comparisons and draw valid conclusions. It is important to be aware, however, that no matter how diligently data are collected or how carefully they are analyzed, crime statistics are at best only suggestive in what they reveal about crime. It is also important to recognize that

**random error**
An error in data collection that occurs because of an intervening variable that could not have been foreseen.

**systematic error**
An error in data collection that the researcher has been able to anticipate and account for.

**crime funnel**
A metaphor referring to the decreasing number of crimes processed at successive levels of the justice system, from law enforcement, through the courts, to corrections.

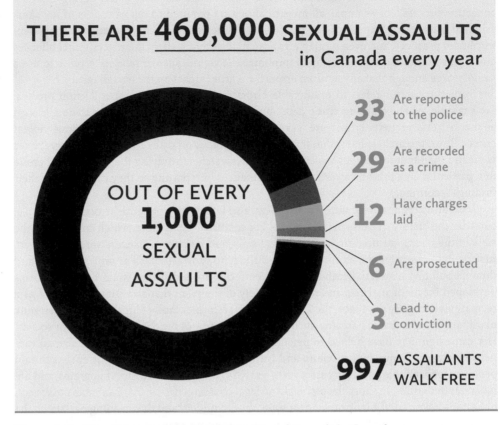

**Figure 2.3    The Crime Funnel Applied to Sexual Assault in Canada**

*Source*: H. Johnson, 2012. Based on research by Dr. Holly Johnson, copyright of YWCA Canada, used with permission.

the statistics gathered by official sources are primarily *descriptive* rather than *explanatory*: the information is almost exclusively about *what* is happening, not *why* it is happening.

Criminologists have long debated the value of official data sources. Their views often depend on what they believe to be the motivation for releasing official data. The consensus model, or the moderate/conservative view, maintains that state releases official crime data to make itself accountable to its citizens and because the public wants the information. Those of the conflict perspective noted earlier (and described in greater detail in Chapter 8) argue that official sources serve the interests of the state by justifying its efforts to expand its control over society—the activity referred to earlier in the chapter as *net-widening*. Conflict theorists suggest that instead of providing data that might help to explain the causes behind crime, the state selectively focuses attention on data that suggest a need for more laws, stricter enforcement, more police officers, and so on—that is, data that serve the state's own goals and objectives.

## 4. Theoretical Knowledge and Crime

**operationalization**
The defining of criminological concepts or phenomena in such a way that they can be observed and measured scientifically.

Theoretical concepts are supposedly based on scientifically verifiable and reliable observations. Yet, the operationalization of these concepts—in other words, how they are defined in terms of specific operations, measurement instruments, or procedures—is often subject to criticism. An operational definition is sometimes referred to as the indicator or measure of a construct. For example, what exactly do we mean by "binge drinking"? In 2014, citing a recent study, a CBC report stated that 1 in 25 Canadians aged 12–14 "binge drank" in the previous year (Machold, 2014). The *variable* that corresponds to concept of binge drinking could be the frequency of heavy episodic drinking; the *indicator* could be how often within the previous week or two weeks the individual was observed consuming five or more drinks containing alcohol in a row. Setting these criteria would enable a researcher to devise an operation definition of binge drinking.

As numerous researchers have pointed out, theoretical knowledge can have a direct impact on public opinion and social policy. By way of example, beginning in 1965, a growing volume of literature in the area of developmental psychology (see Chapter 6) showed that young people develop cognitive skills sooner than was once believed. This then new theoretical knowledge provided some of the critical information that led to the replacement of the 1908 Juvenile Delinquency Act—written at a time when juvenile delinquents were seen merely as misguided children in need of the state's kindly, parental guardianship—with the 1984 Young Offenders Act, which views young offenders as more accountable for their actions. This act has, in turn, been superseded by the 2003 Youth Criminal Justice Act (YCJA), which strikes a balance between accountability and reintegration (Green, 2013).

Theoretical perspectives in other areas of inquiry, besides those specific to the study of crime and criminality, also have much to contribute to criminology. Theories of knowledge are one example. In order to understand crime and criminality, it is important to realize that how we form our perceptions of crime affects how we think about (re)solving problems related to crime or social risk. The complexity of human behaviour means that criminological knowledge needs to be interdisciplinary, embracing theories that bridge the social and physical sciences. Without this integration of theory, criminology's ability to move forward as a science will be greatly hampered.

## Ethical Dilemmas in Criminological Research

This chapter has addressed different aspects of how we form our perceptions of reality and acquire knowledge. By now, you have probably deduced that the questions of how we acquire knowledge and what it means are surrounded by controversy. Wherever our knowledge comes from—personal experience, the media, official sources, or theoretical constructs—it should pass the same test of meaningfulness, verifiability, and reasonableness before it can be accepted. This is especially important given the potential political and social implications of criminological findings.

How then do criminologists rationalize the disclosure of findings that they believe to be meaningful, verifiable, and reasonable? Consider the following findings from a 2010 Angus Reid public opinion survey. The survey found that:

- 62 per cent of respondents favoured capital punishment;
- 31 per cent believed that rapists should be put to death;
- 65 per cent believed that mandatory minimum sentences are appropriate and effective as deterrents; and
- over 60 per cent expressed skepticism about the value of halfway houses, parole, and rehabilitation (Makin, 2010).

Are these results meaningful, reliable, and valid? Should they be taken seriously by a criminologist?

Although criminologists strive to remain objective in their research, their research endeavours rely on funding that comes, increasingly, from government sources (e.g. Public Safety Canada, Correctional Service Canada, the Social Science and Humanities Research Council) as opposed to the private sector and independent foundations like the Law Foundation and the

Napoleon Belanger / Library and Archives Canada / C-014078

The execution of Stanislaus Lacroix in Hull, Quebec, in 1902 was the last public execution in Canada. Although the death penalty was abolished in 1976, some studies have shown that the majority of Canadians today favour its return. Do you want to see Canada bring capital punishment back?

Canadian Women's Foundation (see Murphy & Stenning, 1999). Since researchers' goals must be more or less in line with those of their funding agencies, this shift has influenced not just what criminologists study but the angle of criminological inquiry.

It is important to recognize the power of an applied discipline. As we have seen, crime affects us all, either directly or indirectly. Therefore, criminologists must not only be aware of the ethical implications of sharing their findings, but also be prepared to defend their work in the light of public scrutiny, given how the media might use the information. For example, a presenter at a Canadian criminology conference claimed to be able to detect a propensity for criminal behaviour in children as young as 4. Such a claim carries huge implications for how we raise children and at what point the state might intervene in the guardianship of a child. Can, or should, a child with criminal tendencies be rehabilitated before he or she has even committed a crime? These are weighty questions. The point is that criminologists need to be mindful about not only what they say but how they say it. As discussed at the close of Chapter 1, scientists have a moral, ethical, and social responsibility to examine their goals and the implications of their findings.

Finally, all researchers—not just medical doctors—would do well to adopt the physician's oath as famously expressed by the Greek father of medicine Hippocrates (460–377 BCE): "Above all do no harm."

## Summary

- While the public's knowledge of crime is often naive and limited, public perceptions of crime can have a direct influence on criminal justice policy.
- The general public gains its knowledge of crime from four primary sources: personal experience, mass media, official sources, and theoretical constructs. Each of these has both strengths and weaknesses.
- Concepts of crime have historically been subject to paradigm shifts; this shows that crime is a relative construct.

- While the mass media undoubtedly influence our understanding of crime, conventional perspectives on crime and criminality (such as sociology and psychology) have never adequately explained how media influence behaviour. An interdisciplinary approach is necessary to address these and other issues in order to formulate policies that will balance individual freedoms with the protection of society.
- Ethical dilemmas surrounding what questions should be studied, as well as when and how information about crime should be shared and used, represent a growing area of concern and interest among criminologists.

## Discussion Questions

1. Where does your knowledge of crime come from? How accurate do you think it is? How does that knowledge affect your fear of crime (or lack of fear)? How does it influence your perceptions of crime?
2. What kinds of challenges do public perceptions of crime pose for criminologists and policy-makers? How could these challenges be rectified?
3. Which of the four primary sources of data do you consider superior? Why?
4. Do you have a Crime Stoppers program in your area? If you had information that could assist the police, would you come forward? Would your answer to that question be influenced by the offer of a reward? Do you agree with the concept of Crime Stoppers? Why or why not?
5. How can the public and the media benefit from an integrated approach in criminology?

## Key Concepts

conflict theory

crime funnel

empiricist

*Juristat*

left realism

moral panic

net widening

operationalization

paradigm shift

random error

rationalism

reliability

sampling

systematic error

validity

## Key Names

René Descartes (1596–1650)

David Hume (1711–1776)

Immanuel Kant (1724–1804)

John Locke (1632–1704)

## Weblinks

**Online Newspapers**

Browse current and archived issues of a wide range of Canadian newspapers.

www.onlinenewspapers.com

**Ipsos Canada**

Ipsos Canada conducts surveys on a wide range of social, economic, and political issues.

www.ipsos.ca

**Canadian Crime Stoppers Association**

The national website for the Canadian Crime Stoppers Association.

www.canadiancrimestoppers.org/home

# Chapter 3

## Measuring Crime and Criminal Behaviour

© Chuck Mason / Alamy Stock Photo

It ain't so much the things we don't know that get us in trouble.
It's the things we know that ain't so.
"ARTEMUS WARD" (CHARLES FARRAR BROWNE, 1834–67),
CITED IN HUFF, 1954

## Learning Outcomes

After reading this chapter, you should be able to

- Understand the reasons for collecting crime data;
- Identify the main methods of counting crime;
- Demonstrate familiarity with the official and unofficial crime collection methods and their limitations; and
- Recognize the importance of an interdisciplinary, multi-methods approach when collecting information on crime and criminal justice.

## Introduction

As we saw in Chapter 2, the public tends to believe that crime rates are higher than is actually the case. Perreault and Brennan (2010) point out that rates of self-reported victimization have remained stable since 2000, and that official crime statistics show decreases since the mid-1990s in both the incidence and the severity of crime, which in fact are at their lowest levels since 1973. Yet the "tough on crime" Safe Streets and Communities Act (2012) suggests there is a disconnect between what official data tell us what the federal government tells us. That is to say, despite the fact that crime rates have declined since the mid-1990s, the new act's harsh new measures for punishing criminals would suggest that crime is a greater problem today than it has been previously. Whatever its real or perceived prevalence, crime is a complex phenomenon.

Another important aspect of the crime picture is the cost of maintaining the various elements of the criminal justice system, including law enforcement agencies, courthouses, and correctional facilities. In 1961, total federal spending on police, courts, and corrections was around $4.38 per Canadian; by 1980, it was $16.85 per Canadian. In 1990, total justice expenditures reached $7.7 billion (Griffiths & Verdun-Jones, 1994), and by 2012 the annual budget for the criminal justice systems of the provincial, territorial, and federal governments was over $20.3 billion. Based on real per capita expenditures between 2002 and 2012, and the fact that crime rates dropped from almost 8,000 incidents per 100,000 population to just under 6,000 per 100,000 (even though the per capita costs increased from around $384 to $480 over the same time period—an increase of 23 per cent), one might be tempted to suggest that such expenditures lower the crime rate. However, the current crime rates are only marginally lower than in the 1960s when the CJS budget was a fraction of today's budget. The biggest increases in expenditures between 2002 and 2012 are attributed to growing costs at the provincial corrections level (Story & Yalkin, 2013).

While Chapter 2 focused on the qualitative, subjective, and ideological understanding of criminological phenomena, this chapter will focus primarily on the quantitative, objective, and empirical side of the equation. The main methods of obtaining crime data will be examined in terms of their strengths and weaknesses. We will conclude with a look at the importance of applying the scientific method of research when counting and using crime data. First, however, we will discuss the purpose of gathering crime data.

## Why Criminologists Need Data: Five Key Purposes

Criminologists use crime data to conduct research that can be used to inform public policy. Without valid (i.e. accurate) and reliable (i.e. consistent) data, researchers would be unable to answer such questions as: *Who is most likely to be a victim of a particular crime?*, *What is the*

**crime data**

The information collected to measure the frequency and severity of criminal events.

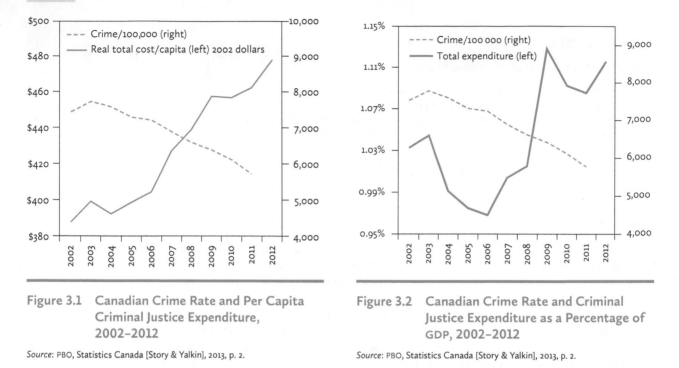

Figure 3.1    Canadian Crime Rate and Per Capita Criminal Justice Expenditure, 2002–2012

*Source*: PBO, Statistics Canada [Story & Yalkin], 2013, p. 2.

Figure 3.2    Canadian Crime Rate and Criminal Justice Expenditure as a Percentage of GDP, 2002–2012

*Source*: PBO, Statistics Canada [Story & Yalkin], 2013, p. 2.

*social and financial impact of crime on society?*, *Are there differences in crime rates across Canada?*, and *How can these differences be explained?* To obtain an accurate picture of what is happening in society, it is essential not only that the data gathered be accurate but that the method of data collection be valid, reliable, and appropriate. Nettler, who taught for many years at the University of Alberta, observed that criminological data serve five key purposes (1987, p. 36):

1. *Description.* The first step toward understanding, explaining, and ultimately predicting crime and criminality is the ability to describe criminal phenomena accurately. Criminal statistics also serve as a barometer of community well-being.

2. *Explanation.* Criminological theories explain crime patterns and trends. Theories enable researchers to make testable predictions based on empirical data. Researchers rely on *quantifiable* (i.e. observable and measurable) data to test their theoretical hypotheses. Then, based on the empirical findings, researchers are able to determine whether or not their theoretical assertions are supported.

3. *Evaluation.* The criminal justice system is expensive to operate, and financial accountability has become a major issue among policy-makers and their constituents. To assess what we are getting for our money and how well it works, we need accurate data.

4. *Risk assessment.* While crime may appear to be everywhere, we know that this is not true. By measuring criminal activity in relation to time, setting, location, and other social and environmental characteristics, criminologists are able to calculate the relative risk of being victimized according to an array of variables or factors (see Box 3.2). For example, men are more likely to be victims of homicide, serious assault, and robbery, while women are more likely to be victims of sexual assault (Perreault & Brennan, 2010). Risk assessment for the elderly has become an important area of study in recent years, as the proportion of elderly people in Canada, relative to the rest of the population, continues to grow.

5. *Prediction.* From both humanitarian and utilitarian perspectives, it would be better to prevent a crime before it happens than to punish the individual responsible after the fact. Historically, social scientists have been intrigued by the possibility of predicting human behaviour. Others are interested in questions such as whether youth peer courts, in which punishment for young people who have committed an offence is meted out by their peers (see Peterson, 2009), represent a viable alternative to conventional/traditional youth courts. Another "hot" Canadian research topic in recent years has evolved along the lines of how best to respond to human trafficking (see e.g. Kaye, Winterdyk, & Quartman, 2014). The list of phenomena that researchers attempt to predict is virtually endless.

---

**BOX 3.1**  **FACTS AND FIGURES**
**REGIONAL VARIATIONS IN RISK**

According to the 2009 General Social Survey conducted by Statistics Canada, "about 7.4 million Canadians, or just over one-quarter of the population aged 15 years and older, reported being a victim of a criminal incident in the preceding 12 months. This proportion was essentially unchanged from that reported in 2004" (Perreault & Brennan, 2010). The data showed that people living in western Canada were at greater risk of victimization than those living in eastern Canada. How do you think this might this be explained?

---

In short, the collection of crime data is essential to the reliability and validity of criminological research. However, as we learned in Chapter 2, there are ethical, methodological, and theoretical limitations in the use of some research data, which means that any crime data—and conclusions drawn from such data—should be viewed with caution and be carefully reviewed before they are widely reported.

---

**BOX 3.2**   **A CLOSER LOOK**
**What an Environmental Criminologist Does**

Using data to predict and prevent crime is a proactive approach that stands in contrast to the reactive, punishment-minded, crime-control approaches of the past, illustrating how the use of crime data changes over time. Thus, environmental criminologists, predicting that criminals will try to avoid being seen, seek to prevent crime by altering environmental factors such as street lighting and storefront visibility. Kim Rossmo, a graduate of Simon Fraser University and former student of environmental criminology experts Paul and Patricia Brantingham, developed a computer-mapping technique known as *geographic profiling*, which is used to predict where various categories of offenders live or work, based on crime-site information. This technique relies on innovative research on the spatial behaviour of criminals (see Rossmo, 2013). Unlike the more conventional approaches to studying the "why" of crime, geographic profiling focuses on the "where."

Do you usually take the same route to and from school every day? Do you usually shop at the same store for your groceries? The theoretical foundation of geographic profiling assumes that offenders limit their travel to distances and areas familiar to them. Therefore, because we (i.e. potential

Kim Rossmo, now faculty at the geographic profiling division of Texas State University, standing in front of a graph made using the algorithm he developed to analyze locations of serial crimes.

victims) typically engage in predictable journey patterns, a prospective offender may become familiar with our mobility patterns and capitalize on the opportunity to commit a crime (Rossmo, 2000). Although initially developed to identify serial murderers and rapists, geographic profiling has also been used to help thwart potential acts of arson, bombing, and robbery (Wortley & Mazerolle, 2008).

Chandler Prude / Texas State University

BOX 3.3        REALITY CHECK

### Can Criminologists Really Predict Criminal Behaviour?

Developing reliable and valid prediction models is as much an art as a science. Monahan (1981) was among the first to point out the risks in predicting human behaviour. Based on his review of psychiatric predictions of dangerous behaviour, Monahan concluded that they produced false positives two times out of three.

Often, prediction appears to be little more than chance, about as accurate as flipping a coin. However, as Bogomolov et al. (2014) report, with sufficiently large and numerous datasets, it is now possible to predict, with reasonable accuracy, crime in a geographic space (see also Box 3.2).

Current research still tends to focus primary on risk and protective factors as they help to explain *why* a problem or a crime exists (Public Safety Canada, 2014b). But as Canadian researchers Hoge, Andrews, and Leschild (1996, p. 419) caution, as important as the study of risk and factors has become in understanding and explaining crime, "there has been no evidence of interaction between risk and protective factors." In other words, human behaviour is complex, and there is no simple solution for preventing delinquency and/or crime. Therefore, any future prevention-based research that uses risk and protective factors needs to take into account the relative efficiency and cost-effectiveness of any "solutions."

---

**false positive**
An incorrect test result, showing the presence of a condition that does not exist in reality.

## Official Sources of Crime Data

*There are three kinds of lies: lies, damned lies, and statistics.* (attributed to Benjamin Disraeli, 1804–1881)

Many people mistrust official crime statistics. As Darrell Huff (1954, p. 8) once cautioned, "the secret language of statistics, so appealing in a fact-minded culture, is employed to sensationalize, inflate, confuse, and oversimplify." Nevertheless, statistics are an essential source of information for social scientists and policy-makers.

The most common measures of crime are the official statistics collected primarily by the various elements of the criminal justice system (CJS): police, courts, and corrections. The stats are used not only by the CJS and academics but by community organizations such as mental health and social service agencies that deal with alcohol and drug abuse and thus rely on official data to conduct research and make informed policy decisions.

### Police Statistics

Today, police reports are the most frequently used source of official crime data. This makes sense, given that the police are usually the first point of official contact for those reporting a crime.

Police data typically consist of criminal events that are known to the police. But not all crimes are necessarily detected, reported, or processed by official criminal justice agencies. If a crime is not detected, it will obviously go unreported; sometimes crimes are detected but not reported; and in some cases crimes that have been reported are not recorded for a variety of reasons (including e.g. emotional distress of the victim; see Boyce, Cotter, & Perreault, 2014). This unknown quantity of criminal activity is called the dark figure of crime (see Box 3.4). Why do certain types of crime more often go undetected and unreported than others? What can be done to improve the detection and reporting of crime? The dark figure of crime has become a major area of study in itself.

The collection of police data in Canada was begun in 1920 by the Dominion Bureau of Statistics, which was created in the 1918 Statistics Act. Data were submitted on a voluntary

---

**dark figure of crime**
Crime that goes undetected, unreported, or unrecorded, and is not included in official sources.

basis—as time and interest demanded—by the provinces for the purpose of tabulating the crimes known to the police forces of communities with populations of 4,000 or more (Worton, 1998). As crime rates increased, it became necessary to standardize police data and include more detailed information. The Uniform Crime Reporting (UCR) system was introduced in 1962 (see Table 3.1 and Box 3.5). The results were collated and published by Statistics Canada in the annual Crime and Traffic Enforcement Statistics and can be found today in the *Juristat* publications produced by the Canadian Centre for Justice Statistics (CCJS; see p. 58 below). The crime categories conform to a set of criteria developed in co-operation with the Canadian Association of Chiefs of Police (Brennan & Dauvergne, 2011). The UCR is a standardized survey, used by all police departments across the country, that collects and collates crime data and makes them available to a range of users, including government departments, scholars, the media, special interest groups, and students.

| BOX 3.4 | WHAT DO YOU THINK? |
|---|---|

### The Dark Figure of Hate Crime

The Government of Canada defines a hate crime as an act that "was motivated by bias, prejudice or hate based on the race, nationality, colour, religion, sex, age, mental or physical disability or sexual orientation of the victim" (Roberts, 1995, p. 7). However, as Roberts observes, there are no reliable data on the true extent of hate crimes in Canada. What are some possible reasons that hate crimes go undetected, unreported, or unrecorded?

**Uniform Crime Reporting (UCR)**
The system used to document criminal activity substantiated by police, providing a continuous historical record of crime and traffic statistics reported by every police agency in Canada since 1962.

**Canadian Centre for Justice Statistics (CCJS)**
The agency responsible for collecting and compiling crime data on a wide range of criminological and criminal justice topics.

### Table 3.1 An Example of Police Statistics: Excerpt from the 2014 Uniform Crime Reporting Survey

| | |
|---|---|
| All violations (Canada) | 2,052,191 |
| All Criminal Code violations (including traffic) | 1,923,039 |
| All Criminal Code violations (excluding traffic) | 1,793,534 |
| Violent Criminal Code violations | 369,359 |
| Homicide | 516 |
| Attempted murder | 617 |
| Sexual assault (levels 1–3) | 20,735 |
| Assault | 212,923 |
| Robbery | 20,924 |
| Criminal harassment | 19,653 |
| Uttering threats | 62,387 |
| Other violent violations | 31,604 |
| Property crime violations | 1,100,403 |
| Breaking and entering | 151,921 |
| Theft of motor vehicle | 73,964 |
| Theft over $5,000 (non-motor vehicle) | 14,258 |
| Theft under $5,000 (non-motor vehicle) | 474,879 |
| Mischief | 264,841 |
| Other property crime violations | 120,540 |
| Other Criminal Code violations | 323,772 |
| Disturb the peace | 103,266 |
| Administration of justice violations | 171,897 |
| Other violations | 48,609 |
| Criminal Code traffic violations | 129,505 |
| Impaired driving | 74,781 |
| Other Criminal Code traffic violations | 54,724 |
| Federal Statute violations | 129,152 |
| Drug violations | 103,757 |
| Other Federal Statutes | 25,395 |

*Source:* Statistics Canada summary table: Crimes, by type of violation, and by province and territory, CANSIM table 252-0051 and Catalogue no. 85-002-X.

## BOX 3.5   FACTS AND FIGURES  UNIFORM CRIME REPORTS AND THE CRIME SEVERITY INDEX

The original UCR survey included the *aggregate* (i.e. total) counts of crime provided by police departments on a monthly basis. However, these counts did not distinguish between crimes that were merely attempted and crimes that were successfully carried out. In addition, the survey instructed that if a criminal incident involved several offences, only the most serious of them would be counted. As a consequence, the survey underreported the actual number of offences committed.

To correct these deficiencies, in 1988 a revised UCR survey was introduced that included an incident-based reporting system. Now data are collected on the criminal event, the offender, and the victim on an incident-by-incident basis. Consequently, the UCR data are much richer today than in the past.

The Crime Severity Index was created by Statistics Canada in 2006, in response to a request from the Canadian Association of Chiefs of Police for "a new measure of police-reported crime that would address the limitations of the traditional crime rate" (Wallace, Turner, Matarazzo, & Babyak, 2009, p. 8). The principle behind the CSI was to give serious crimes greater weight than less serious crimes in the data. As a result, changes in the rate of more serious crimes will have a greater impact on the CSI than on traditional crime data found in the traditional crime-reported data (i.e. the UCR) (Crime Severity Index, 2012; see Table 3.2). The Violent Crime Severity Index is a separate version of the CSI that measures only violent offences, which are crimes that involve the physical violation of a person, including homicide, assault, and sexual assault, among other offences.

### Table 3.2   Excerpt from the 2014 Crime Severity Index

|  | 2014 Crime Severity Index | Change from 2013 CSI (%) | Violent Crime Severity Index | Change from 2013 Violent CSI (%) |
|---|---|---|---|---|
| Canada | 66.66 | −3.80 | 70.22 | −4.94 |

*Source:* Statistics Canada summary table: Crime Severity Index, by province and territory, CANSIM table 252-0052 and Catalogue no. 85-002-X.

Police crime statistics are divided into three categories:

1. *Summary offences* carry a maximum penalty of six months in jail and/or a fine not exceeding $5,000 (unless a different penalty is specified).
2. *Indictable offences* carry a maximum penalty of life imprisonment and no maximum fine.
3. *Hybrid offences* consist of crimes such as impaired driving and theft under $5,000, which the Crown may choose to prosecute as either summary or indictable.

### Judicial Statistics

Historically, court records were the first type of official crime statistics to be collected. Beginning in the early nineteenth century, information was gathered on the number of charges and convictions that appeared before the courts, as well as on the offender's sex, income, education, and occupation. Before long, researchers began to use these judicial statistics to describe trends and patterns such as the spatial and temporal distribution of crime (i.e. where and when crime occurs) and the distribution of the 17 most common crimes by age and gender (Elmer, 1982).

In 1876, the Canadian government began to collect judicial statistics, which remained the primary source of national crime statistics until the late 1960s. Until 1960, the government relied on the provinces to voluntarily submit their crime statistics, but the 1960 Royal Commission on Government Organization (also known as the Glassco Commission) strongly endorsed a centralized approach to gathering national statistics. Such an approach was subsequently adopted, only to be stopped in 1971 because of federal–provincial disputes over jurisdiction and cost. National judicial data were not collected again until the CCJS was established in 1981.

In recent years, CCJS reports have tended to focus on themes such as hate crime, homicide, young offenders, family violence, and home invasion, rather than providing general summaries of crime across Canada (see Figure 3.3). This is largely due to the fact that the CCJS draws its profile report from the General Social Survey GSS. Although Statistics Canada has one of the largest websites in the federal government, the shift in crime data representation makes it difficult to measure and/or discuss general trends and patterns such as

- average length of sentences;
- types of sentences and/or outcome (including alternative options such as restorative justice or community service); and
- variations in sentencing practices between provinces, which might lead to research into possible explanatory factors relating to politics or other factors.

Another source of crime-related information is the Statistics Canada bulletin called *The Daily*. Published since 1932, *The Daily* is a brief report released every day (at 8:30 a.m. EST, in

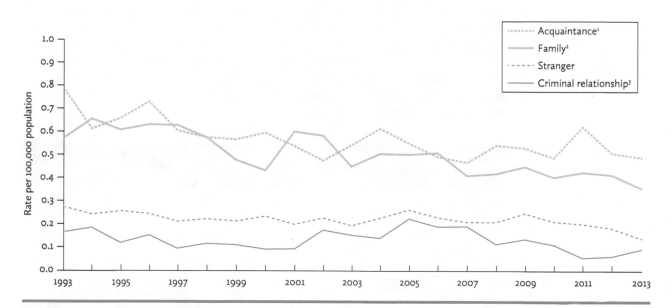

Figure 3.3  Example of CCJS Judicial Statistics: Excerpt from the Homicide Survey, 2013

1. Includes casual acquaintances; close friends; current and former boyfriends/girlfriends and other non-spousal intimate relationships; neighbours; business relationships (legal); and authority figures.
2. Includes current and former spouses (legal, common-law, same-sex, and opposite-sex); parents and children (including biological, adopted, step, and foster relationships); siblings; and other extended family members.
3. Includes, for example, sex workers, drug dealers and their clients, loan sharks, and gang members. Although prostitution is not illegal in Canada, many acts related to sex work are prohibited, such as public communication for the purpose of prostitution, living off the avails of prostitution, and operating or using a bawdy house.

*Source*: Cotter, 2014, p. 13. Statistics Canada, Canadian Centre for Justice Statistics, Homicide Survey.

both English and French), covering a broad spectrum of topics and issues. In 2013–14, there were 10 issues devoted to judicial matters including police personnel and expenditures, the victim services survey, and correctional services key indicators).

## Correctional Statistics

**correctional statistics**

Data on people being held in federal and provincial corrections facilities, including age, sex, offence, and prior convictions.

Although English prison statistics date back to 1836, the data originally appeared only in appendices to special reports. It was not until 1856 that correctional statistics became a regular component of criminal statistics. The data collected included age, gender, education, number of prior convictions, occupation, and birthplace. After 1963 these data were published separately as *Prison Statistics*. Since the establishment of the CCJS in 1981, however, statistics on correctional services have been published annually in the *Juristat* bulletins, which, in addition to producing a variety of justice-related reports on a range of topics and issues, provides in-depth analysis and information on the numbers of persons being held in federal and provincial corrections facilities, those charged awaiting trial, and those placed under supervision (see Table 3.3). Limited demographic information on offenders is also provided (e.g. age, gender, & ethnic background), along with data on federal and provincial corrections expenditures. *The Daily* also publishes occasional bulletins on corrections.

Between 2006, when Stephen Harper became prime minister, and 2011, the corrections budget increased by 86 per cent (Davis, 2011). Was this rise related to the PM's "tough on crime" stance? Canada's correctional investigator, Howard Sapers, has suggested the budget increase reflects, in part, the cost of holding inmates for longer sentences, under tighter conditions (Davis, 2011). Can we continue to sustain such costs? Are there more effective and efficient alternatives? While public protection is central to the correctional system's mandate, even Canada's justice department, in its guide to crime prevention, notes that "building more prison cells to lock up more people for longer periods of time is not an effective response or a greater guarantee for safer communities" (National Crime Prevention Centre, 1998, p. 26). Examining statistics on former prisoners who return to criminal behaviour after release is essential if we are to develop effective corrections policy.

| Table 3.3 Example of CCJS* Correctional Statistics: Average Counts of Youth under Correctional Supervision, by Type of Supervision, 2012–2013 | | | |
|---|---|---|---|
| **Type of Supervision** | **Number** | **Per cent** | **Rate*** |
| **Custody** | | | |
| Sentenced custody | 638 | 5 | 34 |
| Secure custody | 351 | 3 | 19 |
| Open custody | 287 | 2 | 15 |
| Pre-trial detention | 707 | 5 | 38 |
| Provincial director remand | 26 | 0 | 1 |
| **Total custody** | **1,371** | **11** | **73** |
| **Community supervision** | | | |
| Probation | 10,498 | 81 | 577 |
| Community portion of a custody and supervision order | 404 | 3 | 22 |
| Deferred custody and supervision order | 327 | 3 | 18 |
| Intensive support and supervision program | 305 | 2 | 17 |
| **Total community supervision** | **11,534** | **89** | **634** |
| **Total correctional services** | **12,904** | **100** | **685** |

*Rates are calculated per 100,000 youth population (aged 12–17).

*Source:* Excerpted from Perreault, 2014. Excerpted from Statistics Canada, Canadian Centre for Justice Statistics, Youth Corrections Key Indicator Report.

A young offender speaks to his probation officer. The Youth Criminal Justice Act seems to support alternatives to incarceration for young offenders.

The Correctional Service of Canada also offers some statistical data. For example, a review of its annual *Quick Facts* bulletins (see www.csc-scc.gc.ca/publications/005007-3000-eng .shtml) shows that incarceration rates are increasing and that the correctional system is becoming both more punitive and more expensive. This kind of information leads criminologists to look for more effective and efficient alternatives.

## What Do Official Data Measure?

The British criminologist Leslie Wilkins once noted that official crime data do not, strictly speaking, reflect criminal events (Wilkins, 1965): rather, they reflect the responses of the police, the courts, and the correctional system to social behaviour with respect to a particular set of offence categories defined by the Criminal Code. In other words, from a social constructionist perspective, official statistics are collected primarily to meet the collectors' own needs and reflect the collectors' attitudes regarding what is important.

As we saw in Chapter 2, the fact that the volume of recorded criminality is always smaller than that of actual criminality has been attributed to the "crime funnel." Hence, the extent to which the funnelling effect takes place and accurately reflects the true extent of crime is subject to considerable debate. At one end of the debate, researchers such as Chambliss (1988), adopting a *critical* or *left-realist* perspective, argue that official statistics are highly unreliable because of competing social factors and political interests. Evans and Himelfarb, for their part, concluded their review of UCR data by noting that "we can probably learn something about crime from these data, but [given the relative dark figure of crime] we are not sure how much" (1992, p. 78). And Nettler (1987, p. 49) observed that when the various modes of counting yield similar results, confidence in public records increases; however, "judgment is required" when using or interpreting the data because of the inherent limitations of official data.

| Table 3.4    Police-Reported Crime Rates, 2002–2012 (Select Years) | | | | | | | | |
|---|---|---|---|---|---|---|---|---|
| | Total Crime | | Violent Crime | | Property Crime | | Other Criminal Offences | |
| Year | Number (millions) | Rate (per 100,000) | Number (× 100,000) | Rate (per 100,000) | Number (millions) | Rate (per 100,000) | Number (× 100,000) | Rate (per 100,000) |
| 2002 | 2.35 | 7,512 | 451 | 1,441 | 1.5 | 5,080 | 316 | 991 |
| 2004 | 2.42 | 7,600 | 448 | 1,404 | 1.6 | 5,123 | 342 | 1,072 |
| 2006 | 2.35 | 7,244 | 451 | 1,386 | 1.5 | 4,808 | 341 | 1,049 |
| 2008 | 2.20 | 6,617 | 444 | 1,331 | 1.4 | 4,519 | 345 | 1,037 |
| 2010 | 2.09 | 6,137 | 439 | 1,287 | 1.3 | 3,824 | 350 | 1,027 |
| 2012 | 1.94 | 5,588 | 415 | 1,190 | 1.1 | 3,414 | 343 | 984 |

*Source:* Perreault, 2013a, pp. 26–8.

Based on the *absolute numbers* in Table 3.4, we might be tempted to conclude that violent crime fell only slightly between 2002 and 2012. However, when we take into account the fact that the population has increased, the actual *rate* (i.e. the number of incidents per 100,000 population) declined notably over the stated period. So, has Canada become safer since 2002? Are our crime prevention and crime-fighting initiatives working? Or are the declines in violent and property crime rates due to changes in demographic or social structure, or some other social factor? While crime data offer interesting descriptive information, they do not explain why changes occur. This is where scientific inquiry and theoretical knowledge come into play.

Despite their limitations, official data can serve as useful indicators; it's all a matter of how and for what purpose the data are being used. Since crime data do not explain themselves, adopting an interdisciplinary and theoretical approach to using and interpreting official counts of crime is often helpful. While theories have their own shortcomings, they offer reasonably objective means to study crime and its control when they are used as part of a structured approach that uses observable and measurable concepts that can be tested.

One thing is certain: currently there is no sure way of reliably assessing the gap between official crime data and actual crime. Jeffery (1990) offered a scathing assessment of how we measure crime, suggesting that "if we had a radar system or an emergency medical system that operated at the level found in the criminal justice system, we would not be alive for very long" (p. 125).

## Factors Affecting Crime Data

Official crime counts are subject to fluctuation resulting from a variety of factors that influence the collecting and processing of crime data. They include the following.

### 1. Media Coverage

According to research by Marsh and Melville (2009), among others, media coverage of crime can influence crime counts. Focusing on certain crimes or crises draws public attention and affects the reporting rates. As we noted in Chapter 2, media coverage can serve as a barometer of public opinion.

### 2. The Dark Figure of Crime

Fattah (1997) notes that the dark figure of crime—that portion of crime that goes undetected, unreported, or unrecorded—may fluctuate over time and even within settings because of changes in variables such as police enforcement practices, victims' willingness to report their victimization, and public attitudes toward the criminal justice system.

### 3. Changes in Recording Procedures

From time to time, the statistics provided by certain police services or courts may be misleading, whether because they are incomplete or because they are more complete than usual due to varying administrative and/or a divergent range of practical matters (see e.g. Boyce, Cotter, & Perreault, 2014). While Statistics Canada notes these instances, they are seldom discussed by the media, and are sometimes ignored even in academic accounts of crime. Among the reasons for under- or over-reporting are the following:

- *Changes in the number of police forces/officers.* Reports from Ontario's RIDE program and its counterpart in Alberta, "Check Stop," both of which conduct regular campaigns designed to apprehend impaired drivers, show that more people than usual may be charged during a campaign, even if no more people than usual are actually driving impaired during that period.
- *Changes in police/court administration.* Policy mandates at the municipal, provincial, or federal level may change (e.g. from a crime-control model to a community-based prevention model).
- *Changes in the legal definition of crime.* For example, consensual homosexual activity was decriminalized in 1969, and the numbers of people criminally prosecuted decreased.
- *Changes in the population base.* As noted earlier, both the media and the police will sometimes report crime statistics using absolute numbers, which are more likely to attract public attention. This is despite the fact that such figures are meaningless unless they are linked to population size. Only crime rates—that is, the number of incidents relative to some unit of population—should be used when drawing comparisons.

In Canada, as in many other Western countries, crime reports use units of 100,000 people for most crime statistics, although units of 1,000 and 10,000 may be used for certain crime categories (e.g. violent crimes among youth and crimes in the less populated regions of the North) for which the population base is smaller. To calculate the crime rate, the following formula is used:

$$\text{Rate per 100,000} = \frac{\text{number of reported crimes}}{\text{total population}} \times 100,000$$

Even so, the base rates are still subject to several technical problems. First, in Canada, a major census is undertaken every five years (most recently in 2011). In each five-year interval between censuses, fertility, emigration, and immigration rates can fluctuate enough to distort the crime rate. Other ways of calculating base rates have been suggested: for example, using counts of the population at risk rather than total population (Boggs, 1965); calculating break-and-enter rates in terms of the number of dwellings; basing motor-vehicle thefts on the number of vehicles; and basing sexual assault rates on the population of women and girls. However, since the circumstances surrounding victims of crime are not consistent, these strategies also have their limitations.

A final technical problem arises when the way police collect data changes, making historical comparisons difficult. The most obvious such change occurred in 1962, when the system for reporting Canadian police statistics was completely reorganized, and the UCR survey was introduced.

- *Changes in public reporting patterns.* Depending on the type of offence, only around 30 per cent of recorded crimes are the result of police observations or intervention. Yet the Canadian Urban Victimization Survey (CUVS), which is conducted every five years through the General Social Survey (GSS), found in the 2009 cycle that only 42 per cent of recorded crimes were reported by the victim or another member of the public. Therefore, public reporting patterns can have a dramatic impact on crime counts.

In summary, as crime rates rose through the twentieth century, it became increasingly important to establish a comprehensive and centralized system that would coordinate criminal justice data and address community justice needs. The Canadian Centre for Justice Statistics was the national response.

## Canadian Centre for Justice Statistics

When the UCR was introduced in 1962, many believed the new official crime counts would be more comprehensive and reliable than those produced by earlier recording methods. However, as crime rates increased between 1962 and 1988, and as the growing mass media fed and stoked the public's curiosity about crime, people began to call for more details, more information, and more ways to document criminal acts and behaviour. Self-report and victimization surveys, introduced in the late 1960s and early 1970s, were products of this call for more information, but with them came the concept of the dark figure of crime, as it became increasingly evident to criminologists and others that official data were limited.

Between 1974 and 1981, several task forces and advisory boards attempted to reorganize the national data collection methods in an effort to meet both federal and provincial needs. This process culminated in the opening of the CCJS in 1981. Today, crime and criminal justice data are gathered by the CCJS and published in the *Juristat* bulletins. Each issue is devoted to a particular topic. Some recent issues have been devoted to the following topics:

- family violence in Canada
- homicide in Canada
- police-reported cybercrime in Canada
- verdicts of not criminally responsible on account of mental disorder in adult criminal courts
- police-reported hate crime
- family law cases in the civil courts
- police resources in Canada
- shelters for abused women in Canada.

These special topical publications not only inform administrators within the criminal justice system about relevant issues but also fulfill one of the centre's objectives, which is to satisfy the "public's right to know." In addition, the CCJS undertakes studies in a variety of specific areas, which are then published as part of the *Juristat* (see Box 3.6). As several researchers have noted, however, the CCJS continues to experience difficulties in trying to meet the needs of different users. The following are among the key limitations:

- There is no national information on court decisions.
- There are inconsistencies in the way provinces report, as well as count, their crime incidents.
- Data on crime incidents, arrests, charges, convictions, and dispositions lack depth.
- Reports provide little insight into crime and criminal behaviour.
- There are no reports on white-collar crime, organized crime, victimless crime, or other types of non-conventional crime.

---

**Canadian Urban Victimization Survey (CUVS)**
The first major attempt to survey Canadians who had been victims of crime, conducted in the 1980s.

**General Social Survey (GSS)**
A Statistics Canada survey used to regularly gather data on social trends and to provide information on specific policy issues of current or emerging interest.

**victimization survey**
A data collection technique used to gather unofficial information from victims of crime on incidents that have usually occurred within a predefined period of time.

---

**BOX 3.6** **FACTS AND FIGURES** THE BEST OFFICIAL SOURCE OF CANADIAN JUSTICE INFORMATION

Although the topics can vary slightly from year to year, the CCJS regularly provides information on subjects such as the following:

- adult correctional services
- motor vehicle theft
- youth court statistics
- national trends in intimate partner homicides
- justice spending
- victimization

- family violence
- legal aid
- young offenders
- police administration.

*Juristat* publications can be found in most college and university libraries or obtained by e-mailing info@fedpubs.com. You can even contact them by phone (toll-free) at 1-888-433-3782. Although each issue has a nominal cost, most universities have subscriptions and access is free to students and faculty.

---

Nevertheless, the Centre does try to provide information that is of value to policy-makers, criminal justice administrators and planners, those who evaluate justice programs and projects, and the media, as well as the public. And it has had a major impact on the study of crime and criminal justice in Canada.

In summary, the official data-gathering techniques in Canada have evolved over the years, and both the quality and the variety of the data have improved considerably since the establishment of the CCJS. In the future, improvements in search technology and other technical advances will likely make the data faster and easier to access. However, it is important to remember that criminological data are useful only to the extent that they can be applied or used within a theoretical context. While the CCJS provides data on a wide range of topics, not all the data necessarily serve a theoretical function, providing little more than descriptive information. Hence, students are encouraged to familiarize themselves with other significant sources of data. Among the more conventional unofficial sources upon which criminologists have come to rely are victimization surveys, self-report data, and observation data.

## Unofficial Sources of Crime Data

Every crime involves both an offender and a recipient of the offence, and in certain situations crime data can be obtained from either or both. Data obtained directly from the recipient of the offence are formally known as *victimization data*; from the offender, as *self-report data*. A third source of unofficial data involves observational methods. Without unofficial data, the crime picture would be incomplete, since unrecorded crimes (i.e. the dark figure) are not reflected in official statistics.

**unofficial data**
Data collected using unofficial methods (e.g. self-report surveys, victimization surveys, and observational techniques), usually by academics or research organizations, with no specific regularity, for their own purposes rather than to inform the public.

### Victimization Data

*Victimization: An Emerging Field*

> [In 2009] 27% of Canadians aged 15 and older said they had been a victim of a criminal incident in the 12 months before the survey. This proportion was unchanged from 2004. (Statistics Canada, 2010a)

Victimology is an immensely interesting area of investigation within criminology, yet one that is still underdeveloped here in Canada. Even in 2014, most Canadian criminology programs offered victimology only as an elective course.

As early as 1947, Sutherland (1947) pointed out that the public is always the victim of a crime. Sacco and Kennedy (1998, p. 44) complemented Sutherland's observation by identifying three "stages" essential to describing a criminal event that also draw on the relationship between victim and offender. *Precursors* of the event are the "situational factors that bring people together in time and space." *Transactions* are the "interactions among participants" that define the outcomes of their event. The *aftermath* consists of the consequences, including the public reaction (which can lead to changes in the law).

Today, victimization surveys are used in many countries. For example, in the United States the annual National Crime Survey (NCS)—recently renamed National Crime Victimization Survey (NCVS)—involves randomly surveying a representative selection of 100,000 households twice a year. General areas of coverage include costs of crime to victims, the nature and extent of criminal behaviour, probabilities of victimization risks, and victim precipitation of crime and culpability. The NCVS survey is comparable to the British Crime Survey conducted in the United Kingdom.

### *Limitations of Victimization Surveys*

As useful as victimization surveys are at tapping into the dark figure of crime and providing insight into the impact of crime on victims, they are not without limitations. For example:

- Respondents may forget about crimes—especially less serious ones.
- Respondents may be mistaken as to when the incident occurred.
- Respondents may not feel comfortable disclosing certain facts and/or details.
- Respondents may not fully understand the questions.
- There may be variations in how different social groups of respondents reply to the questions; for example, studies indicate that better-educated respondents have better recall.
- Conducting such surveys tends to be both time-consuming and costly.
- Acquiring stable estimates of less common crimes requires larger samples, which add to the already high cost.

As researchers increasingly recognize the importance of gathering data on crime from a range of sources—including official sources such as police data and unofficial sources such as offender and victim accounts—many of these limitations are likely to be addressed. Also, as we move away from what Karmen (2013) calls "offenderology" and become more victim-conscious, integrating victimization into theoretical perspectives, the refinement of victimization surveys is likely to continue. Sociologist Jack Katz (1988), for example, expressed the view that criminologists need to broaden their objective and deterministic perspective of deviance. To this end, the critical left-realist theoretical perspective makes extensive use of victimization data when testing its theoretical tenets, in the belief that in order to understand crime one needs to consider the offender, the state, and the victim (see e.g. Lee, 2007). Similarly, feminist researchers have not only used victimization data but also developed ways of looking into behaviours not covered in traditional victimization surveys (Tombs, 2007). And from 1989 until 1997, the Leiden University in the Netherlands coordinated an international survey of victimization suffered by businesses, which will have both theoretical and policy implications. The various victim assistance programs now operating in Canada will undoubtedly help ensure that the study of victimology becomes a major force in criminological research.

## Self-Report Data

Thorsten Sellin (1931) was one of the first North American criminologists to argue that in order to understand crime, it is important to start by asking about the offender's behaviour and motivation. Since Sellin's article, **self-report studies** have been conducted with a wide variety of sub-populations, from inmates and young offenders to judges, lawyers, law enforcement officers, business people, and senior citizens.

Self-report studies take a pragmatic approach to the enumeration of criminal behaviour by asking respondents simply whether or not they have ever committed a crime (as defined in the survey). Based on the responses, the scores are cross-analyzed against the fundamental demographic and socioeconomic characteristics of the respondents, such as age, gender, known criminal record, and social class. These data are then used to assess both the validity of criminal justice statistics as a crime severity index and the validity of criminological theories based on inferences drawn from those patterns.

### Findings of Self-Report Studies

The flavour of self-report studies has changed over the years. One of the earliest self-report studies was conducted at Texan Christian University by Austin Porterfield (1943), who invited students to participate in a survey on deviant behaviour. While most of his findings might appear trivial or benign by today's standards—79 per cent of male students admitted to having used abusive language, and 77 per cent confessed to having launched spitballs—Porterfield observed a strong gender bias in favour of males: in other words, males committed more delinquent acts than females.

Other early self-report studies offered criminologists some fruitful insights. For example, they revealed that the gap between official and self-report data varied by age, gender, offender type, and race, and that offenders who were not part of the official database (i.e. who hadn't ever been caught) tended to commit a wide variety of offences, rather than specializing in one type of offending behaviour. In Canada, where only about one-quarter of all serious, chronic young offenders are officially apprehended, self-report studies can help to shine a light on the dark figure of unreported and/or undetected offending committed by young people (Winterdyk, 2015).

In Canada, self-report surveys have been limited and tended to focus on youths and adolescents (see e.g. Savoie, 2007; Sprott & Doob, 2008).

### Limitations of Self-Report Studies

Despite a comparatively long history, self-report studies have been fraught with methodological problems. Until recently, few studies were standardized, as they were often carried out at different times by researchers with different interests. Brutus, Aguinis, and Wassmer (2012) conducted a meta-analysis of self-report studies conducted between 1982 and 2007. They noted that self-report studies were susceptible to errors related to validity, and they offered a number of cautionary recommendations for those using this sort of data.

Another limitation of self-report studies has been that they seldom use comparable questions, areas, or time frames. These drawbacks render the studies almost useless for any assessment of the efficacy of criminal justice statistics. Thornberry and Krohn (2000), among others, have identified several other factors that bring into question the reliability of self-report surveys. These include the following:

- Respondents may mistrust the interviewers.
- Respondents may not answer truthfully because of embarrassment.
- Those who feel a deep sense of guilt may not disclose their behaviour.
- Respondents may exaggerate the truth, especially if they are young.
- Respondents may simply have forgotten.

As a result of a number of methodological limitations, self-report studies are plagued by reliability or dependability problems, are of doubtful validity, and have led researchers to

**self-report studies**
Surveys in which individuals are asked to voluntarily disclose whether they have ever committed an offence, yielding stores of unofficial crime data that can shed light on undetected and underreported types of crime (e.g. youth crime).

draw unfair and incorrect inferences. However, various methodological protocols are available to help researchers minimize these constraints. For example, in 2009, Canadian researchers Knobe, Trocme, MacLaurin, and Fallon conducted a national study on child abuse and neglect. In order to ensure the reliability of their measuring instrument (the Canadian Incidence Study, or CIS), they examined their findings for *test–retest reliability*, measuring certain items in the study a second time under identical conditions to see if the findings were fairly consistent from the first test to the second.

In summary, self-report studies have improved steadily and should be considered reasonably reliable, though they remain less reliable when they invite respondents to disclose sensitive information on very serious offences or potentially embarrassing circumstances. Researchers now need to expand the research-topic base. For example, our knowledge of self-reported adult crime, self-reported youth victimization, and self-reported crime among minority ethnocultural communities is very limited. Access to such information could be readily be gained through the use of self-report studies, which are relatively easy to administer among such specific populations. Criminologists' use of self-report studies could also be improved with a more interdisciplinary approach: for example, they could include questions regarding biological and environmental factors that are of interest to growing numbers of researchers today.

## Observational Data

The final approach that is regularly used to obtain accurate data on crime is field research. As Jackson (2012), among many others, has commented, you simply cannot gain insight into offenders' motives by sitting at your desk analyzing data or reading crime surveys. Sometimes it is more informative to meet with offenders in their own setting, in order to observe and understand their behaviour from their perspective.

This **qualitative research** approach was pioneered by the German sociologist **Max Weber**, who emphasized the importance of understanding how individuals interpret their own actions and the actions and reactions of others. Weber called this approach *Verstehen* (German for "understanding"), meaning an effort to understand an event by placing oneself in the participant's situation and trying to see it through his or her eyes.

Over the years, a number of studies have used the field research techniques of observation and qualitative interviews to study crime and criminals. For his book *Crime as Work* (1973), for example, Letkemann interviewed 45 Canadian bank robbers and burglars in an effort to describe and explain their lifestyle, and more recently Schulenberg (2014) published an article on Canadian police decision-making using observational information gathered primarily through surveys.

The two most common observational methods are field observation and participant observation. The objective of field observation is to collect data (i.e. observe people or conduct interviews) about a specific phenomenon in the environment in which it occurs. While the methodology can be somewhat haphazard, the information obtained can be enlightening (Jackson, 2012).

Field observation is the least obtrusive of the observational techniques. We have probably all engaged in it at some time or other—whether hanging around a crime or accident scene to observe the sequence of events or simply sitting at a coffee shop and watching life pass by. Field research can provide rich and detailed information. Observing verbal and non-verbal interactions, as well as elements of some theoretical paradigm that you might be testing, can produce important insights.

The second technique, participant observation, is most commonly used by cultural anthropologists, although the Chicago School—the group of researchers associated with the University of Chicago's sociology department during the early twentieth century—used it to

**qualitative research**
Research designed to study characteristics that cannot be measured or counted.

*Verstehen*
Sociologist Max Weber's term for the effort to understand both the intent and the context of human action.

produce some classic sociological studies (see Theodorson, 1982). As the term suggests, participant observation involves a researcher taking part in the activity or social group he or she is studying, usually over an extended period of time, although degrees of involvement vary. Some participant observers become completely immersed in what they are observing. In a classic illustration of this approach, John Howard Griffin, the author of *Black Like Me* (1961), had his skin artificially darkened so that he could blend in with the black people whose lives he wanted to observe. More recently, Bourgois and Bruneau (2000) used participant observation to study Montreal's needle exchange program for drug addicts. By observing the program first-hand, they were able to conclude that better risk-reduction strategies are needed to ensure effective help for vulnerable street addicts.

*Advantages of Observational Techniques*

As Hamm (1998) notes, field research enables researchers to transcend abstract theoretical analysis by immersing themselves in the real-life meanings and emotions surrounding criminal activity. It can also be useful for gathering data on social processes over time. In social settings (e.g. inmate–guard interactions), observation enables data collection on at least three levels (DeWalt & DeWalt, 2011):

1. the activity itself, the activities surrounding it, and their meaning
2. the dynamics of the participants and their interrelationships
3. the setting in general

*Limitations of Observational Techniques*

Observational data have strong "face validity": that is, since they reflect only what the researcher has observed, they appear reliable. However, this appearance may be only superficial. For one thing, such data are subjective, since the type of information gathered depends on the observer's biases, personal interests, and mental and physical limitations. For another, sample sizes tend to be considerably smaller than in the other unofficial and official means of data collection. As a result, there is no allowance for generalizations beyond the study group.

Observational techniques also raise serious ethical questions. The "Tearoom Trade" study of homosexual activities by Laud Humphreys (1970) has become a classic case in field research ethics. Humphreys's doctoral research involved observing male homosexuals meeting in public washrooms without obtaining their consent; he was allowed to observe their behaviour in return for acting as a "watchqueen," or lookout, warning them when someone else was approaching. He also used police registers to find names and addresses of his research subjects, using licence plate numbers that he had recorded while following the men to their cars. A year later, he visited some of the subjects' homes to conduct follow-up interviews in the guise of a health researcher (Neuman, 1997, p. 447). Was this a violation of their privacy and personal liberty? Humphrey admitted to being less than candid with his respondents. (See Babbie, 2004, for a more detailed discussion.) Is this practice of deception acceptable? Either way, the point is that collecting data through observational methods can be subject to controversy.

Another drawback of observational research is that it tends to be much more labour-intensive than administering victimization or self-report surveys. In addition to placing great demands on their time, it requires observers to operate on two levels simultaneously, immersing themselves in what they are observing while remaining detached from it. Imagine going to your favourite sporting event and being asked to observe without getting personally involved—like a broadcaster or sports reporter. Ethical dilemmas can arise if observers find themselves in situations where an event of which they strongly disapprove occurs. Surveying a sample of members of the American Society of Criminology a number of years ago, Longmire

(1983) found that 63 per cent reported that they had experienced ethical dilemmas when conducting research, some of which included observational research (p. 340). In one notable instance that Longmire describes, researchers involved in what is known simply as the Wichita Jury Study tape-recorded federal jury deliberations without gaining informed consent of the jurors (Longmire, 1983, p. 334). The most common (9 per cent) ethical dilemma surrounding participant observation pertained to issues around confidentiality.

To minimize potential negative impact on their subjects, researchers involved in participant observation must follow some basic guidelines, as summarized by Jackson (2012):

- Never harm participants.
- Ensure that participation is voluntary.
- Maintain the anonymity and confidentiality of participants.
- Be honest at all stages of the study.

If you are interested in substantive issues regarding ethics in criminology and criminal justice policy, the journal *Criminal Justice Ethics* offers a broad selection of relevant articles.

## Validating Findings

Both official and unofficial data sources have their strengths, but no single method of data collection can measure any phenomenon with complete reliability and validity. Therefore, researchers need to validate their findings. As criminology becomes more interdisciplinary, it is becoming increasingly common to examine phenomena of interest from more than one perspective and then compare the results. This technique, known as **triangulation**, is based

**triangulation**
The use of multiple data sources or research methods to investigate a topic, with the goal of producing more reliable findings.

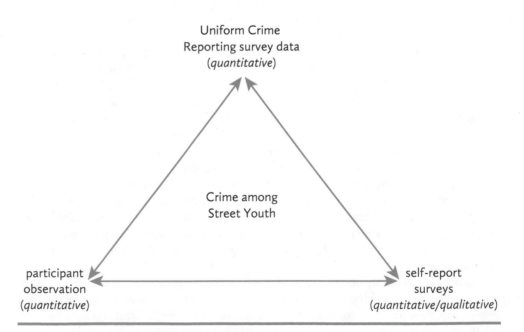

**Figure 3.4    An Example of Triangulation Analysis Using Qualitative and Quantitative Methods**

*Source*: Adapted from CX Partners, www.cxpartners.co.uk/wp-content/uploads/2009/11/triangulation.jpeg

on the principle that using different methods to measure the same thing should produce similar results, whereas using the same method to measure different things should produce different results.

Triangulation has enabled criminologists to illuminate the dark figure of crime. To develop his typology of cheque forgers, for instance, Letkemann (1973) used three different sources of information: subject interviews, police records, and a review of related literature. A similar method was used by Boyd (1988), who used capital case files from the national archives, official data from the CCJS, and interviews of 40 men and women serving time for first- or second-degree murder to develop his typology of murderers in Canada. Totten (2012) used a similar approach to formulate his typology of gangs in Canada.

Even with a multi-method strategy, nothing in the social sciences can be predicted with one hundred per cent accuracy. However, use of the appropriate strategies can reduce invalidity and allow researchers to take some degree of confidence in their findings. This is why, when writing reports, researchers always use statistical techniques to objectively determine the margin of error in their data and lend objective support to their conclusions.

## How Data Are Used

Up until this point in the chapter we have been looking at how crime data are collected. We will now turn to how criminologists analyze and use these findings.

### Correlation

One of the oldest formal techniques used to understand any criminal phenomenon consists of looking for factors with which it may be associated. A correlation (or direct correlation) is a relationship between two or more *variables*, or characteristics, that appear to be associated. If an increase in one variable is associated with an increase in another, there is a positive correlation; if the increase is associated with a decrease in another variable, there is a negative correlation. It is important to note that the existence of a direct correlation does not imply a *causal relationship*, meaning that the change in one variable is *causing* the change in the other; however, it does prompt researchers to examine why and how the variables appear to correlate. For example, some criminologists have claimed to find correlations between crime and economic conditions, crime and the amount of violence on television, and even crime and certain body types. Once a correlation has been established, criminologists attempt to find out whether the association somehow contributes to or causes a change in the phenomenon under investigation.

*Cause* implies that the occurrence of one event is directly affected by the presence of one or more variables. Most people, for example, believe in the concept of causality: that if you pierce your arm with a needle, you will bleed, or that if you tell a good joke, people will laugh. Yet some yogis and Sufi masters appear to have the mental control to prevent themselves from bleeding, and people might not laugh at a joke they don't understand. In other words, nothing is ever perfectly predictable. As the social anarchist Paul Feyeraben (1986, p. 55) writes, "no theory ever agrees with all the *facts* in its domain, yet it is not always the theory that is to blame." For this reason, researchers generally prefer to express the apparently causal relationships between two or more phenomena in terms of *probability* rather than cause and effect. Measuring the probability that certain effects will occur when certain causes are present involves the use of various statistical techniques.

The stronger the degree of association between the variables measured, the greater the likelihood that the relationship will be considered true or valid. When researchers propose

**correlation (or direct correlation)**
A statistical relationship between two or more variables.

**positive correlation**
A direct correlation in which an increase in one variable is associated with an increase in the other variable.

**negative correlation**
A direct correlation in which an increase in one variable is associated with a decrease in the other variable.

**causality**
The idea that one event is the result of one or more other events.

**hypothesis**
An idea or assertion about a phenomenon, a situation, or a relationship between variables that a researcher sets out to prove or disprove.

to test the relationship between two or more variables, they formulate a hypothesis, which is usually a declarative statement about the relationship (for example, "If you were abused as a young person (*cause*), then your chances of becoming an abuser yourself are greater (*effect*) than if you had not been abused"). Theory consists of the constructs that attempt to explain a set of propositions or statements.

## The General Aims of Research

No matter which data-gathering and analytical techniques they use, researchers strive to accomplish four basic aims.

### 1. Discovery

To the uninitiated, research findings sometimes seem to state the obvious. One of the first observations of this kind I came across as a criminology student was the conclusion that if you associated with a "negative element" (i.e. bad kids), it would increase your chances of becoming delinquent. How original, I thought—go figure! However, in addition to verifying the "obvious," researchers often seek to understand exceptions to the apparent rule. For example, why doesn't everyone who associates with a "negative element" become delinquent? Similarly, while "justice" has centred on punishment since the dawn of time, in the 1990s researchers began to explore the possibility that a different approach might also be effective. It was then that the concept of restorative justice—a sentencing model based on restitution and community participation, aimed at reintegrating offenders back into the community—started gaining momentum. By examining data through different lenses, researchers began discovering alternatives to the punishment model.

**restorative justice**
A sentencing model that emphasizes restitution and community participation, aimed at reintegrating offenders back into their communities.

### 2. Demonstration

Suppose you wanted to argue that restorative justice was more effective than retribution. It wouldn't be enough to simply state your claim: you would need to put it to the test—that is, you would need to demonstrate it. For example, a growing body of literature has demonstrated that restorative justice, because it is community-centric, has some enduring success in rehabilitating offenders (see e.g. London, 2011).

It's important to recognize that demonstration cannot prove anything: at best, it can only be consistent with a hypothesis. The fact that we might be able to demonstrate a correlation between, for example, the notion that fear of crime correlates to the safety precautions a person takes does not mean there are no alternative explanations that express similar correlation between the two variables in question.

### 3. Refutation

While science provides the objective tools to test ideas and gradually move closer to the truth, it can also be used to refute existing beliefs. For example, research conducted in the 1960s and 1970s by Fattah (1972), among others, challenged the longstanding belief that capital punishment was an effective deterrent to people who might be thinking of killing another person or persons. These studies were instrumental in the campaign that led Canada to abolish the death penalty in 1976. Similarly, studies on boot camps refuted the notion that hard work, harsh discipline, and a regimented lifestyle deter young offenders from reoffending (Cowles & Castellano, 1995). The highly publicized "Scared Straight" program, in which older prison inmates were used to frighten young offenders out of a life of crime, was also recently refuted after over 30 years of practice (Nissen, 2011). Box 3.7 summarizes a refutation of the success of using punishment as a means of social control.

**BOX 3.7** **REALITY CHECK**

## Refuting the Merits of Punishment

Fattah (1998) uses the following points (paraphrased here) to refute the idea that punishment is an appropriate justice model:

1. *Punishment is ineffective.* Countries like the United States, Iran, Saudi Arabia, and China, with their high execution rates, have among the world's highest incarceration rates.
2. *Punishment achieves nothing.* It does little more than breed anger, hostility, resentment, and antagonism; violence breeds violence.
3. *Punishment is costly.* The financial costs have been escalating year after year.
4. *Punishment is degrading, humiliating, and stigmatizing.* Any form of deprivation of liberty is degrading and humiliating.
5. *Punishment is never personal or individual.* Although we might be imprisoning the offender, we are also having an impact on his or her family, friends, and social network. Punishment extends beyond the offender's immediate circle.
6. *Punishment treats human beings as a means to an end.* While punishment may have some cathartic effects on the public, it does little for the person being punished and is not always satisfying for victims either. The person is sacrificed to achieve some other goal.
7. *Punishment looks at the past.* Punishment is retributive in nature. It is retrograde in its approach and does little for the offender's future well-being.
8. *Punishment perpetuates rather than settles conflicts.* Punishment serves to generate further animosity and

Ezzat Fattah, a Canadian pioneer in the field of restorative justice and victimology, and founder of the School of Criminology, Simon Fraser University.

Simon Fraser University Archives. Media and Public Relations Office fonds, F-61-1-2-0-45.

antagonism among the parties involved instead of settling conflicts.

9. *Punitive penal sanctions amount to punishment of the victim.* By its very practice, not only does punishment serve to further victimize the victim but society may also lose, since it doesn't always accept the sanction.

Fattah uses these points to argue in favour of the restorative justice model.

Do these arguments make sense to you? Do you think society would accept the abolition of the punishment model?

### 4. Replication

The more frequently you can confirm an observation, the greater will be its predictability and consistency. Academic journals are full of studies that replicate previous studies using different participants, different settings, and/or additional measures. For example, Sutherland's differential association study (see Chapter 8) has been replicated hundreds of times (see Williams & McShane, 2012).

At the same time, however, social scientists are trained to be skeptical and to question existing knowledge. Thus, as new evidence and/or insights are gained, theories are subject to being refined or modified.

Finally, however sophisticated and structured research methodology may appear to be, it can also be described as an art—one that requires a certain amount of creativity and practice to perfect (Palys & Atchison, 2013). It is also important to recognize that the flexibility of research design is limited by factors such as cost, time, and practicality.

## Summary

- Crime data, from both official and unofficial sources, are essential to explaining crime trends and patterns, as well as to developing criminological theory and formulating social policy.
- Each of the various data sources has its strengths and weaknesses; the choice of which to employ typically depends on the resources available, along with the researcher's training and theoretical bias, as well as the nature of the phenomenon under study.
- Triangulation is a practical and effective method that can increase the validity of research findings. As Simon (cited in DeKeseredy & Schwartz, 1996, p. 148) observed, "a research method for a given problem is not like the solution to a problem in Algebra. It is more like a recipe for beef stroganoff; there is no one best recipe."
- An interdisciplinary and multi-method approach is recommended for both the collection and the interpretation of criminological information.

## Discussion Questions

1. Why are crime data essential to the study of crime? What are some of the major problems associated with the different sources of crime data?
2. In addition to measuring the volume of crime across Canada, the Crime Severity Index (CSI) takes into account the difference in severity between crimes, which is given by the average sentence for the offence. Do you think the CSI is a good indicator for crime in Canada?
3. How can the various sources of information on criminal events be used to verify or distort crime rates?
4. Identify some criminological/criminal justice policy decisions that appear to have been ill informed. How might such outcomes be avoided?
5. Examine the media coverage of two or three different types of crime currently in the news and then look at the official data on the crimes in a recent *Juristat* bulletin. Is the media coverage consistent with the official data? What might account for the differences? What implications might this have for criminal policy?
6. Which do you think is more useful: UCR data or self-report study data? Why? Which do you think is more predictive of high-risk behaviours and/or reoffending? Based on your answers, how might we determine the best intervention strategies?

## Key Concepts

Canadian Centre for Justice Statistics (CCJS)
Canadian Urban Victimization Survey (CUVS)
causality
correlation (direct correlation)
correctional statistics
crime data
dark figure of crime
false positive
General Social Survey (GSS)
hypothesis

negative correlation
positive correlation
qualitative research
restorative justice
self-report studies
triangulation
Uniform Crime Reporting (UCR)
unofficial data
*Verstehen*
victimization survey

## Key Names

Ezzat Fattah (b. 1929)
Kim Rossmo (b. 1955)
Max Weber (1864–1920)

## Weblinks

**Environmental Criminology Research Inc.**
An excellent Canadian source for those interested in geographic profiling.
www.geographicprofiling.com/geopro/ref-request.htm

**Statistics Canada: Uniform Crime Reporting Survey (UCR)**
A detailed overview of the Uniform Crime Report Survey.
http://www23.statcan.gc.ca/imdb/p2SV.pl?Function=getSurvey&SDDS=3302

**Statistics Canada: Crime and Justice**
Links to recent justice and crime statistics from Statistics Canada.
http://www5.statcan.gc.ca/subject-sujet/theme-theme.action?pid=2693&lang=eng&more=0&MM

**Home Office (United Kingdom)**
The UK Home Office offers a wealth of data on crime in Britain.
www.homeoffice.gov.uk

# Chapter 4

## Victims and Victimology with Jesse Cale*

Nisarg Lakhmani / Shutterstock.com

I am a man; more sinn'd against than sinning.
SHAKESPEARE, *KING LEAR*, ACT III, SCENE 2

* Dr Jesse Cale is Senior Lecturer in the School of Social Sciences
at the University of New South Wales in Sydney, Australia

## Learning Outcomes

After reading this chapter, you should be able to

- Understand the role of victimology in the study of crime;
- Describe the key theories of victimology;
- Identify some of the key findings regarding victims of crime;
- Discuss the new challenges of victimology;
- Identify the range of government services for victims.

In recent years a number of male celebrities, including Stephen Collins, Ray Rice, Bill Cosby, Shane Sparks, and Jian Ghomeshi, have been accused of using their positions to sexually exploit women. The allegations have been widely discussed on social media, and the public has formed strong opinions even in the absence of formal charges. Under such circumstances, how can the rights of the people involved in such cases—not just the accused and their accusers, but their families and friends—be protected? How might public statements made by those involved influence the judicial proceedings? Is there a risk that victims who come forward may be further victimized in the process?

Such cases demonstrate the complexity of victimology. Victimization takes many forms and can carry substantial repercussions for the individuals involved, and the repercussions often extend to their families, communities, and even society as a whole. Studying victimization experiences can assist in the development of theories that can inform prevention efforts, the development of legislation and policy, and the allocation of resources to assist victims. On the other hand, victimization data can also be used politically in ways that raise fundamental questions about human rights.

## Introduction

By definition, every crime has consequences, whether material or personal loss, physical suffering, or emotional distress. Victimization can create the conditions for a wide range of adverse outcomes, including in some cases antisocial behaviour on the part of the victim. Several Canadian researchers have shown that those who have been victims of abuse and/or neglect as children are at increased risk of becoming offenders themselves (MacIntyre, 2013; MacLaurin & Worthington, 2013), and of committing certain types of crimes, such as sexual offences (Cale, Plecas, Cohen, & Fortier, 2010; Cale, Leclerc, & Smallbone, 2014).

The World Society of Victimology defines victimology as

> the scientific study of the extent, nature and causes of criminal victimization, its consequences for the persons involved and the reactions thereto by society, in particular the police and the criminal justice system as well as voluntary workers and professional helpers. (cited in van Dijk, 1999, p. 6)

In this chapter, we will focus on victims and their relationship to the criminal and the criminal justice process. We will also examine how the needs of victims are being addressed and becoming a major focus within Canadian criminology and criminal justice policy and practice.

**victimology**
A sub-field of criminology that focuses on the relationship between victims and perpetrators of crimes, against the backdrop of social institutions such as the criminal justice system.

## The Roots of Victimology

In early Germanic law, those who caused the injury or death of a person were required to pay compensation, known as *wergeld* (literally "man money"), to victims or their families and clans.

In time, however, this system was replaced by harsh physical punishment (often the death penalty). It was the inhumane treatment of offenders that gave rise to criminology, which, as the discipline developed, continued to focus almost exclusively on the perpetrators of crime, leaving victims largely forgotten until the twentieth century.

Although writing about the victim appeared in a number of early works by such criminologists as Beccaria (1764), Lombroso (1876), and Garofalo (1885), one of the first to recognize the importance of the victim was **Benjamin Mendelsohn**, a Romanian defence lawyer who began developing a typology of victims in the late 1930s. Mendelsohn is now commonly referred to as the "father" of victimology. However, in Marvin Wolfgang's view it was **Hans von Hentig** (see Box 4.1) who, above all, drew attention to "the role of the victim in the duet of crime" (cited in Schafer, 1968, p. v). Hentig's landmark work, *The Criminal and His Victim*, was published in 1948.

The idea that "many criminal deeds are more indicative of a offender–victim relation than of the perpetrator alone" (von Hentig, 1948, p. 384) led early researchers to focus their attention on the relationship between perpetrators (von Hentig's "offender") and their victims ("victim"). This focus led to what is sometimes referred to as "blaming the victim," the notion that somehow victims contribute to their own victimization.

In 2013, Global News reported on a survey conducted by the Canadian Women's Foundation, which revealed that victim-blaming still occurs in Canada, especially in cases of sexual assault. Reporting on the findings, which were compiled by a Halifax-based organization, Lau (2013) stated that one in five Canadians believed that woman may unwittingly and/or inadvertently provoke or encourage their sexual assault (i.e. their victimization) by being drunk. Another 15 per cent of those surveyed thought women provoked their victimization by flirting, and 11 per cent believed that wearing a short skirt might have encouraged their sexual assault. The notion of victim-blaming was highlighted around the same time by the suicide of Nova Scotia teen Rehtaeh Parsons, who took her life after a photo taken while she was allegedly being raped by four boys was posted on social media. Parsons had reported the incident to police, but the failure to get the case to trial led to accusations of bias and victim-blaming on the part of police and Crown prosecutors (Ross, 2013).

## BOX 4.1    PROFILE   Hans von Hentig

A German criminal psychologist strongly opposed to Nazi social and political ideology, Hans von Hentig left Germany for the United States in the late 1930s. Within a few years he published an article in which he suggested that in some cases "the victim . . . contributes amply to the commitment of the crime" (von Hentig, 1940, p. 308). This was followed by his seminal book, *The Criminal and His Victim* (1948), which used a sociobiological perspective to explain the relationship between criminal and victim. It was instrumental in helping to move the role of the victim into the discussion of criminal justice; ironically, however, he never used the term *victimology* in his work.

Von Hentig identified several "general classes of victims"—among them women, ethnic minorities, the young, the elderly, people with mental and physical disabilities—and observed that these classes of victims tended to share certain physical characteristics with the perpetrators of the crimes committed against them. He believed, as a result, that understanding the role of the victim in crimes could result in more effective crime prevention.

Later criminologists regarded Hentig's theory with scepticism, given its basis in *determinism*, the view that human behaviour is influenced by factors seen as external to free will. However, his approach was championed by several other pioneers in victimology, including the American Stephan Schafer, Willem Nagel in the Netherlands, and Ezzat Fattah in Canada. In honour of his memory and contributions to the field, the World Society of Victimology has, since 1982, given out an award in his name to the person who has made the most significant mark in victimology.

The early "victimologists," as Mendelsohn (1937) characterized them, were concerned mostly with theorizing the causes of crime, including the victim's role. The following decades saw the growth of empirical research into specific types of victimization, including victimization associated with homicide (Wolfgang, 1958), robbery (Normandeau, 1968), rape (Amir, 1971), and blackmail (Helworth, 1975).

At much the same time, the political and ideological shifts in Western societies that emphasized the rights of disadvantaged groups such as women and ethnic minorities led to criticism of theoretical victimology as "the art of blaming the victim" (Ryan, 2010, p. 11). Although practitioners argued that, on the contrary, their work was directed toward assisting potential victims from becoming victims—a preventative approach—the field now took on a more applied character, focusing on "assisting crime victims, alleviating their plight and affirming

Patrick Doyle/The Canandian Press

In 2014, the men's varsity hockey program at the University of Ottawa was suspended for two seasons in response to allegations that several players had been involved in a sexual assault. Two players were later charged.

their rights" (Fattah, 2000, p. 25). Meanwhile, the feminist movement was drawing attention to the issues of sexual assault, particularly intimate partner violence, and how the legal system had failed female victims (Fattah, 2000). This shift broadened the scope of victimology to include a humanitarian dimension, and set the stage for connections between scholarly research and political activism. Today the victims' rights movement that emerged from the feminist stance provides an important platform for advocates of gay, lesbian, and transgender rights, and scholarly research documenting victimization experiences in those communities (Haskell & Burtch, 2010).

As an applied science, victimology has confronted many of the same challenges as criminology in trying to bridge the gap between theory and practice. After the dramatic changes in theoretical orientation of the 1970s, the 1980s and 1990s represented a period of consolidation, data gathering, and theory testing. These decades were also characterized by the introduction of new victim protection legislation, victim compensation, victim assistance and a wide range of service programs, and policy changes on many levels.

Perhaps most importantly, the study of victimology gained formal recognition in 1985, when the General Assembly of the United Nations adopted the *Declaration of Basic Principles of Justice for Victims of Crime and Abuse of Power*. In framing the declaration, the UN recognized the plight of millions of victims around the world. This recognition was due, in part, to a growing body of research on the nature, causes, and consequences of victimization, and was bolstered by important evidence garnered from the introduction of victimization surveys around the world. Irvin Waller, from the University of Ottawa, was instrumental in both drafting this declaration and bringing it into existence. His passion for the rights of victims is reflected in three recent books (Waller, 2008; Waller, 2010; Waller, 2014) that call for a realignment of criminal justice budgets in order to direct more resources toward support for victims. Since the late 1980s, Canada has been at the forefront in this area, and Canadian institutions have been home to some of the world's leading victimologists, among them Ezzat Fattah, Tammy Landau, Hanna Scott, and Jo-Anne Wemmers.

## Victimization Surveys

As victimologists began to shift from theoretical speculation toward more empirical evaluation of their ideas following the 1950s, new instruments were needed to collect the necessary data. The victimization survey (VS) became the dominant method of inquiry. Such surveys ask respondents whether they have been the victim of a crime (usually within a fixed period of time, such as the previous year); those who say they have been the victim of a crime may then be asked questions about their victimization experiences and their impressions how the various elements of the criminal justice system (CJS) dealt with their case.

### Advantages and Disadvantages

Although Uniform Crime Reporting (UCR) data and victimization surveys both provide information on crime, they approach the subject from very different perspectives: they focus on different populations (offenders and victims), and they make/have different assumptions about the reliability and validity of their data. While VS data are useful for determining the prevalence of different types of victimization (e.g., violent, sexual, and property crimes), they cannot tell us anything about the numbers of perpetrators (see Walklate, 2000), which is information that can be obtained from UCR data. (What these data show is that a small proportion of offenders are responsible for a majority of victimization incidents: see Scott, 2011.) There are benefits, then, to each of these two data sources, which should be seen as complementary.

Evans and Leger (1979) enumerated several of the benefits of victimization surveys, which offer superior insight into

- the extent and distribution of selected crimes—victimization surveys generate data that provide a more complete picture of crime, including the dark figure, than may be possible based on official sources;
- the impact of selected crimes, such as injury and cost to victims (financial, emotional, and physical)—such information is not available through the UCR;
- the risk of victimization—victimization surveys can unearth information not only on factors that affect a person's risk of being victimized but also on perceived risk of criminal victimization; and
- the victim's perception of the functioning and effectiveness of different aspects of the criminal justice system, which can be contrasted with the perceptions of non-victims.

But as useful as VS data may appear to be, measurement in the behavioural sciences is never perfect; criminologists are often forced to ask themselves whether the questions can tell us enough to justify the time and money invested in developing policies based on them. Another important question is whether reporting the results of victimization surveys might create unexpected anxiety and fear of crime in the public. For example, the sale of house alarms closely parallels media coverage of theft-related victimization. Heightened awareness of the risk inadvertently triggers the sale of house alarms. Ironically, it is usually the people most in need of protection (young people and low-income groups) who are least able to afford such preventative devices.

Although the use of victimization surveys has become more common in recent years, the results at times provide more questions than answers (Landau, 2006). For example, measuring crime through surveys of the general population is problematic because crime (especially serious and/or violent crime) is relatively infrequent, and crime victimization is not evenly distributed across the population. Moreover, individuals who are more difficult to reach, such as those with no fixed address and no (mobile) phone access, or those who are hospitalized or incarcerated, are rarely included in such surveys. This is especially important given that some of these individuals are at an elevated risk of victimization (e.g. homeless youth: see O'Grady, 2014). Similarly, surveys do not typically include tourists or visitors who are victimized during their stay.

## Canadian Victimization Surveys

Growing policy interest since the 1980s has led criminologists to produce a greater volume of research on victims over the past three decades. It was early in the 1980s that Canada conducted the Canadian Urban Victimization Survey (CUVS: see Chapter 3), which involved telephone interviews with some 60,000 randomly sampled respondents over the age of 17 in seven different cities: Vancouver, Edmonton, Winnipeg, Toronto, Montreal, Halifax/Dartmouth, and St John's. The survey covered seven categories of crime:

- assault
- sexual assault
- motor-vehicle theft
- household theft (i.e. break-and-enter)
- theft of personal property
- robbery (i.e. theft under threat of force)
- vandalism

**General Social Survey (GSS)**

A series of annual surveys by Statistics Canada designed to gather information on social trends and specific policy issues (e.g., victimization).

**Violence Against Women Survey (VAWS)**

A 1993 survey of Canadian women aged 18+, which examined women's safety inside and outside the home, focusing on issues such as sexual harassment, sexual violence, physical violence, and perceptions of fear.

In 1988, Statistics Canada began conducting a victimization survey as part of its General Social Survey (GSS). The GSS replaced the CUVS and introduced a more standardized and consistent format for gathering victimization data. Data on perceptions of personal safety were collected in 1988 and 1993, and on victimization in 1999 (see Box 4.2). In 2000, Statistics Canada switched to an annual survey; however, the GSS focuses on a different topic each year, (e.g. health and well-being, work and education, social support, or victimization). Today's surveys are conducted by random-digit dialling (RDD) and computer-assisted telephone interviewing (CATI) and take approximately 45 minutes of the respondent's time to complete.

The cross-Canada Violence Against Women Survey (VAWS), conducted in 1993, was designed "to overcome the limitations of traditional survey techniques in uncovering the nature and complexity of violence against women in intimate partner relationships" (Landau, 2006, p. 52). It involved telephone interviews with more than 12,000 women aged 18 and older. The questions focused on experiences of physical and/or sexual violence after the age of 16 as well as perceptions of personal safety. About half of the respondents reported that they had experienced at least one incident of violence since the age of 16; the perpetrators were typically males who were known to them. The VAWS has been the only study of its kind in Canada, but issues related to violence against women in Canada—such as fear of crime, stalking, sexual assault, and spousal violence—were also explored in the 1999 GSS and as part of the Victims Services Survey in 2009–10 (Sinha, 2012).

Since 2001–2, the federal government has conducted annual surveys on family violence. In 2012, an issue of Statistics Canada's periodical *Juristat* reported that the victimization rate for persons 18–24 years of age was 14 times higher than the rate for seniors (2,226 per 100,000 versus 157 per 100,000). Young people under the age of 18 accounted for 21 per cent of all victimizations reported to the police; 60 per cent of those who were victims of sexual offences; and 20 per cent of those who were victims of physical assault (see Figure 4.1, page 78).

Peter Power / Getty Images

A candlelight vigil in Montreal marked the twenty-fifth anniversary of the murder of 14 female engineering students at Montreal's École Polytechnique in 1989. The "Montreal Massacre," which is commemorated every year on 6 December—the National Day of Remembrance and Action on Violence Against Women—gave rise to such initiatives such as the 1993 Violence Against Women Survey (VAWS).

## BOX 4.2 FACTS AND FIGURES HIGHLIGHTS OF THE GSS, 1988–2009

- Strangers committed 45 per cent of robberies in 1988; 67 per cent in 1993; 51 per cent in 1999; and 60 per cent in 2004. Men were generally at greater risk of being robbed than were women. After 1999, robbery rates increased by 44 per cent, but remained stable between 2004 and 2009. This increase reflected an increase in the numbers of women who reported being victims of robbery. By 2009, women and men reported similar rates of robbery victimization.

- Strangers committed 26 per cent of assaults in 1988; 38 per cent in 1993; 25 per cent in 1999; and 44 per cent in 2004. Young adult males made up the vast majority of violent offenders. Women have consistently been far more likely to be victims of sexual assault than men, and similar rates of sexual victimization among women were reported in the 1999, 2004, and 2009 GSS. As well, the risk of violent victimization decreases with age: 21 per cent of those aged 16–24 were victims, versus 3 per cent of those aged 65 years and older. These findings have been consistent for several cycles of the GSS. Between 1993 and 2009, the overall rate of victimization for physical/sexual assault remained virtually unchanged.

- Since 1988, those living in urban settings have consistently reported higher rates of victimization than those living in rural settings.

- Overall, property crime increased steadily between 1993 and 2009. This finding stands in contrast to UCR data indicating that these crimes have been declining since the early 1990s. The discrepancy can likely be explained in part by differences in reporting practices.

- In 2001, 87 per cent of Canadians believed that the police were doing a good job in general, but the support dropped to 69 per cent when respondents were asked if they were satisfied with police responses to crime.

*Sources:* Besserer & Trainor, 2000; Besserer, 2002; Gannon & Mihorean, 2005; Perreault & Brennan, 2010.

### Table 4.1   Self-Reported Victimization, 1999, 2004, and 2009

| Year | Total Violent Victimization Number of incidents (thousands) | Rate per 100,000 | Total Household Victimization Number of incidents (thousands) | Rate per 100,000 | Theft of Personal Property Number of incidents (thousands) | Rate per 100,000 |
|---|---|---|---|---|---|---|
| 1999 | 2,691 | 111 | 2,656 | 218 | 1,831 | 75 |
| 2004 | 2,751 | 106 | 3,206 | 248 | 2,408 | 93 |
| 2009 | 3,267 | 118 | 3,184 | 237 | 2,981 | 108 |

*Source:* Statistics Canada, 2009. General Social Survey.

## The International Crime Victims Survey

The International Crime Victims Survey (ICVS) has been conducted six times between 1989 and 2005, when the final comprehensive cycle was completed in some 80 countries (van Kesteren, van Dijk, & Mayhew, 2014). With each survey, the methodology has been refined to ensure more representative samples, and the resulting data allow international comparisons of crime. Although financial limitations and various political factors have made it difficult to retain a consistent number of participating countries from the developing world (see van Kesteren, et al., 2014), the following are among the highlights from the various survey cycles that Canada has participated in:

- Between 1989 and 2004–5, Canada, the United States, Australia, and several European countries showed a downward trend in victimization rates.
- Consistent with the official crime rates, self-reported rates of victimization have declined since 2000.

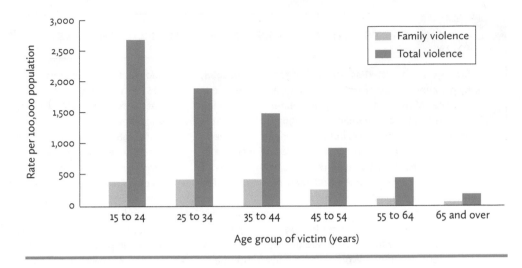

**Figure 4.1    Victims of Violent Crime in Canada by Age Group**

*Source*: Statistics Canada, 2011. Family Violence in Canada, Catalogue no. 85-224-X, p. 27.

- Based on a secondary analysis of the ICVS data (Farrell et al., 2011, cited in van Kesteren et al., 2014), the first crime to show a decline was car theft, followed by break-and-enter. Victimization involving assault also declined, but not as rapidly as some of the other more conventional crimes (e.g. robbery, theft).
- The fact that the drop in reported crime was fairly universal, in the analysis of van Kesteren et al. (2014), undermines claims that declines in individual countries can be attributed only to their efforts in areas such as law enforcement, the judiciary, corrections, or economic conditions. A more nuanced explanation is required.
- ICVS findings over several cycles show no evidence to suggest that prior victimization leads to fear of crime among Canadians. A recent survey of Canadian students by Hincks and Winterdyk (2015) lends support to these findings.

---

| BOX 4.3 | WHAT DO YOU THINK? |
| --- | --- |

## Does Crime Make You Angry or Afraid?

One of the reasons for conducting victimization surveys is to measure the fear of crime among the people surveyed. Yet, as often happens in a relatively new field of study, the concepts used to describe the phenomenon in question may not be adequately *operationalized*, or defined.

Jason Ditton and his colleagues (1999) conducted a study in which they explored the "fear of crime" concept. Based on interview data, they found—contrary to expectations—that more people reported feeling anger at "the prospect of criminal victimization" than fear of it (Ditton et al., 1999, p. 98). They speculated that anger may stem from the general perception that crime is increasing and

that the CJS is not able to effectively fulfill its mandate. They concluded that it might be worthwhile to concentrate on the nature and meaning of anger in the context of victimization. They reasoned that such a focus might help clarify the difference between being angry about the threat of criminal victimization and being afraid of it (Ditton et al., 1999). Their research has helped to highlight the conceptual complexity of both terms and the need to research anger as it relates to risk of victimization.

How important is the distinction between being angry about the risk of victimization and being fearful? Do you think one emotional response might be more debilitating than the other when it comes to perceived risk of victimization?

**Table 4.2    Victimization Rates from the International Crime Victims Survey, Select Countries, 1989–2000**

| Country | Number of Offences per 100 Inhabitants | | | |
| --- | --- | --- | --- | --- |
| | 1989 | 1992 | 1996 | 2000 |
| Canada | 47.9 | 51.3 | 44.1 | 40.4 |
| England & Wales | 28.7 | 51.9 | 56.5 | 54.5 |
| Finland | 22.2 | 34.1 | 30.4 | 28.6 |
| Netherlands | 46.8 | 55.2 | 58.5 | 48.1 |
| All countries | 20.2 | 22.1 | 24.2 | 21.3 |

Note: Includes the following offences: car theft; theft from car; car vandalism; motorcycle theft; bicycle theft; burglary; attempted burglary; robbery; personal thefts; sexual incidents; assaults and threats.
*Source:* Van Kesteren, J.N., Mayhew, P. & Nieuwbeerta, P. (2000) 'Criminal Victimisation in Seventeen Industrialised Countries: Key-findings from the 2000 International Crime Victims Survey'. The Hague, Ministry of Justice, WODC, p. 178.

Although these and other surveys have helped to shed light on crime, reported and un-reported, they have not been without their critics. In particular, concerns have been raised about methodologies. For example, does the fact that surveys tend to question only people in urban centres affect the results? Researchers have made concerted efforts to address such shortcomings. For example, **Jan van Dijk** (see Box 4.4) is attempting to standardize the manner in which the data are recorded in order to make the surveys consistent between countries. Because of the diligence of those who engage in victimization research, victimization surveys have slowly gained acceptance and have had a modest impact on the development of policies to address crime. Innovative methodological designs are also being used to access unique populations. Researchers from the University of Cincinnati have developed large-scale victimization surveys based on nationally representative samples of college students, often with a focus on sexual assault (see Fisher & Lab, 2010). Similar surveys have been conducted in Canada.

## Victim Characteristics

Virtually every victimization survey gathers social and demographic details that differentiate victims from non-victims and/or identify those who might be at greater risk of victimization based on various characteristics.

| BOX 4.4 | PROFILE    Jan van Dijk and the ICVS |
| --- | --- |

Jan van Dijk was introduced to victimology in the early 1970s, after he was asked to take over the class taught by his graduate supervisor, noted Dutch criminologist Willem Nagel. Nagel had left some unfinished notes on victims of violent crime, and van Dijk followed up on the research, eventually working on various victimology projects for the Dutch government and related studies for the United Nations; helping develop the first comprehensive national Dutch victimization survey; and being regularly consulted by the Dutch government. In 1987, he became the founding president of the Dutch National Association of Victim Support.

Van Dijk was instrumental in the creation of the International Crime Victims Survey, which has become the world standard for such surveys. In addition, he has spearheaded initiatives within the United Nations that address the rights of victims, and has played a major role in the World Society of Victimology, which offers a comprehensive collection of literature and information on victimology-oriented work on its website (www.victimology.nl).

## Age

According to the 2009 General Social Survey, just over 25 per cent of the Canadian population over the age of 15 reported having been the victim of a criminal incident in the previous 12 months. Young people aged 15–24 had the highest rates of victimization, while those 65 years of age and older had the lowest victimization rates across all major categories—sexual assault, robbery, physical assault, and theft of personal property (Perreault & Brennan, 2010). Perreault and Brennan (2010) report that proportionately, "people between the ages of 15 and 24 years were almost 15 times more likely than those aged 65 and older to report being a victim of a violent victimization." In accordance with the lifestyle theory and routine activity theory, there also appears to be a strong correlation between lifestyle, age, and victimization (see Payne, 2011). For example, adolescents and young adults tend to stay out later at night, frequent public places such as bars and restaurants, and just hang out in groups far more than adults. Payne (2011), among others, reports that almost half of all victimizations occur in or around a private dwelling, and nearly one-third in public places such as pubs and parking lots (Perreault, 2013b).

In one of the first Canadian studies to examine victimization and fear of victimization among the elderly, Brillon (1987) reported that fear of crime seemed to increase progressively among older age groups. Several years later, Weinrath and Gartrell (1996) reported similar trends in their Alberta-based study, and a more recent study by Ogrodnick (2007) reinforces the findings. Ironically, however, as noted earlier, Perreault and Brennan (2010) report that those aged 65 and older are at considerably lower risk of being victimized than younger age groups. Again, consistent with the lifestyle theory and/or routine activities theory, one explanation is that their physical, financial, and social circumstances can lead the elderly to *feel* more vulnerable than they actually are.

One of the more alarming findings from victimization research is the degree to which children may be at risk in their homes. In 1984, the Badgley Report documented that young people were more commonly victims of sexual abuse in the home than had previously been thought. The report also highlighted that children are more likely to be sexually abused by people known to them, including family members, than by strangers. Various studies point out how difficult it is to provide reliable estimates of child abuse in general and sexual abuse specifically. However, a comprehensive study in 1998 reported that approximately 45 per cent of all cases involving children investigated by welfare staff involved substantiated cases of abuse (see Box 4.5).

## Gender

Gender is a major factor in certain crimes. According to the 2004 GSS and consistent with UCR survey data from 2011, women in Canada are more likely than men to be victims of sexual assault and theft, although men are more likely to be victims of crimes such as robbery and assault (Nault, 2014). Overall, women were more likely to be victimized than men, although only by a slight margin (189 versus 183 per 1,000). However, a preponderance of evidence shows that sexual assaults and spousal violence are dramatically underreported to police (for further discussion of the various policy and prevention/intervention implications of these findings, see Artz, Stoneman, & Reitsma-Street, 2012; Faith, 2002).

Recently, there has been considerable media and political attention given to the confluence of gender and sexual violence on college and university campuses. In 2013, the Canadian Federation of Students in Ontario put out a fact sheet warning about the prevalence of sexual assault on Canadian college and university campuses (CFS, 2013). Drawing on some older evidence (DeKeseredy & Kelly, 1993), the bulletin noted that four out of five Canadian undergraduate students claimed to have experienced violence in a dating relationship. The following year, the issue of campus sexual violence gained national prominence when pro-rape chants

| BOX 4.5 | **A CLOSER LOOK** |
|---|---|
| | **The Canadian Incidence Study of Reported Child Abuse and Neglect** |

The Canadian Incidence Study, or CIS, is a national study that estimates the incidence of child maltreatment (physical, sexual, and emotional abuse and neglect) in Canada on the basis of investigations by child welfare services. To date, only three cycles of the study have been completed (1998, 2003, 2008). For the 2008 cycle, the CIS tracked 15,980 child maltreatment investigations, which make up nearly 15 per cent of an estimated 235,842 investigations into child maltreatment conducted in Canada in 2008. Because the conditions at the time of each of the survey periods differed—for instance, in terms of the political climate and public awareness of the issue—any direct comparisons should be viewed with a degree of caution. Notwithstanding the methodological issues, in 1998 the rate of investigations was 21.47 per 1,000 children in Canada. By 2003, the rate had nearly doubled to 38.33 per 1,000 children, and by 2008 it had climbed slightly more, to 39.16 per 1,000 children. The two most frequently occurring categories of maltreatment were exposure to intimate partner violence and neglect—roughly 34 per cent of all the study cases (Trocme et al., 2010, p. 17).

The 2008 cycle included children of Aboriginal heritage. They were included because they "were identified as a key group to examine because of concerns about their overrepresentation in the foster care system" (Trocme et al., 2010, p. 18). Children of Aboriginal heritage represented 22 per cent of the substantiated cases. As the authors of the study point out, the fact that the CIS captures only cases reported to child welfare suggests that child abuse is far more widespread than statistics indicate (Trocme et al., 2010, p. 22).

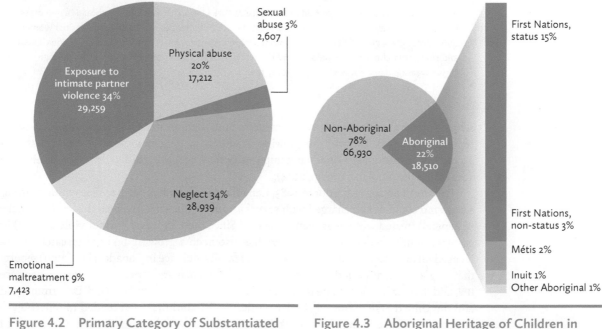

**Figure 4.2   Primary Category of Substantiated Child Maltreatment in Canada, 2008**

Note: Total estimated number of substantiated investigations is 85,440, based on a sample of 6,163 substantiated investigations.

*Source*: Public Health Agency of Canada. Canadian Incidence Study of Reported Child Abuse and Neglect – 2008: Major Findings. Ottawa, 2010. p. 4. © Her Majesty the Queen in Right of Canada, 2010.

**Figure 4.3   Aboriginal Heritage of Children in Substantiated Child Maltreatment Investigations in Canada, 2008**

Note: Based on a sample of 6,163 substantiated investigations.

*Source*: Public Health Agency of Canada. Canadian Incidence Study of Reported Child Abuse and Neglect – 2008: Major Findings. Ottawa, 2010. p. 5. © Her Majesty the Queen in Right of Canada, 2010.

at St Mary's University in Halifax were captured and posted to social media. This episode was followed a year later by an incident involving misogynistic Facebook posts by several dentistry students at Dalhousie University in Halifax. (The CBC maintains an interactive timeline of sexual assaults on Canadian campuses, drawn from incident reports from 87 post-secondary

In 2011, a Toronto police officer told an audience at York University that women should "avoid dress-ing like sluts" to avoid victimization. To protest this stereotyping, as well as violence against women more generally, a group of women organized a march that they called the Slut Walk. The idea spread, and similar marches are now held around the world. In this photo from a Toronto walk, the sign reads "I was wearing pants + a sweater, was it my fault too?"

schools across the country: www.cbc.ca/news/multimedia/interactive-campus-sexual-assault-reports-1.2944538). Despite the growing attention to gender violence in Canadian post-secondary institutions, Canadian campuses appear to have paid only token attention to addressing the problem (Brown, 2014).

It is worth noting that prior to 1983, Canadian law did not recognize rape within marriage: a husband could not be charged with sexual assault of his wife. In effect, the law (like society in general) treated women as men's property. Since then, intimate partner violence (IPV) has garnered much-needed attention. There has also been a growing body of research that has focused on male victims of IPV. In his study of family violence in Canada, Hoff (2001) reported that over a five-year period of study, 8 per cent of women and 5 per cent of men experienced IPV, and that the incidence rate for men had increased over the study period. Data from Britain and the United States showed similar results. Hoff found that men tended to report IPV far less than women, and that this was likely a reflection of social norms. Thus, it is reasonable to conclude that those figures are likely vast underestimates. To report intimate partner violence is to run the risk both of societal stigma and of further assault by the partner; it can also have negative implications for children and family stability, although not reporting IPV can have similar consequences.

## Household Income

The GSS includes a summary of victimization according to household income. The 2009 data showed that Canadians with household incomes of $100,000 or more were more likely (237 per 1,000 households) than others to have their houses vandalized or broken into. This is con-sistent with findings in the 2004 GSS cycle. Needless to say, the higher a household's income, the more inviting its contents will be to prospective offenders. The rate of victimization among those in the higher income brackets was one-and-a-half times greater than among those with household incomes under $20,000 (Perreault & Brennan, 2010).

## Marital Status and Sexual Orientation

The effect of marital status on risk of victimization varies by crime type. On the one hand, marriage and childbearing are turning points in life that decrease the risk of both criminality and victimization for many types of crime because of associated changes in lifestyle. Although marriage also has the potential to increase the risk of other types of victimization, such as intimate partner violence, the 2009 GSS showed that violent victimization rates were higher among single people and those in common-law relationships than among those who were married. Other groups with higher rates of violent victimization included Aboriginal people and self-identified homosexuals. Gay and lesbian individuals experience victimization at a rate 2.5 times higher than heterosexual individuals (see Figure 4.4). The latter results reflected those of an earlier Canadian study on sexual orientation and victimization (Beauchamp, 2004).

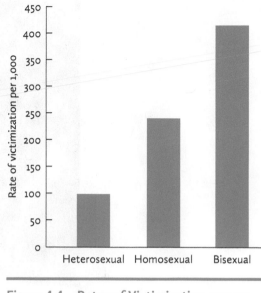

Figure 4.4    Rates of Victimization among Heterosexuals, Homosexuals, and Bisexuals

*Source*: Data from Beauchamp, 2004, p. 8.

## Race and Ethnicity

Because the issue of race and ethnicity is politically sensitive, it can be a difficult topic to study in relation to victimization data. Studies have shown correlations between non-white ethnicity and certain types of victimization, including violence and property crime. However, in both Canada and the United States, these relationships are heavily influenced by additional factors such as social status and poverty. At the same time, unlike in the United States, in Canada the government does not release crime statistics broken down by ethnic background of the victims or the perpetrators, and so it is difficult to gain insight into this type of victimization (Owusu-Bempah, 2013). The problem is further compounded by the fact that refugees who have fled their homelands because of persecution may not trust official agencies enough to report that they have been victimized. Thus, it is often difficult to gain the accurate information needed to address the victimization experiences in some ethnic communities.

Beyond these broad conclusions, the relationship between ethnicity/race and victimization in Canada can also be understood through a more open lens in the way Elias (1993) and Walklate (2006), among others, have proposed. Such efforts would be aided by the introduction of systematic race-based criminal justice data collection, and the public release of such data (Owusu-Bempah, 2013).

The situation of Canada's Aboriginal people with respect to victimization is particularly troubling (see Perrault & Brennan, 2010). The concept of Aboriginal victimization can be extended to include not only criminal victimization but also overrepresentation in the criminal justice system and in systemic social problems, including poverty, high unemployment, poor education, substance abuse, and family disintegration (see Corrado, Cohen, & Cale, 2004). The origins of these adverse conditions have often been traced to historic policies of the Canadian government, such as the policy of removing Aboriginal children from their families and placing them in residential schools. Although the last residential school closed in 1996, the social consequences persist, and Aboriginal people are still all too often victims of racial discrimination. For example, a 2013 report on abusive policing in northern British Columbia details

Trevor Hagan/CP

Rinelle Harper, a 16-year-old Aboriginal victim of sexual assault, addressed the Assembly of First Nations in December 2014 to call for a national inquiry into Canada's missing and murdered Aboriginal women. Aboriginal women and girls are three times more likely than their non-Aboriginal counterparts to be victims of violence.

violent treatment of Indigenous women and girls by the RCMP, including the case of a 17–year-old girl who was punched repeatedly in the face and called a "stupid Indian" by RCMP officers who responded to her call for help when she was being chased by gang members (Human Rights Watch, 2013). The connection between race/ethnicity and victimization remains a controversial and politically charged issue.

## Repeat Victimization

The term "born criminal" was coined by Cesare Lombroso in the late 1800s. Are there likewise born victims? Many of us know someone who seems to suffer from "bad karma," and in a similar way, criminologists have noticed that there are some people who seem particularly prone to experiencing victimization. Aromaa (1974) detected a pattern early on, finding that about 25 per cent of victims of violence were repeat victims. More recently, Kilpatrick and Acierno (2003) argued that, based on the results of their extensive study, the best predictor of future victimization is past victimization. In fact, 4 per cent of victims experience 44 per cent of offences. How do criminologists account for this?

It's not impossible to become a repeat victim simply by chance—to be in the wrong place at the wrong time more than once. There are also certain accidents of birth that give greater plausibility to the notion of the born victim, for we know that those who grow up in certain socioeconomic circumstances have a greater likelihood of being victims of crime. For this reason, the term "born victim" has been replaced in more recent criminological literature by concepts such as "predispositions," "propensities," "proneness," and "vulnerability." These terms refer to the role, whether passive or active, that repeat victims seem to play in their own victimization. In many instances, repeat victimization appears to involve an interaction among factors such as age, sex, personality, occupation, and, perhaps most important, lifestyle. Some of these are social characteristics that people have little or no control over.

Understanding repeat victimization is complicated by the fact that young people (those most likely to be victimized) often do not report their victimization experiences to officials. According to a Toronto-based youth crime and victimization survey, more than half of those who reported being victimized in the past 12 months admitted they had not reported the incidents (Tanner & Wortley, 2002). In partial recognition of this trend, various theoretical models and victim typologies have been developed to explain how various factors converge to increase the likelihood of victimization (see Perreault, 2013a).

## Theoretical Models and Victim Typologies

In many ways, victimology has come full circle. Initially, its focus was on describing types of victims and victimization and trying to explain them without much evidence. Today the field is rich with data that are being used to test old ideas and re-forge them into evidence-based theories of victimization with the goal of developing effective prevention strategies.

### Victim Precipitation Theory

Because the early victim typologies developed by Mendelsohn (1956) and von Hentig (1948) were not based on any empirical evidence, they receive little attention today. However, they reflected the notion that certain people, because of certain distinguishing characteristics and/or their actions (or inaction), presented themselves as potential targets of crime. A common, current example of this way of thinking is the idea that women provoke sexual victimization by dressing provocatively. This line of research is now referred to as victim precipitation theory.

Mendelsohn's typology, the "correlation of culpability (imputability)," focused on the extent of the victim's contribution to the crime. He identified six victim types, including such "completely innocent" victims as children or those who are victimized while unconscious, and such "simulating/imaginary" victims as those who are paranoid, senile, or otherwise detached from reality; today, those who subscribe to conspiracy theories and portray themselves as victims of those in power would fall into the latter category.

Schafer (1968) argued that von Hentig's typology was more sophisticated because he recognized the interaction between biological, psychological, and sociological factors that contribute to victimization. In effect, von Hentig proposed that victims are not "born" but "made." Examples of his types include

- young victims, who because of their age tend to be weak and inexperienced both physically and intellectually and therefore at increased risk of certain crimes such as sexual assault or kidnapping;
- female victims, who tend to be physically weaker than (typically male) offenders;
- minority victims, who are subject to racial prejudice and are often victims of hate crime; and
- "tormentor victims," who actively provoke others to lash out against them.

Not surprisingly, empirical research along these lines has been controversial. In 1958, Wolfgang found that in approximately one-quarter of violent incidents that ended in homicide, the victim had unwittingly played a role in instigating the sequence of events. Amir (1971) found similar proportions and drew parallel conclusions regarding women who were sexually assaulted. Such research can have real-world consequences; the findings may provide information for preventing victimization in the future, but they can also be used to reduce the legal culpability of perpetrators and thus diminish the likelihood of justice for victims. As a consequence, these ideas have been contextualized in more complex models that take into account various factors beyond the victims themselves.

**victim precipitation theory**
The theory that some people make themselves targets for victimization, through their actions or inaction.

## Lifestyle Model

**lifestyle theory/model**
The theory that some people experience a greater risk of being victims of crime because of their lifestyle habits and patterns of behaviour.

One of the first important empirical victimization models was the lifestyle theory (or model) developed by Hindelang, Gottfredson, and Garofalo (1978), who suggested that the risk of victimization is significantly correlated with lifestyle. Put quite simply, the more active and social you are, the greater your risk of being victimized, particularly if you engage in certain types of activities. For example, university students may take part in risky behaviours such as excessive drinking and/or drug use, which put them at considerably greater risk of crimes such as theft and assault (see e.g. DeVoe et al., 2002).

The lifestyle model shares many similarities with opportunity models of offending, which attribute the risk of crime/victimization partly to demographic, social, and economic conditions or situations (see Chapter 8). For example, young people who go out to a bar in Halifax or Winnipeg are at greater risk of being assaulted than those who go camping with their parents in Northern British Columbia. Three related hypotheses have been derived from the lifestyle model:

1. The *equivalent groups hypothesis* suggests that the offender and victim share certain characteristics. This hypothesis seems most valid in relation to personal victimization (i.e. violence). GSS data indicate that victims and their offenders are typically close in age.
2. The *proximity hypothesis* suggests some people knowingly place themselves at risk by choosing a high-risk lifestyle (e.g. frequenting certain bars or hanging out with gangs). Such individuals do not actively encourage their own victimization, but they make bad choices.
3. The *deviant place hypothesis* asserts that some areas are simply more conducive to criminal activity than others. For example, if you were not intoxicated but missed your bus stop late at night and ended up in an area that is home to nightclubs, gang activity, and drug

iStock.com/wundervisuals

The lifestyle model theory correlates the risk of victimization with an individual's lifestyle. Among other things, the theory proposes that the more active your social life, the greater your risk of being victimized.

dealing, your risk of experiencing some form of victimization would increase regardless of any precautions you might have taken.

## Routine Activity Theory

Another conceptual model that has become popular in victimology is Cohen and Felson's (1979) routine activity theory, or RAT (see Figure 4.5 and Chapter 8). This theory posits that any crime requires the convergence of three elements:

- the presence of a motivated offender or offenders
- the availability of a suitable target (i.e. a victim or victims)
- the absence of a "capable guardian" (i.e. someone who could intervene to prevent the crime from being committed)

Although primarily a theory of criminal behaviour, RAT also applies to victims because it focuses on the routine activities of both parties. Several parallels can be drawn between RAT and lifestyle theory. For example, Cohen and Felson (1979) argued that criminals typically do not go to great lengths to create criminal opportunities; rather, they come across them in the course of their day-to-day activities. In the context of victimization, this suggests that differential risk of victimization is primarily a function of differential exposure to offenders.

Fattah (1991) suggested that specific elements of lifestyle theory and routine activity theory should be combined to assess the relative contribution of factors such as opportunity, individual risk factors, motivated offenders, exposure and associations, dangerous times/places, dangerous behaviours, high-risk activities, defensive and avoidance behaviours, and structural/cultural proneness. As of 2015, researchers have not taken up the challenge.

While theories of victimology have made significant advances since the 1940s, it is important not to make victims into scapegoats. To this end, policy development must be guided by sound evidence-based theory. No single theory can explain all forms of victimization. Still, the different theoretical perspectives can serve as foundations for research that can help us to understand and reduce victimization.

**routine activity theory (RAT)**
The theory that the risk of victimization increases when there is (1) the presence of motivated offenders, (2) an availability of suitable targets, and (3) the absence of capable guardians.

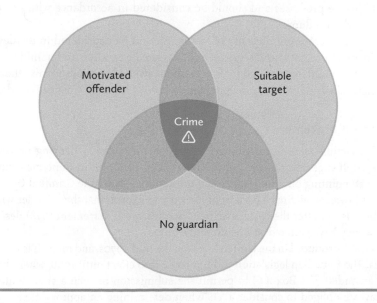

**Figure 4.5   Routine Activity Theory**

*Source:* Based on image by P. S. Burton via Wikipedia CreativeCommons.

# From Theory to Practice: The Emergence of Victims' Rights

*Tears shed for the accused are traditional and "trendy," but has the law none for the victim of crime, the unknown martyr?* (Justice Krishna Iyer of the Supreme Court of India, cited in Rao, 1988, p. 213)

In 2003, the federal, provincial, and territorial ministers responsible for justice endorsed a renewed version of the 1998 *Canadian Statement of Basic Principles of Justice for Victims of Crime* (Justice Canada, 2003). However, it was not until April 2015 that the Office of the Federal Ombudsman for Victims of Crime was finally able to enact the *Victims Bill of Rights Act*. In addition to entrenching many of the principles of justice for victims of crime, the new Act includes four main rights for victims. They include the right to information, the right to protection, the right to participation, and the right to restitution (Canada, 2015).

Reflecting the influence of the UN *Declaration of Basic Principles of Justice for Victims of Crime and Abuse of Power* (1985), these principles are to be respected in laws, policies, and procedures initiated at all levels of government:

1. Victims of crime should be treated with courtesy, compassion, and respect.
2. The privacy of victims should be considered and respected to the greatest extent possible.
3. All reasonable measures should be taken to minimize inconvenience to victims.
4. The safety and security of victims should be considered at all stages of the criminal justice process, and appropriate measures should be taken when necessary to protect victims from intimidation and retaliation.
5. Information should be provided to victims about the criminal justice system and the victim's role and opportunities to participate in criminal justice processes.
6. Victims should be given information, in accordance with prevailing law, policies, and procedures, about the status of the investigation; the scheduling, progress and final outcome of the proceedings; and the status of the offender in the correctional system.
7. Information should be provided to victims about available victim assistance services, other programs and assistance available to them, and means of obtaining financial reparation.
8. The views, concerns, and representations of victims are an important consideration in criminal justice processes and should be considered in accordance with prevailing law, policies, and procedures.
9. The needs, concerns, and diversity of victims should be considered in the development and delivery of programs and services, and in related education and training.
10. Information should be provided to victims about available options to raise their concerns when they believe that these principles have not been followed (Justice Canada, 2003).

## Victim Impact Statements

**victim impact statement (VIS)**
A statement presented by the victim (or a spokesperson) during the sentencing phase of a trial to inform the court of the personal impact of the offender's behaviour.

Traditionally, victims were not permitted to participate in the sentencing process. For example, in 1982, Justice Beverley McLachlin (now Chief Justice of the Supreme Court) refused such a request, pointing out that victims had no standing under the Criminal Code (Burgess, 2010). Today, however, victims have a right not only to expect that the offender will be justly punished but also to offer the court a written victim impact statement (VIS) describing the harm or loss they have suffered as a result of the crime.

The VIS was introduced in the United States in the mid-1970s, and today it is used in all but a few states. The Canadian legislation did not come into effect until 1988, when the Criminal Code was amended (see Box 4.6) to permit the submission of such a statement. Canadian courts today are obliged to consider a VIS when determining an appropriate sentence for a convicted criminal. Victims' rights were further extended in 1995, when Bill C-37 was proclaimed, allowing the presentation of VIS in youth courts.

Although the Criminal Code is a federal law, the lieutenant governor in council of each province directs how a VIS is to be prepared. In Alberta, for example, the VIS program is provided by police services and such non-profit organizations as Victim Services Alberta. In New Brunswick, VIS forms are provided by the provincial Department of Public Safety, which can assist victims with preparation of the statement.

While victims have the option of reading their statements in court, the intention is not to provide an opportunity for them to seek retribution or express their emotions to the offender and/or the court: it is simply to give the court information about how the crime has affected the victims' lives. However, a study by Dugger (1996) suggested that the submission of a VIS can be conducive to retribution in that it gives the victim an opportunity to confront the offender in court. Roberts and Edgar (2006) found that across three Canadian jurisdictions, many judges reported that they felt victim impact statements were useful in providing information relevant to sentencing principles. However, whether victims have a right to influence the sentencing of an offender, especially in an adversarial justice system where crime is considered an offence against the state and is punished by the state, is controversial in itself.

---

**BOX 4.6**

**A CLOSER LOOK**
## What the Criminal Code Says about Victim Impact Statements

### SECTION 722

(1) For the purpose of determining the sentence to be imposed on an offender or whether the offender should be discharged pursuant to section 730 in respect of any offence, the court shall consider any statement that may have been prepared in accordance with subsection (2) of a victim of the offence describing the harm done to, or loss suffered by, the victim arising from the commission of the offence. . . .

(4) For the purpose of this section and section 722.2, "victim," in relation to an offence,

   (a) means a person to whom harm was done or who suffered physical or emotional loss as a result of the commission of the offence; and

   (b) where the person . . . is dead, ill or otherwise incapable of making a statement referred to in subsection (1), includes the spouse or common-law partner or any relative of that person, anyone who has in law or fact the custody of that person or is responsible for the care or support of that person or any dependant of that person.

---

## Victim Assistance Programs

### Victim Compensation and Restitution

In 1968, Schafer observed that there is no country "where a victim of crime enjoys the expectation of full compensation or restitution for the injury, harm, or loss he suffered" (1968, p. 162). In Canada, victims have the right to seek financial redress for crimes they have experienced. The court can order an offender who has been found guilty to financially compensate victims for their losses: this is referred to as *restitution*. By contrast, *compensation* refers to payments made directly by the state to victims in compensation for financial losses and/or other suffering. In theory, these forms of redress seem highly appropriate, but in reality, there are several barriers to successful compensation of victims. For instance, the offender may be unable to afford payment, or there may be difficulty enforcing a payment order. Victims may have to meet very restrictive criteria to be eligible for payments, and in many cases victims are unaware of the restitution/compensation process altogether (Policy Centre for Victims Issues, 2004).

Some progress has been made in the area of compensation; however, budgetary restraints lead most governments to limit both the amount of compensation and the number of eligible victims. According to Fattah, state compensation is essentially token in nature—a symbolic gesture to appease victims—and some countries make a deliberate effort not to publicize the fact that they offer compensation schemes at all (2000, p. 35).

On an optimistic note, the Canadian government has amended the Criminal Code over the years to increase the minimum amount a victim may receive and to extend the grounds for compensation to psychological harm in addition to bodily harm. With the enactment of the Canadian Victims Bill of Rights (Bill C-32) in April 2015, a number of amendments came into effect; among them are the following:

> Section 16: Every victim has the right to have the court consider making a restitution order against the offender.

> Section 17: Every victim in whose favour a restitution order is made has the right, if they are not paid, to have the order entered as a civil court judgment that is enforceable against the offender. (cited in Groot, 2014)

### Court Services

Both directly and indirectly, the *Canadian Statement of Basic Principles of Justice for Victims of Crime* endorses the provision of services required to assist victims and address their (special) needs with respect to attending court and dealing with the criminal justice system process in general. Services can include transportation to and from court and the provision of a counsellor to accompany the victim in court and answer relevant questions.

### Victim Service Programs

As of 2014, every province and territory offered some form of victim/witness assistance program. The programs vary in their nature and organization, depending on local needs, conditions, and resources. Consider, though, the Calgary Police Service's Victim Assistance Support Team (VAST) as an example of what such a program provides, including:

- Volunteer support seven days a week, 24-hours a day. Programs include hospital and home visits, court accompaniment, restitution requests, victim impact statements (VIS), court preparation, and trauma support.
- Information, including answers to questions on subjects such as whether an arrest has been made, when the case will be tried, how to file a VIS, and how to report additional stolen property.
- For victims who might be in need of additional services, referrals to services such as counselling agencies, distress/crisis lines, the public trustee, and the medical examiner's office.

### Public Education

The federal Department of Justice supports various provincial and territorial initiatives designed to inform the public about the law and how it affects them. In addition, specific victim assistance projects offer information and assistance to certain types of victims. One example are the recent efforts by Public Safety Canada to prevent bullying (i.e. acts of intentional harm, repeated over time). Their bullying prevention website points out that "roughly 6% of students aged 12–19 report bullying others on a weekly basis, 8% report that they are victims of bullying weekly . . ." (Public Safety Canada, 2008, p. 2). The website offers a number of educational programs that have been shown to work in preventing or reducing the incidence of bullying in school settings. Similar educational programs can be found for domestic violence, identity theft, and fraud, among other crimes. As the adage goes, being informed about one's potential risk can go a long way to reducing one's risk of possible victimization.

### Crisis Intervention

There are many victim service programs to provide specialized assistance to those who have experienced a negative impact—emotional, psychological, and/or financial—from crime. In Ontario, for example, the Victim Crisis Assistance and Referral Services (VCARS) works with

---

**BOX 4.7        WHAT DO YOU THINK?**

### Male Victims of Domestic Violence

For two decades, Calgary resident Earl Silverman advocated for male victims of domestic violence in his city, and for several years he used his own home as what was thought to be Canada's first "safe house" for men fleeing abusive relationships. By March 2013, however, he was forced to sell the house; a month later, one day after he finished packing ahead of the move, he was found dead in the garage.

According to a suicide note, he had been unable to secure funding to keep the house open from either the provincial or the federal government. A former victim of intimate partner violence himself, he had been supporting 15 men and two children in the house when he was forced to sell (Gerson, 2013).

Does this story make you rethink any assumptions you might hold concerning the relationship between gender and domestic violence?

---

local police services to provide immediate help, and the Ministry of the Attorney General has a website where residents can locate a wide range of services. In addition to crisis intervention, organizations that deal with victims of crime offer empathy, understanding, and validation of victims' feelings of anger and hurt.

Yet there are still areas where improvements are needed. For example, the Canadian Women's Foundation reported that in 2015, "more than 6,000 women and children are staying in shelters because it's not safe for them to be at home" (Canadian Women's Foundation, n.d.). A few years earlier, a report by Statistics Canada counted 601 shelters (with roughly 11,820 licensed beds) for abused women in 2012, and a snapshot survey found that 379 women and 215 accompanying children were turned away from shelters on 18 April 2012, in most cases because the facilities had no room for them (Mazowita & Burczycka, 2014). Furthermore, while there are numerous government and publicly funded initiatives to support female victims of intimate partner violence, there are at most a handful of organizations and shelters for men, the majority of them privately funded and under-resourced (Gerson, 2013; see Box 4.7).

### Victim–Offender Reconciliation Programs

Victim–offender reconciliation programs reflect the gaining influence of the restorative justice movement. Although restorative justice has been informally practised for centuries in various cultural settings around the world (including among Australian Aboriginal people and First Nations in Canada), it has entered the mainstream only in recent decades.

The Mennonite Church began to set up victim–offender reconciliation programs in North America in the early 1970s. By the mid-1990s there were well over 300 of them in the United States, about 20 in Canada, and more than 500 in Europe and Britain (Price, 1996). Many of these programs are run by volunteers, and it is difficult to obtain reliable data from them. However, the spread of the programs indicates that many communities are trying to respond to the needs of both the victim and the offender.

### The Future of Victimology

The victim is no longer the forgotten factor in a criminal event. In 2000, Fattah predicted that victimology would slowly move beyond the simplistic notion of "an innocent victim and a guilty offender . . . to the more realistic and defensible view of two human beings caught in a web of intricate social relationships and human emotions" (p. 39). To this we might add Landau's observation that "home, schools, and communities, must be more central sites for

© Ruby / Alamy Stock Photo

A therapist works with a refugee victim of torture in an innovative garden therapy program.

reform ... as it is here where victimization, criminalization, and the conditions that create and sustain them are most powerful" (2006, p. 126).

Today, both criminology and victimology increasingly incorporate restorative justice concepts, which offer new ideas about offender–victim relationships and our responses to crime (see Landau, 2006). The restorative justice model is having a profound influence on justice paradigms. For example, the Youth Criminal Justice Act explicitly incorporates restorative justice practices such as family group conferences in certain circumstances. Various studies have shown that satisfaction among both victims and offenders who participate in restorative justice initiatives tends to be fairly high, lending support to the idea that it is more productive to focus on restoring social harmony than on punishing transgressions (see Wemmers, 2002).

While victimization data have improved significantly in breadth and volume over the years, they still do not provide all of the details that are crucial to understanding the dynamics between victims and offenders, and the origin of crime generally. Criminology researchers need to continue to improve official Uniform Crime Reporting data, self-report data from offenders, and victimization data by collecting more details about crime events.

Based on current trends, the coming years are likely to see increased emphasis on research into such subjects as the consequences of victimization and the effectiveness of victim assistance programs. In Canada, the government's focus on victims' rights, evident in Bill C-32, suggests that such research will find support. At the same time, it is important to keep in mind that there is a political dimension to the state's interest in victims. A number of years ago, Canadian criminologist Brian MacLean (1992), using a critical criminological perspective, argued that the study of victims can represent an excuse for the state to increase social control by increasing the public's awareness about their prospective risk of being a victim of a crime.

The shift toward including victims in the criminal justice system has helped bring a more balanced approach to the study of all the parties affected by a crime. The approach is closely aligned with restorative justice practice, which "promotes mediation and emphasizes healing the wounds of those affected by conflict and crime, including victims, offenders, and communities" (Scott, 2011, p. 256). In this way, victim studies are living up to the view expressed by Elias (1986) some 30 years ago, that victimology is about examining not just criminal justice but social oppression in multiple forms.

## Summary

- The study of victims has become a major focus in recent years.
- Those at greatest risk of criminal victimization are young people, people living in lower socio-economic settings, and those leading risky lifestyles.
- Among the dominant theories of victimization are victim precipitation theory, lifestyle theory, and routine activity theory.
- Among the practical applications of victimology theory are victim impact statements, public education programs, and victim–offender reconciliation initiatives.
- In recent years, victims' rights have been recognized in restorative justice initiatives as well as in various compensation and/or restitution programs.
- Despite the growth in victim services, gaps remain in both coverage and service availability.

## Discussion Questions

1. Why do you think victims of crime have come to figure more prominently in the study of criminology? Do you think the attention is warranted? Explain.
2. Should all victims be eligible to receive some sort of compensation and/or restitution, or only those who are victims of certain types of crimes?
3. Which of the theories of victimization outlined in this chapter seems the most plausible to you? Explain why, with an example.
4. Explain the basic assumptions of routine activity theory and the lifestyle model. Discuss how these theories may or may not be supported by examining victimization data.
5. How would you go about designing a policy to reduce victimization among those groups most likely to experience it?
6. What additional role, if any, do you think the criminal justice system should play in addressing the needs and rights of victims?
7. To what extent has the study of victims and victimization in Canada grown from the examination of the criminal justice system to a perspective that places victims within the larger human rights context?

## Key Concepts

General Social Survey (GSS)
lifestyle theory/model
routine activity theory (RAT)
victim impact statement (VIS)

victimology
Violence Against Women Survey (VAWS)
victim precipitation theory

## Key Names

Benjamin Mendelsohn (1900–1998)
Jan van Dijk (b. 1933)
Hans von Hentig (1887–1974)

## Weblinks

**Policy Centre for Victim Issues**
Operated by the federal Department of Justice, the Policy Centre for Victim Issues offers government publications on victims of crime, as well as news updates, details of related legislation, and links to resources at the provincial level.
www.justice.gc.ca/eng/cj-jp/victims-victimes

**Canadian Resource Centre for Victims of Crime (CRCVC)**
The aim of this advocacy organization is to "ensure the equitable treatment of crime victims in Canada." The site offers information about CRCVC as well as online publications and links.
crcvc.ca/en

**VAOnline**
A comprehensive directory of victim services across Canada.
www.vaonline.org/prov.html

**VOMA—Victim Offender Mediation Association**
A comprehensive list of victim–offender mediation and related associations around the world.
www.voma.org/links.shtml

# PART II
## Criminological Theories and Approaches

# Chapter 5

## Major Schools of Modern Criminological Thought

Frank Gunn/CP Images

Study the past if you would define the future.
CONFUCIUS

## Learning Outcomes

After reading this chapter, you should be able to

- Discuss the two major and two minor schools of criminological thought and their impact on current understandings of crime, criminals, and criminal justice;
- Recognize the pioneers who have contributed to criminological reform in Canada and internationally;
- Appreciate the importance of an interdisciplinary approach; and
- Recognize the need to include crime prevention in an interdisciplinary model of criminology.

## Introduction

In this chapter, we will examine the history of the classical criminological schools of thought and some of the major contributors to the discipline in greater depth. By familiarizing yourself with the fundamental ideas of each school, you will gain a better appreciation of how criminology and its sub-areas have evolved into an interdisciplinary field of study.

We will address two major schools of criminological thought—the classical and the positivist—and two minor schools—the neoclassical and the neopositive (or social defence). We will also touch on the environmental perspective, which, although it is not generally considered a school of criminological thought, is being embraced by a growing number of criminology scholars as well as by the Canadian criminal justice system.

## The Classical School

### The Roots of Penal Reform

The classical school of criminology emerged in response to the harsh, retributive nature of punishments inflicted on criminals in Europe into the eighteenth century. Despite the existence, in some places, of compensation systems such as *wergeld* (see Chapter 3) and the establishment of certain basic legal principles (such as the 1215 Magna Carta, which gave all "free men" in England the right to a fair trial), justice often amounted to little more than private vengeance, and punishments often resembled ritualistic torture. Even relatively minor crimes were subject to the death penalty, often carried out by burning at the stake.

### The Enlightenment

The Renaissance brought the spread of more rational, scientific, and humanistic ways of thinking. By the eighteenth century, traditional doctrines of absolute obedience to authority were increasingly challenged—to the point of political revolution in the American colonies (1775–83) and France (1789). The prevailing concepts of justice were also challenged. One of the leading figures in this ideological shift was Cesare Bonesara, Marquis of Beccaria, more commonly known as **Cesare Beccaria** (see Box 5.1).

### Beccaria's Key Ideas

Beccaria embraced the concept of free will, arguing that most potential offenders would be deterred if three basic conditions were met:

**classical school of criminology**
A perspective premised on the belief that potential criminals, as rational beings capable of free will, will be deterred by the threat of swift, severe punishment.

## BOX 5.1      PROFILE  Cesare Beccaria

Born to an aristocratic family in Milan in 1738, Cesare Beccaria studied law, and after graduating joined a circle of intellectuals interested in literary and social issues. It was through this society that he became acquainted with the work of philosophers such as Francis Bacon, David Hume, and Jean-Jacques Rousseau (whose revolutionary 1762 treatise *The Social Contract* argued that the people collectively were sovereign, and that the state existed only to carry out the people's will). He then became part of a new group of reformers who called themselves the *Accademia dei Pugni* (the "Academy of Fists").

Having visited prisons to see for himself the need to address penal issues, Beccaria wrote his essay "On Crimes and Punishments," which he published anonymously in 1764. Initially, the work was not widely embraced; in fact, in 1765 it was banned by the Pope for its "extreme rationalism" (Bernie, 1991). However, in time Beccaria's plea for ending torture drew international support. The French philosopher Voltaire invited him to Paris, and a number of foreign governments sought his assistance with the revision of their criminal codes. Although it proved to be Beccaria's only major work, the essay has been heralded as the foundation of the classical school of criminological thought.

- certainty of punishment;
- swiftness of justice; and
- fair penalties proportionate to the severity of the social harm done.

To this day, many criminal justice systems, including Canada's, struggle to ensure that these essential conditions are met (see e.g. Dandurand, 2009). For example, in her evaluation of the British Columbia criminal justice system, Cowper (2012) identified a number of barriers to ensuring the efficiency, swiftness, and fairness of sentencing, including lengthy court case processing times and discretionary authority by various officials in the justice system.

Beccaria's doctrine is characterized by four general principles:

1. equality
2. liberty
3. utilitarianism
4. humanitarianism

### 1. Equality

Beccaria believed that all offenders must be treated equally, without consideration of personal character or motive. He felt that there was no justification for individualized punishment: regardless of who the criminal was, punishment must be determined only by the "public injury" done (1764 [1963], p. 70) to society and not by the sensibility of the criminal.

### 2. Liberty

To ensure that everyone was protected from potential abuse of power by the state, Beccaria believed that "only the law can decree punishment for crime" (1764 [1963], p. 13). Furthermore, no one should be deprived of public protection before his or her guilt had been determined (1764 [1963], p. 30).

### 3. Utilitarianism

Given that the primary goal of any sovereign is the greatest happiness for the greatest number of people, the purpose of punishment should be not individual retaliation and retribution but "to instill fear in other men" (1764 [1963], p. 41) to deter them from offending. Beccaria saw punishment as being necessary as a deterrent, arguing that "it is better to prevent crimes than to punish them. This is the ultimate end of every good legislation" (1764 [1963], p. 93).

### 4. Humanitarianism

Punishment, in Beccaria's opinion, should be not only fair but humane. Beccaria opposed torture and cruel punishment, including the death penalty (1764 [1963], pp. 45–52).

## An Enduring Influence

It has been more than 250 years since Beccaria's classic work was first published, yet the humanitarian principles he espoused remain the foundation of criminal justice policy in many countries. It has even been suggested that these principles inspired the Eighth Amendment of the US Constitution, famously forbidding "cruel and unusual punishments." Some dispute the influence of his work. Newman and Marongiu (1990), for instance, argue that because the sociopolitical conditions of the day helped establish a platform for Beccaria's ideas, these ideas are not as profound as the works of other greater reformists such as Voltaire and Bentham. Maconochesi (1973, p. 48) has likewise suggested that Beccaria never even intended to produce a comprehensive theory on penal justice, and only meant to offer a modest but "logically constructed penological system." Even so, Beccaria's influence on justice policy and the foundation his work gave to various theoretical approaches—social control, social learning, and rational choice (see Chapter 8)—should not be overlooked. His influence on criminology makes his work worthy of close reading to this day.

Among those who carried forward Beccaria's ideas was **Jeremy Bentham** (see Box 5.2). In his *Introduction to the Principles of Morals and Legislation* (1789), Bentham developed the philosophy known as utilitarianism, according to which "the greatest happiness of the greatest number is the measure of right and wrong." Punishment in itself is harmful, but according to the doctrine of utilitarianism, could be justified if it prevented more social harm than it produced.

Like Beccaria, and along with other British philosophers of the day (most notably John Stuart Mill), Bentham subscribed to the concept of free will. He believed that humans, as rational, pleasure-seeking individuals, constantly weigh the probabilities of pleasure against the risks of present and future pain. He therefore believed that the threat of punishment would deter would-be criminals by teaching them to fear the loss of freedom that would inevitably follow the commission of a crime (see Box 5.3). He even developed a quasi-mathematical formula, which he called the "felicific calculus," for calculating how much pain was needed to dissuade someone from committing an offence. To Bentham, penitentiaries (semantically linked with the word *penance*) were not places of punishment but places of reform, where offenders could be conditioned to discontinue their criminal ways out of fear of future imprisonment.

utilitarianism
The concept that any law should be of the greatest benefit to the greatest number of people.

## Evaluation of the Classical School

Does fear of punishment really prevent crime? Overall, the research on deterrence theory is inconclusive (Freedman, 2004). Some early studies reported that under certain circumstances, deterrence does appear to be effective (see Gibbs, 1975). For example, Williams and Hawkins (1986) found that the fear of arrest could act as a deterrent, especially when linked to the indirect social costs of arrest. They identified three types of social cost:

1.  *commitment costs* (an arrest may have an adverse effect on future opportunities, such as employment)

| BOX 5.2 | PROFILE   Jeremy Bentham |
|---|---|

A leading proponent of the doctrine of utilitarianism, Jeremy Bentham was a central figure in a reform movement that helped mitigate the severity of punishments for offenders; abolish usury laws; and remove the "exclusionary laws of evidence" (Geiss, 1973, p. 66), so that evidence could not be introduced if it violated a defendant's constitutional rights. He was instrumental in introducing principles of crime prevention into the judicial process (ibid.).

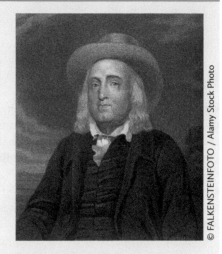

© FALKENSTEINFOTO / Alamy Stock Photo

In 1799, Bentham embodied his ideas on penal reform in a prison design that he called the *Panopticon*, a literally "all-seeing" facility. The intent behind the octagonal design was to enable a guard to keep an eye on all cells from a central control area, while making prisoners constantly aware that they might be under observation: this, he believed, would allow for constructive supervision and reform. Although no such institution was ever built, some early American prisons were modelled after Bentham's design, and some Canadian institutions for young offenders (e.g. Huron County Gaol (Jail) in Goderich, Ontario, open 1839–1972) have incorporated a modified version.

Elevation, section and plan of Jeremy Bentham's Panopticon penitentiary, drawn by Willey Reveley, 1791. From The works of Jeremy Bentham vol. IV, 172-3

Mary Evans / Peter Higginbotham Collection

Bentham designed the Panopticon [*left*] with the idea that if inmates felt they were being watched at all times, they would be less likely to act out. Among the prisons modelled after it is the one in Joliet, Illinois [*right*].

2. *attachment costs* (an arrest can result in harm to personal circumstances)
3. *stigma* (an arrest can damage one's personal and/or public image)

Overall, however, Akers and Sellers (2013) conclude that the correlations found "between the perceptions of risk and subsequent offenses are too weak to validate deterrence theory." Even when a modified version of deterrence theory came into fashion (Cornish and Clarke's rational choice theory: see Chapter 8), its supporters were unable to clearly define what is meant by the "reasoning criminal" (Akers & Sellers, 2013). The classical doctrine also seems questionable when it comes to the reform and rehabilitation of criminals. Rates of *recidivism*

| BOX 5.3 | **A CLOSER LOOK** <br> **Deterrence Theory** |
|---|---|

A cornerstone of the classical school, **deterrence theory** is based on the premise that individuals have free will and are rational in their thinking: therefore, they will fear the punishment that is sure to follow the commission of a crime. Like learning theory, deterrence theory maintains that behaviour is governed by its consequences.

Zimring and Hawkins (1975) identified two levels of deterrence: *specific* and *general*. In the first case, individual offenders learn through punishment to associate a specific behaviour pattern with a specific painful stimulus; this is called

*associative learning*. In the second case, non-criminals learn to avoid criminal activity from the experience of punishment of those who have offended; this is called *imitative learning*.

Even if deterrence is effective with most people, there may be "conditional" circumstances in which legal threats of punishment work only on those who are interested in conforming to the norms of society (see Schmalleger, 2014). Overall, it is difficult to prove the effectiveness of deterrence because only those who have not been deterred come into contact with the CJS.

(reoffending) among both adults and young offenders across Canada and internationally (see Deady, 2014), are discouraging for those who believe in the ability of a first punishment to discourage further criminal acts (see Newark, 2013).

Despite its virtues, the classical perspective failed to acknowledge individual differences, motivation, and situational circumstances (Geis, 1973). **Michel Foucault**, perhaps the most influential modern-day revisionist on the subject of punishment, argued that punishment should not be seen simply as "the independent development of legal or economic institutions" but should be seen as part of an integrative and/or interdisciplinary framework (Barak, 2009, p. 87). That is to say, punishment is an interrelationship between power, knowledge, and the body that is affected by factors such as economics, social development, political ideologies, and changing mass communication: there is no one-size-fits-all model. Consider, for example, a woman who kills her physically abusive partner: should she receive the same punishment as someone who kills for greed? While some maintain that "the law is the law" (remember Beccaria's principle of equality), others argue that individual circumstances may call for compassion and discretion. Mannheim summarized the problem with the classical perspective when he described it as "too static and sterile to guide further progress" (1973, p. 35).

**deterrence theory**
The belief that the threat of punishment can prevent people from committing a crime.

| BOX 5.4 | **A CLOSER LOOK** <br> **The Influence of the Classical School on Canadian Legislation** |
|---|---|

Some of the major tenets of the classical school are entrenched in Canada's constitution, the Criminal Code, and the Youth Criminal Justice Act. These include the following:

- the idea that humans have free will
- the concept of utilitarianism
- civil rights and due process of law
- rules of evidence and testimony
- accountability for one's misdeeds
- *determinate* (i.e. fixed) sentences
- swift justice and certain punishment
- use of the threat of punishment as a deterrent

- the rejection of capital punishment.

These elements reflect the importance of fair, proportionate punishment and due legal process in Canada.

After reviewing the main elements of the classical school of criminological thought, how well do you think our CJS does in maintaining social order? If you could, would there be any aspects of the CJS you would change to improve the efficiency of its operations?

Out of these criticisms of the classical school emerged the neoclassical perspective, which we will examine shortly. First, however, we will look at the second major school of criminological thought: positivism.

## The Positivist School

### The Roots of Positivism

In the latter half of the nineteenth century, a new school of criminological thought emerged in Italy, describing itself as "positivist." The term was coined by **Auguste Comte**, the French philosopher who is generally recognized as the founder of sociology. He used the term "positivist" to describe what he considered the final stage of social development, in which metaphysical explanations would be replaced by a rational, scientific view of the world (Williams & McShane, 2013).

There had been earlier attempts at scientific explanation of human behaviour, of course. The sixteenth-century Italian scholar Giambattista della Porta, also known as Giovanni Battista Della Porta, popularized the ancient pseudoscience of physiognomy, according to which it was possible to judge a person's character from his or her facial features; thus, someone whose face resembled that of a lion, or a sheep, would have the characteristics associated with that animal. More than a century later, Franz Joseph Gall and Johann Spurzheim pioneered the study of phrenology, mapping "bumps" on the skull that they believed were related to behaviour, especially abnormal behaviour (see Chapter 6). And by the mid-1800s, two statisticians had conducted research in a manner approaching positivism. Examining the available social statistics, Adolphe Quetelet and André-Michel Guerry observed "variations in crime rates by climate and season and...the same age and sex differences we find among criminals today" (Williams & McShane, 2013, p. 30). Their work anticipated the emergence of the Chicago School of sociology and criminology, whose related theories all assumed that we are social creatures and that our behaviour is a product of our social and physical environment (see Chapter 8).

### Lombroso and His Contemporaries

The positivist school of criminology was first embraced by three men: **Cesare Lombroso** and his students **Raffaele Garofalo** and **Enrico Ferri**. It is Lombroso, however, who is most often recognized as the father of modern criminology (see Box 5.5).

Lombroso's ideas regarding criminality were influenced by Charles Darwin's evolutionary theory, Rudolf Virchow's ideas on organic regression, and Paul Broca's methods of describing and classifying anatomical features, but he grounded his thinking in Comptian positivism, which emphasized the need for facts that could be observed and measured. He based his theory of biological determinism in criminality on the concept of atavism (see Box 5.6). He used the term *atavistic* to characterize those individuals who, because of certain morphological (bodily) characteristics, were considered throwbacks to some earlier period of human evolution. Lombroso believed that the cause was hereditary. Among the physical malformations (he called them "criminal stigmata") he catalogued were an asymmetric face, an excessively large jaw, eye defects, a large nose, large ears, a receding forehead, long arms, and swollen lips. These physical anomalies, which Lombroso thought could be either inherited or acquired through insanity, syphilis, epilepsy, or alcoholism (Martin, Mutchnick, & Austin, 1990), could render an individual incapable of living within the social norms of society.

The idea that some physical anomalies can indirectly contribute to criminal behaviour reflected Lombroso's recognition that environment can also play a role in an individual's

**positivist school of criminology**
A school of criminological thought whose adherents use the scientific method to measure behaviour, and advocate rehabilitation over punishment.

**determinism**
A doctrine that denies free will while maintaining that our decisions are decided by predictable and/or inherited causes that act on our character.

**atavism**
A biological condition supposedly rendering an individual incapable of living within the norms of a society.

| BOX 5.5 | PROFILE | Cesare Lombroso, Father of Modern Criminology |

Born in Verona, Cesare Lombroso obtained a medical degree at the age of 24 and volunteered as an army physician. With time on his hands, he decided to take anatomical measurements of soldiers from different regions of Italy. In the process he found a positive correlation between those who had tattoos and those who were involved in some infraction of either military or civilian law. He later obtained permission to study mental patients and began to solidify his theory of criminality. Many of his ideas and observations were first published in *L'uomo delinquente* (*The Criminal Man*) in 1876. By its fifth edition in 1896, the book had expanded from 256 to 1,903 pages and attracted international acclaim.

It was at the University of Turin, with the assistance of his students Garofalo and Ferri, that Lombroso refined his general theory that criminals could be distinguished from non-criminals by various physical anomalies, which he considered to be *atavistic* or degenerative in origin. With William Ferrero, he also wrote the first book on women criminals, *The Female Offender* (Wolfgang, 1973).

At his request, on his death in 1909, his brain was placed in the Institute of Anatomy at the University of Turin.

Mary Evans Picture Library / Alamy

development. In many respects, Lombroso was the first true interdisciplinary criminological thinker. Although Lombroso found numerous correlations between physical appearance (e.g. narrow-set eyes, deep voice, double chins, etc.) and criminal activity, he did not take into account the possible effects that social labelling (e.g. bullying, teasing, etc.) might have in triggering anti-social behaviour among those "labelled" as different or even evil. In Chapter 7, we will discuss a theme related to Lombroso's notion of the "born criminal" when we explore the issue of geographic profiling.

Lombroso's findings have been largely discredited: needless to say, we no longer believe that someone born with, say, large ears is predisposed to a life of crime. But Lombroso's use of the scientific method and his belief in the possibility that behaviour might be determined in part by factors outside the control of the individual charted a new course for criminology and laid the groundwork for many later theories based on biological and psychological principles (see chapters 6 and 7).

Ferri and Garofalo, both lawyers by training, not only contributed to the development of Lombroso's ideas but also introduced some significant elements to the understanding of criminal causality. For example, Ferri argued that crime was caused by multiple factors: physical (e.g. geography, climate), anthropological (e.g. age, gender, race, bio-social conditions), and social (e.g. customs, economic conditions, population density, religion) (Williams & McShane, 2013).

## Evaluation of the Positivist School

Which came first: the chicken or the egg? Or, in the case of traditional approaches to crime prevention, which is more important:

| BOX 5.6 | WHAT DO YOU THINK? |

### Can You Spot a Criminal?

The Italian positivists attempted to shift the focus away from the themes of free will and rational choice to focus on the individual biological and mental traits that may predispose people to crime. What do you think: could there be biological or psychological markers that distinguish "bad" people and "mad" people? Consider, for example, psychopaths, who, while capable of appearing "normal," are typically characterized as lacking a conscience (i.e. "mad") and are unable to show empathy. They tend to be manipulative (i.e. "bad") and volatile, and they often engage in criminal conduct. Are these traits apparent enough to "spot"?

1. changing such social factors as lack of opportunity, peer pressure, or early childhood socialization, based on the classical model of social reform via the law; or
2. changing such individual factors as diet, substance abuse, or genetic or constitutional conditions, through treatment?

Do certain "criminal types" exist? Are there "constitutional crime markers," or what have become known generically as criminogenic "risk factors"?

Both the classical and positivist schools have supporters, and both continue to have an impact on criminal justice systems and criminological research today. And although Hackler (2007, p. 109) suggests that "neither of these schools serve us well in terms of reducing crime," positivist ideas continue to have an influence on the judicial process. Thus, in recent years, judges have become more willing to take into account genetic conditions, dietary influences, and biochemical imbalances when deciding how harsh or lenient a sentence certain offenders deserve (see Baudes-Rotger & Gallardo-Pujol, 2014). Correction programs continue to experiment with "better" treatment programs for particular types of offenders (e.g. sex offenders). In addition, certain crime-fighting strategies that involve social engineering (e.g. increased street lighting and subsidized housing for the poor) are based on the **deterministic** principle of trying to mitigate the conditions that "cause" criminal behaviour. Finally, with the growing acceptance of an interdisciplinary perspective, recent positivist-based research in the biosocial, bioenvironmental, and biopsychological arenas, as well as in urban planning, has produced some promising findings (see Chapter 6). Some of the lines of inquiry that are positivist in character draw on sociobiology (Mednick & Christiansen, 1977; Wilson, 2000) and evolutionary theory (Walsh & Ellis, 2007).

> **deterministic**
> Based on or involving the belief that events and behaviour are caused by prior events and conditions existing outside the realm of free will.

Nevertheless, biological, psychological, and sociological determinism has been challenged on four key issues:

- weakness of methodology
- limited application to the understanding of white-collar crime, organized crime, and political crime
- a general fear that positivist-based policies will be intrusive and possibly lead to totalitarianism
- failure to distinguish clearly between the roles of environment and heredity (Schafer, 1976; Cullen & Wilcox, 2010)

## The Rule of Law versus Science

By 1900, the two primary schools of criminological thought had both made their marks on criminology and criminal justice. Table 5.1 illustrates how their principles have been applied in the criminal justice system today.

Although Table 5.1 suggests that the criminal justice system integrates the two schools of thought, in practice the CJS is based primarily on the classical legal doctrine: the decisions of police, lawyers, and judges are based on the law, not the behavioural sciences. And while corrections systems are mandated to offer rehabilitation programs, they are usually unable to provide the required quality of treatment because of underfunding, insufficiently trained staff, and overcrowding (Goff, 2014). The lack of integration that Jeffery (1973) noted between the criminal justice system (law) and criminology (science) means that there is no common model of criminal justice by which the three elements of the CJS operate toward a common goal through common strategies (also see Krason, 2014). It is essential to recognize this inherent conflict, as it plays a significant role in how we study crime and criminal behaviour.

| | Law (classical ideology) | Science (positivist ideology) |
|---|---|---|
| **Table 5.1** | **Law and Science in Conflict** | |
| Philosophy | • free will<br>• utilitarianism<br>• hedonism<br>• crime is a product of social pathology | • determinism<br>• the individual is subject to external forces<br>• crime is caused by individual pathology or abnormality |
| Problem | • crime is a product of poor decision-making on the part of a calculating offender exercising rational thought | • crime is a product of defects in an offender's physical or psychological makeup, combined with prevailing social conditions beyond the individual's control |
| Solutions | • maintain order via social reforms<br>• deterrence<br>• minimal discretion<br>• due process/legal rights<br>• crime can never be completely eradicated<br>• operate in the best interests of society | • evidence-informed research and intervention/treatment<br>• treatment at an individual level (e.g. rehabilitation or resocialization), or intervention at a social level<br>• sentencing and rehabilitation with a view of individual mitigating circumstances<br>• operate in the best interests of the offender |

## The Neoclassical School

The ideas of the neoclassical school of criminology were pioneered in the mid-1800s by **Luigi Rossi** in Italy and **René Garraud** and **Henri Joly** in France. While endorsing the major principles of the classical school, these thinkers departed from it in two fundamental respects:

1. They rejected the rigidity of the classical system of punishment.
2. They called for a degree of subjectivity when assessing criminal responsibility—that is, discretion.

Although basing its main constructs on classical school traditions, the neoclassical school did not receive much attention from criminologists until the late 1980s, when—in line with the growing influence of the rational choice theory, drift theory, and social control theory, among others (see Chapter 8)—rising crime rates led the public to begin demanding longer prison terms, a return to corporal punishment, and even reinstatement of the death penalty. Such a policy of just deserts is based on the premise that those who commit crimes make a rational choice to do so, and therefore deserve to be punished (see Box 5.7).

The neoclassical school, like the classical, assumes that individuals choose to commit crimes after calculating that the potential rewards outweigh the potential risks (Cornish & Clarke, 1986). Today, this perspective is generally classified under the rubric of *rational choice theory*, which assumes that criminals base their decisions on the perceived attractiveness of a target, the absence of guardianship, and level of motivation (Clarke & Felson, 1993).

Among those who were instrumental in promoting neoclassical thinking was James Q. Wilson. Wilson (1975), recalling Beccaria and Bentham, argued that since it seems impossible to identify the root causes of crime, policy-makers should focus on improving deterrence. In addition, Wilson declared that justice should be swift and punishment both certain and proportionate to the severity of the crime.

For Wilson (1975), the more Draconian the sentence (see Box 5.8), the greater the chance of negotiating a plea bargain (see Verdun-Jones, 2012). Plea bargaining is characteristic of the neoclassical approach, providing an incentive for the accused to plead guilty in return for some benefit, such as a reduced sentence, as well as allowing the court to acknowledge that different individuals may be treated differently before the law. In addition, the growing

**neoclassical school of criminology**

A school of criminological thought that believes that some accused offenders should be exonerated or treated leniently in light of situations or circumstances that make it impossible to exercise free will.

**discretion**

The power of an authority to exercise his or her judgement in a particular case instead of having to follow specific rules.

**just deserts**

The idea that an individual who commits an offence chooses to do so and therefore deserves to be punished for it.

**plea bargain**

An arrangement between the defence and prosecution in which the accused agrees to plead guilty in return for some benefit, such as a reduced sentence.

BOX 5.7      REALITY CHECK

## The Singapore Experiment

Singapore has one of the most punitive penal codes in the world. In 1994, it drew considerable media attention when Michael Fay, an 18-year-old from Ohio, received a four-month prison sentence and four lashes for defacing automobiles with spray paint. Although the media have questioned the rationale behind Singapore's policy, the evidence suggests that it works: overall crime rates in the US were between 200 and 380 per cent higher than those in Singapore (Weichman, 1994). According to official sources, Singapore's crime rate between 2005 and 2013 dropped fairly consistently, from 843 incidents per 100,000 to 584 per 100,000 (Singapore Police Force, 2014).

### Table 5.2   Homicide Rate and Number of Incidents, Singapore, 2001–2011

| Year | Rate* | Incidents |
| --- | --- | --- |
| 2001 | 0.8 | 30 |
| 2002 | 0.5 | 22 |
| 2003 | 0.6 | 24 |
| 2004 | 0.5 | 19 |
| 2005 | 0.5 | 21 |
| 2006 | 0.4 | 17 |
| 2007 | 0.4 | 18 |
| 2008 | 0.4 | 18 |
| 2009 | 0.5 | 25 |
| 2010 | 0.4 | 19 |
| 2011 | 0.3 | 16 |

* per 100,000 population

Source: United Nations Office on Drugs and Crime. UNODC Homicide Statistics, 2012.

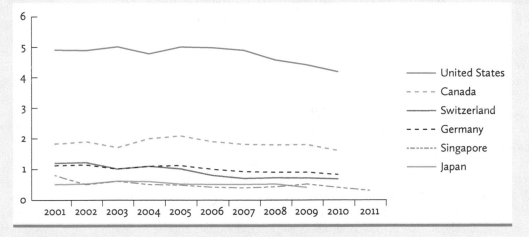

**Figure 5.1   Homicide Rates\* 2001–2010, Select Countries**

* per 100,000 population

*Source*: Based on data from  United Nations Office on Drugs and Crime. UNODC Homicide Statistics, 2012.

Based on the statistics presented in this textbox, do you think there may be merit in the just deserts approach to criminal punishment?

acceptance of several sociological theories such as differential association and identification (see Chapter 8) have served to support such neoclassical assertions that crime can be understood only through an understanding of individual differences in age, gender, social class, etc., of the perpetrator(s).

| BOX 5.8 | **A CLOSER LOOK** |
|---|---|
| | Capital Punishment |

In 621 BCE, Athenian law was written down for the first time by the Greek statesman Draco. This codification had the benefit of making the administration of law less arbitrary. So why does the term *Draconian law* carry such pejorative connotations? Because it prescribed death for virtually every offence, from murder to minor theft.

Although Canada eliminated capital punishment in 1976, the last execution took place 14 years earlier, in 1962. During that span, from 1962 to 1975, the murder rate increased by nearly 70 per cent; yet after capital punishment was eliminated, the murder rate began to decline. By 2001, it had decreased by roughly 30 per cent, and by 2013, the murder rate was lowest it had been since 1996 (Statistics Canada, 2014b). Ironically, many people, from citizens to police associations, still support reinstatement of capital punishment, even though it would violate the 1982 Charter of Rights and Freedoms (Brennan, 2012).

Whether death is a "cruel and unusual" punishment or the only suitable penalty for some crimes has been subject to numerous philosophical, moral, and political debates.

How do you feel about capital punishment? Can it be justified under certain circumstances?

Today the neoclassical perspective emphasizes the deterrent effect of punishment. However, the literature on deterrence, both specific and general, has not confirmed its effectiveness (see e.g. Doob, Webster and Gartner, 2014). Various government studies have shown that approximately 40 per cent of prisoners return to criminal activity upon release. And in the 33 states that still have recourse to capital punishment for some offences (as of 2015), such offences are still committed. On the other hand, a pilot study in Edmonton in 2010 showed statistically fewer collisions and related fatalities in districts where the speed limit was dropped from 50 to 40 kilometres per hour (Pona, 2012), leading one to wonder whether it is the law or the sentence that has the greater bearing on the crime rate.

## Towards an Integrated and Interdisciplinary School of Thought

As we saw in Chapter 1, the cost of the Canadian criminal justice system increases each year. And the expensive treatment programs introduced since the early 1990s, coinciding with the introduction of the risk-need-responsivity model (see Andrews, Bonta, and Hoge, 1990), have not proved particularly effective. To make any significant progress, criminology must find a way to bridge the theoretical differences between the various schools of thought. Sociologists and psychologists need to know the law and work with lawyers, while lawyers need to know more about the behavioural sciences. Most criminology programs in Canada are staffed by people from a variety of disciplinary backgrounds and therefore have the capacity to offer interdisciplinary training focused on prevention. These ideas and themes will be revisited in various forms throughout the chapters that follow.

### Prison Reform

We have already noted that corrections and incarceration have not always been as we know them today. One pioneer who had a significant impact on penal reform was Scottish-born naval captain **Alexander Maconochie**. In Australia, he is probably best remembered for his services at the prison colonies on Norfolk Island and Van Diemen's Land (Tasmania). It was while serving as the private secretary to the lieutenant governor of the latter that Maconochie formulated many of his penal reform policies, a number of which were put into practice.

The treatment and transportation of English convicts in Van Diemen's Land, which Maconochie witnessed first-hand, led him to point out "that cruel and harsh punishment debase not only the victim, but also the society which employs them," and argue that the objective should be "to reform the offender so that he should leave prison capable of useful citizenship, and a better man than when he entered the prison gates" (cited in Barry, 1973, pp. 86–7). Five ideas for prison reform that Maconochie proposed were considered novel at the time:

1. Sentences should be measured not by time but by the ability of a prisoner to complete a specified quantity of labour.
2. The quantity of labour should be determined by the gravity of the offence and the degree to which the prisoner improves himself (there were no female prisons at the time).
3. While in prison, all prisoners should earn everything they receive.
4. When working in groups, all prisoners should be answerable for one another's conduct.
5. As prisoners near their release dates, attention should be given to preparing them for release into society.

Maconochie introduced a variety of novel practices, such as allowing prisoners to use proper utensils, providing educational and spiritual services, and granting other privileges. In essence, Maconochie recognized that prison was not a place to punish but a place to serve one's punishment. Barry (1973) summarizes Maconochie's major contributions in four points:

1. *reward*—prisoners must earn their release through industrious labour and good conduct
2. *individual influence*—if it is to offer constructive support, a prison should not have more than 300 inmates, or 100 for more serious offenders
3. prisons should provide for gradual release (e.g. through halfway houses)
4. there should be strict supervision after discharge (see Box 5.9)

Many of Maconochie's reform ideas were tried in Canada's penal system at one time or another. However, other reformers have also made their mark in the history of penal reform. For example, John Haviland was the architect and builder of Eastern State Penitentiary, which constituted a radical shift away from previous prison designs. It was designed to accommodate opportunities for reforming inmates rather than merely confining them. Haviland's prison design was used in building a number of the earlier prisons in Canada. **John Howard** (see Box 5.10) was instrumental in establishing prisoner advocacy groups. French lawyer Charles Lucas laid the groundwork for maximum and minimum sentences and a system for the classification of inmates based on their moral improvement as determined by the prison disciplinary

---

**BOX 5.9     FACTS AND FIGURES** CONFINEMENT IN CANADA'S MOST NOTORIOUS PRISON

The opening of Kingston Penitentiary, in 1835, marked the beginning of the prison industry in Canada. Before it was built, there was considerable debate over whether the purpose of confinement should be *punishment* or *reformation* of the prisoner, the former being consistent with the classical school perspective, the later with the positivist perspective. The Brown Commission of 1848–9 produced the first major report calling for more humane treatment of prisoners. Over the years, Kingston Penitentiary housed many of Canada's most notorious offenders, including Clifford Olson, Paul Bernardo, Roger Caron, and Russell Williams. The prison was finally closed in September 2013 and is now a National Historic Site.

| BOX 5.10 | PROFILE John Howard |
|---|---|

John Howard was born into financial independence and became a generous philanthropist. However, his life was not an easy one (Schafer, 1976). Health problems and personal hardships seemed to strengthen his determination to improve the well-being of others less fortunate.

Howard's interest in prisons began in 1755, when, en route to Lisbon, Portugal, to help earthquake victims, he was captured by the French (then at war with England) and imprisoned in France. On his release, he returned to England and was elected high-sheriff of Bedfordshire. He used his position to study English prisons as well as

those in Belgium, France, the Netherlands, Germany, and Switzerland. The experience left him distraught, and in 1777 he self-published *The State of the Prisons*, in which he called for the classification of prisoners according to their risk of reoffending, the introduction of vocational training, the provision of constructive work opportunities, and more humane treatment of inmates in general.

The organization most commonly associated with prisoner advocacy, the John Howard Society, was founded in Toronto in 1867. It is a living testament to the significance of his pioneering ideas.

board (see Normandeau, 1970). Lucas also emphasized the need to separate adults from young offenders. Many of his ideas can be seen today in Canada's correctional system (see Winterdyk and Weinwrath, 2013).

## Modern Law Enforcement

Policing in the Western world can be traced to roughly 1035, when the Danish King Canute set up a system in which all males over the age of 12 were bound by law to keep the peace. Until the 1700s law enforcement came under the purview of the sovereign and was somewhat informal in structure (see Box 5.11). With the advent of the Industrial Revolution, the problems that society faced could no longer be dealt with on an informal basis. The solution that emerged was the creation of a bureaucracy—the foundation of modern policing (see Stansfield, 1996).

**Sir Robert Peel** is often recognized for his ideas on policing, but he also had a distinguished career in British politics as the champion of political equality for Roman Catholics, founder of the modern Conservative Party, and prime minister of the United Kingdom (1834–5 and 1841–6).

In 1829 Peel reorganized London's metropolitan police force, instituting uniforms and strict discipline, banning the bearing of firearms, and establishing the fundamental principles that still govern policing today. For example:

- The power of the police depends on public approval of their actions and behaviour.
- Maintaining the respect of the public means securing their co-operation to respect societal laws.
- The police must demonstrate absolute impartiality, courtesy, and friendly good humour.
- The police must use minimal force when trying to restore and/or enforce the law.

Peel's officers became known as "bobbies" (i.e. "little Roberts"), and his system was quickly adopted throughout England, although some argued that this expansion was simply an attempt by government and other power brokers

| BOX 5.11 | FACTS AND FIGURES THE ROOTS OF POLICING |
|---|---|

Remember those old Westerns where the "sheriff" had to round up his "posse"? The word *sheriff* comes from "shire reeve," the old English term for the official appointed by the king to enforce the laws in each shire (or county). The word *posse* comes from *posse comitatus*: Latin for "power of the county." The position of *constable* (from Latin, "officer of the stable") was created in 1285 through the Statute of Winchester. Constables assisted the king in suppressing riots and other violence.

Police officers in the United Kingdom do not carry firearms on regular duty.

to control and suppress the poor. The first Canadian police force was established in Toronto in 1835 (Griffiths, 2015).

## Legal Reform

Since the Code of Hammurabi (*c.* 1772 BCE) law has been the cornerstone of criminal justice. Law is the formal means of maintaining social control, for without it there is no crime, and without crime there cannot be any punishment—principles that can be traced to Beccaria.

There have been many great legal reformers since Bentham. Among them was the American **Isaac Ray**, America's foremost writer on forensic psychiatry in the nineteenth century (Overholser, 1973, p. 177). At a time when law was interpreted strictly and there were few cases in which the courts would consider mitigating circumstances, Ray argued that the legal definition of insanity was too limited in its scope that lawyers were ill equipped to assess mental disorders, and that expert medical testimony was required in cases involving insanity pleas. Ray also argued that criminals could experience temporary interruptions in their ability to reason, which could be treated as a form of mental illness he called moral insanity. A staunch supporter of phrenology, he posited that perhaps the brain was compartmentalized, and that a person who would act rationally in some situations might behave quite differently in others.

One of the founders of the American Psychiatric Association (APA) in 1844, Ray helped to bridge the gap between law and medicine and pioneer an integrated and interdisciplinary approach. In recognition of his contribution, the APA presents an annual award to lawyers or psychiatrists who promote a closer working relationship between law and medicine.

The American legal scholar Charles Doe (1830–1896) also called for law and medicine to work more closely together. He clarified the meaning of *criminal responsibility*—that is, the ability to appreciate the nature of an unlawful act and know that it is wrong. The Spanish legal scholar Pedro Montero (1861–1919) also had a significant impact on North American law. He

**moral insanity**
A form of mental illness in which the offender's ability to reason is temporarily interrupted. It is the basis of modern verdicts of temporary insanity or "not criminally responsible" for offenders whose crimes were the product of a mental illness.

SergeBertasiusPhotography/Shutterstock.com

## BOX 5.12 — FACTS AND FIGURES — A BRIEF TIMELINE OF CANADIAN POLICING

**1651** — Quebec City establishes a watchman system; Upper Canada establishes both a constabulary and a watch-and-ward system (whereby men on watch during the night hours would raise the "hue and cry" to summon assistance from the citizens around to ward off criminals or assist in apprehending them): all three innovations are designed to organize police and help them maintain law and order over the general population 24 hours a day.

**1729** — The Royal Newfoundland Constabulary is founded; it is now the oldest police force in Canada.

**1759** — The English system of policing is imposed on French Canada.

**c. 1830** — Rose Fortune patrols Annapolis Royal's waterfront, becoming Canada's first (unofficial) female police officer.

**1835** — Toronto establishes Canada's first municipal police department.

**1864** — The Western Frontier Constabulary is formed to protect Canadian neutrality during the American Civil War.

**1868** — The Dominion Police Force is created out of the Western Frontier Constabulary to protect government buildings, naval yards, railways, and political leaders in eastern Canada.

**1873** — Parliament establishes the North West Mounted Police (NWMP) to keep the peace in the West.

**1908** — Regina becomes one of the last major centres to establish a police force.

**1910** — Alex Decoteau joins the Edmonton Police Department and becomes the first Aboriginal police officer in Canada.

**1912** — The first official female police officers in Canada are hired by the Vancouver police department.

**1919** — The NWMP and Dominion police merge to form the RCMP.

**1921** — The RCMP acquire their first aircraft for aerial surveillance.

**1923** — The Canadian National Police Service (also known as the railway police), is established.

**1923** — The first bulletproof vests are issued to Canadian detectives in Toronto.

**1952** — "Policewomen" begin to receive the same training as men, and are slowly allowed to go on patrol duty and work in the same departments with their male counterparts.

**1969** — The last Arctic dog-sled patrols are replaced with motorized vehicles such as snowmobiles.

**1972** — The Canadian Police Information Centre (CPIC) begins providing all police agencies across Canada with access to information about known criminals, stolen property, registered firearms, and stolen vehicles.

**1974** — Thirty-two women are sworn in as the RCMP's first female uniformed members.

**1981** — The Commission of Inquiry Concerning Certain Activities of the RCMP (the McDonald Commission) investigates allegations of wrongdoing by members of the RCMP; it leads to the creation of CSIS (the Canadian Security Intelligence Service) in 1984

**1989** — The RCMP first uses DNA analysis in its investigations.

**1994** — The Commission of Inquiry into Policing in British Columbia (the Oppal Commission) recommends, among other things, that municipal forces use 9-mm semiautomatic handguns and adopt the community-based policing philosophy.

NSA Documentary Art Collection, acc.no. 1979-147/56 - Rose Fortune, ca. 1774-1864

Canada's first female police officer, Rose Fortune (1774–1864), was born into slavery in Virginia and came to Canada with black Loyalists who were promised land in Nova Scotia after the American Revolution.

Canadian Press/ Mike McLaughlin

Luka Magnotta, shown here in a courtroom artist's drawing, pleaded not guilty for the murder of Jun Li, which was recorded and broadcast on several websites. Although Magnotta's lawyer closed his argument with the repeated phrase "la folie, c'est la folie" ("insanity is insanity"), Magnotta was convicted, and he withdrew his application for an appeal in February 2015, despite various judicial errors in jury instruction.

argued that judges and lawyers should be trained in the social sciences—especially sociology and psychology—in order to better prevent crime and cure criminals.

In Canada "insanity" is no longer accepted as a legal defence. Instead, an accused can be found "not criminally responsible [NCR] on account of mental disorder." As part of its "tough on crime" agenda, the federal government recently revised the approach to issuing this verdict with the Not Criminally Responsible Reform Act. The act addresses concerns raised by victims of crime with respect to accused persons found not criminally responsible on account of mental disorder (see Box 5.13).

---

**BOX 5.13**

### A CLOSER LOOK
## The Not Criminally Responsible Reform Act

Part of the former Harper government's Plan for Safe Streets and Communities, the Not Criminally Responsible Reform Act (NCRRA) came into force on 11 June 2014 and is intended to focus courts' attention on victims and public safety. It has three main components:

1. placing public safety at the forefront of decision-making in cases where a verdict of not criminally responsible (NCR) is being considered;

2. creating a high-risk designation under which an NCR accused must be held in custody and cannot be considered for release until the designation is revoked by a court; and

3. ensuring that victims' rights and needs are considered in decisions regarding accused persons found NCR; ensuring the victim is notified when an NCR accused is discharged; and "allowing non-communications orders between an NCR accused and the victim" (Prime Minister of Canada, 2013).

## Criminalistics

Until fairly recently, criminologists in North America paid little attention to what happens between the time an offence is committed and the time the offender is sentenced. The phase of the justice process when crime is detected and investigated was generally seen as peripheral to criminology. This inattention reflected the fact that for a long time sociology and psychology were deemed the only acceptable approaches to studying crime and criminality. However, to achieve an integrated and interdisciplinary perspective, criminology must embrace all aspects of the criminal justice process.

Criminalistics is the science of crime detection and investigation. **Alphonse Bertillon** is generally acknowledged as the first modern-day criminalist to apply this anthropological technique to law and criminology. While working for the Paris police department, Bertillon used a variety of instruments to make precise measurements of physical features (head length and width, foot, middle finger, etc.), which were then recorded on cards and filed according to an elaborate system. He also refined and standardized the process of photo identification (i.e. the "mug shot"), photographing the suspect's head and shoulders both from the front and in profile. Meanwhile, Sir Francis Galton (1822–1911), a cousin of Charles Darwin, popularized the use of fingerprinting, which was officially adopted by Scotland Yard in 1901 (Saferstein, 2010). Both techniques are still in use today.

While North American criminologists focused on psychology and sociology, European criminology has been dominated by the legal profession. Austrian lawyer **Hans Gross** observed that while the police were good at maintaining order, many were less adept at solving crimes, often relying on evidence from informers who were engaged in criminal activity themselves. Gross saw first-hand how poorly prepared many court cases were. How could a case be fairly tried without adequate evidence?

In his *Manual for the Examining Justice* (1883) Gross wrote that every criminal case should be treated as a scientific problem, and that every effort should be made to use scientific

**criminalistics**
The science of crime detection and investigation, including such areas of specialization as weapons and DNA analysis.

Forensic analysis is the application of science in the service of law enforcement. While today we consider this the most logical way to solve a crime, forensic science is expensive, and therefore its use is still limited.

investigation techniques to discover who, what, where, when, why, how, and with what. He provided detailed descriptions and illustrations for investigative strategies based on medicine, ballistics, chemistry, microscopy, anthropometry, fingerprinting, rape investigation, and serology, among other areas. Gross also argued that experts in these fields should testify in court, and developed several new methods of examining material evidence that technology has since refined (Grassberger, 1973).

Modern crime investigation techniques including DNA matching, fingerprinting, photo identification, voiceprint identification, hair and fibre analysis, and crime scene analysis can be traced to Gross's pioneering work. These techniques fall into the broad category of criminalistics known as *forensic science*, which is essentially "the application of science to law" (Saferstein, 1998, p. 1). For many, the term *forensic* conjures up images of TV dramas like *CSI* or *Criminal Minds*, in which the main characters work either in crime labs, analyzing evidence, or in the field, searching for clues and trying to get into the minds of heinous criminals.

In the real world, the use of sophisticated forensic technology is limited by financial restraints. However, the RCMP does have a system for tracking the nation's most serious crimes. Introduced in the 1980s, ViCLAS (Violent Crime Linkage Analysis System) is a database that now contains information on more than 300,000 cases. It is also used in a growing number of foreign jurisdictions (ViCLAS, 2013), making it possible for law enforcement agencies around the world to share scientific evidence. As Grassberger concludes in his biography of Gross, scientific evidence "is the hope of any wrongfully suspected person, and it is feared by any offender conscious of guilt" (1973, p. 316).

## (New) Social Defence Movement: Humanistic Criminal Policy?

In 1973, Mannheim, referring to the work of French judge of the Supreme Court and former professor in the faculty of law at the University of Paris **Marc Ancel**, speculated that a fourth school of criminological thought might be emerging, called the school of (new) social defence (see Box 5.14).

Before it was anglicized by eminent British criminologists including Leon Radzinowicz, the term was used by the Italian legal scholar Enrico Ferri, who argued that punishment should be based on individual and social considerations. The term was new, but the concept behind social defence was not: it was present in all the writings of such criminal law reformers as Voltaire, Beccaria, Bentham, and others, who protested against the retributive nature of European justice systems in the 1700s (Schafer, 1976). That is, they asserted that punishment should not be applied for its own sake, but for the sake of society, noting that the concept of punishment was inspired by a Christian ideal of charity and redemption (Ancel, 2001). In this sense, C.R. Jeffery (1990) argues, the concepts and principles of social defence might be more accurately described as neopositivist, since the primary focus of social defence was that punishment should serve to address the individual's transgression and ensure protection of society.

One of the first countries to adopt the principles of social defence into its criminal law was Sweden (Ancel, 2001). The social defence movement also informed United Nations policy, when in 1948 the organization established guidelines for the prevention of crime and the treatment of offenders (Joyce, 2006).

The concept of social defence recognizes that the state has a right to protect itself and society against individuals who choose to break the law, but it also speaks to the need to protect the rights of citizens—including offenders—against the potential arbitrariness of the courts. Today, the social defence model is more widely supported in Europe and the United Nations than in North America. It is characterized by its focus on crime prevention, a theme emphasized by many criminologists and criminal justice practitioners.

**neopositivist school**
An approach to criminal justice popular between the 1930s and 1960s, which focused on the development of rational penal policy, emphasizing the systematic resocialization of offenders through treatment and rehabilitation.

| BOX 5.14 | **A CLOSER LOOK**<br>Principles of Social Defence |
|---|---|

The following points are adapted from Ancel's (2001) revised book and Enrico Ferri's ideas of social defence (Sellin, 1973).

1. Social defence is not deterministic: rather, it is based on the notion that an offender can be deterred from reoffending.
2. It disapproves of a rigid classification of offenders into types and stresses the uniqueness of human personality.
3. It believes in the importance of moral values.
4. It appreciates that society has a duty to offenders, but it also sees that society has a right to be protected; in this sense, it sees the rehabilitation of offenders, designed to prevent reoffending, as striking a balance between the needs of society and of the offender.
5. Although it uses all the resources of modern science, it refuses to be dominated by science.
6. Its aim is not to punish offenders but to protect society from further criminal acts.
7. Penal policies should be tailored to the resocialization needs of the individual, rather than taking a collective approach.
8. Resocialization requires a *humanization* of criminal law, so that individual self-confidence and sense of personal responsibility can grow and human values can be respected.
9. The humanization process should be based on scientific understanding of the phenomenon of crime and the offender's personality (Ancel, 1994).

## Prevention and Environmental Criminology

In the 1970s, C.R. Jeffery called for a new interdisciplinary perspective focused on prevention, which would transcend the classical and positivist schools of criminology. Jeffrey explained: "The Classical School said 'reform the law.' The Positive School said 'reform the man.' The environmental school would say 'reform the environment'" (as cited in Mannheim, 1973, p. 498).

### Crime Prevention

*An ounce of prevention is worth a pound of cure.*

Traditional theories have not been able to fully explain, understand, predict, or suppress crime. It is a cheerless fact that numerous law enforcement practices, correctional protocols, and legal reforms have failed. Criminology needs to move away from the reactive and antiquated notion that punishment will prevent crime and protect society. Crime prevention can be achieved only through understanding what law is, why laws make some human behaviour a crime, and what influences human behaviour.

The notion of crime prevention is nothing new. Anyone who has visited Europe, Africa, or Asia will have seen centuries-old buildings that incorporate elementary yet highly effective crime prevention strategies, such as moats around castles or houses without street-level windows facing onto the street. In many older quarters, especially in southern Europe and parts of Africa, residential buildings share an interior courtyard that allows for natural surveillance.

Preventing crime is not just a matter of installing sophisticated locks and expensive alarm systems, leaving a radio on and using a light timer, and having someone cut your lawn and pick up your mail while you are away. These strategies, all part of crime prevention through environmental design (CPTED), work reasonably well to prevent property-related crime but are ineffective in preventing crimes against the person (Jeffery, 1990). In several Canadian provinces a new approach to crime prevention is being introduced, with a focus on engaging and mobilizing communities in target risk areas (see Russell & Taylor, 2014). And with growing recognition that conventional reactive strategies are not working, the concept of crime prevention is gaining traction (see Box 5.15).

Shared courtyards that allow for natural surveillance, such as this one in southern Italy, are a common architectural feature in many parts of the world.

## Key Ideas

A pioneer of the crime prevention model was **Clarence Ray Jeffery** (see Box 5.16), who argued that in order for a crime to occur, three key elements must be present: motivation, skill, and opportunity. In terms of prevention, skill and motivation are difficult to combat. How can

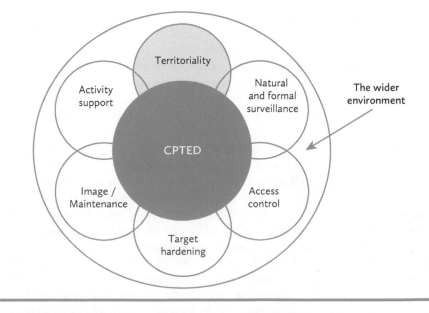

**Figure 5.2    Crime Prevention through Environmental Design (CPTED)**

Adapted from Moffat, 1983, p. 23.

---

| BOX 5.15 | WHAT DO YOU THINK? |
|---|---|

### Is Community Engagement an Effective Crime Prevention Strategy?

In 2010, after engaging in a province-wide consultation process, the Alberta government's Safe Communities Secretariat introduced a program called "Alberta's Crime Prevention Framework." Backed by a $60 million budget, the program promoted a shift from law enforcement to a more balanced approach designed to

- support an increased emphasis on the prevention of crime;
- foster collaboration and integration among government ministries, other levels of government, and community partners; and
- identify a process for engaging communities and stakeholders as an integral part of the government's crime prevention efforts.

For the first three years (2010–13) organizations could submit prevention-oriented proposals for funding consideration. By January 2013, some 88 projects had received funding for a three-year pilot program, to be assessed annually. However, in late 2013, following a change in leadership, the Alberta government suspended the Safe Communities Initiative Fund indefinitely.

Since 2011 the provincial government of Saskatchewan has funded a similar program, called "Building Partnerships to Reduce Crime" (document available at www.justice.gov.sk.ca/PCS-Partnerships). As of 2015, the program appeared to be going strong.

Take a look at the Saskatchewan document and discuss your impressions with classmates. How innovative is this program? How well does it support the "pillars" of intervention, prevention, and suppression?

---

you, for instance, prevent someone from learning how to hotwire a car or hack a computer? Likewise, it is difficult to eliminate the innumerable motivations that might lead someone to commit a crime. For this reason, Jeffery and other crime scholars believe that the focus of crime prevention efforts should be reducing opportunities presented by the social and physical environment.

---

| BOX 5.16 | PROFILE   Clarence Ray Jeffery |
|---|---|

Jeffery's academic career was marked by controversy, as he challenged many conventional views on crime and criminality in North America. While a member of the Department of Psychology at Arizona State University, he developed a version of social learning theory based on B.F. Skinner's principles of behaviour modification (see Chapter 7). A student of Edwin Sutherland (see Chapter 8), he nevertheless essentially rejected all of Sutherland's theory in the 1960s, suggesting that it could be replaced with a single statement of "operant conditioning": that in order for a response to occur, a stimulus is required. In time, Jeffery developed this idea into a sociobiological theory of crime according to which criminal behaviour is the result of an interaction between biology, the brain, and how it processes information in the social and physical environment.

In his 1977 book *Crime Prevention through Environmental Design*, he argued that all behaviour lies in the brain.

In 1963 Jeffery started the newsletter *Criminologica*, and in 1970 he became the founding editor of *Criminology*, which is now the official journal of the American Society of Criminology (ASC). In 1978 he was elected president of the ASC, and he later served on the advisory board of *Crime Times*, a publication that emphasizes research linking criminality and behavioural problems to brain dysfunction. Many of his ideas can be found in his textbook *Criminology: An Interdisciplinary Approach* (1990).

Although initially not well received, Jeffery's ideas of crime prevention and his warning that we must be proactive in addressing crime risk opportunities have become mainstream thinking and standard within criminal justice policy.

## Pioneers of Criminology in Canada

Before we move on to examine the different theoretical perspectives in criminology in the next several chapters, let us take a look at some of the pioneers of the discipline in this country. Their varied international experience has had a noticeable impact on Canadian criminology and criminal justice.

### Tadeusz Grygier, Champion of the Social Protection Code

**Tadeusz Grygier** was the champion of the Social Protection Code, which called for a fair and flexible justice system that promoted principles of rehabilitation and embraced a humanitarian approach. Born and raised in Poland, Grygier was sent to a Soviet gulag during the Second World War. The harsh experience influenced his efforts to champion a humanitarian approach to justice. After his release, he studied at the London School of Economics under the likes of Hermann Mannheim (law and criminology), Sir Karl Popper (philosophy and statistics), and Sir Raymond Firth (anthropology). Grygier's doctoral thesis on oppression (informed by his gulag experience) led to a position in the criminology program at the University of Toronto. In 1967, he moved to the University of Ottawa, where he set up both a research centre and a master's program in criminology, as well as a professional degree program in correctional administration. In 1980, he was instrumental in establishing the school's undergraduate program in criminology. His academic interests were diverse but almost always focused on social justice, fair sentencing, and correctional practices. As he noted, "a criminal law oriented to the past cannot help us to build a just, peaceful and safe society"; only a legal system based on fairness and humanitarian principles can ensure a just society.

### Denis Szabo, Father of Canadian Criminology

Born and raised in Hungary, **Denis Szabo** was educated there and in Belgium. Upon graduating, he taught sociology in France until 1958, when he joined the sociology department at the University of Montreal. The criminology program that he established there in 1960 was Canada's first, and, along with the research centre that Szabo founded in 1969, is now internationally recognized. In 1969 Szabo founded the journal *Criminologie*. He has received numerous international awards, including the distinguished Sutherland award from the American Society of Criminology. He believes that criminology is inseparable from criminal policy: one cannot be studied without proper consideration of the other.

### Ezzat A. Fattah, Champion of Victimology and Restorative Justice

Originally from Egypt, **Ezzat Fattah** left his legal practice in the late 1950s to study at the Institute of Criminology in Vienna. There, under the influence of Roland Grassberger, he became interested in victimology. In 1964 he moved to the University of Montreal to further his studies under the distinguished psychiatrist, medical historian, and criminologist Henri Ellenberger and continue his work in victimology. In 1974 Fattah was invited to set up a criminology program at Simon Fraser University in British Columbia; the first in western Canada, it is now the largest English-language criminology program in the country. In addition to his contributions to victimology, Fattah has been a champion of human rights through Amnesty International and was instrumental in Canada's repeal of the death penalty. More recently, he has been involved in various restorative justice initiatives. Although he retired in 1997, he continues to write and travel extensively, sharing his ideas on human justice.

Courtesy of SFU News, Simon Fraser University. Used with permission

Paul and Patricia Brantingham, with their son Jeffrey Brantingham (who also works on criminal modelling).

## Patricia L. Brantingham and Paul J. Brantingham, Environmental Criminologists

**Patricia Brantingham** and **Paul Brantingham** were both born in the United States. Patricia studied theoretical mathematics at Barnard College and earned a PhD in urban planning at Florida State University, while Paul obtained a Juris Doctor degree and a criminology diploma from Cambridge University. After their paths crossed, they combined their knowledge of planning, criminology, and math and applied it to the study of environmental influences on crime. Inspired by the work of C.R. Jeffery, a mentor of Paul's, they developed the field of environmental criminology. Since moving to the School of Criminology at Simon Fraser University in 1977 they have become the leading authorities on environmental criminology in this country while garnering international recognition for their work.

## Summary

- Although criminology is an evolving discipline, (neo)*classical* and (neo)*positivist* principles are still dominant, and many criminological theories reflect their influence.
- Criminology has moved from being *reactive* to being *proactive* in its approach to crime. It has also become increasingly interdisciplinary, seeing criminal behaviour as the result of various social, economic, individual, environmental, and biological factors.
- Criminological ideas, as illustrated by the work of the pioneers of criminology, are subject to change. This should serve as a caution: what may be "true" today may not be true in the future.

## Discussion Questions

1. Why is knowledge of criminological history important?
2. How might the classical and positivist approaches to the study of crime complicate our ideas about how to implement criminal justice policy?
3. Which of the pioneers covered in this chapter do you feel has made the most significant contribution to criminology as it is practised today? Why?
4. Discuss the ideas and work of the Canadian pioneers. How do their ideas reflect Canadian issues?
5. Which of the four major schools of criminological thought do you think offers the best approach for the study of crime and crime control?

## Key Concepts

atavism
classical school
criminalistics
determinism
deterrence theory
discretion
just deserts

moral insanity
neoclassical school
plea bargain
positivist school
neopositivist school
utilitarianism

## Key Names

Marc Ancel (1902–1990)
Cesare Beccaria (1738–1794)
Jeremy Bentham (1748–1832)
Alphonse Bertillon (1853–1914)
Patricia L. Brantingham (b. 1943)
Paul J. Brantingham (b. 1943)
Auguste Comte (1798–1857)
Ezzat Fattah (b. 1929)
Enrico Ferri (1856–1929)
Michel Foucault (1926–1984)
Raffaele Garofalo (1851–1934)
René Garraud (1849–1930)

Hans Gross (1847–1915)
Tadeusz Grygier (1915–2010)
John Howard (1726–1790)
Clarence Ray Jeffery (b. 1921)
Jules-Charles-Henri Joly (1839–1925)
Cesare Lombroso (1835–1909)
Alexander Maconochie (1787–1860)
Sir Robert Peel (1788–1850)
Isaac Ray (1807–1881)
Luigi Rossi (1787–1848)
Denis Szabo (b. 1929)

## Weblinks

**Crime Prevention**
Public Safety Canada's crime prevention page has links to news releases, reports, and resources relating to crime prevention.
www.publicsafety.gc.ca/cnt/cntrng-crm/crm-prvntn/index-eng.aspx

**Keeping Community in Community Policing**
This article in *Blue Line* magazine—a resource of law enforcement officials—provides the background of community policing in Canada.
http://blueline.ca/articles/keeping_community_in_community_policing

**Criminal Behaviour and Learning Theory**
C.R. Jeffery's 1959 article provides a rich account of the historical development of criminology.
http://scholarlycommons.law.northwestern.edu/jclc/vol56/iss3/4

# Chapter 6

## Biosocial Approaches to Crime

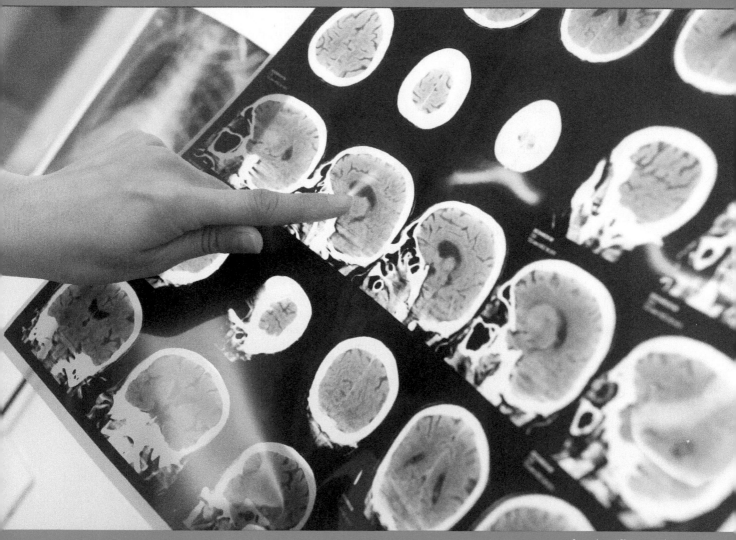

sfam_photo/Shutterstock.com

I have called this principle, by which each slight variation,
if useful, is preserved, by the term Natural Selection.
CHARLES DARWIN (1859, ch. 3)

## Learning Outcomes

After reading this chapter, you should be able to

- Appreciate the value of a biosocial perspective on crime and the effect of environmental factors on crime;
- Describe the research dedicated to biosocial variables and their possible correlations to crime;
- Understand the concept of epigenetics;
- Recognize the importance of an interdisciplinary theory that includes biological, social, and psychological dimensions.

## Introduction

Biological explanations of criminal behaviour have received limited attention in North America, where criminology has been dominated by sociological perspectives. When they have been addressed, they have often been lumped together with psychological explanations. The early positivists (*c.* 1920s) recognized that behaviour could be influenced by both internal and external factors. The internal factors are those arising from *nature*, or biology; the external factors are those arising from *nurture* (socialization and/or environment). Similar views were expressed in James Wilson and Richard Herrnstein's frequently cited work *Crime and Human Nature* (1985), and Shah and Roth (1974) warned that failure to adopt an interdisciplinary perspective would leave the dominant sociological explanations incomplete and inadequate.

Supporters of the biological perspective argue that criminology must take into account the role of heredity, and the importance of physical as well as social factors in the environment. In this chapter we will examine various biological factors that have been linked to criminal behaviour. They fall into two groups: those assuming a direct heritable link and those associated with some external or environmental factor; the latter are described as biosocial factors. After presenting an overview of some of the most important biology-based explanations of crime, we will look at the recent theoretical developments and briefly speculate on the future of theories rooted in biology.

The following observations illustrate the importance of environmental (*external*) and natural (*internal*) factors in understanding aggression, violence, and suicide in society. We will elaborate on many of these findings later in the chapter.

**biosocial factors**

Factors resulting from the interaction of individual biological and social characteristics (i.e. determinants), which predispose individuals to certain behaviours.

- Children of families on welfare show twice the rate of psychiatric disorders as that of children from better-off families, and have serious difficulties, such as alcoholism and criminality, in adulthood (NCPC, 2012).
- A study on the prevalence of mental problems among male federal inmates revealed that a significant number of those surveyed met the criteria for antisocial personality disorders. However, according to the findings of the correctional investigator, Howard Sapers, most of these inmates were handled as security risks, rather than being given treatment for their disorders (MacCharles, 2013). Bill C-10, the Safe Streets and Communities Act (2013), calls for tougher sentences rather than treatment, meaning that inmates with mental problems are even less likely to receive the rehabilitative support they require (Mackreal, 2013).
- Comparing 41 murderers to 41 matched control participants, Raine, Buchsbaum, and LaCasse (1997) found that murderers had significantly lower levels of glucose uptake in

the brain. A more recent longitudinal study, drawing on the work of **Adrian Raine** (who is one of the leading researchers on neurocriminology), found that the amygdala (a part of the brain considered the seat of emotion) of violent offenders was significantly deformed when compared with that of non-violent offenders (Moskowitz, 2011).

## The Foundations of Biological Determinism

According to Schafer (1976, p. 50), the late 1800s and early 1900s were the "golden age of criminal biology," when biological determinism prevailed. Biological determinism is the idea that individual characteristics, physical and mental, are governed solely by heredity. Some of the pioneering research on criminals involved the study of physical attributes, or somatotyping (literally "body-typing"). An association between physical appearance and behaviour has long been a staple of fiction, epitomized in Robert Louis Stevenson's 1886 novel *The Strange Case of Dr Jekyll and Mr Hyde*, which portrays the evil Hyde as a grotesque throwback to a primitive stage of human development. The persistent belief that criminals can be identified based on certain unique characteristics continues to inspire stories in which psychological dispositions are somehow mirrored in physical features (but see Box 6.1).

### Early Theories of Physical Appearance

Stereotypes regarding the physical appearance of "bad guys" go back a long way: Socrates himself was said to have thought that unsavory characters were recognizable by their physical features (cited in Vold & Bernard, 1981, p. 52). One of the earliest "scientific" attempts to validate this idea was the study of physiognomy (from the Greek *phys*, "nature," and *gnomon*, "judge, interpret"), practised by those who believed they could judge a person's character by his or her facial features. Among the telltale features described by Johann Kaspar Lavater, who produced four works on physiognomy, were "shifty" eyes, a "weak" chin, and an "arrogant" nose.

**Franz Joseph Gall** was among the first to develop the theory of *phrenology*, according to which mental faculties and character, including criminal tendencies, were reflected in the irregular surface of the cranium, or skull. While Gall identified 26 such faculties, his collaborator **Johann Gaspar Spurzheim** expanded the list and took the concept to North America (Bernard, Snipes, & Gerould, 2010). Although the theory reflected a biological-determinist perspective, Spurzheim acknowledged that criminal tendencies could be held in check through intellectual and moral development—in other words, he allowed for some measure of free will to control the behavioural tendencies associated with the shape of the skull.

In the late 1800s and early 1900s, phrenology was widely used in American penitentiaries. As science developed, however, the concept was discredited. Because of a lack of scientific evidence, quasi-sciences such as phrenology and physiognomy have largely—though not entirely—disappeared (see Box 6.2).

**neurocriminology**
The study of the interaction between social and biological factors as they relate to crime.

**biological determinism**
The idea that individual physical and mental characteristics are governed solely by heredity

**somatotyping**
The practice of attempting to draw connections between a person's behaviour or temperament and the individual's body type or physique.

© AF archive / Alamy Stock Photo

In the 1931 film adaptation of *The Strange Case of Dr Jekyll and Mr Hyde*, the good and evil personas of the protagonist (played by Frederic March) were dramatically different.

BOX 6.1     WHAT DO YOU THINK?

## Can You Judge People by Their Appearance?

In Shakespeare's play *Julius Caesar*, Caesar notes that Cassius has "a lean and hungry look" and remarks that "such men are dangerous." Have you ever judged someone's character on the basis of his or her physical appearance? Do convicted murderers like Robert "Willie" Pickton of the infamous pig farm killings outside Vancouver, or Luka Magnotta, who posted his killing and dismemberment of Jun Lin online, or HIV killer Johnson Aziga—look like criminal types? Why do we rely so much on the way people look when forming preliminary opinions about their character?

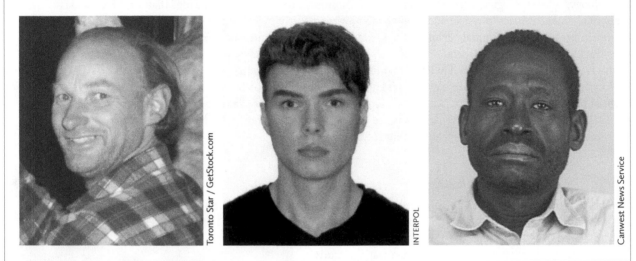

BOX 6.2     REALITY CHECK

## Quasi-science

Phrenology represented an early attempt to understand the relationship between physical characteristics and criminal behaviour. Today, such quasi-scientific means of predicting behaviour from physical characteristics have largely disappeared. Yet certain similar practices that rely on physical features or markings still exist. Iridology, for instance, is a means of diagnosis by examination of the iris of the eye. And many people still subscribe to deterministic practices such as astrology and the calculation of biorhythms, which link patterns in mood and personality to the time of year a person was born.

Do you ever read your horoscope? If so, how much stock do you put in it?

### Anthropological Measurement

*The widely held supposition that physique is irrelevant to behaviour and personality is downright nonsense. Your carcass is the clue to your character.* (E.A. Hooton)

Although Lombroso is the most famous proponent of the idea that criminals can be identified based on their physical attributes, he was not alone in this view. For example, **Charles Buckman Goring**, in *The English Convict* (1913), compared 3,000 recidivist criminals with a control group consisting of soldiers, hospital patients, and university students (Bernard, Snipes, & Gerould, 2010). Goring's examination of 37 mental and physical traits (including nasal contours, eye and hair colour, and head circumference) "led him to believe that a defective state of mind combined with poor physical condition unavoidably makes a person a criminal personality" (Schafer, 1976, p. 51). Drawing on parental (father–son) and fraternal (brother–brother) resemblance comparisons, he concluded that criminality has a hereditary link.

Goring's contribution to criminology lies not in the specifics of his findings but in the later research his work inspired. Unlike his predecessors, Goring did not restrict his explanation of crime to either the environment or heredity. Instead, he suggested that criminal behaviour might be the result of interaction between the two, one that could be summarized as follows:

Crime = Heredity + Environment

While Goring was unable to explain this interaction, his idea became the basis for numerous later studies, including some that have contributed to criminological theories today (see Williams & McShane, 2013). Few criticized Goring's findings until Harvard anthropologist **Earnest A. Hooton** raised questions about Goring's anthropometric findings. A pioneer of constitutionalism (explained below), Hooton was greatly influenced by Goring's methodological and statistical analysis, but he himself did not argue that physical differences *caused* crime. Instead, he believed that physical differences, together with social and environmental factors, could be used to *predict* crime. As cited in Vold and Bernard (1981, p. 62), Hooton reported that

- criminals were inferior to non-criminals in nearly all their bodily measurements;
- low foreheads, nasal anomalies, compressed faces, narrow jaws, and thin lips suggested general constitutional inferiority; and
- tattooing was more common among criminals than among non-criminal control groups.

In spite of his impressive sample size (some 17,000 individuals), Hooton's methodology came under criticism. He was also accused of confirmation bias, interpreting the results in a way that confirmed the assumptions he held at the outset of his study. Edwin Sutherland, Robert Merton, and Ashley Montagu all pointed out that even if heredity did play some role, what was inherited was never made clear.

## Body Types and Criminal Behaviour

While Lombroso tried to establish a relationship between temperament and physical characteristics, this line of inquiry is most often associated with **Ernst Kretschmer** in the 1920s and **William Sheldon** in the 1940s. Kretschmer believed that people fell into two fundamental personality groups:

- *cycloids*, who were manic-depressive in temperament and made up 10–20 per cent of the criminal population; and
- *schizoids*, who were lanky asthenics (i.e. tall and thin and weak) and made up 50–90 per cent of the criminal population (Vold, Bernard, & Snipes, 1998).

He also identified three body types:

- *asthenic* (as noted above: lanky and weak—typically schizoid);
- *pyknic* (short, rotund, and soft—typically cycloid); and
- *athletic* (strong, broad, and muscular).

Although Kretschmer's work was challenged for its lack of empirical rigour, Sheldon (see Box 6.3) set out to refine and improve on it. A physician, he based his theory of *constitutionalism* on the belief that human embryos are made up of three tissue layers: endomorph (inner), mesomorph (middle), and ectomorph (outer). Based on his psychological training, Sheldon constructed corresponding temperaments.

| BOX 6.3 | PROFILE  **William Herbert Sheldon** |
| --- | --- |

After finishing medical school at the University of Chicago, Sheldon visited Europe, where he met Ernst Kretschmer. He then began to do research on somatotypes at Harvard, where he met another pioneer of constitutionalism, Earnest Hooton. In time, he came to believe that biology formed the basis not only for psychology and psychiatry but also for religion. In sum, Sheldon believed that the body, mind, and spirit were all biologically determined.

Sheldon's first major work, *The Varieties of Human Physique* (1940), was devoted to somatotyping, and his second, *The Varieties of Human Temperament* (1942), provided guidelines for assessing personality and temperament based on physique (Martin, Mutchnick, & Austin, 1990, p. 133). His final book on somatotypes, *Atlas of Men: A Guide for Somatotyping the Adult Male at All Ages* (1954), consisted mainly of photographs, with little theoretical explanation.

The relationships among the three body types (a) and temperaments (b) were as follows:

1. (a) *endomorphic*: heavy-set and soft in appearance, with smooth, soft skin and small bones
   (b) *viscerotonic*: extroverted, easy-going, and fond of the "good life"

2. (a) *mesomorphic*: predominantly muscular, strong-boned, and lean
   (b) *somotonic*: assertive in manner and quite active in behaviour

3. (a) *ectomorphic*: thin, pale, and delicate, with small bones, fine hair, and sharp noses
   (b) *cerebrotonic*: introverted complainers, troubled by insomnia and chronic fatigue (list adapted from Vold, Bernard, & Snipes, 1998, p. 47)

Recognizing Kretschmer's theoretical limitations, Sheldon did not consider the three types to be mutually exclusive: rather, he saw them as interrelated to varying degrees. To quantify this assertion, he used a seven-point scale to describe individual subjects: "1" meant a virtual absence of the mental or physical trait, while "7" represented a preponderance of the trait. Thus a person with the score 6–1–4 would be a strong endomorph with no mesomorphic and some ectomorphic attributes. Sheldon found that most "delinquent" youths were predominantly mesomorphic. He did not use "delinquent" in the sociological or legal sense; instead, his notion of delinquency derived from the young person's somatotype. Using different schematic arrangements, he identified different types of delinquency. For example, he used the term "biological delinquents" to describe those youths who possessed mesomorphic attributes.

Support for William Sheldon's findings came from a 1956 study by Sheldon Glueck and Eleanor Glueck involving 500 chronic delinquents and 500 non-delinquents. The Gluecks added a fourth constitutional type—balanced—and also used a multi-factor approach.

Body-type theories eventually lost credibility because they were not able to provide convincing evidence regarding the influence of biological factors. In any case, to think simply in terms of biology, without taking environment into account, would be counterproductive to understanding the complexity of human behaviour. Future studies might explore possible connections between biology and environment: for example, might body type combine with social factors to promote violent and/or antisocial behaviour? Who are typically the bullies in public school? Who usually starts trouble? Perhaps, as suggested by Beaver (2012) and others, there are biosocial traits that can be identified.

# Genetic Research

In spite of the criticisms levelled at the positivists, the belief that physiological and behavioural tendencies have a constitutional foundation continued to evolve (see Wasserman & Wachtbroit, 2001). The positivists were spurred on by the development of new methods of measurement. One research area that required the discovery of an appropriate scientific measurement instrument was the possible link between criminal behaviour and an abnormal number of gender chromosomes.

Sex chromosomal abnormality is a biological defect in one of the 23 pairs of chromosomes that each human possesses. It may be inherited, or it may be the result of some chromosome mutation either at the time of conception (i.e. meiosis) or during the development of the fetus in the uterus (from exposure to radiation, for example). In the genetically normal female, both chromosomes resemble X's (hence their name). By contrast, the normal male has an XY pairing, with the Y chromosome smaller than the X.

For reasons not yet fully understood, sex chromosomal abnormalities occur when there is improper separation of the chromosomes during meiotic cell division (see Box 6.4) According to Herrnstein (1989a), this occurs in less than one-tenth of 1 per cent of the male population. There are several known combinations of abnormal numbering of sex chromosomes, two of which have been reported to be associated with criminal behaviour. The possible sex chromosomal types include the following:

- XX: normal female
- XY: normal male
- XO: Turner's syndrome (female only)
- XXY: Klinefelter's syndrome (male only)
- XYY: a male condition generally referred to as the supermale syndrome
- OY: an embryo that does not survive

The first of the criminal sex chromosomal abnormalities to be discovered was the XXY type, or Klinefelter's syndrome. While Dr Harry Klinefelter first described the condition in 1942, it wasn't until the 1950s that researchers began to identify males with the extra X chromosome. The syndrome is reported to be associated with degeneration of the testes, sterility, breast enlargement, tallness and thinness, and social and/or school learning problems. Alcoholism, homosexuality, frustration-based outbursts, and overrepresentation among the mentally challenged have also been reported among those with the XXY variation (Beaver & Walsh, 2011). It is probably the most common chromosomal variation in humans, occurring in approximately 1 in every 500 to 1,000 live-born males.

Research by British cytogeneticist Patricia Jacobs and her associates in 1965 drew considerable criminological interest when she found that a disproportionate number of incarcerated males had the XYY constellation. These men were characterized as being exceptionally tall, being more introverted, and having a strong propensity toward violent and criminal behaviour. Their findings, however, were based on a limited sample size and should therefore be viewed with caution (see Anderson, 2007).

---

| BOX 6.4 | FACTS AND FIGURES
WHO ARE STRONGER:
MEN OR WOMEN? |

Geneticists note that the male is the weaker of the sexes. From birth to death, males are more prone to birth defects, adolescent diseases, mental illness, heart attacks, behavioural problems, learning disabilities, and criminal behaviour. Depending on the type of crime, males are significantly more likely to face criminal charges than are women. According to Richards (2009), the ratio is around 3:1.

Can you think of any crimes or offences where women perpetrators might outnumber men? How might you explain this from a biosocial perspective?

**XYY chromosome
theory**
The theory that the extra
Y chromosome found in
some males predisposes
them to criminal or
antisocial behaviour.

The case that first drew public and academic attention to the XYY chromosome theory, positing a link between the extra Y chromosome and violent behaviour, was that of Richard Speck, who in 1968 was convicted of killing eight Chicago nurses. Because of his physical size and emotional instability, he was suspected of having an extra Y chromosome. However, he was never tested for the condition during the trial, and years later it was discovered that he did not in fact have it (Fox, 1969). Nevertheless, there were other international trials throughout the 1960s that put forward the XYY condition as the basis for a plea of insanity (Shah & Roth, 1974). Although experts testified that the men in question were genetically predisposed to be criminally dangerous, the courts did not consider the syndrome a valid excuse.

There are only a handful of recent studies into genetics and criminal behaviour. A notable one focused on an extended Dutch family, and found that the structural gene for monoamine oxidase A (MAOA), a neurochemical in the brain believed to be associated with aggressive criminal behaviour, was prevalent among a number of males in the family (Brunner et al., 1993). More recently, Anderson (2007, p. 72), in a consideration of individuals involved in genocide, cautioned about drawing any causal conclusion between genetics and antisocial behaviour. Today, one of the few places where mainstream criminology supports research into possible links between genetics and aggression is Denmark, which has kept meticulous records on twins since the late 1800s (see e.g. Nelson, 2006; the importance of twin studies is discussed in the next section). This is unfortunate: the XYY pattern may be too rare to represent a major factor, but that should not prevent criminologists from recognizing the role that biological factors might play in criminal behaviour, which remains fertile ground for research.

## Twin and Adoption Studies

Of the biological lines of investigation described above, none have been able to

- clearly delineate the biological influence;
- account for possible intervening variables such as IQ, emotional instability, EEG (i.e. brain) patterns, and the like;
- pinpoint the stage of development during which biological factors begin to exert their influence on behaviour; or
- determine why the influence is not the same for all people who possess a given biological characteristic.

These methodological criticisms aside, the possibility that the environment might interact with genetics to influence behaviour also needs to be explored. Two lines of inquiry that have tried to clarify the relationship between biological and environmental factors involve twins (identical and fraternal) and adoption.

Fraternal twins are the products of two eggs fertilized by two separate spermatozoa and genetically are no more alike than any other siblings, whereas identical twins are the product of a single fertilized egg and therefore share identical genes. While identical twins may have many traits (both physical and psychological) in common, however, careful attention reveals differences (Beaver & Walsh, 2011). This suggests that, in addition to heredity, the environment also plays a role, although it has not been clearly defined.

One of the first twin studies to focus on criminality was conducted by the German scientist Johannes Lange in the late 1920s (cited in Schafer, 1976). Using 30 sets of twins selected because one of each pair was known to have been incarcerated, Lange found that the relative concordance rate (i.e. rate of agreement across key physical and personality traits) was significantly higher among twins who were identical (i.e. monozygotic, or MZ) than among twins who were fraternal (dizygotic, or DZ). Based on these findings, he suggested that there was evidence for inherited criminal behaviour. Although no study has found a concordance rate of 100 per cent for identical twins, their rates are always significantly higher than for DZ twins (for a comprehensive review, see Rowe, 2002; Anderson, 2007). Given the consistent differences between MZ and DZ twins, it seems fair to conclude that the differences indicate some degree of genetic predisposition for some form of antisocial behaviour, with MZ twins being more alike in the types of antisocial behaviour they engage in (Rowe, 2002; see Box 6.5). With better biometric measurement techniques to measure human biological traits, thanks in large part to more advanced statistical methods, twin studies are likely to make increasingly important contributions to genetic research on crime.

| BOX 6.5 | WHAT DO YOU THINK? |
|---|---|

### Can You Blame Your Parents?

*Heredity is one of the reasons that parents with problems often have children with problems.* (J.R. Harris, 1998, p. 294)

Do you agree with this statement? If so, what theoretical implications does it raise?

Another method for determining the role of heredity in criminality is to compare the records of adoptees with those of their biological and adoptive parents. One of the first such studies, undertaken by Fini Schulsinger in the early 1970s, focused on psychopathic adoptees who were matched with non-psychopathic adoptees on the basis of age, gender, social class of adoptive family, and age of transfer to adoptive home (Schulsinger, 1972). The incidence of psychopathy among the biological relatives of the psychopathic subjects was more than twice that among the biological relatives of the control group (14.4 per cent to 6.7). What might account for the difference?

Summarizing their findings from a longitudinal study of 344 families with two or more children and looking at the possible influences of inherited genetic factors, Rowe and Farrington (1997, p. 197) observed that "unless criminologists routinely adopt behavioural genetic research designs that estimate genetic components in environmental effects (e.g. twins or adoptive studies), no unambiguous evidence can be obtained for family environmental effects on children's criminality." A few years later, Rowe (2002) attempted to unravel this puzzle by reviewing twin studies. He estimated "that 38% of the individual differences in delinquency were heritable, that 28% were due to shared environment, and that 34% were due to non-shared environment" (p. 30). The findings by Rowe, and others, show that the closer the family similarities (e.g. among twins), the greater the likelihood for behavioural similarities (e.g. antisocial behaviour).

In summary, although the research evidence pointing to a genetic link between identical twins and criminality is suggestive, it is not conclusive. The limited number of international studies indicate that while heredity does play a role, environment also has an influence, and it has not yet been clearly understood. Yet, Stoff and Cairns (1996, p. 7) note that children are more vulnerable to environmental factors than are adults and suggest that "common environment may play a more important role than it does for adults." In his summary of the research on twin studies, **Richard Herrnstein** (1989a) concluded that the evidence suggests a more complex chain of connections between the influence of genetic affects and constitutional and environmental factors on the likelihood for criminogenic behaviour. Yet, as Anderson (2007, p. 118) concludes: "more studies are needed to identify the gene(s) and their alleles or variants that are involved in different problems."

Before we move on, let us briefly reflect on the impact of biological determinism on the study of crime. We have explored a variety of heritable factors that have been, and in some cases continue to be, linked to criminal behaviour. While earlier notions such as phrenology, somatotyping, and physiognomy have been largely discredited, there may be elements of these perspectives that should not be completely discarded. Until a satisfactory theory comes along, criminologists should continue to entertain all new and old ideas and subject them to scientific scrutiny.

Later in this chapter, in a section called Contemporary Biosocial Theories, we will look at some of the main biology-based explanations that have been advanced more recently and that continue to influence criminology. Instead of relying strictly on inheritance as the sole determinant or predictor of crime, many of them point to a combination of inherited and internal and external mediating factors. Before that, we will examine two other frequently researched factors—intelligence and personality—that have been examined as possible predisposing factors for criminogenic behaviour. These factors have also been subject to the inherited, environmental, or acquired debate.

## The Brain and Behaviour

*How a person behaves is determined largely by how he thinks. Criminals think differently.*
(S.E. Samenow, 1984)

### Intelligence

The possibility that criminal behaviour might be related to mental abnormality was first proposed by the German psychiatrist **Gustav Aschaffenburg**. Since then, a considerable volume of evidence has shown that criminals have an average IQ of about 91–93, compared to 100 for the general population (see Herrnstein, 1989a; Miller 2009; Quay 1987).

In 1905 the French team of Alfred Binet and Theodore Simon developed an early version of what would become the Stanford-Binet IQ Test. It was translated into English in 1908 by **Henry Herbert Goddard**, an American psychologist and proponent of eugenics, who established the first laboratory for the psychological study of the intellectually challenged. His most famous work, *The Kallikak Family: A Study in the Heredity of Feeble-mindedness* (1913), traced the genealogy of one of his patients back to a Revolutionary War soldier and the "feeble-minded" woman with whom he supposedly had a son before marrying a respectable Quaker woman. Identifying 480 people descended from the "feeble-minded" mistress and 490 from the respectable wife, Goddard claimed to find evidence of mental problems, prostitution, and criminality among a significant number of the former, and very few among the latter. Goddard concluded "that crime is the result of low-grade mentality; primarily feeblemindedness, which is an inherited quality" (cited in Schafer, 1976, pp. 60–1). As a result of his findings, Goddard was asked to help draft the first American law mandating special education for the intellectually challenged.

Goddard's claims also prompted efforts to prevent "feeble-minded" women from reproducing. In the 1920s, for example, both Alberta and British Columbia passed legislation allowing the involuntary sterilization of persons classified as "mentally deficient." In Alberta alone, almost 3,000 men and women (although disproportionately more women) were sterilized before the government finally repealed the legislation in 1972. In 1999, more than 800 victims successfully sued the province, which responded with a formal apology and over $142 million in compensation (Grekul, Krahn, & Odynak, 2004).

In reality, and contrary to Goddard's claims, intelligence does not predict delinquency or crime as well as environmental factors do. McCord and McCord (1959) were among the first to suggest that the extent of parental discipline, family cohesion, religious upbringing, and exposure to positive peer and social opportunities are better predictors of criminal behaviour. Still, perhaps we should not completely dismiss the relationship between intelligence and criminal behaviour. For example, Gordon (1987) demonstrated a correlation between an individual's high verbal IQ score and a low probability of delinquent behaviour, especially when combined with high socioeconomic status (SES) (Walsh & Hemmens, 2013). Quay (1987) argued that a lower IQ places youths at social risk, while Beaver and Wright (2011) add that a lower IQ is often associated with poor parenting and is linked to unfavourable socioeconomic conditions.

In short, it is difficult to dismiss the possibility of a correlation between IQ and crime. More research is needed to determine the mechanisms by which low IQ predisposes individuals to crime and the extent to which low IQ is a product of the social and cultural environment, as opposed to early brain dysfunction.

## Personality

Walsh and Hemmens (2011, p. 234) define personality as "the relatively enduring, distinctive, integrated and functional set of psychological characteristics that results from an individual's temperament interacting with his or her culture and personal experience." How do we acquire personality? Most people would probably say that personality is the product of innate psychological factors. However, like language, personality may also have a biosocial foundation.

Because of poor methodology and flawed measurement, early research found little or no relationship between the personalities of offenders and those of non-offenders. The biological/biosocial component of personality is still not well understood because measurements of personality have not been standardized and at best measure only approximations of personality (see Herrnstein, 1989a). In recent years, however, an abundance of evidence has suggested that most offenders' personalities are distinctive, though not necessarily abnormal.

Perhaps the strongest link between personality and criminality appears in the work of **Hans Eysenck**. In the 1970s, Eysenck developed an influential model of personality which included three dimensions of personality: psychoticism, extroversion, and neuroticism. Using the personality scale he developed, Eysenck claimed to be able to predict a person's propensity to commit a crime based on his or her scores across the three dimensions (Akers & Sellers, 2013).

Personality and intelligence tests are premised on standardized psychological assessment of observable and measurable indicators, which are seen to be acquired primarily through one's life experience(s). Herrnstein (1989a), however, suggested that the different aspects of personality (e.g. emotional, intellectual, and structural) may have different heritabilities. In other words, it may be possible that, combined with environmental cues (i.e. experience and context), certain inherited personality traits predispose individuals to criminal behaviour. If that is the case, personality and intelligence are likely not produced by the environment alone but by interaction between the environment and the brain.

## Substance Abuse

Extreme drunkenness has been used as a legal defence for various crimes. However, in 1994, in a case referred to as *R. v. Daviault*, the Supreme Court ruled that extreme intoxication can be used only if the suspect's behaviour is akin to automatism. While the drunkenness defence is based on legal principles (sections 1, 7, and 11(d) of the Charter of Rights and Freedoms), any malfunctioning of the brain must be biochemical in nature.

In their study of incarcerated federal offenders in Canada, Brochu et al. (2002) found that the substance most commonly used/abused before incarceration was alcohol. And although it was not the only substance they used, two of Canada's most notorious serial killers, Clifford Olson and Robert Pickton, were known to have been excessive drinkers prior to incarceration (see Box 6.6).

| Table 6.1 | Top 5 Narcotic Substances Used by Canadians (%), 2013 | | |
| --- | --- | --- | --- |
| Rank | General Population (aged 15+) | Youth (aged 15–24) | Adults (aged 25+) |
| 1st | Alcohol (78.4) | Alcohol (70.0) | Alcohol (80.0) |
| 2nd | Cannabis (10.2) | Cannabis (20.3) | Cannabis (8.4) |
| 3rd | Cocaine/Crack (1.1)* | Hallucinogens (3.9)* | Cocaine/Crack (0.7)* |
| 4th | Hallucinogens (0.9)* | N/A (suppressed) | Hallucinogens (0.4)* |
| 5th | Ecstasy (0.6)* | N/A | N/A (suppressed) |

*Figures should be interpreted with caution because of the small sample size.
*Source:* Health Canada. Canadian Alcohol and Drug Use Monitoring Survey, 2013.

Given the dominant sociological perspective in North America, increasing rates of substance abuse and experimentation have been explained from a social constructionist perspective, which views society as a constructed representation of reality in which the world has no underlying objective character (see Pfuhl & Henry, 1993). However, a perspective grounded in biology may have greater predictive and explanatory potential as far as crime and substance abuse are concerned.

The effects of alcohol and drugs (both legal and illegal) on metabolic processes and the central nervous system have been extensively studied. For example, Cadoret (1995) showed that the chance of alcohol abuse by an adoptee whose biological parent was an alcoholic was statistically high. Having an alcoholic in the adoptive home also increased the risk of alcohol problems in the adoptee, but not to the same extent. As more sophisticated techniques have

iStock.com/Thinkstock.com

Alcohol, though legal in Canada, has been more strongly linked to incarceration than any illegal substance. Do you think that alcohol is a dangerous drug? Should it be more carefully regulated?

| BOX 6.6 | **FACTS AND FIGURES** SUBSTANCE ABUSE AND CRIME |
|---|---|

A growing body of literature shows a link between substance abuse and criminal behaviour. Consider, for example, the following points, compiled from the website of the Canadian Centre on Substance Abuse (CCSA—www.ccsa .ca/eng/Pages/default.aspx):

- Impaired driving is the most prominent factor contributing to serious road crashes.
- Based on data from 2006, the CCSA estimated the total societal cost of substance abuse to be $39.8 billion, or $1,267 for every Canadian.
- Alcohol causes over $14 billion annually in economic harm—yet anyone over the age of 18 can legally buy and consume it.
- Canada's youth (18–24 years of age) have the highest self-reported rate of marijuana use among all Canadians surveyed. It is estimated that marijuana use accounts for $8.2 billion of the $40 billion spent on illicit drugs.

Among the key findings of a CCSA report on substance abuse in Canadian prisons (Weekes, Thomas, & Graves, 2004) are the following:

- More than 70 per cent of federal inmates have engaged in "problematic use of alcohol or drugs" while in prison.
- Fetal alcohol spectrum disorder (see Box. 6.7) has emerged as a potentially serious problem among inmates, especially Aboriginal inmates. Several institutions now have special units and/or programs for offenders suffering from FASD.
- The three drugs most commonly used by inmates are marijuana, alcohol, and cocaine.

What do you think of the recent legalization of the use and sale of marijuana in Colorado and Washington?

© Mike Clegg / Alamy Stock Photo

Pro-marijuana demonstrators rally in Toronto during a 4/20 event. What are some of the barriers to legalizing marijuana in Canada? What are some of the reasons for keeping marijuana criminalized?

## BOX 6.7

### A CLOSER LOOK
### Fetal Alcohol Spectrum Disorder (FASD)

Fetal alcohol spectrum disorder (FASD) is the term used to identify a range of effects caused in children of women who drank excessively during pregnancy. FASD is associated with below-average intelligence (mean IQ of 68), cardiac defects, central nervous system impairment, growth abnormalities, and certain distinct facial features.

FASD is a particular concern among Aboriginal youths whose parents attended residential schools (see Salmon, 2011; Tait, 2003). In a recent study on the topic, Burnside and Fuch (2013, p. 41) point out that despite all the attention that has been given to the problem, it remains "well documented that Aboriginal children are significantly overrepresented in child care [i.e. foster care] populations across the country, especially in the western provinces." Arguably, the programs are not having their intended impact, in part because the parents and/or guardians of Aboriginal children with FASD are unequipped to deal effectively with the condition.

FASD has been identified as the third-ranking cause of developmental disability, behind Down syndrome and spina bifida).

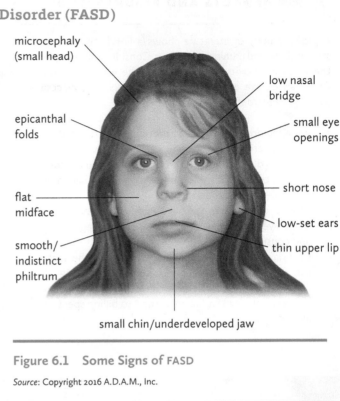

Figure 6.1    Some Signs of FASD

*Source:* Copyright 2016 A.D.A.M., Inc.

been developed, researchers have been attempting to localize the gene(s) responsible and find out how they operate (Raine, 2007). Other investigators have been looking for risk factors or genetic and biological markers for alcoholism and drug use. Marks (2009), among others, for example, cites numerous research conducted over the years that found neurotransmitters in the brain that are related to alcoholism.

In summary, while studies have shown that drugs and alcohol correlate highly with aggression and risk of suicide, homicide, motor vehicle accidents, and domestic violence, a clear causal relationship has not been established. We know that drugs act on the neurotransmitter system of the brain, but research is less clear about the influence of environmental, cultural, gender, and innate differences. Future studies should look at the effects of alcohol and drugs from a multiple-level and interdisciplinary perspective.

### Brain Chemistry

The physicians of ancient Greece believed that the human mind, body, and soul are closely linked. Hippocrates, the father of modern medicine, taught that both health and temperament were determined by the proportions in the body of four fluids, or "humours": blood, phlegm, yellow bile, and black bile. A faint echo of this idea can be seen in the science of endocrinology, which studies hormones (the chemical substances that circulate in the bloodstream and regulate cell activity). In 1928, Max Schlapp and Edward Smith published the first criminological textbook to try to explain criminal behaviour as a product of hormonal imbalances.

Although that idea fell out of favour within a few years (see Bernard, Snipes, & Gerould, 2010), today there is a growing body of literature that relates various behavioural conditions to endocrine imbalances.

It was the German chemist Friedrich Wohler who pioneered the study of endocrine systems (Vold & Bernard, 1981). Excited by the idea that humans are chemical entities, researchers began to identify some of the physiological and psychological effects of the endocrine glands—the glands that produce hormones. Louis Berman (1938, cited in Vold & Bernard, 1981, p. 109) was among the first to develop a chemical–glandular theory of personality differences. The brain is responsible for managing all the hormones released from the pituitary gland, located near the middle of the brain (see Figure 6.2). The hypothalamus is the nerve centre for the autonomic nervous system and the control centre for sex hormones (libido). It is also the seat of our emotional reactions: fear, aggression, hunger, and thirst. Jeffery (1990, p. 200) refers to the functions of the hypothalamus as the "food, sex, fight or flight" syndrome. Below it is the substantia nigra, whose main function is to send signals throughout the body. The brain communicates with itself by neural transmission. The thalamus is the sensory relay location that transmits neural information from the sensory organs to other parts of the brain. The chemical transporters that carry the message along the nerve fibers are the neurotransmitters. How information gets around the brain depends on the amount of each neurotransmitter present at the synapses where the neurons join. Information is transmitted through the neurons via an electrochemical and biochemical impulse (Beaver & Walsh 2011). There are four main types of neurotransmitters.

Neurotransmitters can either increase (excite) or decrease (inhibit) the level of activity of receptor neurons. The primary excitatory neurotransmitters are dopamine (DA) and acetylcholine (ACh), while the two main inhibitory neurotransmitters are serotonin (5-HT) and noradrenalin (norepinephrine) (NE). While considerable efforts have been made to understand how hormonal imbalances lead to problems in many areas (from the prostate gland and female reproduction to sex drive and mental alertness), criminologists have not been overly

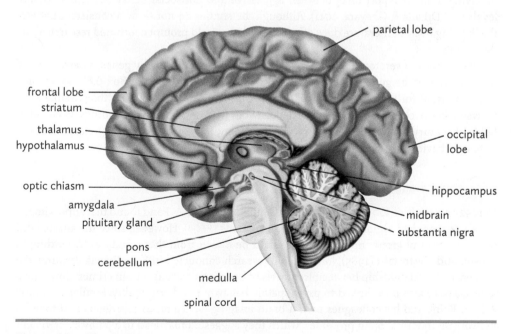

**Figure 6.2   The Brain**

interested in examining the role that such imbalances might play in criminal behaviour. One of the first studies to examine the influence of hormonal changes on female behaviour found that 46 per cent of the subjects (N = 156) committed their crimes either in the four days before or in the four days after menstruation (Dalton, 1961). Although more recent evidence has supported this finding (see DiLalla and Gheyara, 2011; Fishbein, 2000), it is still not clear whether the psychological and physical stress of aggression might trigger menstruation rather than vice versa. Nevertheless, in the 1980s a number of women who had killed men were successfully defended on the grounds that they had been experiencing premenstrual syndrome (PMS) at the time (see Katz & Chambliss, 1995).

As for the effect of hormones on men, a study by James Dabbs (cited in Gibbs, 1995) found that male prison inmates with higher testosterone concentrations were more likely to have committed violent crimes. If hormonal imbalances in the hypothalamus and striatal cortex can affect our health, is it not also possible that certain hormonal imbalances might predispose us to criminal behaviour? Walsh (2002, p. 140) points out that adolescent males have about 20 times more "free" testosterone than females, and that the activation of this hormone is thought to "partially account for the onset of antisocial behaviour among most young men."

Canadian researchers Philippe Rushton and Julie Harris (1994) tested salivary testosterone levels in male and female twins (228 pairs) exhibiting pro-social and aggressive behaviour. They found that testosterone levels were higher among those males who displayed more aggressive behaviour than among those who did not exhibit violence tendencies. The researchers speculated that male violence was largely genetic in origin, whereas female violence was often triggered by environmental factors, and they posited that the gender differences in violence patterns were related to testosterone levels. What remains unclear, however, is the effect of the interaction among biology, gender roles, and socializations.

Finally, there is a growing body of research into the possible link between low serotonin (5-HT) levels and violent or impulsive and suicidal behaviour among criminals and psychiatric patients. While most of this research has been conducted on animals, some recent studies involving humans report links between aggressive and antisocial behaviour and serotonin levels (see DiLalla & Gheyara, 2011). Although the studies do not show a consistent pattern, the growing body of literature does offer results that should prompt continued research along these lines.

Since levels of serotonin in the brain may be partly determined by genes, a percentage of individuals may be genetically predisposed to violent behaviour (see Box 6.8). Issues such as this warrant further research. Increasingly, criminologists are revisiting the possible links between brain chemistry and criminal behaviour and incorporating findings from other fields of inquiry, such as biochemistry and neurology, to form an interdisciplinary theory of human behaviour.

## EEG Abnormalities

In 1952, in a study of 100 serious offenders, Dennis Hill and D.A. Pond found that approximately half of them had abnormal electroencephalograms (EEGs). However, since the authors did not use a control group, no conclusions could be drawn from these findings. According to Wilson and Herrnstein (1985), longitudinal research conducted in Scandinavia confirms the existence of a relationship between low levels of brain arousal and certain crimes. Low arousal levels have also been linked to psychopathic behaviour and criminality. Similarly, in 1997 Adrian Raine and his colleagues used a brain imaging device on 41 murderers and found a network of abnormal brain processes, which they suggested may lead to a pathway of violent behaviour. More recently, research teams headed by Pillmann (1999) and Zukov (2008) found

| BOX 6.8 | **A CLOSER LOOK**<br>**A Misguided "Wonder Drug"?** |
|---|---|

Since low levels of serotonin have been linked to both clinical depression and anxiety disorders, anti-depressant drugs called SSRIs (selective serotonin reuptake inhibitors) are widely used in Canada. Yet such drugs are controversial because of their side effects, especially in young people. In 2011, for instance, a 15-year-old Manitoba youth became the first person in North America to have his murder charge reduced because he had been under the influence of the SSRI commonly known as Prozac (Blackwell, 2011). And Michael Moore, the director and producer of the film *Bowling for Columbine*, has called for an investigation into the possibility that one or both of the perpetrators of the Columbine shootings were taking antidepressants.

In the end, is not all medication to some degree toxic? Have you ever read all the side effects of any medication you were taking? What did you think?

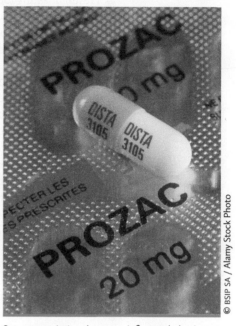

Some prescription drugs can influence behaviour.

© BSIP SA / Alamy Stock Photo

that abnormalities in the left hemisphere—the creative half of the brain—were significantly more common in violent than in non-violent offenders. Perhaps we need to pay closer attention to the possible relationship between criminal behaviour and physical anomalies such as endocrine imbalances and EEG abnormalities.

## Nutrition and Environmental Toxins

*Let food be thy medicine.* (attributed to Hippocrates)

When asked what she would do about violence in Canada if she were given a blank cheque, Dr Marnie Rice, former director of research at Oak Ridge Psychiatric Hospital in Penetanguishene, Ontario, said she would "spend it feeding good food to young mothers-to-be" (Carter, 1995, p. 34). If we are what we eat (and drink, and breathe), then perhaps there is a connection between nutrition and crime. While we may exercise free will in what we eat, we cannot control how certain foods affect our body and brain.

### Diet, Toxins, and Food Additives

There is an abundance of literature showing that chemical imbalances resulting from diet, ingested toxins (e.g. heavy metals), and food additives can influence behaviour (Gesch, 2013; Raine, 1993). Perhaps the most frequently documented example of a nutritional defect that may be a source of crime is hypoglycemia, or low blood sugar (Anderson, 2007). And perhaps the most famous legal case involving diet was that of Dan White, who was charged with murdering San Francisco's mayor and supervisor in 1978 but convicted on the lesser charge of voluntary manslaughter after his lawyer argued that he suffered from "diminished capacities" as a result of eating too much junk food high in sugar, which aggravated a chemical imbalance. This argument came to be known as the "Twinkie defence."

One of the functions of the pancreas is to secrete insulin into the blood system to remove sugar and convert it to fat for future energy use. The brain regulates and controls blood sugar levels in the body. Philpott (1978, p. 128) found that studying blood sugar levels "before and after exposure to addictants in known narcotic, alcohol, and food addicts" showed that "the stress of the addictive withdrawal state" could be consistently related to hypoglycemia (see Beaver & Walsh, 2011).

Among the first to popularize the notion that violent delinquent behaviour might be related to bioenvironmental factors—specifically, dietary factors that produce biochemical imbalances—was **Alexander Schauss** (1988). With several associates, Schauss found that on average juvenile offenders ingested 32 per cent more sugar than youths with behavioural disorders but no criminal records. In 2004, Schauss's research and ideas helped legislators limit the sale of sodas and junk food in Seattle (Saul, 2004). According to a recent CBC report, in 2014 Canadians consumed on average 27 teaspoons of sugar per day (much of it in processed foods), even though the World Health Organization recommends no more than 12 (CBC News, 2014a). And while the concept might seem outlandish to conventional criminologists, students of nutrition have amassed considerable data showing a link between diet and antisocial behaviour.

A growing body of literature has linked certain dietary practices to criminal behaviour and general behavioural disorders:

**attention deficit hyperactivity disorder (ADHD)**
A psychological and/or biological disorder characterized by inability to concentrate.

- In his review of the literature, Adams (1998a) found a link between attention deficit hyperactivity disorder (ADHD) and a diet high in saturated fats. ADHD is characterized by restlessness, hyperactivity, and forgetfulness. It has been related to conduct disorders, sensation-seeking, and early adult offending among delinquents (Farrington, 1994). In 2013 it was estimated that ADHD affects between 5 and 12 per cent of Canadians—including 1.2 million children—and that boys are three times more likely than girls to develop the disorder (Statistics Canada, 2013b).

- Smith, Fairburn, and Cowen (1997) reported that women whose diets are low in the amino acid tryptophan are at greater risk of depression than those with normal diets. (Tryptophan deficiency is commonly found among women with eating disorders: Ross, 2012). Bond, Wingrove, and Critchlow (2001) also found that reduced levels of serotonin (the brain chemical responsible for mood balance) may contribute to aggressive behaviour in women during the premenstrual phase of their monthly cycles.

- According to Schoenthaler et al. (1995), improvements in behaviour that follow a decrease in sugar consumption may be due less to the decrease in sugar than to an increased intake of the vitamins and minerals contained in fresh fruits, vegetables, and whole-grain foods. In the team's 15-week study, two groups of research subjects received different doses of vitamin and mineral supplements (100 and 300 per cent of the US recommended daily allowances), while one group received a placebo. Among those who took the supplements, there was an overall decrease in rule-violating behaviour (a mean reduction of 16 per cent for the group that took the higher dose), while the placebo group had a mean increase in rule violation (20 per cent). The authors concluded that while environment should still be considered when studying violent behaviour, more research is needed into the possibility that nutritional intervention could help to control antisocial behaviour.

- After reviewing several methodologically sound studies and a rich cross-section of related literature, Anderson (2007, p. 286) concludes: "the evidence strongly suggests that something as simple and ordinary as what we eat can have a major impact on our well-being and subsequent behaviour."

The link between diet and public health, though so well established today as to be beyond argument, was not always recognized. Back in 1959, Dr Frank Boudreau predicted that "If all we know about nutrition were applied to modern society, the result would be an enormous improvement in public health, at least equal to that which resulted when the germ theory of infectious disease was made the basis of public health and medical work" (as cited in Williams & Kalita, 1977, p. ix). Yet almost 20 years later, Williams and Kalita criticized the lack of attention that had been given to the role of nutrition in preventing illness. They reported (1977) that in 1975, half the world's population was suffering from some degenerative disease, and the number of children classified as hyperactive, "retarded," or schizophrenic was steadily increasing. Why? The authors blamed dietary habits and environmental pollutants.

More recently, there has been study of the possible connection between nutrition and intelligence. In a 1992 article that appeared in the prestigious medical journal *The Lancet*, Lucas and associates reported that by the age of 8.5, babies born pre-term and fed formula rather than mother's milk had an average IQ score 8.3 points lower than those who had received mother's milk. As Walsh (2009) points out, this is an example of epigenetics: an overlap between biology and sociology in which external factors change the way genes behave. A compelling Canadian example can be seen in the pioneering work of Richard Tremblay and associates. Drawing on data from a longitudinal study starting with 1,000 children in Montreal in 1984 and involving numerous follow-up social and behavioural indicators (including antisocial behaviour), Tremblay observed that there is an epigenetic basis for the transmission of violence (Bokhoven et al., 2006).

Unfortunately, poor nutrition is a problem that continues to afflict many families, and young people in particular, throughout the world. In 2005, Dr Emanuel Cheraskin surveyed more than 1,400 healthy individuals over the age of 20 and found not only that they ate better than less-healthy people but that they consistently consumed between five and nine times the government-recommended levels of nutrients. Yet according to the UN's Food and Agriculture Organization (2014), between 2012 and 2014, an estimated 1 in 9 people globally suffered from chronic malnutrition, mostly in developing countries. And according to the 2014 Hunger Count report (p. 5), produced annually by a network of Canada's food banks, 37 per cent of those who were helped by food banks were children, suggesting that even in this country, many young people are not getting adequate quantities of healthy food. What effect might this have on violent behaviour and crime?

**epigenetics**
The study of genetic modifications caused by external (i.e. environmental) factors that do not alter the DNA sequence but affect how cells "read" genes, effectively turning them "on" or "off."

## Vitamins

Research on the possible links between nutrition and crime includes studies on the effects of an excess or undersupply of vitamins such as C, $B_3$, and $B_6$ (see Box. 6.9) as well as studies on the relationship between food allergies and antisocial behaviour (see Beaver et al., 2013). Related to this is a growing body of evidence linking nutrition to mental development. For example, a recent Danish study found that vitamin C deficiency in pregnant women can have serious consequences for the fetus. In summarizing the study, Kearney (2012) points out that "[e]ven marginal vitamin C deficiency in the mother stunts the fetal hippocampus, the important memory centre, by 10–15 per cent." It appears that the damage is done very early in the pregnancy and cannot be undone, even by taking vitamin C supplements later on (Kearney, 2012).

Furthermore, Bernard Gesch (2005) has found a link between nutritional supplements and criminal behaviour. He conducted a clinical trial with 231 maximum-security young adult prisoners to see whether enhanced nutrition might cause them to commit fewer disciplinary offences. It found that, on average, those who received supplements committed 26.3 per cent fewer offences than those who received placebos (Figure 6.3).

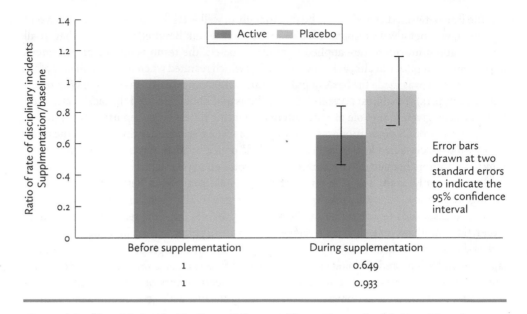

| | Before supplementation | During supplementation |
|---|---|---|
| | 1 | 0.649 |
| | 1 | 0.933 |

**Figure 6.3    Gesch's Study Findings: Effect on Those Treated with Nutritional Supplements for More Than Two Weeks**

*Source*: Data from Gesch et al. "Influence of supplementary vitamins, minerals and essential fatty acids on the antisocial behaviour of young adult prisoners." 181 *British Journal of Psychiatry* (July 2002) 22-28. © 2002 Royal College of Psychiatrists.

## Minerals

Excessive exposure to, or high intake of, common minerals such as cadmium, copper, lead, magnesium, manganese, and zinc has been linked not only to learning disabilities and cognitive deficits but also to aggression (see Marlowe, Bliss, & Schneider, 1994). For example,

- The ancient Greeks are said to have believed that manganese could have harmful effects on humans who had been exposed to the metallic element through extended dermal contact. The Greeks had learned to use manganese to help strengthen their weapons (VRF, 1994).
- In 1989, Cawte and Florence reported that, based on 50 years of data, the incidence of violence and murder was 299 per cent higher on Groote Eylandt, where the heavy metal manganese is mined, than in any other area in Australia. The island produces about a quarter of the world's manganese.
- While exploring whether there was any difference in the levels of toxic chemical substances among prisoners and control groups, Gottschalk and associates (1991) found that the inmates who had committed violent crimes had measurably higher levels of manganese in their hair analysis than did the control group. Manganese lowers the levels of serotonin and dopamine.
- While volunteering at a prison in Illinois, Anthony Walsh, professor of criminal justice at Boise State University, conducted hair analysis on 24 pairs of brothers—one a "good guy" and the other a "boy from hell." The delinquent boys consistently had high levels of copper, very low levels of zinc, sodium, and potassium, and elevated levels of lead, cadmium, and manganese compared to their brothers (Challem, 2001).

Masters, Hone, and Doshi (2005) conducted a comprehensive study of geographic variations in rates of violent crime in the United States. They found that poor diet and deficiencies in vitamins and minerals can cause neurotoxic metals such as lead and manganese to be

BOX 6.9

## A CLOSER LOOK
### Environmental Toxins Inherited

In a follow-up to a study of Canada's 1991 Gulf War veterans and questions about the incidence of birth defects in the children of those veterans, a 2006 report by the American Institute of Medicine confirmed that the children born to veterans of that war were 20 per cent more likely than others to have physical defects. The updated report also concluded that the causes could include exposure to chemical and biological weapons, use of anti-nerve gas pills, toxic fumes from oil fires, and war-related stress (Gulf War and Health, 2006). The report also noted that the findings were consistent with an American study conducted on veterans in Iowa (p. 65).

More recently, researchers at the Center for Reproductive Biology at Washington State University found that exposure to environmental toxins during embryonic development caused adult-onset disease not only in the test animals but in most of their descendants (Winner, 2014). Given the current state of the environment, this is important research.

absorbed into the brain, interrupting normal brain development and functions. Masters et al. also noted that environmental pollutants could interact with poverty, poor diet, alcohol and drug abuse, and social stress to put some individuals at risk for loss of impulse control and increased violent crime (Masters et al., 2005).

In summary, there is a growing body of evidence that links nutrition to crime. However, it is important to note that no single food type, mineral, or vitamin has emerged as the key factor, and most of the evidence suggests that environmental and/or psychosocial factors may play mitigating roles. Nevertheless, the findings do suggest that human behaviour may be altered by what we eat, drink, or breathe. Yet despite the volume of evidence demonstrating a connection between nutrition and violence, the evidence has not yet translated into policy.

## Contemporary Biosocial Theories

Until recently, the biosocial perspective had received minimal support among criminologists, perhaps because the flawed early biological-determinist studies led them to mistrust more recent theories rooted in biology. However, in their edited book on biosocial theories of crime, Beaver and Walsh (2011, pp. 14–15) note that "the biosocial perspective is beginning to gain a significant amount of traction within the field of criminology.... Some leaders in the field ... have even argued that it is now time to abandon a purely sociological approach to crime and replace it with a biosocial approach."

### The Birth of Sociobiology/Biosociology

In 1975, Edward O. Wilson, a professor of zoology at Harvard, wrote a controversial book entitled *Sociobiology: The New Synthesis*. Introducing sociobiology as "a branch of evolutionary biology and particularly of modern population biology," Wilson defined it as "the systematic study of the biological basis of all social behaviour" (1975, p. 4).

Wilson argued that our genetic makeup predisposes us not only to protect our own kin but to eliminate those who appear as threats. However, he was careful to note that "there is no universal 'rule of conduct' in competitive and predatory behavior" (1975, p. 247). So how do we control innate aggression? According to Wilson, "we should design our population's densities and social systems in such a way as to make aggression inappropriate in most conceivable daily circumstances and, hence, less adaptive" (p. 255).

More recently, Raine et al. (1997a) identified four major interactive biosocial (or sociobiological) theories of crime. We will address only three, as the fourth is considered too broad and too difficult to test empirically. All these perspectives emphasize the need for theory to become integrated and interdisciplinary in nature.

## Mednick's Biosocial Theory

For **Sarnoff Mednick**, all behaviour is triggered by the autonomic nervous system (ANS). He believed that we are all occasionally prone to do things that violate the norms, values, and rules of society. The reason most of us do not follow through on these impulses is that we learn to control them as part of our socialization process and our desire to avoid punishment. We become law-abiding as we learn to fear punishment, and as we learn to avoid fear, the behaviour gets reinforced.

Mednick theorized that those whose ANS recovers quickly from fear easily learn socially proscribed behaviour, whereas those whose ANS recovers slowly have difficulty learning to inhibit antisocial behaviour. Thus, learning non-criminal behaviour involves both individual abilities (ANS response rate) and environmental factors ("consistent and adequate punishment for aggressive acts"). Absence of these factors strongly predisposes a person to antisocial behaviour.

## Eysenck's Biosocial Theory

As early as 1964, in his then-controversial book *Crime and Personality*, Eysenck was the first to argue that being an introvert as opposed to an extrovert was an inherited trait, and that the former were more prone to cause antisocial behaviour when they interacted with various socialization processes. As Raine et al. (1997a) explain, Eysenck further theorized that, combined with autonomic and central nervous system characteristics, these biological factors affected the individual's responsiveness to punishment and propensity for antisocial outcomes. More specifically, Eysenck found that extroverts experienced cortical under-arousal and were less responsive to punishment than were introverts. In other words, punishment is less effective with extroverts, even though our correctional system is fundamentally premised on incarcerating (i.e. punishing) offenders for their crimes. However, even though Eysenck provided compelling evidence to show that criminals scored higher than the general population on extroversion, neurotics, and psychopathy, some of the contemporary research suggested that there are no 'true', or absolute, extroverts or introverts, and therefore more research is needed to clarify the merits of such personality traits (see Mischel, 1995; Muncie, 2009).

## Moffitt's Biosocial Theory

life course theory
An integrated theory used to identify factors that predispose individuals to criminal activity, which involves the study of changes in the offending pattern of an individual over the course of his or her life.

While her work has also been aligned with the life course theory (see Chapter 8), **Terrie E. Moffitt** proposed that "the biological roots of antisocial outcomes are present before or soon after birth" (Raine et al., 1997a). Relying on longitudinal data from her New Zealand study, Moffitt theorized that congenital factors such as heredity and perinatal complications produce neuropsychological problems in the infant's nervous system. These deficits then manifest themselves in childhood complications ranging from poor motor skills development to poor memory and temperamental difficulties.

Moffitt's theory asserts that while some children may be born with neuropsychological deficits, a deficient social environment might also predispose a child to perinatal complications, poor nutrition, and abuse—which, in turn, may result in some biological deficiency.

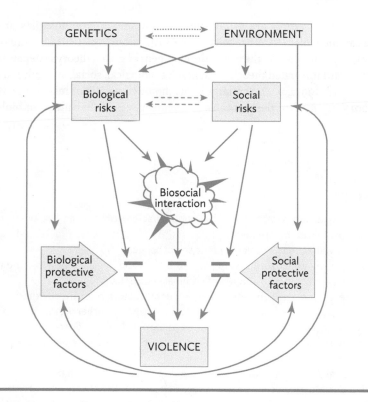

**Figure 6.4    Heuristic Biosocial Model of Violence**

*Source*: Raine, Brennan, & Farrington, 1997a, p. 15.

According to Raine et al. (1997a), the biosocial theories we have just discussed offer solid support for a biosocial approach. They build on the strengths of existing models while providing a broader framework in which to study biosocial interactions. Furthermore, as can be seen in Figure 6.4, they do not have violence as the only outcome variable. Behaviour that results in violence is the outcome of a complex interaction of social and biological factors, both of which need to be considered when attempting to understand violence or any other form of criminal behaviour. Figure 6.4 clearly illustrates this interdisciplinary, interactive, and integrated approach to understanding deviant behaviour.

## The Future of Explanations Rooted in Biology and Genetics

Biology continues to be something of a dark horse in criminology. Most of the theories we have looked at focus on physical conditions—aberrant genes, hormones, and so on—and there is limited support within society for overt manipulation of such conditions. Genetic engineering, for example, raises many ethical and policy concerns (see e.g. Resnik & Vorhaus, 2006). And while the biosocial and related biopsychological and bioenvironmental perspectives appear to be transcending the more traditional criticisms, for the most part they are still unable to explain precisely how, and to what extent perhaps, psychological or social factors interact with biology. Perhaps Moffitt summarized the biological position best: "I would prefer that the basic research be conducted for the goal simply of generating new knowledge and that the individuals who are in charge of deciding how [biological] research can be applied would be a separate group from the scientists" (cited in Ghosh, 2002).

While biological factors are gaining recognition among criminologists, it is clear that they alone cannot explain criminal behaviour. As American Society of Criminology president James Short, Jr, put it in 1996, "the future development of causal theory is dependent upon our movement toward integrated theories that involve biological, social, and cultural dimensions" (cited in Wellford, 1997a, p. 4). Similarly, in his thorough update of related literature, Scott C. Johnson (2013) argues that "the root causes of crime may lie deep within our biology."

## Summary

- Biological explanations of criminal behaviour first emerged in an era when social control took the form of retribution and "just deserts." The implications of racial and class bias in the eugenics movement had not yet become social concerns.
- Most of the early explanations were plagued by methodological problems, and none of them produced a satisfactory explanation of criminal behaviour.
- In the case of criminal behaviour, environmental factors (nurture = experience + context) seem to be inseparable from biological factors (nature). In other words, biology might affect experience or context, but environment also influences biology. Therefore both sets of factors need to be studied, and we need to recognize that behaviour has many possible causes spanning the life and social sciences.
- The biological perspective does not assume that social control can be exercised only through law and order. Much current research is based on an interdisciplinary approach that emphasizes individualized treatment through various biological and environmental intervention strategies.
- Among the newer explanations rooted in biology, the biosocial perspective has received particular support. There are currently different models, but they all take an interdisciplinary approach to the study of criminal behaviour.

## Discussion Questions

1. At a time when a growing body of research suggests that criminal behaviour may have a biological basis, which issues pose the greatest problems for criminology? How might we overcome these problems?
2. Describe the major theories discussed in this chapter. In each case, what are the relative strengths and weaknesses? What are the primary differences between the early and more recent biology-based approaches? Which theory do you think has the most explanatory power? Why?
3. Might other aberrant behaviours have a biological basis? To what extent might psychopathic behaviour be the result of an interaction between brain function abnormalities and social or familial factors?
4. To what degree do you think that biology-based explanations of crime, past and current, have been grounded in scientific principles?
5. How does the biogenetic perspective reflect an interdisciplinary approach to the study of criminality? What are its strengths and weaknesses?
6. How might the various components of theories rooted in biology be incorporated into an interdisciplinary criminological perspective? Which components do you think would be the most important?

## Key Concepts

attention deficit hyperactivity disorder (ADHD)
biological determinism
biosocial factors
epigenetics

life course theory
neurocriminology
somatotyping
XYY chromosome theory

## Key Names

Gustav Aschaffenburg (1866–1944)
Hans Eysenck (1916–1997)
Francis Joseph Gall (1758–1825)
Charles Goring (1870–1919)
Henry Herbert Goddard (1866–1957)
Richard Herrnstein (1930–1994)
Earnest Hooton (1913–1954)

Ernst Kretschmer (1888–1964)
Sarnoff Mednick (1928–2015)
Terrie Moffitt (b. 1955)
Adrian Raine
Alexander Schauss (b. 1948)
William Sheldon (1898–1977)
Johann Gaspar Spurzheim (1776–1832)

## Weblinks

**Crime Times: Linking Brain Dysfunction to Disordered/Criminal/Psychopathic Behavior**
Although last published in 2010, this online journal offers a diverse and very useful summary of research into biology and crime.
www.crimetimes.org

**Canadian Centre on Substance Abuse**
The Canadian Centre on Substance Abuse offers up-to-date information on issues ranging from consumption patterns and their economic impact to crime and laws related to drug use and abuse.
www.ccsa.ca

**BCA: The Biosocial Criminology Association**
Established in the early 1990s, the BCA is the premiere organization solely dedicated to the advancement of biosocial criminology. Their website offers a range of resources.
www.biosocialcrim.org

# Chapter 7

## Psychological Perspectives

De Visu/Shutterstock.com

[T]here is now much evidence to discredit the type of sociological theory
so prominent and widely accepted . . . ; criminals require socialization
by properly planned [behavioural] conditioning treatments.
H.J. EYSENCK (1964, pp. 12–13)

## Learning Outcomes

After reading this chapter, you should be able to

- Recognize the impact that psychology has had on the understanding of criminal and antisocial behaviour;
- Appreciate the complexity of human behaviour;
- Outline the major psychology-based theories of criminal behaviour;
- Describe some of the most important treatment methods that have been proposed; and
- Appreciate the importance of learning theories for understanding criminal and antisocial behaviour.

## Introduction

In casual discussions of crime and its perpetrators, people will often say things like, "She must be really warped to have done something like that," or "He clearly needs some serious help." As we saw in Chapter 5, these perspectives reflect the positivist assumption that behaviour is not freely chosen: rather, it is determined by a variety of factors, internal and/or external. In this chapter we will examine explanations of criminal behaviour that focus on psychological factors.

Until recently, psychological approaches to understanding criminality were not always distinct from the biological approaches discussed in the previous chapter. In fact, Schafer (1976) situated biological and psychological approaches on a continuum between nature and nurture, and as recently as 10 or 15 years ago, introductory criminology textbooks typically grouped them together. Today, however, with the growing volume of research in both the (socio)biological and psychological arenas, it makes sense to separate the two perspectives. As criminology becomes more interdisciplinary, biological and psychological theories now warrant individualized discussion.

We will begin with a look at the oldest known explanation of deviant behaviour: demonic possession. Then we will review several of the main psychological explanations of criminal behaviour. As in the other theory chapters (6 and 8), the objective is to provide an overview of key theories, not a detailed examination. What follows, then, is a cross-sectional introduction to psychological theories, which—although most also acknowledge the influence of social and/or environmental factors—identify individual factors as the primary causes of criminal behaviour.

In this chapter we will look at four major psychological theories, or orientations:

- psychodynamic
- cognitive
- moral development
- behavioural personality

These four orientations fall into two broader theoretical categories, emphasizing (1) intra-psychic factors, and (2) learning theories. As diverse as these perspectives are, they all tend to "focus their examinations on basic components of human nature, such as appetites and aversions, motives and emotions that are viewed as characteristic of the human species" (Barak, 1998, p. 127).

Before we examine these scientific approaches to the psychology of criminal behaviour, we'll take a brief look at some of the earliest deterministic explanations of the criminal mind, rooted in religion, superstition, and the supernatural.

## Supernatural Explanations

*The devil made me do it.* (Comedian Flip Wilson, 1933–1998)

Among the regular characters played by Flip Wilson on his popular 1970s variety show was "Geraldine," who would blame the devil whenever she got into trouble. The idea was that she had been possessed by an evil power beyond her control. Although the line was always good for a laugh, there is a grain of truth in most jokes, and the idea of demonic possession is a very old and still engrained myth.

In his thought-provoking book *The Soul's Code*, James Hillman (1996) used the term "bad seed" to describe a psychopathic criminal. Using examples ranging from Adolf Hitler to the serial killer Jeffery Dahmer (the "Milwaukee Cannibal"), Hillman argued that there are "bad seeds"—people who seem to be born psychopaths, without a soul. Many of his ideas recall Lombroso's notion of the "born criminal" (see Chapter 5). In keeping with the positivist model, Hillman describes how the evil in such people can be exorcized by "redressing the balance between the psyche's weakness and the daimon's [i.e. the soul's] potential" (1996, p. 242).

Throughout history, people have believed in the existence of supernatural powers, both of good and of evil. Although the first refutation of the existence of demons was written in 1533—its author, the Dutch physician and occultist Johann Weyer, argued that those thought to be possessed were in fact mentally ill—the superstitious belief in demonic possession persisted until the Enlightenment and has not entirely disappeared (see Box 7.1). Among those most frequently suspected of being possessed were the poor and those (mostly women) believed to be witches. According to Pfohl (1994, p. 39), it has been estimated that a million people, mostly women, were burned at the stake for practising witchcraft. Were these people possessed by the devil? Or were they scapegoats of a fearful, superstitious culture?

Like the idea of crime, the idea of "evil" is relative and evolutive (see Chapter 1). In ancient times there appears to have been a general consensus that evil was associated with criminal behaviour. However, as societies evolved, so did the understanding of evil. Today, what used to be called "evil" is more likely to be understood in terms of individual psychology. For example, one modern way of interpreting "evil" behaviour is to see it as "a response pattern that a person has found to be effective, or thinks to be effective, in certain circumstances" (Bartol & Bartol,

**demonic possession**
Control of an individual by a supernatural spirit or power, typically identified as the cause of deviant or criminal behaviour.

---

**BOX 7.1    REALITY CHECK**

### Modern-Day "Possession" and Mental Health

The notion that people can be possessed by evil spirits still exists today. One of the most infamous serial killers of all time, Ted Bundy, confessed that he believed his heinous crimes of sexual assault and murder were driven by an alien force and fuelled by his infatuation with violent obscenity. In 2012, the Roman Catholic Diocese of Saskatoon was contacted by a woman who feared that her uncle had been possessed by the devil; the man's behaviour returned to normal after a priest offered blessings. Also fairly recently, a woman on an Edmonton train was caught on video

behaving erratically before exploding in a sudden, unprovoked fit of rage at a fellow passenger; in the video of the attack, another passenger can be heard exclaiming, "She's possessed!" (Zavan, 2014). Finally, Neuner et al. (2012) investigated the relevance of a local variant of spirit possession in a group of people aged 12–25 in war-affected regions of northern Uganda. The "Lord's Resistance Army" used a form of spirit possession, to control abducted child soldiers by instilling fear and obedience.

Do you think the behaviour of people suffering from mental health problems could be symptomatic of being "possessed" in some form or manner? Explain.

Granger, NYC — All rights reserved.

For centuries, burning at the stake was the standard punishment for many crimes, including witchcraft and *heresy* (dissent from the official teachings of the Roman Catholic Church). This image shows women and children burned alive in 1556 for the "crime" of being Protestants.

2010, p. 174). In other words, maybe "evil" behaviour is simply a *maladaptive* (i.e. inappropriate) coping mechanism.

The notion that someone must possess, or be possessed by, an "evil mind" to commit a crime has also been refined over the years. Today it is not enough for the criminal justice system to determine that the crime (the *actus rea*) was committed by the person accused of it: in order to find that person guilty, the law requires the prosecution to show that the act was committed with *mens rea*: criminal intent. In other words, the accused must be found criminally responsible for the action. We do not punish people for committing a crime if they were "incapable of appreciating the nature and quality of the act … or of knowing that it was wrong" (Criminal Code s.16, ss.1). (We will discuss the issue of criminal responsibility in more detail later in this chapter.)

In summary, supernatural forces and metaphysical explanations have been used throughout the ages to account for behaviour. Likewise, religious organizations and the state historically used the idea of evil as a justification for social control, attributing wrongdoing to supernatural agencies that could be suppressed only through horrific punishment. With the emergence of the positivist school of thought (see Chapter 5), religious explanations of deviant behaviour were replaced by scientific approaches.

## Early Psychological and Intrapsychic Approaches to Crime

### Introduction to Psychiatric Aspects of Crime

Scientific interest in the psychological dimensions of criminal behaviour emerged in the mid- to late 1800s. A number of scholars played a key role on bridging aspects of psychology with law. Jeffery (1973) identified three essential contributors to this development (see also Box 7.2).

| BOX 7.2 | PROFILE　James Mark Baldwin: The Father of Canadian Psychology |
| --- | --- |

Born in South Carolina, James Mark Baldwin studied theology and philosophy at Princeton before travelling to Germany to study with Wilhelm Wundt, one of the early pioneers of experimental psychology. In 1889 Baldwin was appointed professor of metaphysics at the University of Toronto, where he established the first psychology laboratory in the British Empire. Although his work did not directly involve the study of crime, he did groundbreaking work on child development and was among the first to apply Darwin's theory of evolution to his own ideas on development, which in turn influenced the later work of Lawrence Kohlberg and Jean Piaget (see page 157).

1.  **Henry Maudsley**, an English medical doctor described as brilliant, believed that criminals were "morally degenerate"—lacking in moral development. He played an instrumental role in laying the legal framework for diminished responsibility as a result of mental disease. He once said: "criminals go criminal, as the insane go mad, because they cannot help it" (cited in Scott, 1973, p. 755). In the 1970s, his ideas helped to inform the basis of Canadian prison education programs.
2.  **Isaac Ray**, the most influential forensic psychiatrist of his time and one of the founders of the American Psychological Association (APA), wrote extensively on the subject of "moral insanity" (see Chapter 5). He considered it a "disease . . . never established by a single diagnostic symptom" (cited in Overholser, 1973, p. 183). In 1951, the APA named an award in his honour, recognizing him for outstanding work that furthers the relationship between law and medicine.
3.  **Gustav Aschaffenburg**, a German pioneer of psychiatric criminology, argued that we are influenced less by heredity than by our social environment (von Hentig, 1973). After being dismissed as dean of the Bonn Law School in 1935 he moved to the United States, where his work contributed to the idea that criminal behaviour is not pathological but a form of socially maladaptive behaviour.

criminal personality

A personality type characterized by such traits as antisocial behaviour, social immaturity, and nervous systems that do not condition well, believed by some to be typical of criminals but also capable of being corrected.

psychodynamic theory

Freud's theory that behaviour—including criminal behaviour—is an expression of internal conflict stemming from unresolved, often unconscious experiences during childhood.

Nearly a century later but building on the foundational ideas of these pioneers, two well-known American psychologists, Samuel Yochelson and Stanton Samenow (1976), conducted an intensive study of criminally insane patients in a Washington, DC, hospital. Based on their findings and drawing on the earlier work of Hans Eysenck (1964), they posited there may be a criminal personality, or at least a different thinking pattern among criminals. The idea that there might be something "wrong" with the minds of criminals lent support to the notion that wrongdoers should be required to undergo treatment of some kind.

Psychological explanations of criminal behaviour can be divided into two major theoretical categories: those that emphasize intrapsychic (internal psychological) factors and those that emphasize learning factors (Webber, 2010). Although the learning theories are more widely accepted today, we will begin with Freud's intrapsychic approach, as it was one of the first influential theories to treat individual personality as an observable and measurable factor in criminal behaviour.

## Freud's Intrapsychic Approach: Psychodynamics

Perhaps the best-known intrapsychic perspective is the psychodynamic theory developed by **Sigmund Freud**, which combines Kantian rationalism and the Lockean notion that behaviour is the result of sensations and experiences. According to this model, criminal behaviour is the result of internal conflicts and tensions that emerge in early childhood because of developmental problems and/or problems in interactions with parents.

Freud (see Box 7.3) believed that the mind has three levels of consciousness—subconscious (the id), preconscious (the superego), and conscious (the ego)—that represent different drives and aspects of personality (see Figure 7.1). How we behave as adults depends on how we process our early childhood experiences, traumatic or otherwise.

The id is innate, present in us from birth. It is unconscious, consisting of the most basic biological urges: for food (the will to live), for sex (pleasure), and for survival (aggression). It is also amoral. Driven by the "pleasure principle," it demands immediate gratification and seeks to avoid pain and unpleasant experiences. The power of the id can be used to explain how some people are driven to steal or fight for their survival—out of necessity. As Freud noted, the id is the life source, or *eros*, our creative side, and the basis for both positive and negative aggression. However, because of the id's self-centred focus, we start life in a state of amorality. The humanist-oriented existential psychologist Rollo May (1969) would later refer to the id as "will."

The ego and superego, by contrast, are products of individual learning experiences through childhood, adolescence, and adulthood. The ego—literally the "I," or reality principle—represents an adaptive outgrowth of the id. Based on early childhood experiences, the ego learns to weigh the consequences of acting on the id's impulses; thus, it serves as the control mechanism that keeps behaviour within the boundaries of social convention.

The other unconscious aspect of personality, the superego, arises out of the relationship between our early life experiences and external influences: the moral values of our parents and the community at large. The superego is an indicator of our socialization process as it serves to help regulation, through self-reflection in a particular cultural and social milieu. This notion is well illustrated in Aichhorn's classic book *Wayward Youth* (1935). In addition to defining delinquent groups according to the id and the ego, Aichhorn noted that those with criminal superegos belong to criminal groups or identify with a delinquent father—a very sociological orientation of criminality, according to Webber (2010). The superego is the "psychic police officer" (Bischof, 1964) that polices the id through conscious thought. Redl and

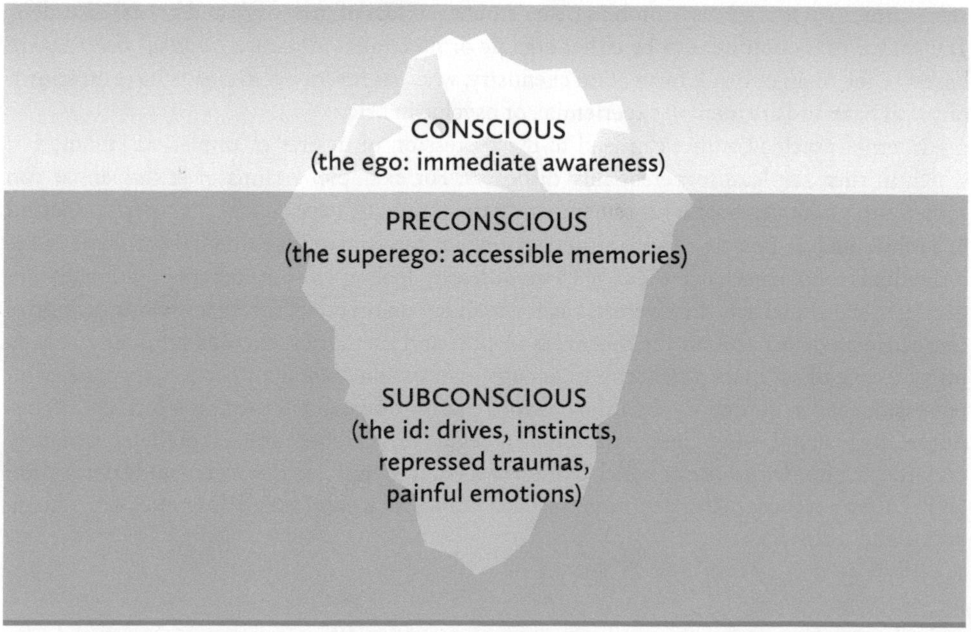

**id, ego, superego** The terms used by Freud to refer to what he believed to be the three basic elements of personality. The id represents primitive, instinctual urges; the superego is the moral and ethical dimension of personality; and the ego is the rational, conscious dimension that mediates between the id and the superego.

**CONSCIOUS**
(the ego: immediate awareness)

**PRECONSCIOUS**
(the superego: accessible memories)

**SUBCONSCIOUS**
(the id: drives, instincts,
repressed traumas,
painful emotions)

**Figure 7.1    Freud's "Iceberg" Model of Consciousness**

BOX 7.3

**PROFILE   Sigmund Freud:
The Father of Psychoanalysis**

Born in 1856 in what is now the Czech Republic, Freud was raised in Vienna, where he would live almost all his life. He studied medicine, specializing in neurology, and eventually opened a private practice. Many of his patients were women suffering from "hysteria," which he came to attribute to sexual factors. The treatment he developed consisted of encouraging patients to talk about whatever came into their minds—a method that he later described as "free association." When the Nazis overran Vienna in 1938, Freud fled to London, where he died the following year.

Although many of Freud's theories, especially regarding gender and sexuality, have now been discredited, and his work has been widely criticized for its lack of scientific rigour, his influence on later psychological theory has been profound.

Sigmund Freud (1856–1939) believed that criminal behaviour stemmed from internal conflict among the different aspects of an individual's personality.

Wineman (1951) coined the term "delinquent ego" to describe young people who, because of inadequate ego and superego development, are able to rationalize their delinquent aggression. They also reported that such youth lack close personal relationships with adult figures.

The three aspects of personality—id, ego, and superego—can be in conflict. In fact, they usually are in conflict to some degree. Among the more common forms of intrapsychic conflict are neuroses such as anxiety, phobias (fears), amnesia (loss of memory), and sexual disorders. The source of the conflict can be either organic or functional in nature. *Organic disorders* are based in the brain or result from brain chemistry, whereas *functional disorders* have no known physical base and are mental, experiential, or psychic in origin.

Internal psychic conflict can lead to the repression of desires or unpleasant memories, which in turn can lead to personality disorders. For example, victims of sexual abuse can sometimes go for years without remembering the traumatic experiences they were subjected to as children (see Box 7.4). Those repressed feelings can lead to fundamental problems in the individuals who experience them, such as difficulty feeling close to others or difficulty engaging in the sexual acts they were subjected to. If left unattended, the unconscious memories can cause anxieties around the repressed desires and memories. Victims are then likely to resort to one of six main defence mechanisms—repression, denial, projection, displacement, regression, and sublimation—in order to avoid confronting the reality of their hidden desires. According to Freud, when the mental anguish begins to negatively affect their behaviour, they are suffering from *neuroticism*, which expresses itself in symptoms that can include depression and anxiety, psychosomatic symptoms (e.g. insomnia, back pain, weight loss, etc.), or hallucinations and delusions.

## Freudian Explanations

In accordance with the basic assumptions underlying Freudian theory, human behaviour is inherently antisocial and delinquent, and criminal behaviour is an indication of a personality

| BOX 7.4 | **A CLOSER LOOK**<br>Freud and Human Psychosexual Development |
|---|---|

Freud argued that since the id represents the core of the personality and is the dominant force at birth, it is early childhood experiences that most directly affect later psychological development. In particular, Freud believed that since sex is an instinctual need, how we progress through the five stages of child development significantly influences our psychosexual development. The stages are as follows:

1. Oral (birth–age 1): The first stage is centred on the pleasure of sucking and eating. Manifestations in later life include gum chewing, smoking, passivity, and dependence.
2. Anal (ages 1–3): The second stage, which includes the toilet-training period, focuses on control and elimination. Manifestations in later life can include compulsive behaviour, stinginess, and excessive concern with order.
3. Phallic (ages 3–5): Children at this stage discover their genitals and derive pleasure from masturbation. This is also the stage when boys form an attachment to their mothers and begin to compete with their fathers: Freud called this the *Oedipus complex*, after the Greek tragedy in which the son unknowingly kills his father and marries his mother. The son normally resolves the conflict by identifying with and obeying his father. This is a superego development.

4. Sexual latency (ages 6–13): The fourth stage is characterized by repression of sexual feelings and interest in others of the same sex (boys play with boys and girls with girls).
5. Genital (age 13 and beyond): In this final stage the superego has developed enough for the young person to behave in culturally, socially, and morally prescribed ways.

According to Freud, problems experienced during any of these phases could trigger psychological problems that could lead to unacceptable and even criminal behaviour. The methods used to determine whether a person is experiencing problems are dream analysis and free association. Freud, along with many of his followers, believed that our dreams contain many of the repressed feelings and hostilities that our conscious mind (i.e. the superego) would normally not allow to surface for fear of embarrassment or some other unpleasant experience.

If criminal behaviour is the result of a personality conflict/disorder, should offenders still be held responsible? Do you reflect on your dreams?

conflict. Freud believed that all humans are driven by two fundamental instincts: one toward pleasure and life, the other toward destruction and death. Although the id and ego generally serve to moderate the destructive urges, they do not always succeed. When destructive urges prevail and express themselves in criminal acts, the ego can lead criminals to feel the need for punishment, but the id will usually prevent them from confessing—unless, as Freud noted, the person "suffers" from an overdeveloped superego. In effect, a person commits a crime in order to be punished and thereby relieved of guilt. Therefore, according to Freud, the guilt comes *before* the crime. In time, however, the superego may compel individuals to relieve their guilt by admitting what they have done.

We see this process at play among criminals on death row in the United States, who are given the opportunity to spend time with a chaplain before they are executed. Halleck (1967), among others, observed that many criminals will readily confess all at this time and then express relief. Consider, too, the case of the New York serial killer who, from 1990 to 1993, came to be known as the "Zodiac copycat" killer because, like the original Zodiac killer (who was never caught), he would leave an encircled cross with three sevens at the scene of each crime. After he was arrested in 1996 for wounding his half-sister, Heriberto "Eddie" Seda was asked to write his version of what had happened. One of the attending detectives thought Seda's writing style was very similar to that of the Zodiac killer and that the signature symbol he used at the end of his letters appeared identical. The cumulative evidence eventually led to his conviction in the Zodiac copycat killings as well. Although never proven, psychoanalytical interpretation suggests that this type of behaviour is a classic example of the Freudian battle between the driving and restraining forces in the psyche.

As summarized by Warren and Hindelang (1986), Freudian explanations of criminality hold that:

- Criminal behaviour is the product of an uncontrolled id. It is a form of neurosis—an unconscious, internal conflict that is expressed through an overt act.
- Criminal activity may be an alternative way of satisfying needs that were not fulfilled by the criminal's family.
- Some criminal and delinquent behaviour is the result of traumatic (non-pleasurable) experiences, the memories of which the offender has repressed.
- Some forms of delinquent behaviour may be the result of displaced hostility and/or an unconscious desire for punishment.
- Criminals have an unconscious need to alleviate their sense of guilt and anxiety.

**psychoanalysis**
Freud's approach to treating internal conflict and tension that results from certain unresolved, often unconscious childhood experiences.

Since the mid-twentieth century Freudian theory has been widely challenged, as has the Freudian treatment modality of psychoanalysis. One of the most pointed criticisms was written by Hans Eysenck (1985; see below). Eysenck argued that Freud's work lacked an objective scientific foundation and was based on persuasive reasoning garnered through his subjective perspective. According to Sulloway (1979), however, as a neurologist, Freud can in many ways be considered a founding father of the psychobiology of mind–body healing and personality. In fact, Freud's approach can be described as interdisciplinary in nature, as he placed a strong emphasis on biological and social as well as psychological factors. Today, some researchers still seek to validate the theoretical assertions of the psychoanalytic approach. And since no other theory has yet been able to explain all aspects of criminal behaviour, perhaps Freudian theory still deserves consideration.

## Learning Theories

"Learning theory" is a broad category of psychological study that comprises various schools focusing on different aspects of the learning process. In this section we will focus on three primary types of learning theory as they apply to crime: *cognitive*, *moral development*, and *behavioural*.

### Cognitive Explanations

**cognition**
The mental processes through which we organize our thoughts and make sense of the world around us, including attention, perception, memory, and language.

In psychology the term cognition refers to the mental processes—including attention, perception, memory, and language—through which we organize our thoughts and make sense of the world around us, Jeffery (1990, p. 213) offers the following illustration of the mentalistic/cognitive model of human behaviour:

$$\text{environment} \longrightarrow \text{mind} \longrightarrow \text{behaviour}$$

How the mind processes sensory experiences is based on the premise of free will and intentionality. From the cognitive perspective, criminal behaviour is the result of faulty or irrational thinking.

*Frustration–Aggression Theory*
Antisocial behaviour is often attributed to aggression resulting from frustration. When people perceive that they are being prevented from achieving their goals, their frustration is likely to turn to aggression. For example, a growing concern in many North American cities is road rage (see Box 7.5), which occurs when a driver's temper flares up at the slightest provocation, such as being cut off by another driver.

## BOX 7.5    REALITY CHECK

### Road Rage

In 2014 a two-year-old boy and his father in Surrey, BC, were pepper-sprayed by an irate driver after the father shouted at the driver to slow down (CBC News, 2014b). Unfortunately, such incidents are not as uncommon as one might think.

The issue of road rage began to draw attention in the late 1990s. In 1997, Vest, Cohen, and Tharp reported that road violence in the United States had increased by 51 per cent since 1990. In the cases they studied, 37 per cent of offenders had used firearms, and 35 per cent had used their cars. In a 1998 his article on road rage, Coyle (1998) cites a Canadian expert, Dr Lorne Korman, in describing road rage as a reaction to perceived violation of the driver's personal space, facilitated by the fact that being in a car reduces the risk to the offender by giving him or her a degree of anonymity and the chance to make a quick escape.

The modern frustration–aggression conception of criminality can be traced back to the work of John Dollard and associates, who in 1939 linked the Freudian idea of *Thanatos*—an innate drive toward disintegration (i.e. a death wish), whereby aggressive energy accumulates within and from time to time must be drained—with "the methods and concepts of an emerging behavioural perspective of human behaviour" (Andrews & Bonta, 2010, p. 111). Andrews and Bonta (2010) highlight five elements of the study by Dollard et al. (1939):

1.  Aggression is always a consequence of frustration. Strasburg (1978) observed that communication problems are more common among violent young offenders than among non-violent offenders. He also noted that speech and language disorders are more common among young males than among young females. Frustration results from a negative reaction toward a valued outcome. There are two types of aggression (Feshbach, 1964). *Hostile aggression* is expressed or acted out (e.g. through insults or physical assault), while *instrumental aggression* occurs when offenders weigh their options in order to obtain their desired outcome—using just enough coercion to gain another person's compliance.
2.  The risk of aggression escalates with the degree of outside interference, the frequency of frustrating experiences, and the intensity of the event that instigated the frustration.
3.  The greater the perceived risk of punishment for an aggressive act, the greater the likelihood that the act will not be committed. This is one of the premises of the classical doctrine: certainty of severe punishment can serve as an effective deterrent.
4.  If directing aggression toward the actual source of frustration could result in additional harm, then it is likely to be redirected. Rather than take your aggression out on the police officer who has ticketed you, you might go home and vent your frustration on your partner.
5.  Once frustration has been vented, there is a temporary reduction in the desire to act out aggressively. This is referred to as *catharsis*. You feel better after getting it off your chest—at least for a while.

Although criminological knowledge was still in its infancy in the 1930s, the frustration–aggression theory was thought to provide a viable explanation for most criminal acts, and it was the primary theoretical perspective to justify the use of the treatment—otherwise known as the "rehabilitation" model—that predominated until the 1960s (see Anderson & Bushman, 2002). Similarly, Andrews and Bonta (2010) note that the frustration–aggression model is still regularly used, in Canada, in treatment programs that focus on anger management.

Subsequent research on the frustration–aggression perspective by Leonard Berkowitz (1962) both updated and refined the theory. For instance, Berkowitz divided criminal personalities into

BOX 7.6

**A CLOSER LOOK**
**Modelling**

Canadian-born **Albert Bandura** and his doctoral student Richard Walters conducted a number of studies on aggression and violence that were based on a learning model. Bandura (1965) identified three kinds of learning:

1. *Observational learning* is based on modelling, in which the observer imitates the behaviour of figures with whom he or she identifies. Thus, children may mimic the behaviour patterns of their parents, or of their favourite television characters.

2. *Response stimulation* is similar to the "monkey see, monkey do" tendency some people engage in. For example, children may mimic television characters from their favourite programs or they might mimic (expressive) words and/or gestures they hear or see from their parents. Research has shown that viewing violent or sexually explicit movies can stimulate a desire to mimic that behaviour.

3. *Vicarious reinforcement* refers to the way our attitude toward a model is affected by the consequences of the model's behaviour. We are more likely to emulate behaviour that succeeds or is rewarded than behaviour that fails or is punished. Studies have shown that young offenders become more aggressive after seeing a sympathetic character who has been subjected to "unwarranted" aggression use "warranted violence" against the aggressor. These stereotypes are often played out in the wrestling world, where the "hero" is beaten into near defeat before rising to take revenge on the bad guy.

Bandura and Walters (1959) argued that while violence and aggression may result from neurological mechanisms and/or brain damage, most types of aggression in young people are caused by emotional arousal, which is learned behaviour stimulated by certain environmental cues. They also note that the presence of positive or negative reinforcement affects the likelihood that violent behaviour will be repeated (see classical conditioning on p. 159). These ideas are very similar to those put forward in sociological learning theories (see Chapter 8).

two main classifications: individual and socialized. Whereas the individual offender's behaviour is a product of persistent, intense episodes of frustration resulting from unmet needs, the socialized offender's behaviour is a result of learning, conditioning, and modelling (see Box 7.6).

How can we measure frustration, aggression, or feeling better? How does the mind process sensory stimuli (the triggering observation)? How intense does a stimulus need to be to trigger a response? Are some environmental factors more important than others? The frustration–aggression model cannot answer these questions because the mind can never be directly, empirically observed (Webber, 2010). Nevertheless, the mind–body dualism assumed by the model is congruent with two key elements of criminal law: the concepts of *mens rea* and *actus reus* (see Box 7.7).

In summary, the frustration–aggression model is based on social learning theory, which is part of cognitive psychology. While Dollard et al. (1939) understood social learning as a matter of imitation, Bandura emphasized observation. Other variations on the social learning model

BOX 7.7

**A CLOSER LOOK**
**Not Criminally Responsible**

In 2008 Vince Li beheaded a fellow passenger on a Greyhound bus in Manitoba. At his trial the judge accepted the defence argument that Li was not criminally responsible (NCR) because diminished mental capacity left him without *mens rea*, or the ability to recognize the wrongness of his actions: therefore, he was sentenced to a high-security mental facility rather than prison. A recent study conducted for Justice Canada found that only 8 per cent of all NCR cases involved serious violence, and only 15.5 per cent of those cases involved women (Mental Health Commission of Canada, 2013).

Do you think a victim of post-traumatic stress disorder (PTSD) who commits a serious crime might qualify for a "not criminally responsible" defence?

include modelling and symbolic interactionism (see Chapter 8). However, as Jeffery (1990) among others has observed, we do not all respond in the same way to similar stimuli. Therefore, a possible limitation of social learning theory is that it takes into account neither individual biological factors, such as genetics or brain chemistry, nor learning differences. In Chapter 8, we will see that sociologists interpret social learning differently than psychologists.

## Moral Development Explanations

"Kids have no respect for people or property." "How could anyone do such a heinous thing!" Statements like these may well reflect elements of another learning-based theory of crime: moral development theory. Can you remember when you were five or six years old and perhaps had an older sibling? Do you recall that despite the age difference, you thought everyone should get "equal shares"? As you got a few years older, do you remember being able to recognize that your older sibling did more work around the house and therefore "deserved" more? This is a simple example of the way our sense of morality develops in stages as we mature. As with most theoretical constructs, there are different theories of moral development, but a central theme in all of them is their focus on individuals' development and developmental stages of a sense of morality and responsibility.

The Swiss psychologist **Jean Piaget** was the founder of the mental and moral development theory. Piaget hypothesized that there are four primary stages of mental development (see Table 7.1). He believed that children progress from being self-focused in their mental awareness to being able to understand and integrate their outer environment. Thus, as they mature, children learn to process moral-conflict situations in an intelligent manner.

*Moral Development and Criminality*

Piaget did not address delinquency or criminality directly; it was the American psychologist **Lawrence Kohlberg** who applied the concept of moral development to criminality. Kohlberg (1969) theorized that all individuals pass through a common series of stages in which they develop their moral reasoning skills. As we progress through the stages, we learn to make decisions about right or wrong and determine the ethically/morally acceptable course of action based on circumstances.

Kohlberg divided moral development into three levels, each with two stages of moral reasoning (see Table 7.2). For example, adolescents typically reason at the conventional level. At this level, they accept the values and rules of society and therefore try to abide by the laws. However, according to Kohlberg and his colleagues, most young offenders (and criminals in general) reason at the preconventional level. They might know that it's against the law to commit break-and-enter, but they think only in terms of the chances of getting caught breaking in and being punished for it. By contrast, the reasoning of a youth at the postconventional level of moral development would include respect for the rights of others.

**moral development theory**
The theory that morality develops in stages.

| Table 7.1   Piaget's Moral Development Theory | | |
| --- | --- | --- |
| **Stage** | **Age Range** | **Description** |
| Sensorimotor | birth–age 2 | Learning to respond to the environment; developing motor skills. Self-focused mental awareness. |
| Preoperational | ages 2–7 | Learning language, drawing; abstract thought still difficult. |
| Concrete Operational | ages 7–11 | Developing logical thinking and problem-solving. |
| Formal Operations | ages 11–15 | Learning to deal with abstract ideas and process theoretical and hypothetical questions. Showing signs of moral reasoning. Able to understand and engage in higher-order reasoning. |

| Table 7.2    Kohlberg's Levels of Moral Reasoning | | |
| --- | --- | --- |
| Level of Moral Development | Stage of Reasoning | Approximate Ages |
| Preconventional "do's and don'ts" | • **Stage 1:** Right is obedience to power and avoidance of punishment.<br>• **Stage 2:** Right is taking responsibility and leaving others to be responsible for themselves. | birth–age 10 |
| Conventional | • **Stage 3:** Right is being considerate: "uphold the values of other adolescents' and adults' rules of society."<br>• **Stage 4:** Right is being good, with the values and norms of family and society at large. | adolescence and adulthood |
| Postconventional | • **Stage 5:** Right is finding inner "universal rights" balance between self-rights and societal rules—a social contract.<br>• **Stage 6:** Right is based on a hgher order of applying principles to all humankind, being non-judgmental, and respecting all human life. | age 20 and over |

*Source:* Adapted from Kohlberg, 1986, pp. 57–8.

Kohlberg theorized that not everyone makes it through all the stages of moral development or progresses at the same rate, and that incomplete moral development was a major reason for criminal and deviant behaviour. Studies by Kohlberg and his associates (1973), among others, found that moral reasoning ability was significantly less developed in both adolescent and adult offenders than in non-criminals of the same social background.

It is not surprising that moral development theory has been an important cognitive theory for criminology (see Vozzola, 2014). Drawing on Kohlberg's ideas, Steven Duguid (1979) developed a training module to help Canadian inmates develop their moral reasoning skills through a series of interactive exercises that incorporated various classical and contemporary philosophical reflective activities. His model had modest success.

In spite of its pragmatic appeal, Kohlberg's theory has had its critics. For example, it does not clarify whether a lower level of moral reasoning predisposes an individual to offend, or whether someone who has already offended might be predisposed to avoid further development of their moral reasoning. Nor does it address possible reasons for delayed or incomplete moral development, such as peer pressure, family conflict, or biochemical imbalances.

Gilligan (1982) argued that Kohlberg's theory is biased in favour of males and that there are variations in moral standards between men and women. Women, she suggested, tend to be more care-oriented while men are more justice-oriented when making moral decisions. This difference has never been clearly explained.

A final criticism pertains to the difficulty of quantifying moral development. Although the evidence suggests that the level of moral reasoning is related to behaviour in general, the theory is not able to associate particular types of criminal behaviour with particular stages of moral development, and the correlations reported in many studies are quite low (Gibbs, 2014).

## Behavioural Explanations

Most psychological theories of crime maintain that human behaviour is the product of interaction between an internal personality variable and situational variables existing outside the individual. However, in their review of the literature Bartol and Bartol (2010, p. 85) note that "much crime research and theory neglects situational variables in favour of dispositional factors," meaning that this research focuses primarily on an individual's self-beliefs.

An exception to this limited frame of reference lies in the behavioural approach. Of all the psychological theories, behavioural psychology is perhaps the most economical and elegant (Jeffery, 1990). Proponents of behavioural learning theory focus on specific behaviour rather than abstract concepts such as attitudes, interests, past experiences, or individual personality patterns (see Figure 7.2). They believe that an individual's behaviour is learned, shaped, and reinforced primarily by external factors, not by inherent personality traits.

Behaviourists see crime as the result of learned responses to life situations—responses that are not necessarily abnormal or morally immature. For example, the wife who kills her abusive husband (or, as in a recent case from Nova Scotia, who hires someone to kill her abusive husband: see Makin, 2013), or the starving survivors of a plane crash who resort to cannibalism do not necessarily commit those acts because they have some personality pathology or maladaptive personality trait; these are simply conditioned responses to external situations.

There are two basic behavioural models of associative learning: *classical conditioning* and *operant conditioning*. We will consider these in turn.

### Classical Conditioning

Stimulus–response (S–R) theory originated with the pioneering work of **Ivan P. Pavlov**, who won the Nobel Prize in physiology and medicine in 1904. Pavlov demonstrated that if he repeatedly presented a dog with both a piece of meat (the unconditioned stimulus) and the sound of a tuning fork (the conditioned stimulus), eventually the sound alone would elicit salivation (the conditioned response): in other words, the conditioned response could be induced by the conditioned stimulus in the absence of the unconditioned stimulus. This type of learning was referred to as conditioned response (CR), Pavlovian conditioning, or classical conditioning (see Box 7.8). The model was interpreted to mean that the subject (the dog or, by extension, a person) has no control over the situation or over what happens to it (Bartol & Bartol, 2010).

There are four kinds of classical conditioning, defined by the relationship between the conditioned and unconditioned stimuli (Lavond & Steinmetz, 2003):

- *Simultaneous conditioning* occurs when the conditioned stimulus (CS) and unconditioned stimulus (UCS) occur together. For example, to treat a paraphiliac (see Box 7.9) such as a child sex offender, a picture of a child (CS) might be presented to the offender accompanied by an electric shock, a noxious smell, or an aversive taste (UCS) to extinguish any sexual arousal (CR).
- *Delayed conditioning* occurs when the CS precedes the onset of the UCS and may continue after the commencement of the UCS. With pedophiles, a picture may be displayed to see

**behavioural learning theory**
A psychological theory maintaining that all behaviour is learned through some type of external stimulus (negative or positive).

**classical conditioning**
A process of behaviour modification in which a subject comes to respond in a particular manner to a previously neutral stimulus that has been repeatedly presented along with an unconditioned stimulus that elicits the desired response.

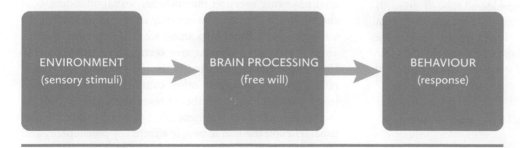

Figure 7.2    Simplified Model of Behavioural Learning

Mark Stivers

**avoidance learning**

A form of behavioural learning in which the individual learns to associate an undesirable behaviour with punishment and therefore to avoid it.

**psychopathy**

A personality disorder characterized by lack of empathy and remorse, an inability to learn from experience, low arousal levels, and antisocial behaviour; a growing body of literature suggests that many chronic criminal offenders suffer from some degree of psychopathy.

**low arousal**

A condition in which an individual experiences lower than normal emotional arousal to external stimuli, often leading to restlessness, impulsivity, and sensation-seeking.

if it elicits a reaction before the shock is administered. The picture and shock may stay on together until the patient's sexual reaction subsides.

- *Trace conditioning* occurs when the CS is terminated before the onset of the UCS: there is a delay between the two stimuli.
- *Backward conditioning* occurs when the UCS precedes the CS; however, Adams (1976, p. 94) notes that "little or no conditioning is found with backward conditioning... so it is dubious as one of the main kinds of conditioning."

Classical conditioning is often used in a treatment modality called avoidance learning or aversion therapy. By associating the fear of punishment with the crime or the behaviour, the offender is taught to avoid and "extinguish" the behaviour (Domjan, 2014).

Over the years, behaviourists have compiled a considerable volume of literature demonstrating that aversive stimulation has a strong effect on behaviour. Maletzky (1991, p. 90), after reviewing aversion therapies for sexual offenders, concluded that the "techniques not only were highly effective but also provided a framework upon which to develop theories about the origin of maladaptive sexual approach disorders." However, aversion conditioning is less effective with pedophilia, psychopathy, and other conditions associated with low arousal. In fact, a number of researchers have found that the autonomic nervous system (ANS) does not respond in the usual reflexive manner in people affected by psychopathy and other disorders linked to low arousal, including ADHD and antisocial personality disorder (Bartol & Bartol, 2010).

**BOX 7.8    REALITY CHECK**

### Pavlov on Psychology

Although Pavlov is described as the father of classical conditioning, he considered himself primarily a physiologist and, ironically (given his contribution to the discipline), had little respect for psychology. He once said, "it is still open to discussion whether psychology is a natural science . . . at all" (cited in Adams, 1976, p. 91).

What do you think: is psychology a "natural" science?

| BOX 7.9 | **A CLOSER LOOK**<br>Paraphilias |
|---------|----------------------------------|

The term paraphilia refers to recurrent and extreme sexual fantasies, urges, and behaviours involving dangerous or unusual objects, activities, or situations—typically ones that most people do not consider sexually arousing.

Among the paraphilias categorized in the fifth edition of the *Diagnostic and Statistical Manual of Mental Disorders* (*DSM-5*, released in May 2013) are humiliation (sadomasochism), sexual attraction to non-human animals or material objects (e.g. shoes or underwear), and pedophilia.

One recent case of pedophilia involved a Roman Catholic deacon in Beaconsfield, Quebec, who was also a spokesperson for his church on issues of child abuse. In December 2012, the deacon was charged with possession and distribution of child pornography after police seized more than 2,000 photos, as well as computers and hard drives (Beaudin, 2012).

The American psychologist Seymour Halleck (1967, p. 176) observed that the line between what is legally defined as a sex crime and what society considers sexual deviation "is almost incomprehensibly muddled by value judgements,

conflicting concepts of normality and an aura of secrecy." For example, in the 1960s, intercourse outside marriage was illegal in 10 American states. Halleck also pointed out that many of the sex offenders he had treated readily confessed their "sins." This led him to wonder whether they should be treated solely as criminals, or rather as people with deep personal troubles over which they felt shame and guilt and for which they wished to be punished.

In 2007 Arrigo conducted a study for the CSC on the role that paraphilias might play in certain types of offence (e.g. cruelty toward animals, setting fires, destroying property, and general disregard toward others). Aside from acknowledging the role that paraphilias appear to play in motivating certain offenders, it was also acknowledged that the literature is still relatively lacking because researchers tend to focus more on the offence as opposed to the factors that may be responsible for triggering the crime(s). However, Arrigo suggests studying the cognitive processes underlying those who are diagnosed with paraphilia can help to better inform intervention and treatment models.

Noted Canadian psychologist Robert Hare (b. 1934) and German-born behavioural psychologist **Hans Eysenck** are among the researchers to focus on the role that factors related to social learning, such as poor parenting and an impoverished learning environment, play in psychopathology. Although their models differ slightly, both have argued that psychopathic and antisocial behaviour is linked to a breakdown in inhibition and/or the ability to process information. Other psychologists have pointed out that psychopaths suffer from a lack of empathy—the capacity to put oneself in another person's shoes (see e.g. Blair, 2003). Yet in spite of the growing volume of research on criminal psychopaths, Bartol and Bartol (2010) conclude that there is much we still do not understand about them, and treatment programs have been only marginally effective.

The esteemed, albeit controversial, Eysenck coupled his personality/temperament theory of criminality (Table 7.3) with classical conditioning to suggest that the problem with criminals is that they have not been conditioned to behave in a socially accepted manner. For example, the break-and-enter offender, based on his or her personality traits, may not be

**paraphilia**

A condition characterized by abnormal sexual desires, typically involving activities, situations, or objects that most people do not consider sexually arousing.

**pedophilia**

A psychological disorder in which an adult (or older adolescent) is sexually aroused primarily by underage (usually prepubescent) children.

| Table 7.3 | Eysenck's Personality Theory of Criminality | | |
|-----------|---------------------------------------------|---|---|
| **Personality Trait** | **Neurobiological Influence** | **High Scores** | **Low Scores** |
| extraversion | Reticular activating system; central nervous system | Stimulation-seeking | Stimulation avoidance |
| neuroticism | Autonomic nervous system | Nervous, unstable | Stable, calm |
| psychoticism | Excessive androgen | Tough-minded | Tender-minded |

*Source:* Bartol & Bartol, 2005, p. 100.

BOX 7.10     FACTS AND FIGURES  THE *DSM-5*

In the early 1840s the US census began collecting data on "idiocy/insanity." In time, the numbers of categories for mental disorders multiplied, as did efforts to develop a standard guide that would facilitate not only the collection of statistics but the diagnosis and assessment of patients. The first *Diagnostic and Statistical Manual of Mental Disorders* (*DSM*) was published in 1953 and listed 106 distinct diagnoses; by the end of the century, it had undergone several major revisions, and the number of diagnoses had nearly tripled to 297 documented in the revised text of the fourth edition, known as *DSM-IV-TR* (2000). This edition has since been superseded by the *DSM-5*, published in May 2013. The latest edition is not without its critics. Vocal among them is Allen Frances (2012), emeritus professor of psychology at Duke University and chair of the *DSM-IV* task force. He argues

that it essentially medicalizes normality, giving a big boost to drug companies that benefit when normal behaviours are identified as conditions that should be treated medically. Various medical boards and associations in Canada have similarly expressed their concern that the *DSM* sets a dangerous precedent for "massive over-diagnosis and harmful over-medication" (Frances, 2012).

Among its more controversial changes, the *DSM-5* named new diagnoses for those who overeat once a month over a three-week span ("binge eating disorder") and those who accumulate objects they are unable to part with ("hoarding disorder"). What are the benefits and dangers of adding new diagnoses?

deterred (UCR) by the presence of a house-alarm sticker (UCS). Based on Eysenck's theory, the alarm decal may not be critical enough to deter certain offenders, even though it might deter other potential offenders.

### Operant or Instrumental Learning

While **John B. Watson** is often recognized as the father of experimental psychology and behaviourism (Bartol & Bartol, 2010), **B.F. Skinner** has been one of the most influential behaviourists in North America (see Box 7.11). Although Skinner agreed that human cognition exists, he maintained that it could not be scientifically studied because, without a physical basis, it could not be observed and measured.

Skinner believed that human behaviour is not the product of free will: rather, it is situational, determined only by stimuli to which we simply react. However complex a given environment might be, careful research can identify the triggers behind any behaviour that occurs therein. Even the simplest decision—say, what to eat for breakfast—is not a matter of free choice but a response to a stimulus of some kind. Do you agree? This principle, known

**behaviour modification**

A psychological theory and treatment that focuses on changing not personality (i.e. trying to make people "good") but behaviour, relying on a system of rewards and punishments.

BOX 7.11     PROFILE  **B.F. Skinner**

Burrhus Frederic Skinner was born in 1904 and raised in Susquehanna, Pennsylvania. Determined to become a writer, he majored in English at university, but when he proved unable to make a living by writing he went back to school to study psychology at Harvard University. Upon graduating in 1931 he quickly became a leading figure in experimental psychology. In addition to numerous academic works, Skinner wrote a utopian novel entitled *Walden Two* (1948), in which he described a model community based on

the principles of behaviour modification. In 1971 Skinner detailed his conception of determinism in *Beyond Freedom and Dignity*.

On the value of punishment, Skinner (1971, p. 66) wrote, "the trouble is that when we punish a person for behaving badly, we leave it up to him to discover how to behave well, and he can then get the credit for behaving well." Instead, he argued, it is the environment that should be given the credit for changes in the person's behaviour.

as operant conditioning (i.e. behaviour is the result of an individual's response to an external stimulus or event), forms the basis of behaviour modification. In accordance with the theory, the most powerful element of behavioural therapy is reinforcement.

We can probably all recall times when we changed our behaviour in response to some reward or punishment. In grade school, if you earned stars for doing well on a test, you might have been motivated to study even harder for the next one; and if you were given a detention for skipping school, you might have decided not to do that again. Behavioural psychologists have applied this general principle to the treatment of antisocial/criminal behaviour. The key to initiating change is reinforcement through either positive (i.e. rewarding desirable behaviour) or negative (i.e. punishing undesirable behaviour) reinforcement (Bartol & Bartol, 2010).

One common positive reinforcement strategy used in correctional settings is the token economy, in which "tokens" such as poker chips, points, or stamps are given to inmates as symbolic rewards whenever the desired response occurs. The tokens can then be exchanged for reinforcers of value to the inmate (such as food or permission to watch a favourite TV program).

Negative reinforcement is designed to extinguish undesirable responses by creating a negative association between the response and the discriminative stimulus. As noted above, negative reinforcement (i.e. aversion therapy) has been used in a variety of treatment programs for sex offenders.

Reinforcement is not always delivered in the same manner. The two basic methods involve the use of different schedules, as follows:

- *ratio schedules* – Reinforcement occurs after a specific number of responses regardless of time frame.
- *interval schedules* – Reinforcement is delivered on a schedule independent of the number of responses.

Some of the key aspects of behaviour modification (BM) are as follows:

- The first step is to define the problematic behaviour (e.g. shoplifting) within a social, cultural, economic, etc., context.
- Unless the underlying problem can be identified, behaviour cannot be properly changed. For example, some people may turn to shoplifting to alleviate tension when they feel stressed.
- Treatment usually involves drawing up a contract that specifies contingency elements (i.e. what each party expects to gain from the situation), such as house arrest, a curfew, having to report in every day at a predefined time, etc.
- The aim of the program is to shape the behaviour of the offender using either a positive approach (e.g. earned remission, praise, "tokens" that can be put toward a reward of choice) or a negative one (e.g. fines, lockdown, loss of privileges).

In their extensive review of Canadian correctional programs, Gendreau and Ross (1987) identified a number of advantages and disadvantages of treatment based on operant conditioning. The advantages include the following:

- There is no need to dwell on past experiences.
- Because patients must focus on their current behaviour, they cannot use past experiences or events to explain or excuse their behaviour.
- BM-oriented programs do not require trained therapists to administer them.

**token economy**

A strategy used by behavioural therapists to reinforce a desired behaviour by rewarding the participant with poker chips, gold stars, or other "tokens."

Among the elements that are considered limitations of the behavioural treatment approach, Vito, Maahs, and Holmes (2006) found the following issues:

- Negative reinforcement, in which rewards are withdrawn, may be used simply to gain control of "troublemakers" rather than to treat them or offer a constructive learning opportunity. It may even be unconstitutional, as all offenders are entitled to an opportunity to reform their behaviour.
- Adequate steps may not always be taken to protect the rights of the inmates.
- Behaviour management programs tend to create artificial situations that do not resemble the natural environment in which the patient must live. Thus, as Vito et al. (2007, p. 132) observed, "not all good behaviours are rewarded."

In summary, behavioural learning stands in stark contrast to most of the other learning-based theories. The model—in both its classical and operant conditioning versions—asserts that behaviours change in response to the stimuli in the individual's environment. Behaviourists do not assume that behaviour is rooted in an inherently abnormal personality.

Treatment programs based on the behavioural approach were popular in the 1970s (see e.g. Gendreau & Ross, 1987). In the 1980s, however, ethical and practical concerns led certain areas of the criminal justice system, in particular corrections, to move away from the behavioural approach (see Goggin, Smith, & Gendreau 2013). Nevertheless, in keeping with other theoretical trends in criminology, behaviourism has evolved to embrace a more interdisciplinary model of learning.

## The Place of Psychology in Criminology Today

Theories of criminal and delinquent behaviour rooted in psychology tend to have little regard for the contexts within which people act. As Schissel and Brooks (2008) note, protocols for treatment and intervention require that a person be labelled as potentially criminal or at risk of committing an offence based on an assortment of assessment tools that lack reliability and validity (see Cao, 2004). Furthermore, the assessment tools used for evaluation tend not to take into account factors such as age, social class, culture, gender, or race (Schissel & Brooks, 2008). Some have also criticized psychological approaches on the grounds that they focus on "defective" or "abnormal" personalities or personality traits (Akers & Sellers, 2013).

None of the psychological approaches outlined in this chapter have been able to identify a single criminal personality type, although efforts continue to identify a cluster of traits that might account for certain types of offenders. Psychological explanations have been able to explain geographic or temporal variations in crime rates and have helped us to understand variations in crime rates by age, race, gender, and social class through one or more of the theoretical perspectives. Finally, they have also provided insight into the various arousal mechanisms that are, or can be, influenced by the social environment. Of course, psychological perspectives also play an important role in the criminal justice system's efforts to determine the criminal responsibility of defendants.

Most crime-prevention initiatives today focus either on modifying the environment in which crime occurs or on encouraging social development initiatives by providing individuals with choices that help them live productive and crime-free lives. However, there remains an established body of research dedicated to rehabilitating offenders. Such work is premised on the belief that we are rational beings who can be "trained" to see the negative implications of our offending behaviour. And even though the success rate is estimated to be only 8–10 per cent (Andrews & Bonta, 2010), efforts to improve psychological rehabilitation continue.

# Summary

- The roots of psychological theory can be traced to the ancient notion that criminal behaviour is the result of demonic possession.
- Psychological explanations are premised on the deterministic principle that the causes of criminal behaviour lie within the individual.
- Proponents of psychological approaches subscribe to the assertion that a medical/positivist model of treatment and intervention is most effective.
- Intrapsychic explanations see criminal behaviour as the result of internal conflict and tension among various aspects of the individual personality.
- Cognitive explanations see criminal behaviour as the product of choice based on how the individual processes sensory experiences; frustration is seen as a key trigger of antisocial behaviour.
- Moral development theories see criminal behaviour as the product of either poor learning or compromised cognitive processes.
- Behavioural explanations attribute criminal behaviour to situational rather than dispositional variables. (For a summary of the various schools of thought see Box 7.12.)
- The main criticism of psychological theories is that they pay minimal attention to the relative nature of crime.
- Psychological intervention and treatment require the categorization of various behaviours as unacceptable.
- Most of the tools used to measure psychological phenomena are of questionable value.

---

**BOX 7.12**    **FACTS AND FIGURES** A SUMMARY OF PSYCHOLOGICAL PERSPECTIVES ON CRIME

| Perspectives | Theorists | Causes/Core Elements |
|---|---|---|
| **Supernatural** | | |
| demonic possession | | evil spirits |
| **Intrapsychic** | | |
| psychodynamic theory | S. Freud | unconscious conflicts |
| | A. Aichhorn | childhood experiences |
| | | defence mechanisms |
| | | anger |
| **Learning** | | |
| cognitive theory | S. Yochelson | the individual's thoughts, feelings, beliefs, and |
| | S. Samenow | perceptions |
| frustration–aggression model | J. Dollard et al. | the individual is prevented from achieving a goal |
| social learning | A. Bandura | the individual's association with others who engage in crime/deviance |
| moral development | J. Piaget | people with lower levels of moral reasoning will |
| | L. Kohlberg | engage in crime/deviance and/or violence |
| behavioural conditioning | B.F. Skinner | people commit crime as a result of a failure to |
| | H. Eysenck | provide positive stimuli |

## Discussion Questions

1. There has been an increase in the number of offenders who appear to be suffering from some mental or emotional disorder. How might you explain this trend from a psychological perspective? Use at least two different theoretical models.
2. What are the main strengths and weaknesses of the major psychological theories discussed in this chapter? Which theory do you think has the most explanatory power? Why?
3. What challenges might exist in accepting any one type of psychological theory over another type?
4. Is there a "criminal personality"? How do the different theoretical orientations compare in terms of identifying specific personality traits that might be common to the majority of criminals?
5. Despite the challenges discussed, how might psychological factors help to explain differences in crime rates across Canada over time, and in conjunction with factors such as gender, age, and social class?
6. How might psychological components be incorporated into an interdisciplinary criminological perspective? Which components do you think would be the most important?

## Key Concepts

avoidance learning
behaviour modification
behavioural learning theory
classical conditioning
cognition
criminal personality
demonic possession
id, ego, superego

low arousal
moral development theory
paraphilia
pedophilia
psychodynamic theory
psychoanalysis
psychopathy
token economy

## Key Names

Gustav Aschaffenburg (1866–1944)
Albert Bandura (b. 1925)
James Baldwin (1861–1934)
Hans Eysenck (1916–1997)
Sigmund Freud (1856–1939)
Lawrence Kohlberg (1927–1987)

Henry Maudsley (1835–1918)
Ivan Pavlov (1849–1936)
Jean Piaget (1896–1980)
Isaac Ray (1807–1881)
B.F. Skinner (1904–1990)
John Watson (1878–1958)

## Weblinks

**Schizophrenia Society of Canada**
Although it doesn't deal with crime specifically, the website of the Schizophrenia Society of Canada offers lots of interesting information about an illness that many criminals seem to suffer from.
www.schizophrenia.ca

**Drivers.com**
This website offers a variety of links to discussions of the social aspects of road rage, as well as an Australian paper on the significance of road rage.
www.drivers.com/topic/31

**Psychology Today**
The popular magazine *Psychology Today* regularly prints various current and topical articles about psychology and crime.
www.psychologytoday.com/blog/inside-the-criminal-mind

# Chapter 8

## Sociological Perspectives with Nick Jones[*]

John Lehmann/The Canadian Press

The sociological imagination enables us to grasp history and
biography and the relations between the two within society.
C. WRIGHT MILLS (1959, p. 12)

[*] Nick Jones is an associate professor in the Department
of Justice Studies at the University of Regina.

## Learning Outcomes

After reading this chapter, you should be able to

- Discuss the contributions that sociologists have made to the study of crime;
- Identify the major sociological perspectives;
- Understand the strengths and limitations of the major sociology-based perspectives on crime; and
- Better appreciate the need for an interdisciplinary approach.

**social structure**
Consistent and stable patterns of social interaction.

In Chapter 1 we saw that "crime" refers to the violation of criminal law, while "deviance" is used (primarily by sociologists) to refer to the violation of social norms. Both criminality and deviance are widely recognized as social problems. As social beings, humans are shaped by their social environment, and—as the prominent American sociologist C. Wright Mills (1959) observed—the problems of individual people are rooted in the social structure (see Box 8.1) and their interactions with it. This general perspective has dominated the study of crime and deviance in North America.

Although the contributions to criminology of other disciplines (including biology, economics, political science, and psychology) are gaining greater acceptance, sociology is still the dominant discipline in criminology. No discipline has had a greater influence, either on criminal justice policy or on the theoretical understanding of crime. While a comprehensive introduction to sociological perspectives on crime is well beyond the scope of this book, in this chapter we will present a cross-section of some of the major theories.

According to Johnson (1995, p. 269), "sociology is the study of social life and social behavior, especially in relation to social systems, how they change, the consequences they produce, and their complex relation to people's lives." Those social systems include the educational system, the political system, the health system, and the criminal justice system.

We will begin with a brief introduction to the three main sociological approaches to crime and deviance. Then we will discuss a few of the most important theories they have produced, and conclude with a look at some more recent theories.

---

**BOX 8.1**

**A CLOSER LOOK**
**A Sociological Approach to Crime**

Sociologists suggest there are two central questions in the study of criminology. According to Barkan (2011, p. 3), they are as follows:

1. Why do crime rates differ across locations and over time?
2. Why do crime rates differ according to the key dimensions of structured social inequality: race/ethnicity, class, gender, sexual orientation, and (dis)ability?

One sociological answer to these questions can be found in the routine activity theory (Cohen & Felson, 1979)

introduced in Chapter 4, which suggests that the reduction in property crime in the 1990s was due to a reduction in suitable targets, as debit and credit cards replaced cash and the price of home security systems fell. In other words, the decline in crime was a product of changes in the social environment.

One of the fastest growing crimes today is identity theft (see Chapter 9). How many pieces of ID do you carry with you? What precautions, if any, do you take to prevent your identify from being stolen?

## Sociological Approaches

As we saw in Chapter 5, **Auguste Comte**, the founder of the positivist school of philosophy, is also recognized as the founder of sociology. The positivists advocated the study of social phenomena based on "systematic observation and the accumulation of evidence and objective facts within a deductive framework"—that is, following the "scientific method" and moving from the general to the specific (Williams & McShane, 2013, p. 29). Comte instilled in sociology the notion that human behaviour is a function of forces beyond the control of the individual—that is, forces of social structure.

Thus, sociology starts with the idea that all behaviour is shaped by the social structure and/or social dynamics (i.e. social change). The sociological perspective generally asserts that individuals are socialized into the existing social structure as they internalize society's norms, or social expectations. This generally promotes conformist behaviour. However, pressures within the social structure can lead some people *not* to conform, and instead to engage in deviant behaviour.

What a given society considers acceptable is defined through two types of norms: *prescriptive* (telling us what we should do) and *proscriptive* (telling us what we should not do). Some norms are informal, in that there are no written laws defining them: they are simply a long-established part of the social environment. However, as societies become more complex and develop more formal structures, it becomes necessary to convert some norms into formal laws (Einstadter & Henry, 2006). In addition, norms may change over time as a society evolves: what was once considered acceptable may come to be prohibited, and vice versa.

One of the founding fathers of sociology, **Émile Durkheim**, encapsulated these ideas when he observed that even in a society of saints there would be deviance. He believed that human groups will always make rules, and that every group will have some members who break some of the rules—that is, engage in crime and/or deviance. Although the exact reasons are not always clear, according to Durkheim individual behaviour is the product of the social environment rather than intrinsic traits. For example, Durkheim would suggest that even a child who is very good at keeping secrets (an intrinsic trait) will tell a best friend's secrets in order to win acceptance from the broader group (the social environment). Furthermore, Durkheim believed that people are innately self-serving and the most rational thing for people to do is reap as many benefits as possible from society. Similarly, as the English political philosopher Thomas Hobbes also argued, humans are intrinsically self-centred, and without a hegemonic social structure to keep human nature in check, there would be chaos, a "war of all against all." If so, then criminal laws, as well as the uncodified laws that govern cultural norms and values, are essential to maintain social order.

Theories of social order can be classified in terms of two paradigms: *consensus* and *conflict*. Those in the first group subscribe to Durkheim's understanding of society as a set of interrelated parts, each of which contributes to the overall functioning of the whole. According to this consensus, or *functionalist*, paradigm of society, there is a general consensus surrounding the underlying moral framework that Durkheim called the *collective conscience*. This framework is what defines a society's values and norms, as well as its response when those values and norms are violated. In the consensus view, the collective consensus of society defines behaviour that does not conform to it as deviant.

By contrast, the second group of theories subscribe to the conflict paradigm. Derived primarily from the writings of Karl Marx, conflict theories see society not as a largely consensual whole but as an assortment of disparate groups competing for power and resources. From this critical perspective, it is society's most powerful who define what or who is deviant, typically in a way that best satisfies their own interests.

Flickr.com/jmith1

Taking up two seats on the bus or subway during rush hour isn't against the law, but it does go against the collective conscience and thus represents a breach of a societal norm. What are some of the reasons someone might engage in this sort of deviant, norm-breaking behaviour? How might other passengers sanction this behaviour to reinforce the norm?

The third approach, *symbolic interactionism*, can be traced to the work of **Gabriel Tarde**, who focused less on the social order than on the social processes through which (criminal) behaviour is learned—notably imitation and interaction (i.e. similar to Aristotle's laws of learning) with others in the individual's social environment.

As sociology developed, these three fundamental perspectives on society gave rise to three major ways of thinking about criminal and deviant behaviour: as the product of the social structure, as the product of social conflict, and as the product of social processes. The rest of this chapter will provide an overview of the most important theories within each of these approaches.

## Social-Structural Theories

*In the first place crime is normal because a society exempt from it is utterly impossible.* (Durkheim, 1895, cited in Jacoby, 1994, p. 65)

The social-structural tradition is the oldest and most fundamental of the main sociological perspectives. It tends to look for the root causes of crime in social institutions such as the family, organized religion, and the economic, education, and political systems. For example, in his recent book on gangs in Canada, Totten (2014) points to structural elements—poverty, dysfunctional families, unemployment—as factors that influence a young person's decision to join a gang.

Social theorists suggest that gangs provide a social structure for those who lack such structure in other areas of their lives, such as family, school, or employment.

## The Human Ecological School

The first sociology department in North America was established in 1892 at the University of Chicago. Not surprisingly, given the location, the early Chicago School focused on urban life. Among its most influential members were **Robert E. Park** and **Ernest W. Burgess**, who borrowed concepts from the field of plant ecology—including dominance, invasion, and succession—and applied them to the city. Although their research was primarily sociological, their ideas became the basis of the human ecological school of criminology, an important sub-discipline.

Park and Burgess envisioned the city as "a series of distinctive concentric circles radiating from the central business district" (Williams & McShane, 2013, p. 59). Their concentric-circle theory divided the city into five zones, each characterized by different social and organizational elements. Zone 1, the central business district, was characterized by light manufacturing, retail trade, and commercial recreation, while Zone 5, the outermost ring, was a relatively wealthy residential–commuter area (see Figure 8.1). Zone 2, just outside the central business district, was characterized as a zone in transition from residential to industrial/commercial use—an area of cheap, rundown rental housing and growing numbers of factories, where newly arrived immigrants would stay for a time before moving on to more permanent homes in Zones 3 (working-class) and 4 (middle-class residential).

### Shaw and McKay's Social Disorganization Theory

In the 1930s, two other Chicago sociologists, **Clifford R. Shaw** and **Henry D. McKay**, examined the spatial distribution of crime, delinquency, tuberculosis, poverty, and infant mortality in the city over three time periods (1900–6, 1917–23, and 1927–33) and found a pattern consistent with the concentric-circle model (see Figure 8.1): the rates were all highest in Zone 2 and declined in each successive circle (Shaw & McKay, 1942).

**ecological school of criminology**

A sub-discipline of criminology that studies how elements of the physical and social environment interact to create a criminal environment.

**concentric-circle theory**

An early human ecological theory, according to which cities develop from the inner city to the suburbs in a predictable series of concentric rings, each of which encompasses a particular set of social and environmental characteristics.

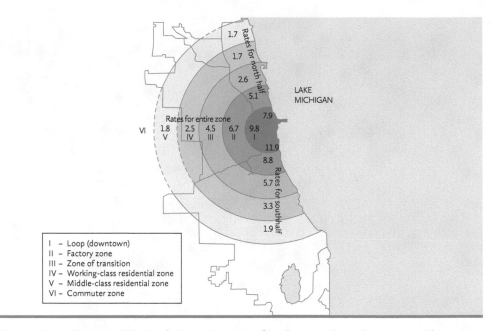

**Figure 8.1    Shaw and McKay's Zone Rates\* of Male Juvenile Delinquents, Chicago (1927–1933)**

Note: The zone rates represent the rate per 100 youths (aged 10–16).
*Source*: Adapted from Clifford R. Shaw and Henry D. McKay, *Juvenile Delinquency and Urban Areas* (Chicago: University of Chicago Press, 1942), p. 69.

Building on the work of Burgess and Park, Shaw and McKay theorized that the differing rates of delinquency could be attributed to differences in the physical and social environment across the geographic area. In essence, the more stable and homogeneous the neighbourhood was, the greater the likelihood of a stable community. Hence, according to Shaw and McKay, crime and delinquency "had its origin in the juvenile's 'detachment from conventional groups'" (Vold, Bernard, & Snipes, 1998, p. 143). High rates of delinquency in Zone 2 (the oldest section of a city) reflected "social disorganization": a breakdown of social control in an environment characterized by social and economic instability, a legacy of failing by businesses and industry, and a deterioration of housing. The fact that the delinquency rates in Zone 2 had remained high over time, as different immigrant groups moved in and out, lent support to Shaw and McKay's **social disorganization theory**, suggesting that ethnicity was not a factor. In other words, it was not the personal characteristics of the residents that led to the social breakdown, but the characteristics of the environment itself, such as a lack of "social capital" (i.e. social networks), which discouraged residents from working together to address problems. Williams and McShane (2013, pp. 68–9) list four elements that contribute to social disorganization:

- low economic status
- ethnic diversity
- high mobility (residents moving in and out of the area)
- family disruption

Shaw and McKay also investigated the process by which a subculture of delinquency develops in a neighbourhood over time. According to their **cultural transmission theory**, delinquency is a socially learned behaviour that is passed down from one generation of residents to the next.

**social disorganization theory**

A sociological theory that sees deviance and crime as consequences of a breakdown of social control in environments characterized by social and economic instability.

**cultural transmission (or deviance) theory**

A sociological theory that sees deviance as a socially learned behaviour that is transmitted through successive generations, especially in disorganized urban settings.

Two later theories that incorporated Shaw and McKay's idea of delinquent subcultures are outlined in Box 8.2. More recently, sociologists have expanded the idea of subcultures to include such groups as anarchists, computer hackers, drug addicts, extreme religious groups, and organized crime groups.

Until the late 1930s, the concentric-circle theory enjoyed considerable success as studies of other American cities (e.g. Richmond, Virginia; Baltimore, Maryland; Los Angeles, California; etc.) showed delinquency patterns similar to those reported by Shaw and McKay in Chicago. However, as the social structure and urban design of cities changed, the social ecological approach shifted from a focus on individual crimes to a focus on the geographical location of crime, and from physical characteristics of the environment (e.g. dilapidated structures) to social traits (e.g. high mobility of residents, diverse cultural mix, high rates of disease, etc.) (Deegan, 2014). For example, during the pre-automobile era, mobility patterns tended to be confined more than they are today. With the growing popularity of automobiles, our social structure has changed, people have become much more mobile, and our awareness and use of space has become more fluid. Thus, the traditional ecological approach could no longer adequately explain criminal behaviour. Nevertheless, it laid the foundations for environmental criminology (see Chapter 5).

Among the first to suggest that opportunities for crime could be reduced by modifying the physical environment was Jane Jacobs, in *The Death and Life of Great American Cities* (1961). Others expanded on her ideas, including people like Oscar Newman (see below) and C.R. Jeffery (see p. 181). Their work marked the emergence of the environmental model known as *crime prevention through environmental design* (CPTED), which in Canada eventually gave rise to an approach known as *crime prevention through social development* (CPTSD) (see Chapter 14).

*More Recent Applications of Ecological Principles*

As Paul Brantingham and Patricia Brantingham (1984, p. 18) have observed, there has been a "shift from the sociological to the geographical imagination"—that is, a shift in focus from how people perceive and interact with their *social* environment to how they perceive and interact with their *physical* environment. Routine activity theory (see p. 190) is one example of this shift. Another can be seen in the work of the American architect Oscar Newman, who was among the first to note how crime rates in residential areas vary depending on the residents' relationship

---

**BOX 8.2**   **FACTS AND FIGURES** OTHER SUBCULTURAL THEORIES

- **Albert K. Cohen**, who studied under Robert Merton and Edwin Sutherland, developed a theory to explain male delinquent subcultures in working-class neighbourhoods. In his classic 1955 book *Delinquent Boys: The Culture of the Gang*, Cohen suggested that delinquency among lower-class males was the product of the "status frustration" they experienced when confronted with the middle-class values promoted by the public school system. Unable to attain these values and status through the methods prescribed by the school, they sought alternative, criminal means to gain status among others experiencing the

same frustration. Totten (2012, 2014) has drawn on Cohen's theory to explain youth gangs in Canada.

- Among the first to attempt to explain the high rates of interpersonal violence between members of certain subcultures within the larger community culture were Marvin Wolfgang and Franco Ferracuti. In *The Subculture of Violence: Towards an Integrated Theory of Crime* (1967) they argued that certain segments of society embrace idiosyncratically violent values as a way to achieve and maintain status (i.e. their honour). Having internalized pro-violent values, the members of these subcultures are able to justify frequent violent behaviour without experiencing guilt.

© Toronto Transit Comission 2016. Reproduced with permission of the Toronto Transit Commission.

The Toronto Transit Commission embraces crime prevention through environmental design. This recently renovated subway station entrance incorporates many features of CPTED, including large windows, bright interior and exterior lighting, open space, and benches for public seating, all making for a "natural surveillance" system that assists in preventing crime.

with their physical environment. In a later edition of his acclaimed book *Defensible Space* (1972; 1996), Newman presented updated information on how to build or refurbish urban communities to prevent crime by reducing the unattended space that offers opportunities for criminal behaviour. The intent is to promote a sense of ownership and responsibility through the physical design and layout of homes, office buildings, and other structures that make up the community. For another example of how the principles of the ecological school have been put into practice, see Box 8.3.

The ecological school and its various theoretical derivatives have played a major role in crime prevention strategies. In their review of the ecological school, Akers and Sellers (2013)

---

**BOX 8.3**

**A CLOSER LOOK**
**Kim Rossmo**

Kim Rossmo, a Canadian scholar currently teaching in the United States, has applied the principles of geographic mapping to the study of violent serial and sexual crimes. He developed a sophisticated computer program system called Rigel that is used for geographic profiling. Combined with investigative police work, this program has been used to locate a number of serial killers and rapists (see Rossmo, 2009, 2013).

An important feature of Rossmo's software is its ability to analyze data on an ongoing basis. As new information is obtained, the program recalibrates to construct a new "geoprofile." Then, as the profile database evolves, the number of possible scenarios can be narrowed to pinpoint the home base of the offender. In addition to combining elements of environmental criminology and routine activity theory to the real world of police investigation, Rossmo's work shows the importance of combining academic research with concrete criminal justice issues. Like DNA analysis, geographic profiling is a vital new strategy for combatting crime.

point out how social disorganization theory and cultural transmission theory are similar to the theories of social control, differential association, situational choice, routine activities, and human ecology, among others (for a complete list of related theories, see Einstadter & Henry, 2006). For example, neighbourhoods characterized by social disorganization provide fertile territory for crime and delinquency. Such areas tend to have a lack of behavioural control mechanisms, and this allows for the (easier) cultural transmission of delinquent values.

### Summary and Evaluation

The ecological approach drew on both biology and human geography. It assumed that particular characteristics of the physical and social environment can precipitate crime—that human behaviour is a product of the social environment and that the environment defines the boundaries of our cultural values and behaviour.

The ecological school has provided some powerful explanatory models for crime and has had a lasting influence on North American sociological criminology. Its influence can be seen in Frederic Milton Thrasher's work on youth gangs in the 1920s, in Edwin Sutherland's formation of the differential association theory in the 1930s and 1940s, and in Howard Becker's labelling theory in the 1960s.

However, there are questions that ecological models do not answer. The lack of clear theoretical clarity makes it difficult to accurately measure what is meant by "social disorganization" (SD). The theory offers no explanation as to why middle-class crime occurs, or why some youths are insulated from a delinquent career. As well, according to Cao (2004), economic status, ethnic heterogeneity, and residential mobility have not been very reliably and accurately measured. Cao points out, however, that many newer studies of SD (e.g. Bursik, 1988; Osgood & Chambers, 2000) have refined the concepts and the measuring methods. It is likely that this re-orientation of SD will continue and is worth further exploration.

## Anomie/Strain Theory

A second major social-structural theory centres on the concept of anomie. Durkheim used the term to refer to a condition of "deregulation" or "normlessness" in society. Two propositions are central to Durkheim's thesis:

1. Social organization is necessary to keep undesirable humans tendencies in check.
2. Where social order breaks down and social norms lose their influence, anomie develops and crime increases significantly (Durkheim, 1951, cited in Wright & Fox, 1978, pp. 135–6).

In recent years, anomie has been identified as one of the defining characteristics of the emerging "precariat" class, made up of people whose precarious jobs (part-time or temporary, with few if any employment benefits) provide little or no predictability or security. According to Standing (2013, p. 33), members of the precariat experience the four A's of anger, anomie, anxiety, and alienation, and have played a large part in the Occupy movement.

Durkheim argued that all societies are initially characterized by homogeneity in the "lives, work, and beliefs of their members" (Bernard, Snipes, & Gerould, 2010, p. 126). These simple "mechanical" societies are self-sufficient and autonomous, with little division of labour. As societies evolve and become more complex, with increasing labour specialization and heterogeneity, there is a need for different kinds of laws—both mechanical (such as penal laws and the Criminal Code) and organic (oriented around restitution)—to maintain social order.

Durkheim regarded crime as a natural and inevitable element of society, and he recognized two types of criminals emanating from the anomic breakdown in homogeneity: altruistic

**anomie**

Durkheim's term for a state of deregulation, breakdown, or normlessness in society, usually attributed to decreased homogeneity; an anomic social environment is conducive to crime.

© Moviestore collection Ltd / Alamy Stock Photo

In *V for Vendetta* (2005), Hugo Weaving plays a self-proclaimed freedom fighter willing to commit murder and vandalism to overthrow a government that he believes is corrupt. What "real world" figures fit the altruistic profile today? Consider the eighteenth-century English highwayman and horse thief Dick Turpin, or WikiLeaks, the not-for-profit organization whose aim is to reveal private (and potentially embarrassing) government and corporate documents.

criminals and common criminals. The altruistic criminal is unable to integrate due to a decline in economic well-being, and is offended by the rules of society and seeks to change them for the better. The more typical offender is the common criminal, who rejects the norms of society and intentionally violates laws with little regard for the rights of others (Bernard et al., 2010). Together, altruistic and common criminals produce the social ills of their community.

Although compelling, Durkheim's theory lacked empirical evidence, and it leaves important questions unanswered. For example, why do only a minority of people in an anomic society resort to crime? And what determines the kinds of crimes that individual offenders choose to commit?

In spite of its conceptual limitations, Durkheim's thesis found wide support at a time when sociology was the dominant perspective for the study of human behaviour in Europe. Some 60 years later, the American sociologist Robert Merton modified and applied the theory to deviance in general.

### *Merton's Strain Theory*

It was in his seminal article "Social Structure and Anomie" (1938) that **Robert K. Merton** expanded and modified Durkheim's concept and began to develop his own explanation of crime. Rejecting the earlier tendency "to attribute the malfunctioning of social structure primarily to those of man's imperious biological drives which are not adequately restrained by social control," Merton (1938, p. 672) argued that there are "certain phases of social structure ... in which infringement of social codes constitutes a 'normal' response."

Merton (1968) based his theory of "social structure strain" on four assumptions:

1. All modern societies have a core of common values.
2. The majority of the members of modern societies have internalized (i.e. accepted) their own society's values.
3. The most significant values are those that channel energy toward the achievement of certain success goals.
4. All members of a society do not have an equal opportunity to use socially approved means to attain socially approved goals.

According to Merton's strain theory, anomie is not an individual problem, but rather the product of these structural factors. He identified five distinct "modes of adaptation" to the goals and means approved by society:

1. **Conformity.** Without conformity there would be no social order. Most people, regardless of their social and personal circumstances, are conformists. For example, someone who pursues postsecondary education as the means of obtaining a well-paying job would be considered a conformist. Conformists have internalized both the goals of their society and the means prescribed for achieving them.
2. **Innovation.** This mode is adopted by people who accept the goals of society (e.g. getting an education) but either lack or reject the socially accepted means of achieving them. Therefore, they use illegitimate (sometimes illegal) means to achieve those goals: thus an aspiring student might sell drugs to help pay for her education. Theft, prostitution, and pornography distribution could all be seen as examples of innovation in this sense.
3. **Ritualism.** Individuals who adopt a ritualistic approach accept the goals prescribed by society but do not put any effort into pursuing them. An example might be the student who attends school because society expects it, and does well enough to pass but does not attempt to improve, let alone excel. Although they are not motivated to "get ahead," ritualists tend to respect the norms of hard work and honesty.
4. **Retreatism.** This mode applies to people who reject both society's goals and the accepted means of achieving them. Retreat or withdrawal can be the response when the socially approved means to achieve the socially approved goal (e.g. working to learn a skill that will lead to a well-paying job) is perceived as unlikely to result in success. Retreatism offers an escape route for people who are essentially social dropouts.
5. **Rebellion.** Rebels reject the system in its entirety. Instead of finding ways to live within it, they seek to replace it. Some go beyond political protest and resort to the extreme violence of terrorism. This category could account for the four young men from London, Ontario, who allegedly took part in the al-Qaeda–linked attack on the Tigantourine gas facility in Algeria in 2013.

**strain theory**
Sees emotional turmoil and conflict as resulting from individuals' inability to achieve socially approved goals through legitimate means.

In accordance with Merton's theoretical principles, the lower classes should be disproportionately represented among the criminal population, because they have limited opportunities to reach their goals legitimately. Based on a review of more than 100 studies, Braithwaite (1981) found general support for the assertion that lower-class people commit more crimes than those in other social classes. However, the studies did not explain why all lower-class people do not resort to crime. In response to these and other challenges, Thornberry and Farnsworth (1982), among others, have suggested that the model also needs to take into account such factors as race, gender, intelligence, access to adequate salaries, and legitimate opportunities to obtain and acquire the goods that many others have. However, according to Cao (2004), incorporating a wide variety of other factors makes the model too complex to be of much practical use. Instead, a number of researchers have proposed variations on Merton's theory.

© Dorset Media Service / Alamy Stock Photo

Surveillance footage of the brothers responsible for the Boston Marathon bombings of 2013—an example of rebellion, according to Merton's theory of social-structural strain. Why do structuralists like Durkheim and Merton view terrorism as a natural and inevitable product of a complex society? Do you agree with the structuralist position?

### Agnew's Strain Theory

Notable among the various attempts at refining Merton's theory is that of Robert Agnew. As Akers and Sellers (2013, p. 187) explain, Agnew "approached the revision of anomie/strain theory from a micro-level social psychological perspective." Agnew's general strain theory holds that strain is caused by failure to achieve certain material goals, and he identified three general forms of strain:

1.  strain caused by failure to achieve positively valued goals;
2.  strain caused by the removal of positively valued stimuli from the individual; and
3.  strain caused by the presentation of negative stimuli (Agnew & White, 1992).

Agnew's theory offers a more comprehensive account of the cognitive, behavioural, and emotional adaptations to strain, since it acknowledges that individuals have differing abilities to cope with stress, based on past experience, peer influence, temperament, financial resources, and so on.

While his theory addresses some of Merton's limitations, Agnew's version of general strain theory failed to clearly measure the types of strain that limit the ability of a person to achieve positively valued goals such as money or status (see Mazerolle & Maahs, 2000).

### Summary and Evaluation

It is clear that Durkheim's and Merton's ideas about anomie have had a major impact on sociological criminology. In general, the anomie theory has "drawn attention to the interplay between social structure, cultural context, and individual action" (Cao, 2004, p. 79).

While the anomie theory tries to explain the relationship between social conditions and deviance, it does not explain why particular people commit particular crimes, or why most young people who have engaged in crime eventually become law-abiding adults (Siegel, Brown & Hoffman, 2013). Nor does it effectively explain violent crimes such as assault, rape, and homicide (Barkan, 2011). It has also been criticized for not addressing middle-class and white-collar crime (Hirschi & Gottfredson, 1987).

There have been successful revisions and extensions of the theory: Albert Cohen's theory of status frustration, developed in his influential book *Delinquent Boys: Culture of the Gang* (1955), is one; another is the popular subculture-based differential opportunity theory of Richard Cloward and Lloyd Ohlin, which in the 1960s emphasized the role of strain in blocking access to legitimate opportunities. With these and more recent developments, the anomie/strain perspective will likely continue to draw a strong following (see Box 8.4 for an example of recent research). However, future research will need to

- determine to what extent social factors either precipitate or predispose some people to criminal behaviour;
- more clearly operationalize the level of strain that differentiates criminal from non-criminal behaviour;
- examine how strain works at the aggregate and individual levels; and,
- explain the process by which some previously stable neighbourhoods become "disorganized" and how they might return to a stable/organized state.

---

**BOX 8.4**

**A CLOSER LOOK**
Strain Theory and Hate Crime

Hate crime, which we will examine in more detail in Chapter 9, is a growing global concern. According to Jeffrey Ross (1995, p. 166), rates of hate crime rise during "hard economic times and consequential loss of jobs and inflation." While the Criminal Code (ss. 318–19) prohibits dissemination of hate literature in Canada, the relative anonymity of the Internet has encouraged this form of hate crime activity. Those most targeted by hate crimes (minorities, particularly recent immigrant groups) are often blamed by the perpetrators for stealing jobs and creating economic hardship (see Chapter 9). However, Allen and Boyce (2013) report that hate crime has declined in recent years, and that the number of successfully prosecuted cases in Canadian courts is comparatively small.

Why do you think youth and young adults are responsible for most of Canada's hate crime incidents?

---

## Policy Implications of Social-Structural Theories

Social-structural theories see crime as the product of macro social conditions. Policies based on such theories typically seek to prevent crime by improving those conditions—for example, by increasing socially acceptable opportunities for meaningful employment.

However, there is little evidence that these policies have succeeded. Although poverty decreased in the United States by roughly 23 per cent between 1963 and 1993, the crime rate rose nearly 350 per cent over the same period (Walsh & Ellis, 2007). And efforts to alleviate poverty among Aboriginal people in Canada also appear to have had no direct effect on crime rates: a 2013 report from Canada's Correctional Investigators Office shows that since March 2005, the federal inmate population has increased by 17.5 per cent. Over the same period, the Aboriginal inmate population grew by 47.4 per cent, and the population of black inmates grew by over 75 per cent. These groups now make up 22.8 per cent and 9.8 per cent of the total incarcerated population respectively (Correctional Investigator Canada, 2014, p. 2).

We will now shift our attention to two broad but popular sociological theoretical perspectives. First, we will provide an overview of a range of theories related to social process, which, unlike the social-structural theories discussed above, tend to focus on micro-level factors as opposed to macro-social indicators. This section will be followed by an overview of some of the more contemporary radical and critical theories, among which we will cover conflict, peacemaking, and feminist theories. Although these theories may not be as well established as the social-structural or social-process theories, they have played a notable role in how researchers attempt to respond to crime and deviance.

## Social-Process Theories

The father of sociology in the United States, **Charles Horton Cooley** (1902), coined the term "looking-glass self" to describe how our self-concept depends on how we imagine others perceive us. Do you care about what your friends think of you? If so, you understand the foundation of the social-process approach. Social-process sociologists embrace the perspective known as symbolic interactionism (SI), according to which an individual's identity and self-concept exist only in the context of society. In other words, our social being is the product of our interactions with others in our social environment, and our self-identity depends on who those others are and how we communicate with them. There are arguably six main social-process theories:

- differential association
- social learning

**symbolic interactionism (SI)**
A sociological approach to studying behaviour focusing on the symbolic value of words and gestures in everyday social interactions.

- social bond
- social control
- labelling
- neutralization

## Sutherland's Differential Association Theory

**differential
association (DA)
theory**
A sociological theory
that holds that criminal
behaviour is socially
learned through
frequent exposure to
negative influences.

**Edwin H. Sutherland** first outlined his theory of differential association (DA) in the third edition of his textbook *Principles of Criminology* (1939)—one year after Merton published his article on social structure and anomie. Conceptually, DA is a refinement of Tarde's nineteenth-century concept of imitation (Martin, Mutchnick, & Austin, 1990). Sutherland explained crime as a function of a learning process that could affect any individual in any culture (see Box 8.5).

Sutherland believed that people learn how to commit crimes primarily through social interaction. The more intimate the contact, the more likely it is that the behaviours will be imitated. The theory is based on nine fundamental principles:

1. Criminal behaviour is learned through cultural transmission.
2. Criminal behaviour is learned in direct interaction with other persons in a process of communication.
3. The principal part of the learning of criminal behaviour occurs within intimate personal groups. Vicarious exposure (e.g. through TV shows) may provide the "script," but the motivation comes from intimate personal relationships.
4. The process of learning criminal behaviour includes (a) learning the techniques of committing the crime, and (b) learning the specific direction of motives, drives, rationalizations, and attitudes.
5. The specific direction of motives and drives is learned from definitions of legal codes as favourable or unfavourable.
6. A person becomes delinquent because of an excess of definitions favourable to violation of law over definitions favourable to the law. For example, when young people talk about engaging in some deviant act, their attitudes about the legitimacy of the act begin to shift.
7. Differential associations may vary in frequency, duration, priority, and intensity. The extent to which criminal behaviour is learned depends on the frequency with which the message is reinforced.
8. The process of learning criminal behaviour involves all the mechanisms that are involved in any other learning.
9. While criminal behaviour is an expression of general needs and values, it is not explained by those general needs and values, since the motives for criminal behaviour are not the same as those for conventional behaviour.

| BOX 8.5 | PROFILE   **Edwin Hardin Sutherland** |
|---------|-----------------------------------------|

It was while teaching in the sociology department at the University of Illinois that Sutherland wrote his now classic introductory textbook *Principles of Criminology* (1924). Sutherland went on to complete three revisions, and after his death a former student, Donald Cressey, published six more. Among Sutherland's other noteworthy publications are *Twenty Thousand Homeless Men* (1936), *The Professional Thief* (1937), and *White Collar Crime* (1949).

In summary, DA is a micro-level theory that combines psychological understandings of learning with symbolic interactionism. It sees criminal behaviour as the product of interaction between operant conditioning and social group relations and environmental factors.

While Sutherland's textbook is considered a classic in its field, DA theory has met with varying degrees of support. When Matsueda (1992) attempted to measure the three key concepts (definition favourable to criminality, attitude toward peers, and attachment to deviant friends) he found a relatively low reliability coefficient.

### Variations on Differential Association Theory

Most social-process theories assume that people engage in crime as a result of learning and socialization experiences with significant others. This idea is reflected in Jeffery's (1965) theory of differential reinforcement (DR), which is based on the ideas of conditioning history, lacking of opportunity, satiation, the profits of crime being reinforcing in themselves, and the absence of punishment. However, unlike Skinner's theory of operant conditioning (Chapter 7), Jeffery's theory simply takes for granted the existence of constant stimuli in the environment, and posits that it is the lack of opportunity or satiation that affects whether or not the stimuli are reinforcing. "Criminal behavior is operant behavior; that is, it is maintained by the changes it produces on the environment," writes Jeffery (1965, p. 295). In the case of theft, for example, "the reinforcing stimulus is the stolen item."

Another variation on Sutherland's theme was developed by Robert Burgess and Ronald Akers (1966). In an effort to make DA theory more testable and to clarify the learning processes involved, they developed a theory that they called "differential association-reinforcement." Like Jeffery's theory, it drew from Skinner's behavioural principles. Although Reed Adams (1973) argued that it misused the principles of operant conditioning and therefore might mislead criminologists and sociologists unfamiliar with them, in Siegel's view (1995, p. 213) it was important because it "consider[ed] how both the *effectiveness* and *content* of socialization condition crime."

According to Akers and Sellers (2013), people learn social skills through operant conditioning that is controlled by stimuli that follow the behaviour (see Chapter 7). Through cues they receive in interactions with significant others, they learn to evaluate and adjust their behaviour (in terms of frequency, length, timing, etc.). Following initiation, criminal and/or deviant behaviour is reinforced by exposure to deviant models and by differential association with deviant peers. Consider this scenario for example: Three young people visit their local convenience store, and one of the youths—"Youth A"—decides he "deserves" a treat. One of the friends—"Youth B"—believes it would be acceptable to obtain the treat by stealing. B's illegal behaviour is reinforced by the approval of his friends. The behaviour might escalate if B is not interrupted—that is, caught.

In time Akers came to see the theory as "more closely aligned with cognitive learning theories" such as Bandura's (Akers & Jennings, 2009, p. 324), and since the publication of his book *Deviant Behaviour: A Social Learning Approach* (1973), it has been generally known as *social learning theory*.

There are a number of questions that none of the variations of social-process theory answer. For example:

- How might personality and/or biochemical makeup predispose some to learn criminal behaviour and not others?
- Why do some people who learn criminal behaviour patterns never engage in criminal acts?
- How do the techniques and behaviours originate?
- Why are children are more apt to model behaviour than adults?

**differential reinforcement (DR) theory**
A sociological theory that sees crime as a learned behaviour reinforced by its consequences.

Nevertheless, the theories of differential association and social learning will likely continue to play a vital role in criminological inquiry.

## Labelling Theory

Although the theoretical perspectives discussed so far in this chapter are able to explain serious crime in general terms and locate its causes either in individuals or in the social environment, none of them addresses two fundamental questions:

- Why do some behaviours come to be defined as normative while others are defined as deviant?
- What are the individual/psychological and social consequences of being identified as a criminal or delinquent?

**labelling theory**

A sociological explanation of crime that proposes that negative labelling can predispose people to feel like outcasts, increasing the likelihood of further deviant or criminal behaviour; also known as *societal reaction theory*.

Labelling theory addresses these questions. Integrating social-process and structural explanations, it adopts a symbolic-interactionist perspective.

As we have seen, no act is criminal unless the law defines it as such. Similarly, according to labelling theory, no individual is inherently criminal. Unlike traditional sociological theories, labelling theory adopts a "relativist" definition, seeing crime and deviance not as properties of specific behaviours or individuals but as products of the way others, and society in general, regard them (Barkan, 2011).

Labelling theory originated in the 1950s, when a number of social scientists—observing that the egalitarian ideals North Americans had fought for abroad were not being upheld on the home front—began to ask some probing questions. For example,

- How do certain behaviours come to be defined as deviant or criminal?
- Why do society and the criminal justice system seem to discriminate and apply official labelling and sanctions?
- What are the effects of labelling on continued criminality, or on those individuals who are labelled?

The theory gained wide support in the 1960s, after **Howard S. Becker** published his book *Outsiders* (1963). Becker argued that once individuals have been "tagged" as criminals, the stigma attached to the label can make it difficult for them to reintegrate into society: for example, a criminal record tends to make it hard for an "ex-con" to find legal employment (Rhodes, 2008). In short, labelling theorists suggest that labelling creates a self-fulfilling prophecy. Furthermore, the heavier the sanction, the less likely it is that the individual will be able to shed the stigma. This is the reasoning behind recommendations that the justice system use sanctions other than imprisonment for youth in particular.

The fact that certain groups are labelled as more crime-prone than others supports the notion that the law is both selectively created and selectively enforced. For example, it is well documented that Canada's Aboriginal people are overrepresented in the criminal justice system and that they receive more severe sentences than non-Aboriginal people for similar offences (see generally Bonta, LaPrairie, & Wallace-Capretta, 1997).

**moral entrepreneurs**

Individuals who use their power and/or influence to shape the legal system to their advantage.

Labelling theory focuses attention on the process of rule-making and, in particular, the role played by moral entrepreneurs, who use their power and/or influence to shape the legal system to their advantage, typically by drawing attention to issues that they have identified as social problems in need of being addressed (Becker, 1963).

## Primary and Secondary Deviance

As Lemert (1951) points out, central to labelling theory is the distinction between primary and secondary deviance. Primary deviance is behaviour that is contrary to societal norms but has not been recognized as such (Lemert, 1951). In other words, primary deviants may engage in deviant acts, but they are not considered deviant or "bad" people. For example, an office worker who takes home a few of the company's pens without being detected may not even recognize that he has committed theft, and if detected is unlikely to be stigmatized. However, if that behaviour is repeated, or if it escalates in other ways, the company may be forced to institute a new policy about office supplies, including penalties for those who remove supplies without permission or for personal use. The office worker is then likely to face more serious consequences for his behaviour, including labelling. If that happens, he may respond by internalizing the stigma and committing more serious theft. This *deviance amplification* (Lemert, 1951) would be an example of secondary deviance. The transition from primary to secondary deviance is summarized in Box 8.6.

As Lemert noted, secondary deviance sets in after the community, or society, has become aware of a primary deviance—real or perceived. The individual takes on the self-concept of "deviant" or "criminal," which predisposes him or her to engage in further deviance. In other words, secondary deviance—criminal acts the individual otherwise would not have committed—involves a process of resocialization into a deviant role.

## Summary and Evaluation

How likely would you be to marry someone you knew had "done time"? Would you want your children to associate with a junkie or a known gang member? Your answers to these questions bring us to the heart of labelling theory, which argues, essentially, that if you view and treat people as criminals, they will come to commit criminal acts.

Although labelling theory has found many supporters, it has also had its critics. Various researchers, for example, have shown that the stigma of crime does not necessarily result in escalation of criminal behaviour (see Schwarz, 2003). In addition, Schur (1972) points out that labelling theory does not explain primary deviance, while Nettler (1984) suggests that labelling does not necessarily affect everyone in the same way. Gibbons (1994) goes so far as to argue that labeling theory isn't a theory at all—only "a collection of 'sensitizing' notions."

**primary deviance**
Acts or behaviour that run counter to societal norms but that have not been socially recognized or labelled as deviant.

**secondary deviance**
Deviant acts or behaviour that result from labelling.

---

| BOX 8.6 | **A CLOSER LOOK**<br>**From Primary to Secondary Deviance** |

1. A person commits a deviant or criminal act. If undetected, this deviance remains primary.
2. Society responds in a retributive or punitive way to reinforce the label.
3. Once labelled, the individual commits more infractions (secondary deviance), which in turn draw additional attention. The deviance cycle begins to escalate in frequency and/ or intensity.
4. The labelled individual develops more hostility and resentment toward criminal justice agents.
5. The legal system responds by further labelling and stigmatizing the offender, further limiting his or her options.
6. As other options become increasingly restricted, the offender comes to see himself or herself as deviant.
7. The probability of future deviant acts increases (via *deviance amplification*) as the stigmatized offender's identity and self-concept come to revolve around deviance.

However, as we have seen in previous chapters, no one theory can be expected to address all issues. Labelling theory has done much to enrich the study of crime and deviance, and it has given rise to a number of new approaches to the study of crime and criminality. As we will see in Chapter 14, for example, Braithwaite's reintegrative shaming theory (introduced in the 1980s) and the broader restorative justice approach both reflect the influence of labelling theory (see Gavrielides, 2012).

Still, it is worth keeping in mind the following questions, which are among those that labelling theory has so far not been able to answer:

- Why do people become involved in deviance in the first place?
- Can an individual reject a label once it has been applied? Is it possible to see oneself as a good person after having done a bad thing?

For a brief overview of some other social-process theories, see Box 8.7.

## Summary and Evaluation

In summary, social-process theories include social learning theory, social bond theory, social control theory, labelling theory, and reintegrative shaming (see Chapter 14). These micro-level theories assume that everyone has the potential to violate the law; and they all emphasize the importance of social interaction (i.e. culture and social organization) in crime causation. They examine all aspects of the life experience, from birth through adolescence and into adulthood,

---

**BOX 8.7    FACTS AND FIGURES   OTHER SOCIAL-PROCESS THEORIES**

- **Neutralization theory.** The key tenet of Gresham Sykes and David Matza's 1957 theory is that offenders learn to neutralize the moral constraints that cause most of us to be law-abiding citizens. In fact, the theory can be regarded as an extension of Freud's notion of defence mechanisms, which he articulated as part of his psychoanalytical theory (Chapter 7). The process of neutralization, which serves to rationalize criminal behaviour, has five components:

  1. denial of responsibility (*I didn't do it.*)
  2. denial of injury (*No harm was done.*)
  3. denial of victim (*He/she deserved it.*)
  4. condemnation of the authorities (*They are always out to get me.*)
  5. appeal to higher principles or authorities (*I didn't do it for myself.*)

- **Social bond theory.** Travis Hirschi's theory is based on the idea that people form bonds with their social institutions, and that the stronger the bonds, the less likely one is to become deviant/criminal. The theory identifies four main types of bonding:

  1. attachment
  2. commitment
  3. involvement
  4. belief

Although both popular and empirically supported, according to Schulz (2006) this theory neglects the influence of the structural variables that can affect opportunity and/or family stability; fails to recognize a causal order; and has less direct policy impact than strain theory.

- **Social control theory.** Though reflected in the work of several key sociologists, including Albert Reiss (1961), Walter Reckless (1970), and David Matza (1964), a more recent expression is found in the classic 1990 book *A General Theory of Crime*, by Hirschi and Michael Gottfredson, who moved away from the classic social bonding formulation and argued that criminal behaviour is the product of a breakdown in self-control sparked by exposure to criminal opportunities—temptations that appear to have minimal risk of detection and apprehension (Gottfredson & Hirschi, 1990).

for social conditions, individual circumstances, and life experiences that lead to crime and deviance. Social-process theories commonly use self-report instruments as they can more clearly approximate the meaning of social-process concepts and offer a more nuanced perspective to inform crime control/prevention policies.

We will now look at some more recent theories rooted in sociology.

## Radical and Critical Theories: Conflict, Peacemaking, Feminist, and Left-Realist

A number of radical and critical theories emerged on the heels of labelling theory in the 1960s (Manski & Nagin, 2011). They centre on social conditions, ranging from social and political unrest to situations involving gender, race, and class discrimination.

There are several primary streams of the critical perspective. In this section, we will briefly examine four of the most important:

- conflict theory
- peacemaking theory
- feminist perspectives
- left-realism

### Conflict Theory

According to conflict theory, a social theory rooted in the teachings of Karl Marx, crime is the product of the conflict that naturally exists in every society at every level, from the individual to the group. Its origins are both instrumental (abuse of power and/or the use of coercion by those with power/influence) and symbolic (e.g. our communications and interactions form reality as we know it). Conflict theory challenges the social context that it holds responsible for conditions such as poverty, racism, and sexism resulting in the unfair conditions and treatment of marginalized groups.

For policy-makers, conflict theory presents some practical challenges. For example, rather than attempting to explain crime and offer resolutions, its proponents identify the sources of social conflict and social processes through which definitions of deviance and crime are created and enforced. Conflict theorists point to discriminatory practices within the criminal justice system, discrimination against the lower classes, and discrimination in the ways in which laws are created and used to support the status of those who make them. Yet in spite of their charges against the system, conflict theorists generally call for peaceful evolution, rather than revolution, to eliminate social conflict and improve the existing criminal justice system. Conflict theory reached its height in Canada in the early 1980s. Among the key Canadian contributors to the field have been Tullio Caputo, Thomas Fleming, Brian MacLean, and Robert Ratner.

One of the few conflict theorists to propose concrete measures to reduce crime was Austin Turk (1995). He recommended that governments stop building more prisons, since they have proven to be breeding grounds for "better" criminals while doing little to rehabilitate offenders, as well as decriminalizing public-order offences such as recreational gambling and consensual sexual activity (see Box 8.8). Unfortunately, these ideas have received scant attention from policy-makers.

By the early 1990s the conflict perspective had begun to give way to other perspectives, including peacemaking theory, feminism, left-realism, and cultural criminology (see below).

**conflict theory**
A social theory that sees crime as the product of social and/or economic disparities in society and suggests that people resort to criminal activity in response to division and competition.

**BOX 8.8        WHAT DO YOU THINK?**

## Do You Agree with Canada's New Prostitution Laws?

In 2014 the federal government passed Bill C-36 (the Protection of Communities and Exploited Persons Act), which creates new offences for clients and pimps engaged in prostitution but does not criminalize the prostitutes themselves. The government created this legislation in response to a Supreme Court ruling that had struck down the old anti-prostitution laws on the grounds that they

unduly increased the physical risk to prostitutes and therefore violated the charter right to security of the person. As John Lowman, one of Canada's top experts on prostitution, noted in an interview: "We're trying to fix complex social issues with a very ham-fisted approach."

How do you think a conflict theorist would explain the causes of prostitution? What about a proponent of labelling theory? What solutions might each one propose? How do you think we as a society should handle prostitution?

## Peacemaking Theory

Former conflict theorists **Harold E. Pepinsky** and **Richard Quinney** have been strong advocates of this relatively new (early 1990s) school of thought in North America (Cullen, Wright, & Blevins, 2011). Dissatisfied with the traditional conflict perspective, both Quinney and Pepinsky searched for a "radical humanistic understanding of social existence and human experience" (Friedrichs, 1991, p. 102). They recognized that even though most people prefer peace to violence, sometimes violence seems unavoidable. But is it necessary? Or natural?

Quinney and Pepinsky argue that the traditional criminal–non-criminal dualism, pitting "us" versus "them," has done little to alleviate the crime problem. No matter how we define crime and punishment, we cannot punish acts, only the actors (Pepinsky, 2000). As the esteemed Norwegian criminologist Nils Christie observed, "you're more likely to see that a person's soul is not embodied in any single act, and that you cannot punish an act without contaminating a complex actor" (cited in Pepinsky, 1991, p. 107). Hence, there can be no justification for using punishment to resolve disputes, and people should not be labelled or "pigeonholed" based on acts they have committed. Peacemaking theory, like all conflict-based theories, posits that fundamental changes in the structure of society are required if crime is to be reduced.

Pepinsky and Quinney, among other advocates of peacemaking theory, point out that the criminal justice system is based on the "warlike" principle of vengeance (see Braswell, Fuller, & Lozoff, 2001). They see punishment as no less violent than crime. However, Pepinsky adds that non-retaliation alone is not enough. He argues that we all need to be participants in the democratic process, which involves the social process by which empathy prevails over the use of violence (i.e. punitivity)

Judging from the main anthologies on the subject, the peacemaking model has not been widely embraced (see Cullen, Wright, & Blevins, 2011). But perhaps it is making itself felt in more practical ways—for example, in the support that the concept of restorative justice has attracted in recent years (see Chapter 14).

**peacemaking theory**
A humanistic approach to crime control that emphasizes reconciliation through mediation and dispute settlement, rather than punishment and retribution.

## Feminist Perspectives

Even though Lombroso himself wrote a book on female criminality more than a century ago, female offenders were largely ignored in criminology until the late 1960s. Typically, criminologists studying crime among women and girls focused only on crimes such as prostitution and shoplifting. According to Leonard (1982), theoretical criminology failed to address women's crime because the discipline was dominated by men trying to explain male patterns of crime and delinquency. However, this changed in the 1970s, when the women's movement brought women's issues to the forefront. **Freda Adler's** *Sisters in Crime* and Rita Simon's *Women and Crime*, both published in 1975, were the two pioneering and influential works on the subject. Both Adler and Simon attributed the growth in women's crime to the emancipation of women in the 1970s. Although this interpretation did not sit well with other feminists, who found the interpretation too narrow and biased, and who believed it simply served to reinforce the androcentric views that had dominated criminology (Daly & Chesney-Lind, 1988), Adler's and Simon's ideas, along with those of other feminists, challenged the assumptions underlying traditional research on gender and criminal justice.

In the late 1980s, Daly (1989b) argued that criminology had not felt the impact of feminist thought except in the areas of rape and intimate partner violence, and that in general criminologists did not find women's crime sufficiently interesting as a topic for study, largely because women remained significantly underrepresented in the criminal justice system. On the other hand, Herman Schwendinger and Julia Schwendinger (1991) listed a number of significant innovations in legal discourse introduced by proponents of the feminist perspective:

**feminist perspective**
A general term for any of a variety of sociological approaches to the study of crime that focus on female offenders and victims, emphasize the patriarchal bias in society, and call for greater equality between the genders both in the criminal justice system and in theory construction.

- **Universalization of rape laws.** In January 1983, as a result of relatively low numbers of tried cases, Canada's existing rape law was repealed and replaced with the general offence of assault. The new law consisted of three new categories:
   1. sexual assault (s. 246.1 CCC)
   2. sexual assault with a weapon, threats to a third party, and bodily harm (s. 246.2)
   3. aggravated sexual assault (s. 246.3) (see Chapter 4)

- **Redefinition of gender crimes.** Changes in women's gender roles were reflected in the increase in women's rates of criminal involvement.
- **Redefinition of gender relations in criminology.** Feminist research has helped criminological theory move beyond male-dominated perspectives. Among the leading Canadian scholars in this area are Ellen Adelberg, Dorothy Chan, Dawn Currie, Shelley Gavigan, and Rita Gunn.
- **Increased awareness that women are handled differently from men throughout the criminal justice system, from the point of arrest through judicial process to incarceration.** For example, a report released by the Correctional Investigator (2012) points out that while Aboriginal people in Canada are disproportionately represented in crime statistics overall, the number of Aboriginal women held in institutions is even more disproportionate. As of 2012, the number of Aboriginal women in Canadian prisons had increased by over 80 per cent over the previous 10 years (Correctional Investigator, 2012).
- **A call for new measurement and methodological strategies that might better capture and explain women's experiences of oppression and discrimination.**

Depending on one's source, there are three or four primary strands of feminism and feminist theory. Sally Simpson (1989) identifies three, while Williams and McShane (2013) add a fourth. All "share a concern with identifying and representing women's interests, interests judged to be insufficiently represented and accommodated within the mainstream" (Williams & McShane, 2013, p. 606); moreover, all have made significant contributions to criminological theory and criminal justice practices.

1. **Liberal feminism.** Liberal feminists advocate for women's equality and freedom of choice. They see gender inequality in most spheres of influence, including education, politics, the

law, and the workplace, and call for "men and women to work together to 'androgynize' gender roles . . . and eliminate outdated policies and practices that discriminate against women" (Simpson, 1989, p. 607). Adoption of this approach, they argue, would eliminate inequality and promote greater social harmony.

2. **Socialist feminism.** Proponents of this perspective combine radical and Marxist principles (see below). They see gender oppression as an inherent feature of capitalist societies and criminality as a by-product of the class system. For socialist feminists, the only solution is a society free of gender and class stratification. They feel that the existing social structure explains why men are more likely to commit violent street crimes, while women are more likely to commit property and vice crimes (Simpson, 1989).

3. **Radical feminism.** Supporters of radical feminism believe that women are subordinated by a patriarchal system rooted in male aggression and desire to control women's sexuality. They believe that "sex, not gender, is the crucial analytical category" (Williams & McShane, 2013, p. 261): that is, that "female subjugation is universal and originates in the biological differences between men and women" (Hinch, 1994, p. 6). They see men as using the law to exercise control over women. Radical feminists believe that eliminating male domination will reduce both female crime rates and male violence against women.

4. **Marxist feminism.** Marxist feminists believe that gender oppression is "secondary to and reflective of class oppression" (Simpson, 1989, p. 607). It is because the capitalist system exploits subordinate groups that women are relegated to lower occupational status than men and receive lower pay for equal work. From the Marxist perspective, capitalism has a direct influence on female crime. Women are more likely, than men, to commit property offences and sex offences such as prostitution.

Today, feminist perspectives are sometimes classified among the "new" gender-based theories (see van Gundy, 2014). In fact, Barak (1998, p. 163) has noted a tendency for the different feminist perspectives to become more inclusive and focus on "the commonalties of gender, power, and conflict." All criticize the traditional male-centred approaches to studying crime, and all seek to develop gender-sensitive interpretations of deviance.

How significant the feminist perspective will be in explaining crime and delinquency is still not clear. However, as Barkan (2011, p. 248) suggests, "without full consideration of gender and its intersection with race and class, the study of crime and criminal justice will remain incomplete."

### Left-Realism

**left-realism**

A theoretical approach that focuses on crime prevention strategies and the implications of crime control policies rather than the causes of crime.

Historically, most conflict and radical criminologists have tended to blame capitalism for crime. However, as the conventional versions of the conflict and radical perspectives evolved (see above), a number of radical theorists began to criticize the prevailing views held by conventional conflict and radical theorists. Their key proponents include Richard Quinney, Walter DeKeseredy, John Lea, Elliot Currie, Tony Platt, and Jock Young, among others.

Relying primarily on victimization data, the left-realists suggest that conflict theorists have ignored the poor and the working class, focusing instead on crimes of the ruling (upper) class. They have also charged that the radical criminologists have developed weak crime control strategies. In partial response, the left-realists argue that crime is not only a *real* problem but a conundrum that also exists among the lower socio-economic classes.

There are six basic premises of the realistic perspective:

1. The material, political, and ideological impact of crime on the maintenance of capitalism makes crime a real problem.

2. In order to understand the impact of crime, we must look at the reality behind the outward appearance that crime has on society.

3. In order to address crime, we should focus on crime control by encouraging community involvement through various crime prevention initiatives

4. Since all criminal acts involve a victim and an offender, we must come to understand the relationship between the two in order to more effectively determine the best response.

5. Police should not be autonomous from society. They need to be integrated in the community, both responsive and responsible to it.

6. Victimization surveys provide a more realistic picture of crime than official statistics do.

Left-realism, according to Matthews (1992), can be summarized as consisting of four central elements, all of which share common themes with those identified by Lea and Young above. They include the following:

1. a commitment to detailed empirical investigation; left-realists rely heavily on victimization data

2. the independence and objectivity of criminal activity

3. the disorganizing effect of crime: all crimes are serious

4. the possibility and desirability of developing measures to reduce crime

Left-realists feel that the best way to combat crime is through crime prevention (see Chapter 14), which involves improving the socioeconomic conditions underlying crime, relying more on community-based policing, providing victim compensation, using imprisonment only for those who pose a "real" threat to society, and increasing police surveillance (and social integration) in those areas where crime is a problem.

## Evaluation

Although the left-realist perspective is now some 20 years old, it may represent what the Norwegian criminologist Nils Christie (1997, p. 13) refers to as an "oversocialization within criminology." As Williams and McShane (2013) among others have suggested, until fairly recently, criminological theory has not advanced much. Those who espouse such a view point out that although official crime rates in Canada have been declining, little has actually been accomplished in the area of crime control. In fact, Christie (1997, p. 13) argued that the impact of criminology on crime control can perhaps best be described as "dull, tedious, and intensely empty as to new insights."

Nevertheless, despite any prospective promise that left-realism might hold, Canadian criminologist Robert Menzies (1992) accuses left-realism of being gender-blind and ignoring violence against women, as well as largely overlooking issues of corporate crime. Meanwhile, Canadian criminologists Walter DeKeseredy and Barbara Perry (2006) further suggest that left-realism is too willing to inflict punishment as a tool of social control while deflecting responsibility from the capitalist system. And finally, former University of Guelph sociologist Ronald Hinch (2003) argues that the perspective has a poor conception of the working class and points out that members of the working class often shift roles from offender to victim and vice versa.

Some of the more recent attention given to the left-realist perspective has shifted to what Matthews (2010) calls "critical realism." While still acknowledging that crime is a social contract, critical realism argues that there are objective aspects of crime and its effects that cannot be understood simply in terms of language and discourse. Hence, as Matthews and others have suggested, the perspective does not offer a "theory of either criminal justice or crime that can be empirically validated" (Akers & Sellers, 2013, p. 243).

## Summary and Evaluation

The critical theories view crime as the product of inequality in a society where crime is defined by those with power. Thus from the critical perspective the only way to achieve the change required to prevent crime is through major social reform, in some cases bordering on revolution. Only through aggressive social reform is it possible to correct the social and/or economic inequalities that are seen as the root causes of crime.

Can such change be achieved? To expect a dramatic reversal of existing social and political conditions is unrealistic. However, we have seen the emergence of what Lynch and Groves (1989, p. 128) refer to as "middle-range policy alternatives" such as the abolition of mandatory sentences, prosecution of corporate crime, increased employment opportunities, and an increasing shift toward community-based alternatives to incarceration.

While critical theories appear promising, they are still unable to explain why some people become offenders and others do not. Hence, while the social conflict–based approaches are important, they need to be linked with other disciplinary perspectives such as biology and psychology. In this way, the elements of the individual, the group, and society can be incorporated into an interdisciplinary explanatory model.

# More Recent Theories

In addition to the other approaches discussed in this chapter, there are several more recent perspectives that are worth exploring. In this section we will take a brief look at two of them: rational-choice and cultural theories.

## Rational-Choice Theories

An early example of rational-choice theory in criminology was the routine activity theory (RAT) developed by **Lawrence Cohen** and **Marcus Felson**, introduced in Chapter 4. Like the classical theory of Beccaria, it assumed that the decision to commit a crime is a rational choice, based on the offender's assessment of the likely costs and benefits. Routine activity theory is intuitively strong, and policy based on it can be readily adopted. Many crime prevention programs today focus on practices such as "target hardening" (e.g. installing deadbolts on doors and security bars on windows) and public education.

Other iterations of the "rational-choice" perspective include the following.

- **Lifestyle theory** (Hindelang, Gottfredson, & Garofalo, 1978). As we saw in Chapter 4, lifestyle theory argues that risk of victimization is to some extent a function of lifestyle, in particular the social settings that the individual frequents and his or her position in the social structure (the higher the status, the lower the risk of victimization). According to the theory, potential victims make a rational choice when deciding whether or not to place themselves in a situation of vulnerability, leading Akers and Sellers (2013) to ask whether the lifestyle model simply expands on rational-choice theory.
- **Rational-choice theory** (RCT) (Cornish & Clarke, 1986). Essentially a variation on deterrence theory, which itself draws on the classic theoretical work of Beccaria and Bentham, RCT views crime as both offence- and offender-specific. Offenders rationally assess the level of skill required to commit the act, the personal gain to be obtained from the act, and the risk of detection/apprehension. RCT is grounded on the "expected utility" principle: the offender decides to commit the crime as a result of a rational decision-making process that takes into account the expected benefits and risks.

- **Life-course theory** (Nagin, Farrington, & Moffitt, 1995). Initially proposed by Karl Mannheim in the 1930s in his PhD dissertation, this interdisciplinary theory maintains that behaviour can be affected by major events, experience, or awareness, or "turning points" that occur at different stages of life, putting an individual into the position of having to respond or not respond. For example, an alcoholic who frequently drives while drunk may have an epiphany one day—perhaps having narrowly avoided a serious accident—and realize he or she needs help. When these events are positive they help people accumulate social capital and are life-sustaining. However, negative experiences can increase the likelihood of delinquency (see Delisi & Beaver, 2014). Among the factors that can interact with life events to predispose youth to criminal behaviour are neuropsychological problems, poor communication skills, and poor nutrition.
- **Routine conflict theory** (Kennedy & Forde, 1999). This theory, based on Kennedy and Forde's (1995) survey of over 2,000 respondents from Alberta and Manitoba, argues that the behaviour of both offenders and victims is a product of rational choice based on learned repertoires for responding to conflict. Both the Canadian Urban Victimization Survey and the General Social Surveys suggest that these repertoires are influenced by characteristics such as age, gender, income, race, and social class. The theory combines sociological and psychological factors.

## Cultural Criminology

Cultural criminology developed out of the postmodern and deconstructionist movements and took root in the United Kingdom in the mid-1990s (see Ferrell, 1994, 1995), with critical criminologists such as Schwartz and Friedrichs (1994) helping to generate interest in it. **Jeff Ferrell** provides a succinct description:

> Cultural criminology explores the many ways in which cultural dynamics intertwine with the practices of crime and crime control in contemporary society; [it] emphasizes the centrality of meaning and representation in the construction of crime as momentary event, subcultural endeavor and social issue. (Ferrell & Hayward, 2011)

Among the research topics that cultural criminologists have examined is the media's role in creating *moral panic*—widespread concern about an issue involving a deviant behaviour whose seriousness and frequency have been greatly exaggerated. Other common themes among cultural criminologists are how the media negatively portray teenage girls using socially disapproving/condemnatory images and how poverty is perceived in a wealthy society as an act of exclusion—the ultimate humiliation in a consumer society (DeKeseredy, 2011).

Criticisms of cultural criminology include the following (DeKeseredy, 2011):

- It is more political than analytical.
- It overemphasizes subcultures and "outlaws"—groups that might be merely resisting change—and underemphasizes more traditional forms of crime and deviance.
- Its methodology tends to be subjective and/or narrow in its cultural focus.

So far the academic impact of cultural criminology has been limited. Nevertheless, since 2005 the journal *Crime, Media and Culture* has provided a forum for exploration of the "relationship between crime, criminal justice, media and culture," and the University of Kent in the UK has a centre and website dedicated to cultural criminology. Arguably, the leading cultural criminologist in Canada today is Stephen Muzzatti at Ryerson University in Toronto, whose

THE CANADIAN PRESS/Galit Rodan

Cultural criminologists look at how visual representations of crime shape public perceptions. In 2013, a Toronto police officer shot a knife-carrying 18-year-old on an otherwise empty streetcar. The incident caused widespread outrage when video captured by bystanders was made public on YouTube. Video evidence was critical to a rare charge of second-degree murder against the officer. How does this incident illustrate a "democratization" of the way crime is presented?

primary research interest is the connections among globalization, late modernity, consumer culture, and transgressive and/or criminal behaviour.

This chapter has reviewed a variety of theories rooted in sociology, each offering its own unique explanation of crime and deviance as well as its own approach to crime control. While most of them meet the general criteria for "good theory" (see Akers & Sellers, 2013), none of them can claim to have produced a solution to the crime problem. However, it is possible that combining sociological insights with those from other disciplines will help us develop more effective policies.

## Summary

- Sociology originated in Europe and took root in North America at the University of Chicago in the early twentieth century.

- Sociological theories of crime focus on social forces and processes.
- Social-structural theories focus on the macro-level forces (e.g. anomie, strain, social disorganization) that can lead to criminal behaviour.
- Social-process theories focus on the micro-level interactions through which criminal behaviour is learned. Theories include differential association, social learning, and labelling.
- Critical criminology encompasses a variety of theories that focus on social conflict and unequal power relations based on race, gender, and social class.
- Contemporary sociological theories include rational-choice and cultural criminology.

---

**BOX 8.9**    **FACTS AND FIGURES** A SUMMARY OF SOCIOLOGICAL PERSPECTIVES ON CRIME

| Perspectives | Theories | Focus/General Themes |
|---|---|---|
| **ecological school** (also known as **Chicago School**) | • concentric-circle theory<br>• social disorganization theory<br>• cultural transmission theory<br>• crime prevention through environmental design (CPTED) | • sees crime as a product of the relationships between humans and their physical and social environments |
| **social-structural theories** | • anomie<br>• strain theory<br>• general strain theory | • see crime as the product of the pressures exerted on individuals by social structures |
| **social-process theories** | • differential association<br>• differential association-reinforcement theory<br>• labelling theory | • associate crime with the identity constructed through interaction with others |
| **critical theories** | • conflict theory<br>• peacemaking theory<br>• feminist theories<br>• left-realism | • focus on identifying and reducing structural inequalities that perpetuate discrimination based on factors such as gender, race, and social class<br>• focus on crime prevention, alternative data source other than official statistics |

---

## Discussion Questions

1. To what extent do you think crime is the product of structured social inequality related to factors such as race/ethnicity, social class, and gender? Which of these factors do you think are most important for understanding crime? Why?
2. Describe the major theories discussed in this chapter. What are their strengths and weaknesses? Which theory do you think has the most explanatory power? Why?
3. To what extent do you think the new and emerging contemporary theories of criminology can contribute to our understanding of crime?
4. How might sociological perspectives be incorporated into an interdisciplinary criminological perspective? Which components do you think would be most important?

## Key Concepts

anomie
concentric-circle theory
conflict theory
cultural transmission theory
differential association (DA) theory
differential reinforcement (DR) theory
ecological school
feminist perspective
labelling theory

left-realism
moral entrepreneurs
peacemaking theory
primary deviance
secondary deviance
social disorganization theory
social structure
strain theory
symbolic interactionism

## Key Names

Freda Adler (b. 1934)
Howard Becker (b. 1928)
Ernest Burgess (1886–1966)
Albert Cohen (1918–2014)
Lawrence E. Cohen
Auguste Comte (1798–1857)
Charles Cooley (1864–1929)
Émile Durkheim (1858–1919)
Marcus Felson (b. 1947)
Jeff Ferrell

Henry McKay (1899–1980)
Robert Merton (1910–2003)
Robert Park (1864–1944)
Harold Pepinsky (b. 1945)
Richard Quinney (b. 1934)
Kim Rossmo (b. 1955)
Clifford Shaw (1896–1957)
Edwin Sutherland (1883–1950)
Gabriel Tarde (1834–1904)

## Weblinks

**LaMarsh Centre for Child & Youth Research**
York University's LaMarsh Centre involves faculty and students in interdisciplinary research in a variety of topics affecting infants, children, adolescents, and emerging adults.
http://lamarsh.info.yorku.ca

**Division on Critical Criminology—American Society of Criminology**
This site provides links to sources of information on peacemaking, restorative justice, and related social conflict theories.
http://critcrim.org/peacemaking.htm

**University of Kent—Cultural Criminology**
The site of the cultural criminology centre at the University of Kent.
http://blogs.kent.ac.uk/culturalcriminology

# PART III

## Different Types of Crime

# Chapter 9

## Violent Crime

Couperfield/Shutterstock.com

Murder! Rape! Robbery! Assault! Wounding! Theft! Burglary! Arson! Vandalism!
These form the substance of the annual official criminal statistics on indictable offences. . . .
[T]hey constitute the major part of "our" crime problem. Or at least, we are told so daily by
politicians, police, judges, and journalists who speak to us through the media
of newspapers and television. And most of us listen.
STEVEN BOX (1983, P. 1)

## Learning Outcomes

After reading this chapter, you should be able to

- Describe the main types of violent crime;
- Identify the trends in rates of different violent crimes;
- Understand that there is no single, definitive explanation of the causes of violent crime;
- Appreciate how crime data can be used to explain patterns of violent crime and devise social policy;
- See the importance of applying an integrated and interdisciplinary approach to using crime data; and
- Appreciate the benefit of using comparative criminology to gain further insight into the study and control of violent crime.

## Introduction to Violent Crime

Anyone who follows the news would think that violence and violent crime are omnipresent and that our world is more dangerous than ever before. Consider some of the sensational violent crimes that have received extensive media coverage in recent years:

- In January 2012, Montreal residents Mohammad Shafia, his wife Tooba Yahya, and their son Hamed were found guilty of first-degree murder in the 2009 deaths of Zainab, Sahar, and Geeti Shafia and Rona Amir in a suspected honour killing.
- In February 2012, Dustin Paxton was convicted of aggravated and sexual assault in the torture of his Calgary roommate.
- In May 2012, a jury found Michael Rafferty guilty of the 2009 abduction and murder of 8-year-old Victoria Stafford from Woodstock, Ontario.
- In April 2013, Luka Rocca Magnotta was convicted of first-degree murder, among other charges, in the 2012 death and dismemberment of Chinese student Lin Jun.
- In May 2013, Dellen Millard was charged with first-degree murder in the death of Ancaster, Ontario, resident Tim Bosma, who disappeared after giving a test drive to two men interested in buying a used truck; Millard was later charged with murder in connection to the deaths of his father, Wayne Millard, and former girlfriend Laura Babcock.
- In June 2014, Kathryn and Alvin Liknes and their grandson Nathan O'Brien went missing from the couple's Calgary home; a month later, a man known to the family, Douglas Garland, was arrested on three counts of murder.

As shocking as these incidents are, violent crime is hardly unique to modern times. Historian Will Durant (1953, p. 590) quipped that in sixteenth-century Rome, assassins could be bought almost as cheaply as religious indulgences. Eisner (2003), in a fascinating study of long-term trends in violent crime, shows that rates of murder and assault today pale in comparison to historical rates of these violent offences in several major European cities. Likewise Gurr (1981), in a review of historical trends in violent crime, points out that the incidence of violent crime since the mid-1850s is much lower than in earlier times. This is largely attributable to cultural and demographic changes that have brought increasing rates of urbanization, higher levels of overall wealth and prosperity, and thus greater attention to combatting crime (see e.g. Carrigan, 1991). And indeed, despite some geographic variation, Canadians overall have felt relatively safe in recent years (Brennan, 2013).

In the next two chapters, we will focus respectively on violent crime and property crime, both of which fall under the category of *conventional crimes*, which we defined in Chapter 1. (*Non-conventional crimes*, which include organized crime and cybercrime, will be discussed in chapters 10–13). Chapter 9 will examine three major violent crime offences—homicide, sexual assault, and robbery—and several "new" forms of violent crime: abduction, hate crime, stalking, and terrorism. Throughout this chapter, keep in mind that the general observations and conclusions are more important than the numbers themselves. Although violent crime represents only around 10 per cent of all Criminal Code incidents, it commands considerable media and public attention. In 2013, there were 383,945 reported incidents of violent crime, compared with over 1.2 million property-related infractions (Boyce, Cotter, & Perreault, 2014). But given most people's fascination with violent crime and the fact it can potentially result in the most serious harm (both emotional and physical), we will examine it first.

As we noted in Chapter 1, the meaning of crime depends on one's perspective. Rather than focus on the various interpretations of crime, we will base our observations in this chapter on factual data. In so doing, we will focus primarily on those categories of violent crime that are documented by Statistics Canada (e.g. assault, sexual assault, murder, armed robbery, etc.). However, we will also examine, especially in the feature boxes scattered throughout this chapter, examples of other violent offences that fall outside the categories of violent crime identified by Statistics Canada (see e.g. Box 9.2).

**abduction**

The illegal apprehension of another person for the purpose of financial gain, retribution, or personal or political gain.

**hate crime**

A crime in which the perpetrator's conduct is motivated by bias, hatred, or prejudice regarding the actual or perceived race, colour, religion, national origin, gender, disability, or sexual orientation of another group or individual.

---

## BOX 9.1     WHAT DO YOU THINK?

### How Safe Do You Feel?

Between 1962 and 1992, the rate of violent crime in Canada quadrupled (Hendrick, 1996, p. 1; Figure 9.1). However, between 2003 and 2014, the violent crime rate declined by 35 per cent (Boyce, Cotter, & Perreault, 2014; Figure 9.1). Also in 2014, the Violent Crime Severity Index fell to its lowest point since it was introduced in 2001—30 per cent lower than the peak rate in 2006 (Figure 9.2).

> How concerned are you about the threat of violent crime? What factors affect your level of concern? (For example, where you live, whether you are male or female, what regular activities might put you at greater risk.)

**Figure 9.1   Police-Reported Rate of Violent Crime, Canada, 1962–2014**

*Source:* Statistics Canada (2014), "Police-reported crime statistics, 2014," *The Daily* (22 July).

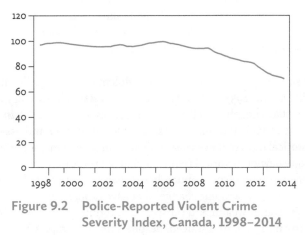

**Figure 9.2   Police-Reported Violent Crime Severity Index, Canada, 1998–2014**

*Source:* Statistics Canada (2014), "Police-reported crime statistics, 2014," *The Daily* (22 July).

Given that we will be relying mostly on official data, it bears reminding that, as we observed in Chapter 3, these statistics have limitations and do not necessarily represent the "real" picture. As well, it is not possible to discern from official violent crime data exactly who is committing these crimes and why; this area deserves immediate and closer attention from researchers and policy-makers.

**violent crime**

A general category of crime that includes homicide, attempted murder, robbery, assault, and other mostly indictable offences that involve the physical violation of a person.

## Violent Crime Rates and the Cost of Crime

While the incident rate of violent crime has been decreasing over the past decade, the financial cost of crime to Canadians has been increasing (see Table 9.1). In the 1970s, the per capita cost of administering justice was approximately $170 (Griffiths & Verdun-Jones, 1994). By 1994–5, the cost per Canadian had risen to $324, for a total of nearly $9.4 billion spent on police, courts, corrections, legal aid, and criminal prosecution (CCJS, 2002, 22(11), p. 14). By 2000–1,

---

**BOX 9.2    REALITY CHECK**

### Hate-Motivated Violence

Under Sections 318 to 320 of the Criminal Code, there are four specific forms of hate crime:

1. advocating genocide
2. publicly inciting hatred
3. wilfully promoting hatred
4. mischief in relation to religious property

In May 2013, Toronto police launched a hate crime investigation into an incident involving a man who was caught on a security camera as he both verbally assaulted and spat on a woman who was entering a mall. The apparent motive was that she was wearing a hijab ("Spitting," 2013). In a 2011 report, Brennan and Dauvergne state that while the percentage of visible minorities in Canada grew by 27 per cent between 2001 and 2006, over 50 per cent of hate-motivated incidents were associated with racial or ethnic differences or differences in religious affiliation. And while we might think the phenomenon is new, Canada has a long history of hate-motivated violence toward Aboriginal people and racialized ethnic minorities. In an early documented incident, in 1907, a mob attacked local Chinese and Japanese communities in Vancouver, causing extensive damage to property and, reportedly, several casualties ("Data on hate-motivated violence," 1995).

Not all hate-motivated crimes tried in Canadian courts have their origins in Canada. In July 2013, the case of Jacques Mungwarere ended when he was sentenced after being convicted of war crimes. Mungwarere was a Hutu teacher in Rwanda, accused of organizing the executions of minority Tutsi in the country; he had escaped to Canada after the genocide. Désiré Munyaneza, who was

Nevil Hunt/Metroland Media

Under the Criminal Code, even graffiti can be considered a hate crime if it is judged to reflect wilful promotion of hatred or mischief in relation to religious property. This graffiti on a sign at the site of a future Muslim community centre in Ottawa is evidence of the need for these protections in Canada, despite our reputation for tolerance.

living in Toronto, was the first man arrested and convicted in Canada for war crimes, also in relation to his role in the Rwandan genocide (Aubrey, 2013).

Although often difficult to prove, hate-motivated crimes reflect a gross violation of human rights and dignity. Through its legislation, Canada has taken bold steps to uphold the fundamental rights of all Canadians while supporting international criminal justice to ensure that perpetrators of hate crime—especially crimes against humanity—are not free of impunity.

How does hate crime differ from other forms of violent crime?

| Table 9.1 | The Cost of Administering Justice by Sector (Billions) | | |
|---|---|---|---|
| | 1990–1 | 2000–1 | 2011–12 |
| Police | $5.24 billion | $6.80 billion | $7.90 billion |
| Courts | .77 | 1.00 | 2.60 |
| Legal aid | .41 | .51 | .76 |
| Youth corrections | .43 | n/a | n/a |
| Adult corrections | 1.79 | 2.10 | 2.20 |
| **All sectors** | **8.52** | **11.10** | **20.30** |

*Source*: Statistics Canada, Canadian Centre for Justic Statistics, Justice Spending in Canada, 1997, 17(3); Statistics Canada, Catalogue nos. 85-225-XIE, 85-403-XIE, 85F0015XIE, 85-211-XIE and 85-402-XIE.

the per capita cost had climbed to $362 (total budget: $11.1 billion), and a decade later, it sat at $480 (with a total budget of over $20 billion!). In 2013, a report by the Parliamentary Budget Office showed that spending on the justice system had risen by 23 per cent from 2002 to 2012, while Canada's crime rate had decreased by exactly the same proportion during the same time span (Mackrael, 2013). Figure 9.3 shows the changing cost of policing alone, expressed in constant 2002 dollars (to correct for the effects of inflation and deflation), from 1993 to 2003; the same figure shows the trend in Criminal Code incidents during the 10-year period.

When we take a moment to compare our violent crime trends with those of other countries, the picture may seem less alarming. Since a majority of Canadians live within 200 kilometres of the American border, most of us have probably spent some time reading (or hearing) about the crime problem in the United States. By all counts, violent crime is a much more serious problem there than it is in Canada (see Box 9.3).

Changing demographics, economic recession and restructuring, and increasing drug use might for some of the similarities in international trends, but they do not explain variable rates. More sophisticated, integrated models are required to explain these differences. In the meantime, there is considerable merit in having criminologists conduct comparative research and apply their theories to comparative data (see Barbaret, 2004).

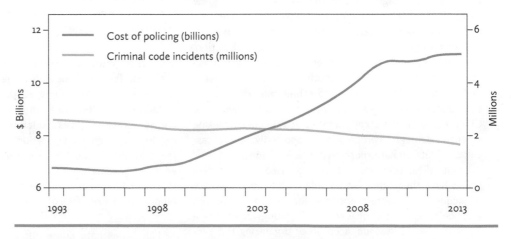

**Figure 9.3   Cost of Policing\* and Number of Criminal Code Incidents in Canada, 1993–2013**

\* Expressed in constant (2002) dollars.
*Sources:* Statistics Canada. Police resources in Canada, 2014. Cat. no. 85-002-X.

## BOX 9.3 FACTS AND FIGURES WHY IS CANADA LESS VIOLENT THAN THE UNITED STATES?

Being next-door neighbours to the United States, Canadians are often drawn to making comparisons between the two countries. Canada and the US have many things in common—the predominance of the English language, the ability to trace the inhabitants' heritage to European and Aboriginal peoples, the consumer-oriented cultural outlook, and the general outlines of the criminal justice system, among others. Yet they differ on a number of economic, social, and political counts, and notably, the crime rates in the two countries are dramatically different. As indicated in Table 9.2, violent crime rates in the United States over the past decade were significantly higher than in Canada, despite the overall decline in violent crime in both countries.

A variety of reasons have been offered to account for these differences.

- Canada has less inequality than the United States has.
- Canada's gun control legislation is much stricter than that of the United States.

- Handgun ownership is considerably lower in Canada than in the United States.
- Canada was settled in a more peaceful fashion than the United States was. Canada's North West Mounted Police helped ensure a peaceful settlement in the West, in stark contrast to the way the American West "was won." As a Canadian columnist observed a few years ago, "the Canadian cowboy's most beloved possessions were his horse and saddle, not his gun" (Simonds, 1996, p. 51).
- Along these lines, Canada's constitution and independence were obtained without the civil war or revolution that created a legacy of proud gun ownership as a defence against threats of the state in the US.

Can you think of any other possible explanation for the different violent crime rates between Canada and the United States?

### Table 9.2 Rates of Violent Crime in Canada and the United States, 1993–2013

| | VIOLENT CRIME RATE PER 100,000 | | | | | |
| | Canada | | | United States | | |
| Crime | 1993 | 2003 | 2013 | 1993 | 2003 | 2013 |
|---|---|---|---|---|---|---|
| Homicide | 2.2 | 1.7 | 1.4 | 9.5 | 5.7 | 4.5 |
| Aggravated Assault | 146 | 152 | 140 | 440 | 295 | 229 |
| Robbery | 104 | 101 | 66 | 256 | 143 | 109 |

*Sources:* Statistics Canada, 2014. CANSIM table 252-0052; Federal Bureau of Investigations, 2014.

## "Causes" of Violence

How do we account for the violence? Researchers have been preoccupied with trying to understand, explain, and control different forms of violent behaviour since criminology was established as a disciplinary study in the 1800s. Yet, aside from providing descriptive information and advancing a variety of theoretical interpretations, criminologists have not been able to explain what specifically causes violent crime.

Criminologists have, however, identified certain factors that can exacerbate the violent tendencies that lead to violent crime. These include the following:

1. abusive families
2. competing cultural values
3. the availability of firearms

4. gang motivation
5. human instinct
6. personality traits
7. regional values
8. substance abuse

Numerous articles can be found describing how these various factors contribute to violence in society, and many of them have been incorporated into theoretical explanations.

One of these explanations is the *deterministic model*, which focuses on human instinct and personality traits. This model was made popular by theorists such as Sigmund Freud and Konrad Lorenz, who argued that we possess a basic instinct for violence. Other explanations have focused on social structures (e.g. abusive families), social forces (e.g. gangs and regional values), and anomie (which can lead, for example, to substance abuse). However, no one theory has been able to completely explain the *etiology*—that is, the causes—of violence. As we have noted before, criminologists are increasingly aware that interdisciplinary approaches to explaining crime may prove most promising. To date, insufficient research has been conducted in this area to bear out whether this line of inquiry will prove fruitful. Nevertheless, it is incumbent on criminologists to explore new theoretical directions if violence, in its diverse forms, is to be curbed.

Let us now examine some of the trends and patterns of violent crime in Canada. We will begin with the most deadly of these: homicide.

## Homicide

**homicide**
The act of causing the death of another person, whether directly or indirectly, by an unlawful act or by negligence; culpable homicide is a criminal offence, while non-culpable homicide is not.

Under section 222 of Canada's Criminal Code, "a person commits homicide when, directly or indirectly, by any means, he causes the death of a human being." The law goes on to define specific elements of *culpable* and *non-culpable homicide*. In Canada, non-culpable homicides are those considered legally justified (e.g. those committed in self-defence), while culpable homicide refers to murder, manslaughter, and infanticide.

Students reading about homicide for the first time might ask, what is the difference between *homicide* and *murder*? Are they synonymous? While both terms pertain to the death of a human being caused by another, murder refers more narrowly to the unlawful, often planned, and deliberate taking of another person's life, whereas homicide is a more general term that, in addition to murder (both first- and second-degree), encompasses other ways of causing death, such as infanticide and manslaughter.

The *Criminal Code* divides homicide into four sub-categories: (1) first-degree murder, (2) second-degree murder, (3) manslaughter, and (4) infanticide. Aside from infanticide, the basis for placing murder in a subcategory is the offender's intent and the nature of the act that causes someone to die (see Box 9.4).

### Homicide Rates, Trends, and Patterns

Between 1990 and 2001, the homicide rate in Canada steadily declined and, after a small spike in 2005, has fallen to its lowest rate since the mid-1960s (Figure 9.4). Among the highlights from the most recent data in violent crime are the following (Perreault, 2012; Boyce et al., 2014; Boyce, 2015):

- Since 2000 there has been a shift away from firearms as the primary means of homicide: while gun-related killings still account for approximately two-thirds of homicides in Canada, the proportion of stabbing homicides has increased over the past 15 years.

---

| BOX 9.4 | **A CLOSER LOOK**<br>Categories of Culpable Homicide |

Section 222 of the Criminal Code distinguishes between culpable and non-culpable homicide. Non-culpable homicide includes deaths caused in self-defence and is not a criminal offence. On the other hand, culpable homicide is a criminal offence and includes murder, manslaughter, and infanticide:

- *First-degree murder* includes: (a) the planned, deliberate killing of another person; (b) the killing of an on-duty police officer or prison guard; (c) the killing of another person in the course of committing sexual assault, hijacking or terrorism, criminal harassment, or crimes on behalf of a criminal organization.
- *Second-degree murder* includes the unplanned but deliberate killing of another person, as well as all murder that falls outside the category of first-degree murder.

- *Manslaughter* is the unintentional killing of another person, even if it results from an intention to cause harm.
- *Infanticide* is the intentional or unintentional killing of a newborn child, through deliberate actions or through acts of omission (i.e. negligence).

Although these sound like well-defined categories, the distinctions between them—especially between first- and second-degree murder and between second-degree murder and manslaughter—are frequently subject to debate among law-enforcement officials and the courts.

> Why do you think law enforcement officials and the courts might find it difficult to clearly identify which type of murder they are dealing with?

---

- The majority of homicides continue to be committed by someone known to the victim, and approximately three-quarters of all homicides were solved in 2013.
- The risk of being killed by a stranger has remained relatively stable over the past decade, although the gap between murders by strangers and murders by friends/relatives/acquaintances has narrowed since 1981.
- The number of gang-related homicides increased dramatically between 1991 and 2008, followed by a slow decline since. In 2013, Saskatoon, Edmonton, and Winnipeg had the highest number of gang-related homicides.

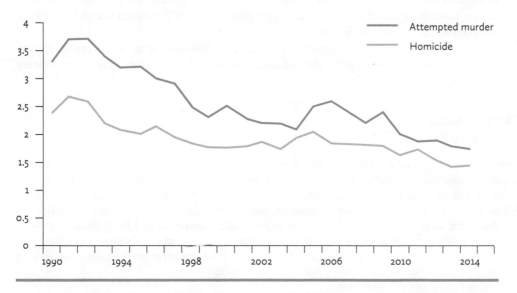

**Figure 9.4    Rates of Homicide and Attempted Murder in Canada, 1990–2014**

Note: Rates per 100,000 population.
*Sources:* "Canada's crime rate: Two decades of decline" (2014), *The Daily*: Canadian Megatrends (Ottawa, ON: Statistics Canada); Boyce, 2015.

| Table 9.3   Homicide Rates for Selected Countries, 2012 | |
|---|---|
| Honduras | 90.4 |
| Jamaica | 39.3 |
| South Africa | 31.0 |
| Mexico | 21.5 |
| Brazil | 25.2 |
| Rwanda | 23.1 |
| Barbados | 7.4 |
| Russia | 9.2 |
| United States | 4.7 |
| Chile | 3.1 |
| India | 3.5 |
| Canada | 1.6 |
| Greece | 1.5 |
| Hungary | 1.3 |
| France | 1.0 |
| Australia | 1.1 |
| Sweden | 0.7 |

*Source*: UNODC Homicide Statistics 2013.

- In 2014, and for the seventh year in a row, Manitoba had the highest provincial homicide rate (3.43), followed by Alberta (2.52) and Saskatchewan (2.13). The highest rates of homicide occurred in the three territories—Nunavut (10.93), Yukon (8.22), and Northwest Territories (6.88)—while the lowest rate belonged to Newfoundland and Labrador (0.38).
- In 2013, intimate-partner homicides remained well below the peak reached in 1991.
- In terms of homicides by occupation, taxi drivers were at the greatest risk of being killed, followed by police officers and jewellers.
- Internationally, Canada's homicide rate is well below that of countries such as Russia and the United States but generally greater than that of most European countries (see Table 9.3).

## Why Do People Kill?

How do we explain the most feared and most serious of violent crimes—murder? First, the wilful killing of one person by another can occur under a wide range of circumstances—during an episode of domestic violence, in times of war, as a result of postpartum depression, because of temporary insanity, in response to aggravating circumstances, as a hired killing, or for morally justifiable reasons (Fiske & Rai, 2015). Likewise, the motivation for killing another can vary significantly depending on the nature of the murder. Hence, Silverman and Kennedy (1992, p. 5) observe that while the media want simple answers to explain homicide rates to their viewers, listeners, and readers, the reality is that "these crimes need to be understood in all their complexity, especially when it comes to planning ways of preventing their occurrence."

This does not stop criminologists, and others, from speculating about the causes of murder, and whether the etiology of violence (including homicide) rests within the social structure

---

**BOX 9.5**  **A CLOSER LOOK**
### The Female Serial Killer

In 2012, police in Indonesia arrested a 29-year-old Filipino woman for killing and cannibalizing humans. During her interview, the woman confessed to having killed and eaten more than 30 girls as well as her husband. She had kept their meat in the refrigerator and had even served human meat to guests who were not aware of what they were eating.

This is a highly sensational and unusual case, but women serial killers are not a recent phenomenon. Yet relatively little is known about this category of serial killers. While researchers have developed typologies for male serial killers, there is insufficient data to offer similar explanations

for women who kill repeatedly. Hickey (1991) suggests that female serial killers represent only about 8 per cent of American serial killers and 16 per cent of serial killers internationally (the United States has been home to roughly 85 per of the world's known serial killers). Because they are no less lethal than their male counterparts but harder to detect, Hickey refers to them as *the quiet killers* (see Kelleher & Kelleher, 1998).

Why do you think we seem to know so little about female serial killers?

of society or within the personality or biological makeup of the perpetrator. Silverman and Kennedy (1992) suggest that there are two classes of theories that deal with homicide. The first class involves "individual social interaction and conflict." Among the theories under this classification are Hirschi's social control theory (see Chapter 8) and its newer derivations (for example, the general theory of crime and the power–control theory). Also included is routine activity theory (see Chapter 4). Theories in the second class focus on the level of society. Silverman and Kennedy explain that in accordance with these theories, crime is subject to the effects of the economy, inequality, and social disorganization in the environment. They cite a variety of studies that support the relationship between the presence of such factors and homicide rates.

Certain questions, however, remain unanswered by these explanations. For example, with regard to economic inequality, how extensive does this inequality have to be before murder rates increase? Also, what are some of the mediating preventive elements, and to what extent can economic inequality be used to explain the different types of homicide? Similar criticisms can be made of the social disorganization condition. For example, Blau and Blau (1982, cited in Silverman & Kennedy, 1992, p. 60) found a high correlation between rates of divorce and crime. But what is not clear is the level at which crime rates "suddenly" increase. For instance, to what extent do support groups for divorcees mitigate crime rates? These and other factors related to social disorganization have not been carefully studied.

Aside from these two classes of theories, there are a host of alternative approaches to explaining homicide. These include some of the micro-level approaches (such as the socio-biological perspective), biology-based explanations, psychological approaches that emphasize the role of moral frustration, and psychological theories that emphasize particular psychiatric disorders (see Rhodes, 2000; Totten & Kelly, 2002).

As with the two main classifications mentioned above, this last group of theories may be able to explain some types of murder, but each of these theories, given its narrow theoretical perspective, is limited in its coverage. Until criminologists begin to recognize the complexity of human behaviour and the importance of applying an interdisciplinary approach to the study of murder, or any crime, we will have to settle for interesting but limited theoretical explanations (see Box 9.6).

## Summary

Contrary to what one might imagine based on the media's coverage of sensational murders, homicide is still a comparatively infrequent phenomenon in Canada, with a rate that has, for the most part, been declining since the mid-1990s. Certain variables in the homicide rate—including geographic location, gender, and age—have remained fairly consistent for years.

Explanations for why people kill cover the spectrum from sociological and psychological to biological and socio-biological perspectives. In light of our current limited ability to understand and develop social policies that can reduce homicide rates, however, what may be needed is an integrated and interdisciplinary approach that deals with ecological factors, lifestyle factors, motivations, personalities, and social settings. But developing a model based on these principles to profile offenders remains a major challenge to criminologists (see e.g. Adams, 2007).

Only when criminologists gain a better understanding of the characteristics of people who kill (i.e. typology of killers) can they recommend, and subsequently implement, sound policies to apprehend, detect, punish, or treat offenders and to protect citizens. In the meantime, the criminal justice system should not put too much stock in profiling or relying on criminal typologies to identify and/or catch certain types of killers.

We will now turn our attention to the violent crime of sexual assault.

**general theory of crime**
A sociological perspective asserting that criminal behaviour is a product of defective socialization processes that make it difficult for a potential offender to exercise self-control.

**power–control theory**
A sociological perspective that focuses on how power dynamics, patriarchy, and gender role socialization within the family contribute to delinquency and crime.

BOX 9.6 **REALITY CHECK**

## Homicide and Capital Punishment

Capital punishment was officially abolished in Canada in 1976, 14 years after Arthur Lucas and Ronald Turpin became the last people to be executed in Canada. Since then there have been efforts to reinstate the death penalty for certain capital offences, notably in 1987, when the motion was introduced and debated in the House of Commons, and in 1999, when Conservative MP John Reynolds's private member's bill (Bill C-467) was narrowly defeated.

Toward the end of the twentieth century, a national survey revealed that between 65 and 75 per cent of Canadians supported the provisional use of capital punishment, for such offences as the killing of a police officer while on duty (Honeyman & Ogloff, 1996). The last Canadian executions, which took place at Toronto's Don Jail on 11 December 1962, were for offences involving the murders of law-enforcement officials (Turpin was hanged for shooting and killing a Toronto police officer, Lucas for killing an undercover narcotics agent).

As of 2015, capital punishment remains a legal sentence in 31 American states, and the question of whether to extradite prisoners in Canadian prisons to stand trial in states where the death penalty is in use has frequently been a contentious issue. One such case involved suspected American serial killer Charles Ng. Following an arrest for shoplifting in San Francisco in 1985, he escaped police custody and fled across the border to Calgary. Shortly after arriving in Calgary he was arrested for shooting a department store security guard who had caught Ng in the act of shoplifting. Ng fought extradition to the United States on the grounds that being deported to a country that uses the death penalty would violate rights enshrined in Canada's Charter of Rights and Freedoms. His constitutional challenge ended in 1991, when the Supreme Court ruled he could be returned to California. In 1998, he stood trial for the killing of 12 people. He was eventually found guilty on 11 counts of murder and was sentenced to death in 1999. As of 2015 Ng remains on death row in California's San Quentin State Prison, where he awaits death by lethal injection.

The notifications of the last two people to be executed in Canada were posted on the Don Jail door on the evening of 11 December 1962. Protestors demonstrated for hours outside the jail prior to the notification. When the declarations were posted, the crowd tried to push past police to read the papers before dispersing.

The last Canadian executed in the United States was Stan Buckowski of Toronto. After being convicted of killing a California woman, he was gassed in San Quentin in 1952. A number of Canadians are currently on death row in the United States, including Thomas McCray, Tony Dameron, Robert Bolden, and Ronald Smith. Smith, who pleaded guilty in the shooting deaths of two Montana men in 1983, initially asked for and was given the death sentence but then changed his mind and has been fighting the sentence ever since. His most recent appeal concerns the constitutionality of Montana's use of the drug pentobarbital for lethal injection (Graveland, 2015).

Should Canada honour its extradition treaty with the United States even in cases where it may result in the execution of an offender?

## Sexual Assault

As the examples in Box 9.7 illustrate, sexual assault cuts across all social classes and ages in North America. The perpetrator of a sexual assault can be unknown to the victim, but more commonly an assault is carried out by a relative, a neighbour, a co-worker, or even, as the sampling of recent cases in Box 9.7 shows, figures in positions of authority. Sexual assault is an issue that the courts may not be taking as seriously as they should, despite the legal measures that have been introduced.

In 1983, under Bill C-127, the Criminal Code was revised with the addition of sections 271 and 272, which replaced the offences of rape and indecent assault with the current offences of sexual assault, aggravated sexual assault, and sexual assault with a weapon. The new framework allows police to arrest a suspect when they have "reasonable and probable grounds" to believe that an assault was committed.

The Criminal Code recognizes three levels of sexual assault:

1. *Level 1 assault* (s. 271): There is no serious bodily harm or physical injury to the victim. This type of assault is also known as *common assault*.
2. *Level 2 assault* (s. 272): A greater degree of force or threatened force (e.g. with weapon) is used, and a degree of bodily harm, such as broken bones, bruises, or cuts, is involved. A slap across the face does not constitute a level 2 assault.

---

**BOX 9.7**   **REALITY CHECK**

## Whom Can You Trust?

### A JUDGE?

- In June 2004, a former British Columbia provincial court judge was sentenced to seven years on charges of sexual assault causing bodily harm and breach of trust. His victims, who ranged in age from 12 to 16, were Aboriginal girls from poor communities who had run afoul of the law (Saltman, 2008).

### A POLICE OFFICER?

- In July 2014, officials in Saint John, New Brunswick, revealed that a former police officer was likely responsible for sexually assaulting or abusing more than 260 children over a 25-year period. The victims—mostly boys but also some girls—were typically vulnerable children from low-income neighbourhoods who were lured to isolated sites with gifts and alcohol (Chai, 2014).

### A TEACHER?

- In August 2014, a Quebec physical education teacher was convicted of sexual exploitation and assault for carrying on a two-year sexual relationship with one of her male students, who was 15 at the time the relationship began (Woods, 2014).
- In May 2015, a private school teacher in Calgary was sentenced to five years in prison after pleading guilty to two sex-related charges involving a student who was 14 at the time their relationship began; the sentencing judge characterized the behaviour as "monstrous" (Martin, 2015).

### A PRIEST?

- In May 2015, a Romanian Orthodox priest in Toronto pleaded guilty to seven charges of sexual assault and admitted to having abused his position in the church to assault at least three other women, all in their twenties and thirties. In one instance, he threatened to curse for generations the family of a woman who had rebuffed his advances (Pazzano, 2015).

### A PARAMEDIC?

- In June 2015, a former paramedic was convicted of sexually assaulting a 71-year-old woman in her home in Hants County, Nova Scotia. The offender and his partner had been dispatched to the home to attend to the victim's husband after a fall (Fairclough, 2015).

### A DOCTOR?

- In February 2014, an anaesthesiologist at a Toronto hospital was sentenced to 10 years in prison for sexually assaulting 21 of his female patients while they were semiconscious on the operating table (Hasham, 2014).
- In April 2015, an Edmonton-area doctor was found guilty of sexually assaulting a female patient during a routine medical exam (CBC News, 2015a).

### A COACH?

- In June 2015, former Western Hockey League coach Graham James, who had already been convicted of molesting five of his players while with the Swift Current Broncos, pleaded guilty to another charge of sexual assault involving a different victim (CBC News, 2015b).

3.  *Level 3 assault* (s. 273): The victim is disfigured, maimed, wounded, or has his or her life endangered. This type of assault is also known as *aggravated assault*.

A host of other sexual offences are described or explained in the Criminal Code. They include sexual interference (s. 151); sexual touching (s. 152); sexual exploitation (s. 153); incest (155); anal intercourse (s. 159); bestiality (s. 160); and the related offences of committing indecent acts (s. 173) and corrupting morals (s. 163).

### Sexual Assault Rates

As with most conventional crime categories, the number of reported incidents of sexual assault declined by 4 per cent between 2011 and 2014, following a fairly consistent trend that parallels those for other types of violent since the 1993 (see Figure 9.5). When considering Figure 9.5(b), keep in mind that the absolute numbers are quite small: in 2014, the number of level 2 sexual assaults reported to police was just 319; the number of Level 1 sexual assaults reported was just 105. The vast majority of the 20,735 sexual assaults reported in 2014 were for the least serious class, shown in Figure 9.5(a).

As with all crimes in a country as vast and diverse as Canada, there were geographic differences. While most provinces and territories experienced a drop in the rate of reported sexual assaults between 2010 and 2014, Yukon experienced an increase of just over 20 per cent during that period, though it still had among the lowest number of actual recorded incidents in Canada. Indeed, one should be mindful that given the relatively small populations in the three territories, any small changes in the number of offences can result in dramatic shifts in the rate and/or percentage of change between years. Even so, the rate of Level 1 sexual assault per 100,000 population is far higher in the territories than in Canada overall (see Box 9.8). Consider that in 2014,

- there were 20,311 reported incidents of Level 1 sexual assault in Canada, for a rate of 57.15 per 100,000 population;
- there were 77 incidents in Yukon, for a rate of 210.90;

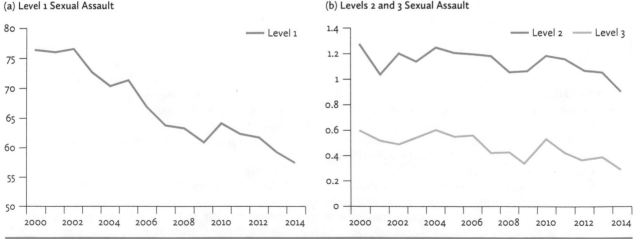

**Figure 9.5    Rates of Sexual Assault (Levels 1–3) in Canada, 2000–2014**

Note: Rate is per 100,000
*Source:* Statistics Canada CANSIM Table 252-0051.

## BOX 9.8 · REALITY CHECK

### How Can We Explain High Rates of Sexual Assault in the North?

While one might assume that the high number of sexual assaults in the North occur exclusively among the region's Indigenous people, the facts sometimes speak to other problems in the three territories. For example, in 2012 in Baker Lake, Nunavut, a long-serving RCMP officer, who is not Aboriginal, was charged with sexually assaulting a local woman while he was on duty ("Nunavut Mountie," 2013). The officer's account differed from that of the alleged victim, and given that there was no other evidence—there were no surveillance cameras at the Baker Lake detachment—the officer was ultimately found not guilty. However, the presiding judge chastised the guard for showing a lack of reasonable judgment for undertaking a search of the prisoner without a female officer present, and cautioned that if more female guards weren't properly trained, the RCMP should expect more charges of excessive force and sexual assault ("Nunavut Mountie," 2013). The case highlights the way that Aboriginal women in the North are vulnerable by virtue both of their gender and of their Aboriginal status.

Why do you think Aboriginal women might be at greater risk of sexual assault than women in mainstream Canadian society? What other women in Canada might be at greater risk for sexual assault?

- there were 143 incidents in Northwest Territories, for a rate of 327.81; and
- there were 180 incidents in Nunavut, for a rate of 492.00 (Statistics Canada CANSIM Table 252-0051).

According to the 2004 General Social Survey, women between the ages of 15 and 24 were significantly more likely to be victims of sexual assault than those aged 55 and over. Alarmingly, despite falling rates of sexual assault overall since 1993, the number of sexual violations against children increased by 6 per cent between in 2012–13 and again in 2013–14, with year-over-year increases in seven provinces and territories (Boyce, 2015, pp. 3 & 35). The category of sexual violations against children includes sexual interference, invitation to sexual touching, sexual exploitation, luring a child via a computer, and making sexually explicit material available to a child to facilitate any of the aforementioned offences. It does not include child pornography, which is treated as a separate category of offence.

### Interpreting Trends in Reported Sexual Assaults

While the overall decline in the rate of sexual assault is encouraging, the fluctuating trends need to be seen in the context of several factors that either promote or discourage reporting of sexual assault incidents. For example, there are a number of Canadian studies, corroborated by results from the GSS, indicating that sexual assault is greatly underreported (Brennan & Taylor-Butts, 2008; Perreault & Brennan, 2010). The reasons victims of sexual assault give for not reporting these crimes include the following:

- "The incident wasn't important enough" to report.
- The incident was "of a private matter."
- The incident was being dealt with "in another way." (Brennan, 2012)

Moreover, surveys conducted by various sexual assault clinics across the country have found that many victims lack faith and trust in the justice system, which is why they do not report sexual assaults. Cultural barriers to reporting crime may also play a role in some communities.

Recent legislative changes have made it easier to report sexual attacks, a development that could produce an increase in the number of reported incidents; however, these same changes have also broadened the sentencing options and increased the severity of punishments, thereby adding to the deterrent effect. Overall, the research does not support the premise that the law alone can account for slight fluctuations in the trends. Instead, some recent work by Johnson (1996a, pp. 146–7) suggests a number of alternative explanations for the fluctuations, including the following:

- The 1970s and 1980s saw significant changes in the social, economic, and political status of women, making them more likely to report cases of sexual assault.
- The media during this time gave increasing attention to the rights of victims, especially women.
- Sexual assault/rape support centres became more accessible to more women, offering counselling services and information on how to report offences to police.
- An increasing number of hospitals added specialized teams trained to support and assist victims of sexual assault.
- Victims of childhood sexual assault were encouraged to come forward as adults to report crimes that had taken place many years previously.
- Women's groups lobbied intensively for the passage of the rape reform legislation.

Yet in spite of the Criminal Code amendments and all the public awareness programs and support services, the gap between official counts and Statistics Canada's Violence Against Women (VAW) survey findings reflects the fact that "very few cases of sexual assault are

Now an annual event marked around the world, the White Ribbon Campaign began in Canada in the wake of the École Polytechnique shooting as a response by men to the issue of male violence against women. Resources dedicated to supporting victims of sexual assault and domestic violence appear to be growing, yet cases of sexual assault continue to be greatly underreported. How might we explain this?

Graham Hughes/The Canadian Press

reported to the police" (Johnson, 1996a, p. 143). This is also in spite of the federal government's designation of 6 December as the National Day of Remembrance and Action on Violence Against Women, in memory of the 1989 shooting of 14 women by a lone male shooter at Montreal's École Polytechnique.

## Characteristics of Perpetrators and Victims of Sexual Assault

The characteristics of the sexual predator accord with the generally held notions about such offenders. For example, in 2002, over 40 per cent of sexual offenders were drinking at the time of the incident. Women under the age of 18 were the most common victims of sexual offences (61 per cent), and most sexual assaults (64 per cent) occurred in a private residence. Most victims were assaulted by someone they knew—an acquaintance (41 per cent of cases), a friend (10 per cent), or a family member (28 per cent). Only 20 per cent were assaulted by strangers.

Meanwhile, males made up only 15 per cent of victims of sexual assault overall. Boys under the age of 12 made up 29 per cent of the male victims (CCJS, 2003, 23(6)). More recently, a 2012 report by Statistics Canada revealed that although it was the second year in a row of a reported decrease in sexual offences, about 14,000 children and teens reported that they had been victims of sexual offences. Children and teens account for more than half (55 per cent) of all victims. Of these victims, 72 per cent were victims of level 1 sexual assaults. As in 2002, girls were more likely than boys to report abuse, with 341 of every 100,000 Canadian girls reporting abuse, compared to 75 per 100,000 Canadian boys. Also, similar to 2002, in 88 per cent of cases, the victim knew the accused ("Police-reported sexual offences," 2014).

In a survey conducted by Angus Reid on behalf of the Canadian Women's Foundation, 20 per cent of respondents, of all ages, said they believed that women provoke their own sexual assaults in cases when they've been drinking or wearing provocative clothing (CWF, 2013); 23 per cent of those holding this view were between the ages of 18 and 34. The study has also found that 15 per cent of Canadians believed women could encourage or provoke sexual assault by flirting with a man (CWF, 2013). The persistent pattern of victim blaming is a factor that hinders many victims from coming forward and reporting their victimization. However, while not implying a causal link, a number of studies have shown that young women who have many sex partners are at greater risk of being sexually assaulted than those who have fewer sex partners (Fergusson, Horwood, & Lynskey, 1997).

Efforts to explain sexual violence vary greatly, but the more common theoretical orientations are those that relate sexual assaults to the offenders' personal pathologies. For example, in a meta-analysis of over 80 recidivism studies, two Canadian researchers (Hanson & Morton-Bourgon, 2005) found that among adult and adolescent male sexual offenders, the primary predictor of sexual assault was antisocial orientation (i.e. antisocial personality, antisocial traits, and a history of rule violation). The study also revealed that the risk factors for persistent sexual assault offenders was slightly different from those for one-time offenders, and included negative family backgrounds (Hanson & Morton-Bourgon, 2005). Overall, the analysis revealed that the risk factors, although having a relatively low predictive value, are nevertheless related to the offender and not the victim.

**recidivism**
The act of reoffending (esp. repeatedly) on the part of a convicted criminal.

Sociological studies, meanwhile, point to such factors as the social learning processes within lower-class subcultures, where violence may be seen as a way of life, and the mass media, which often depict the sexual exploitation of women in ways that reinforce such actions (Gregory & Lees, 2012). Does violence really breed violence? Nettler pursued this line of inquiry in his 1982 book *Killing One Another*. The anecdotal evidence gleaned from watching sporting events or kids in the playground during recess would lead us to conclude that, yes, violence does breed violence! Drawing on the social learning model, Nettler came to the same conclusion.

Conversely, feminist theorists (see Chapter 8) consider sexual violence to be the product of deep-rooted patriarchal traditions in which men are encouraged to dominate all aspects of life, including women. In this view, women are seen as little more than property to be used and sexually exploited. In line with such a perspective, various studies have shown that women who have attained higher levels of education tend to be at greater risk of sexual victimization than those with less education (Crowell & Burgess, 1996). Why should this be so? One explanation is that men who commit sexual violence feel particularly threated by better-educated and more successful women, who are less likely to behave with the subservience these offenders consider appropriate in a patriarchal society. Thus, the behaviour of these offenders comes from a desire to subjugate successful women and assign them to the inferior role they believe is appropriate.

Even biology and sociobiology have offered their interpretations of sexual violence. Drawing on the notion of evolution, sociobiologists assert that men have an innate drive to create offspring. The lower the degree of certainty of doing so, the greater the man's tendency to turn to inappropriate sexual behaviours such as rape, child molesting, voyeurism, or collecting pornographic material (see Holmes, 1991). More recently, McKibbin, a leading authority on sexual violence, argued that something more nuanced than this evolutionary psychological approach was necessary to understand the complex social, biological, psychological, and evolutionary factors that should be taken into account when trying to understand and respond to people who commit rape (McKibbin et al., 2008).

**date rape**

A form of sexual assault that involves unlawfully coercing sexual interactions with someone against his or her will within the context of a dating relationship.

Unfortunately, the varied explanations provide little consensus on which to base new social policy to curb the problem of sexual violence. Furthermore, some of the "newer" forms of sexual assault—such as elder abuse, child abuse, and date rape—present unique challenges to researchers. Take the issue of date rape, which has been subject to growing awareness and discussion in recent years (see Box 9.9). Although Statistics Canada has conducted an annual family violence survey since 1995, there have been no recent national data on assaults by a date or boyfriend since the 1993 General Social Survey reported that 12 per cent of women had been assaulted by a dating partner. Meanwhile a widely reported Internet statistic of

---

**BOX 9.9**

**A CLOSER LOOK**

## "No Means No" and Affirmative Consent: Student-Led Campaigns to Fight Dating Violence

In North America, the issue of date rape first gained front-page attention when Katie Koestner went public with her story in 1991. She had been sexually assaulted by a fellow student at a US college.

In the early 1990s, the Canadian Federation of Students started the "No Means No" campaign to shine a light on the epidemic of dating violence among teens and young adults, and to put a stop to date rape on college and university campuses. The "No Means No" approach, which emphasized that "no" represents an unequivocal rejection of sexual advances, has since been superseded by the notion of affirmative consent, which requires the person initiating sexual contact to gain the other party's consent to continue. Affirmative consent recognizes that *not saying no* is not the same as *saying yes*, and it makes the person initiating a sexual encounter responsible for ensuring that it

is consensual, rather than placing this responsibility on the person being approached.

Although initially designed to raise awareness on post-secondary campuses, the affirmative consent campaign has grown and is now part of the curriculum in some high schools across the country. However, because each province's sex ed curriculum is determined by its own provincial Ministry of Education, there is no national approach to raising awareness about consent and the dangers of dating violence.

What is the differences between "no means no" and affirmative consent?

Darryl Dyck/The Canadian Press

While there have been national pushes for university campus sexual assault prevention programs in the United States, in Canada the issue is being tackled provincially. What steps have been taken at your school to deter or prosecute perpetrators of sexual assault and to support victims of sexual assault?

questionable reliability suggests that between 50 and 80 per cent of teens in the United States have known someone who was involved in a violent dating relationship (see e.g. New York City Alliance, 2012). Somewhere between these two statistics lies the true extent of date rape, which criminologists have yet to fully uncover.

In summary, while incidents and rates of sexual assault have generally declined since the mid-1990s, sexual violence remains a pressing issue. Campaigns to combat and raise awareness about sexual assault—in the home, in public, and on campus—have had the double effect of reducing the prevalence of this crime while emboldening victims to come forward and report cases of sexual assault, including those that happened many years earlier. The result is a cloudy picture for criminologists, who are encouraged to embrace this complex phenomenon from a multidisciplinary perspective—for as all the evidence has shown, there is no one explanation or solution.

We will now turn our attention to the violent crime of robbery.

## Robbery

On 10 September 1904, Canadian Pacific Railway train No. 1 was robbed just after it left Mission, BC. This was Canada's first train robbery, and the ring leader, Billy Miner, was credited with using the phrase "hands up" (Veltri, n.d).

In his book on robbery in Canada, Desroches (2005) describes robbery as one of the most feared crimes common to large urban centres because of "its sudden nature and the threat of death or serious injury." Robbery entails a double element of fear: fear of losing one's property and fear of suffering physical harm. Next to murder, robbery easily attracts our attention, perhaps because of its lack of predictability. But robberies are not that common: in 2013, robberies accounted for only about 6 per cent of all violent crimes in Canada (Boyce et al., 2014), and from 2013 to 2014, the robbery rate fell by over 6 per cent, from 66.1 (per 100,000 population) to 58.9 (see Figure 9.6).

Robbery, as defined in section 343 of the Criminal Code, has certain broad characteristics. Section 343 states that

Every one commits robbery who:

(a) steals, and for the purpose of extorting whatever is stolen or to prevent or overcome resistance to the stealing, uses violence or threats of violence to a person or property;

(b) steals from any person and, at the time he steals or immediately before or immediately thereafter, wounds, beats, strikes or uses any personal violence to that person;

(c) assaults any person with intent to steal from him; or

(d) steals from any person while armed with an offensive weapon or imitation thereof.

This definition clearly reflects the notion that robbery is an act of violence. Normandeau (1968) pointed out that in the United States, in contrast, robbery is more commonly associated with property-related crimes or burglary than with violence. There robbery is defined as "the unlawful taking or attempted taking of property that is in the immediate possession of another by force or threat of force or violence and/or by putting the victim in fear" (Normandeau, 1968, p. 64). Desroches (2005, p. 6) further notes that the penal code of some states defines robbery as a property crime rather than an offence against the person.

The unfortunate news is that there are many different ways a person can be robbed, including the following:

- commercial robbery
- highway robbery

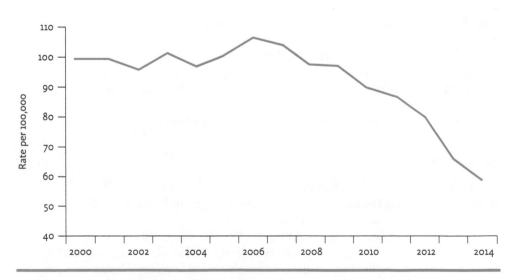

**Figure 9.6    Robbery Rate in Canada, 2000–2014**

*Source:* Statistics Canada CANSIM Table 252-0051.

- street robbery (i.e. mugging)
- armed robbery (i.e. with force, using a weapon)
- strong-armed robbery (i.e. with force but without using a weapon)
- identity theft
- drug-related robbery
- home invasion (see Box 9.10).

Research shows that the various types of robbery differ not only in terms of practicalities, such as the method used (or *modus operandi*), but also in terms of offender traits and motivation for the crime.

In this section, in addition to examining recent trends with regard to robbery in Canada, we will look at some of the different types of robbery and of robbers. We will see that certain types of robberies are more prevalent than others, and that not all robbers are "cut from the same cloth."

## Characteristics of Robbery and Robbers

As Erickson (2003), among others, has noted, most robbers are not specialists who engage in robbery as their only criminal activity. Most are amateur petty criminals and opportunists. However, as with any type of crime, there are some who are specialists at robbing and are careful with their planning and selection of targets (Willis, 2006). According to Dauvergne (2010), some 90 per cent of all robberies are committed by young males (aged 12–24), and money is the item most commonly stolen (37 per cent). Other popular items include jewellery and personal electronic devices—items that are easy to sell for quick profit.

In 2014, there were 20,924 robberies in Canada, for a rate of 58.87 per 100,000 people—a 47 per cent decline from 2006, when the robbery rate peaked at 106.36 (see Figure 9.6 above). A detailed breakdown of robberies committed in 2008 (Dauvergne, 2010) showed that while commercial or institutional robberies (of banks, gas stations, jewellery stores, liquor stores, and other retail outlets) had declined, residential robberies and robberies committed in public had increased or remained stable. Over half of the robberies in 2008 occurred on the street or at an outdoor location, and commercial robberies accounted for around 39 per cent of all robberies (see Figure 9.7).

The use of firearms in committing robbery is on the decline: firearms were used in 20 per cent of robberies committed in 1998 and just 14 per cent committed a decade later, in 2008 (Dauvergne, 2010). And as with all other types of crime, there are regional variations: while the robbery rate declined in seven provinces between 2013 and 2014, it went up in Saskatchewan, Newfoundland and Labrador, and Prince Edward Island (which, nevertheless, had just 27 reported robberies—the lowest total of any province; Boyce, 2015, Table 6).

## "Causes" of Robbery

Clermont (1996) has suggested that a high unemployment rate among males in the 15–24 age group might explain the robbery trends. Tracking Canadian robbery rates and the unemployment rates between 1978 and 1993, Clermont showed that in the early 1980s, an increase in robbery rates coincided with a rise in unemployment for young males. Similarly, as unemployment rates dropped in the late 1990s, so did the robbery rates.

What Clermont did not take into account are the different types of robberies. For example, it is important to distinguish between opportunistic robberies—those committed on impulse, sometimes just for excitement—and "professional" robberies, committed by serial burglars

**BOX 9.10**

### A CLOSER LOOK
## How Common Are Home Invasions?

In January 2014, two men broke into the home of a Surrey, BC, family, where they attacked the adult residents and "terrorized" the couple's three children. The family may have been targeted because of their East Indian background: the RCMP allege that, based on the evidence, the modus operandi was very similar to that used for home invasions in South Asia, and concluded that the crime may have been committed by someone of East Indian background against a family that was well known within the East Asian community. Gold, cash, and passports were reportedly stolen (Luis & Puri, 2014).

Because of the sensational nature of such incidents, home invasions frequently make front-page news. But how common are they? A statistic offered freely online—particularly by alarm companies—suggests there have been 289,200 home invasions annually in Canada "for the past five years"—a shocking number! However, a closer look suggests this is not a credible statistic at all: in 2014 in Canada, for example, there were just 151,921 cases of breaking and entering (Boyce, 2015), and home invasions make up but a small subset of that offence.

The home invasion is a relatively recent phenomenon in criminological research. In a 2002 bulletin issued by the Canadian Centre for Justice Statistics, Kowalski (2002) noted that because there was then no agreed-upon definition, it was difficult to accurately measure the incidence of home invasions in Canada. Nevertheless, that same year, Canada's justice minister, Anne McLellan, introduced amendments to the Criminal Code to toughen sentencing provisions for home invasions. Accordingly, section 348.1 of the Criminal Code now states that for a person convicted of breaking and entering,

> the court imposing the sentence on the person shall consider as an aggravating circumstance the fact that the dwelling-house was occupied at the time of the commission of the offence and that the person, in committing the offence,
> (a) knew that or was reckless as to whether the dwelling-house was occupied; and
> (b) used violence or threats of violence to a person or property.

In other words, in setting the sentence for someone convicted of breaking and entering, the court would have to take into account whether the offender knew or might have known that the residents were home and whether the offender used force. It is important to note that this is a sentencing provision, and home invasion is not recognized as a separate crime within the Criminal Code.

By 2010, there was still no universally accepted definition for home invasion, as a Statistics Canada report (Dauvergne, 2010) explains:

> Residential robberies are sometimes associated with the term "home invasion." Using data from the UCR survey, home invasion can be defined in two ways. The first "narrow" definition simply includes all robberies that occur in a residential dwelling. . . . The second "broad" definition includes robberies that occur in a residential dwelling as well as break and enters that have an associated violent offence.

Using the "narrow" definition, the report indicated that the rate of police-reported home invasions had increased by 38 per cent between 1999 and 2005 before levelling off for the rest of the decade. The rate for the "broad" definition, while higher, showed a similar pattern of increase to 2005 before achieving a stable rate (Table 9.4). Overall, the total number of home invasions in Canada in 2008, based on these rates, was roughly 7,400 using the "broad" definition and 3,050 using the "narrow" definition—a far cry from 289,200! Statistics Canada has not released data on home invasions since 2010.

| Table 9.4    Rates (per 100,000) of Police-Reported Home Invasion, Canada, 1999–2008 | | |
|---|---|---|
| Year | "Narrow" Definition[1] | "Broad" Definition[2] |
| 1999 | 7.5 | 19.3 |
| 2000 | 7.2 | 19.4 |
| 2001 | 7.4 | 20.4 |
| 2002 | 8.1 | 21.0 |
| 2003 | 8.6 | 20.7 |
| 2004 | 9.0 | 21.3 |
| 2005 | 10.3 | 22.8 |
| 2006 | 9.4 | 21.8 |
| 2007 | 9.2 | 22.2 |
| 2008 | 9.1 | 22.1 |

[1] Robbery within a residence.
[2] Robbery in a residence or break-and-enter in a residence with any violent offence.
*Source:* Statistics Canada, Canadian Centre for Justice Statistics, Incident-based Uniform Crime Reporting Survey.

Why do you think home invasions are not treated as a separate offence in Canada's Criminal Code?

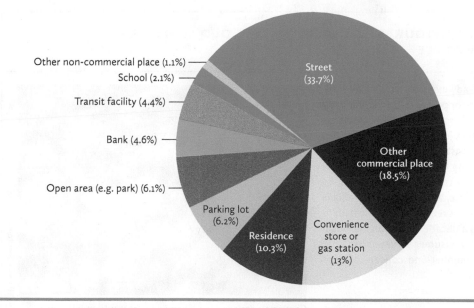

**Figure 9.7   Police-Reported Robbery by Location, Canada 2008**

Notes. Examples of "Other commercial places" include grocery stores and pharmacies. Examples of "Other non-commercial places" include community centres, hospitals, and churches. "Residence" includes private dwelling units and other private property structures.
*Source:* Adapted from Dauvergne, 2010, Chart 5.

who depend on robbery for their livelihood. There are also robberies committed by compulsive or "addict" robbers. The profiles of the individuals committing each of these types of robbery may differ. Clermont also did not demonstrate that young men between the ages of 15 and 24 were directly accountable for the changes in the robbery rate. More recently, Neumayer (2005) provided data to support the notion that the incidence rates of robbery does *not* relate directly to changing levels of social inequality.

Some criminologists have approached robbery from a perspective similar to that of routine activity theory. They have found that robberies are more likely to occur in areas having certain "geosocial attributes"—a feature that lies somewhere between an offense characteristic and an area attribute (see e.g. Dunn, 1976). This approach is somewhat interdisciplinary, as it acknowledges both environmental factors and social attributes within an area (see Box 9.11). For example, in 2014, Manitoba had the highest provincial rate of robberies at 119 per 100,000 population; PEI had the lowest, at 18 per 100,000 (Boyce, 2015, Table 6). This shows that the two provinces have very different geosocial attributes that make robbery a far more likely occurrence in Manitoba than in PEI. Meanwhile Wright and Decker (1997) found that personal robberies tend to involve victims who are likely to produce a higher return for the robbers' efforts, and Miller, Cohen, and Wiersema (1998) found that robbers tend to choose their victims based on perceived vulnerability.

In a comprehensive overview of robbery in Canada, Desroches (2005) concedes that we know very little about what motivates someone to commit robbery and what motivates a robber to target a particular victim. Using rational choice theory, Desroches reasons that an offender's rationality is "limited to what seems reasonable at the time, given their financial needs and the limited alternatives and opportunities open to them" (2005, p. 106). But why, then, do some people turn to certain forms of criminal activity while others in the same predicament do not? How does one measure "rationality" and "what seems reasonable," and what constitutes a robber's "financial needs"?

## BOX 9.11    FACTS AND FIGURES    IDENTITY THEFT: OLD WINE IN A NEW BOTTLE?

For all their benefits, rapid advances in technology have brought ever-increasing ways for people to be victimized by crime. Among these is the crime of identity theft, which, as an RCMP slogan warns, "doesn't just happen in the movies." It has been described as the fastest-growing form of robbery today, and indeed, identity fraud was among the few non-violent offences that increased from 2013 to 2014, by approximately 8 per cent (Boyce, 2015, Table 5). Canadians now spend on average 600 hours reclaiming their lost identity, as opposed to 175 hours a decade ago, at an individual cost of up to $2,000. In fact, consumer surveys show that identity fraud remains the number-one concern of consumers today (idAlerts, 2013).

Pabkov/Shutterstock.com

How concerned are you about identity fraud? What measures, if any, do you take to guard against it?

Consumers are constantly warned to protect their PINs when withdrawing cash or paying by debit card. How realistic is this as a preventative method, given the sophisticated ways of stealing and using someone else's PIN?

The perceived seriousness of robbery is reflected in the fact that more than 80 per cent of those convicted of robbery are incarcerated. Of those, over 75 per cent are placed in federal institutions (Desroches, 2005). Rather than diminishing rates of robbery, we are witnessing an increase in new forms of robbery—carjacking, sea piracy, and so on—that will be reviewed in the next section.

A Canadian report from 1995 indicated that "the age of onset of criminality for armed robbery offenders was, on average, 12, while occasional armed robbery offenders didn't tend to begin their criminal career until 15" ("A profile of robbery," 1995, p. 3). The study further pointed out that association with robbers and/or thieves, "both during adolescence and during adulthood" seemed to be more strongly correlated to the likelihood of a person's engaging in that form of crime than for other types of offenders. These findings are consistent with what we might expect based on differential association theory. However, this interpretation may be too simplistic, as the report fails to clearly define what is meant by "association"; nor does it explain how "association" was empirically measured.

In summary, robbery tends to capture the public's and mass media's interest because it carries the double-edged threat of physical injury and loss of property. There is much that can be said about the nature, extent, characteristics, and motivations of robbery, based mostly on correlations between robbery and various aspects of social, individual, and cultural variables.

However, we have also seen that no criminological theory can clearly link a causal explanation to any specific set of variables. For example, why is it that female robbers' chief motivation is financial gain? Why do female robbers tend to act in response to external circumstances such as intoxication, financial need, or peer pressure (see Fortune, Vega, & Silverman, 1980)? None of the criminological theories appears able to provide a clear answer. When it comes to social policy and robbery prevention, criminologists can offer little—and what they do offer should be used with considerable care (see Box 9.12).

| BOX 9.12 | **A CLOSER LOOK**<br>The Vancouver Robbery Prevention Program for Convenience Stores |
|---|---|

In the early 1970s, convenience store robbery was becoming a serious concern. The convenience store chain 7-Eleven (first opened in 1927) became one of the first companies to conduct studies to learn why convenience stores had become prevalent targets and what could be done to diminish their risk of being targeted. Based on the findings, employees were taught how to deter robberies by reducing the amount of cash kept in the register and removing signage from store windows to improve visibility of the cashier's desk from the street. These measures were based on a modified environmental crime prevention model.

After implementing the changes, the chain observed a 30 per cent decrease in robberies in its study area of southern California. The Robbery Information Program (RIP) for convenience stores quickly spread, and Vancouver became one of the first cities in Canada to adopt it. The RIP was designed to proactively deter store robberies and to make it easier for employees to identify thieves.

The pilot study had a positive impact on those stores that participated. These stores averaged lower financial losses per incident. As well, there was a marked decline in the number of injuries to staff, and staff were generally better informed about the procedures that should be followed in case of a robbery. One of the limitations of the RIP was a low rate (less than 20 per cent) of store compliance (Roesch & Winterdyk, 1985).

The concept of robbery prevention has since expanded and has led to the use of security systems like those used in homes and closed-circuit TV surveillance cameras. Although there are no comparable data in Canada, there are over 135,000 convenience stores in the United States with some 100 million visits per day, and convenience stores still account for around 8 per cent of all robberies. And while the robbery incident rates have declined since the 1970s, given the number of convenience stores, there is still room for researching and improving crime prevention strategies.

What measures could variety stores adopt to decrease robbery?

In the final section, of this chapter, we will explore some of the 'newer' and less conventional forms of violence.

## "New" Forms of Violence

So far, we have examined the more traditional forms of violent behaviour. In recent years, however, there has been an increase in other forms of violence. Here we will concentrate on honour killing, hate crimes, sea piracy, and terrorism.

### Honour Killings

Canada's demographic and cultural mix is more diverse today than it has ever been. Since seeing a dramatic increase in the arrival of immigrants during the early 1900s, Canada has been one of the most receptive Western countries when it comes to welcoming immigrants. These immigrants come from all corners of the world, bringing cultural practices and traditions that greatly enrich Canada's social fabric. However, some practices may be in conflict with Canadian norms, values, and laws, presenting challenges not only for new immigrants but also for Canada's legal system.

In the early 2000s, the subject of honour killings came into public consciousness, primarily through the media, which reported some sensational accounts of domestic homicide carried out supposedly in an effort to preserve a family's reputation. A notable instance, mentioned briefly at the start of this chapter, occurred in 2009, when a Montreal-area couple and their son, all recently arrived from Afghanistan, were charged with first-degree murder in the deaths of the couple's three daughters and the father's first wife. During the trial, it was alleged

**honour killing**
Homicide committed against a relative (usually female) who has supposedly brought dishonour upon the family, typically through a relationship with a person of whom the family does not approve.

that Mohammad Shafia and Tooba Yahya strongly disapproved of the daughters' behaviour, particularly the eldest daughter's relationship with a young Pakistani man, which they viewed as immoral and an act of dishonour upon the family name. The trial featured expert testimony from a witness who linked what the judge would later call a "twisted sense of honour" to the Shafias' cultural and religious beliefs (Mehta, 2015). In 2012, Mohammad, Tooba, and their son Hamed were found guilty of four counts of first-degree murder.

According to Professor Amin Muhammad (2010) at Memorial University in Newfoundland, there have been over a dozen known honour killings in Canada since 2002. By contrast there have been hundreds of such killings in the United States and Great Britain (Boesveld, 2012). The phenomenon is reportedly more widespread in Islamic parts of the Middle East. For example, according to Onal (2008, p. 253), between 2000 and 2005 in Turkey, 2,806 women were victims of honour killings while 5,375 others committed suicide "in the face of family pressure."

The Shafia case, and others like it, raise a number of sensitive but important issues. For instance, is it right to draw connections between supposed honour killings and a certain strict interpretation of the Qur'an and the body of Islamic law known as Sharia? In 2015, the Shafias appealed their murder convictions, citing, among other things, the "highly prejudicial" testimony of the expert witness and rejecting any claim that they "had a disposition to commit family homicide as a result of their cultural background" or "a different set of cultural beliefs" (Mehta, 2015). Muhammad points out that there is in fact no justification in the Qur'an for killing of any kind, but that some followers of Sharia law have twisted the wording of passages that refer to "protecting" women, taking them as licence to control women. Another question is whether honour killings should be viewed separately from other acts of domestic violence.

While honour killings may not be pervasive in Canada, they speak to the need for criminologists to be sensitive and aware of the pioneering work that Thorsten Sellin did on culture conflict in the late 1930s. Sellin (1938) argued that value clashes can become root causes of criminal behaviour. Part of the challenge is how to identify such potential conflicts. How many suicides of women with origins in cultures where honour killings are acknowledged practices are the result of dishonouring the family? How do we respect cultural differences while ensuring compliance to the norms and values of Canadian society? How do families steeped in a cultural tradition retain their family's integrity, especially among like-minded community members?

## Hate Crime

The conventional violent crimes covered earlier in this chapter are acts of an interpersonal nature that involve targets regardless of their ethnic background, physical characteristics, religious beliefs, or skin colour. Hate crime is an interpersonal violent crime that is motivated by bias against victims who may be characterized by a particular physical or social trait.

According to Statistics Canada (Allen, 2014), in 2012, there were 1,414 hate-motivated incidents reported to police. The most targeted groups were homosexuals and black people. Some 51 per cent of all hate crimes were racially or ethnically motivated, while 30 per cent were motivated by religious hatred, and 13 per cent were related to sexual orientation (Allen, 2014). Given that visible minorities make up roughly 38 per cent of the population and that same-gender relationships have increased by 42 per cent between 2010 and 2013 (Allen, 2012; Allen & Boyce, 2013), there is little question that the face of Canada is changing quickly, bringing the extremes of, on the one hand, greater awareness and acceptance, and on the other hand, greater resistance in the form of extreme prejudice and hate.

Hate crimes are addressed in sections 318 and 319 of the Criminal Code, which concern the use of propaganda to promote genocide and the communication of ideas to incite hatred

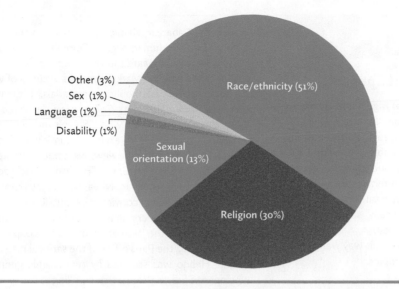

**Figure 9.8    Motivation for Police-Reported Hate Crimes in Canada, 2012**

*Source:* Statistics Canada, Canadian Centre for Justice Statistics, Incident-based Uniform Crime Reporting Survey.

of any identifiable group. In 1996, in response to the growing concern about hate crime, section 718.2 of the Criminal Code, which deals with principles of sentencing, was amended to allow courts to take into consideration whether the offence was "motivated by bias, prejudice, or hate based on race, national or ethnic origin, language, colour, religion, sex, age, mental or physical disability, sexual orientation, or any other similar factor" (s. 718.2(a)(i)). The amendment now allows courts to regard hate motivation as an aggravating circumstance when setting a sentence. While hate crime is generally classified as a crime of violence, it can also be a property-related offence.

Hate crimes can be divided into three types based on the motives for the crime:

- *Thrill-seeking hate crimes.* Occasionally, a group of hate-mongers decides to "raise a little hell" by terrorizing ethnic or other minorities and/or violating their property. The perpetrators derive a sadistic sense of satisfaction from threatening and/or terrorizing their targeted group. In June 1997, the family dog of a Filipino sailor seeking refugee status in Canada was killed and the family threatened. Why? On arriving in Halifax, the sailor's fellow Filipino crew members had reported to authorities that they had witnessed six Taiwanese officers throwing three stowaways overboard in the year before (Purdy, 1997). The attack on the family dog was an attempt to scare a visible-minority family out of the community and silence the sailors so they would not testify in court against the perpetrators, who, apart from harbouring racial hatred, found it exciting to instill fear in the family.

- *Reactive hate crimes.* When an "outsider" is seen as a threat, he or she may become the victim of a reactive hate crime committed by someone acting out of a misguided sense of righteousness and loyalty to the community. For example, in November 2009, a Calgary teen spray-painted swastikas and anti-Semitic messages on a Holocaust memorial and two synagogues (Lungen, 2010); the teen pleaded guilty to charges including promoting hatred. The rate of reactive hate crimes may increase with high-profile events involving the targeted group. For instance, some US states have reported increases in anti-gay hate

| BOX 9.13 | WHAT DO YOU THINK? |
|---|---|

## Hate Crime or Freedom of Speech?

Section 2 of the Canadian Charter of Rights and Freedoms guarantees freedom of expression to all Canadians. However, this freedom is not without limits. Publicly expressed opinions must be reasonable and within the public interest; opinions expressed publicly can be considered hate speech if they are extremely severe and hateful, unless they are good-faith interpretations of religious doctrine or opinions expressed ironically, sarcastically, or to encourage public discussion (Butt, 2015).

Is restricting freedom of speech in this way warranted? Consider some of the following examples.

- In the early 1980s, an Alberta public school teacher and Holocaust-denier, James Keegstra, was charged with hate speech for preaching anti-Semitism in his classes. His 1984 conviction was overturned by the Alberta Court of Appeal, but in 1990 the Supreme Court of Canada upheld the conviction, arguing that infringing on Keegstra's freedom of expression was constitutional if it prevented the dissemination of hate propaganda.
- In 1992, the Supreme Court overturned the conviction of another Holocaust-denier, Ernst Zundel, who was charged with spreading false news after publishing a pamphlet called "Did Six Million Really Die?" In this case, the court found that because the pamphlet, though seriously flawed, was unlikely to incite violence against an identifiable group, the conviction contravened Zundel's right to freedom of expression.

- In 2007, the Canadian Islamic Congress sent a complaint to the Ontario Human Rights Commission concerning articles that appeared in *Maclean's* magazine. The author of the articles, Mark Steyn, was accused of writing provocatively Islamophobic materials. Ultimately, the federal Human Rights Commission dismissed the complaint, stating that while Steyn's articles were "obviously calculated to excite discussion and even offend certain readers," the views were not "extreme" as defined by the Supreme Court ("Human rights," 2008).
- In 2010, two brothers in Nova Scotia, Nathan and Justin Rehberg, were convicted of public incitement of hatred (as well as criminal harassment) for setting a burning cross on the lawn of an interracial couple.
- In January 2015, the Paris office of the satirical magazine Charlie Hebdo was stormed by two Islamic gunmen, who opened fire on the newsroom, killing 12 and wounding 11. The attack was intended to avenge the publication of cartoons featuring the prophet Muhammad. In the wake of the shooting, many Canadian news outlets chose not to publish the controversial cartoons.

Arguably, hateful expression can have a traumatic impact on its (directly or indirectly) intended target. Hate/bias expressions, like bullying, can create fear and even incite further violence.

Why do you think Canadian newspapers chose not to reprint the controversial Charlie Hebdo cartoons? Do you think the decision sent the wrong message about freedom of speech or the right message about censoring material that some would consider offensively anti-Islamic and even blasphemous?

crimes following landmark court rulings advancing LGBT rights (Clark-Flory, 2015), and some commentators have attributed the 2012–13 increase in anti-Muslim hate crimes in Canada to the rise of the Islamic State (ISIL or ISIS) overseas (Connolly, 2015).

- *Mission hate crimes.* White-supremacist groups, such as the Ku Klux Klan, Identity Church, Aryan Nations, and various skinhead groups, think it is their duty to rid the world of those who are not white. They see it as their mission, and their right, to seek out and eliminate people who they believe threaten their religious beliefs, racial purity, and power. Neo-Nazi skinheads, for example, have been associated with "gay bashing," "Jew bashing," and attacks on certain East Indian groups. Marc Lépine, who killed 14 women at Montreal's École Polytechnique, believed he was "fighting feminism" by targeting women who were becoming educated to enter professions traditionally dominated by men. Like a number of mission hate offenders, Lépine committed suicide after carrying out his so-called mission.

Although hate crime in Canada arrived with European colonization, the concept of hate crimes has arguably always been a part of societies characterized by social, cultural, and/or ethnic diversity. Examples of hate crime as it is defined in the Criminal Code can be found in the earliest French settlers' dealings with Aboriginal people after Samuel de Champlain established the first permanent settlement at Quebec in 1608 (Carrigan, 1991).

Can the roots of hate crime be found in social, individual, political, or biological traits? The research provides no clear answers. As a result, policy-makers face major dilemmas when attempting to address the problem. For example, amendments to the Criminal Code are not likely to affect individuals who are driven by a warped sense of social justice or natural superiority. Educational programs may sensitize some of us to certain issues, but the history of prejudice and hostility is a long one.

Whatever its cause, hate-motivated violence offers a gloomy commentary on humanity. Hate crime deserves our concerted attention so that constructive social policy measures can be introduced to combat the problem.

## Robbery on the High Sea

When we hear about piracy and armed robbery at sea, most of us probably think of incidents occurring in East Africa (in the Gulf of Aden and off the coast of Somalia) or Southeast Asia (in the Western Indian Ocean). However, armed robbery of this kind also occurs closer to home. In 2012, a panel of naval and legal experts at a conference in Halifax warned that "piracy not only costs the shipping industry billions of dollars each year and threatens international and national safety but has had dire effects on the crews, many of whom are treated for post-traumatic stress disorder" (Nanji, 2012).

So how common are cases of piracy in Canada? Fortunately, Canada has not had any recent cases of high-seas piracy. However, Canadian ports such as Halifax have had ships arrive in harbour bearing the scars of having been attacked at sea. There are also recorded cases of Canadians working on international oil drilling and exploration platforms who have been subjected to attacks by "sea pirates" (Nanji, 2012).

Canada's Foreign Affairs Department has contributed over $75,000 to combatting high-sea piracy internationally and since 2008 has deployed at least three brigades to assist in fighting sea pirates. As Nanji points out in his article, citing government officials, while we might not have sea pirates in Canadian waters, because of our global involvement in fighting this non-conventional crime, Canadians are impacted both directly and indirectly.

One of the biggest challenges facing the international community with regard to sea piracy is which nation-states can and/or are willing and able to assume responsibility for prosecution? For criminologists, it is interesting to explore the factors that appear to trigger incidents of sea piracy. For example, Geiss and Petrig (2011) point out that in the case of Somalia, such acts were likely triggered by the "illicit overfishing by foreign vessels and dumping of toxic waste into Somalian territorial waters, combined with general economic hardship," which forced the local fishermen to explore other ways of making their living.

## Terrorism

Canadian criminologist Gwynn Nettler (1982:227) describes terrorism as "the calculated instilling of fear through cruelty, killing, or the threat of both as a means to obtain or maintain power." In addition to being an act of violence, terrorism is also classified as a political crime, as terrorists usually reject the goals and objectives of their society and seek to instill their own goals and objectives. Stephen Schafer (1976) called terrorists "convictional criminals" as a way of characterizing the political convictions underlying their illegal behaviour.

Overall, attempts to define and describe terrorism have been somewhat broad and subject to interpretation. For example, if you were an ardent environmentalist and put spikes

**terrorism**
The use of propaganda, violence, or dangerous acts against an organization or state in order to obtain concessions or rewards for a deeply held personal or political cause.

into trees in an effort to deter logging in an area, could you be considered a terrorist? Or, if a group commits a robbery in order to support their revolutionary cause (as have members of the white-supremacist organization Aryan Nations), should the act be treated as a crime of political terrorism or simply as an armed robbery? In the aftermath of the September 11 terrorist attacks, Canada, along with many other countries, introduced legislation to deal with acts of terrorism. In 2001, Bill C-36 enabled the courts to deal more effectively with terrorist threats. The bill created the Terrorist Financing Act and amended the Criminal Code and other acts. In addition to providing clearer definitions of terrorism and terrorist groups, these changes allowed the government to restrict the financing of terrorist groups and prompted new strategies for identifying and curbing money laundering. In May 2015, the Conservative government, with help from the Liberals, passed Bill C-51, the Anti-Terrorism Act, which gave the Canadian Security Intelligence Service more power to gather and act on information, while also making it a crime to encourage someone to carry out an act of terrorism. Many of these legal changes comply with the various United Nations conventions on terrorism. For example, Operation Apollo, established in 2001 by the Canadian government, involved committing some 2,000 troops (air, sea, and land) to combatting terrorism on foreign soil.

Whatever form they take, politically motivated crimes against a sovereign state have occurred throughout history. Some of the more recognizable people to be considered political criminals in their time include Socrates, Joan of Arc, Martin Luther King, Jr, and Canada's own Louis Riel, who led Métis on the prairies in a campaign against the federal government during the late 1800s.

Recent cases of terrorism on Canadian soil include the violent campaign waged by the Front de Libération du Québec, which involved the kidnapping in 1970 of two politicians, one of whom was killed, and two attacks that occurred within days of each other in 2014: the killing of Warrant Officer Patrice Vincent in Saint-Jean-sur-Richelieu, Quebec, and the shooting of Corporal Nathan Cirillo as he was guarding the National War Memorial on Parliament Hill. The largest mass murder in Canada's history was the 1985 bombing of Air India flight 182 from Toronto to New Delhi, which killed all 329 passengers and crew; Inderjit Singh Reyat, a Canadian national associated with the Sikh militant group Babbar Khalsa, remains the only person convicted in the deadliest act of terrorism in Canada's history. Box 9.14 describes other recent examples of international terrorism.

In recent years, terrorism has not only increased internationally but has also evolved into new and deadly forms. Today, terrorists have access to and occasionally use such deadly weapons as chemical and biological warfare; many can also use nuclear threats. Cyberterrorism is an emerging phenomenon with the potential to wreak havoc on government and commercial infrastructure. Overall, however, the number of recorded incidents of terrorism in Canada declined from 126 to 72 between 2012 and 2013, representing a drop of 44 per cent (Boyce et al., 2014).

### Typologies of Terrorism

The difficulty in defining terrorism is reflected in the varied typologies used to describe it. Simple dichotomous models include Jeffery's (1990) classification according to the target of the terrorists' violence: (1) *violence against foreigners* and (2) *violence against the citizens of one's own country*.

Paul Smythe (1996) offers a three-tiered model, classifying terrorist groups as follows: (1) *ethnic separatists* and *emigrant groups* (e.g. Armenians and Sikhs); (2) *left-wing radical groups* (e.g. the Squamish Five in British Columbia); and (3) *right-wing racist groups* (e.g. Heritage Front groups). These groups are usually a combination of Jeffery's groups 1 and 2 as they are not averse to using violence, and all of Smythe's groups actively recruit new members.

---

**BOX 9.14**

**A CLOSER LOOK**
**Some Recent Examples of Terrorism**

- March 1995: Shoko Asahara, leader of Japan's Aum Shinrikyo ("Supreme Truth") sect, places several canisters of deadly sarin nerve gas in the Tokyo subway. The gas kills 10 people and injured over 5,000. The Asahara incident is an early example of a new type of terrorism perpetrated by what are socially characterized as extremist groups.
- April 1995: Timothy McVeigh, an anti-government terrorist, detonates a truck full of explosives in front of a government building in Oklahoma City, Oklahoma, killing more than 160 people and injuring over 600.
- November 1998: Steve West, Alberta's energy minister, lashes out against so-called eco-terrorists, who have been targeting the oil and forestry industries as well as electrical utilities across the province. Between 1996 and 2001, there are approximately 160 acts of eco-terrorist vandalism causing $2 million in damage. The frequency of such incidents declines markedly after 2003, to next to no cases by 2012 (Su & Yang, 2014).
- September 2001: Muslim extremists crash four commercial jets in the United States: two into New York's World Trade Center; one into the Pentagon in Washington, DC; and one into a farm field in Pennsylvania. Close to 3,000 people die in the carefully planned 9/11 attacks.
- November 2008: In a coordinated series of shooting and bombing attacks, members of the Pakistan-based militant group Lashkar-e-Taiba carry out a four-day campaign of terror in Mumbai, India, killing more than 160 people and wounding over 600.

- 2011–15: The Middle Eastern state of Syria is rife with car bombings, rocket attacks, and other terrorist killings carried out by various *Takfiri* (Sunni Muslim) groups, notably the Islamic State of Iraq and the Levant (ISIL). The attacks cripple the country's infrastructure and lead eventually to all-out civil war.
- July 2011: Anders Breivik, a xenophobic, far-right extremist, kills 8 people with a car bomb in the Norwegian capital of Oslo before shooting 70 participants at a summer camp run by the Workers' Youth League.
- April 2014: Boko Haram, a Muslim extremist group that has been carrying out terrorist kidnappings and killings in northeastern Nigeria since 2009, seizes 276 girls from a school in the town of Chibok. Some are fortunate to escape, but over 200 remain in captivity, possibly sold into slavery, forced into marriage, or killed.
- April 2015: Gunmen representing Al-Shabaab, an extremist militant group based in Somalia, storm a university in Garissa, Kenya, killing 147 students, most of them Christian.
- November 2015: In a series of coordinated attacks, Islamic gunmen and suicide bombers kill 130 people and wound 360 in Paris and its suburb Saint-Denis. Locations of the attacks include a number of popular entertainment venues, including the Stade de France, the Bataclan concert hall, and cafes and restaurants.

Virtually every day, a terrorist attack of some form—typically a suicide bombing or a car bombing—takes place somewhere in the world.

---

Finally, Johnathan White (2013) suggests five fairly broad types of terrorism: (1) *revolutionary terrorism*, whose perpetrators use violence to invoke fear in those in power (e.g. the Palestinian Liberation Organization and Iranian-backed Hezbollah); (2) *political terrorism*, which is directed at specific individuals or groups who oppose the terrorists' ideology (e.g. Aryan Nations and other supremacy-oriented groups); (3) *nationalistic terrorism*, whose perpetrators are intent on promoting their own minority ethnic or religious factions (e.g. the Provisional Irish Republican Army); (4) *non-political terrorism*, which champions particular religious or social causes (e.g. abortion groups, Greenpeace, Animal Liberation Front); and (5) *state-sponsored terrorism*, which tends to involve repressive political regimes that rely on force and violence to force compliance (e.g., the death squads in Nigeria, Brazil, Guatemala, and Iraq, among others).

Regardless of the typology used, attempts to control terrorism through law or the use of force have usually not resulted in satisfactory resolutions. In addition, as Smythe (1996, p. 19) notes, the face of terrorism is changing; today, there is "faction sponsored terrorism;

An Aryan Guard supporter at a White Pride rally in Calgary. Racially motivated hate crimes in Canada are thankfully not common but can be disturbing reminders that there is work to be done to understand what causes people to participate in mission-motivated hate crimes, and how to prevent these crimes.

| Table 9.5    Typologies of Terrorism | | |
|---|---|---|
| **Theorist** | **Method of classification** | **Categories** |
| C.R. Jeffrey | Target of violence | 1) violence against foreigners<br>2) violence against the citizens of one's country |
| P. Smythe | Source of motivation | 1) ethnic separatists and immigrant groups<br>2) left-wing radical groups<br>3) right-wing racist groups |
| J. White | Source of motivation (broader definitions) | 1) revolutionary terrorism<br>2) political terrorism<br>3) nationalistic terrorism<br>4) non-political terrorism<br>5) state-sponsored terrorism |

Jeff McIntosh/The Canadian Press

issue-motivated terrorism; and crime-related terrorism," as well as state-sponsored terrorism, environmental terrorism, and criminal terrorism, to name just a few emerging forms. Terrorism will likely be a major area of interest to criminologists in the future as cultures, ideologies, and religious ideas continue to come closer together in our global community.

The emergence of the "new" forms of violence provides impetus for criminologists to attempt to better understand the purpose, meaning, characteristics, and theoretical causes underlying such acts. Violence seems to be evolving and spreading throughout society. We must recognize the problems that new forms of violence pose, work toward understanding their causes, and develop social policy and support programs to ameliorate the problems.

In the aftermath of 9/11, the international community, including Canada, introduced both legal and justice-oriented measures to combat the potential threat of terrorism. Canada's Liberal government introduced the Anti-Terrorism Act in 2001, granting government and the courts greater powers to fight and prosecute cases of terrorism. Controversially, it lacked a "sunset clause," or a provision that would set a time limit on the period for which the rights of an individual suspected of being involved in terrorism could be suspended. In 2015, the Conservative government passed the controversial Bill C-51, which expanded the scope of Canada's intelligence-gathering agency CSIS to monitor suspected terror groups.

In addition to expanding its anti-terrorism legislation, in 2003 the government formed the new super-ministry of Public Safety and Emergency Preparedness in an effort to consolidate resources and streamline the efforts of combatting terrorist threats. This initiative involved combining the Canadian Border Services Agency and the Canada Customs and Revenue Agency in an effort to have a more effective system for responding to potential terrorist threats. The new super-ministry of Public Safety was formed in 2005 and in many respects is similar to the American Department of Homeland Security. Public Safety Canada now includes five different criminal justice service agencies, all in the name of trying to ensure the safety of its citizens.

A 2006 report prepared by the Fraser Institute, a conservative think tank, sharply criticized Canada's response to the threat of terrorism and called for a number of policy reforms (Collacott, 2006). Specifically, it pointed to Canada's limited efforts at preventing terrorist fundraising, to its lax immigration laws, and to its lack of commitment to building bridges with the Muslim community.

As the nature and forms of terrorism continue to evolve, the question for criminologists may be whether we ever learn to predict its occurrence and ultimately control or prevent it. In doing so, we must determine where to draw the line between, on the one hand, protecting Canadians and honouring human and civil rights, and on the other, suspending rights and freedoms in the interest of combatting terror.

---

**BOX 9.15          WHAT DO YOU THINK?**

### Trying to Define a Terrorist

Perhaps you saw the 2012 movie *Zero Dark Thirty*, which portrays a slightly distorted account of the hunt for and eventual killing of Osama bin Laden (1957–2011), considered the mastermind behind al-Qaeda's September 11 terrorist attacks. Having evaded capture for over a decade, bin Laden was finally located and killed in May 2011. In a survey poll conducted by the Pew Research Centre shortly after bin Laden's assassination, 63 per cent of Pakistanis said they disapproved of his killing (Pew Research Center, 2011). In his various speeches and issued *fatwas*, bin Laden had condemned the Americans for plundering Muslim resources and interfering in the politics of Islamic countries. He was an idealist who was labelled a terrorist in many parts of the Western world but who commanded a strong and loyal following among his followers.

Was bin Laden a terrorist or a crazed idealist?

## Summary

- Although the rate of violent crime has fluctuated over time, statistics indicate that since the mid-1990s, the rates of most violent crimes have been in decline. The rates today are, however, greater than those first recorded in the 1960s.
- Not all types of violent crime have declined. And, aside from traditional forms of violent crime, we are witnessing new forms of violence for which official statistics either are not yet kept or are very limited. Media reports often reflect the fact that violence takes many forms and can be found almost anywhere.
- Criminologists tend to prefer viewing violent crime in traditional legalistic terms, using conventional disciplinary explanations to describe it. Yet, as reflected elsewhere in this text, criminologists may have to deviate from these traditional frameworks in order to begin viewing and interpreting violent crime as a problem rooted in behaviour.
- Describing the extent and nature of violence in our society is not enough: criminologists must embrace an interdisciplinary approach toward understanding the dynamics of violence and violent behaviour and in this light examine the various forms violence can take.

## Discussion Questions

1. What can the violent crime statistics tell us about the crime trends and patterns in Canada? How has the picture changed in recent years? Why do you think it has changed?
2. Who is primarily responsible for committing violent crimes? Are there any common denominators? What are some of the major explanatory models for the different types of crimes covered in this chapter?
3. Are there any common causal factors that can be used to explain violent crimes?
4. Why are the crimes covered in this chapter referred to as *conventional* crimes? How do they differ from *non-conventional* crimes?
5. Collect at least a dozen articles related to "new" forms of violence. What do they tell us about the nature and extent of the problem? What kinds of solutions, if any, are offered? Do these forms of violence pose a more serious threat to society than traditional forms?

## Key Concepts

| | |
|---|---|
| abduction | honour killing |
| date rape | power–control theory |
| general theory of crime | recidivism |
| hate crime | terrorism |
| homicide | violent crime |

## Weblinks

**Statistics Canada: Crime and Justice**
This page allows you to browse Statistics Canada data on a range of specialized topics, including correctional services, family violence, and legal aid, or consult one of the many crime-related Stats Can publications, including *Juristat*. Some databases may involve a cost, but most college and university libraries have free access for academic purposes.
http://www5.statcan.gc.ca/subject-sujet/theme-theme.action?pid=2693&lang=eng&more=0&MM

**A Handbook for Police and Crown Prosecutors on Criminal Harassment**
This online handbook, published by the Canadian Department of Justice, contains information on the offence of criminal harassment, including guidelines for police and Crown prosecutors on investigating and prosecuting cases of criminal harassment.
www.justice.gc.ca/eng/rp-pr/cj-jp/fv-vf/har/part1.html

**Crime Statistics in British Columbia, 2014**
The BC Ministry of Justice's Police Services Division provides an annual detailed overview of crime in the province. Search other provinces for similar websites.
www.pssg.gov.bc.ca/policeservices/shareddocs/crime-statistics.pdf

**Stalking Resource Center**
The American National Center for Victims of Crime maintains this site, which offers information on stalking laws by state, statistics on the incidence of stalking crime, and resources for victims.
www.victimsofcrime.org/our-programs/stalking-resource-center

**United Nations Office on Drugs and Crime**
The UNODC has information on a range of international crime topics as well as resources for those keen to participate in various anti-crime campaigns.
www.unodc.org

You can use your favourite search engine to easily locate violent crime statistics for virtually any country, as well as reports on any type of violent crime.

# Chapter 10

## Property-Related Offences

Jacob Lund/Shutterstock.com

Greater Vancouver is proportionally [given its size and population] the
worst metropolitan area in Canada for property crime . . . [costing] industries,
businesses, government and insurance organizations more than $128M annually.

VANCOUVER BOARD OF TRADE (2003)

## Learning Outcomes

After reading this chapter, you should be able to

- Identify the major forms of property crime and discuss their general trends;
- Understand that there is currently no absolute explanation of the causes of property crime;
- Appreciate the importance of using crime data to understand property crime trends and patterns, explain crime, and recommend social policy;
- Defend the importance of applying an integrated and interdisciplinary approach when using crime data; and
- Recognize the benefit of using comparative criminology to lend further insight into the study and control of property crimes.

While violent crimes may be somewhat foreign to most of us, most people can readily relate to property crime. For example, have you ever taken something that didn't belong to you? Perhaps when you were younger you pinched some change from your parents' piggy bank or snuck some alcohol from the liquor cabinet; maybe you went so far as to take a chocolate bar from the neighbourhood convenience store without paying. Property crime ranges from these relatively innocent acts to far costlier and sometimes more sophisticated—even professional— activities such as shoplifting, bank robbery, vandalism, graffiti, break-and-enter, forgery, and arson. As with violent crime, criminologists have studied the wide range of property offences in an effort to understand what motivates them and how best to prevent them. After all, property crime is the most common and prevalent form of criminal activity documented by official crime statistics (see Figure 10.1).

Property crime is unique among criminal activity in that it can carry a degree of prestige, bringing attention and even acclaim to those who practise it. Think of some of the outlaws and gangsters whose exploits have been immortalized in popular film and literature:

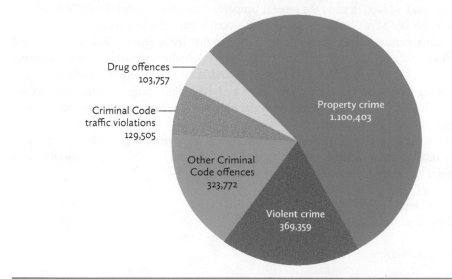

**Figure 10.1   Police-Reported Crime for Selected Offences, Canada 2014**

*Source:* Adapted from Boyce, 2015, Table 5. Statistics Canada, Canadian Centre for Justice Statistics, Incident-based Uniform Crime Reporting Survey.

## BOX 10.1     PROFILE  Ken Leishman, "Gentleman" Bandit

In the 1960s and 1970s, a Manitoba bank robber named Ken Leishman acquired almost folklore status and was dubbed "the Flying Bandit" and "the Gentlemen Bandit" by the media because of his reputation for never harming anyone during his holdups. After his capture and imprisonment, he even managed to escape—twice—gaining greater notoriety and celebrity.

Following his release in 1975, the community of Red Lake, Ontario, named him president of the town's chamber of commerce, and he set up his own air service business. He died while conducting a mercy flight in 1979, and his remains were never found (Schroeder, 1997). Leishman's life and times were later chronicled in *Bandit*, a book by Wayne Tefs (2011).

University of Manitoba Archives & Special Collections, Winnipeg Tribune fonds, PC 18 (A.81-12), Box 9, Folder 299, Item 11.

What is it about bank robbers and other property criminals that we find so compelling?

Butch Cassidy and the Sundance Kid; Jesse James; Bonnie and Clyde; Ma Barrow; John Dillinger; Baby Face Nelson; Pretty Boy Floyd; the Stopwatch Gang. The list goes on and on.

**property crime**

The broad range of offences involving property, including breaking and entering, fraud, theft, and motor-vehicle theft.

As we saw in the last chapter, violent crime, while it captures a lot of public and media attention, occurs infrequently compared with crimes against property. In 2014, property crime accounted for almost 80 per cent of all non-violent crimes reported to the police (not including traffic offences) and occurred at a rate almost three times that of violent crime (3,096 per 100,000 population for property crime, versus 1,039 for violent crime; Boyce, 2015, p. 18 and Table 2b). Nationally the rate of property crime has been decreasing: the 2014 rate of 3,096 was 40 per cent lower than the rate of 5,123 recorded 10 years earlier (Boyce, 2015, Table 1b; see Box 10.2). In fact, in 2014 the rate for property crime was almost the same as what it had been in the late 1970s and early 1980s (CCJS, 2004, 24(6)). The 10-year drop in the rate of property crime mirrors a dramatic 39 per cent drop in the Crime Severity Index (CSI), from a rate of 104.1 in 2004 to 66.7 in 2014 (Boyce, 2015, Table 1a). At the regional level, while all provinces except BC (+7 per cent), Alberta (+1 per cent), and Manitoba (0) experienced a decline in property crime from 2013 to 2014, Saskatchewan had the highest property crime rate (5,628) and Quebec had the lowest rate (2,101), with the national rate being 3,096 per 100,000. The same regional trend applied for the CSI (Boyce, 2014, Table 2a).

Crimes against property take various forms, but all have an economic element to them, since they involve either the theft and/or destruction of property. In this chapter, we will focus on five major conventional forms of property crime:

- break-and-enter
- fraud and identity theft
- theft
- motor-vehicle crime
- arson

For each of these forms we will examine offender and victim characteristics, the impact it has on society, and the relevant policy implications and prevention strategies.

---

**BOX 10.2** **FACTS AND FIGURES** THE PRICE OF YOUR IDENTITY

We live in a society that values material goods, and for the most part, we value who we are. News stories about people fighting, and even killing, to illegally obtain certain goods (for example, running shoes, cellphones, vehicles) are not infrequent, and these stories can prompt us to take extraordinary measures to protect our material goods. Increasingly, we are also going to great extremes to protect what might be considered our greatest non-material good: our identity. We use complicated passwords, we safeguard our PINs, and we would seldom share these codes or write them down for fear of having them found and used to access our personal information. Yet while the overall rate of property crime has fallen over the past decade, identity fraud and identity theft are offences on the rise, with the rate of identity fraud increasing by 8 per cent between 2013 and 2014 (Boyce, 2015, p. 18). Owing in part to the dramatic increase in identity fraud and theft, in January 2010 the Uniform Crime Reporting survey was amended to include these new violations, which had previously been recorded under the general category of fraud. Identity theft is the illegal collection or acquisition of another's personal information so that it can be used for criminal purposes;

identity fraud is the illegal use of another's personal information for fraudulent purposes.

Though fraud and identity fraud are quite different, they both involve theft and reflect society's preoccupation with wealth, material goods, and clandestine ways to obtain them. Just as we enjoy the things we actually possess, so, too, do we derive satisfaction from our ability to purchase things. Both our possessions and our ability to obtain possessions become targets for criminals. And while property crimes are legally considered less serious than violent crimes, victims of theft and identity theft often suffer a tremendous sense of personal violation and emotional distress.

Have you ever had your home broken into or had something personal stolen from you? How did it make you feel? Victims of theft sometimes feel a sense of distress out of proportion to the value of the item(s) taken—was this the case for you?

---

## Break-and-Enter

The terms break-and-enter (B&E) and burglary are often used interchangeably. Is there a difference? Essentially, burglary is an older common-law term, still in legal use in the United States and England; in Canada we use the modern term *break-and-enter* (see Box 10.3). Legally, they are comparable, except that in the United States a burglar might use force if the individual encounters someone in the course of committing the crime. Technically, in Canada, such an act would be classified as a robbery, which is a theft associated with violence. A break-and-enter, meanwhile, does not have to involve theft: it can be associated with any indictable offence, such as vandalism.

In Canada, the critical difference between robbery and breaking and entering is the presence, or lack, of a person-to-person confrontation. Unlike robbery, a break-and-enter does not involve face-to-face contact or the threat of force because it is undertaken when the resident or owner of the property entered is not present. For this reason, breaking and entering is considered a property crime, whereas robbery, which involves contact between victim and offender, is considered a violent crime (see Chapter 9). The term *home invasion* (sec. 348.1 Criminal Code) is sometimes used to characterize a break-and-enter carried out by an offender who knows the residents of the dwelling are or may be home and who uses forced confinement, violence, or threats of violence (e.g. assault or battery) against them. Technically this sort of crime would be considered robbery, since it involves the threat or use of force; for this reason, it is not considered a separate offence in Canada's Criminal Code, but is merely an aggravating circumstance to be taken into account during sentencing (see Box 9.10 in Chapter 9).

**identity theft**
The act of illegally obtaining an individual's personal information for criminal purposes.

**identity fraud**
The illegal use of the name and personal information of another person (living or dead) for fraudulent purposes.

**break-and-enter (B&E)**
A form of property crime that involves the illegal entry or attempt to trespass into a building or dwelling without permission and with the intent of committing a theft or an act of violence.

BOX 10.3

### A Closer Look
### Redefining Burglary

Under old English common law, burglary was an offence only if it was "breaking and entering of a dwelling during the night with the intent to commit a felony." Canada used this classification and description until the law was amended in 1985. The new law no longer specified that burglary had to be in a dwelling (that is, businesses and other non-residential properties were included), and the amendment omitted the specific time frame of "night time" (Carrigan, 1991). Today in Canada, the term *burglary*, although no longer used in the Criminal Code, is still used informally to refer to such offences as damage to buildings, safety deposit boxes, safe boxes, etc.

Compared to robbery then, breaking and entering is a more passive, non-violent crime that might not even necessarily involve stealing. Does that mean that victims of break-and-enters are less victimized than the victims of other crimes? Hardly. Apart from the considerable emotional distress caused by having one's home or property violated, the victim of a break-and-enter may face significant financial costs. Consider a couple of very high-profile cases. In 1995, the official residence of then prime minister Jean Chrétien and his wife was broken into. Following a lengthy investigation into the property's security system, in 1998 the residence was given a significant "security boost" at a cost of $417,629 (Naumetz, 1999).

In 2004, vandals broke into the historic Lougheed Mansion in Calgary, entering through an unlocked window. They caused $150,000 worth of damage (Myers, 2004). Indeed, breaking and entering is an offence that carries a significant cost.

## Patterns and Characteristics in Break-and-Enters

In 2014, there were 151,921 total police-reported cases of breaking and entering, the lowest number in over 35 years (Boyce, 2015). In fact, since 1993, when there were 406,421 incidents, the number of B&E's has fallen by a remarkable 63 per cent (see Figure 10.2).

Winnipeg Tribune fonds, PC 18 (A.81-12), Box 9, Folder 299, Item 11.

Why might a building such as Lougheed House, located in the Beltline district of downtown Calgary, be targeted for break-and-enter? What type of burglar would be attracted to this target?

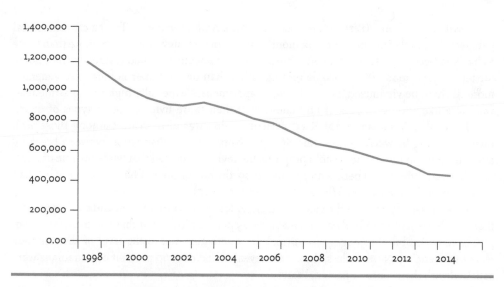

**Figure 10.2    Break-and-Enters in Canada, 1998–2014**

*Sources:* CCJS, 2004, 24(5):11; Statistics Canada CANSIM Table 252-0051.

There are three categories of B&E's: residential, business, and those involving other "non-residential private structures, such as detached garages, sheds, and storage and transportation facilities" (CCJS, 2004; Boyce et al., 2014). Unfortunately, Statistics Canada does not regularly provide a breakdown of break-and-enters using these categories. However, based on available data, we know that since 2000, residential break-and-enters have outnumbered commercial B&E's, and that both categories are in marked decline (see CCJS, 2004, 24(5)); Perreault & Brennan, 2010).

How can we account for the significant drop in cases of breaking and entering reported to police? Part of the reason may lie in the increasing use and improved quality of security devices and services available to residential and commercial property owners (Gannon & Taylor-Butts, 2006). Fedorowycz (2004) suggests that rising insurance deductibles could also result in fewer incidents being reported to police, therefore creating a misleading impression of the true extent of property crime. To overcome this "dark figure" of property crime, it is helpful to consider self-report findings such those obtained from the General Social Survey (GSS). Data from self-reported victimization portion of the 2009 GSS (conducted only once every five years) suggest that between 2004 and 2009, the number of break-and-enters in Canada actually increased 21 per cent, although the 2009 rate was roughly equal to the rate in 1999. Nevertheless, the difference in the trends found in GSS self-reported B&E's and police-reported B&E's is worth noting (Perreault & Brennan, 2010).

Research in the United States suggests that the rate of break-and-enters is on the decline in that country as well. In addition to the factors noted above for Canada—more widespread use of superior security systems, and a reluctance to make insurance claims for minor B&E's—the research suggests that the decline in the number of break-and-enters can be attributed to growing use of crack cocaine. The illegal street drug is a cheaper alternative to heroin, which has been partly responsible for high rates of property crime among addicts looking for cash to support their habit (Hagan, 2013). In fact, based on per capita rates of breaking and entering, Belleville, Ontario, and Prince George and Langley, BC, rank within the top 10 per cent of all North American cities, based on data from 2010 ("Canada's most dangerous cities," 2011).

According to 2009 data from the Uniform Crime Reporting survey and the General Social Survey, Canadians were more likely to be victims of a break-and-enter if they rented rather than owned their home (Perreault & Brennan, 2010). And interestingly from a criminological perspective, people who had lived six months or less in their new home were more than twice as likely to become a victim of a house break-in than someone who had resided in their home for ten years or more. While people renting rather than owning their homes were generally more likely to be victimized, people living in apartments—especially high-rise apartments—were less likely to be victims of household theft than those living in other types of dwelling (Perreault & Brennan, 2010). Risk of victimization was also greatest among those with incomes falling between $40,000 and $99,000. Note here the distinction between breaking and entering and theft of household property: the review indicated that while the rate of B&E's had changed little overall between 1999 and 2009, the rate of theft of household property had gone up over the same decade (Perreault & Brennan, 2010).

Not surprisingly, most of the victims felt anger followed by frustration and confusion after their residence had been broken into. Just over 25 per cent indicated that the crime had compromised their ability to engage in normal daily activities due to the level of distress they were experiencing. Nevertheless, the survey revealed that over 60 per cent of Canadians were satisfied with their sense of personal safety.

In a unique study, Wright and Decker (1994) managed to interview active burglars, rather than those who were incarcerated, and reported that efforts to reduce B&E rates through *target-hardening* (for example, installing better locks and home security devices; also see Chapter 14) were not very effective. The primary reason was that most homeowners eventually become careless about maintaining their security devices. In addition, even if a home alarm is functioning, most burglars spend less than five minutes in a house—much less time than it takes an alarm company to have police dispatched to respond.

In an earlier study, Rengert and Wasilchick (1985) found that experienced burglars were more systematic in selecting their targets and would take time to "case the joint." They looked for subtle clues (such as closed windows, no lights, mail in the mailbox, etc.) to gauge whether or not a home was a good target. They also took into account the location of the target, the ease of escape, and their general familiarity with the area. That said, the consensus in the literature today is that most break-and-enters are committed by opportunistic young offenders. A Vancouver study found that a small core group of 40–50 criminals—the majority of them young men aged 18–24—were responsible for a significant proportion of property crimes in the city (Vancouver Board of Trade Information, 1997). Both reports note that the primary underlying causes of break-and-enters are social factors, such as economic need and substance abuse and addiction.

Burglars who are opportunists do not want to spend a lot of time planning, do not want to make noise, and prefer to commit their crimes undetected: they are not as brazen as burglars who might stage a burglary in broad daylight—in the guise of a moving company, for instance. Therefore, it is not surprising that opportunistic burglars target houses on the edge of an unoccupied area far more than those situated within a residential development. Rhodes and Conly (1981) found that residential burglars usually live within approximately 2 kilometres of their target (compared to 3.4 kilometres for robbers and 1.9 kilometres for rapists). Similar results were reported by O'Leary (2011), who further notes that understanding *criminal distance decay*—the observed relationship between the distance of a target from the offender's home and the likelihood the offender will attack that target—is important for police in identifying potential offenders.

In 2004, the CBC reported on a new trend of thieves from urban settings going into the country to commit break-ins. This trend speaks to the notion that break-ins are crimes of opportunity and rational choice. As more people move to the country, they create new opportunities for offenders. A 2013 news release by the RCMP in northern Alberta suggests that rural homeowners are become aware of the problem: the release quotes the victim of a break-and-enter as saying, "It has us second-guessing the decision to move to the country" (Hudson, 2013). Wright and Decker (1994) found that the summer months account for about 30 per cent of annual B&E's. Why is that? Summer is the time of year when school is out and people are taking their holidays, leaving their homes unoccupied and, as a result, less secure. Consistent with rational-choice theory, the majority of B&E's take place between 6 p.m. and 6 a.m., when people are either out or asleep.

One element that Statistics Canada does not provide in their publications about burglaries is information about B&E typologies. A number of typologies have been devised by criminologists. Among them is Walsh's (1977) typology involving five types of burglars that range from least to most organized. The classifications are self-explanatory and include, in order, junkies, juvenile burglars, young burglars, known burglars, and professionals. Young burglars, for example, are usually in their late teens or early twenties; their level of planning and organization is not as sophisticated at that of the professionals, but they are typically on their way to becoming professionals.

## Clearance Rates and Explanations

Crime *clearance rates*—the proportion of reported crimes solved by police—often tell us something about the nature of a crime and how effective crime prevention or intervention strategies are. In 2010, the B&E clearance rate was 16.7 per cent, which was well below the overall weighted clearance rate (39.4 per cent) and much lower than the clearance rate for other major offences (see Figure 10.3). In fact, the clearance rate for all property crime was just 23.5 per cent, lagging far behind the clearance rate for violent crime (72.2 per cent). Fortunately for police, when B&E offenders are ultimately caught, they can usually be tied to a string of similar crimes, and will often plead guilty to multiple charges as part of a plea bargain arrangement (Wright & Decker, 1994).

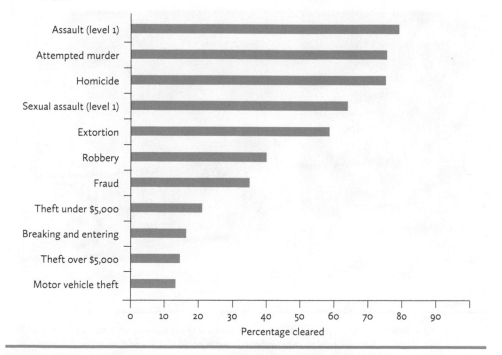

**Figure 10.3   Clearance Rate by Selected Offence, Canada 2010**

*Source:* Statistics Canada, Canadian Centre for Justice Statistics, Uniform Crime Reporting Survey.

As noted earlier, the principal model used to explain breaking and entering is rational-choice theory, which posits that the offender weights the potential costs and rewards of the act against the likelihood of being caught (Cromwell, Olson, & Avary, 1991). So, for example, break-and-enter crime is more likely to occur in urban centres where it is easier to convert stolen goods into cash (e.g. through pawnshops). Pawnshops serve as "primary distribution centres for stolen goods" (Vancouver Board of Trade, 1997), and thus make up an important part of a city's informal symbiotic support network that serves to perpetuate B&E's.

Bursik (1995) suggests that burglars rely primarily on environmental cues, targeting homes that they are familiar with, that are less visible to neighbours and passersby, and that have a general appearance of affluence and that appear unoccupied. The police regularly offer the public crime prevention tips that focus on many of these issues. For example, if you are going to be away, have someone collect your mail and cut your lawn. Do not leave recorded message on your land line indicating that you have gone on vacation. Also, mark your belongings and post the decals in a visible place. These precautions cannot guarantee you will never be a victim of a break-and-enter, but they reduce your risk. However, as Reppetto (1974) observed, these measures are likely to produce a *crime displacement effect*, meaning that the crime is not actually prevented: instead, the criminal will simply target an "easier" home.

In summary, while B&E's do not involve generally involve direct confrontation, they are often traumatic for the victim. They also pose a serious problem for the criminal justice system, not to mention insurance companies. And while they are one of the most prevalent crimes, their clearance rates are extremely low. They are difficult to solve because research shows that in most cases, and in contrast to many other crimes, there is no prior relationship between the offender and the victim. It is true that some theories provide sound explanations for burglaries, but they have failed to produce meaningful programs or strategies to abate them. As Greenberg (1996, p. 165) observed, "fears about public safety among the general public appear

© Justin Minns / Alamy Stock Photo

Displaying a "Beware of Dog" sign—even if you don't have a dog—is one way to encourage a burglar to try your neighbour's house instead. What other strategies could you use to discourage someone from targeting your home, be it a house, apartment, or condo?

to be on the rise. Clearly, restoring public faith in the justice system should be at or near the top of the Canadian agenda." How are the police going about this? By tackling the most serious crimes while making B&E's, which are generally difficult to solve, a low priority.

## Fraud

There are 16 sections (ss. 380–96) in the Criminal Code dealing with various aspects of fraud. Fraud is the act of taking money or property unlawfully from another person by means of deception, falsehood, or cheating. It can take many forms. For example, imagine you purchased a used car from someone who claimed it had never been in an accident. Having bought the car in good faith, you later learned that it had indeed been in a serious accident. The transaction through which you acquired the car would then be considered fraudulent. Another example: people with little money and an inclination to invest in the stock market often appreciate the value of buying penny stocks, which typically carry share prices under a dollar. But buyer beware: in 2013, four Canadians and five Americans were caught after having fraudulently stolen some $140 million from unsuspecting investors through an international penny stock scheme. The Canadian perpetrators of this *securities fraud* face up to 20 years of imprisonment ("4 Canadians charged," 2013).

In this section, we will deal only with property-related fraud. Many fraud cases could easily fall under the general heading of white-collar crime or organized crime, discussed in Chapter 11, since they are committed by businesses and professionals. Typically, property-related fraud

**fraud**
The unlawful use of cheating or deception for financial gain.

---

| BOX 10.4 | **A Closer Look**<br>**The Lure of Money and Power** |

- In 2005, two Saskatchewan women—one of them a provincial government employee—were charged with fraud in connection with the disappearance of over $460,000 from the Saskatchewan Environment Department ("Former gov't employee gets 15 months," 2008). Brenda Oates, a high-ranking civil servant, was eventually found guilty, sentenced to 15 months in prison, and ordered to repay nearly $434,000 for her participation in a scheme that involved false invoices and expense claim forms. Her sister, a minor participant in the fraud, was also found guilty and ordered to repay $26,000. The money was supposedly used to support Oates's gambling addiction.

- In September 2011, the Competition Bureau of Canada laid charges against five individuals from Montreal for their alleged involvement in a fraudulent telemarketing scam involving $172 million worth of products (McFarland, 2011). The accused were charged with using deceptive telemarketing and misleading representations to secure sales of office supplies and other goods, which they then sold at markedly inflated prices. In 2015, three of the accused were fined and given conditional sentences (Competition Bureau, 2015a).

- During the 2011 federal election, there were reports of

automated phone calls directing voters to the wrong polling station on election day. The robocall scandal, as it came to be known, gained national attention and sparked a three-year investigation into complaints lodged in 261 ridings across Canada. In April 2014, the Commission of Canada Elections said there was sufficient evidence to support a charge in only one case, connected to the campaign office of a Guelph-area Conservative Party candidate. The candidate's communications director, Michael Sona, was charged with wilfully preventing or endeavouring to prevent an elector from voting (Bryden, 2014). Sona was found guilty in August and later sentenced to nine months in jail and a year of probation (Payton, 2014).

- In July 2007, the Competition Bureau launched an investigation into allegations of price-fixing among several chocolate manufacturers operating in Canada. The investigations led to charges against three companies: Nestlé, Mars, and ITWAL (a national network of independent wholesale distributors). Proceedings against the latter two organizations were stayed in 2015, but Nestlé pleaded guilty to a criminal charge of price-fixing and was fined $4 million (Competition Bureau, 2015b).

© Photos 12 / Alamy Stock Photo

Leonardo DiCaprio portrayed the famous fraudster Frank W. Abagnale in the motion picture *Catch Me If You Can* (2004). In this promotional photo, DiCaprio speaks to the real Abagnale.

includes cheque fraud, credit card fraud, and "other" fraud, which may involve breach of trust, false pretences, forgery, mail fraud, identity theft, antivirus scams, telemarketing fraud, fraudulent manipulation of the stock exchange, or counterfeiting.

In the 1960s the FBI pursued and finally caught one of the most flamboyant and successful fraudsters in American history: Frank W. Abagnale. He later wrote a book titled *Catch Me If You Can*, which in 2004 was made into a popular movie by the same name. Between the ages of 16 and 21, Abagnale made more than $2.5 million through forgery and, without proper

---

**BOX 10.5**    **FACTS AND FIGURES** NEW "WEAPONS" FOR FIGHTING ECONOMIC CRIME

In 2004, the RCMP set up a website where people could report economic crimes including identity theft, credit card fraud, marketing fraud, and "advance fee" fraud (where a stranger asks for financial help to transfer a much larger sum of money from a fictitious African bank account). The website has grown to become the hub for the Canadian Anti-Fraud Centre, or CAFC. The site provides tips on avoiding the latest Internet frauds affecting businesses and individuals, including

- dating scams, where the victim is contacted through a dating website and asked for gifts or money;

- emergency scams, where a senior is contacted by a young person claiming to be a relative in need of immediate funds to get out of trouble; and
- prize scams, where the victim is notified by e-mail or phone of a large lottery prize that will be released after a small upfront fee has been received.

The site also lets citizens report spam and other e-mail violations, including phishing, malware, and deceptive marketing, via www.fightspam.gc.ca.

credentials, acted as an airline pilot and even an attorney, among other professions. His release from prison was conditional on a promise to share his knowledge with government and businesses to help them prevent fraud. In a 2004 interview Abagnale claimed it is "2,000 times easier to do today" ("Identity theft, fraud so easy 'it's absurd,'" 2004).

## Patterns and Characteristics of Fraud

The rate of fraud in Canada declined steadily from 1991, when it peaked at 487 police-reported incidents per 100,000 population, to 225 per 100,000 in 2012. The rate rose slightly in 2013 (to 227) and 2014 (to 231). It is worth noting that identity fraud is now a separate criminal offence (section 402.1 of the Criminal Code), and since 2010, Statistics Canada has counted cases of identity fraud separately. Between 2011 and 2014, the rate of identity fraud climbed by 6.5 per cent, and it is one of the fastest-growing crimes not just in Canada but globally (Boyce et al., 2014).

While the media have sometimes reported that the dollar value of losses through fraudulent activities rivals the dollar values normally associated with organized crime, this cannot be corroborated by Statistics Canada reports, which do not consistently provide such a breakdown (McPhie, 2006). We do know that total losses through fraudulent activities exceeded $200 million in 2003, down from $227 million in 1999, but that the estimated losses from mass-marketing fraud and identity fraud alone surpassed $10 billion in 2012, a year in which close to a million Canadians fell victim to consumer mass-marketing frauds (Kreiter, 2012, p. 15).

As for the methods used in fraudulent acts, McPhie (1996, p. 167) observes that most frauds are still carried out "by individuals or small groups who pass bad cheques; who use found, stolen, or altered credit or bank cards; or who misrepresent themselves in some manner during financial transactions." The people charged with fraud are generally older than those accused of other property crimes, such as breaking and entering. However, as with most profitable crimes, fraud is increasingly becoming a crime associated with organized crime. A 2012 RCMP report claims that in 2012, organized criminals were responsible for nearly 80 per cent of mass-marketing fraud, nearly 90 per cent of large counterfeiting scams, and nearly 90 per cent of all mortgage frauds (Kreiter, 2012, p. 5). In fact, the same report notes that commercial fraud is ranked the most serious concern for law enforcement agencies across the country, ahead of gun violence and gun-related crimes; terrorism ranked the lowest among of all potential concerns (Kreiter, 2012).

As with all crimes, there are geographical variations in fraud across the country. Unfortunately, no regular data are collected within Canada. However, several years ago, Statistics Canada produced a report indicating that Saskatchewan had the highest rate of reported incidents (540 per 100,000), while Newfoundland and Labrador and Quebec had the lowest rates (291 and 250, respectively) (CCJS, 1998, 18(11)). No studies have been conducted to examine or explain the variations, but we can assume that the differences are the result of a mix of social, cultural, and personal circumstances. For example, we know that people within certain social and demographic groups (e.g. seniors, recent immigrants, and people who are less comfortable with new technology) are frequently targeted by fraudsters, so regions with higher-than-average concentrations

---

**BOX 10.6          WHAT DO YOU THINK?**

### Will You Be a Victim of Fraud?

According to Kreiter's (2012) report on behalf of the RCMP's Commercial Crime Branch, only 1 per cent of Canadians did *not* expect to be victims of fraud, while 80 per cent of those who *had* been victimized felt helpless in resolving their problem and believed their offender would likely go unpunished.

Is fraud inevitable? What do you do to reduce the risk of becoming a fraud victim? Do you expect to be a victim of fraud one day regardless of the precautions you take?

of people within those social categories may see higher-than-average rates of fraud. Note that in contrast to other forms of crime we have considered so far, in which the offender and victim occupy the same geographic space, fraud often happens remotely (e.g. remote access scams via phone or the Internet), meaning that a resident of, say, Halifax could be the victim of a fraud carried out by someone living halfway around the world.

Fraud, in general, is one type of crime in which youth is not well represented. In 2003, the rate of fraud committed by young people was only 108 per 100,000, compared to 294 for adults (CCJS, 2004, 24(6)). Certain kinds of fraud involve sophisticated processes and costly technology that young people may not have access to. Consider, for instance, *synthetic identity fraud*, a growing trend that in 2014 cost Canadians over $1 billion. It involves the production of thousands of fraudulent driver's licences, using real information (e.g. social insurance numbers) and fake identities. The driver's licences enable the fraudsters to apply for credit cards, passports, and other documents that can be used for financial gain or for carrying out other crimes (McInnes-Rae & Gollom, 2014). Among adult fraudsters, women are more likely to be involved in fraud than in other, more violent crimes, and they are most likely to engage in—and be caught committing—cheque fraud. Gobeil and Barrett (2007) report that women convicted of fraud have a high rate of recidivism.

Unlike crimes such as robbery and homicide, fraud—and the methods used to commit it—changes or, as described in Chapter 1, *evolves* with the times. Perhaps this is because a crime that depends on outsmarting rather than overpowering victims is always in need of new tricks to keep ahead of public awareness campaigns and other crime-prevention efforts. Perhaps, too, it is a crime that adapts easily to our new ways of doing things. Consider online dating. With the ever expanding use of social media to get and stay connected, it may come as no surprise that online dating sites have become a haven for fraudulent scams that lead to lost money and broken hearts. In 2012, the Canadian Anti-Fraud Centre reported that online dating scams had become the number-one source of fraud against Canadians, costing in excess of $17 million in 2011, despite the fact the number of victims is smaller than for other forms of fraud (Mertl, 2012). Are we too trusting? Does a willingness to sacrifice safety in the search for romance make us vulnerable? If so, anti-fraud groups have some common "red flags" to watch for. If a person you meet online has too many excuses for not meeting in person, or if he or she is unwilling to talk about financial issues too early in the dating phase, you could be dealing with a scam artist (Mertl, 2012).

Indeed, there appears to be no limit to the creativity of scams used to defraud innocent victims. In the 1990s, numerous fraud scams involved postcards mailed out to homes informing the residents, "One of the following prizes is being held in your name!" At face value, it suggested the recipient was guaranteed a wonderful prize—an exotic trip, an expensive automobile, a large sum of cash, and so on. To claim the prize, the recipient was instructed to call a 1-900 telephone number—at a cost of $9.90. Subsequent investigation revealed that the chances of winning any of the prizes were extremely low; if the exotic trip was in fact available, the

## BOX 10.7    REALITY CHECK

### Is Fraud Violent?

Although fraud is classified as a non-violent crime, some of the documented results of being a victim of fraud suggest otherwise. For example, Kreiter (2012) reports that falling victim to fraud has been associated with marriage breakups and spousal violence; physical and emotion harm inflicted on children in the family; and depression and even suicide among the victims.

Ian Law / Shutterstock.com

These fraudulent handbags claim to be made by a well-known purse design company but are in fact fakes. Is such crime victimless? Who is harmed by the selling of fake designer merchandise?

winner had to pay his or her own airfare at greatly inflated prices through participating travel agencies (Remar, 1991). Similar scams are done with live sex lines, which charge at posted "regular long-distance rates." What they fail to mention is that the calls are run through a foreign country where the rates are considerably higher.

These and other scams, involving false advertising, bogus celebrity endorsement offers, price fixing, telemarketing swindles, and the ever-popular fakes and knockoffs are all designed to capitalize on people's greed and the ability of the perpetrator to win the victim's trust or confidence. Another strain of fraud preys on our better nature and the desire to help those in need, such as the stranger whose car broke down on the way to visit his mother in hospital and who now needs $50 for a cab. Along these lines is what has become known as the *grandparent scam*, which targets seniors. A young, college-aged caller claiming to be the senior's grandchild needs money transferred immediately in order to get out of jail or some other kind of trouble. "Just don't tell Mom and Dad," the caller implores; "they'll just freak out." Seniors are targeted for a number of practical reasons: scammers often get their numbers from "lead sheets" acquired from data collection agencies, and these lead sheets contain more land-line numbers than cellphone numbers (Streshinsky, 2014). Seniors are more likely to be at home during the day and are more likely to have a land line. Other factors, according to Streshinsky (2014), are the "geographic and psychological distances that usually exist between a grandparent and a grandchild: grandparents aren't likely to know the day-to-day details of their grandkids' lives" and aren't in a position to quickly verify the story. The grandparent scam isn't new, but anecdotal evidence suggests that cases are on the rise. However, incidents of this kind that exploit our vulnerability are underreported, since victims are often embarrassed to admit that they have been duped.

## Explaining Fraud

In his classic study of cheque forgers, Edwin Lemert (1953) observed that most forgers are naive and tend to commit the offence out of economic need. He also found that they tend not to be involved in other forms of property crime and to be older than most property offenders.

Has forgery evolved as a crime? In 1986, Trembley noted that there had been an increase in the number of professional forgers who had developed sophisticated schemes and were sometimes working in teams. As cheques have fallen out of favour, forgery has given way to telephone and online fraud. Consistently, though, the elderly are among the preferred targets of scam artists (McPhie, 1996, p. 173). As noted above, seniors are easily accessible; some of them are looking for a little extra income on their fixed pensions; and many are reluctant to report their victimization because of embarrassment (Brennan, 1999). RCMP reports reveal that seniors are particularly prone to telephone fraud scams.

Other explanations emphasize techniques of *neutralization*. In the case of business fraud, perpetrators rationalize their actions by claiming that businesses make so much money that they will not be hurt by a "little" loss. As for fraudulent transactions with people,

### BOX 10.8 | FACTS AND FIGURES
### CANADA: MASS-MARKETING FRAUD HAVEN

RCMP reports suggest that there are hundreds of telephone fraud businesses operating in Canada. Project COLT, established by the police in 1995 to counter phone fraud and mass-marketing fraud, estimates that phone fraud generates about $70 million a year in North America. The techniques used vary, but they usually involve offering a significant reward that the victim can claim once he or she has paid a nominal registration fee. In a variation on this scam, in 2013 a group was found to be impersonating Canada Border Securities agents and requesting personal information payments over the phone.

Have you ever received a suspicious e-mail from your bank requesting you to update your banking information. Have you ever received an email offering you a credit load even if your credit rating is not very good. Or have you ever bought something online at such a good price that you "just had to buy it"? These are all known forms of fraud.

offenders might rationalize that if certain people are naive enough to fall for the false pretence, they deserve to be taken advantage of.

In summary, fraud is a commonly occurring form of property crime that can also take the form of organized criminal activity and white-collar crime (see Chapter 11). The total value of financial losses incurred through fraud is not known because of the high rate of unreported incidents. However, based on available data, it is clear that fraud costs individuals, organizations, and the government billions of dollars every year. And while the overall official rate for fraud may have declined in recent years, new forms of fraud may simply be one step ahead of police detection.

As long as most Canadians value economic success, it will be difficult to develop social policies that significantly reduce crimes of fraud. Meanwhile, although certain target-hardening programs have been devised, some criminals seem to be one step ahead in finding new twists to the old "snake oil" scam.

## Theft

There are 14 sections in the Criminal Code dealing with theft, ranging from theft of cattle (s. 338) to theft by spouse (s. 329) to theft with intent to deprive (s. 322). The large number of sections implies that theft is considered a serious form of property crime and that tremendous variety exists in methods of committing theft. Even before Confederation, theft was one of the more common crimes reported to police (Carrigan, 1991). In general terms, theft refers to the unlawful taking of property from the possession of another. However, unlike robbery, theft does not involve the use or the threat of force or overt deception.

**theft**
A property crime that involves the unlawful taking of property or a service that belongs to an in individual or a business, typically without any intention of returning it.

### Patterns and Characteristics of Theft

Theft offers an excellent illustration of how crime is, as we discussed in Chapter 1, both *evolutive* and *relative*. When the Canadian Criminal Code was first enacted, theft was known as *larceny* (derived from the Latin *latro*, "robber"). One of the earliest common-law offences, the crime of larceny was created by English judges to try a deter people from stealing other people's property. Later, in Canada, it was defined as *theft* and later subdivided into theft under $200 and theft over $200. The amount was raised to $1,000 in 1986 and, most recently, to $5,000 in 1995 (see Box 10.9). These changes reflect our social economy and the relative value of goods. And while general comparisons can be made over time, these comparisons should be viewed

---

| BOX 10.9 | **A Closer Look**<br>**The Difference between "Theft Over" and "Theft Under":**<br>**Strange but True** |
| --- | --- |

One of my former research assistants who used to be employed by a bank shared with me an interesting story she had been told by colleagues at the bank. During a low-key bank robbery, a teller was passed a note by the robber demanding $4,999.00, which he was given. The bank employees speculated that the robber requested this amount in case he was later apprehended, believing that this would result in a charge of theft under instead of the more serious charge of theft over. In fact, the crime of theft under is technically defined as "theft of $5,000 and under," which means the lesser charge would still have applied if he had been caught with an even $5,000!

Why does it make sense to recognize two types of theft, differentiated by the value of goods stolen? Knowing that one charge will result in a tougher sentence than the other, do you think the current $5,000 threshold for theft over and theft under is reasonable? Can you think of cases where it might not make sense?

with caution, since not all property has increased equally in value. Therefore, when the trends in theft are described here, the terms *theft over* and *theft under* will be used, without specifying an amount. Note that motor-vehicle theft is treated as a separate category, as we shall see shortly.

Between 1993 and 2003, there was an 84 per cent decline in the rate of theft over incidents reported to police (see Table 10.1). While there was a declining trend in the rate of theft overall, a good part of the drop occurred after 1995, when the threshold for theft over was raised from $1,000 to $5,000. The rate has continued to drop ever since. Likewise, the rate of theft under has steadily declined (following a small jump immediately after 1995), though it still accounts for the largest number of property-crime offences.

It is well documented that rates of theft, like other forms of crime, vary according to patterns of social and economic factors across the country (see Figure 10.4). When examining Figure 10.4, it is worth noting that Yukon's high rate of theft over (71 per 100,000) is based on just 26 reported incidents; Ontario, by contrast, has a much lower rate (30 per 100,000) but leads all provinces and territories with 4,122 reported incidents, accounting for nearly 30 per cent of the national total. The same is true for cases of theft under, where Ontario's modest rate of 1,156 per 100,000 is based on 158,194 reported incidents; the next closest total is BC's 113,042, although BC's rate of 2,441 per 100,000 is the highest of any province.

Canadians enjoy the freedom and independence that owning a motor vehicle offers them. In a recent study published by the World Bank, Canada ranked very near the top with a rate of 607 automobiles per 1,000 citizens. Higher rates of ownership were found in countries like Australia (692), Italy (672), and the United States (802), but compare these totals with

### Table 10.1 Police-Reported Rates of Theft Over and Theft Under*, 1993–2013 (Select Years)

| | Thefts per 100,000 | |
|---|---|---|
| Year | Over | Under |
| 1993 | 408 | 2,680 |
| 1998 | 78 | 2,366 |
| 2003 | 61 | 2,214 |
| 2008 | 50 | 1,663 |
| 2013 | 41 | 1,343 |

Note: The threshold for theft under and theft over was raised from $1,000 to $5,000 in 1995, resulting in a small spike in cases of theft under and a sharp decline in cases of theft over; see explanation in the text.
*Sources*: Hendrick, 1996, Table 2; CANSIM Table 252-001.

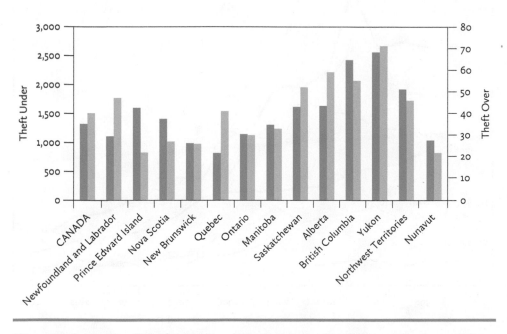

Figure 10.4   Rates of Theft Under and Theft Over by Province and Territory, 2014

*Source:* CANSIM Table 252-0051.

those of countries at the other end of the spectrum, including Bangladesh (3), Rwanda (5), and Myanmar (6). In 2014, thefts of motor vehicles in Canada were more common than cases of theft over, with a rate of 208 per 100,000 (versus the theft over rate of 40 per 100,000) (Boyce, 2015). Overall, the rate of vehicle theft has dropped by over 60 per cent since 2003 (Boyce et al., 2014). The decline can be attributed to a number of factors, including the use of OnStar tracking devices in most new cars; the introduction of the "bait car" program, in which vehicles equipped with special surveillance technology are parked in high-theft areas in order to attract and apprehend thieves (see Dauvergne, 2008); and the highly successful Winnipeg Auto Theft Suppression Strategy (WATSS) (see Box 10.12 on page 250). Introduced in 2005, WATSS was key to reducing the number of vehicle thefts per day in Winnipeg from 24 in 2005 to 3.5 in 2012—this in spite of a growing population (Preventing Auto Theft, 2013). Figure 10.5 shows that while vehicle theft has declined overall, several major Canadian cities experienced an increase in the early 2000s. We will consider motor-vehicle theft in greater detail later in this chapter.

Not since around 2004 has Statistics Canada provided a detailed breakdown of theft by item stolen. However, there is anecdotal evidence that bicycle theft has been on the rise across the country. For example, according to a report by Calgary Police Services (2015), over 1,000 bikes were stolen each year in Calgary between 2010 and 2014. In 2014, the number jumped to 1,821 from 1,051 in 2010—a 73 per cent increase (Calgary Police Services, 2015). The report also observed that the highest rate of bicycle thefts occurred in the downtown commercial core, where there is the highest concentration of bicycle commuters and bike couriers. Of all the city's bike thefts, 76 per cent were classified as crimes of opportunity, involving bikes left visible and unattended—even if locked. Only 19 per cent of bicycle thefts occurred during break-and-enters (Calgary Police Services, 2015). Unfortunately, the report does not provide any information on the percentage of bikes recovered. With increasing bicycle use nationwide, it stands to reason that there is a correlative increase in bicycle theft. However,

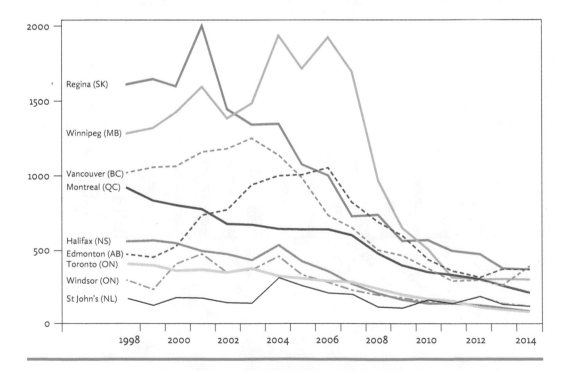

**Figure 10.5    Motor-Vehicle Thefts in Nine Canadian Cities, 1998–2014**

*Source:* Statistics Canada CANSIM Table 252-0051.

because bicycle theft is a low priority for police forces in most major cities, and because bikes are seldom recovered, many thefts go unreported, making it difficult to know precisely the extent of the problem.

Similarly, the theft of laptops, cellphones, and other portable devices has spiked in recent years. The increases are likely due to three factors in particular: availability, limited surveillance, and relative difficulty in relocating the stolen item. However, there has been an equal proliferation of crime-prevention responses (see Box 10.10).

The kinds of theft we have considered so far affect individuals and their possessions. Retail theft presents a different set of challenges for criminologists specializing in crime prevention. According to a 2009 CBC documentary, 80 per cent of Canadians had shoplifted something at least once in their life (Macdougall, 2013). Buckle and Farrington (1984) suggest that shoplifting is so prevalent because of its low risk of detection: less than 1 per cent of shoplifters were caught, according to the data they studied. However, accurate counts of shoplifting are difficult to establish because many businesses blend shoplifting losses into what they call *inventory shrinkage*—a category that also includes bookkeeping errors, damage to merchandise, and employee theft. Although shoplifting occurs every day, the Christmas season is prime time for shoplifting and fraud. Given the staffing cutbacks in some retail outlets, the problem may grow even worse, although most major department stores now have hidden security cameras and have hired their own in-house security staff (see Box 10.11).

Although male and female rates of victimization by theft were nearly equal in 2009, younger women were more likely to be victimized than their male counterparts. Not surprisingly, living in an urban setting places a person (regardless of age) at greater risk than living

---

**BOX 10.10**  **FACTS AND FIGURES** THE PRICE OF PURSUING A HEALTHIER LIFESTYLE: PREVENTING BICYCLE THEFT

The city of London, England, saw bicycle use increase by some 83 per cent between 2000 and 2007. In the United States, bicycle sales increased by 20 per cent between 1992 and 2006 (Johnson, Sidebottom, & Thorpe, 2008). Unfortunately, there are no readily available data on bicycle sales in Canada, but consumer report statistics that group the sale of bicycles with other sporting goods have shown a steady increase in sales since 2000, and many municipalities have introduced bike-sharing programs where bikes can be rented for short periods and then returned to designated bike-sharing stations. Montreal was the first city in North America to introduce such a program, in 2005.

To reduce the risk of having your bike stolen there are now a number of education programs and devices available to bike owners. They include such items as bike lockers and shelters, improved bike parking furniture, security cameras, and much stronger locking devices.

Image courtesy Børge A. Roum

Bike lockers such as these ones, found on the campus of the University of British Columbia, are effective in combatting bicycle theft, but they are not without drawbacks: relative to standard bike racks they are costly to install and require considerable space. What do you think is the best solution to combatting bicycle theft?

Do you own a bicycle? If so, has it ever been stolen? What do you to reduce your risk of having your bike stolen?

**BOX 10.11**

**A CLOSER LOOK**

## The Amateur vs Professional Shoplifter

In a pioneering study on shoplifting, Mary Owen Cameron (1964) developed a typology of shoplifters, which was subsequently refined and expanded by others, including Ronald Holmes (1983). Three principal types of shoplifters are as follows:

- The *snitch* is an amateur pilferer. This is the most common type of shoplifter and is usually a "respectable" person, in Cameron's description. Cameron believed that snitches are not driven by impulsive urges but usually respond to an opportunity that has been preceded by a stressful experience. When caught, older persons usually change their behaviour, while youths are less likely to be deterred (Klemke, 1978). Cameron estimated that snitches made up nearly 90 per cent of all shoplifters.
- The *booster* or *heel* is the professional shoplifter who may steal for personal interest, like the snitch, but more often intends to resell the stolen merchandise. Boosters usually sell the stolen goods at half to one-third the original retail cost. However, some boosters will "steal to order," carrying out jobs for others interested in obtaining specific merchandise.
- The *kleptomaniac*, identified by Holmes (1983), is driven to steal not for material gain but for the thrill and arousal gained from the experience. Kleptomaniacs are usually women, though there are exceptions. Holmes notes that only a small percentage of shoplifters fit this category. More recent support for this observation can be found in Klemke's study (1992).

Contrary to popular opinion, even though men typically commit more shoplifting offences than women, it is one of the crimes with the smallest gender gap of all offences (Hirtenlehner, Blackwell, Leitgoeb, & Bacher, 2014).

in rural settings. This general trend, however, does not reflect the fact that theft rates in the Yukon, which is mostly rural, are very high (Perreault & Brennan, 2010).

Overall, it might be fair to speculate that given the prevalence of theft, the current sentencing dispositions are not having a deterrent effect on offenders—especially young offenders (see Carrington & Moyer, 1998). Are the dispositions too lenient or are we simply using an ineffective approach to apprehending thieves? Criminologists need to examine such issues. However, it might also be the case that public apathy undermines crime prevention efforts. Most people view theft as a nuisance rather than a real threat (unless they are the victims); with limited resources, criminal justice agencies may simply be mimicking public apathy. For example, in 2004 there was a rash of thefts of inflatable likenesses of the character SpongeBob SquarePants from roofs of various Burger King fast-food outlets in the United States. The pop icon was a hot item on eBay, and the inflatables were selling for as much as US$1,000. In addition to being a financial burden, the thefts represented a nuisance to Burger King. Nevertheless, the company did not actively pursue the missing inflatables; as a media spokesperson commented, "at the moment, it is a sort of very amusing phenomenon" ("Inflatable SpongeBobs," 2004).

### Explaining Theft

In his study of college students, Klemke (1992) found that nearly 60 per cent of those surveyed had been involved in at least one shoplifting offence. Katz (1988) suggests that students participate in shoplifting as a release from boredom rather than out of financial need. Shoplifting in this case falls into the category of crime for thrills, in which people commit acts that are "sensually compelling" (Katz, 1988). In a 1995 study involving almost 2,000 respondents, McCarthy (1996) found that males and adolescents were more likely than females and adults to report getting a "high" from an object they considered stealing. How can we account for such a strong psychological response to a coveted object, and how does this high relate to rates of theft? An interdisciplinary perspective would certainly aid in addressing these two as yet unanswered questions.

Any general explanation of theft must consider cultural as well as individual factors. Consider the case of East Germany, which from 1961 until 1989 experienced a low rate of crime under the tight control of the governing communist regime. In 1989, when the Berlin Wall—built to keep out negative Western influences—was opened up and eventually dismantled, there was a sharp rise in shoplifting (along with other forms of criminal activity). As Cooper (1996) explains, "While familiar structures were discredited almost immediately, no new ones emerged to take their place, leaving a sort of anarchic vacuum. . . . The fear they [communist police and security forces] had nourished for decades disappeared; a liberated but confused citizenry took 'freedom' to mean 'anything goes.'" Indeed, theft in the form of looting is often a by-product of the "anarchic vacuum" produced by rioting when citizens take to the street in violent protest, whether over controversial court decisions (such as the 1992 Rodney King verdict in Los Angeles) or disappointing sports results (in Vancouver, for example, following the Canucks' Stanley Cup losses in 1994 and 2011). Along these lines, Klemke (1992) proposes anomie—the state of social normlessness and society breakdown—as one possible explanation for theft. He also considers strain theory, which suggests that people who become frustrated by their inability to attain the North American dream break the law for economic gain.

In summary, theft is one of the oldest crimes and one of the first common-law crimes codified by English judges. Throughout our history, the criteria of theft have undergone various updates reflecting social and financial change. Other than theft from motor vehicles, shoplifting is the most common type of theft in Canada. Explanations have ranged from stealing for the thrill to *neutralization*—the sense of justification for their crimes that offenders feel based on their belief that the store already makes enough profit. Individuals at risk of being victimized by theft tend to be high-income earners, homeowners, and urbanites, as well as people who are young, people who are single, and people who are well educated.

Attempts to control theft have focused on target-hardening strategies such as using hidden cameras or undercover security staff to monitor vulnerable areas, placing tags with electronic devices on high-ticket items, and securing some small, expensive items to racks. Overall, these and other criminal justice measures appear to have had little impact on overall rates of theft.

## Motor-Vehicle Crime

In August 2013, the *Financial Post* reported that Canadian auto sales had reached a record high with over 26,000 motor vehicles sold in July alone (Deveau, 2013). And as we saw earlier this chapter, Canada ranks well within the top 10 countries with regard to per capita vehicle ownership. Indeed, Canadians—like their American neighbours—love their automobiles and spend billions every year maintaining and nurturing them. Given what Canadians invest in automobile purchases and maintenance, it is not surprising that cars, trucks, and SUVs are attractive targets for theft and other motor-vehicle crime (MVC)—including carjacking, joyriding, and vandalism—among both restless adolescents and big-time organized crime groups (see Box 10.12).

The Criminal Code deals with the theft of a motor vehicle under the subheading "Offences Resembling Theft" in section 335. Regardless of the high value Canadians place on their vehicles, the taking of a motor vehicle without consent is punishable with only a summary conviction. However, in response to the problems associated with stolen vehicles (insurance costs, personal loss, risk the stolen vehicle will be used to damage property or to carry out other crimes, etc.), in 2011, the government introduced four new Criminal Code offences in an effort to control vehicle theft. They include separate offences for

- motor-vehicle theft (s. 333.1);
- altering, removing or obliterating a vehicle identification number (VIN) (s. 353.1);
- trafficking in property obtained by crime (s. 355.2); and
- possession of property obtained by crime for the purpose of trafficking (s. 355.4).

**motor-vehicle crime (MVC)**

A broad range of offences involving a car, truck, or SUV, including theft *of* a vehicle but also theft *from* a vehicle and criminal damage to a vehicle.

## BOX 10.12    REALITY CHECK

### Motor-Vehicle Theft: Big Business

In September 1996, the Ontario Provincial Police (OPP), in co-operation with several regional police forces and Canada Customs, successfully smashed a sophisticated ring of car thieves that involved at least six members, leading to the recovery of 95 luxury vehicles valued at $2.5 million, destined mostly for Vietnam. The gang paid youths and adults anywhere from $300 to $500 per vehicle to steal cars for a Mississauga import–export business (Mitchell, 1996).

The head of the OPP anti-theft team pointed out that Ontario at the time had the highest rate of motor-vehicle theft (MVT) in Canada, having increased by 100 per cent since 1990. And as Figure 10.5 (p. 248) shows, rates of vehicle theft in several major Canadian cities continued to rise into the early 2000s.

In the early 1990s, recovery rates for stolen vehicles was 95 per cent, but this figure fell to 61 per cent in 1999. Why? Police officials point to the proliferation of organized

vehicle theft beginning around 1995. Vehicle theft is no longer undertaken by thrill-seeking adolescents: it is a lucrative enterprise undertaken by organized crime gangs.

If recovery is difficult, then prevention may be the best option. Witness the city of Winnipeg, which in 2004 reached an all-time high in MVT: an average of 24 vehicles *per day*. In 2005, the city introduced a crime prevention program called the Winnipeg Auto Theft Suppression Strategy, or WATSS for short. Despite another peak in auto theft in 2006, the city saw its daily rate of motor-vehicle theft fall to 3.5 per day in 2012—an 85.4 per cent decrease!

Strategies for preventing motor-vehicle theft are often undertaken on a municipal basis. Research the programs your city might have in place to prevent MVT. Do you think there should be a national strategy in place to prevent MVT, or does it make sense to apply different approaches in different municipalities?

## Patterns and Characteristics of Motor-Vehicle Crime

In this section, we will look at some of the general patterns and characteristics of motor-vehicle crime, in particular motor-vehicle theft. We will also examine some of the strategies that have been introduced to combat the problem.

Motor-vehicle theft is defined as the unauthorized use of a motorized vehicle (an automobile, a bus, a van, a truck, or a motorcycle) for the purpose of joyriding, short- or long-term transportation, profit, and/or the commission of another crime. Motor-vehicle crime refers to the broader range of offences involving a motor vehicle that includes theft *from* vehicles, theft *of* vehicles, criminal damage to vehicles, and vandalism.

After a relatively stable period between 1981 and 1987, the rate of motor-vehicle theft (MVT) rate increased by 62.7 per cent between 1988 and 1993. Starting in 1994, the rate began to nudge up (CCJS, 2004, 24(6):10) and saw dramatic fluctuations in some Canadian cities in the early 2000s (see Figure 10.5, p. 248). However, as with most categories of violent and non-violent crime, MVT has experienced a dramatic drop over the past 10 years (see Table 10.2). Between 2004 and 2014, MVT dropped by over 60 per cent to a rate of 208 per 100,000 population. But while MVT is down overall in Canada, there remain considerable regional variations (see Figure 10.6). What the data do not tell is why these regional differences exist. Is it perhaps that people in certain provinces and territories are more trusting and don't lock their vehicles?

### Table 10.2    Rate and Number of Motor-Vehicle Thefts in Canada, 1996–2014 (Select Years)

| Year | Thefts per 100,000 | Thefts (total) |
|------|--------------------|----------------|
| 1996 | 607 | 180,123 |
| 1998 | 550 | 165,920 |
| 2000 | 522 | 160,315 |
| 2002 | 516 | 161,912 |
| 2004 | 532 | 169,977 |
| 2006 | 487 | 158,638 |
| 2008 | 378 | 125,568 |
| 2010 | 272 | 92,506 |
| 2012 | 225 | 78,068 |
| 2014 | 208 | 73,964 |

*Sources:* CCJS, 2003, 23(1):10; 2004, 24(6)10; Boyce et al., 2014; Statistics Canada CANSIM Table 252-0051.

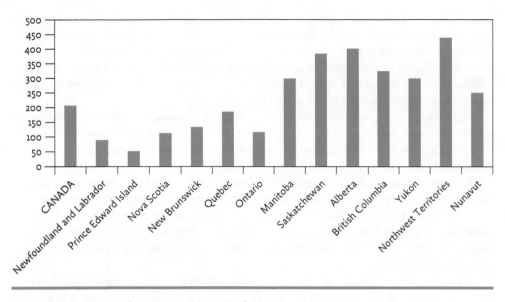

**Figure 10.6    Rate of Motor-Vehicle Theft, by Province and Territory, 2014**

*Source:* Statistics Canada CANSIM Table 252-0051.

Or do they tend to own older-model vehicles that don't have the modern anti-theft devices? Are there other ways to explain these trends?

## Explaining Motor-Vehicle Crime

In 1996, Canada's rate of MVT exceeded that of the United States, and by 2000, Canada's rate was 26 per cent higher than the American rate (CCJS, 2003, 23(1):4). The Canadian and US rates are relatively close today: 223 versus 229 per 100,000, respectively, in 2012 (FBI, 2015). So why are motor-vehicle crimes so prevalent in North America, and what draws people to become involved in MVC?

Based on his review of the literature, Morrison (1996) cites a number of common explanations for motor-vehicle crime in North America. For example, vehicles are stolen or vandalized, especially by young people, because of the symbolic value of having something of status (a car is undeniably a status symbol in North America's consumer culture). In their research on types of auto theft, McCaghy, Giordano, and Henson (1977) developed a typology that includes the following kinds of motor-vehicle crime:

- *Joyriding.* This refers to short-term theft, usually by young people, for the purpose of having fun. A number of years ago, a Statistics Canada *Juristat* report noted that when young people are involved in MVT, approximately 76 per cent of the thefts are for *joyriding.* The report also reveals that young people are more likely to steal vehicles in July and August, during the summer holidays (CCJS, 2003, 23(1):5). However, research shows they rarely are suspected or apprehended.
- *Profit-motivated MVT.* This kind of vehicle theft is usually carried out by organized crime groups that specialize in stealing and modifying cars for quick resale, sometimes overseas.
- *MVT for short- or long-term transportation.* Vehicles may be stolen by someone simply needing to get from point A to point B, possibly in the course of committing another crime. In this case, the stolen vehicle is usually left abandoned and is sometimes vandalized in the process. Sometimes valuable parts will also be removed for future illegal resale.

Another typology for MVC could be simple vandalism, carried out by an envious offender who wants to deprive the vehicle's owner of a privilege that is inaccessible to the offender (see Box 10.13). The action provides the offender with a sense of power. Motor-vehicle crime may also be motivated by peer pressure or boredom or the desire for a reward for returning the vehicle. MVC also includes theft *from* vehicles, which is all too likely when potential victims leave their valuables insecure and in plain view.

Light, Nee, and Ingham (1993) found that offenders who steal vehicles for profit develop a dependency on this type of income. However, they found that most youths involved in MVT simply grow out of the activity. It is not the legal sanction that deters them but simply growing up.

Borrowing from Felson's routine activity theory, Trembley and associates (1996) suggest that the motivation of joyriders could be better understood by undertaking a cross-sectional analysis of joyriders' responsiveness to structural features or urban environments. However, the authors point out that the process of developing a fruitful explanatory model requires "a much more detailed investigation of the routine activities and concerns" of all the factors that could be involved.

A number of years ago, Karmen (1979) raised a number of interesting questions about the motivation of motor-vehicle crimes. He pointed out that it is important to understand not only the relationship between motor-vehicle thieves or vandals and their victims but also the role that the automotive industry plays in the design and security of cars. For example, why are cars easy to damage but expensive to repair? Why are cars still relatively easy to steal? Does the automotive industry have a stake in car theft and vandalism, he asked? Surveys indicate that most people are willing to pay higher purchase prices for effective security features.

In recent years, several automakers have taken steps to target-harden their vehicles. In 1997, Ford, in its Taurus model, introduced an electronic key that eliminates the ability to hotwire a car. Several leading automakers have equipped cars with GPS and Boomerang devices that

What theories of criminology support the idea that leaving valuables in plain sight—such as on the seat of a car—increases the chances of theft?

---

**BOX 10.13 · FACTS AND FIGURES** RESPECT VERSUS ENVY

Criminologists rely on anecdotal evidence as well as statistical data. This story, which comes from my own experience, reveals something about the nature of motor-vehicle crime.

I used to own a relatively high-end sports car, which was constantly subjected to minor (but costly) acts of vandalism while I was living in Vancouver: "keying," in which a key is used to scratch the paint; theft of the hood ornament; removal of the wheel decals; and so on. After several years—and several thousand dollars' worth of repairs—I sold the car.

At around the same time, I visited Italy, and had the opportunity to travel in a very expensive Italian-made sports car. Knowing the history of my car troubles, the owner, and friend, offered to engage in a small experiment to prove a point about respect. At his insistence, we parked the car outside the hotel in a busy part of town for the entire evening without locking the doors. Nothing happened!

> Why do you think the car in Italy was left untouched? What do think might have happened, if anything, had the same car been left unlocked in the city where you live?

---

enable the vehicle to be tracked via a satellite to pinpoint its location. Both systems include a monitoring fee. A passive arming system includes immobilizers that shut off the electrical circuit when the car is shut down and prevents the car from being started without a special coded key. There are also numerous mechanical devices (such as The Club, a relatively inexpensive mechanical barrier system that attaches to the steering column) that can be used to reduce the risk a car will be stolen. The "Denver boot," a wheel-clamp device dating back to the mid-1940s, has been used not only to reduce the risk of theft but—by parking authorities—to immobilize a car that has been illegally parked. Other recent efforts that have been introduced across Canada include the Bait Car Program, where police-owned decoy vehicles are set up with GPS and surveillance tracking devices to target potential problem areas where cars are being stolen. In 2006, British Columbia introduced a program called Project No Free Ride, which allowed the courts to recover the financial costs associated with MVT through civil litigation. Finally, in 2009 the Criminal Code (ss. 331, 354–5) was amended to create stiffer penalties for motor-vehicle theft and to also allow harsher punishment for those who steal cars for resale. And while MVT may still be quite prevalent, nationally around 80–85 per cent of stolen vehicles are recovered and returned to their registered owner or insurance company.

When one takes into account all the target-hardening measures that have been introduced and tried over the years, perhaps it is time to consider an alternative strategy. For example, crime prevention strategies should consider both the types of vehicles being targeted and the motivation of the perpetrator.

In summary, motor-vehicle crimes have decreased in recent years. The patterns vary geographically. The characteristics and motivations of offenders are also varied. The problem of motor-vehicle crime is not unique to Canada or North America. Sophisticated professional car-stealing rings serve as reminders that all the security devices and safety programs that have been introduced have curbed, but not solved, the problem.

As long as we continue to value automobiles and as long as the average cost of vehicles remains high, the opportunity for motor-vehicle crime will not go away. We need to not only focus on security measures but also better understand the motivation behind motor-vehicle crime. This will require an integrated and interdisciplinary approach. In the meantime, we might want to explore what countries with low rates of MVC are doing and adopt some of their methods.

## Arson

**arson**

A form of vandalism that involves the destruction of one's own or another's property through the use of fire or an explosion.

Sections 433 to 436.1 of the Criminal Code pertain to the legal definition and parameters of arson. While not classified as a property crime, arson is defined as the destruction of property through the use of fire or an explosion. Arson can be committed on another person's property or on one's own property, either for fraudulent purposes or by negligence. Once considered a form of vandalism, arson has increased in frequency and seriousness to the point where it has now been defined as its own offence. It remains far less common than theft or other types of property or economic crime, but the motivations for it tend to be more diverse (see Box 10.14).

### Patterns and Characteristics of Arson

Between 2002 and 2009, the rate of arson incidents reported to police remained stable, varying from 40 to 43 cases per 100,000 population. But between 2003 and 2014, the percentage of arson attacks dropped by 41 per cent, including a drop of 21 per cent between 2012 and 2013 (Boyce et al., 2014; Figure 10.7). Yet despite its relative infrequency, the damage caused by intentional fire-setting can be enormous. For example, a 2011 fire started by vandals in Slave Lake, Alberta, caused over $700 million in property damage. Likewise, the sentences for arson can be lengthy. In 2013, in the largest eco-terrorism case in US history, a Canadian woman who described herself as a zealous environmental activist pleaded guilty to setting over 20 fires in the western United States. The penalties she received for each count ranged from 27 months to 157 months (Carson, 2013).

Men and boys are far more likely to be charged with arson than are women and girls, making up 86 per cent of charged offenders. In addition, while the median age of male fire-setters is 19, for women it is almost double that: 33 years (Gannon & Pina, 2010). Why is there such a gender-based age difference? Moreover, why are the areas targeted by arsonists typically

---

**BOX 10.14**    **A CLOSER LOOK**
### The Many Faces of Arson

The following stories represent a cross-section of incidents that reflects the diversity of the reasons for committing arson.

- In February 1997, about 500 tradespeople, many unemployed, descended upon the site of a new apartment development in Sydney, Nova Scotia, and set it ablaze to protest the use of non-unionized workers in the construction ("Protest by arson," 1997).
- In 2004, a 39-year-old man was charged with torching a Quebec band chief's home over political differences in the Mohawk community of Kanesatake, Quebec. The chief had fired the community police chief shortly before the incident. Reports indicate that some 40 people stood by and watched the house burn ("Arrest in Kanesatake," 2004).
- In July 2014, three teens in Gatineau, Quebec, were charged with arson in connection to a 2013 incident in which a food truck was set ablaze. The truck,

which belonged to a non-profit organization that provides warm meals to the homeless, had been used to gather food for the region's needy ("Three Gatineau teens," 2014).
- In April 2015, a Quebec man was found guilty of setting fire to his home in Gentilly for the purpose of defrauding his insurance provider (Mailhot, 2015).
- In November 2015, fire was deliberately set to a mosque in Peterborough, Ontario. Police investigated the case as a hate crime, given that it occurred just days after Islamic terrorists had attacked several sites in Paris, France, killing over 120 people.

To what extent do you think intentional fire-setting can be an instrument of power? Consider the fact that children and adolescents are more prone to fire-setting than adults are. How might we best prevent arson?

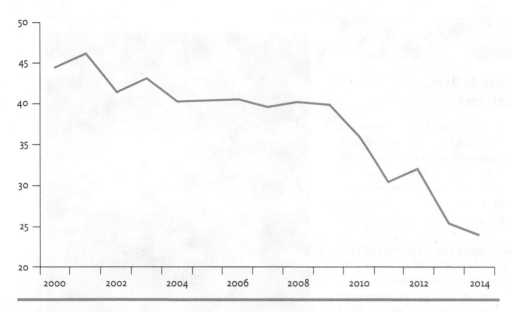

**Figure 10.7    Police-Reported Cases of Arson in Canada, 2000–2014 (Rate per 100,000)**

*Source:* Statistics Canada CANSIM Table 2522-0051.

economically depressed? And why are vacant buildings and companies with ongoing labour problems so often targeted? To help us find answers to these questions, it helps to understand the different types of arson and the motivations underlying such acts.

In his study of young arsonists, Wayne Wooden (1991) identified four categories of juvenile arsonists:

1.  The *playing with matches fire-setters* are children, usually between the ages of 4 and 9, who start a fire accidentally while playing with matches (or other incendiary devices) carelessly left around.
2.  The *crying for help fire-setters* tend to be a little older (aged 7–13) and set fires to reduce anxiety or stress. The source of such feelings is usually related to family-based issues such as divorce, abuse, death, or domestic strife. These youths have difficulty expressing their pain, so they act it out.
3.  The *delinquent fire-setters*, aged 14–18, set fire to property in retaliation for some criticism they might have received. Gaynor and Stern (1993) found that delinquent fire-setters are mostly males (10 for every female) characterized by anger, antisocial personalities, and a lack of regard for social rules and norms.
4.  The *severely disturbed fire-setters* are youths who have some personality disturbance. These fire-setters are likely to set numerous fires. The word *pyromaniac* is sometimes used to describe them.

In 1995, Swaffer and Hollin studied a group of adolescent fire-setters, including boys and girls, and came up with some slightly different categories. Although their sample size was small—only 17 adolescents—the results are nevertheless interesting. Five youths said they set fires out of "revenge." Three said they set fires either to conceal a crime or because of peer pressure. What is interesting to note is that all three of the girls reported self-injury as their motivation.

Pioneering FBI profilers such as John Douglas note that the commision of arson at a young age may be symptomatic of greater problems to come. With Mark Olshaker he studied

## BOX 10.15    WHAT DO YOU THINK?

### Arson: Mischief, Vandalism, or Aggravated Vandalism?

Under English common law, arson was broadly defined as "the malicious and willful burning of the house or outhouse of another man" and was generally classified as a form of vandalism (Working Paper 36, 1984, p. 5). However, as societies evolved and the meaning of property became more sophisticated, there arose a desire to legally enunciate the gravity of the act (*actus reus*) and its underlying intent (*mens rea*).

In response to the increase in arson attacks, the Law Reform Commission of Canada was asked to clarify why arson should be treated differently to vandalism. The commission offered five recommendations in "an attempt to eradicate the complexities and redundancies of an area of law, which despite some unique problems, may be clearly and simply enunciated in our new *Code*" (Working Paper 36, 1984, p. 29).

The recommendations set out to treat arson as an aggravated form of vandalism that carries a higher maximum penalty. In 1985, the recommendations were incorporated in the Criminal Code amendments. Today, arson is treated more seriously than mischief or vandalism, reflecting the emotional and personal value we place on our property.

Jen Grantham / ThinkStock

A three-alarm fire burns through a Toronto-area Roots clothing store and the apartments above it. Once considered a form of vandalism, arson is now defined as its own offence. Why do you think arson was given its own classification?

Do you agree that arson should be treated more seriously than vandalism and mischief?

common features in the early lives of rapists and other violent offenders. Together, they identified a "homicidal triad" that consisted of three "prongs": arson/fire-setting, cruelty to animals, and enuresis (bedwetting) at an inappropriate age (Douglas & Olshaker, 2000). Douglas and Olshaker (2000) assert that when adolescents engage frequently in two or more of these behaviours, it should be a warning that greater criminal acts may lie ahead. They substantiated their arguments by reviewing the history of several notorious violent offenders, including David Berkowitz, better known by his nickname Son of Sam, who started over 2,000 fires before evolving into a serial killer (Douglas & Olshaker, 2000).

Not unlike young offenders, adults commit arson for a variety of reasons, though adult arsonists tend to have very different motivations than adolescent fire-setters. The most common form of arson among adults is *arson for profit*. For example, the owner of a failing business might torch his or her building to claim insurance money. However, many insurance companies today require a thorough fire inspection before insuring buildings in an effort to make it more difficult to file fraudulent claims. Another motive for adult fire-setting is *revenge* (Somers, 1984). This is the most common motive for serial arsonists and involves retaliation for some injustice or imagined injustice.

In addition, some psychologists state that adult fire-setters commonly suffer from personality disorders. Webb and her colleagues (1990) argued that most adult arson should be viewed as evidence of a mental health problem—not as a criminal act. The emotionally disturbed pyromaniac often sets fires in an attempt to cover up or destroy evidence of another crime. Vito and Holmes (1994, p. 315) cite an example in which a man set fire to his house after killing his wife, hoping to incinerate the evidence; however, the fire department was able to put the fire out and find his wife's remains.

## Explaining Arson

In addition to studying the motivations of individual arsonists, criminologists have designed a number of theories to explain fire-setting more broadly. In their review of the literature, Putman and Kirkpatrick (2005) identify eight different theories that have been used to explain fire-setting. These range from opportunity theory and strain theory (see Chapter 8) to risk assessment theory. Virtually all of the theories assert that the underlying motive is either *instrumental* (calculated to benefit the perpetrator) or *expressive* (committed spontaneously out of anger, jealousy, frustration, etc.) and that the origin for the acts is usually *external*, meaning that something about the situation or the environment triggers the arsonist's fire-setting urges.

Finally, organized crime groups and political terrorists are also known to use arson. Between 1976 and 1980, Cecil Kirby, a member of the Satan's Choice motorcycle club, carried out over 100 contract crimes for the Mafia in Canada. The crimes he committed included arson, assault, bombing, and attempted murder (Carrigan, 1991). The Provisional Irish Republican Army is probably the terrorist group best known for its use of arson.

According to research by Pettiway (1988), arson patterns can be explained by environmental and ecological theories. Pettiway found that the rate of arson was significantly related to the age of the housing: the older the house, the greater the likelihood of arson. Stahura and Hollinger (1988) approached arson using routine activity theory. They found that arson rates were related directly to criminal motivation (based on socioeconomic status, employment status, age, etc.), criminal opportunity (based on the presence of older housing, as noted above, or the presence of commercial/industrial buildings), and guardianship (based on the extent of police resources and the number of women officers).

In summary, arson, although not legally defined as a property offence, involves the wilful destruction of private or public property. While the rate of arson has declined since 2009, the cost of arson remains extremely high. As a result, different agencies, including fire departments and insurance companies, devote considerable resources to investigating and preventing arson, but their efforts could be supplemented by contributions from criminologists, who need to better understand the motives underlying arson attacks.

## Summary

- Property crimes are generally committed with the aim of providing financial reward to the offenders. Offenders are either amateurs capitalizing on an opportunity or professional criminals. Most offenders are young males.
- Most property crimes (in particular, theft) have evolved over time, reflecting social and economic changes, and may readily cross over into other crime classifications, such as violent crime (theft), organized crime (arson), or white-collar crime (fraud).
- Most theories relating to property crime are grounded in sociology, and the policies resulting from them have had a questionable impact in reducing property crime incidents. Most property crime prevention approaches have focused on target-hardening strategies, which have

been marginally, if at all, successful. An integrated and interdisciplinary approach may be more effective, focusing instead on other environmental, political, and individual factors motivating property-related criminality.

- The nature of property crime has evolved beyond the conventional categories of simple theft, arson, and so on. We are experiencing new variations of property crime that are having a broader impact on society.
- Despite the fact that conventional crime rates have been declining, current rates are still alarmingly high when compared with earlier rates. Social policies should endeavour to incorporate interdisciplinary and integrated approaches in their efforts to study and remedy such crimes.

## Discussion Questions

1. What can the property crime statistics tell us about crime trends and patterns in Canada? Has the picture changed in recent years? Why?
2. Who is primarily responsible for committing property crimes?
3. Are there common denominators for property crime offenders?
4. What are some of the major explanatory models for the different types of crimes covered in this chapter? Are there any common causal factors that can be used to explain both violent and property crimes?
5. Collect at least a dozen media articles related to the "new" forms of crimes against property. What do they tell us about the nature and extent of the problem? What kinds of solutions, if any, are offered? Do these forms of property crime pose a more serious threat to society than traditional forms?

## Key Concepts

arson

break-and-enter

fraud

identity fraud

identity theft

motor-vehicle crime (MVC)

property crime

theft

## Weblinks

**2015 Facts of the Property and Casualty Insurance Industry in Canada**
The Insurance Bureau of Canada provides annual statistics on claims relating to property crime and motor-vehicle theft.
http://assets.ibc.ca/Documents/Facts%20Book/Facts_Book/2015/FactBook-2015.pdf

**Scams and Fraud**
Hosted by the RCMP, this site offers information on fraud, scams, telemarketing, identity theft, and related property and personal crimes.
www.rcmp-grc.gc.ca/scams-fraudes/index-eng.htm

**Canadian Anti-Fraud Centre**
This site provides tips on avoiding and reporting a host of online and other frauds, including dating scams, emergency scams, prize scams, phishing, and deceptive marketing.
www.antifraudcentre-centreantifraude.ca

**Alberta Municipal Affairs: Fire Statistics Reports**
The Alberta Fire Commissioner issues regular reports with statistics relating to damage and loss of life from fires in the province.
www.ofc.alberta.ca/fire-statistics-reports

# Chapter 11

## Organized Crime, Corporate Crime, and Cybercrime with Mike B. Beke*

bikeriderlondon/Shutterstock.com

The reason crime doesn't pay is that when it does,
it is called a more respectable name.
LAURENCE J. PETER

\* Mike Beke is an associate with the international
evaluation company Blomeyer & Sanz, based in Spain.

## Learning Outcomes

After reading this chapter, you should be able to

- Describe the nature and significance of organized crime;
- Discuss the various types of organized crime groups operating in Canada;
- Assess the extent of corporate crime in Canada and the difficulty in regulating it;
- Talk about the causes of corporate crime and evaluate what can be done to regulate corporate crime; and
- Describe the evolution of cybercrime and discuss the various motivations of cybercriminals.

## Introduction

In Chapters 9 and 10 we dealt with conventional crimes, or "crimes of the street"—violent crimes and property crimes. These conventional crimes are typically (but not always) committed by individuals or small groups from the middle and lower socioeconomic classes. Information on violent and property-related crimes is dutifully recorded, and the data are made readily available through official police records and Statistics Canada, as we have seen over the last two chapters.

There are, however, other forms of crime whose impact can be more devastating and that can present very different challenges to criminologists. In this chapter, we will examine the characteristics, methods, motives, and trends of these non-conventional crimes and review some of the major theoretical perspectives used to explain them. In addition, we will examine some strategies that criminologists have recommended for thwarting non-conventional criminals and what the state has done to deal with these powerful groups and their illegal activities.

Organized crime and corporate crime are typically committed by powerful and influential groups or individuals. Likewise, computer-mediated crime, or cybercrime, while once associated with solitary hackers acting out of mischief and not as part of a larger criminal conspiracy, is increasingly being carried out by sophisticated criminal groups. Because of the status or power that these groups and individuals hold, the impact of these crimes can be very costly in both human and financial terms. These crimes can also have a transnational dimension, which makes them difficult to combat.

## Organized Crime

While the public's image of organized crime usually involves Colombian drug cartels, the Italian Mafia, the Asian Triads, and motorcycle gangs (see below), organized crime can also involve reputable, well-established, and apparently legitimate businesses. In this section, we will examine some of the conventional and non-conventional forms of organized crime.

### History of Organized Crime

Since the days of hunting and gathering, human beings have been interested in acquiring goods of one sort or another. As societies moved from subsistence farming to mercantile practices based around the exchange of goods and services, people learned how to capitalize— legally and illegally—on the value of commercial goods (Wright & Fox, 1978).

Piracy is among the earliest examples of organized crime. Some of the ancient Phoenicians (*c.* 1200–146 BCE) roamed the Mediterranean Sea and plundered ships. From the close of the eighth century, the Vikings of Scandinavia were known to practise acts of piracy throughout France, Scotland, England, and Ireland. However, the most famous examples of piracy occurred during

---

**organized crime**
Illegal activity conducted by individuals or groups acting in consort, typically involving extortion, fraud, theft, smuggling, or the sale of illicit products.

**corporate crime**
Illegal activity conducted by employees and/or officers of a business, either for individual gain or to benefit the company.

**cybercrime**
Any crime that involves the use of computer technology or the Internet.

---

**BOX 11.1**  **FACTS AND FIGURES** RECENT EXAMPLES OF ORGANIZED CRIME IN CANADA

- July 2002: After an 18-month investigation, Canadian, American, and Caribbean police and customs officers smash one of Canada's largest-ever drug-smuggling rings, seizing $95.7 million in drugs. The largest raid, which involves members of the Hells Angels Motorcycle Club, takes place at the Port of Halifax (Aldred, 2004).
- August 2004: The RCMP concludes that a series of brazen heists of cigarettes and tobacco, once thought to be the work of lone-wolf street-corner thugs, is in fact the work of organized gangs (Brewster).
- 2012: A Sûreté du Québec investigation into drug trafficking in the province ends with the arrest of 90 people on 300 charges, as well as the seizure of over 200 kg of cocaine, 62 kg of cannabis and hashish, 150

firearms, 400 kg of explosives, and roughly $1.5 million in cash, according to Criminal Intelligence Service Canada (CISC, 2014).
- 2013: Following a year-long investigation, the RCMP arrests over 30 people involved in running an offshore gambling website used to profit from illegal gaming and to launder the proceeds of other crime generated in Canada (CISC, 2014).
- September 2014: Police and prosecutors break up a major drug trafficking network in eastern Canada. The investigation, code-named Operation J-Tornado, led to the seizure of large quantities of cocaine, heroin, and marijuana, as well as firearms, drug paraphernalia, and cash, and the arrests of 29 people in Saint John, Halifax, and Laval ("Organized crime sting," 2014).

---

the 1600s, when flamboyant, swashbuckling pirates with eye patches and bandannas ranged the seas to pillage European ships carrying goods to and from colonies in the New World. While sea pirates continue to operate today, notably off the northeastern coast of Africa, most of today's pirates need not ever leave their homes as long as they have access to the laptops they use to steal and distribute online content, including music, movies, software, and banking information.

Historically, Canada and the United States have shared more than the world's longest border. Brodeur (cited in Koenig, 2003, p. 47) points out that there is certainly evidence of cross-border "associations of criminals *organizing* crime." As we delve into the subject of organized crime, this is an important point to keep in mind: that unlike other forms of criminal activity that are carried out close to home, organized crime is very much a transnational phenomenon, involving international networks of individuals or groups involved in the illegal movement of goods and, in the case of human trafficking, even people.

## Defining Organized Crime

**Howard Abadinsky** (2012), one of the leading North American authorities on the subject, is critical of past attempts at defining organized crime. He suggests there is no ideal type of organized crime that we can pinpoint, but that organized crime in fact exists as a "degree" of criminal activity or as a point on the "spectrum of legitimacy." Nevertheless, several writers have attempted to define organized crime and organized criminals. Here is a sampling:

> Any group having a corporate structure whose primary objective is to obtain money through illegal activities, often surviving on fear and corruption. (Interpol, 1988)

> Economically motivated illicit activity undertaken by any group, association, or other body consisting of two or more individuals, whether formally or informally organized, where the negative impact of said activity could be considered significant from an economic, social, violence generation, health and safety, and/or environmental perspective. (Porteous, 1998)

BOX 11.2     REALITY CHECK

## Cracking Down on Organized Crime

In September 2002, the federal, provincial, and territorial ministers responsible for justice pledged to make combatting organized crime a national priority (Public Safety and Emergency Preparedness, 2003). This was just months after the federal government had amended the Criminal Code to clarify the meaning of organized crime and crime groups.

Students today can easily find academic books and articles on organized crime, a subject firmly embedded in our cultural consciousness thanks to the vast number of movies and shows whose stories revolve around the subject. Yet it wasn't until February 2002, with the passing of Bill C-24, that a simplified definition of organized crime was added to the Criminal Code, along with three new offences relating to organized crime, tougher sentences for those involved in criminal organizations, and special measures to protect those who assist in apprehending and/or prosecuting members of a criminal organization. According to section 467.1 (1) of the Criminal Code, a criminal organization is any group that

(a) is composed of three or more persons in or outside of Canada; and

(b) has as one of its main purposes or main activities the facilitation or commission of one or more serious offences that, if committed, would likely result in the direct or indirect receipt of a material benefit, including a financial benefit, by the group or by any of the individuals who constitute the group (Criminal Code of Canada, sec. 467.1).

The section notes that "a group of persons that forms randomly for the immediate commission of a single offence" is not considered a criminal organization.

> Do you think that the Criminal Code definition of a criminal organization matches your understanding of the term? Does it leave out anything you would have expected to be included?

[T]he illegal activities carried out by structured groups of three or more persons for a prolonged period of time and having the aim of committing serious crimes through concerted action by using intimidation, violence, corruption, or other means in order to obtain, directly or indirectly, a financial or other material benefit. (Council of Europe 2002, p. 6)

[A] continuing criminal enterprise that rationally works to profit from illicit activities that are in great public demand. Its continuing existence is maintained through the use of force, threats, monopoly control, and/or the corruption of public officials. (Albanese, 2014, p. 4)

Other definitions, while they vary in their precise terminology, tend to share several themes: (1) the supplying of illegal goods and services; (2) the involvement of predatory crime (carried out by gangs and terrorist cells); and (3) the transnational dimension.

Organized crime is a broad concept that encompasses a wide range of activities and methods. As Beare (1996, p. 266) explains, one of the challenges to offering a single definition is the difficulty of "captur[ing] the essential aspects of the 'process' that certain criminals use in carrying out criminal activity." This leads to another challenge for criminologists: as Loree (2004, p. 10) points out, since each nation "creates its own legal definition of organized crime, [it] complicates international collaboration, data collection, and analysis."

Appreciating the difficulty in giving organized crime a single, all-encompassing definition, Abadinsky (2012), along with several other scholars, has focused on identifying a set of attributes that are commonly found among organized crime groups. Among other things, organized crime groups are:

- *non-ideological*—most organized crime groups have no political affiliation, with goals that are not directly motivated by political concerns;
- *hierarchial*—they feature a chain of command, with three or more permanent positions of authority typically existing within the group;
- *defined by limited or exclusive in membership*, sometimes based on ethnic, racial, or kinship ties, or shared criminal history;
- *perpetuous*—these groups constitute an ongoing criminal conspiracy designed to persist over time;
- *organized through specialization or division of labour*—members have specific areas of responsibility and defined roles (e.g. enforcers, soldiers, money movers);
- *monopolistic*—organized crime groups strive for hegemony (dominance) over a geographic area, thereby restraining competition and increasing their own profit; and
- *governed by rules and regulations*—virtually all organized crime groups require their members to take an oath of secrecy: for example, members of the Japanese yakuza used to have to submit to having a joint of their little finger removed, and some gangs require new members to undergo hazing or beatings by fellow members, while others require a criminal act as part of their initiation.

What kinds of activities are criminal organizations involved in? We will discuss specific kinds of organized crime activity throughout the chapter, but the following list gives an overview of the main activities recognized by the RCMP and Interpol:

- alien smuggling
- armed assault
- car theft
- drug dealing
- fraud
- trafficking in humans, radioactive material, and weapons
- robbery and smuggling of precious and antique goods
- exploitation through prostitution
- chemical terrorism
- gambling
- embezzling from industries and financial institutions
- infiltration and control of private and commercial banks
- control of black markets

Even from this sampling of crimes one can readily see how organized crime groups can represent serious business enterprises and pose a serious threat to the economic stability of countries.

## Organized Crime Groups in Canada

We will now turn to several of the more prominent types of organized crime groups that exist in Canada today. Although they may differ in their orientation, all of these groups share many of the characteristics that Abadinsky (2012) identified and defined.

According to the Canadian Public Safety website, as of 2009 there were 157 organized crime units across Canada (Organized Crime Research Unit, 2014). A study commissioned in 2010 deemed that such a response was necessary because the "increasing sophistication of criminal organizations and the multi-jurisdictional nature of organized crime demand an equally sophisticated law enforcement and regulatory response" (Organized Crime Research Unit, 2014). While acknowledging the invaluable service the units serve in combatting

BOX 11.3     REALITY CHECK

## Did the RCMP Assist Organized Criminals?

Between 1990 and 1994, an undercover RCMP operation inadvertently helped Colombian drug traffickers and their associates import and sell almost 5,000 kilograms of cocaine with an estimated street value of $2 billion. A follow-up report revealed that the sting operation had failed as a result of insufficient officer staffing levels, a reluctance of senior RCMP officials to respond to requests for assistance, and—perhaps most alarming—internal security breaches by at least two corrupt officers. The RCMP fiasco ultimately helped "the clandestine drug pipeline between Colombia's cocaine cartels and Canadian biker gangs and Italian Mafia gangs that import, distribute and sell cocaine to users and addicts in Canada" (McIntosh, 1998, p. A2).

In 2007, the RCMP completed an internal investigation focusing on corruption within the force over an 11-year period from 1995 through 2005. The results of the investigation—dubbed Project Sanction—were summarized in a report that was kept private until 2014, when the RCMP was forced to release it to The Canadian Press following an access-to-information request. The report identified 322 cases of corruption within the Mounties, including 12 cases involving organized crime. The report attributed the corruption to "poor guidance, lack of adequate supervision, or a combination of life pressures that culminated in a desperate decision" ("RCMP tracks its own," 2014). The RCMP reports that since introducing their new recruitment screening protocols in 2007, the number of corruption incidents among new recruits has dropped significantly (Bronskill, 2014).

What do you think causes some police officers to engage in unlawful activity themselves?

organized crime, the report offered three key recommendations for improving the work of the units: (1) finding ways to measure and evaluate the success of integrated units; (2) learning what effect the integrated units have on their priority target crimes; and (3) investigating how these initiatives benefit all partners.

### Aboriginal Crime Groups

**Aboriginal crime groups**

Organized crime groups started or operated in Canada by Aboriginal people, involved in crimes ranging from cigarette smuggling to illegal gambling.

Once thought to be little more than low-level groups of thugs lacking formal structure, Aboriginal crime groups—such as Indian Posse, Redd Alert, Alberta Warriors, and Native Syndicate—have been drawing increasing attention since the early 1990s as a result of their escalating involvement in criminal activities (Totten, 2012). Beare (1996, p. 272) describes the organized criminal activity of Aboriginal people as "a perfect example of a 'manufactured' organized crime problem," since certain groups seek out illegal ventures by which to attain their goals as a result of perceived limited economic opportunities and of being marginalized on a number of social levels. And while most Aboriginal crime groups are street gangs, falling between "wanna-be" groups and criminal business organizations in terms of their sophistication and formal structure (Grekul & LaBoucane-Benson, 2006, p. 16; Totten, 2012), Aboriginal groups have been involved in very serious organized crime activity. The following are some recent examples:

- In 2003, several prairie-based Aboriginal gangs were working with more established gangs—such as the Hells Angels and various Asian gangs—in selling drugs at the street level (Dolha, 2003). In 2004, there were an estimated 300 Aboriginal gang members incarcerated in the prairie region.
- In April 2014, the RCMP reported that organized Aboriginal gangs were caught in a raid along the Canada–US border, which resulted in 25 arrests. The report also noted that the gang members caught had links with the Mafia. During the raid the police seized

40,000 kilograms of tobacco worth $7 million on the black market. In addition, investigators also seized more than $450,000 in cash ("Tobacco smuggling," 2014).

Because of tax exemptions, as well as certain other rights and their location near the US border, Aboriginal organized crime groups can make a profit of over a million dollars with a single tractor trailer loaded with 1,200 cases of cigarettes (Nickerson, 2004). Such opportunities, which yield relatively easy profits, have made intervention difficult. The difficulty of controlling smuggling and other criminal activities among First Nations people is compounded by the fact that many reserves have their own police forces by agreement with the federal government; for this reason, they fall outside the jurisdiction of the RCMP or local provincial force.

What can be done? Because these are crimes of opportunity, they are particularly difficult for law enforcement agencies to monitor and combat. In 1994, the sale of illegal cigarettes had become such a critical problem that the federal government dramatically reduced taxes on legal cigarettes in an effort to eliminate the demand for black-market products. However, in 2001, Ottawa, recognizing the significant risk of tobacco products to Canadians' health, reversed its policy and raised the price of cigarettes by $4 a carton, while allocating $480 million for anti-smoking programs and programs to combat cigarette smuggling. In 2014, a package of 20 cigarettes ranged in price from a low of $3.16 in Ontario to a high of $5.87 in Newfoundland and Labrador. The price differences are largely attributable to different tax

Mark Taylor

Richard Wolfe at his kitchen table in Fort Qu'Appelle, Saskatchewan, shortly after serving 15 years for attempted murder. Wolfe, along with his late brother Daniel (in the picture), co-founded the Indian Posse street gang. What factors do you think make gang membership attractive to young Aboriginal people?

levies. While the anti-tobacco measures have received public support, the higher prices now charged for legal cigarettes have stimulated the market for cheaper, illegal products.

In 2000, Ovide Mercredi, former National Chief of the Assembly of First Nations, prepared a report in which he called for initiatives that promote a path of healing and positive contribution in the community for gang members, based on a model of restorative justice (see Chapter 14). However, the best solution to fighting Aboriginal crime organizations may lie in ending the persistent marginalization of Canada's Aboriginal people and providing them opportunities to attain a socioeconomic standard and lifestyle that are more appealing than what can be gained from gang membership. Many of these ideas are captured in the report of the Truth and Reconciliation Commission, released in December 2015.

### Cartels

**cartel**
An association of manufacturers or suppliers who have entered into an informal agreement to fix prices, to limit supply, and minimize competition by various means, some of which may be illegal and may involve violence.

A cartel is an informal association of independent commercial enterprises designed to limit competition. The term was coined in the late 1800s by the Austrian economist Friedrich Kleinwächter, who used it to refer to "the alliance of enterprises." Since then, the term has taken on a more sinister meaning that encompasses the illegal business practices and sometimes violent criminal behaviour that are associated with cartels. In a special report in *Criminal Justice International* (1994) the cartels were described as a new breed of international organized crime

AP Photo/Eduardo Verdugo, File

Mexican drug lord Joaquín Archivaldo Guzmán Loera, shown during his arrest in February 2014, rose to power as the head of the Sinaloa Cartel during the 1980s. In 1993, Guzmán (or "El Chapo," as he is known) was arrested and sentenced to 20 years for murder and drug trafficking. In 2001, he escaped a maximum-security prison after bribing his guards. Despite multi-million dollar rewards offered by the Mexican and US governments for information leading to his arrest, he evaded capture for 13 years. In July 2015—just 16 months after this photo was taken—El Chapo again escaped from a maximum-security prison, this time through an underground tunnel. He remained at large until January 2016, when he was captured shortly after a secret meeting with Hollywood actor Sean Penn, who had interviewed the drug lord for an article in *Rolling Stone* magazine.

that transcends nations. Cartels are seen as threats to democracy, national security, and international development. The 1994 report estimates that in the early 1990s there were over 2,600 organized cartels operating around the world. How widespread are cartels? Consider that in 2014, Alberta Mennonites with generations-old roots in Mexico were suspected of bringing cocaine from Mexican drug cartels into Canada (Grant, 2014).

Although the Colombian cartels emerged in the early 1980s and 1990s under the notorious drug lord Pablo Escobar, their highly sophisticated operations since the early twenty-first century have made them textbook examples of the threat posed by transnational crime groups capable of co-opting entire governments. Even so, their practices have in recent years been eclipsed by the escalating violence of Mexican drug cartels, which have taken ownership of the far-reaching networks and drug routes into the United States and beyond (Grillo, 2012). The Mexican cartels are very powerful and, in some regions, extremely violent. Their work is largely responsible for a spike in the national murder rate, which rose from just over 2,000 in 2006 to over 12,300 in 2011 (Grillo, 2012). Their sophisticated infrastructure, ability to corrupt officials, and preparedness to defend their illicit market will not readily succumb to government raids and the odd arrest.

Other powerful drug cartels include certain Nigerian operations, the Japanese yakuza or Boryokudan groups, and Jamaican groups known as posses (see Totten, 2014). While these groups originate abroad, their reach is global. According to Vancouver police, the business model for many Mexican cartels is to have high-ranking members stationed in countries like Canada to arrange shipments of cocaine and other drugs into the country (Bolan, 2014b). Among the newer cartel groups in Canada and the United States are the Russian organized crime groups (see Box 11.5).

Cartels are a prime example of the changing face of organized crime. Once little more than glorified regional gangs, they have evolved to become international threats to national economies and the political stability of states. Changes in the global economy and political instability in various parts of the world have created an environment favourable to the spread of these criminal organizations. The widespread and international nature of many cartels poses a major problem for those attempting to combat them. Most solutions require co-operation between law enforcement agencies across jurisdictions and international borders (Smyth, 2001; Nores & Swan, 2010). Criminologists should also explore proactive and interdisciplinary approaches in their efforts to understand and address the problem.

**illicit market**

The market for illegal goods and services (e.g. prostitution, illicit drugs, contraband computer software, off-market cigarettes), typically made up of otherwise law-abiding citizens and serviced by organized crime groups.

---

| BOX 11.4 | **A CLOSER LOOK** |
|---|---|
| | **Cocaine: A Medicinal Drug?** |

Cocaine—the most lucrative of drugs trafficked by Colombian and Mexican cartels—is derived from the leaves of the coca shrub, which has grown naturally in the Andean highlands since 1500 BCE and which has historically been used for medicinal and restorative purposes. John Pemberton believed in the plant's curative effects when he included coca leaves in the tonic he invented in 1886; today we still know it as Coca-Cola, although coca leaves have not been part of the recipe for over a century.

Abuse began after 1862, when a German chemist was able to extract an alkaloid that he labelled cocaine. Its potent properties were soon being touted as a "magical substance" by Sigmund Freud in 1886. Today, cocaine is used in a variety of legally sold pharmaceutical products. However, in 1961, a treaty ratified by 125 nations introduced a ban on producing or processing cocaine—except for medicinal purposes. It was shortly thereafter that cocaine became the drug of choice and a marketable item for organized crime groups (McCarthy, 2011).

What are your thoughts about legalizing "illicit" drugs? How might we prevent the trafficking of cocaine and other illicit drugs?

---

**BOX 11.5**

**A CLOSER LOOK**

## The Russian "Mafiya"

*The law cannot keep up with crime which is no doubt the biggest industry in Russia. (Moscow Times, cited in Goodwin, 1995, p. 3)*

Organized crime in eastern Europe traces its roots to the 1970s and 1980s, when it became increasingly involved in the black-market supply of Western consumer goods that were otherwise unavailable in Europe's communist countries. However, it was in 1991, when the Soviet Union collapsed, that organized crime began to flourish in Russia and the countries of the former Soviet bloc. In 1991, the Russian Ministry of the Interior reported that there were at least 785 organized crime groups operating throughout Russia; by 2000, their numbers had swelled to 5,600—a growth of over 700 per cent (Finckenauer & Waring, 2001). Over roughly the same period, murder rates rose 25 per cent each year.

The US Central Intelligence Agency (CIA) now estimates that more than "half of Russia's 25 largest banks have illegal ties to Russian organized crime," which stands as a major impediment to both economic and institutional reform in the country (Gupta, 2010, p. 133). What is more, since 1991, the Russian Mafiya has been moving beyond national borders, placing agents in Western countries including Canada. A recent CSIS report suggests that a number of Russians applying for immigration status in Canada have ties to organized crime groups, and a 2006 report published jointly by the RCMP, the US Federal Bureau of Investigation (FBI), and the US Drug Enforcement Administration (DEA) notes that Toronto is a hub of eastern European organized crime in Canada concerned particularly with the diamond trade in the North (Canada/US Organized Crime Threat Assessment, 2006, p. 7). The report explains that Russian Mafiya groups working abroad tend to feature an *autorityet*, an authority and decision-maker who administers funds, and a *krisha* (literally "roof"), a sponsor who provides protection in exchange for a cut of the profits.

---

### Ethnic Crime Groups

According to the most recent Statistics Canada data on the topic (Chui & Flanders, 2013), Canada is home to over 200 different ethnic groups, and visible minorities make up almost 20 per cent of the population (Table 11.1). Some of these groups come from war-torn areas where violence, corruption, and extortion have become a way of life, and due to these reasons as well as significant cultural and ethnic differences, they may not assimilate as readily as other groups. On arriving in Canada, members of these groups may occasionally bring their conflicts with them. Their activities may receive a fair bit of attention, while those of members of certain other minority groups may go largely unnoticed because of the image the group projects (see Box 11.6).

Pace (1991) and, more recently, Abadinsky (2012) have observed that ethnicity may affect a group's tendency toward violence, its market of specialization, and its accessibility to legitimate markets. Different ethnic groups are thus involved in different types of criminal activities and use different strategies when engaging in criminal behaviour.

Asian triads, Vietnamese gangs, Albanian mafia, and Caribbean gangs can be found in most provinces. However, the greatest amount of ethnic gang activity takes place in British Columbia, Ontario, and Quebec (Totten, 2012). Influenced by social and political circumstances in their ancestral countries, these groups are known for their violence, manifested in, for example, drive-by shootings, home invasions, and extortions.

Among the more serious ethnic organized crime groups in Canada are Asian-based crime groups, whose roots can be traced all the way back to the first wave of Chinese immigrants, predominantly goldfield or railroad workers in the mid-1800s (Malinowski, 1997). In 2002, an Alberta solicitor general's report expressed concern about the possible influx of Asian criminals after the Chinese takeover of Hong Kong in July 1997. The wealth of many new Hong Kong immigrants in Canada could make them prime targets for extortion, drug trafficking, and other activities of Chinese crime groups. In 2015, the federal court of appeal upheld a deportation order in the case of Lai Tong Sang, an alleged Asian organized crime boss who had been living in Canada for 17 years. Lai was alleged to be the leader of the Shui Fong triad in Macau, but he reportedly left the island to escape a violent turf war between rival gangs (Dhillon, 2013).

Vietnamese gangs, including United Bamboo, Born to Kill, Viet-Ching, and AOC, are known for their violence and general disregard for law enforcement (Helfand & Osborne, 2003). In Canada, they often prey on members of their own communities through extortion and robbery, taking advantage of immigrants who are unfamiliar with Canadian ways and who, because of their cultural background, are afraid to go to the police (Carrigan, 1991). Many gang members see going to jail as better than being in a refugee camp. The exact extent of these groups' involvement in organized crime is not known because it is suspected that a significant number of their activities go unreported. One Vietnam-born police officer estimated that as much as "75 per cent of the crime committed by the Asian community [in Canada] is not reported" (Carrigan, 1991, p. 194).

In one of the first studies to explore the Vietnamese criminal organization in Canada, Prowse (1994, p. 2) observed that "the most powerful gang is the most violent gang; with violence, you get power, and with power, you get money." Criminal activities among Vietnamese gangs first came to the attention of Canadian authorities in the early 1980s, but these groups were often mistaken for Chinese triads. Starting in the 1990s, their level of violence escalated, and they have since "undergone a transformation from loosely structured crime groups . . . to well-armed and semi-structured criminal organizations" (Prowse, 1994, p. 5). Although formed in the 1990s, the FOB ("Fresh Off the Boat") gang and its eventual splinter group the FKs ("Fresh Killers") were engaged in major gang rivalry warfare in Alberta, resulting in a number of daytime drive-by shootings and the eventual death of some 25 gang members, before police were able to intervene and dismantle both gangs in 2013 (Grant & Bakx, 2013).

| Table 11.1 Ethnic Origin* of Canadians, Based on Results of the 2011 National Household Survey | |
| --- | --- |
| **Ethnicity** | **Responses** |
| North American | 12,906,490 |
| Canadian | 10,563,805 |
| Aboriginal | 1,836,035 |
| American | 373,575 |
| Québécois | 193,885 |
| Other North American | 150,590 |
| European | 20,157,965 |
| British | 11,343,710 |
| French | 5,077,215 |
| Western European | 4,439,950 |
| Eastern European | 3,142,775 |
| Southern European | 2,798,395 |
| Northern European | 1,164,425 |
| Asian | 5,011,220 |
| East & Southeast Asian | 2,650,000 |
| South Asian | 1,615,925 |
| West Central Asian & Middle Eastern | 778,465 |
| African | 766,735 |
| Caribbean | 627,590 |
| Latin, Central, and South American | 544,380 |
| Australian, New Zealand, & Pacific Islands | 74,875 |

* Includes all results, whether respondents claimed a single ethnic origin or more than one ethnic origin.
Source: Statistics Canada, *2011 National Household Survey: Data tables*, Statistics Canada cat. no. 99-010-X2011028.

### Outlaw Motorcycle Gangs

In 2014, there were 688,204 registered motorcycles and mopeds in Canada, according to Statistics Canada (CANSIM Table 405-0004). Despite a common belief that all bikers are involved in criminal gangs, most of these vehicles are owned by upstanding biking enthusiasts who may attend the odd Harley Davidson motorbike convention but who do not engage in any form of criminal activity. In fact, the number of bikers involved in crime is so low that they are sometimes referred to as "one percenters," a name derived from the claim (attributed to the American Motorcycle Association) that 99 per cent of motorcyclists are law-abiding citizens.

The Hells Angels are the most notorious outlaw motorcycle gang (OMG) operating within the "one percent" (see Box 10.7). Its members often own Harleys and may attend some of the conventions, but the orientation of the club is decidedly criminal, involved primarily in narcotics trafficking. In 2014, Manitoba became the first province to declare the Hells Angels

BOX 11.6    REALITY CHECK

## The Mennonite Drug Pipeline

Known for their commitment to pacifism, hard work, and traditional religious observances, North American Mennonites are, for the most part, law-abiding people, the most conservative of whom still speak German, avoid modern technology, and seldom stray far from their tightly knit communities. However, no ethnic, religious, or social group is immune to the temptation of criminal opportunities.

In May 1997, three Mennonites from southern Ontario were charged with operating a very sophisticated drug smuggling operation between Mexico and Canada after they were caught with marijuana valued at over $8 million during a series of police seizures between 1991 and 1997. Each of the three men received seven years for conspiracy to import narcotics and five years for possession of narcotics ("Mennonite drug pipeline expanding," 1997).

More recently, Mennonite migrant workers in southwestern Ontario have been charged in cocaine trafficking operations (O'Brien, 2014). Many of those involved hold dual Mexican–Canadian citizenship and travel seasonally between their homes in Mexico and Ontario's farm belt, where they find work during the summer months. As noted earlier in the chapter, police in Alberta have broken up Mennonite-run cocaine pipelines into the province from Chihuahua, where some Canadian Mennonite families have ties that date back generations to when their ancestors were forced to leave Canada to find work in Mexico. These recent incidents show that while there is at least a 20-year history in Mennonite drug smuggling, harder drugs are now the focus of operations.

How might we explain Mennonite involvement in drug trafficking?

© Horizons WWP / TRVL / Alamy Stock Photo

Outlaw motorcycle gangs, such as the Canadian chapter of the Hells Angels, use a combination of legitimate businesses like real estate, online gambling, and bar management to hide their more illegal activities, such as prostitution, pornography, and drug dealing, from law enforcement.

a criminal organization, a move designed to fast-track legal proceedings against the group and its members (prosecutors in that province no longer have to prove in every trial that the Hells Angels are in fact a criminal group). The legislation also makes it easier for provincial enforcement officials to seize property as the proceeds of crime, which is why, according to an expert on OMGs, the Hells Angels and other criminal biker gangs have been selling off assets like their clubhouses and renting space to hold their meetings (Bolan, 2014a).

Other OMGs in Canada include the Outlaws, the Bandidos, Satan's Choice, Quebec's Rock Machine, and the Red Devils, Canada's oldest OMG, operating in the greater Hamilton area. These gangs engage in drug trafficking, prostitution, contract killing, and (more recently) the cultivation and distribution of hydroponic marijuana. They also own bars and strip clubs (primarily for laundering the proceeds of their criminal activity) and are involved in extortion and intimidation of rival bar owners. According to research conducted at the US Institute for National Strategic Studies, the extent of the illicit global economy is between $1.69 and $1.92 trillion annually; OMGs account for a portion of this, stemming from their various illegal activities (Miklaucic & Brewer, 2013).

Wolf (1991), using a sociological framework, investigated the lives and subculture of bikers. He noted that most of the members came from the lower classes and working classes, where they experience a sense of *anomie*—Durkheim's term for a lack of purpose and identity (see Chapter 8). Becoming a member of a bike gang allows people who feel alienated and dissatisfied to romanticize their mundane lives. With the backing of fellow members, they become a part of a wild and countercultural existence, acting out a form of rebellion. The patches or gang colours they wear and the bikes they ride (typically a Harley Davidson with an engine of a particular size) add a comforting sense of order and ritualism to their lifestyle. These practices allow members to express their loyalty to their gang and recognize fellow members. They also intimidate non-bikers, which can enhance the self-esteem of gang members. Bikers also have their own jargon (see Box 11.8), which reinforces their sense of community and internal cohesion while separating them from outsiders in the mainstream culture.

Wolf suggests that OMGs persist partly because they represent an outgrowth of a capitalist system in which certain members of the working class feel alienated. Within the deviant subculture of the gang, these people are able to share a common set of social norms that are usually in contrast to those of society at large. Adoption of such norms draws social rejection and further reinforces rebellious attitudes and behaviours.

---

**BOX 11.7** | **A CLOSER LOOK**
### Hells Angels

Formed by the Bishop family in the late 1940s, in Hollister, California, the Hells Angels Motorcycle Club was made up mostly of ordinary individuals who were looking for a little recreation and excitement after the war. They called themselves the Pissed Off Bastards of Bloomington and formed the first American Motorcycle Association. It was only after a member of the group was arrested and not released that the group became more violent and renamed itself the "Hell's Angels" (see Caine, 2012; Langton, 2010). Historically they have been involved with violent crimes, including drug dealing, trafficking in stolen goods, extortion, and prostitution. They expanded into Quebec in the 1980s and 1990s, but by 2015 they had some 31 chapters across the country with an estimated 400-odd members (Humphreys, 2015). Today the club has over 100 chapters operating in 30 countries.

---

**BOX 11.8** | **FACTS AND FIGURES** HOW TO RECOGNIZE A MEMBER OF AN OUTLAW MOTORCYCLE GANG

By the language they use, including the following terms:

- *AFFL*: "Angels Forever, Forever Loaded."
- *Angels' Bible*: Harley Davidson motoring manual, frequently used for their private weddings and torn up for divorce proceedings.
- *Back pack*: Full colours (i.e. emblems or insignia) tattooed on a member's back.
- *Chopper*: Chopped or cut-down motorcycle with all unnecessary equipment, such as front brake and fender, stripped off.
- *Crash truck*: A van, panel truck, or converted school bus that follows or precedes the bike run and picks up broken-down bikes.
- *Filthy few*: Denoting a biker who has killed for the gang.
- *Full patch*: Denoting a biker with full club membership.
- *Hawg*: (1) Law enforcement officer, also known as "the man"; (2) Harley Ownership Group
- *Mama*: Any woman sexually available to all club members.
- *Patch over*: A situation where a stronger major club takes over defeated or probationary clubs; this can be accomplished peacefully or through war.

- *Suck to the Bulls*: Talk or act friendly toward a police officer.

By the tattoos or patches they wear, including the following:

- *1%*: Denoting a biker's status as a "one-percenter," or outlaw.
- *13*: Denoting a biker's involvement in the illegal sale and distribution of marijuana or methamphetamine (from the initial letter *m*, the thirteenth letter of the alphabet).
- *22*: Denoting a rider who has served time in prison.
- *24*: Having drunk 24 beers in less than 8 hours.
- *81*: Hells Angels (from the initial letters *h* and *a*, the eighth and first letters of the alphabet).
- *666*: Denotes a member who has engaged in acts of violence (666 is traditionally the sign of the devil).
- *\**: Tattooed between the thumb and forefinger, asterisks are used to indicate how many times the wearer has been in prison.

*Source*: Adapted from Lemay, 1994, p. 39.

What Wolf does not explain is why more working-class people do not join motorcycle gangs or other subcultural groups. Why don't women become involved more in subcultural groups? Are violent subcultural groups a product of social conditions, or is it possible that individual biological factors are also involved? After all, very few societies have ever been crime-free, and gangs, mobs, and organized crime groups seem to have existed since the beginning of recorded history.

Motorcycle gangs have become very sophisticated in their criminal activities, and many now have international operations (see Scaramella, Brenzinger, & Miller, 1997). In North America, where the Hells Angels have a very strong presence, the gang is involved in prostitution, the illegal drug trade, money laundering, fraud, and trafficking in weapons. It is believed that the Italian Mafia hires bikers as "musclemen" to protect Mafia bosses, intimidate rivals, and carry out hired killings. The Mafia has also allegedly employed bikers to move drugs and carry out violent tactics such as bombings and arson (Totten, 2012).

During the 1990s, OMGs made headlines repeatedly, thanks to a violent turf war in Quebec and the takeover of the Grim Reapers by the Hells Angels in Alberta. These were signs that certain OMGs were becoming stronger. Yet in spite of some high-profile raids and arrests, police in Canada have struggled to diminish the strength and spread of outlaw motorcycle gangs. Why is this the case? First, law enforcement agencies are limited in what they can do when a biker gang moves into town: other than harassing bikers with tickets for minor traffic violations, the police are unable to prevent them from moving about as they please, even if the group is suspected of involvement in criminal activity. Recently, in fact, police forces have had to deal with legal constraints and court rulings that are undermining some of their efforts (Caine, 2012).

The second challenge facing law-enforcement agencies is that OMGs are gaining strength at a time when many police departments are facing cutbacks. In provinces such as Alberta and Quebec, there is a dearth of investigators and tactical analysts that can be deployed in the fight against biker crime (Caine, 2012). Biker gangs, on the other hand, are becoming larger, better organized, and more sophisticated. Yves Lavigna (1996), a noted Canadian expert on OMGs, compares the Hells Angels and similar motorcycle gangs in North America to the ethnic gangs found in other parts of the world. They draw recruits from among the social outcasts and rebellious youths found in the least prosperous social class: Lavigna states that bikers have their roots in what he calls "white trash"—the lowest socioeconomic class, found typically in rural areas and made up primarily of people of white, European descent. But behind the image of the rough-hewn, lawless biker—the "rebel without a cause"—is a tightly governed criminal network with significant resources at its disposal. As Hall and Richards (2004) explain, biker gangs typically consist of a vertical chain of command with at least three tiers. Because of their sophisticated organizational structure, they are able to continue operating in spite of the loss of key members (to prison, or to a hit by a rival gang). And, as is common among organized crime groups, they are prepared to use violence and bribery as a means of creating and maintaining their existence and monopoly over certain criminal activities (Scaramella, Brenzinger, & Miller, 1997). Finally, OMGs have a clearly defined set of rules and regulations that govern membership, making them both difficult to join and difficult for law enforcement to infiltrate (Abadinsky, 2012).

As recently as 2012, in a report titled *The State of Organized Crime*, the federal government acknowledged that the growing sophistication of organized crime, including biker crime, was making it difficult to combat. The only way to fight sophisticated crime is with sophisticated methods. This requires an integrated approach involving co-operation among all the elements of the criminal justice system and the support of society. Neither the police nor the law can stop the growth of organized criminal activities alone. Nevertheless, the Canadian Security Intelligence Service (CSIS) has made combatting OMG and organized crime in general a major priority. The service's budget grew from $248 million in 2001–2 to $540 million in 2011–12

(CSIS, 2014; see Figure 11.1). Yet, despite the increase in resources, the agency's success in stopping biker gangs has arguably been minimal.

### The Italian Mafia

It is believed that *La Cosa Nostra* (the formal name of the Mafia, translated as "our thing" or "our cause") originated during the ninth century on the island of Sicily, when Arab invaders tried to oppress the original inhabitants. To survive, the inhabitants sought refuge in the hills of the island. The word *Mafia* means "refuge" in Arabic. Subsequent attempts to force out the native inhabitants of the island led Sicilian families to form a secret society with its own infrastructure. Members were required to take an oath on initiation with the intention of creating a sense of family based on ancestry and Sicilian heritage. To this day, the oath includes five fundamental principles:

- *omerta*: a code of silence, or a vow never to reveal any Mafia secrets or expose Mafia members under the threat of torture or death;
- total obedience to the boss, or "don";
- a "no questions asked" promise to assist any befriended Mafia member;
- a vow to avenge any attack on members of the family, because an attack on one is an attack on all; and
- a vow to avoid any contact with the authorities. (Dilger, 2012)

The Mafia grew into a strong organization that used extortion, intimidation, and other forms of crime to advance its cause. When Mafia members did not get their way, they resorted

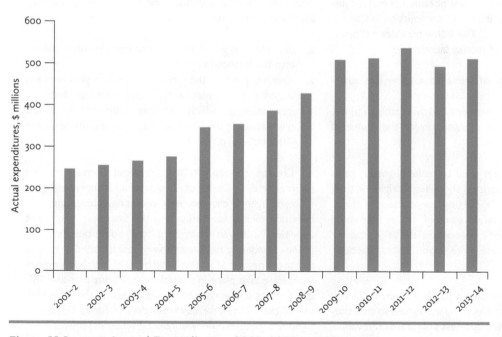

**Figure 11.1   CSIS Annual Expenditures, 2001–2002 to 2013–14**

In the decade from 2001–2 to 2011–12, CSIS enjoyed a 217 per cent increase in expenditures to combat organized crime and terrorism. Is it working?

Note: Includes salaries, operating expenditures, and construction costs
*Source:* Canadian Security Intelligence Service, 2014, p. 52; Ljunggren, 2014.

to violence to force compliance. Soon families began to compete for power and territory, leading to the emergence of organized crime families so often depicted in the movies. Al Capone, Charles "Lucky" Luciano, Bugsy Siegel, and Meyer Lansky have all been subjects of various gangster films.

Today, in Italy, the Mafia poses a serious problem for the government. Its *modus operandi* has evolved over time, and it now operates in concert with other organized crime groups. For example, in recent years, the Mafia has formed alliances with Colombian drug cartels and outlaw motorcycle gangs as a means of facilitating international drug trafficking.

In Canada, traditional Italian-based organized crime has been reported in every province, with the greatest concentration in the major urban settings of southwestern Ontario and Montreal, and, to a lesser extent, in Calgary and Vancouver (CISC, 2004). Although the primary

---

**BOX 11.9**

## A CLOSER LOOK
## Money Laundering

Section 462.31 of the Criminal Code (CC) provides a wordy and cumbersome definition of the offence known as *laundering the proceeds of crime*. According to the CC, a person is guilty of this offence if he or she "uses, transfers the possession of, sends or delivers to any person or place, [etc.] . . . any property or any proceeds of any property with intent to conceal or convert that property or those proceeds, knowing or believing that all or a part of that property or of those proceeds was obtained or derived directly or indirectly as a result of the commission in Canada of a designated offence . . ." The RCMP provides a simpler, three-point explanation of money laundering:

1. It converts proceeds of crime to another less suspicious form.
2. It conceals the criminal origins and ownership of funds.
3. It creates a legitimate explanation for the source of funds. (RCMP, 2013a)

It is, then, any transaction used to make ill-gotten gains look "clean" in order to conceal their illegal origins. A thief who sells stolen goods is laundering the proceeds of crime. Because they deal with larger sums of money that could attract notice when spent or deposited in a bank account, organized crime groups use more sophisticated practices, including the following:

- Depositing illegally obtained funds incrementally into the bank accounts of a legitimate business so that they appear to be part of the business's natural daily revenue. Businesses such as restaurants and bars are frequently used, since they have high volumes of daily cash sales, which are harder than credit card sales to document, making them better for concealing stolen money.
- Setting up a shell company and declaring any illegal funds as legitimate revenue. The anonymous nature of

the company makes it useful for concealing the identities of the individuals involved.

- Using money obtained illegally to purchase real estate or to invest in stocks, which are quickly sold to make the profits appear legitimate.
- Owning or controlling banks, which are used to make large deposits appear legitimate.

Regardless of the scheme, money laundering typically involves three steps:

1. *placement*, in which money obtained illegally is placed into the financial system;
2. *layering*, in which the money is put through numerous transactions to create a legitimate audit trail; and
3. *integration*, in which the now laundered funds are placed back in the financial system by legitimate means (FINTRAC, 2013).

Created in 2000, FINTRAC (Financial Transactions and Reports Analysis Centre of Canada) is an independent government agency charged with detecting, preventing, and deterring money laundering and the financing of terrorist activities. But as Van Koningsveld (1998) points out, the art of money laundering has become very sophisticated thanks to (1) the opening up of international borders, which lets money laundering take place in multiple jurisdictions that are difficult for any one agency to monitor, and (2) the increasing use of the Internet for quick transfers of funds. Effectively fighting organized money laundering schemes requires international co-operation and the establishment of databanks of all companies and their *beneficial owners*—in money laundering, these are the people who are involved directly in the movement of illegal funds but who are not listed as the company owner. As Van Koningsveld states, "the weakest link is the problem of identification of the beneficial owner."

specialization of these groups has been drug trafficking and protection rackets, they have also been known to engage in, among other crimes, illegal gambling, loan-sharking, union racketeering, counterfeiting, vote buying, and money laundering (Gambetta, 2009). Of particular concern to law enforcement agencies is the Mafia's "extensive investment in legitimate businesses," which "are used to invest their profits, to serve in a money laundering capacity, and as a cover or front for criminal operations" (Beare, 1996, p. 271).

In spite of a few sensationalized cases in which big-time mobsters have been arrested and prosecuted, or even killed (e.g. Nick Rizzuto, Jr, in Montreal in December 2013; Carmine Verduci in Toronto in April 2014), efforts to weaken the influence of the Mafia in Canada have not been very successful (see Box 11.10). When arrested, Mafia members usually obtain relatively light sentences by plea-bargaining, since they have access to the best legal talent available. While in prison, they tend to be model prisoners, still able to continue their entrepreneurial activities, and are usually paroled as soon as they become legally eligible. Better policing, the use of informants, and successful prosecution bring occasional success, but the impact of these has been minimal (Cedilot & Noel, 2012).

## Explaining Organized Crime

We have examined a variety of organized crime groups in Canada and seen that organized crime is pervasive and has a dramatic impact on the social economy of the country. We also noted that organized crime groups have become more sophisticated over the years, matching new efforts by

**protection racket**

A criminal arrangement, associated especially with the Mafia, in which a business is provided with protection from sabotage, vandalism, robbery, and other crime, in exchange for a regular fee, typically paid to someone who has threatened violence or other retribution if the "client" rejects the service and refuses to make the payment.

---

### BOX 11.10 | A CLOSER LOOK
### Investigating Mafia-Related Incidents

In December 2009, 42-year-old Nick Rizutto, Jr, son of the alleged Montreal Mafia crime boss Vito Rizzuto, was gunned down in the middle of the day on a street in the Montreal neighbourhood of Notre-Dame-de-Grâce. His death was the first in a series of executions targeting the Rizzuto clan that occurred while Vito—considered by many the most powerful Mafia boss in Canada—was serving a 5-year prison term in the United States. In May 2010, Rizzuto associate Agostino Cuntrera was assassinated in broad daylight, less than two weeks after Vito Rizzuto's brother-in-law Paolo Renda disappeared. In November 2010, Nicola "Nick" Rizzuto, Sr—father of Vito and grandfather of Nick, Jr—was shot in his Montreal home.

The killings were seen as part of a power struggle between the Sicilian faction of the Montreal Mafia, headed by the Rizzutos, and the Calabrian branch, led by the Contronis. The turf war did not end with the killing to Rizzuto, Jr. A series of deaths following Vito Rizzuto's release from prison are considered revenge killings (Lamberti, 2014). Notable among these are the suspicious deaths of Giuseppe De Vito and Carmine Verduci. De Vito, a one-time Rizzuto associate, was part of the Calabrian faction that mounted a coup against the Rizzutos during Vito's time in prison. Six months after being sentenced for mob-related crimes in December 2012, he was found dead in his jail cell with traces of cyanide in his blood. Carmine

Verduci, a known member of the Calabrian underworld, was shot outside a café in the Toronto community of Woodbridge in April 2014 (Lamberti, 2014).

Law enforcement officials have had some success in battling the Mafia in Quebec. In June 2014, the RCMP conducted a raid that resulted in the arrest of 31 alleged Mafia members. The Mounties were later forced to apologize to the National Congress of Italian Canadians for giving the sweep the code name "Project Clemenza," after one of the lead characters from the novel and movie The Godfather. The complaint accused the force of promoting negative stereotypes of the Italian community (Banerjee, 2014). In November 2015, the Quebec Commission of Inquiry on the Awarding and Management of Public Contracts in the Construction Industry, also known as the Charbonneau Commission, identified ties between organized crime groups, including the Mafia and the Hells Angels, and corrupt public officials responsible for awarding lucrative construction contracts (Edwards, 2015).

For interesting details on the Mafia, see Mobsters, Gangsters and Men of Honour: Cracking the Mafia Code (2004), by Pierre de Champlain, an RCMP intelligence analyst. For a closer look at the Mafia in Quebec, see André Cédilot and André Noël's book Mafia Inc: The Long, Bloody Reign of Canada's Sicilian Clan (2012).

law enforcement and criminal justice agencies to counter organized crime. These efforts include the involvement of research organizations such as the Nathanson Centre on Transnational Human Rights, Crime, and Security. Established in 1997 at York University's Osgoode, the centre aids in the fight against international organized crime by "studying ... and constantly querying the relationship between crime, security, and human rights, as informed by transnational perspectives." In 2006, Public Safety Canada produced the *National Agenda to Combat Organized Crime*, which brings together law enforcement agencies at all levels to develop unified strategies to more effectively address the spread and complexity of organized crime.

Hackler (2007, p. 308), acknowledging the wide variety of theories that have been put forward to explain organized crime, argues that organized crime groups should be seen as "cancers that invade and destroy healthy societies." Because of the economic consequences of most organized criminal activity both on government and on private business, the cancer analogy has become a popular interpretation. It enables governments to justify taking extreme measures, such as enacting the War Measures Act, passing special legislation to control outlaw motorcycle gangs, exercising special provisions for screening new immigrants, confiscating property, and so on. The assertion is that through aggressive crime control and intervention efforts, organized crime can be rooted out—or at least controlled.

Criminologists have also used a functionalist approach that sees organized crime as a normal adaptive response to the structural organization of society. As Einstadter and Henry (1995, p. 145) explain, organized crime emerges in response to societal deficiencies caused by "(1) the division of labour, (2) the nature and distribution of occupational roles, and (3) the opportunities available to obtain them." For groups such as the Mafia, Colombian cartels, and Aboriginal crime groups—whose members often come from the lower working class, where there are limited opportunities for upward mobility—the functionalist approach offers a plausible, albeit tenuous, explanation. However, the functionalist perspective does not explain crime groups such as the Yakuza in Japan, the criminal tribes of India, and the roving pickpocket gangs of Paris (Hackler, 2007). Furthermore, traditional explanations such as social disorganization, anomie, and subcultural theories cannot readily explain why so many more men than women participate in organized crime (though see Schwartz & Steffensmeier, 2010, for a discussion and explanation of gender differences).

As a macro approach, the functionalist theories are good at focusing on the *criminogenic* conditions of societies—in other words, the factors that lead people generally to take up crime—but they are less adept at explaining the more micro social processes by which individuals choose to become involved in organized crime. In addition, the functional perspective, in accordance with its principles, assumes that organized crime performs some function. Remember that functionalist theories view society as a living organism, in which each component plays a role in promoting growth and survival. When applied to organized crime and society, however, this is a tautological argument and not necessarily true. For example, if organized crime is *dysfunctional* to the stability of society and the state, then how could we reason that organized crime contributes to the evolution and expansion of society rather than its ultimate demise?

In terms of the criminogenic conditions, organized crime is fluid. Its existence is more dependent on public and official readiness to co-operate with its illegal activities than on legislation or lack thereof. As Potter (1994, p. 147) observes, organized crime does not *produce* the desire for vice (taking drugs, buying or selling sex, gambling, and so on); rather, "it merely fills an already existing social gap."

Should criminologists, then, study which vices should be legalized as a means of crime control? It is possible that organized crime does serve a functional symbiotic service, as governments are still able to operate with varying degrees of corruption? If we legalized drugs, gambling, prostitution, and other vices (other countries have experimented with such measures), would this serve to lessen organized crime's power and related problems? Whether such solutions would help or merely generate new problems is not clear, and it is the subject of considerable debate. However, criminologists could engage in comparative studies and evaluations involving countries that have legalized certain activities that remain illegal in Canada to see whether such measures might work. Kappeler, Blumberg, and Potter (2004) point out that the existence of laws against consensual crimes simply creates the opportunity for organized crime, both nationally and internationally (see Box 11.11). Furthermore, it would also be prudent for researchers to engage in an integrated and interdisciplinary approach because organized crime is an evolving phenomenon that takes many forms. Criminologists need to view organized crime in terms of how society has structured its economic, political, and social resources to create an environment in which organized crime can both thrive and evolve. We also need to recognize that organized crime has become more complex and sophisticated and that a different level of response to combatting it is therefore required.

**consensual crimes**
Unlawful activities involving willing participants who have given consent to their involvement.

## Comparing Organized Crime Groups to Other Organizations

As noted above, from a functionalist standpoint, organized crime groups have a role to play in administering unlawful economic activities like prostitution and illegal drug sales that governments have been unable or unwilling to control. In fact, when we consider the hierarchical administrative structure of some larger criminal organizations, their sophisticated bureaucracy, and their internal regulations, it is easy to draw comparisons between organized crime groups and governments, which share many of the same administrative, operational, and organizational traits.

A principal difference, of course, is that we don't normally associate our governments with criminal activity. But given the similarities between governments and crime groups, it is perhaps not surprising that some governments, or levels of government, sometimes engage in behaviour that is illegal. Just as organized crime bosses are insulated by the group's large network of officials and operatives, illegal government activities are often difficult to detect or trace thanks to elaborate government architecture (DiLorenzo, 2012). There are also countries where government corruption and illegal activity are rampant, and where violence and intimidation—hallmarks of organized crime—are used to keep citizens in line. DiLorenzo (2012) uses a robust understanding of economics to show how countries like Austria, among others, have systematically and regularly engaged in organized crime, while governments in Nigeria, Cambodia, and Myanmar (to cite just a few cases) have been completely taken over by organized crime groups. Closer to home, the Charbonneau commission of inquiry

**transnational crime**
Crime that involves activities or transactions that violate the laws of more than one country.

---

| BOX 11.11 | **A CLOSER LOOK** |
|---|---|
| | **The Effects of Globalization: Transnational Crime** |

Until recently, organized crime has been largely a regional concern. However, with improvements in transportation and communication technology, organized crime has become an activity that knows no national borders. The more sophisticated organized criminal syndicates are now involved in transnational crime, which includes international drug trafficking, human smuggling, money laundering, terrorism, and other criminal activities that cross national boundaries.

The problem has become so widespread that the United Nations now holds special sessions on transnational criminal activity. A 1998 report for the Canadian

Security Intelligence Service (CSIS) identified 18 transnational crime groups operating in Canada, "including Asian triads, Colombian cartels, Japanese *yakuza*, Jamaican posses, Mafia groups from the USA, Calabria, and Sicily; Russian/Eastern European mafiyas, Nigerian crime groups, and major outlaw motorcycle gangs" (CSIS, 1999). It would not be surprising to learn that the number has grown well beyond 18 since the report was released. It is partly for this reason that criminologists have recently published scholarly works that focus solely on transnational crime (see Reichel & Albanese, 2014).

into the awarding of government contracts and influence peddling in Quebec's construction industry found that organized crime was deeply embedded in the political process, and that corruption and collusion were "far more widespread than originally believed" ("Charbonneau commission," 2015).

It is also worth considering terrorist organizations in the context of organized crime. While the principal aims of terrorist organizations are political, they are sustained by funds that may be raised using illegal methods characteristic of organized crime groups. Abadinsky (2012) states that the terrorist activities of various Islamic factions have been interpreted as a type of organized crime. Consider the Islamic terrorist group calling itself Islamic State of Iraq and the Levant (ISIL), which aspires to establish an Islamic caliphate in the Middle East. According to a 2015 report by the Financial Action Task Force (FATF), an intergovernmental organization established in 1989 by the heads of G7 countries (including Canada) to investigate money laundering, ISIL is financed largely by illicit proceeds from activities that include bank looting, extortion, human trafficking, and the illegal sale of petroleum and petroleum products. According to the report,

> ISIL manages a sophisticated extortion racket by robbing, looting, and demanding a portion of the economic resources in areas where it operates, which is similar to how some organized crime groups generate funds. This vast range of extortion, including everything from fuel and vehicle taxes to school fees for children, is done under the auspices of providing notional services or "protection." The effectiveness of ISIL's extortion relies on the threat or use of force within its operational territory. (FATF, 2015, p. 12).

An FBI (2015) report draws attention to ISIL's involvement in the illegal smuggling and sale of stolen antiquities and artifacts, describing "industrial-level looting" and warning dealers and collectors to be on alert for illegally obtained objects. While terrorist organizations clearly have

---

## BOX 11.12    PROFILE   Ernesto "Che" Guevara

What one person sees as a fight for freedom may be terrorism in the eyes of another. Perhaps the most famous of all "terrorists" was the notorious guerrilla leader Ernesto "Che" Guevara (1928–1967). Guevara met Fidel Castro in 1954 and soon after helped lead the Cuban Revolution, which led to the overthrow in 1959 of the US-backed Cuban dictator Fulgencio Batista. Adopting the practice of guerrilla warfare, he became known as "Che," an Argentinian expression for "buddy." During the revolution he was frequently described by the Batista regime as being involved in organized crime. In 1965, Guevara left Cuba to fight for revolution elsewhere. He was captured in Bolivia and executed in 1967. His remains were returned to Cuba, where he was treated as a national hero. Today, he continues to be a controversial symbol of revolution, variously celebrated as a champion of the poor oppressed by capitalist regimes and reviled as a ruthless terrorist responsible for the execution of many people deemed "traitors" and war criminals, often without due process.

© MARKA / Alamy Stock Photo

"Heroico." Cuban photographer took the now iconic picture of the "heroic guerrilla fighter" in Havana, Cuba, in 1960. How should Che Guevara be remembered today: as revolutionary, terrorist, organized criminal—or all of the above?

aims that set them apart from organized crime groups, the range of activities described here shows obvious similarities between the revenue-generating practices of a terrorist group like ISIL and those of certain organized crime groups we have considered in this chapter.

Whatever their similarity to governments or terrorist organizations, organized crime groups are widespread and increasingly heedless of national boundaries. The economic impact of organized crime is far greater than that of conventional crime, and attempts to control it have done little to hamper its growth. The relationship between business and criminal organizations takes us to another form of non-conventional crime: corporate crime.

## Corporate Crime

### What Is Corporate Crime?

Like organized crimes, corporate crimes are committed by powerful groups in society. Organized crime groups and corporate crime offenders share several characteristics identified by Abadinsky (2012). Above all, both are concerned with maximizing the profits of their organization through illegal business practices. The difference is that corporations are legitimate and are run by high-status members of society.

Corporate crime involves illegal acts carried out by employees of a business in order to benefit the financial performance of the corporation. As Kramer (1984, p. 31) points out, such crime is "the result of deliberate decision making by persons who occupy structural positions within the organization. The organization makes decisions intentionally to benefit itself." Many of the officials involved hold prestigious social positions and earn annual incomes well above the national per capita average. In this way, corporate crime differs from many of the conventional crimes reviewed in earlier chapters—particularly break-and-enter, theft, assault, and homicide—which are committed disproportionately by people from lower socioeconomic classes. Yet as Snider (1993, p. 1) observes, "corporate crime . . . actually does more harm, costs more money, and ruins more lives" than conventional crimes. She argues that there are more deaths in a month from corporate crime than there are in a decade from mass murderers.

Carrigan (1991) compiled a list of Canadian companies that have committed an assortment of corporate crimes. The following is a cross-section of the cases and the penalties imposed during the 1980s and the 1990s:

---

**BOX 11.13   FACTS AND FIGURES** WHO ARE THE WORST CORPORATE OFFENDERS?

The Global Exchange is an international human rights organization that in addition to promoting social justice around the world also provides an annual list of its top 10 corporate criminals. The following are their top 3 corporate offenders for 2014:

- **Bayer**, for manufacturing and using bee-killing pesticides, blaming the bee crisis on other causes, exposing farmers to harmful pesticides, and working to monopolize drug prices.
- **Carnival Corporation**, for dumping sewage pollution into oceans, using cheap and air-polluting fuels, evading taxes, and paying unfair wages.
- **Alpha Natural Resources**, for polluting rivers, streams, and groundwater; violating the Clean Water Act; destroying forest and wildlife habitats; and devastating Appalachian communities. ("Top 10," 2014).

Which of the activities described above are actual crimes, and which are merely unscrupulous business practices? Should we distinguish between the two?

## Table 11.2  Perceived Levels of Public-Sector Corruption, 2014: Top 10 and Bottom 10 Countries

| Rank | Country | CPI score |
| --- | --- | --- |
| 1 | Denmark | 82 |
| 2 | New Zealand | 91 |
| 3 | Finland | 89 |
| 4 | Sweden | 87 |
| 5 | Norway | 86 |
| 6 | Switzerland | 86 |
| 7 | Singapore | 84 |
| 8 | Netherlands | 83 |
| 9 | Luxembourg | 82 |
| 10 | Canada | 81 |
| 166 | Eritrea | 18 |
| 166 | Libya | 18 |
| 166 | Uzbekistan | 18 |
| 169 | Turkmenistan | 17 |
| 170 | Iraq | 16 |
| 171 | South Sudan | 16 |
| 172 | Afghanistan | 12 |
| 173 | Sudan | 11 |
| 174 | North Korea | 8 |
| 174 | Somalia | 8 |

Do you think a country's level of public-sector, or government, corruption reflects the amount of corporate or private-sector corruption? If so, where does the fight against corporate crime need to begin?

Note: CPI = Corruption Perception Index.
*Source:* CPI 2014 Brochure © 2014 by Transparency International. Licensed under CC BY-ND 4.0
http://www.transparency.org/cpi2014/results.

**white-collar crime**

Illegal activities such as fraud and embezzlement conducted by employees and officers of a company using their professional status for personal and/or corporate gain.

**victimless crime**

Unlawful activity in which there is no identifiable victim, either because the activity is consensual (e.g. gambling) or because the activity is directed against a corporate entity rather than an individual (e.g. white-collar crime).

- Stone Consolidated Inc. was fined $35,000 for spilling toxic PCB-laced transformer oil.
- Amway Canada was charged with tax evasion and agreed to pay $45 million in an out-of-court settlement.
- Zellers Inc. in Nova Scotia was fined $35,000 for listing sales prices above advertised levels.

Notable, high-profile Canadian cases involve the mining company Bre-X, which saw stock prices soar during the 1990s after gold was fraudulently added to samples taken from its mine in Borneo (Ro, 2014); the theatre company Livent, which fraudulently misstated its financial earnings every quarter from 1993 to 1998 (McFarland, 2014); the former telecommunications giant Nortel, which saw three top executives charged in 2008 with altering financial results to trigger lucrative bonuses (French, 2013); and the newspaper conglomerate Hollinger, which was at the centre of a shareholder-initiated investigation into the activities of its head, Conrad Black, who was convicted in a US court in 2007 of fraud and obstruction of justice. Yet, as one study recently found, Canada is still perceived as relatively free of corruption, in the public sector at least. A Transparency International (2004) report placed Canada tenth on a list measuring 175 countries' perceived levels of public-sector corruption; the report ranked Denmark and New Zealand as the most honest, and Sudan, North Korea, and Somalia as the most corrupt (see Table 11.2).

Corporate crime is a modern-day phenomenon. Only after the emergence of industrialization and the market economy was it possible for corporate crime to manifest itself. And, it was not until **Edwin Sutherland**'s ground-breaking 1949 book *White Collar Crime* that corporate crime became a subject of interest to criminologists. Sutherland's work was based on an analysis of 70 leading American companies operating in the mining, manufacturing, and mercantile sectors. Sutherland's study was focused on the following illegal business practices (Keane, 1996, p. 282):

- restraint of trade
- misrepresentation in advertising
- infringements of patents, trademarks, and copyrights
- violations of labour law
- illegal rebates
- financial fraud and violation of trust
- violations of war regulations

The most common violation, found in 60 companies, was restraint of trade. Sutherland suggested that 90 per cent of the corporations were habitual criminals, and 97 per cent were *recidivists*, meaning that they would reoffend even after having been caught.

While *corporate crime* refers to criminal activities undertaken by or on behalf of a corporate entity, it requires the efforts of individual employees and officers—that is, *white-collar workers*. Hence, the term white-collar crime refers to business-related crime such as embezzlement, fraud, insider trading, bribery, and theft, committed by an offender who takes advantage of his or her professional status for either personal gain or for the benefit of the company. Corporate crime may involve white-collar crime, but it is an organized activity designed primarily to benefit the company, not the individuals involved.

---

**BOX 11.14**

### A CLOSER LOOK
### Is Business Crime Victimless?

In his 1939 presidential address to the American Sociology Society, Edwin Sutherland argued that criminologists needed to extend their focus of study beyond the crimes committed by the social underclass to those of the upper socioeconomic class and upper-class professions. He referred to the latter category of offences as *white-collar crimes*. They represent crimes committed by individuals of respectability and high social status in the course of their professional duties but for their own benefit (Rosoff, Pontell, & Tillman, 2004). White-collar crime, or professional crime, involves the linkage of social status and prestigious occupational standing. Related to white-collar crime is *corporate crime* (also referred to as *business crime* or *elite deviance*), which involves employees in a business setting who intentionally engage in "corporate illegalities on behalf of the corporation and in accordance with formally specified corporate goals" (Gomme, 1993, p. 395).

Both white-collar crime and corporate crime are sometimes described as victimless, since the injured party is typically a large, faceless corporate entity rather than an individual. However, white-collar and corporate crime create many victims, from company shareholders, whose profits decline if executives are embezzling corporate funds, to consumers, if higher prices are being charged to absorb the costs of employee theft. And business crime is widespread. Recently, a global survey by PricewaterhouseCoopers found that 36 per cent of Canadian organizations—mostly in financial services, retail, and communications—had been hit by white-collar crime, a figure that is 1 per cent below the global average (McKenna, 2014). White-collar crime is difficult to detect and prosecute, according to the report, so the best means of combatting it is for companies to implement effective prevention strategies.

Who are the victims of corporate crime and white-collar crime? Is any crime truly victimless?

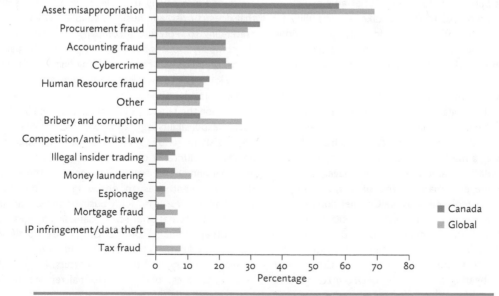

**Figure 11.2   Types of Economic Crime, Canada and Globally, 2014**

*Source:* PricewaterhouseCoopers, 2015, p. 6 (Fig. 2).

Our economic history is rich with examples of corporate crime activities ranging from counterfeiting, embezzlement, forgery, and fraud to regulatory offences (see Snider, 2002). Yet until the pioneering work of Goff and Reasons (1978), Canadian criminologists virtually ignored this area of inquiry, since corporate crime was not seen as "real" crime and since conventional criminological theory was not oriented toward the study of white-collar crime.

Since Goff and Reasons's (1978) landmark study, however, there have been a number of noteworthy studies conducted in an attempt to shed light on, and explain, Canadian corporate criminality (Clinard & Yeager, 2011; Keane, 1996; Snider, 2015). Topics have included

- the nature and impact of crimes against consumers and employees through such activities as price fixing, illegal mergers, industrial espionage, and environmental pollution (Goff & Reasons, 1986);
- the effectiveness of jurisdictional laws in protecting consumers and the labour force (Snider, 2002);
- corporate violence against women (DeKeseredy & Hinch, 1991); and
- the corporate crimes committed by some Canadian banks, brokerages, and companies like Nortel, Magnex, and IBM (Livesey, 2013).

Some criminologists have examined how legislation aimed at preserving a competitive and free-enterprise system has encouraged corporate crime activities while, at the same time,

---

**BOX 11.15    FACTS AND FIGURES** REGULATING BUSINESS CRIME

Most forms of white-collar crime are dealt with not as corporate crimes per se but simply as fraud or embezzlement as defined under the Criminal Code (Snider, 2015). For the most part, regulatory agencies at all jurisdictions ranging from municipal to federal take responsibility for defining corporate offences and identifying violations. The primary jurisdictional body concerned with overseeing corporate transgressions is the Ministry of Consumer and Corporate Affairs.

Until 1986, the most important regulatory statute was the Combines Investigation Act (CIA). Introduced in 1889, the act was intended to enable the state to protect consumers from unethical business practices such as price fixing, establishing a market monopoly, pollution, and safety and health violations, among others. However, only two convictions were ever made under this act, and in June 1986, the CIA was replaced with the Competition Act.

Complaints involving business practices in Canada are filed first with the Competition Bureau, which investigates the complaints and determines which ones have merit. Those that do are brought before the Competition Tribunal for a hearing attended by between two and six judicial members (i.e. judges) and between one and eight civilian or "lay" members. The tribunal decides whether a company has violated its monopoly powers. If so, then the case is tried under civil law.

Every year, the Competition Bureau receives thousands of complaints, the majority of which relate to scams involving fraudulent directory listings (in which companies are duped into paying to be listed in a business directory that doesn't exist) and business supplies (where a fraudster pretending to represent a company's regular supplier sells the company supplies at exorbitant prices). The bureau also warns of business scams targeting individuals, involving phony lottery prizes, work-at-home opportunities, and cure-all products advertised online (Competition Bureau, 2015).

In 2009 the federal government launched its Corporate Social Responsibility legislation, which was renewed in 2014. The legislation is designed to encourage Canadian businesses to voluntarily operate in an economically, socially, and environmentally sustainable manner. The slogan that the government uses to encourage self-monitoring of Canadian businesses is "doing business the Canadian way."

On an international scale, Canada engages regularly with other members of the G10, made up of wealthy industrialized nations that consult and co-operate on economic, monetary, and financial matters. In 1997, the G10 attempted to establish international regulations for several transnational business operations (for instance, electronic banking). However, no consensus could be reached because of "the different approaches that various countries [had] taken to regulations in the field" (Pressman, 1997).

government measures to crack down on illegal business practices have been largely inept. In a similar vein, Gordon and Coneybeer (1995, p. 400) offer several general conclusions about corporate crime:

- While material losses from corporate crime are considerable, we must be mindful, too, of the number of deaths and injuries caused by corporate criminal negligence. Consider, for example, recent data from the Canadian Centre for Occupational Health and Safety: in 2013, there were 902 workplace deaths in Canada, or an average of 2.47 deaths per day. That's consistent with the average annual number of workplace deaths recorded in Canada between 1993 and 2012 (AWCBC, 2013; CCOHS, 2015; see Figure 11.3).
- Criminal law regulating corporate crime is poorly defined, and violators are usually dealt with outside the criminal justice system. Compensation and victim appeasement are common strategies used by corporate offenders to avoid prosecution. Perhaps the best illustration of this is the landmark legislative settlement reached in 1998 between US attorneys general in 46 states and the 4 largest American tobacco producers. The tobacco companies agreed to hefty fines (considered light, on balance, by many anti-smoking groups critical of the deal) and limits on tobacco marketing, in exchange for exemption from private class-action lawsuits.
- Laws designed to prohibit certain forms of corporate behaviour are not only poorly enforced but ineffective as deterrents.
- Because of their symbiotic relationship, governments usually work with corporations in constructing "appropriate" legislation and in determining measures to handle violators.
- The causes of corporate crime involve the complex interactions between individual, organizational, and social structural factors.
- High-quality investigations into corporate crimes by criminologists are stymied by a variety of methodological problems, such as limited access to funding and data and the complexities of corporate businesses.

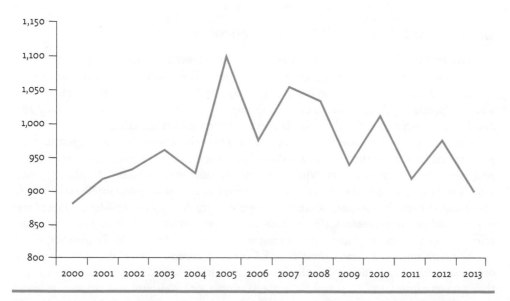

**Figure 11.3    Annual Workplace Fatalities in Canada since, 2000–2013**

*Source:* Association of Workers' Compensation Boards of Canada, 2013, Table 22: Number of fatalities, by jurisdiction, 1993–2013.

© Pierrette Guertin / Alamy Stock Photo

No hard hats, no safety harnesses. . . . Who is criminally responsible in the event of a worker death under these circumstances? Why does or doesn't this fit the definition of a corporate crime?

## Organized and Corporate Crime: Cut from the Same Cloth?

We have examined two different forms of crime by the powerful in society, noting that they share some common operational goals and motivations. The primary difference between the two is that most organized crime involves participants from the middle and lower classes, while corporate criminals often come from the upper class, making them both socially and politically powerful as well as wealthy. However, in their efforts to explain the crimes of the powerful, criminologists have found a number of other characteristics that suggest that the participants in both of these kinds of crime share one important characteristic: they begin with basic criminal propensities. While one might wonder why someone who already holds wealth and power would engage in criminal activity, these types of criminals, like others, simply choose to capitalize on their situation—as opportunity theory suggests—for a range of real or perceived pragmatic reasons. Unlike those involved in organized crime, however, corporate offenders operate under a guise of public trust and legitimacy (Webb, 2004; Freidriches, 2010).

Although no direct comparisons have been made, research shows that participants in organized crime begin their criminal careers early in life, while white-collar criminals begin their careers a little later (Weisburd, Chayet, & Waring, 1990). Weisburd et al. (1990) also found that white-collar criminals are often repeat offenders. Recidivism rates varied from 10 per cent for bank embezzlers to 46 per cent for those engaging in credit card fraud. Goff and Reasons

(1978) suggest that corporate criminals tend to be repeat offenders because of the challenges associated with enforcement, prosecution, and effective deterrence.

## Explaining Corporate Crime

In his landmark 1949 book, Sutherland used his theory of differential association (see Chapter 8) to explain white-collar crime. The theory, however, emphasizes the individual rather than the organization, which—given the general definition of corporate crime—poses a conceptual problem. Therefore, as Clinard and Quinney (1973) suggested, Sutherland's theory is better suited to explaining what we call *occupational crimes*—that is, crimes in which a person takes advantage of his or her occupation, such as fraud, embezzlement, and theft. Is there any real difference between occupational crime and corporate crime? Do criminologists need to make a distinction? Without an individual to initiate it, a corporate crime cannot take place. Hirschi and Gottfredson (1989) appear to recognize this point when they suggest that criminologists do not need separate theories to explain corporate and white-collar crime.

A possible solution for criminologists is to adopt a narrower definition of white-collar crime, limiting it to individual acts conducted in the course of committing corporate or business crime, while regarding crimes committed by individuals for personal benefit as common-law property offences. Accepting this line of reasoning would require using an organizational theory that considers the factors that make up the environmental setting of the corporation, such as market competition, organizational stratification, and profit motivation. The objective of organizational theory is to understand what variations within a business setting allow a company to engage in illegal activities (see Jones, 2012).

In contrast, the conflict perspective focuses on "external factors of influence" (Keane, 1996, p. 283). According to this perspective, businesses in a market economy are motivated to maximize profit, ensure perpetual growth, monopolize their market, and have free rein over their operations. Government regulations only serve to restrict natural growth. From a conflict perspective, capitalism contains the seeds of its own destruction. The price of success for corporations is to "run a tight ship" so as to maximize their profits. So, while companies may not intentionally set out to cause harm, there will always be trade-offs, since the pressure to succeed and excel can create conflict, prompting some to engage in social deviations.

In her study of corporate crime in Canada, Snider (1993) argues that the interests of corporations and the state are not always compatible, and that this can—and does—lead to the creation of distorted public images of "big business." For example, governments are sensitive to public pressure for job creation and keeping unemployment rates down. These are usually major issues during election campaigns. Back in 1997, then BC premier Glen Clark allegedly offered (he was later acquitted of the charges) the lumber industry financial incentives to create more jobs (Pitts, 2013). However, as the lumber industry has become more mechanized in an effort to compete on the international market, it has not needed to employ more people to support itself.

On the other hand, government regulatory bodies have served as watchdogs to minimize the risk of corporations destroying the environment in their zeal to make profits. For example, these bodies have been instrumental in drafting regulations restricting clear-cut logging, setting limits on how close to rivers and streams loggers can cut, setting catch limits for the fishing industry, requiring pollution controls to be placed on emission devices, and so on. Corporations now have to engage in a balancing act between meeting social and environmental obligations and conducting business (see Box 11.16).

Another theory that has a certain level of appeal in explaining corporate crime is Sykes and Matza's (1957) theory of **neutralization**, which has to do with how criminals are able

**neutralization**

The theory that criminals draw on a set of techniques to temporarily neutralize, or suppress, their internal moral obligation to abide by the law, which allows them to overcome their natural hesitation to commit a crime.

| BOX 11.16 | **FACTS AND FIGURES** WHO ARE CANADA'S MOST RESPONSIBLE CORPORATE CITIZENS? |
|---|---|

The independent Canadian media company Corporate Knights has been producing an annual ranking of the top 50 corporate citizens in Canada each year since 2000. The ranking is based on a wide range of indicators, including the amount of carbon emissions the business generates, how reliably they pay their taxes, the diversity of their board of directors, the ratio of CEO to average worker pay, and the amount of employee turnover. Here are their top five Canadian corporate citizens for 2015:

1. Tim Hortons
2. Vancouver City Savings Credit Union (Vancity)
3. Mountain Equipment Co-op
4. Teck Resources
5. Telus (Corporate Knights, 2015a)

The top five most sustainable foreign corporations operating in Canada in 2015 were the following:

1. Biogen Idec, a biotechnology company headquartered in the United States
2. Allergan, a pharmaceuticals company also based in the United States
3. Adidas, the German-based athletic apparel manufacturer
4. Keppel Land, a real estate management company located in Singapore
5. Kesko, a food retailer based in Finland (Corporate Knights, 2015b)

In 2015, *Maclean's* magazine produced a similar ranking of the 50 most socially responsible corporations. Their list is divided by industry; the following are some of the results:

- PepsiCo ranked atop the food and beverage category for its commitment to tackling global water scarcity.
- L'Oréal SA ranked first in retailing and household goods for its dedication to responsible sourcing of raw materials for use in its cosmetic products.
- Intel took the top spot in the technology category for collecting and disclosing detailed environmental impact data for 10 of its manufacturing facilities worldwide. (Smyth, 2015)

It's worth noting that there was some overlap between the rankings presented in the two magazines. Vancity, ranked second on the Corporate Knights list, was the top-ranked company in the *Maclean's* banking category, while Telus, number five on the Corporate Knights list, finished first in *Maclean's* ranking of telecommunications and electronics companies.

How important is a company's social responsibility to you? Would you ever consult a list like the ones generated by Corporate Knights and *Maclean's*? Have you ever been guided by a company's good (or bad) reputation for social responsibility when making a purchase?

to temporarily overcome, or "neutralize," internal values that would otherwise prevent them from committing illegal acts. Despite the fact that Sykes and Matza presented their theory 60 years ago, and in the context of young offenders specifically, it has been picked up and applied to corporate crime by contemporary criminologists including Carl Keane (1996, pp. 228–9), who offers a concise account of how the techniques of neutralization can be applied to the way companies can justify illegal behaviour. We will use the tobacco industry as an example of how the culprit might neutralize any responsibility. The following are the main neutralization techniques:

- *Denial of responsibility.* The tobacco industry does not force people to smoke its cigarettes—smoking is an individual choice. The industry is simply satisfying a market demand, and uses highly visible warning labels on its packaging to help consumers make an informed choice.
- *Denial of injury.* There has never been conclusive evidence proving that tobacco causes cancer. Millions of smokers have lived long and healthy lives and died of natural causes.

Deaths may be attributed to other factors. By placing warning ads on packages, the industry is fulfilling its legal obligation to warn people of the possible hazards.

- *Denial of victim.* Not all smokers die of lung cancer. Smokers who do die may well have been predisposed to getting lung cancer.
- *Condemnation of the condemners.* Why does the government focus on cigarettes when alcohol, sugar, fast cars, and many other products pose equally serious health risks? (This is the "everyone is corrupt" defence).
- *Appeal to higher loyalties.* When the tobacco industry was under attack, a number of people pointed out that the government had been quite happy for years to collect the revenue generated from the high taxes levied on cigarettes. The tobacco industry was supporting the economy. Is it not hypocritical to sanction this industry and yet continue to profit from its profits? Who is the real offender?

Criminologist Stanley Cohen (2001) attributed the fact that there is so little information (official or unofficial) on corporate crime to what he called a *culture of denial*, suggesting that we are all wilfully oblivious to the extent of business crime. Moreover, when someone is caught and charged, the penalty is nominal. For example, after the 1989 *Exxon Valdez* oil spill in Alaska, Exxon was not forced out of business. Similarly, in spite of the overwhelming evidence linking tobacco to cancer, tobacco companies are allowed to continue to produce and market cigarettes. The list goes on.

The various explanations of corporate crime have focused on micro- or macro-level external, internal, or individual factors governing how organizations conduct their business. Each

Although the warning labels on Canadian cigarette packages have gotten larger and more grotesque, one of the few studies to examine the effect of warning ads on cigarette purchases (Argo & Main, 2004) showed they have little effect. Would these warning labels deter you from smoking? Why or why not? And who do you think should be primarily responsible for reducing smoking: the tobacco industry? the government? stores that sell cigarettes? individual smokers? someone else?

approach has its strengths but also its limitations. For example, although neutralization techniques have appeal, they do not in themselves explain crime. Therefore, as some investigators have suggested, a more prudent approach might be to synthesize these findings in an integrated format.

Keane (1996) suggests that one of the underlying themes of most explanations is the concept of *stress*. The idea of stress could be used, for example, to link the micro- and macro-level external, internal, and individual elements. Strain is an *external* factor in the context of the competitive market and the pressure on corporations to compete and succeed. *Internal* stress is experienced by company owners and employees as they try to conduct business within the confines of existing regulations. Individual stress can result from the potential risk of failure or shutdown. In other words, the causes of corporate crime are as complex as the requirements of running a successful corporation.

A more realistic way to integrate macro and micro elements is to apply an interdisciplinary approach. As much as we might want to analyze corporate crime at an organizational level that consists of external, internal, and individual factors, the white-collar offender is still a biological and psychological individual. Without *mens rea* and *actus reus*—which only an individual can possess—there can be no crime. The only difference between conventional types of crime and corporate crime is that the offender commits the crime within the organizational structure of the corporation. Therefore, when studying corporate crime, criminologists must adapt an interdisciplinary approach and integrate biological, psychological, social, and legal levels of analysis.

## Regulating Corporate Crime

There is little doubt that corporate crime has a major social and economic impact. What is more difficult to agree on is how the state should respond to this type of crime. With regard to corporate crime, the state follows traditional punishment rationales of retribution and just deserts—but should it prosecute the individual offender or the corporation? Or should prosecution involve the individual *and* the corporation? In addition, is the traditional approach of shaming the offender (see Box 11.17) effective?

Attempts to control corporate crime are further complicated by the interests of the state. For example, as noted above, penalizing the tobacco industry would result in considerable loss of government revenue. So would banning video lottery terminals and lottery tickets, as these generate millions of dollars in government revenue every year. Yet in regulating, and thereby sanctioning, such activities, the state opens the way for people to become addicted to these vices, and many end up ruining their lives to support their habit.

The criminal justice system has been, and continues to be, largely reactive in its approach to economic crimes. Economic crimes happen because criminals are proactive and are able to take advantage of opportunities. In order to regulate corporate crime, criminologists and criminal justice agencies must learn to be sensitive to international issues, differences in law, differences in law enforcement, changing technology, and market and social trends. For example, the ways in which different countries respond to corporate offenders vary. According to Hackler (2006), government tolerance is lower in Australia, Britain, Japan, and Sweden, while in the United States and Canada corporations have a tendency to resist regulation.

In summary, the economic, social, and political implications of corporate crime are often far-reaching, and yet the public is usually not well informed about these crimes. Unfortunately, methodological problems make the study of this type of crime particularly difficult. Criminologists and policy-makers have a tall order in front of them. At present, we are ill equipped to address economically motivated crime (Kappler, Blumberg, & Potter, 2004).

---

**BOX 11.17**

**A CLOSER LOOK**
### Shame on You! How Effective Is Shaming the Corporate Criminal?

In 1989, **John Braithwaite** introduced his theory of reintegrative shaming in *Crime, Shame, and Reintegration*. This approach has been described both as a general theory of crime and as an integrative explanation of crime. The theory combines elements of "labeling, subcultural, control, opportunity, and learning—the positive and negative aspects of lawbreakers" (Barak, 1998, p. 203).

According to Braithwaite, not all forms of social disapproval are the same. Braithwaite distinguishes between *disintegrative shaming* and *reintegrative shaming*. The former is negative in orientation and does not provide the offender with any opportunity to make amends for his or her behaviour. This type of shaming usually drives the offender into further acts of deviance or criminal behaviour. In contrast, reintegrative shaming involves efforts to bring offenders back into the community. While the offender is expected to experience some remorse for the crime, he or she is given positive opportunities for social reintegration through community involvement.

Braithwaite's ideas have been applied in many settings, but the general concept works best in homogeneous societies such as Japanese society, Aboriginal communities, and other "communitarian" societies that are characterized by a high degree of concern for the welfare of others. Some workplaces fall into this category, which is why the reintegrative shaming approach shows promise in cases of corporate or white-collar crime.

One of the earliest studies related to corporate crime involved interviews with 70 offenders who had been convicted of a corporate crime. Benson (1990) found that most of the offenders had already experienced disintegrative shaming, usually at the hands of the media. But while reintegrative shaming has been incorporated successfully into restorative justice programs for conventional crimes and young offenders, there is little evidence that it has been used successfully in relation to white-collar offenders (see Harris, 2006).

> Why do you think reintegrative shaming would or would not be successful in the rehabilitation of white-collar offenders?

---

The state cannot financially afford to combat the spread of these types of crimes, and criminal justice systems, by themselves, have been slow to change their timeworn and now ineffective approaches. It is time to look beyond our parochial views. In order to combat these crimes, criminologists and criminal justice agencies must collaborate and share their ideas. In addition, since single explanations and strategies will never work, an integrated and interdisciplinary approach will be required.

## Cybercrime: A New Form of Corporate Crime?

Computer technology is so widespread that it is an indispensable part of everything we do, from studying and banking to communicating and listening to music. Crime is no different in terms of its increasing reliance on computers. So far, we have considered computer crime in the context of cyberterrorism (Chapter 9) and e-mail/Internet fraud (Chapter 10). These are both criminal acts that fall within the ever-growing area of criminal activity known as *cybercrime*.

Although cybercrime encompasses conventional crimes like theft and terrorism, it still falls within the category of non-conventional crime, alongside organized crime and corporate crime—criminal activity that has changed dramatically over time and that presents considerable challenges for the authorities. Cybercrime, in fact, has much in common with organized crime and corporate crime:

- Like organized crime and corporate crime, cybercrime is transnational and knows no borders.

**reintegrative shaming**
A correctional philosophy introduced by John Braithwaite that advocates the use of public shaming and/or public acceptance of wrongdoing as a way of having offenders re-enter general society.

- Once associated with the renegade hacker operating alone, cybercrime today is just as likely to be a sophisticated activity involving networks of individuals and coordinated operations.
- Like corporate crime especially, cybercrime can be high-profit and low-risk, and far more costly to society than conventional crimes like motor vehicle theft and robbery.
- Like some forms of organized crime discussed earlier in this chapter, cybercrime can be motivated by a political or activist agenda.
- The scope and complexity of cybercriminal networks make cybercrime very difficult for authorities to control and prosecute.

These are just some of the reasons it makes sense to address cybercrime in this chapter.

In general, cybercrime is any illegal activity that involves the use of computer equipment and technology as the means of committing the crime. It is carried out by computer hackers, who are driven by a variety of motives, including personal profit, protest or revenge, and challenge. Generally speaking, hackers fall into four general categories:

- *Black hats* are hackers with good computer skills and a desire to cause harm, whether for profit, revenge, or sport.
- *White hats* are hackers with good intentions, such as the desire to expose vulnerabilities in secure networks so that they can be patched; for this reason, white hats are sometimes hired as security analysts.
- *Grey hats* perform both defensive and offensive activities.
- *Suicide hackers* are intent on causing harm without any concern about being caught.

**Trojan horse**

A computer program designed to damage to a local computer system when the software is activated by an unsuspecting user while performing another, non-threatening task.

It's fair to say that the profile of the typical hacker has changed dramatically with the evolution of cybercrime. In 1998, a 22-year-old living near Sudbury, Ontario, was charged with hacking into NASA's computer system and causing damage estimated at over $70,000 ("Hacker charged," 1998). The accused, Jason Mewhiney, ultimately accepted a plea deal and served six months in prison for what was essentially an act (albeit a costly one) of computer mischief. He represents the "black hat" likely motivated more by the challenge of breaking into a sophisticated government network than by any desire to profit individually. Hackers in this vein have been known to engage in numerous kinds of attack, including denial-of-service (DoS) attacks, password guessing, identity spoofing, backdoor attacks, and Trojan horse attacks, which involve malicious malware that, when opened by an unsuspecting user, has the potential to destroy files and software (see Box 11.18).

**BOX 11.18   FACTS AND FIGURES ARE CANADIANS VULNERABLE TO COMPUTER VIRUSES?**

Just about everyone has had an encounter with one of those dreaded computer viruses (e.g. ILOVEYOU, Melissa, Flashback, and so on). New viruses seem to emerge daily, requiring updated firewalls and anti-malware to protect our computers from malicious programs like viruses, worms, Trojan horses, and spyware. The good news is that although we continue to hear regularly about new and threatening computer viruses, in 2014 Microsoft announced that only about 14 per cent of Canadian computers were vulnerable to the unauthorized installation of malicious software (Pilieci, 2014). This is well below the global average of around 22 per cent; in countries like India and Vietnam, some 50 per cent of computers were considered to be at risk of being compromised.

Today, close to 20 years after Mewhiney broke into NASA, the typical hacker is likely to be either a criminal entrepreneur—working alone or in tandem with others to attack large companies for personal profit, protest, or revenge—or a "cyberspy" engaged by one company or government to steal information from another. Consider a couple of recent cases. In 2003, a small association of hackers came together on the imageboard 4chan; within five years, they were launching vigilante attacks against the Church of Scientology under the banner Anonymous. The "white hat" group has since launched *hactivist* (i.e. hacker activist) protest campaigns against a wide range of targets including government agencies, child pornography sites, and, quite recently, the extremist group calling itself ISIL. In December 2014, Sony Pictures received international attention when the company's American network was hacked, allegedly by North Korean cyberpirates, on the eve of releasing the movie *The Interview*, a comedy about the assassination of North Korean leader Kim Jong-un. The hackers threatened retaliation against Sony if they released the movie. The movie was almost completely shelved before being given a limited release, demonstrating the power that such an attack can have (Limer, 2014). The case was notable because the hacking was widely viewed as an act of aggression by one state, North Korea, against the commercial interests of another, the United States.

Whether groups like Anonymous are outlaws, watchdogs, or bullies is open to debate. While their motives might be honourable, their practices are illegal, and they are the same ones used by cybercriminals involved in high-stakes forms of corporate crime. Some hacker groups are involved in breaking into computer networks of banks and other big companies to steal files or money. Hackers can engage in identity theft to steal an individual's personal information, giving them valuable access to banking records and other private details. They can also simply neutralize a company's network by flooding it with traffic until a ransom is paid; this is known as a *denial of service (DoS) attack*, or a *distributed denial of service (DDoS) attack* if the traffic is channelled through multiple systems. In one such instance, a Calgary business had to pay the hackers a $500 bitcoin fee to get their service back; however, it paid far more—over $5,000—in IT costs to undo the damage to the system and to safeguard it against any future attacks ("Bitcoin ransom," 2015). Another form of unauthorized access is *media piracy*. Have you ever obtained a copy of software or a movie from a friend and put it onto your computer? The duplication process is relatively simple. More sophisticated piracy ventures might involve businesses copying software and media files and then selling them as the original products—usually at much lower prices.

Legally, sections 342.1 and 430 of the Canadian Criminal Code define computer crime as destroying data, altering data, rendering data meaningless, and/or interfering with someone using legitimate data. However, the likelihood of apprehending and prosecuting offenders is very slim. Offenders tend to be well educated, highly skilled, and young, and the sophisticated practices they use often keep them one step ahead of the authorities. At the same time, law enforcement resources are limited. There is a shortage of RCMP officers trained in computer-related crime techniques, and only about one-half are assigned to commercial crime units across Canada. Members are trained to provide technical guidance and expertise on techniques known to the offenders—but, unfortunately, once an offence has been recognized, it is usually too late.

## Summary

- Organized crime and corporate crime—or simply economic crimes of the elites—are difficult to define. They are subject to change with the passage of time and are often culturally relative, which further complicates the gathering of information and enforcement.

- While organized crime and corporate crime differ in many ways, their *modus operandi* are very similar. Both share the motive of economic gain through illegal means; both strive to monopolize the economy; and both resort to varying forms of threats, intimidation, and deceptions to succeed. As well, the organizational structure of many organized crime groups mirrors the business model.
- Organized crime is becoming increasingly diverse within countries as well as more transnational in its dimensions, coinciding with improved technology and communications.
- Cybercrime shares much in common with organized crime and corporate crime, including its transnational nature, its growing complexity and sophistication, its profitability, and the challenge it presents for law enforcement agencies.
- The rapid expansion of governments and corporations has given rise to an increase in organized crime and corporate crime.
- Traditionally, sociological theories have been used to explain non-conventional crimes like organized crime and corporate crime, but they have had limited success. Criminology must extend its approach to embrace an integrated and interdisciplinary perspective as well as adopting an international and comparative view of organized crime, corporate crime, and cybercrime.

## Discussion Questions

1. What are the similarities and differences between organized crime and corporate crime? How does cybercrime relate to both?
2. Should organized crime, corporate crime, and cybercrime be treated and/or explained differently than conventional crimes (robbery, murder, theft, etc.)?
3. Why is it difficult to detect and prosecute non-conventional crime offenders?
4. Why is it better to apply an interdisciplinary approach to the study of organized crime, corporate crime, and cybercrime?
5. Do outlaw motorcycle gangs serve a useful function in society? Aside from these gangs' high level of organization, why can authorities not stop the expansion of these organized groups? What should criminologists focus on when studying such groups in order to offer sound advice?

## Key Concepts

Aboriginal crime groups
cartel
cybercrime
consensual crimes
corporate crime
illicit market
neutralization

organized crime
protection racket
reintegrative shaming
transnational crime
Trojan horse
victimless crime
white-collar crime

## Key Names

Howard Abadinsky (b. 1941)
John Braithwaite (b. 1951)
Edwin Sutherland (1883–1950)

## Weblinks

**Organized Crime Research**
Public Safety Canada maintains this portal to organized crime research briefs, short summaries of recent research reports on "hot topics in the study of organized crime."
www.publicsafety.gc.ca/cnt/cntrng-crm/rgnzd-crm/rgnzd-crm-rsrch-eng.aspx

**Serious and Organized Crime**
The RCMP provides an excellent overview of organized crime and its impact. This page outlines the agency's strategy for fighting organized crime and links to articles on human trafficking, marijuana grow-ops, and the witness protection program.
www.rcmp-grc.gc.ca/soc-cgco/index-eng.htm

**Assessing the Effectiveness of Organized Crime Control Strategies**
The University of Ottawa's Thomas Gabor prepared this literature review for Canada's Department of Justice to inform the department's evaluation of the Measures to Combat Organized Crime initiative and possible legislative reforms. While the report was prepared over 10 years ago, it remains an insightful policy analysis.
www.justice.gc.ca/eng/rp-pr/csj-sjc/jsp-sjp/rr05_5/rr05_5.pdf

**The Mafia Site**
This non-academic website contains some offensive material but is nevertheless worth the visit for its detailed information about the past and present of the Mafia.
http://mafiasite.8m.com

**Follow the Money: Is Canada Making Progress in Combatting Money Laundering and Terrorist Financing? Not Really**
This 2013 Senate report reviews Canada's fight against money laundering and terrorist financing and offers 18 recommendations to improve the effectiveness of anti-money laundering and anti-terrorist financing strategies.
www.parl.gc.ca/Content/SEN/Committee/411/BANC/rep/rep10mar13-e.pdf

**Multinational Monitor**
Although the online magazine of this corporate watchdog ceased publishing in 2009, it is worth visiting the site for its interesting (albeit out-of-date) articles on such topics as the political economy of the oil and gas industry, the hidden costs of big-box stores, and the 10 international companies with the worst corporate practices—an annual list.
http://multinationalmonitor.org

**Jack & Mae Nathanson Centre on Transnational Human Rights, Crime and Security**
Associated with York University's Osgoode Hall, the Nathanson Centre aims to promote an interdisciplinary program of research into the relationship between crime, security, and human rights. The website offers a searchable bibliographic database as well as many informative links.
www.yorku.ca/nathanson/Links/links.htm

# Chapter 12

## Crimes against Public Order

Ppictures/Shutterstock.com

It is the greatest happiness of the greatest number
that is the measure of right and wrong.
JEREMY BENTHAM (1776)

## Learning Outcomes

After reading this chapter, you should be able to

- Recognize the relationship between law and morality;
- Be familiar with the various types of public-order offences;
- Understand public-order offences such as gambling, prostitution, pornography, and substance abuse;
- Have an awareness of how public-order offences affect society; and
- Appreciate the difficulty in regulating public-order offences.

Over the past several chapters we have seen evidence of an important premise introduced all the way back in Chapter 1: that the criminalization of certain behaviours is *relative* and *evolutive*. Perceptions of what constitutes wrongful behaviour vary widely throughout society and over time. For example, is it wrong for someone to share their home with 50 cats? Were Russian officials in 2012 justified in arresting members of the all-female punk group Pussy Riot for making provocative statements about Russian politics and LGBT rights? Why is marijuana use legal in some parts of North America and not in others? The answers lie in what John Hagan, in his seminal book *Crime and Disrepute* (1994), described as *the relative degree of social harm, social response, and social agreement*. So, when an act or actions exceed a proscribed limit of acceptance (real or imagined), it is sometimes then defined as a public harm.

In criminology, these acts are often referred to as public-order crimes. They are also known by a variety of other names, such as crimes against convention, consensual crimes, victimless vices, and victimless crimes. Public-order crimes are based on moral principles and are

**public-order crimes**
Activities deemed illegal because they are viewed as immoral or harmful, even though the parties who engage in them do so by choice.

Greek supporters of the Russian punk rock band Pussy Riot engage in the sort of protest that got two of the band's members arrested and charged in Moscow in 2012. What does the incident say about the relative nature of crime?

© Konstantinos Tsakalidis / Alamy Stock Photo

consequently subject to controversy. Consider the term *victimless crime*, which implies that no one is harmed by the activity, typically because the activity is consensual. For this reason, some criminologists question whether or not these acts should be considered criminal. Public-order crimes include gambling, prostitution, pornography, substance abuse, vandalism, and graffiti. Would you say that these crimes are victimless?

## Law and Morality

*Good laws lead to the making of better ones; bad ones bring about worse.* (Jean-Jacques Rousseau, *The Social Contract*, Book 3, Chapter XV)

Consider the following questions:

- If it is not against the law to buy lottery tickets, why are other forms of gambling considered illegal?
- If it is legal to have sexual relations with partners of one's choice, why is it illegal to pay someone for such services?
- If the Charter of Rights guarantees freedom of speech and the press, why are some music videos censored?
- If women are allowed to sell their eggs for profit (to donor banks), why is the public at large not permitted to sell their organs?
- Why is same-sex marriage legal today in countries where public support remains mixed (see Box 12.1)?

The primary purpose of the law generally is to protect society by legislating behaviours that "society" (broadly defined) considers immoral and/or socially harmful. However, what is the foundation of morality? As the eighteenth-century German philosopher Immanuel Kant argued, morality cannot rely on religious doctrines. Rather, according to more recent philosophers such as Nils Rauhut (2004), morality must be established on grounds that can withstand skeptical challenges and enrich the lives of all.

These philosophical points have been the subject of extensive debate over the years. How does one determine whether an act presents a clear and immediate harm to those who partake in it? For example, how should criminology respond to certain acts that take place between consenting individuals (gambling, prostitution, and doctor-assisted suicide, for example)? Answers to these questions are complicated by an assortment of related variables. How old are the participants? Is there a greater social and moral issue at stake? For example, does allowing sex workers to solicit their services openly in the streets send an inappropriate message to young impressionable people? Does it promote the entry of the homeless and runaways into prostitution as a means of survival? Does it result in their exploitation? These are questions of morality for which there are no clear-cut answers. As we will see throughout this chapter, it is uncertain whether criminal law can be effectively used to regulate these behaviours.

Since antiquity, social conventions and rules of etiquette have been the guiding principles for maintaining social harmony. As societies evolved, they needed to codify their norms and values in order to maintain a sense of social harmony. This codification resulted in the creation of formal criminal law. Law can be interpreted as subscribing to one of two general theoretical orientations—the *consensus perspective* or the *conflict perspective*—which are not necessarily mutually exclusive.

According to the consensus perspective (see Figure 1.1 on page 7), laws are seen as broadly representing the interests of a given society. In effect, from this view, the function of criminal

**consensus perspective**

A criminological perspective that sees laws as representing the interests of society.

## BOX 12.1    REALITY CHECK

### Homosexuality

Prior to 1968, homosexuality was a punishable crime in Canada. Following two decades of social and cultural changes in the 1950s and 1960s, Bill C-150 was passed in 1969, legalizing the practice of homosexuality. Even so, homosexuality was for some years after viewed as a disease rather than a crime (Duhaime, 1996).

During the mid-1990s, Alberta, Ontario, British Columbia,

and Nova Scotia granted restricted rights to gays and lesbians, and in 2005, Canada became just the fourth country in the world to legalize same-sex marriage. Ten years later, in 2015, the US Supreme Court ruled that state-level bans on same-sex marriage were illegal; the verdict—which found approval among 59 per cent of Americans, according to a CNN survey (Agiesta, 2015)—effectively legalized same-sex marriage nationwide in the United States.

**Figure 12.1    The Legal Status of Same-Sex Marriage Worldwide**

*Source:* Adapted from FreedomToMarry.org. http://www.freedomtomarry.org/landscape/entry/c/international

law is to express a widely held notion of public morality. Conversely, the conflict perspective interprets laws as representing the interests of specific groups, such as vocal minorities and those who occupy positions of power in society. The architects of the Canadian constitution, in 1982, recognized a key dilemma inherent in the law. In formulating the constitution, they attempted to strike a balance between respecting natural law (reflecting utilitarian principles) and the relative and evolving nature of social norms and values. However, the tension between social order and individual freedoms is one that is not likely to ever be resolved in our multi-ethnic, multicultural, and pluralistic society. We will now examine four different types of public-order crimes—gambling, prostitution, pornography, and substance abuse—to demonstrate this issue.

**conflict perspective**

A criminological approach that sees laws as representing the interests of specific groups in society.

In an effort to curb loitering—illegal under section 175.1 of the Criminal Code—some municipalities and businesses are installing spikes, studs, fences, and subtler forms of "hostile architecture" in places where people have become accustomed to sitting, sleeping, or just hanging around. Assess Canada's loitering law from both a consensus perspective and a conflict perspective.

© Guy Corbishley / Alamy Stock Photo

## Gambling

*Gambling is not a healthy commercial activity. It is an activity that shows a society is morally bankrupt.* (Marie Lucie Spoke, Citizens Against Gambling Expansion, 1998 [qtd in Welsh & Donovan, 1998])

Have you ever bought a scratch-and-win card or a raffle ticket? Have you ever played the slots or bet on a horse? Have you ever joined a game of online poker or made a casual bet with a friend? Chances are you've participated in one or more of these activities, maybe on a regular basis or else once or twice, "just for fun" (see Box 12.3, later in this chapter). Why do you think some forms of gambling are considered socially acceptable and quite innocent while other forms have been prohibited by law? What does the law say about gambling? These are questions we will explore in this section.

### Gambling and the Law

Gambling is covered in sections 197–210 of the Criminal Code, where it is referred to as *gaming and betting*. But the distinction between what is defined as acceptable chance-taking and what is defined as illegal has become murkier and murkier since the late 1960s, when certain types of lottery sales were legally approved. Since then, more and more forms of gambling have been legalized. Why? Here are some of the reasons:

- Legalization undermines the exploitation of gambling by organized crime groups.

- The public has become more tolerant with regard to a variety of vice crimes, including gambling. Today, it is possible to buy lottery tickets in every province and territory, and legally operated casinos have been established in various jurisdictions.
- Gaming is a lucrative enterprise in Canada, drawing annual revenues of $15 billion for the provinces (see Figure 12.2), of which nearly half is pure profit (McMahon, 2013). The provinces use these revenues to pay for social programs.
- Casinos operating on traditional First Nations lands give Canada's Aboriginal people an opportunity to benefit economically from a share of provincial casino revenues. In 2014, there were 16 casinos in Canada operated by First Nations peoples (Canadian Tribal gaming, 2014), which generated over $5 billion in annual profits. Note, however, that 11 per cent of Aboriginal people in Canada are considered to have a gambling problem, verus 2.6 per cent of non-Aboriginal Canadians (Goffin, 2013).

By providing so many legal avenues for gambling, are legislative bodies preying on human weakness? Or should we be applauding governments for providing safe environments for an activity that would otherwise be unsafe (and illegal), while diverting revenues from criminal organizations to their own coffers for use in funding social programs? This argument is the essence of the conflict perspective. It is worth noting that governments divert an average of just 1.65 per cent of their gambling revenues to problem gambling (CPRG, 2015, Table K). In addition, moral entrepreneurial groups such as Gamblers Anonymous and the Canadian Foundation on Compulsive Gambling, along with many religious groups, warn about the dangers of gambling. While their reasons may differ, they all agree that the harm done to families and individuals, and the relationship between gambling and crime, are serious issues.

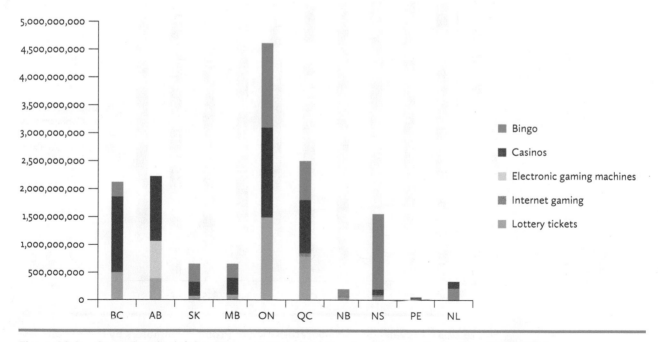

**Figure 12.2    Gross Provincial Government-Operated Gaming Revenue by Source, 2013–2014**

Notes
– Casinos: Data unavailable for New Brunswick.
– Electronic gaming machines: Includes slots and video lottery terminals located outside bingo halls and casinos (i.e. at bars and racetracks).
– Internet gaming: Data unavailable for British Columbia and Manitoba.

*Source:* Data from Canadian Partnership for Responsible Gambling, *2013–2014 Gambling Data & Statistics*, Table E.

## Characteristics and Trends

- In 2013–14 there were approximately 35,000 gambling venues in Canada, including bingo halls, casinos, racetracks, and lottery ticket outlets (CPRG, 2015, Table A). The amount of government-operated gaming revenue that was generated per person 18 years and over in 2013–14 was $496, down from $557 in 2011–12 (CPRG, 2015, Table E).
- Provincial rates of participation in some form of gambling range from 67 per cent in Quebec to 87 per cent in Saskatchewan and Nova Scotia (CPRG, 2015, Table M).
- According to a 2009 report by Statistics Canada, single men spent over 50 per cent more on gambling annually than single women did—$814 compared to $516 (Marshall, 2009, Table 4).
- The provinces with the highest proportions of moderate-risk and problem gamblers are Manitoba (6.1 per cent of the population aged 18+) and Saskatchewan (5.9 per cent); the province with the lowest rate—1.6 per cent—is PEI (see Figure 12.3).

What we often overlook when scrutinizing raw data on gambling are the moral consequences of legalizing different kinds of gambling. What is the social impact? What unintended consequences might result? What is the impact on organized crime?

As we saw in Chapter 11, many organized crime groups are heavily involved in gambling-related activities. Any attempt to estimate the amount of profit criminal groups make from illegal gambling activities would be sheer speculation. Nonetheless, criminal justice agencies are aware of the extent of the problem and prefer instead to direct their attention

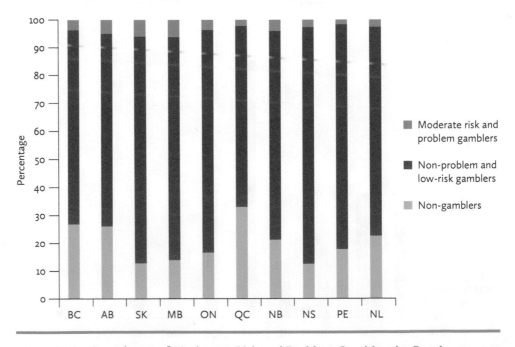

**Figure 12.3    Prevalence of Moderate-Risk and Problem Gamblers by Province, 2013–2014**

Note: Results are based on provincial surveys of adults aged 18 and over using the Canadian Problem Gambling Index, a standardized instrument used to measure problem gambling in the general population.

*Source:* Data from Canadian Partnership for Responsible Gambling. *Canadian Gambling Digest* 2013-2014. August 2015, p. 16.

| BOX 12.2 | WHAT DO YOU THINK? |

## VLTs: Social Benefit or Social Harm?

In 1998, several members of the Alberta legislature raised concerns about how the growing prevalence of VLTs—video lottery terminals—was contributing to problem gambling. In many provinces, including Alberta, the machines are found in bars and lounges, although the concerned MLAs recommended (without success) that they be limited to more traditional gambling sites such as casinos and racetracks.

VLT machines were introduced in Canada in the early 1990s, often replacing traditional slot machines. A 2003 study found that at least 25 per cent of VLT users were either at-risk or problem gamblers (Smith & Wynne, 2004). Yet a 2006 report by the Canadian Gaming Association said that Canada's VLT industry was "well-run and well-regulated by Crown agencies with a high degree of public accountability" (CGA, 2006). The report also pointed out that from 1991, when VLTs were introduced, to 2005, they had generated over $20 billion in revenue for the provinces, and that the provinces had spent a combined $75 million to address problem gambling. (It is worth noting that the CGA is an industry lobby group that speaks on behalf of gaming operators, equipment suppliers, and others involved in regulated gaming.)

In the latest effort to fight problem gambling, Alberta has recently begun introducing new VLTs that "feature new time limits and replace the indefinite betting amount with a $100 maximum" (Kaufmann, 2013). However, the top prize the new machines can award has risen from $1,000 to $2,500, making them more enticing.

VLTs generate revenues that provinces use to fund important social programs. However, they can also encourage financial ruin among gambling addicts. Do you think governments should be involved in regulating—and profiting from—VLTs and other forms of gambling? Can you think of any way to make VLTs safer for problem gamblers?

to understanding and curbing it. Undoubtedly, the recent liberalization of gambling laws throughout North America has reduced organized crime's income from gambling. In response, organized crime groups have turned to other illegal pursuits, such as extortion, illicit drugs, immigration fraud, money laundering, and pornography.

The legalization of many forms of gambling has also sparked a rise in problem gamblers, and the negative social effects have escalated accordingly. Although there are minimal scientific data, there is sufficient research to conclude that gambling is a social vice that threatens public order, increases health care costs, and increases criminal activity.

Those who experience serious gambling addiction are sometimes referred to as *compulsive gamblers*. In Canada, gambling behaviour is typically classified according to the problem gambling severity index (PGSI), shown in Box 12.3 (see also Figure 12.4). Compulsive gambling is generally seen as symptomatic of an emotional or behavioural disorder—low self-esteem, inability and/or unwillingness to accept reality, immaturity, or obsessive/compulsive behavioural patterns. While compulsive gambling behaviour is governed by various environmental, psychological, and social factors, it is possible to identify certain warning signs in the individual. Recent research has shown that problem gamblers frequently struggle with other addictions as well as certain psychiatric disorders (Kim, Grant, Eckert, Faris, & Hartman, 2006; Sacco, Cunningham-Williams, Ostmann, & Spitznagel Jr, 2008).

Gambling is seen as a social problem, and problem gamblers require attention. In January 1957, Gamblers Anonymous (GA) was formed to help people deal with compulsions to gamble. GA operates on the premise that gambling is an illness; that it is progressive in nature; and that it cannot be cured, only managed. Similar to Alcoholics Anonymous, GA primarily advocates that adherence to spiritual principles can help control a behaviour they consider a moral vice. Today, this organization has chapters all around the world.

## BOX 12.3

### A CLOSER LOOK
### The Problem Gambling Severity Index

The following self-assessment test is based on the Canadian problem gambling severity index (PGSI). Your score will tell you if your gambling is really just for fun or if it poses possible negative consequences.

**THINKING ABOUT THE LAST 12 MONTHS . . .**

1. Have you bet more than you could really afford to lose?

   **never   sometimes   most of the time   almost always**

2. Have you needed to gamble with larger amounts of money to get the same feeling of excitement?

   **never   sometimes   most of the time   almost always**

3. When you gambled, did you go back another day to try to win back the money you lost?

   **never   sometimes   most of the time   almost always**

4. Have you borrowed money or sold anything to get money to gamble?

   **never   sometimes   most of the time   almost always**

5. Have you felt that you might have a problem with gambling?

   **never   sometimes   most of the time   almost always**

6. Has gambling caused you any health problems, including stress or anxiety?

   **never   sometimes   most of the time   almost always**

7. Have people criticized your betting or told you that you had a gambling problem, regardless of whether or not you thought it was true?

   **never   sometimes   most of the time   almost always**

8. Has your gambling caused any financial problems for you or your household?

   **never   sometimes   most of the time   almost always**

9. Have you felt guilty about the way you gamble or what happens when you gamble?

   **never   sometimes   most of the time   almost always**

Score the following for each response:

   **0** = never

   **1** = sometimes

   **2** = most of the time

   **3** = almost always

The higher your score, the greater the risk that your gambling is a problem.

   **0** = non-problem gambling

   **1–2** = low level of problems with few or no identified negative consequences

   **3–7** = moderate level of problems leading to some negative consequences

   **8 or more** = problem gambling with negative consequences and a possible loss of control

Source: Problem Gambling Institute of Ontario, www.problemgambling.ca.

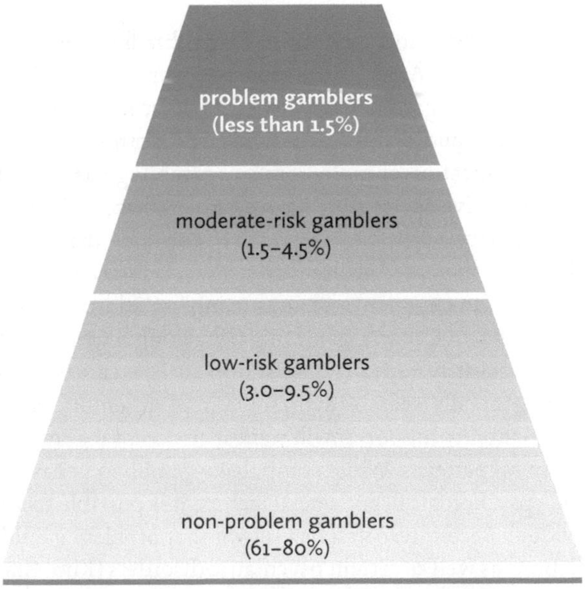

problem gamblers
(less than 1.5%)

moderate-risk gamblers
(1.5–4.5%)

low-risk gamblers
(3.0–9.5%)

non-problem gamblers
(61–80%)

**Figure 12.4   Prevalence of Problem Gambling in Canada**

*Source:* Approximate data ranges based on data from Canadian Partnership for Responsible Gambling. *Canadian Gambling Digest* 2013-2014. August 2015, p. 16.

| BOX 12.4 | **FACTS AND FIGURES** HOW BIG IS LEGALIZED GAMBLING IN CANADA? A SNAPSHOT OF ONTARIO |
| --- | --- |

- Prevalence* of gambling: 82.9 per cent (rank among provinces: 4th)
- Gross government-operated gaming revenue: $4.7 billion (rank: 1st)
- Net government-operated gaming revenue: $1.9 billion (rank: 1st)
- Gross charity-operated gaming revenue: $382 million (rank: 1st)

- Net charity-operated gaming revenue: $155 million (rank: 2nd)
- Prevalence* of moderate-risk and problem gamblers: 3.4 per cent (rank: 5th)
- Percentage of government gaming revenue distributed to problem gambling: 2.01 per cent (rank: 2nd)

\* Based on the percentage of the population aged 18 and over.
*Source:* CPRG, 2015.

## Explaining Gambling

Why do people gamble? The question has been approached from a number of perspectives, but three schools of thought are used most frequently to propose explanations:

- *Biological theories* explain gambling as an impulse-control disorder with a specific biochemical link. Berman and Siegel (1992) cite studies showing that compulsive gamblers have low levels of serotonin and increased responsiveness of the noradrenergic system, associated with poor impulse control.
- *Psychological theories* focus on differences in individual psychological makeup, such as low self-control resulting from adversities experienced during childhood, and suggest that basic emotional needs of gamblers are not being met. This approach also suggests that problem gambling is symptomatic of a broader pattern of sensation-seeking and risk-taking that may be associated with feelings of guilt, emotional isolation, and pain.
- *Learning theories* explain gambling as a learned behaviour that is governed by differential reinforcement patterns.

Explanations of problem gambling behaviours are about as diverse as the methods by which people gamble. What is evident is that gambling is a complex personal, social, and cultural phenomenon that may be best explained by a framework that considers individual (e.g. biological, psychological), social (e.g. societal norms and values) and situational (i.e. availability/accessibility of gambling) characteristics.

## Prevention

A number of researchers have studied the link between the ever growing number of government-run gambling facilities and the risk of problem gambling and associated public health concerns, including psychological problems, suicide, and family breakdown (Afifi, Cox, Martens, Sareen, & Enns, 2010; Bureau du coroner du Québec, 2004; Jacobs, Marston, Singer, Widaman, Little, & Veizades, 1989; Rutsey, 2009). In response to growing concerns, most provinces have introduced a wide range of intervention and prevention initiatives, which can be characterized as either educational or policy-oriented (Williams, West, & Simpson, 2007). However, Williams and Simpson (2008) point out that most of the initiatives are either poorly designed or poorly implemented.

In addition to identifying the characteristics of problem gamblers and those forms of gambling that are the most harmful, criminologists need to closely consider the extent to which gambling is, or is not, a victimless crime. In terms of social policy research, it is necessary to understand whether offering help lines, establishing support groups or programs, and having trained staff at gambling facilities can minimize the damage gambling causes.

© Jruffa | Dreamstime.com

The glitz, glamour, and spectacle of Niagara Falls casinos give gambling an air of excitement and social acceptability. Do you support the increased tolerance of vice crimes in Canada? Or have we gone too far?

---

**BOX 12.5    WHAT DO YOU THINK?**

## Daily Fantasy Sports: Game of Skill or Gambling?

Strict rules govern the ability to place bets on sporting events in North America. For instance, in Canada, it is illegal to bet on the outcome of a single sporting event, like a football game or a horse race. Instead, a sports bettor must make a *parlay*, placing a wager on the outcomes of at least three events, and must be correct on all three in order to win.

Fantasy sports leagues, in which participants compete to assemble the best roster of professional players based on their combined statistics over the course of a season, have long circumvented regulation. Such leagues have traditionally been privately organized and are considered to involve more skill than luck, since they depend on a thorough knowledge of player statistics and a commitment to managing a roster over the course of a full season. Recently, however, online operators that offer daily fantasy sports, in which a much larger pool of participants' draft lineups of players that are judged on their performance in a single game, have attracted scrutiny from government regulators. In November 2015, following a month-long investigation, the attorney general for the state of New York ruled daily fantasy sports to be games of chance, not skill, because they were about "instant gratification" rather than long-term strategy and smart play over the course of several months ("FanDuel & DraftKings deemed 'gambling,'" 2015). New York thus became the second state, after Nevada, to ban daily fantasy sports betting. In December 2015, the attorney general for Illinois followed suit, arguing that the games constitute gambling because daily fantasy players "lack control over the real-world outcomes" (Pramuk, 2015).

> Are fantasy sports really "games of skill" that depend on careful research and long-term strategy, or are they "games of chance" like other forms of sports betting? Is it reasonable to argue that daily fantasy sports and traditional fantasy sports are different, or is this a case of splitting hairs?

---

## Prostitution

You have probably heard prostitution referred to as the "oldest profession in the world," borrowing a phrase attributed to the nineteenth-century English poet and short-story writer Rudyard Kipling (1865–1936). For many people, it is indeed a profession, and a lucrative one at that; however, those who profit the most are too often not the sex workers themselves but the pimps and organized criminals who control the business. This is why many people view prostitution as a serious moral interdiction that exploits some of society's most vulnerable people, primarily young women and girls. Others still accept prostitution as a necessary evil to be tolerated—but not condoned—as long as it occurs in the shadows, out of public view. As we have seen with other criminal activity, context is crucial, as attitudes toward prostitution have changed over time and vary depending on where you live.

Although there is a considerable volume of Canadian literature on sex workers today, most of it did not begin to emerge until the early 1980s. Prostitution became a politically relevant issue when special interest groups such as POWER (Prostitutes and Other Women for Equal Rights), CORP (Canadian Organization for the Rights of Prostitutes), SWAV (Sex Workers Alliance of Vancouver), and Dans La Rue began to draw attention to the needs and rights of sex workers. The battle for the rights of sex workers led to a Supreme Court challenge of Canada's prostitution laws and a ruling, in December 2013, that those laws were unconstitutional. New laws introduced in December 2014 generated criticism, both by opponents of prostitution and by sex workers themselves, and Canada continues to look for a legislative model that will satisfy everyone affected by an industry that has been described variously as dangerous, socially harmful, empowering, and lucrative.

**prostitution**
The practice or occupation of engaging in sexual services in exchange for money.

## The Changing Laws Defining Prostitution

### *The Law in Canada from the Beginning to the Fraser Report (1985)*

In keeping with much of our legal heritage, Canada's first prostitution laws were based on British common law. Prostitution was initially prohibited under vagrancy laws; the first vagrancy act was the Nova Scotia Act of 1759 but has since been frequently amended. The laws were not directed at prostitution per se but at the "nuisance that was created by 'streetwalkers' and 'bawdy-house' activities" (Lowman, 1995, p. 333), and enforcement was superficial. In the historic frontier regions of Canada and the United States especially, red-light districts were openly tolerated by the police (see Brannigan, Knafla, & Levy, 1989).

Prostitution is legally defined in sections 210 to 213 of the Criminal Code, which address such activities as "keeping a common bawdy-house," or brothel; "procuring," or living off the avails of prostitution; and "offences in relation to prostitution," such as stopping a person in a public place for the purpose of engaging in prostitution. Lowman (1995) argues that sections 210 through 212 were intended to protect sex workers from exploitation by third parties, while section 213 was designed to protect the public from the nuisance effects of prostitution. Did the laws work? Many critics argued that the law, rather than promoting the health and security of people involved in prostitution, did little more than prompt sex workers to devise better means of avoiding detection (see Davis & Shaffer, 1994; MacIntyre & Miller, 2016).

In the 1980s, adult prostitution was the focus of a report produced by the Special Committee on Pornography and Prostitution (SCPP), also known as the Fraser Committee. The committee's mandate was to review the status of prostitution and pornography and their related regulatory laws. The report, referred to as the Fraser Report, was released in 1985. One of its recommendations was to amend the outdated 1850 Bawdy House Act (see s. 210 of the Criminal Code). The authors of the report argued that the act represented an outmoded morality law that made criminals of people who might simply be living an alternative lifestyle. Under the law, it was not only illegal to operate a bawdy house (i.e. a place used "for the purpose of prostitution or the practice of acts of indecency," according to section 197 of the Criminal Code); it was also a crime to simply be found in a bawdy house. A key problem with the act was the vague reference to "acts of indecency," which were not clearly defined in the Criminal Code.

The SCPP (1985) reported that only 62 per cent of Canadians surveyed felt that exchanging sex for money was indecent and worthy of disapproval. Indeed, Canadians' acceptance of prostitution has grown over time. In their recent review of public support for legalizing prostitution, Lowman and Louie (2012) observed that between 1984 and 2011 various opinion surveys showed that a small majority of Canadians favoured some form of decriminalization of consensual adult prostitution. This increasing public acceptance of sex work buoyed a series of high-profile court cases that challenged the legal status of prostitution, culminating in a landmark 2013 Supreme Court ruling that Canada's prostitution laws were unconstitutional.

### *Constitutional Challenges and a New Prostitution Law*

Prior to the 2013 ruling, prostitution was, technically speaking, legal in Canada: that is, the simple exchange of money for sexual services was not prohibited by law. What was illegal, as noted earlier, were the following activities:

- owning, operating, or even being found in a "bawdy house," or brothel;
- bringing a person to a brothel;

---

**vagrancy**
The crime of being intentionally unemployed and therefore having no lawful means of supporting oneself or one's family.

**Fraser Report**
A 1985 report of the Special Committee on Pornography and Prostitution (SCPP), frequently called the Fraser Committee, whose mandate was to review the status of prostitution and pornography and their related regulatory laws.

---

**BOX 12.6    FACTS AND FIGURES**
**WHAT DO WE MEAN BY A "RED-LIGHT DISTRICT"?**

The term *red-light district* is used to refer to the part of town where prostitution and other sex-related businesses (such as strip clubs) are concentrated. The expression became popular in North America during the railroad-building era in the 1800s. When visiting a prostitute, a railway worker would hang his red signal light outside the woman's tent, so that if he was suddenly needed for work he could be quickly found (Bullough & Bullough, 1987).

- **procuring**, or living off the avails of prostitution—in other words, acting as an agent, or pimp, for a prostitute; and
- **soliciting**, or communicating and selling sexual services in a public place.

Despite the fact that prostitution itself was not illegal, given these restrictions, it was almost impossible for a sex worker to work without violating laws—or, at least, to work safely (see Box 12.7).

In December 2013, in the case of *Canada (Attorney General) v. Bedford*, the Supreme Court struck down Canada's prostitution laws on the grounds that they made the practice of prostitution—legal in and of itself—extremely dangerous, thereby violating basic Canadian values (Fine, 2013). In the words of the Court, the laws "prevent[ed] people engaged in a risky—but legal—activity from taking steps to protect themselves from the risks" (cited in Fine, 2013). The ban on brothels and pimping had been intended (partly) to prevent prostitutes from being exploited by third parties. However, brothels provide prostitutes with safe, indoor spaces to ply their trade, while those involved in procurement might include bodyguards, drivers, receptionists, and even responsible managers—people, in other words, who could actually make the working conditions of a prostitute safer. Solicitation, meanwhile, was a means of vetting potential clients in advance, and weeding out those who appeared to pose a threat.

The Supreme Court ruling effectively nullified Canada's major prostitution laws, but the Court suspended its ruling for one year, giving the government time to amend its legislation in accordance with the ruling. The government responded with the Protection of Communities and Exploited Persons Act, which came into effect in December 2014. The new law was designed to criminalize those who buy or profit from prostitution, apart from the prostitutes themselves. Under the new law, it is legal to solicit for the purpose of selling sexual services, provided this activity does not take place anywhere where people under the age of 18 might be present. It is also legal to advertise one's own sexual services, but third-party advertising (i.e. in newspapers and on websites) is illegal. It is also illegal to purchase sexual services—a big change over previous laws.

*The Status of Prostitution Under the New Law*

The new laws reflect the government's view that sex workers are "prostitution's primary victims" while "those who create the demand for prostitution, i.e., purchasers of sexual services, and those who capitalize on that demand, i.e., third parties who economically benefit from the sale of those services, both cause and perpetuate prostitution's harms (Canada, Department of Justice, 2014). The aim of the law, stated clearly in a Justice Department technical paper, is to reduce the demand for prostitution "with a view to ultimately abolishing prostitution to the greatest extent possible" (Canada, Department of Justice, 2014). So, at a time

**procuring**

The illegal act of arranging for, recruiting, or forcing a person to act as a prostitute, providing sexual services to another in exchange for money.

**soliciting**

The illegal act of *communicating* with another person in a public place for the purpose of offering or providing sexual services as a prostitute.

---

| BOX 12.7 | **FACTS AND FIGURES** WHAT KINDS OF VIOLENCE DO SEX WORKERS EXPERIENCE? |
|---|---|

From 2006 to 2008, Kate Shannon and a team of researchers at the University of British Columbia studied the prevalence of gender-based violence against female prostitutes in Vancouver. Of the total number of research participants, 70 (30 per cent of those studied) reported that they had experienced client-perpetrated violence. Table 12.1 shows what percentage of those sex workers experienced each of eight different forms of client-perpetrated violence.

**Table 12.1   Types of Client-Perpetrated Violence Reported by Female Sex Workers in Vancouver, 2006–2008**

| Type of Violence | Number (Percentage) of Participants Who Experienced It |
|---|---|
| Verbal harassment | 70 (100%) |
| Physical assault or beating | 47 (67) |
| Rape or sexual assault | 34 (49) |
| Assault with a weapon | 31 (44) |
| Strangling | 19 (27) |
| Abduction or kidnap | 18 (26) |
| Attempted sexual assault | 15 (21) |
| Thrown from a moving car | 14 (20) |
| Other* | 11 (16) |

Notes: In total, 70 out of 237 (30 per cent) of the sex workers studied reported client-perpetrated violence. Median number of incidents: 1 (interquartile range 1–2).
*"Other" responses included being robbed; being held against will or locked in car; and being assaulted under the influence of a date rape drug.
*Source:* Shannon, K., et al. (2009). "Prevalence and structural correlates of gender based violence among a prospective cohort of female sex workers." *British Medical Journal.* 339. Copyright © 2009, British Medical Journal Publishing Group.

when many Western countries have moved away from criminalizing prostitution, Canada is moving in the opposite direction (see Box 12.8).

There is some evidence—anecdotal only at this point—that the law is scaring off some clients who fear arrest now that purchasing sex is illegal (Warnica, 2015). Critics of the new law say that the market for sex services will not diminish but that clients will adopt new, more secretive methods of arranging the purchase of sex, which will put sex workers at risk by making it more difficult for prostitutes to vet new clients. More fundamentally, critics who view sex work as a legitimate profession that should be brought out in the open object to the law's stance on sex workers as victims. Pushing the profession further into the shadows makes prostitution more dangerous, not less so, and diminishes the legitimacy and dignity of what they do. Legalization, they argue, is the only way to make prostitution safe for sex workers.

## Characteristics and Trends

Drawing on a variety of studies, we can identify some of the key characteristics and trends of prostitution in Canada:

- The average age of female sex workers is 28, while the average age of male sex workers is 35. The average age of entry into prostitution among female sex workers is around 15 (Report of the Sexually Exploited Youth Committee of the Capital Regional District, 1997, cited in Bittle, 1999).
- Between 2000 and 2014, the number of official incidents dropped from 5,051 to 1,073 (see Figure 12.5). This should not be taken to mean that prostitution in Canada is on the decline; rather, it reflects police priorities and the difficulty of laying prostitution-related

© STEFFEN SCHMIDT/epa/Corbis

In 2013, the city of Zurich, Switzerland, introduced a new drive-in facility, located on the outskirts of town, where clients, after passing a check-in gate, can obtain the services of a prostitute at a partially enclosed wooden booth like the one pictured here. Is this a model to follow in other countries where prostitution is legal? What do you consider the pros and cons of legalizing prostitution?

---

**BOX 12.8** **A CLOSER LOOK**
**Prostitution in Other Countries**

The following examples illustrate variations that exist in attitudes toward prostitution, age of consent, and related issues in different countries.

- *Australia:* Prostitution laws are set by individual states. For the most part, prostitution is not illegal, but certain forms of prostitution (e.g. street prostitution) may be restricted in some regions. In Victoria, for example, street prostitution is legal but prohibited near schools, churches, and hospitals. The age of consent is generally 16.
- *Costa Rica*: Prostitution is legal, but promoting and facilitating prostitution are illegal. Sex workers are required to be licensed and to carry ID cards. The age of consent is 18.
- *Greece:* Prostitution is legal. Recent provisions have been proposed to require prostitutes to retire at 55,

with the state providing social and medical benefits. Workers are required to undergo health checks every two weeks.
- *Netherlands:* Prostitution has never been outlawed in the Netherlands. Since 1988, prostitutes have joined the Service Sector Union as a legal profession, and sex workers have been required to pay income taxes since 1996. No health checks are required. The age of consent is 16.
- *Vietnam:* In the mid-1970s, after North Vietnam and South Vietnam united, the communist-oriented government began a major campaign to rid the country of prostitution. Today, giant billboards warn against illicit sex, gambling, and other vices, but prostitution is thriving. Authorities attribute the resurgence of prostitution to the emergence of the market economy.

---

charges. The suspension of Canada's prostitution laws in December 2013 helps to account for the sharp decline in 2014.
- In 2012, 1 per cent of those charged in relation to prostitution were between the ages of 12 and 17 (Canada at a Glance 2012, 2013).
- The clearance rate for murders involving sex workers is 34 per cent, compared to 77–85 per cent for homicide victims who are not sex workers (Bittle, 2002).
- Sex workers are a common target for multiple forms of victimization: an earlier study in the 1990s indicated that as many as 80 per cent of female sex workers had been victims of sexual assault (Durkan, 1997).

**clearance rate**
The percentage of reported crimes that are solved over a fixed period of time.

An early Canadian study on prostitution found that sex workers usually enter the profession in one of three ways. First, Lautt (1984) found that the youngest (aged 12–16) are often targeted through exploitation activities of other individuals. Criminals (i.e. street pimps) patrol bus stops, airports, train stations, and other entry points into a city looking for prospective vulnerable young girls and boys who can be manipulated into prostitution with the promise of food and shelter. More recent research suggests this is still often the case. MacLaurin and Worthington (2013, p. 188) report that "a percentage of runaway and homeless youth become involved in prostitution while living on the streets." In effect, these youths do not leave home "with the goal of taking up prostitution, but rather, entering into prostitution occurs as a result of the street situation" (MacLauren & Worthington, 2013, p. 188).

For some young people who experience extreme adversities early in their lives, such as severely dysfunctional families and child abuse, serious personal problems and economic need, entering into the sex trade for money may become a means of survival. In 2015, *Toronto Star* investigative journalist Olivia Carville described how "victims as young as 12 are tricked into the sex trade by 'Romeo' pimps who sell a dream of money, love, and security" (Carville, 2015). According to Carville, girls are drawn into human sex trafficking by men who start off as model boyfriends. The girls are first approached at house parties or, increasingly, online, on

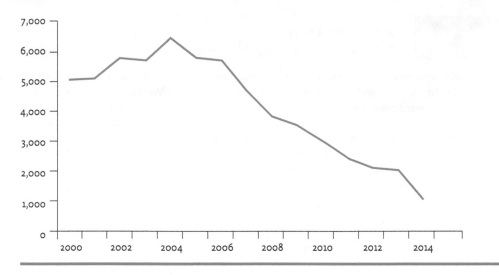

**Figure 12.5     Reported Prostitution Offences in Canada, 2000–2014**

Note: The following violations officially expired on December 20, 2013: bawdy house, living off the avails of prostitution of a person under 18, procuring, obtains/communicates with a person under 18 for purpose of sex, and other prostitution. As a result of the new Protection of Communities and Exploited Persons Act: Bill C-36 (effective December 2014) the following violation codes were introduced: communicate for the purpose of procuring sex near school or playground, stopping motor vehicle/impeding traffic, communicating for the purpose of obtaining sex, communicating for the purpose of obtaining sex <18, material benefit from sexual services, material benefit from sexual services <18, procuring, procuring <18, advertising sexual services, parent/guardian procuring sexual activity <16, parent/guardian procuring sexual activity (16–17), householder permit sexual activity <16, and householder permit sexual activity (16–17). Comparisons of 2014 data to previous years should be made with caution.

*Source:* Statistics Canada CANSIM Table 252-0051.

---

| BOX 12.9 | **A CLOSER LOOK**<br>**Willy Pickton: Canada's Deadliest Serial Killer?** |

Robert "Willy" Pickton is arguably Canada's deadliest serial killer. When the former pig farmer from Port Coquitlam, BC, was finally caught and brought to trial in 2007, he was facing charges relating to the disappearance and murders of 15 prostitutes—although, at the time, prosecutors indicated they had enough evidence to proceed with a total of 22 first-degree murder charges. Following an extensive search of Pickton's property, police found traces of other missing women, and the murder charges increased. The victims were among 60 women—most of them sex workers from Vancouver's Downtown Eastside—who had gone missing between the late 1970s and the late 1990s.

In 2007, Pickton was convicted of second-degree murder of six women; he had been charged with the murders of an additional 20 women, but those charges were stayed in 2010. Pickton was sentenced to life in prison with no possibility of parole for 25 years.

In 2013, lawsuits were filed against the Vancouver Police Department, the RCMP, and Pickton by daughters of three of the women Pickton was convicted of killing. The lawsuits claim that the police failed to properly conduct their initial investigation into the women's disappearances, and that they failed to warn prostitutes working in the Downtown Eastside that a serial killer was believed to be targeting the neighbourhood's sex workers ("Another three victims," 2013).

The Vancouver police estimate that there are some 600 women involved in the sex trade in the city on any given day. Meanwhile, Lowman (1997) estimated that the "murder rate of British Columbia women involved in street prostitution was roughly 60 to 120 times the rate of other adult women."

Why do you think the homicide rate for sex workers is so much higher than it is for the rest of the population? Why do you think the clearance rate for homicides involving prostitutions is so low?

social media sites like Instagram and dating sites like Tinder and Plenty of Fish. They begin a relationship that involves

> romantic dates, the illusion of love and the promise of a future, complete with a house they would own together. Then it's the grooming, the gifts and the hints about how much money she could make working in the sex trade.
>
> Finally, it comes to the "sale," where a pimp convinces a girl to prostitute herself and give him all her money. (Carville, 2015)

Over time, the pimps become abusive to maintain control of their girls. They use violence or the threat of violence, as well as the threat of exposing the girls to their family and friends. They also control the girls' cellphones and e-mail accounts to keep them isolated. The girls, according to Carville (2015), are trapped—physically and psychologically—and are too afraid to run.

A second method of entry into prostitution is through the influence of what Lautt called a "big sister." In this situation, an older sex worker may recruit naive and vulnerable adolescent girls. Lautt suggested that initially, the recruited girls may perceive participation in sex work as "fun" or thrilling because of the associated lifestyle and money, but then this becomes the primary means by which these individuals earn their livelihood (Lautt, 1984). In a recent study, MacIntyre (2012) found that 36 per cent of those involved in prostitution became involved because of someone they knew in the business.

The third main way that sex workers enter the trade according to Lautt (1984) is simply through an independent pragmatic decision, where typically more mature individuals (adults or young adults) choose to engage in soliciting prostitution services out of economic desire or necessity. These women, and occasionally men, likely come from all walks of life, including university students and employed individuals simply seeking extra money, as noted in the 1985 Fraser Report.

## Types of Sex Workers

Several approaches to classifying sex workers have been proposed in the literature. Some of these are based on evidence that, as with other professions, there is a status hierarchy among sex workers. Here we will consider six types of sex workers that have been described. These types vary according to the manner in which the sex workers operate and provide services, and

---

**BOX 12.10**     **A CLOSER LOOK**
**Youth at Risk**

The first piece of legislation introduced to protect young children from being exploited in Canada was the Seduction Act, which came into effect in March 1837. The act enabled the father of a domestic servant who had been seduced by her employer to sue the employer (Bailey, 1991, p. 159). It also amended the common law by making the father liable for the support of his illegitimate child.

Over the next 150 years, laws protecting children from exploitation underwent a number of revisions until the Family Law Act was introduced in 1986. In 1999, Alberta became the first province to put into effect legislation aimed specifically at youth involved in sex work, with the Protection of Children Involved in Prostitution Act (PCIPA). Under revisions to the act, a police officer or any director working under the province's Child Welfare Act may "apprehend and convey the child to a protective safe house" where the child can be confined for a period of up to five days to ensure the safety of the child and assess the risk (www.humanservices.alberta.ca/abuse-bullying/15416.html). The legislation has been criticized for ignoring the broader social and economic conditions that lead to prostitution, particularly among vulnerable young people (Bittle, 2002).

the level of risk involved in each mode of practice. It is important to note that, regardless of the type, many, if not a majority of, sex workers are subject to exploitation by sex traffickers and organized crime groups.

### 1. Streetwalkers

- Are the most visible and possibly most common type of sex workers.
- Are the most commonly researched.
- Are offered the greatest number of intervention strategies.
- Are at the greatest risk of arrest and injury, and the greatest risk of sexual assault, payment evasion, robbery, and exploitation.
- Have a clientele that is garnered primarily through street solicitation.

### 2. Bar Girls

- Operate primarily out of public drinking establishments such as bars and taverns (ranging from seedy watering holes to luxurious hotel lounges).
- Typically work these establishments with co-operation of the management.
- Approach prospective clients and engage in flirtatious discussion leading to an arrangement, thereby avoiding charges of solicitation.
- Experience less police interference than streetwalkers.
- Are considered to maintain a higher social status than streetwalkers.

### 3. Massage Parlour Prostitutes

- Work in parlours that use suggestive or clandestine language and messages to indicate the availability of sexual services; fees charged are comparable to those charged in legitimate parlours to avoid entrapment.
- Rely on clients to request extra (i.e. sexual) services and negotiate fees.
- Are rarely charged by the police because of the clandestine method of operation.

### 4. House Prostitutes

- Work in "bawdy houses," or brothels.
- Are generally considered higher on the social ladder than streetwalkers, bar girls, and massage parlour prostitutes (depending on the nature of the brothel).

### 5. Rap Session Booth Prostitutes

- Converse with clients in adult bookstores or shops that provide private booths (for example, in the red-light districts of Amsterdam and London); such booths are illegal in Canada today.
- Sit behind glass; money is passed through an opening in the booth.
- Remove their clothing for a fee determined according to an informal fee structure; there is no direct sexual contact between the sex worker and the customer.

### 6. Escort Service Prostitutes

- Are also known as "call girls."
- Often keep an exclusive and comparably small and select group of clients.
- Fall outside the legal definition of prostitution, since they do not engage in solicitation; it is incumbent on the client to request "extra" services for an additional fee.
- Are able to advertise their services in magazine or newspaper classified ads, in the Yellow Pages, and online on websites like backpage.com.
- Usually use an escort agency (or have their own) that screens for vice squads and clients considered unsuitable. Prospective clients may be shown photos, video clips,

---

**BOX 12.11**

**A CLOSER LOOK**
**Organized Crime and International Human Sex Trafficking**

In many parts of the world, organized crime and prostitution go hand in hand. In the 1990s, eastern European organized crime groups became heavily involved in human trafficking for the purposes of sexual exploitation (Milivojevic & Pickering, 2013). In 2014, a report by the International Organization of Migration noted that in Moldavia alone, some 25,000 women and children fall victim to trafficking gangs every year (Brinzeanu, 2014).

Tim Stone, in an investigative piece written for *Crime & Justice International*, documented the extent of sex trafficking in the former Soviet bloc. His article describes how young women from impoverished villages of the former Soviet Union were lured into the sex trade by Russian criminal networks using advertisements for dancers, models, orange pickers, waitresses, au pair girls, and even foreign language students (1998, p. 7). As Stone explains, "Wages as high as $1,000 a month are offered to women in order to entice them to leave their homelands," adding that "Promises of such high wages are extremely attractive to Slavic women, considering that the average salary

in the Ukraine is slightly less than $30 a month" (Stone, 1998, p. 7).

Once the women have been recruited, they are taken abroad and told that they must engage in sex work to earn back the money they owe the company for their passage. Those women who refuse to comply are "forced into sexual slavery through physical, mental, and sexual torture" (Stone, 1998). Far from home and afraid of being outed as illegal immigrants, many of the women are unable to escape their lives as indentured sex workers. For the criminal organizations involved in human sex trafficking, the enterprise is more lucrative than trafficking in drugs or illegal weapons as it involves none of the overhead costs associated with those goods.

Compare Tim Stone's description of international human sex trafficking to Olivia Carville's description of domestic sex trafficking (see page 309 above). In what ways are these enterprises similar or different?

---

and/or audio tapes of potential escorts (all for an extra fee) and are guaranteed discretion and confidentiality.

- Are recognized as belonging to a legal operation; therefore, clients can pay with credit cards, cheques, or cash.
- Are seldom targeted by the police because of the privacy of the transactions and because of the relatively high social standing of many of the clients.

## Male Prostitution

Until recently, the subject of male prostitution has been largely overlooked by social scientists. One of the few early studies on the topic was conducted by the American sociologist Albert Reiss (1961). While studying male young offenders, Reiss found that a number of them had been involved in homosexual contact with older men as a means of making money. Yet when questioned, they denied they were ever involved in any kind of prostitution. Reiss's work has helped to perpetuate the myth that most male prostitutes are homosexual.

One of the first Canadian studies on the topic was conducted by Cates and Markley (1992). Their research gave some support to Reiss's earlier general finding that one of the main reasons males engage in prostitution with older males is to find someone who will support them financially. As discussed earlier, financial motivation is also common among female sex workers.

Perhaps most strikingly, a study by Wright (1997), based on extensive interviews, found that 84 per cent of male sex workers in Vancouver were survivors of sexual abuse. He observed that, like many female sex workers, male sex workers experienced a lack of intimacy that made them feel like commodities. Furthermore, most of the male sex workers he interviewed coped with their pain through disassociating from it.

Male sex workers experience many of the same dangers and risks as female sex workers. In a recent study of male sex workers across Canada, MacIntyre (2012), concluded that there is a serious service gap for men who engage in sex work, as well as an information gap, which criminologists should be addressing.

## Explaining Prostitution

Why do individuals become involved in prostitution? The explanations are varied. Based on his review of the literature, Simon Fraser University's John Lowman (1995) noted that theoretical perspectives on the question range all the way from biological positivism to feminist approaches. The Badgley Report, *Sexual Offences Against Children and Youths* (1984), offered a social-psych-ological perspective on prostitution, focusing on such characteristics as family stability, social background, and unwanted sexual acts and/or physical violence. While the report is much acclaimed for its ground-breaking efforts, Lowman (1995) identified a number of limitations of both the report and this particular theoretical approach. For example, he noted that "very little is said about the effect of unemployment structures and the marginal position of youth." He also criticized the report for negating "any kind of structural analysis of the family as a social unit" and for paying too little attention to gender relations (Lowman, 1995, p. 349). Critically, these are elements that are usually examined when using a social-psychological perspective.

In a follow-up to a series of studies on prostitution over the years, Van Brunschot and Brannigan (1997) adopted a social-psychological approach with an emphasis on social control theory. In keeping with other social-psychological studies, the authors found a significant rela-tionship between involvement in prostitution and a history of physical abuse, non-traditional family structures, expulsion from school, and repeated incidents of running away. Similarly, MacIntyre (1994, 2002, 2012) found that almost 75 per cent of male and female sex workers began sex work in adolescence. Furthermore, over three-quarters of those interviewed had been sexually and/or physically abused prior to their involvement in sex work. Consistent with prior studies, running away, school difficulties, and a low self-esteem were common features among those in the study group.

By contrast, the Special Committee on Pornography and Prostitution, working for a con-servative think-tank, presents a political economy perspective on prostitution (Lowman, 1995). Influenced by feminist approaches, this perspective stresses inequalities in job oppor-tunities, earning power, and "sexual socialization as the structural factors responsible for mak-ing prostitution appear to be a choice at all" (Lowman, 1995, p. 349). Hence, prostitution is described as being motivated by economic necessity, with women being the victims of a patri-archal power structure. Brannigan, Knafla, and Levy (1989) found that 77 per cent of women and 84 per cent of men stated that money was their primary motivation for entering the sex trade. However, by contrast, MacIntyre (2013) found that the need for money accounted for only 30 per cent of those who entered the business. Therefore, the empirical support for this perspective is mixed at best.

Some feminists view prostitution as one of the ways in which men exploit women, using them as expendable commodities to be bought and sold. Liberal feminists have argued that some women become involved because they do not have access to legitimate employment opportunities. On the other hand, Marxist and socialist feminists view prostitution as a prod-uct of women being subjugated into the trade. Radical feminists "believe that prostitution is the result of the role women are trained into in the serving of men" (MacIntyre, 2012). Yet, some scholars who espouse a feminist perspective argue that prostitution should be decrim-inalized, pointing to European countries (e.g. Germany, the Netherlands, and Belgium) where sex work has been successfully legalized and regulated (see Halley, Kotiswaran, Shamire, & Thomas, 2005; Weitzer, 2015).

**Badgley Report**
The informal name of the Report of the Committee on Sexual Offences Against Children and Youths, the first major Canadian study on the abuse of children and young people, released in 1984.

**political economy perspective**
Applied to prostitu-tion, the theory that social inequalities force some women to turn to prostitution out of economic necessity.

Another perspective that has received support is the structural-functionalist approach. Drawing on the work of sociologist Kingsley Davis in the late 1930s, functionalism views prostitution as part of our social institution. While it condemns the practice of prostitution on the one hand, functionalism also suggests that it contributes to stability in society by providing men with a sexual outlet. This view reflects a double standard and reinforces the status quo. For example, in 1982, Portugal legalized prostitution, partly in response to the number of upper-class men who saw prostitutes while their wives stayed at home (Geis, 1989). Feminist groups applauded the liberalization of laws but still opposed the exploitation of women. It can be argued that only if the needs of society are equated with the needs of men could prostitution be considered functional.

Finally, Lowman (1997) argues that Canadians need to "cut the hypocrisy and work out what we want prostitution law and social policy to accomplish." Accordingly, he identifies four goals in a decriminalization process:

- prevent sexual procurement of children and youth;
- protect prostitutes from pimp coercion and customer violence;
- encourage prostitute self-employment; and
- protect bystanders from nuisance.

In summary, prostitution, while often called the oldest profession, is also one of the most dangerous ones for workers. In spite of its long history, there are many misconceptions as to who sex workers are and why they enter this profession. While many come from abusive backgrounds and are coerced into prostitution, many also come from respectable backgrounds. Some enter into sex work for economic gain, knowing the risks and avoiding the physical abuse, emotional damage, and addiction issues that often come with sex work. In fact, a recent study in the United States suggests that over one million women rely on prostitution as their primary source of income (Bartol & Bartol, 2012).

This leads inevitably to the question of whether prostitution should be legalized. Legalization offers the opportunity to make sex work safer for prostitutes but also normalizes a practice that too often victimizes vulnerable women. Canada's new laws, enacted in 2014, take the country no closer to legalization; on the contrary, they are designed explicitly to eliminate prostitution by diminishing the demand.

## Pornography

*[I]f true equality between male and female persons is to be achieved, we cannot ignore the threat to equality resulting from exposure to audiences of certain types of violent and degrading material. Materials portraying women as a class as objects for sexual exploitation and abuse have a negative impact on "the individual's sense of self-worth and acceptance." (Regina v. Red Hot Video Ltd (1985) 18 C.C.C. (3d))*

Have you read *The Stone Angel* by Margaret Laurence or *Ulysses* by James Joyce? What about *Lady Chatterley's Lover* by D.H. Lawrence, *Fanny Hill* by John Cleland, or Daniel Defoe's *Moll Flanders*? These books have all been considered obscene at one time or another. Have you ever read erotic fiction online or seen an old copy of *Penthouse* or *Playboy*? These are legitimate media products for those over 18, although there are many pornographic websites and magazines that are illegal in Canada, such as ones containing child pornography. What do you think of the sexually explicit lyrics of Nicki Minaj's "Anaconda," Lil Wayne's "Lollipop," or a multitude of other "dirty rap" songs? Where do we draw the line, in art, between provocative and obscene, sexy and pornographic?

**pornography**
A public-order offence relating to explicit descriptions, or representations of sexual activity, prohibited by law.

Like prostitution, pornography has been around a very long time. Plato, who lived over 2,300 years ago, is sometimes credited with beginning the debate on the role of the arts in society. His simple question concerning the proper function of art continues to be relevant. Pornography was common in ancient Greece, and the term itself comes from the Greek *pornē*, meaning "prostitute," and *graphen*, meaning "to write." The term, therefore, literally means writing about the activities of prostitutes. Today, pornographic material is available in an increasingly large range of formats, thanks largely to the Internet.

*Pornography* is sometimes used interchangeably with the term *obscenity*, derived from the Latin *caenum*, meaning "filth." The difficulty in controlling pornography revolves around the legal definition of obscenity, since law enforcement officials can seize only material that is defined as obscene. The question is, how do you define obscene? Is it something that can be universally defined? In 1987, the US Supreme Court ruled that pornographic material could be judged obscene, and thus banned, if a "reasonable person" could conclude that the work lacked any social value. But as Albanese (1996) points out, the term "reasonable person" lacks objective standards. And despite two presidential commissions, the US Supreme Court is no closer to successfully defining the term. The common theme seems to be the extent to which certain sexually explicit materials are considered to violate social values and norms. Since we live in a heterogeneous society with diverse moral and ethical standards, it may not be possible to reach a consensus on the definition of this issue.

## Pornography and the Law

Crimes pertaining to pornography, or more precisely obscenity, are listed under "Offences Tending to Corrupt Morals" in sections 163 to 169 of Canada's Criminal Code. Section 163 makes it illegal to possess, produce, sell, show, or distribute "any obscene written matter, picture, model, phonograph record, or other thing whatever." (The inclusion of "phonograph records" in the list speaks to the antiquity of the law.) Section 163.1 specifically deals with child pornography. Introduced in 1993, the law prohibits the exploitation of children (i.e. anyone under the age of 18) in any manner that involves explicit sexual activity. The maximum penalty is five years imprisonment. The law also prohibits the importation, selling, or any other distribution of child pornography.

Figure 12.6 shows the trend in police-reported incidents of pornography (i.e. "corrupting morals") and child pornography generally since 2000. Since the start of the twenty-first century, there has been a dramatic increase in the availability of sexually explicit materials online; however, it is clear from the graph that while law enforcement agencies have made a priority of combatting the production and distribution of child pornography, which makes victims of society's most vulnerable, there has been a slight decline in use of the Criminal Code's "corrupting morals" clause (s. 163) to fight other forms of pornography. In fact, when this seldom-used legal provision was invoked in the case of Luka Magnotta in 2012, a criminal lawyer from Toronto described it as an "old-fashioned section of Canada's law" (Russell, 2013).

## Does Pornography Cause Violence?

A turning point in the study of pornography occurred in the late 1960s, when the United States Congress, under President Lyndon B. Johnson, struck a committee to study whether pornography was a social problem in the United States. The committee presented its findings in 1970, in the *Report of the Commission on Obscenity and Pornography*, which stated that pornography was not, in fact, a serious problem, that there was no significant link between exposure to sexually explicit materials and delinquent or antisocial behaviour, and that laws banning the sale and distribution of pornography should be slackened or lifted altogether (Bates & Donnerstein, 1990).

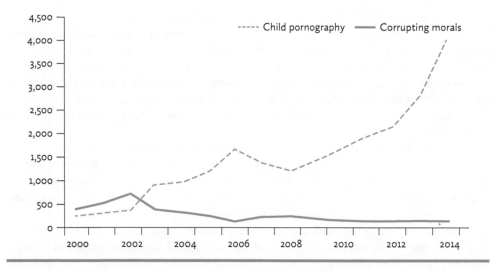

**Figure 12.6   Pornography and Child Pornography Incidents in Canada, 2000–2014**

*Source:* Statistics Canada CANSIM Table 252-0051.

The report was roundly rejected by Congress, the Senate, and newly elected president Richard Nixon, who declared: "So long as I am in the White House, there will be no relaxation of the national effort to control and eliminate smut from our national life" (quoted in Brenner, 2010).

Many thought the issue would quickly die, but hundreds of studies were conducted on this question in the following years, spurred partly by the women's movement and various advocacy groups. A subsequent US Presidential Commission, struck in the early 1980s, concluded that while erotic material may not cause sexual aggression, viewing such material could lead to a greater acceptance of sexual aggression through a "habituation to pornography" (Adler, Mueller, & Laufer, 1991).

---

**BOX 12.12        WHAT DO YOU THINK?**

### The Challenge of Trying to Legislate Morality

Although Canadian law criminalizes the possession, creation, and distribution of child pornography, in 2001 the Supreme Court defended the possession of self-produced materials created for personal use in their ruling in the case of *R. v. Sharpe*.

The case caused considerable controversy, both prior to and subsequent to the high court's final ruling. John Robin Sharpe, the accused, had in his possession self-created writings and drawings of a sexual nature involving children under 14 (the legal age of consent). The court was asked to decide whether or not this constituted possession of child pornography under section 163 of the Criminal Code. The Court held that self-produced visual or written material created for personal use (such as writings, journals, and drawings) and other self-created visual material (such as photos and videos) that do not depict illegal sexual activity and are exclusively for personal use are permissible under the law.

What do you think of the court's ruling?

What do you think, more generally, about punishing consumers, as opposed to producers, of pornography. Consider the comments of former University of Calgary professor and adviser to Stephen Harper Tom Flanagan, who touched off controversy in 2013 when he said, "I certainly have no sympathy for child molesters, but I do have some grave doubts about putting people in jail because of their taste in pictures" (Green, 2013).

Over the years, criminologists have thus shifted the focus from moral issues to the question of whether pornographic material contributes in any way to violence and victimization of women and children (and possibly even of men). There are several ways in which this may be the case. The most obvious perhaps, as Chelsea Draeger (1997) and many others have stated, is that there is ample evidence that many individuals are forced to participate in pornography against their will, and in these cases are being seriously harmed while doing so. However, pornography may contribute to violence and victimization in other, more complex ways as well.

Some researchers argue that exposure to pornography can facilitate expressions of anger and violence (Conklin, 2013). Radical feminists, for example, argue that by objectifying women and by linking coercion and violence with sexual stimulation, pornography leads to an acceptance of violence against women (Berger, Searles, & Cottle, 1991). Despite these suggestions, many studies have shown that there is an inverse relationship between the availability of pornography and the rate of reported rape (Ferguson & Hartley, 2009); in other words, as the availability of pornography has increased, rates of rape and sexual assault have dropped in many countries. In an early article on the topic, Scott and Schwalm (1988) pointed out that after Denmark repealed all bans of sexually oriented material in the late 1960s, sex crimes actually declined in the country. Similarly, Japan has a flourishing pornography trade, and yet its rate of sexual assault is less than one-quarter the rate in Germany or Great Britain and one-fourteenth the rate in the United States (Livingston, 1992). In a 2009 review of recent studies and crime data, Ferguson and Hartley (2009) go so far as declaring that "it is time to discard the hypothesis that pornography contributes to increased sexual assault behaviour." Some research suggests that it may not be the depiction of sexual acts in general but depiction of violent sexual acts specifically that triggers violent behaviour. What is now generally agreed upon is that for those individuals who are already predisposed to sexually offend, exposure to pornography has a positive, or motivating, effect on their behaviour (Seto, Maric, & Barbaree, 2001). In the words of Malamuth, Addison, and Koss, "if a person has relatively aggressive sexual inclinations resulting from various personal and/or cultural factors, some pornography exposure may activate and reinforce associated coercive tendencies and behaviors" (2000, p. 81).

The findings described above lend credence to the idea that sex crimes are related to certain cultural climates. If this is accurate, criminologists need to explore what the possible critical cultural factors are that differentiate countries with high sexual offence rates from countries with low sexual offending rates. Knowing such factors may enable countries to better regulate pornography. We have seen dramatic changes in our society's level of tolerance in terms of acceptable norms and values as well as lifestyle choices—such as gay marriage and the presence of graphic depiction of sex and violence in movies, music videos, and most notably on the Internet. The notion of pornography is a relative concept that poses a major challenge to criminologists interested in studying any associated criminogenic relationship. The fact that pornography not only involves questions of morality but also is closely tied to the notion of constitutional right to freedom of speech and the press further complicates matters.

## Substance Abuse

*She threw into the wine which they were drinking a drug which takes away grief and passion and brings forgetfulness of all ills.* (Homer, *The Odyssey*)

In Chapter 6, we looked at the relationship between the biochemical effects of alcohol and criminal behaviour. We saw that an inordinate number of violent crimes (as high as 65 per cent, according to Single, Robson, Relm, & Xie, 1996) are committed while individuals are under the influence of alcohol and/or drugs. Between 1997 and 2007, the rate of official drug-related offences increased from around 220 to 305 per 100,000: this represented the highest rate in over 30 years (Dauvergne, 2009). And between 2004 and 2014, the total number of drug-related offences increased by 6 per cent, although the rate actually declined during that period (see Table 12.2).

Abuse of alcohol and drugs (both legal and illegal) can affect the sense of public order as a result of the altered behaviour expressed by people under their influence. According to the media, there has been a drug epidemic in North America since at least since the 1960s. A Health Officer's Council of BC report indicated that "for every $5 spent on drug rehabilitation by the Canadian government, $95 is spent on incarceration of drug users" (HOC, 2005) and we spend more than $4 on enforcement for every $1 spent on the health response in dealing with illegal drugs (Haden, 2008). The social, financial, and personal costs of substance abuse remain staggering even though as early as 1987, the Government of Canada launched a five-year, $210-million strategy, the National Drug Strategy, to combat substance abuse.

**Table 12.2  Total Drug Violations in Canada, Actual Incidents and Rate, 2004–2014**

| Year | Actual Incidents | Rate per 100,000 |
| --- | --- | --- |
| 2004 | 97,630 | 306 |
| 2006 | 96,175 | 295 |
| 2008 | 102,271 | 308 |
| 2010 | 109,222 | 321 |
| 2012 | 110,093 | 317 |
| 2014 | 103,757 | 292 |

Source: Statistics Canada CANSIM Table 252-0051.

## History of Substance Use and Abuse

There is virtually no society in which people cannot be found using mind- and mood-altering substances (Schlaadt, 1992). We can find numerous examples of how alcohol has been used throughout the ages in everything from religious rites and social celebrations to simply complementing a meal.

While in ancient times alcohol was not the only *psychoactive substance*—that is, a substance affecting mood or behaviour—in use, it was the most prevalent. Both the Greeks and the Romans had gods of wine (Dionysus and Bacchus, respectively). As the Roman Empire spread throughout Europe, the Romans brought their love of wine and copious consumption with them. The French, Spanish, Germans, and British were quick to embrace the practice and began to cultivate their own vines for wine production. Schlaadt (1992, p. 3) suggests that the eventual downfall of the Roman Empire was due in part to alcoholism (along with greed, corruption, and self-indulgence). After the birth of Christianity, even the Catholic Church used wine in such rituals as the sacrament of Communion. To this day, certain monasteries throughout Europe are known for the alcoholic beverages they produce. Not surprisingly, Europeans brought their drinking habits with them to the Americas. By the nineteenth century, alcohol was both plentiful and frequently used and abused throughout the Western world. North American temperance unions rose up during the nineteenth century, bringing prohibition to select jurisdictions. The United States adopted a nationwide policy of prohibition during the 1920s, which was repealed in 1933, all but ending the temperance movement.

In eastern Europe, there is also a long history of drinking spirits such as vodka. For example, although the consumption rate has steadily declined since 2002, the average Russian still consumes about 13.5 litres of vodka per year (Adomanis, 2013). In Japan, beer has become very popular, especially among men, since being introduced to the country around a hundred years ago, and it is estimated that almost 10 million people in Japan have a potential dependency problem, based on the results of a 2013 health ministry survey (Ito, 2014). As for other parts of the world, there is often limited information available, for various reasons. For example, in Muslim countries, where alcohol is often forbidden, it is difficult to obtain reliable data on the extent of alcohol consumption.

The use of other mind-altering drugs has an equally long history. Egyptian records show that as early as 1500 BCE opium was being used for medicinal purposes. The inhabitants of ancient Peru were known to chew coca leaves, and Native North Americans discovered the use of mescaline as a mood-altering substance. It appears that most cultures have chosen some drug that can be readily found in their area as a socially accepted way for altering the state of consciousness.

It was not until the late 1800s and early 1900s that drug regulation became an issue in North America. Fishbein and Pease (1996) suggest there were two important factors that contributed to this awareness and the subsequent move to regulate drugs. The first was an alarming increase in the rates of addiction. The second was "the association of drug use with minority groups" (1996, p. 11) in increasingly multicultural societies, where Chinatown "opium dens" became a target of moral entrepreneurs warning of the "Yellow Peril" posed by East Asian immigrants.

## Drugs and the Law

Generally, we think of drug abuse as overuse or physical and/or psychological dependency. But, as Blackwell (1988) notes, this definition is ambiguous. For example, what quantity of drinks, joints, or pills is harmful, and is it the same for all people? At what point is a person's drug or alcohol use considered a pattern of dependent behaviour?

The Controlled Drugs and Substances Act replaced Canada's Narcotic Control Act in 1996. The new law covers everything from "possession of substance" and punishment to "forfeiture of proceeds of crime." Schedules I through VIII, which are located at the end of the text of the

A vending machine for medicinal marijuana is pictured at the BC Pain Society in Vancouver, BC. Once it is eventually legalized, where should marijuana be sold—convenience stores? Grocery stores? Liquor stores? All of the above?

Canadian Press/Johnathan Hayward

act, provide a list of all the controlled substances. With respect to this list, what is interesting to note is section 60, pertaining to "amendments to schedules," which reads:

> The Governor in Council may, by order, amend any of Schedules I to VIII by adding to them or deleting from them any item or portion of an item, where the Governor in Council deems the amendments to be necessary in the public interest.

The wording of the section reflects recognition of how new drugs can be manufactured and used in harmful ways. Consider fentanyl, an opioid thought to be hundreds of times more powerful than heroin, which has been linked to an alarming rise in Canadian overdose deaths since 2010 (Sagan, 2015). What is less clear is what constitutes "necessary in the public interest." For example, cannabis was a banned substance that was legalized for medicinal purposes. However, in 2013, the federal government introduced new legislation that prevented people from growing their own marijuana for medical purposes, forcing those users to obtain it from official government-regulated vendors. This led to a sharp increase in the price of medicinal marijuana (Bradshaw, 2013). Is this "in the public interest"?

## Alcohol the Drug

Once it enters the body, alcohol is absorbed quickly and completely. In fact, there are few other drugs that can be as quickly absorbed into the bloodstream. However, absorption and rate of impact are moderated by the concentration of alcohol in the drink, which can range from 5 per cent in regular beer to 40 and 50 per cent in distilled liquor, for example.

The psychological and psychoactive effects of alcohol are well known. For example, one of the serious consequences of continuous drinking is that over time, the body develops a tolerance for alcohol, meaning that more is required to achieve the same effect. As a result, there is an increased tendency to develop a dependency on alcohol to sustain the false sense of well-being. Then, because of the biochemical changes that occur with sustained heavy drinking, drinkers develop withdrawal symptoms when they try to go without. This is where addiction begins to take hold, and the symptoms escalate. Another catastrophic consequence of alcohol addiction is the transference of biochemical changes from mothers to their newborns: babies born to mothers who are chronic drinkers are highly susceptible to fetal alcohol spectrum disorder (May & Gossage, 2011).

Despite its harmful effects, alcohol is not regulated like other drugs. In Canada, it can be legally consumed, in any quantity, by anyone over the age of 18 (17 in some provinces), and while the retail sale of liquor and spirits is limited to provincially owned outlets in most jurisdictions, some provinces allow beer and wine to be sold in privately owned grocery and convenience stores, and some liquor stores in BC and all liquor stores in Alberta are privately owned. Alcohol is illegal when sold and served to underage consumers and when driving is involved. In addition, data on incarcerated Canadians reveal that a significant number of inmates had substance abuse problems and/or were under the influence of alcohol or drugs when committing their offences (Brennan & Dauvergne, 2011), which suggests a strong link between alcohol use and criminal activity, even if alcohol consumption is not in itself illegal.

It is worth considering this information in relation to corporate responsibility and how alcohol is marketed. Many critics of the alcohol industry have commented on how producers are luring young drinkers with sweet, fruit-flavoured drinks that have bright, colourful labels and that resemble the non-alcoholic drinks they are used to drinking. Though some companies add warning labels related to drinking and driving, they take minimal responsibility for promoting the use of their product. Should these companies share responsibility

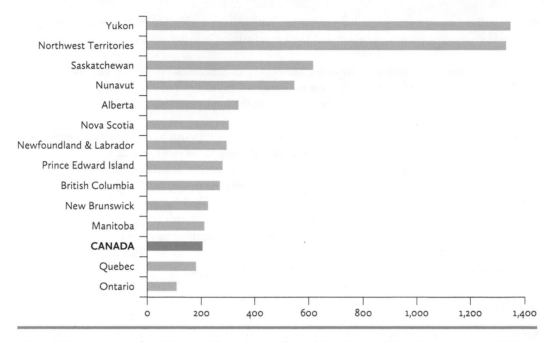

**Figure 12.7    Impaired Driving Incidents, Canada and Provinces, 2014 (Rate per 100,000)**

*Source:* Statistics Canada CANSIM Table 252-0051.

for crimes committed by people under the influence of their products? It also appears that public campaigns initiated by governments (such as Alberta's 2015 "Thanks Alcohol!" campaign) and non-governmental activist groups like MADD (Mothers Against Drunk Driving) have not always served as effective deterrents as most provinces and territories still have rates of impaired driving above the national average (see Figure 12.7).

## Illicit Drugs

There are three broad classes of psychoactive drugs that affect the central nervous system: *stimulants*, *depressants*, and *hallucinogens*. While these categories describe the general effects created by the three classes of drugs, they are not always mutually exclusive. For example, marijuana is known as a *crossover drug*, as it initially acts as a stimulant and then a depressant as the effects wear off. Depending on the potency and amount smoked, it can also create sensory distortions similar to those created by hallucinogens.

Stimulants tend to elevate the user's sense of well-being. Sometimes referred to as "uppers," these drugs keep the user alert and able to resist fatigue. The most common examples are nicotine and caffeine. Other examples include cocaine, crack, and the synthesized drugs called *amphetamines* (e.g. crystal meth and MDMA, more commonly known as ecstasy). Stimulants, like other drugs, vary in potency and addictive properties. According to a study cited by Fishbein and Pease (1996, p. 85), nicotine is the most addictive stimulant drug (nearly 100 per cent of first-time users get addicted), with crack cocaine being a close second. Caffeine is the least addictive of the stimulants (approximately 85 per cent of first-time users become addicted). Methamphetamine, commonly known as *crystal meth* or *speed*, is also highly addictive and causes severe and acute adverse health effects.

Depressants, or "downers," as the term suggests, slow down the central nervous system. They can induce sleep, alleviate pain, relax muscles, reduce anxiety, and create a sense of euphoria. The most common depressant is alcohol. The opiate drugs (heroin, morphine) and barbiturates, antihistamines, PCP (phencyclidine), and a variety of aerosol sprays can act as depressants. Alcohol is the most addictive of the depressants (approximately 87 per cent for first-time users), followed closely by heroin.

Hallucinogens create an altered state of awareness—a distortion of reality. Users of hallucinogens report "out-of-body" experiences such as hearing sounds, seeing images and colours, and experiencing a distortion of time and place. The most popular hallucinogen among Canadians is marijuana, although in the 1960s peyote (a type of cactus) was very popular. Peyote contains mescaline, which can also be made synthetically. Other synthetic hallucinogens include LSD (lysergic acid diethylamide, commonly called *acid*) and PCP (phencyclidine). LSD is derived from a natural fungus known as ergot, which grows on such grains as rye. PCP, also known as *angel dust*, *hog*, or *green*, is easily made, comparatively inexpensive, and the most addictive of the hallucinogens. Stories of hallucinogens causing violent and uncontrollable behaviour seem to have made them less desirable in recent years. However, since the 2000s, there has been a dramatic increase in the use of the powerful synthetic opiate fentanyl. According to an Alberta report, between January and September of 2015, there were 213 fentanyl-related deaths in the province; in 2011, Alberta saw just 6 fentanyl-related deaths (Rieger, 2015).

Table 12.3 presents a breakdown of drugs used by Canadians and the associated costs in dollars and lives. Although the data are 25 years old, the table provides a fascinating snapshot of Canadians' drug use at a time when smoking rates were higher than they are today. What stands out is that Canadians in the late 1980s and early 1990s were more likely to use/abuse legal drugs, which posed much higher health risks. Figure 12.8, meanwhile, shows the changing rate of incidents involving the trafficking, production, and distribution of marijuana, cocaine,

This window display, belonging to a "smart shop" in Amsterdam, advertises "truffles" available for purchase. These truffles are unprocessed psychoactive mushrooms containing psilocybin, and they are legal only through a legislative loophole that allows these "magic truffles" to be sold openly.

Anton Gvozdikov/Shutterstock.com

| Table 12.3 | Canada's Drug Users, Costs, and Attributable Deaths: A Snapshot from 1991 | | | |
|---|---|---|---|---|
| Drug | Annual Number of Users (x 1,000) | Weekly Cost for the Average User ($) | Possibility of Overdose Death? | Annual Number of Related Deaths |
| alcohol* | 16,000 | 10–100 | YES | 3,000–15,000 |
| amphetamines | <100 | 100–500 | YES | <100 |
| cocaine | 300–500 | 10–5,000 | YES | <100 |
| heroin | <100 | 50–5,000 | YES | <100 |
| LSD | <100 | <20 | NO | <10 |
| marijuana | 1,500–2,500 | 10–100 | NO | <10 |
| tobacco* | 6,000–8,000 | 30–100 | NO | 35,000 |
| tranquilizers* | 1,500–2,500 | 0–20 | NO | <10 |

* Denotes drugs that are legal.
*Source*: Used with permission from Boyd, 1991.

and other controlled drugs and substances, including crystal meth, ecstasy, and heroin. The figure shows that while police-reported marijuana offences have dropped significantly since 2010—perhaps reflecting the growing public and police tolerance of marijuana and to the growing use of marijuana for medical purposes—the rate of reported offences for "other" drugs has remained stable, if not increased. This could be explained in part by the growing popularity of such drugs as crystal meth, ecstasy, OxyContin, and fentanyl.

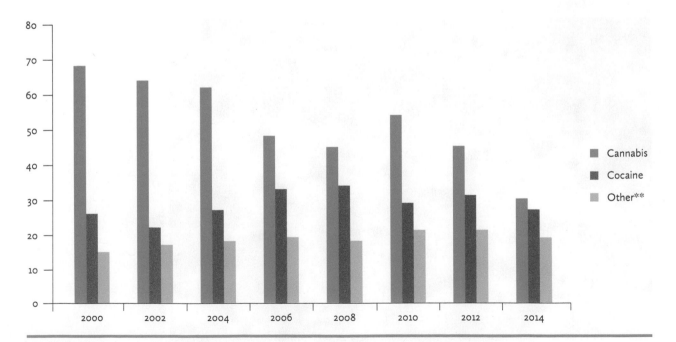

Figure 12.8     Police-Reported Drug Offences,* by Type of Drug, Canada 2000–2014 (Rate per 100,000)

* Includes trafficking, production, and distribution.

** Includes heroin, methamphetamines (crystal meth), methylenedioxyamphetamine (ecstasy), and other substances prohibited under the Controlled Drugs and Substances Act.

*Source:* Statistics Canada CANSIM Table 252-0051.

## Characteristics and Trends

A 2005 Canadian Addiction Survey reported that just over 79 per cent of Canadians aged 15 and older consumed alcohol, and that over 22 per cent of those who drank exceeded the standard for low-risk drinking, defined as (a) fewer than 3 drinks per day, and (b) fewer than 15 drinks per week for men or 10 drinks per week for women (Adlaf, Begin, & Sawka, 2005, p. 20). In addition, 17 per cent of Canadian drinkers engaged in hazardous drinking, and according to a 2007 study, 2.4 per cent of those 69 years of age or younger died of alcohol-related problems (George, 2007). Yet at some level, Canadians are aware of the risks associated with alcohol consumption. In a study comparing attitudes in the United States and Canada, Giesbrecht and Greenfield (1999) observed that Canadians generally supported increases in prevention programs, while 75.5 per cent supported severe intervention programs. Furthermore, 66.7 per cent were opposed to selling alcohol in convenience stores, and 69.5 per cent were in favour of placing warning labels on bottles containing alcoholic beverages.

With the exception of those countries where religion forbids its consumption, alcohol is consumed in great quantities throughout the world. Knowledge about the harmful effects of alcohol has had no significant impact on consumption. As a vice, should we view alcohol as a disease rather than a crime? How should criminologists deal with the latest scientific evidence that suggests that people who use modest amounts of alcohol are less likely to experience health problems such as arteriosclerosis, heart attacks, and strokes?

While there is considerable literature and research on alcohol and tobacco abuse, there is, comparatively speaking, a dearth of information on the effects of illicit drug abuse. According to a 2013 Health Canada study, the rate of use of psychoactive pharmaceuticals decreased modestly among Canadians aged 15 and older, from 26 per cent in 2010 to 23 per cent in 2011 ("Drug and alcohol use statistics," 2013). At one time, Canada was spending more than four dollars on law enforcement for every one dollar spent on the health response in addressing the challenges of illegal drugs (CRS Report, 2008). However, Rehm and colleagues (2006) reported that every dollar spent on treatment will achieve the same reduction in the flow of cocaine as $7.30 spent on enforcement. The authors demonstrate that spending money on treatment is virtually always a more efficient way of combatting drug trafficking than spending money on enforcement. This clearly speaks to the benefit of being proactive (i.e. through crime prevention) instead of reactive (through formal criminal justice).

According to the RCMP, illicit drug use cost Canadian society an estimated $8.2 billion in 2010 (Drug Enforcement Branch, 2011), compared to $1.37 billion just 18 years earlier in 1992 (Single et al., 1996). As with most crime trends and patterns, the cost of abuse varies considerably across the country, but the fact remains that substance abuse causes serious social consequences in terms of health, family disorders, problems in the workplace, and crimes instigated under the influence of drugs.

Research evidence shows a strong link between controlled substance abuse and criminal behaviour. Several studies have found that offenders with a substance abuse problem commit a high percentage of violent crimes (see e.g. Gropper, 1985; Zawitz, 1992) and that drug addicts commit more crimes while under the influence than when sober (Nurco, Cisin, & Ball, 1985). Speckart and Anglin (1986) observed that substance abuse was significantly related to high levels of property crime.

In many respects, the public seems hypocritical in its condemnation of the illicit drug problem in Canadian society, since more Canadians die every year from legal drugs than from illicit drugs (see Box 12.13). As well, the focus shifts from decade to decade. In the 1960s, the evils of marijuana were the main concern; in the 1970s, the focus shifted to hallucinogens such as LSD and PCP; and in the 1980s, cocaine and its synthetic form crack became the main targets of public condemnation. All the while, considerably less public attention was directed at the number one killer drugs: alcohol and tobacco.

It is true that the government has set limits on how alcohol and tobacco can be advertised, but out of fear of losing millions of dollars in revenue from the high taxes levied on these products, and because of Canadians' acceptance of alcohol and a growing tolerance of soft drugs like marijuana, the government is not prepared (or able) to ban them. Boyd (1991), calling Canada "a country of drug takers," is particularly critical of the prevalent attitude that legal drugs are less harmful than illegal drugs.

As for tobacco, it is possible we overlook cigarettes in the conversation on drugs because, apart from the physiological addiction to nicotine, there is no substantial psychomotor or cognitive impairment involved in smoking. In other words, smoking does not substantially alter one's ability to drive, talk, or perform delicate tasks. But smoking is a silent killer and a relatively inexpensive one. Compare the cost of a package of 25 cigarettes (roughly $15) to that of

## BOX 12.13     REALITY CHECK

### The Human and Social Costs of Alcohol and Tobacco Use

In 2002, the abuse of illicit drugs cost between 1,455 and 1,695 Canadian lives, according to a 2006 study by the Canadian Centre on Substance Abuse (Rehm, Baliunas, Brochu, et al., 2006, Table 1), which arrived at these figures using two separate methodologies. These numbers, however, do not even come close the number of deaths attributed to Canada's most deadly drugs: alcohol and tobacco. According to the same study by the CCSA, the number of deaths attributed to alcohol in 2002 was between 8,103 and 9,100, while the number of deaths related to tobacco was roughly 37,200 (Rehm et al., 2006, Table 1).

Not only does tobacco remain the leading preventable cause of death in Canada, it carries a social cost of $17 billion, according to the CCSA (Rehm et al., 2006, Table 2). The CCSA's guidelines, used internationally, factor in such direct costs as hospital care and law enforcement, as well as indirect costs such as productivity losses due to tobacco-related hospitalization or long-term disability. By comparison, alcohol abuse carries a cost of roughly $14.5 billion, while the social cost of illegal drugs is roughly $8 billion (see Table 12.4).

According to Health Canada's 2012 Tobacco Use Monitoring Survey there has been a steady decline in the overall smoking rate among Canadians over the age of 15. Nevertheless, in 2012, an estimated 4.4 million Canadians (16 per cent of the population aged 15 and over) still smoked. Smoking is linked to 2.2 million acute hospital days per year (Reid, Hammond, Burkhalter, & Ahmed, 2012).

Should Canada do more to control the use of tobacco and alcohol, given these drugs' high social costs?

### Table 12.4    The Social Costs of Drugs in Canada, 2002, as Calculated by the CCSA

| | (in millions of dollars) | | | |
| --- | --- | --- | --- | --- |
| | Tobacco | Alcohol | Illegal Drugs | Total |
| Direct health care costs | $4,360.2 | $3,306.2 | $1,134.6 | $8,800.9 |
| Direct law enforcement costs | — | 3,072.2 | 2,335.5 | 5,407.8 |
| Direct prevention & research costs | 78.1 | 53.0 | 16.5 | 147.6 |
| Other direct costs | 87.0 | 996.1 | 79.1 | 1,162.2 |
| Indirect costs: productivity losses | 12,470.9 | 7,126.4 | 4,678.6 | 24,275.9 |
| Total | $16,996.2 | $14,554.0 | $8,244.3 | $39,794.4 |
| Total per capita cost | $541 | $463 | $262 | $1,267 |

Source: Rehm et al., 2006, Table 2. Reproduced with permission from the Canadian Centre on Substance Abuse.

a gram of cocaine ($80–$100), a single marijuana cigarette ($5), or a bottle of spirits ($20 and up). Withdrawal from smoking has been reported to be more difficult than withdrawal from heroin, and the relapse rate is nearly 70 per cent (Canadian Cancer Society, 2013).

## Explaining Addiction

Fishbein and Pease (1996, p. 82) point out that while there are many theoretical explanations for drug use and addiction, "many theories do not distinguish between those factors that contribute to the reasons to first use a drug, reasons to maintain drug use, and reasons for relapse." After reviewing biological, psychological, and a variety of sociological theories of addiction, they note that none of the perspectives is able to address all the factors, suggesting that an interdisciplinary approach is necessary. They embrace the diathesis–stress model, which views behaviour—in this case, compulsive behaviour leading to addiction—as a product of individual biological/genetic factors and personality of the individual, and factors at play in the real and perceived social environment. *Diathesis*, from a Greek word for "disposition," refers to the individual's built-in predisposition to engage in a certain behaviour, which may be touched off by external stressors, leading to the behaviour.

> **diathesis–stress model**
> An approach to studying addiction that views compulsive behaviour as a product of the interplay between an individual's predisposition to the behaviour and stress from life experiences.

Some of the drugs that are considered illicit today were once legal and may even have been used for medical purposes. A conflict theorist might interpret the changing legal status of a particular substance in terms of how that substance presents a threat to the social stability of a group with the authority to legalize or ban it. In other words, the powerful within society might sanction a drug like marijuana only if they could monopolize the making and selling of the drug. From this point of view, the best way to combat an "evil" drug is through thought reform and education.

Drugs present a moral dilemma for society. Whether one subscribes to the psychological position of Erich Fromm—that we learn to desire those things that go along with our economic and social system—or the sociological position put forth by the sociologist Max Weber—that society rewards those who are industrious—it is cultural values that dictate what "pleasure-seeking" outlets are acceptable or unacceptable. If our desire to use drugs can be traced back to earliest recorded history, perhaps the current drug controversies are a reflection of a cultural lag between existing laws and people's changing feelings and values—in other words, between crime and morality.

## Summary

- Although public-order offences represent the "most widespread organization of lawlessness" (Sutherland & Cressey, 1955, p. 230), attempts to legislate issues of morality in a heterogeneous society are controversial and complex. Most people engage in various vices, and many organizations—both criminal and non-criminal—exist to feed society's demands.
- Gambling is an ancient pastime that continues to plague certain individuals and sectors of societies. Gambling generates revenue for governments and various groups but at the same time is a bane for those who become addicted to it. Efforts to explain and control gambling have met with minimal success.
- Both prostitution and pornography have long histories. Once regarded with high esteem, prostitution today is generally considered a social ill. There are those, however—including many front-line sex workers whom some people would consider victims—who would like prostitution brought out of the shadows to make it safer for those involved. Although the subject has endured the full criminological spectrum of theoretical explanations, no theory

has been able to provide a complete understanding of why people enter into prostitution. As the legal landscape in Canada changes, the status of prostitution in society remains murky.

- Substance abuse parallels the trends and patterns of the other vices covered in this chapter. Whether legal or not, all drugs have potential addictive and destructive consequences, and their differentiation in legal status is a social construction.

- Criminologists must bridge the gap between laws and social science when considering public-order offences. They must focus on the acts as they relate to human behaviour from an integrated and interdisciplinary perspective. Only by recognizing the complexity of behaviour in this manner will criminologists begin to understand what such behaviours mean and how to more appropriately respond to them. Even so, it does not necessarily follow that society will be able to control all public-order crimes, nor is it clear that we should even endeavour to do so.

## Discussion Questions

1. Should criminologists advocate for the legislation of issues of morality? If so, what issues need to be taken into consideration when making such a decision? To what extent might trying to control public-order offences contribute to crime rates and the number of people involved in the criminal justice system? To what extent might legislating morality promote the expansion of activities of organized crime groups?

2. To what extent does involvement in any public-order offence imply voluntary participation?

3. Where does one draw the line in defining obscenity? How do these laws affect the right to freedom of speech and expression?

4. Are there moral and/or ethical issues around using marijuana for medical purposes? Is it, in your view, preferable to or worse than alternative methods of relieving chronic pain?

5. Why have conventional theories been relatively ineffective in explaining public-order offences and in helping to formulate effective social policy? How could an interdisciplinary and integrated approach be applied to address public-order crimes?

## Key Concepts

clearance rate                        pornography
consensus perspective                 procuring
conflict perspective                  prostitution
Badgley Report                        public-order crimes
diathesis-stress model                soliciting
Fraser Report                         vagrancy
political economy perspective

## Weblinks

**Canadian Centre on Substance Abuse**
The CCSA aims to address issues of substance abuse that affect the health and safety of Canadians. Its website provides statistics through its reports as well as resources for professionals involved in addiction treatment.
www.ccsa.ca

**Access Canada Justice Network**
Operated by the Centre for Public Legal Education Alberta, the ACJNET website offers information on a wide variety of public-order issues including prostitution, gambling, and substance abuse.
www.acjnet.org

**Marijuana Party**
The official site of the Marijuana Party of Canada contains some interesting information on its political platform, as well as links to related resources. Watch this page as the current federal government moves forward on its promise to legalize marijuana in Canada.
www.marijuanaparty.ca

**Canadian Alliance for Sex Work Law**
Although they do not have a webpage per se, the alliance has Facebook account, which is active and which includes information and current initiatives undertaken by its alliance members.
www.facebook.com/sexworklawreform/

**Take 5: Gambling Support Network**
Designed specifically for those coping with problem gambling—either their own or that of a loved one—the Nova Scotia government's Problem Gambling Services website offers resources for those seeking help and inspirational stories of people who have overcome gambling addiction.
https://gamblingsupportnetwork.ca

# Chapter 13

## Emerging Crime Trends: Transnational Crime, Terrorism, Human Trafficking, and Cybercrime

CP PHOTO/ Ian Barrett

Our lives are not our own. From womb to tomb we are bound to others, past and present,
and by each crime and every kindness we birth our future.

DAVID MITCHELL, *CLOUD ATLAS*

Banking security is everyone's responsibility—the banks' and customers' alike—and we hope that some
of the information we have provided, in some small measure, helps towards saving other people
from experiencing such a cruel, harrowing, and near life-wrecking ordeal.

ANONYMOUS VICTIM OF "VISHING" FRAUD, CITED IN DREW (2014)

## Learning Outcomes

After reading this chapter, you should be able to

• Describe some of the key aspects of new and emerging crime trends;
• Recognize the complexity of the various types of human trafficking and explain why it is both a human rights and a transnational concern;
• Describe different forms of terrorism and cite cases that show how terrorism is changing;
• Explain the various forms of cybercrime and discuss why it is such a concern to criminologists today;
• Appreciate the need for criminology to explore the contemporary and emerging crimes from an interdisciplinary perspective; and
• Discuss the importance of applying a comparative perspective to the study of emerging crime trends.

## Introduction: How Globalization Contributes to Crime

In 2013, the case of Mumtaz Ladha shone a light on a crime few people believed could happen in Canada: human trafficking. A 21-year-old Tanzanian woman had accused Ladha of having lured her from her home in sub-Saharan Africa with the promise of work in a hair salon. Instead, according to testimony given during a sensational 22-day trial, she was enslaved in the wealthy businesswoman's $5 million West Vancouver home, where she was forced to work 18-hour days performing unpaid domestic chores while living on little more than table scraps (Hutchinson, 2013).

The case drew international media attention, making headlines around the world. People wondered how modern-day slavery could be practised in a country like Canada. And then, on 22 November 2013, a BC Supreme Court justice found the defendant, Ms Ladha, not guilty on all of the charges against her, including human trafficking, employing a foreign national without authorization, misrepresenting facts to the High Commission of Canada, and misrepresenting facts to Citizenship and Immigration Canada (Hutchinson, 2013). In fact, in an unwavering decision, the judge characterized Ms Ladha's accuser as an unreliable witness with a motive to lie—namely, the opportunity to remain in Canada as a victim of human trafficking.

Before you conclude that human trafficking is not a crime that occurs in Canada, you should know that in 2014, there were 139 police-reported cases of the crime in Canada, up from just 78 cases in 2013, according to Statistics Canada (CANSIM Table 252-0051). And as we will see later in this chapter, human trafficking is a growing problem not only in Canada but internationally.

Human trafficking is one of a number of crimes we characterize as *emerging crimes*. While some of what we call emerging crimes are indeed relatively new—cybercrime, for example—others are forms of criminal activity with long histories that are simply receiving new or greater attention from criminologists today. These include non-conventional crimes like organized crime, white-collar crime, political crime, and copyright infringement, which have not always received a fair share of criminologists' attention compared with conventional crimes like homicide, robbery, and assault. Until recently, some of these non-conventional crimes were not addressed by the criminal codes of most countries. Therefore, aside from the relative "newness" of these crimes, they pose interesting and unique challenges for criminology and criminal justice systems.

The following quotation might not reflect the views of most criminologists, but it does capture the growing anxiety many law enforcement officials are feeling about the dangers posed by emerging forms of crime:

**cybercrime**
Illegal activity that involves the use of computer technology or the Internet as the target or the instrument of the crime.

**non-conventional crimes**
Illegal acts that most people tend not to associate with crime and that are often not pursued by the criminal justice system, such as organized crime, political crime, and computer crime.

While organized crime is not a new phenomenon today, some governments find their authority besieged at home and their foreign policy interests imperiled abroad. Drug trafficking, links between drug traffickers and terrorists, smuggling of illegal aliens, massive financial and bank fraud, arms smuggling, potential involvement in the theft and sale of nuclear material, political intimidation, and corruption all constitute a poisonous brew—a mixture potentially as deadly as what we faced during the cold war. (former CIA director R. James Woolsey, qtd in Hesterman, 2004, p. 1)

Arguably, crime in general could be described as a "poisonous brew" for the integrity and safety of any society. What is interesting is how these emerging crimes are by-products of two trends that Western society has openly encouraged: globalization and technological change. Organized crime and trafficking are largely transnational crimes: crimes that have the potential to cross international borders. They are the dark side of globalizing processes that make it easier to move goods from one part of the world to another. Likewise, computer crime is the dark side of technological advances that allow us to conduct banking transactions and commercial purchases over the Internet. The vast networks that support emerging crime—geographic networks on the one hand and virtual networks on the other—have made these crimes easier to commit and far more difficult to detect, much less manage or control.

It is against this backdrop that we examine several major types of emerging crimes affecting Canadians, all of them falling under the broad umbrella of *transnational crime*, which is where our discussion begins.

**transnational crime**

Criminal activity that violates the laws of more than one country, such as drug trafficking, terrorism, and human trafficking.

## Introduction to Transnational Crime

In 2013, the Canadian Security and Intelligence Service (CSIS) declared that "technological advances over the past 20 years have made national borders irrelevant to telecommunications

---

| BOX 13.1 | **A CLOSER LOOK**<br>Globalizing Criminal Gangs |
|---|---|

While globalization has promoted the forging of new transnational trading partnerships, giving a boost to many of the world's struggling economies, it has also provided numerous opportunities for emerging crimes that depend on the movement of goods. Consider, for example, how globalization has changed the profile of the criminal gang.

The first generation of criminal gangs were involved in what we call street-level crime, consisting of petty crimes carried out within certain targeted neighborhoods. The second generation of gangs developed regional networks to carry out more sophisticated operations. Drug cartels, triads, the Yakuza,[1] the Mafia (i.e. the American Camorra and the Ndrangheta, whose origins are in Italy), and the Russian Mafiya are organizations that came to dominate criminal markets in the broader regions in which they first formed. The third generation of gangs, operating today, are fully transnational criminal organizations. These organizations tend to monopolize international black markets for illegal drugs and weapons. Many are also involved in human smuggling and trafficking. As with such groups as the organization calling itself Islamic State (ISIL), third-generation criminal gangs may employ paramilitary forces and exercise political control within a particular territory. Their use of social media is an important part of the way they establish and maintain their criminal networks.

Successful businesses—from fast-food restaurant chains to clothing manufacturers—grow by continuously adapting to changing economic environments. In what ways is this also true of successful criminal organizations?

[1] Originating in Japan, the Yakuza are made up of several crime groups, or *Yamaguchi gumi*, and they have been described as one of the most powerful organized crime groups in the world.

and financial transactions, and have enabled the globalization of criminal activity" (Office of Audit and Evaluation, 2013, p. i). As a result, the crime syndicates that had once engaged in illegal street-level activities such as drug trafficking, prostitution, gambling, and extortion have today evolved into criminal quasi-businesses involved in such crimes as arms dealing, large-scale insurance fraud, environmental crime, migrant smuggling, money laundering, and bank fraud. These varied activities fall into the category of *transnational crime*.

Undertaken increasingly by organized crime groups, transnational crime tends to affect countries scoring high on the corruption scale and characterized by unstable politics and civil unrest. However, the impact of such criminal activity presents considerable threats to the public safety, national security, and economic stability of countries like Canada and other countries of the comparatively stable North and West.

Over the course of this chapter, we will consider a number of transnational crimes, including terrorism, human trafficking and smuggling, intellectual property crime, money laundering, and cybercrime. These criminal activities can, and frequently do, occur within a very localized context. For example, an act of domestic (or home-grown) terrorism can involve a lone gunman who travels no further than the end of the street to attack the target. Likewise, money laundering can be undertaken by street-level crime groups operating within a city or even a neighbourhood. What these crimes have in common, however, is that they are increasingly transnational in nature, making them more and more difficult for law enforcement agencies to combat.

## Terrorism

Although crimes including homicide, genocide, bombing, hijacking, police brutality, kidnapping, and arguably war are the most publicized forms of political violence, terrorism did not become a major focus of criminological research until after the events of 11 September 2001, or what we commonly call "9/11." Those old enough to remember the date will likely never forget exactly where they were when they first learned about hijacked jets crashing into the twin towers of the World Trade Center in New York. I was in a cycling shop in Italy. No one was there to greet me when I entered: everyone in the shop was clustered around a wall-mounted TV watching CNN coverage of events so horrible they defied belief. What happened that day was so shocking and grim that I will certainly never forget what the weather was like, where I stood, or how I first felt when I realized what had happened. In essence, this is a principal objective of terrorism: to link a political cause to an act of violence in a way that causes an immediate and lasting impression.

While September 11 was a life-changing moment for nearly anyone who was alive to experience it, it also marked a new age in crime fighting and crime research. It is difficult to believe, given that in 2013 alone there were over 20 academic books, in English, published on the topic, but despite its long history, terrorism had received scant attention from criminologists prior to the twenty-first century. This may be because acts of terrorism were, until then, relatively infrequent and isolated. In addition, during the twentieth century, many terrorist attacks were ignored or even suppressed to keep them out of the news: there was a reluctance to aid the terrorists by drawing attention to their cause or to participate in what has become the sensationalized modern expression of extreme political action.

When terrorism reappeared in the late twentieth century with such groups as the Baader-Meinhof Gang in West Germany, the Japanese Red Army, Italy's Red Brigades, the IRA in Northern Ireland, and various terrorist groups in India, Iraq, and Pakistan (see Johnson, 2009), there was the tendency to regard it as a new phenomenon without precedent. Yet it is safe to say that since 9/11, the rise of al-Qaeda, Boko Haram, al-Shabaab, the Haqqani network,

**terrorism**
The use of propaganda, violence, or dangerous acts against an organization, an agency, or a state for the purpose of obtaining concessions or rewards for a deeply held personal or political cause.

and ISIL have made terrorism a top-of-mind concern not just for academics but for the public generally. Social media have helped terrorist groups ensure their crimes are no longer kept secret, and the Internet has become an important marketing tool that enables terror groups operating locally to find recruits among disaffected young people in all corners of the world. The globalization of terror reflects its evolutive nature. Today we encounter terrorism not just on the news but in popular books, movies, and TV shows. In the twenty-first century, terrorism has gone mainstream.

Despite our heightened awareness of terrorism, there are, as Johnson (2009) notes, many crucial questions that we have yet to answer. For example, why do some people who share the same convictions turn to terrorism while others do not? What is terrorism's true impact on international politics? And what influence, if any, could terrorism have in the future? Criminologists have an important role to play in addressing these topics.

## Defining Terrorism

*Any time bombs are used to target innocent civilians, it is an act of terror.* (US president Barack Obama, commenting on the Boston Marathon bombing in April 2013 [Landler, 2013])

If only it were so simple to define terrorism. In fact, despite its long history, terrorism has no single universally accepted definition. Those definitions that do exist tend to be subject to varying interpretations (see Box 13.3). Consider the following, which is just part of the definition of terrorism in Canada's Criminal Code (s. 83.01):

(b) an act or omission, in or outside Canada,

(i) that is committed
  (A) in whole or in part for a political, religious or ideological purpose, objective or cause, and
  (B) in whole or in part with the intention of intimidating the public, or a segment of the public, with regard to its security, including its economic security, or compelling a person, a government or a domestic or an international organization to do or to refrain from doing any act, . . . and

---

**BOX 13.2    FACTS AND FIGURES WHAT WAS CANADA'S FIRST CASE OF TERRORISM**

In his timeline of terrorist acts in Canada, *Vice* columnist Brian McKenna (2013) begins with the following entry:

1692: French and Iroquois combatants descend on three Mohawk villages south of Montreal, killing the men and sending the women to the Quebec heartland to "populate" the settlements of New France.

He defines terrorism broadly as "a sudden and violent action against civilian people who had no . . . reason to expect such a thing, . . . done to communicate a message of both willingness and desperation" (McKenna, 2013).

Do you agree with McKenna's "broad" definition of terrorism? Is it too broad or too narrow?

To you, does the 1692 incident represent a true case of terrorism, or would you consider it an act of murder, warfare, or even genocide?

(ii) that intentionally
  (A) causes death or serious bodily harm to a person by the use of violence,
  (B) endangers a person's life,
  (C) causes a serious risk to the health or safety of the public or any segment of the public,

---

## BOX 13.3    WHAT DO YOU THINK?

### When Does a Homicide Become an Act of Terrorism?

Nearly every criminology program in Canada now offers a course dedicated wholly or partly to the study of terrorism, yet the rate of terrorist attacks in Canada is rather small. We think of the FLQ crisis of the late 1960s, which culminated in October 1970, when the separatist Front de libération du Québec carried out a 10-day bombing spree and kidnapped British diplomat James Cross and Quebec labor minister Pierre Laporte (who was found dead in a truck of a car after the incident). To quell the violence, the federal government invoked the War Measures Act, an extraordinary measure reserved for times of invasion, insurrection, or war. (The act has not been invoked since.) We also think of the 1985 Air India bombing—Canada's worst act of mass murder—when a flight leaving Canada bound for India exploded over the Atlantic Ocean, killing all 329 people on board, including 280 Canadians. The attack was carried out by a Sikh separatist group based in BC.* We might also think of the foiled "Toronto 18" plot, which involved a conspiracy to bomb Parliament Hill, RCMP headquarters, and nuclear power plants. Of the 18 people arrested in 2006, 11 were found to have links to al-Qaeda and are now in prison.

Where, though, do we situate the 1989 Montreal massacre, in which a man motivated by a hatred of feminism and feminists shot 28 people at the École Polytechnique, killing 14 (all of them women)? Does this fit the definition of terrorism?

What about the October 2014 shooting of Corporal Nathan Cirillo as he stood guard at the National War Memorial in Ottawa? The RCMP and Prime Minister Stephen Harper classified the attack as terrorism, but others attributed the act to mental illness rather than religious extremism. The incident occurred two days after a man used his car to attack two soldiers in Saint-Jean-sur-Richelieu, Quebec, killing one, in what was also described as a terrorist attack. The perpetrator, a recent convert to Islam who showed signs of having become radicalized, nevertheless had no direct ties to any terrorist group.

> Consider both the Montreal massacre and the Parliament Hill shooting: would you describe these as acts of terrorism or as conventional homicide? Does it matter how we label the crimes given that both gunmen died during the events?

* In January 2016, the only person ever charged in the bombing, Inderjit Singh Reyat, was released after having served two-thirds of a nine-year sentence for perjury.

Visitors place flowers and pay their respects at the National War Memorial in Ottawa, where Nathan Cirillo was shot in October 2014.

THE CANADIAN PRESS/Justin Tang

(D) causes substantial property damage, ... if causing such damage is likely to result in the conduct or harm referred to in any of clauses (A) to (C), or

(E) causes serious interference with or serious disruption of an essential service, facility or system. . . .

Briefly, then, terrorism is an act motivated by political or religious ideology intended to inspire fear while causing death or significant injury to one or more people.

## Varieties of Terrorist Crime

### Kidnappings and Hostage-Takings

One of the oldest forms of terrorism is kidnapping, the seizure of a person to be kept as a hostage. The motive for kidnapping is to elicit publicity and to establish a position of bargaining power in the negotiation for political or financial concessions (i.e. a ransom). As noted in Box 13.3, above, it was the kidnapping of two political figures in Quebec that raised the separatist Front de libération du Québec's seven-year bombing campaign to crisis levels. The group's demands included the release of jailed FLQ members and the broadcast of the organization's manifesto.

Today, Westerners travelling in the Middle East and parts of Asia (e.g. the Philippines) are particularly vulnerable to kidnapping by terrorist groups, who may use the hostages to draw attention to their cause or to exchange for the release of political prisoners. Companies doing business in these parts of the world, as well as journalists and aid workers, may go to great lengths to protect themselves and their families from being kidnapped or taken hostage. Some companies even have special insurance for employees who work in high-risk zones where kidnapping is used as a means of extorting money to support their cause.

Recent high-profile instances of political kidnapping include the 2006 capture of Gilad Shalit, an Israeli soldier, by the Palestinian Islamic group Hamas. Shalit was held for over five years before being released in exchange for over 1,000 Palestinian prisoners who had engaged in terrorist activities against Israel (Martin, 2011). More recently, in 2014, Boko Haram, an Islamic jihadist group that had been carrying out a violent terror campaign in northeastern Africa since 2009, came to international prominence when it kidnapped 276 schoolgirls in Chibok, Nigeria. Although the kidnapping sparked international outrage, the girls were not released and are believed to have been kept as brides or sold into marriage or slavery. Meanwhile, Boko Haram drew considerable media attention to its cause, most of it fuelled by a well-meaning but unsuccessful public awareness campaign carried out on Twitter under the hashtag #BringBackOurGirls.

### Hijackings and Skyjackings

The 1950s and 1960s are sometimes called the "golden age of air travel," but as Scott McCartney (2010) explains in an article in the *Wall Street Journal*, the boom in air travel led to a spate of aircraft hijackings (or "skyjackings") in the late 1960s and early 1970s. He reports that in January 1969 alone, eight planes were hijacked to Cuba. After the Popular Front for the Liberation of Palestine hijacked three planes bound for New York in October 1970, US president Richard Nixon ordered air marshals to be on board all flights and introduced X-ray machines to scan for weapons; this led to a dramatic drop in the incident rate of skyjacking (McCartney, 2010). The 9/11 attacks, in which four planes were hijacked, led to another series of security improvements, both on the ground and onboard aircraft. Stricter airport screening measures were put in place almost immediately following the attacks, and all major airlines have introduced security doors to the cockpit, making it very difficult for unauthorized passengers to gain access to the flight controls.

By definition, skyjacking involves taking control of an aircraft in a bid to gain publicity, risk lives for a cause, and use hostages as human shields. These strategies make it difficult to neutralize the event while the terrorists have control of the plane. Hijacking can also involve the forceful takeover of a land transportation vehicle, such as a truck, car, boat, or train. In fact, the last official hijacking in Canada involved a bus. It occurred in 1989, when a Canadian of Lebanese origin, aiming to draw attention "to the plight of Christians in his homeland," commanded a charter bus en route from Montreal to New York. As Thomas (2013) reports, the whole incident ended peacefully on the lawn of Parliament Hill.

### Bombings

You have probably heard of a Molotov cocktail, a crude, improvised incendiary device consisting of a bottle filled with gas and a rag that, once ignited, is thrown toward a target with the intent of setting it on fire. Although these petrol bombs were first used during the Spanish Civil War that began in 1936, the now common term "Molotov cocktail" dates to the Soviet Union's attack on Finland in 1939–40, when the plucky Finns used the devices—which they named in mocking tribute to the Soviet minister for foreign affairs—to withstand the Red Army's assault. Today, the Molotov cocktail is a weapon of choice among upstart rebel groups and riotous protestors. Among terrorists, it is most commonly used by smaller radicalized groups that are not as well organized or equipped as the more formidable terrorist groups (Johnson, 2009).

Bombings are the most common type of terrorist act. Bombing typically involves the use of improvised explosive devices (or IEDs), which are relatively easy and inexpensive to make. An Internet-savvy terrorist can readily find instructions for making simple IEDs online. However,

Associated Press/ Sergei Grits

A protestor prepares to launch a homemade Molotov cocktail at police using a slingshot in central Kiev, Ukraine, in January 2014. The low-tech grenade, popular among violent protestors around the world, can be made using common household items, but better-financed terrorist groups tend to use more sophisticated explosive devices that have greater impact.

just as our efforts to combat terrorism have evolved, so have the bombing devices that terrorists are using. The explosive devices commonly used today are more sophisticated, smaller, and easier to conceal, making them well suited to suicide bombing missions; they also have the capacity to cause greater destruction and loss of life.

One of the deadliest terrorist attacks in recent years occurred in September 2007 in northern Iraq, when four vehicles laden with explosives—including a fuel tanker—were driven into two villages inhabited by members of a minority religious group, the Yazidi. When the explosives were detonated, nearly 800 people were killed and thousands were wounded (Wander, 2010). While no one claimed responsibility for the attack, many attributed it to al-Qaeda, who would later use aircraft as bombs in the September 11 attacks on the World Trade Center and the Pentagon. In both incidents, the terrorists gave up their own lives in the attacks. Indeed, it appears that the rate of suicide bombings is increasing globally. Hunter (2015) reported that between January and August 2015, the number of people killed in suicide bombings was 45 per cent higher than the number of deaths by suicide bomb over the same period in 2014, and that 56 per cent of casualties from IED attacks were the result of suicide attacks. The report was published in August, months before the deadly Paris attacks in November 2015, which involved seven suicide bombers, as well as a shooter, and which resulted in 130 deaths. Hunter (2015) suggests that the suicide attack is a "low-cost, low-tech option" requiring little training, and she warns that such attacks may become more common owing to their popularity among Boko Haram and ISIL, two terrorist organizations that appear to be escalating their terror campaigns.

The most devastating terrorist incident in Canada's past remains the 1985 bombing of Air India flight 182, discussed in Box 13.3, which also ranks among the deadliest terrorist acts ever committed.

## Terrorism: Future Trends

There is no shortage of causes—be they agricultural, social, political, environmental, or economic—to inspire passionate groups of activists. Any group whose protests go unheard or unanswered will look for increasingly public—and sometimes violent—ways to draw attention to their cause. Terrorism can be seen as an expression—an extreme one—of the frustration groups feel when they are not heard. Similarly, as long as there remain divergent values, needs, and expectations in society, terrorists will explore conventional and new means of conveying their message and attracting supporters. And as Johnson (2009) observes, with globalization comes increasing opportunities for competing ideologies to come into contact and to clash.

Should we be afraid? According to University of Ottawa terrorism expert Wesley Wark, Canadians are now "actually safer than ever.... [N]ational counter-terrorism efforts have vastly improved over the last decade, and al-Qaeda has been significantly weakened in many ways since Sept. 11" (quoted in Gillis, 2013). The picture however may not be as promising internationally. Johnson (2009), and others since, has warned that radical Islamic extremism, which was once visible only in certain parts of the Middle East, Asia, and Africa, is branching out, fuelled by new media

## BOX 13.4   WHAT DO YOU THINK?

### Defining Terrorism

As we saw at the outset of this section, *terrorism* is a widely used term that, nevertheless, does not have a universally accepted definition. Confusing the matter is the fact that other terms are sometimes used synonymously or conflated with terrorism: these include *radicalism*, *extremism*, and *jihadism*.

Find different definitions and examples of each of these terms and note any apparent difference and similarities. What conclusions can you draw from your review of these terms, and how—and by whom—they are used?

and other technology that allows it to find supporters in Europe and North America: supporters who will return to countries like Syria to take up the cause of groups like ISIL, or who will, like the three British-born terrorists involved in the 2005 London bombing or the French-born mastermind behind the November 2015 Paris attacks, take up the fight closer to home.

Amid all of this, commentators such as Mueller (2006, p. 29) have cautioned that it is not the damage caused by terrorism that poses a problem but the ill-informed fear and "often hasty, ill-considered, and overwrought reaction" that must be properly managed. In other words, while we should not ignore the potential risk of a terrorist attack, better research and understanding of terrorism could help inform alternative policies that do not feed on perpetuating fear and promoting ideological rifts. Here people like Mueller (2006, pp. 143–4) point to three basic approaches:

1. National security agencies should focus strategically on limited preventive and protective measures.
2. Political leaders should attempt to limit erratic, "knee-jerk," and ill-informed responses to security threats and breaches.
3. Policy-makers should seek to control their instincts to overreact.

After all, picking a fight with terrorist organizations simply gives them the attention and legitimacy that sustains them.

## Human Trafficking and Smuggling

### Human Trafficking

Although it is sometimes referred to as "modern-day slavery," human trafficking is a practice as old as recorded history. Greek terracotta paintings dating back to the fifth century BCE depict scenes of slavery, which was also widely practised by the ancient Romans from at least the second century BCE through the fourth century CE. Overall, history is rife with examples of people being exploited for the economic and/or military gain of many nations.

In 1641, Massachusetts became the first British colony to legalize the practice of slavery, beginning a practice that lasted in North America until 1863, when US president Abraham Lincoln attempted to abolish slavery through his Emancipation Proclamation. In 1948, the United Nations adopted the *Universal Declaration of Human Rights*, designed as a global standard for all nations to aspire to. Article 4 of the document states: "No one shall be held in slavery or servitude; slavery and the slave trade shall be prohibited in all their forms." Slavery

---

**BOX 13.5    REALITY CHECK**

### Slavery in Canada

The average Canadian tends to think of slavery as an American or international problem. But while more people may have been enslaved in the United States than in Canada, Canadians were not innocent in the practice. Consider the following excerpt from a letter, written in 1763 by Quebec governor James Murray to a colleague in New York:

I must earnestly entreat your assistance. Without servants nothing can be done. . . . Black Slaves are certainly the only people to be depended upon. . . . . Pray therefore if possible procure for me two Stout Young fellows . . . [and] buy for each a clean young wife, who can wash and do the female offices about a farm. I shall begrudge no price. . . . (as quoted in Hill, 2007)

continues to be practised in some regions of the world, particularly in India and parts of Africa, and it is estimated that the number of enslaved persons worldwide—in forced labour, chattel slavery, bonded labour, and forced marriages—is between 12 million and 30 million people (Onyanga-Omara, 2016). Nevertheless, the institution of slavery has greatly diminished, or is garnering less attention than human trafficking and smuggling, which make news headlines in the present media environment.

Toward the end of the twentieth century slavery took on renewed international interest thanks to growing concerns over human trafficking: the practice of relocating people from one region or country to another, by means of force or deception, in order to exploit them for prostitution or forced labour. Prior to 2000, there were very few scholarly works on the subject; however, since 2000—when the United Nations adopted the *Protocol to Prevent, Suppress and Punish Trafficking in Persons, especially Women and Children*, also known as the Palermo protocol—there has been a virtual explosion of scholarly books, journal articles, special reports, and book-length studies of the topic. A number of post-secondary institutions have opened human trafficking research centres. To put it bluntly, human trafficking has become a hot topic.

The primary reason for the sudden interest is that human trafficking is considered one of the most grievous human rights violations, affecting mostly (though not only) women and children, robbing them of dignity and innocence, and leaving them scarred for the rest of their lives (see Figure 13.1). Moreover, virtually no country is untouched by human trafficking, whether it be a country of origin, a transit country, or a destination country:

- *Countries of origin* are countries where the victims of trafficking are from. Typically, they are impoverished countries where opportunities are limited and awareness of the risks of trafficking are also limited.
- *Transit countries* are those countries through which victims are sometimes transported or smuggled in order to facilitate entry into the destination country. For example, officials in some countries may be more prone to bribery, making these countries better conduits for human trafficking. Other countries that are considered "low-risk" for human trafficking may be used to disguise the origins of trafficked humans: officials in destination countries will be less suspicious of someone entering from a low-risk transit country than of someone entering directly from a country of origin known to be associated with human trafficking.
- *Destination countries* are those where considerable profits can be made for the perpetrators. They may also be countries where the risk of apprehension and/or prosecution is low.

According to a 2014 report by the United Nations Office on Drugs and Crime (UNODC), in 2010–12, trafficking victims with 152 different citizenships were identified in 124 countries, showing the global reach of human trafficking. Canada is generally characterized as a country of transit or a country of destination, in part because of its low rate of convictions. Consider that since 2000, when human trafficking legislation was enacted, there have been fewer than 50 cases of human trafficking brought to court in Canada and even fewer successful convictions (Kaye, 2013). As Box 13.6 illustrates, Canada can also be described as a country of origin.

While the majority of human trafficking cases involve sexual exploitation, other cases involve forced labour, domestic servitude, forced marriage, forced military service, and the removal of human organs (UNODC, 2014, p. 35). As Figure 13.2 shows, there is a sharp gender difference in cases of human trafficking.

There are three basic elements that characterize all forms of human trafficking:

- *The act.* This refers to the harbouring or receipt of a victim, as well as the recruitment, transportation, and/or illegal transfer of the person.

**human trafficking**
The trade in human beings, carried out through force or deception, for the purpose of sexual exploitation or forced labour.

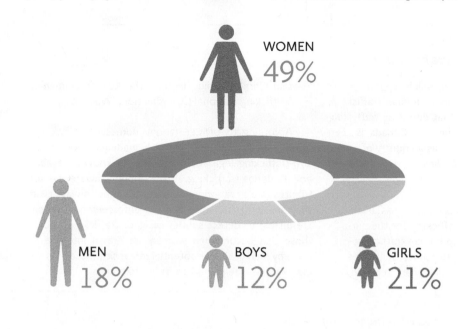

**Figure 13.1   Profile of Human Trafficking Victims, 2011**

Note: For the purpose of this figure, girls and boys are under the age of 18.

*Source:* UNODC, Global Report on Trafficking in Persons 2014 (United Nations publication, Sales No. E.13.IV.1), p. 29.

- *The means.* Human trafficking can involve the abuse of power or the exploitation of a position of vulnerability to adduct a person; it can also involve the use coercion, deception, the threat or use of force, or the giving of payments or benefits to gain control over another person.
- *The purpose of exploitation.* People, mostly women and children, are trafficked primarily for the purpose of commercial sex, including prostitution, stripping, pornography and live-sex shows; as noted above, other motives for trafficking include forced labour, forced marriage, and the sale of illegally harvested organs.

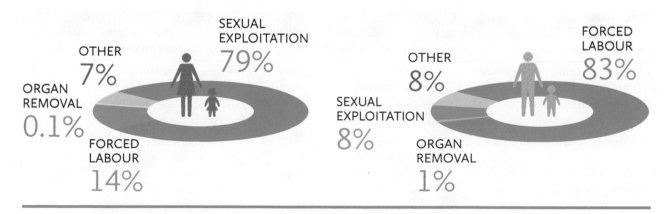

**Figure 13.2   Forms of Exploitation among Female and Male Trafficking Victims, 2010–2012**

*Source:* UNODC, Global Report on Trafficking in Persons 2014 (United Nations publication, Sales No. E.13.IV.1), p. 36.

| BOX 13.6 | **A CLOSER LOOK**<br>Domestic Trafficking |
|---|---|

The Canadian Women's Foundation, which supports young girls and women who are survivors of human trafficking, makes it clear on their website that domestic trafficking occurs inside Canada, despite the fact Canada is seen more as a destination country than as a country of origin. An article that appeared in the *Globe and Mail* elaborates on the situation:

> The majority of human trafficking cases in Canada relate to domestic human trafficking for the purposes of sexual service. Of 46 human trafficking–related convictions as of late June, sentences have ranged from one day to nine years in prison,

said Corporal Nilu Singh of the RCMP's Human Trafficking National Co-ordination. (Woo, 2013)

According to UNICEF (2009), domestic trafficking is enabled by lax law enforcement, inadequate or delayed anti-trafficking legislation, and lack of knowledge about how to define trafficking. A lack of public awareness contributes to a situation where victims are not always aware they are being trafficked and law-enforcement personnel are unable to detect subtler cases of trafficking, such as those that occur when women are drawn into the sex trade by men posing as potential romantic partners on dating websites (see pages 309–11 in Chapter 12).

### Who Is Involved in Human Trafficking

Like other forms of emerging crime, human trafficking can be highly lucrative, with the extent of profits depending on the scale and location of the operation. The UNODC (2014, p. 47) reports that the business of human trafficking—particularly when it involves sexual exploitation—is far more profitable in richer countries than in poorer countries. The organization cites a case in which a Canadian man involved in intimate-partner exploitation—where a man begins dating a woman and then leverages his power over her to force her into the commercial sex trade—earned roughly US$180,000 over a seven-month period of exploiting one woman. The incident illustrates van Duyne and Spencer's (2011) observation that although human trafficking has a very real human element, to the perpetrators of such crimes it is simply economics.

The case reported above offers maximal profit because it involves a relatively rich country (Canada) that is both the country of origin and the destination country. When human trafficking involves transporting people from a poorer country to a richer one, both the costs of the operation and the amount of organization increase. It is for this reason that human trafficking on a transnational scale is often carried out by large organized crime groups (see Table 13.1).

| Table 13.1 Typologies of Human Traffickers | | |
|---|---|---|
| **Small Local Operations** | **Medium Subregional Operations** | **Large Transregional Operations** |
| • Domestic or short-distance trafficking flows | • Trafficking flows within the subregion or neighbouring subregions | • Long-distance trafficking flows involving different regions |
| • One or few traffickers | • Small group of traffickers | • Traffickers involved in organized crime |
| • Small number of victims | • More than one victim | • Large number of victims |
| • Limited investment, limited profits | • Some investments and some profits, depending on the number of victims | • High investments, high profits |
| • No travel documents needed for border crossings | • Border crossings with or without travel documents | • Border crossings always require travel documents |
| • No or very little organization required | • Some organization needed, depending on the border crossings and number of victims | • Sophisticated organization needed to move large number of victims over long distances |
| • Intimate-partner exploitation | | • Operation designed to endure |

*Source:* UNODC, Global Report on Trafficking in Persons 2012 (United Nations publication, Sales No. E.13.IV.1), p. 51.

How are people drawn into human trafficking? The simplest and most common explanation is that traffickers prey on vulnerable individuals, such as people seeking support, living a life of limited opportunity, or trying to escape their social, economic, and/or political situation. These are commonly referred to as *push factors*, since they "push" people into a positon of vulnerability. The corresponding *pull factors*, which are used to entice and entrap victims, are deception and false promises of opportunity, a better life, and so on (Winterdyk & Kaye, 2014).

It is also worth trying to understand who the traffickers are. While there is no single type of trafficker, various sources note that international traffickers commonly share similar ethnicity with their associates and have ethnic ties to the source countries of their victims (Shelley, 2010). The ethnic ties enable the trafficker(s) to build on familiarity and trust to exploit the opportunity.

### Combatting Human Trafficking

One of the issues affecting efforts to combat human trafficking is a lack of capacity to address the problem at a local, national, or international level (Dandurand, 2012). A recent report by the US Department of Justice showed that in spite of increased resources to fight human trafficking, 23 countries failed to comply with the international guidelines in 2011, up from just 12 in 2010 (Pelham, 2011). Along the same lines, the UNODC (2014, pp. 51–2) reports that as of 2014, 5 per cent of the world's countries still do not have legislation that criminalizes human trafficking, and 15 per cent of 128 countries studied did not record a single conviction for human trafficking from 2010 to 2012.

## Smuggling

As with other crimes covered in this chapter, smuggling is not a new crime: it dates back to ancient times, when certain goods and services were unavailable in a particular jurisdiction owing to laws that made them illegal (e.g. prostitution, or drinking for people under a certain age) or prohibitively expensive (e.g. cigarettes or gasoline, as a result of high taxes). Today, the ease of travelling and moving goods across borders has made smuggling an international phenomenon. Strangely, though, most introductory criminology textbooks either don't mention smuggling at all or else give it passing reference, lumped in with theft or drug use. As we will see, the matter is complex enough to warrant its own treatment.

### Types of Smuggling and Smugglers

If I asked you what products are smuggled, drugs would probably come immediately to mind. You might also think of migrants, recalling stories that have been in the news recently. Other common objects of smuggling operations include weapons, nuclear waste, contraband cigarettes, and even endangered animals, as well as any number of other hard-to-get items for which there is a demand and therefore an illegal, or black, market.

Smuggling, like human trafficking, is an activity that often involves organized crime groups. The person doing the smuggling may be a low-level member of the group or else a "mule": an individual, sometimes a tourist, who agrees to conceal an illegal product in a suitcase or carry-on bag and bring it to a destination in exchange for a fee or the cost of transportation. According to Lichtenwald (2003), this is the smuggler who is most easily and commonly apprehended.

In May 2005, the MITRE Corporation developed a computer-simulation program that was capable of modelling the complex adaptive behaviours of smugglers. The program is capable of generating novel smuggling techniques so that law enforcement agencies could devise strategies to combat them. These strategies could be fed into the simulation program to test how successful they might be and to see what methods smugglers might adopt in response.

BOX 13.7    WHAT DO YOU THINK?

## How Should We Fight the Sale of Illegal Cigarettes?

We know that cigarette smoking among Canadians is on the decline. According to a 2015 report by the University of Waterloo's Centre for Population Health Impact (Reid, Hammond, Rynard, & Burkhalter, 2015), the prevalence of cigarette use among Canadians aged 15 and older has fallen from roughly 50 per cent in 1965 to 15 per cent as of 2013 (Reid et al., 2015, p. 14). Nevertheless, illicit tobacco smuggling is a multi-million dollar industry in Canada, one that, according to the RCMP (2013), is growing. How can we account for an increase in tobacco smuggling while tobacco use is in decline?

One of the principal strategies used to discourage tobacco use has been to raise the price of—or, more accurately, the tax on—cigarettes. Nevertheless, as numerous studies have shown, smoking is an addictive habit that is not easy to break—price notwithstanding. The high cost of legally sold cigarettes creates an opportunity for some people to capitalize on this addiction by offering black-market cigarettes at a discounted price. It is a simple response to the supply-and-demand principle.

Do you think it is worth imposing such high taxes on tobacco products to discourage cigarette use even if it contributes to the market for illegal cigarette products? What alternative prevention strategies might be worth exploring?

## Summary

Human trafficking and smuggling are not new crimes but are crimes that have benefited enormously from globalizing processes that have made it easier both to transport people and goods across international borders and to establish the transnational networks needed to manage complex criminal operations. As the growing potential for economic gain combined with the low risk of detection, apprehension, and prosecution make these areas of crime attractive for criminal entrepreneurs, we are seeing new kinds of trafficking (in human organs, for example) and new kinds of smuggling (of nuclear weapons, for instance). Criminology has a role to play in trying to understand these phenomena and developing evidence-informed intervention and prevention strategies by which to better combat these crimes.

## Intellectual Property Crime

Intellectual property (IP) crime occurs when someone infringes on the copyright or trademark on a product in order to produce an illegal copy for profit. For example, producing an illegal copy of a book, a movie, or a painting for sale or distribution is a violation of the copyright governing the work. Producing counterfeit copies of a designer handbag is a breach of product's registered patent and—if the counterfeit is made with the designer label—an instance of trademark theft.

According to the most recent statistics released by the RCMP (2013c), counterfeit clothing and footwear make up 45 per cent of counterfeit products seized in Canada, followed by copyrighted audio-visual and other works (20 per cent) (see Figure 13.3). The main country of origin for counterfeited goods discovered in Canada is China (including Hong Kong), though India, Pakistan, the United States, and Thailand are other source countries for IP-infringing goods arriving in Canada (RCMP, 2013c). What this shows is that IP crime is often transnational, and like other forms of transnational crime that involve the movement of illegal goods across borders, it involves—and brings profit to—organized crime groups.

Why should IP crime concern us? For one thing, it represents an economic threat to those involved in the legitimate production and sale of the goods being copied. It also profits organized crime groups, thereby funding other, dangerous criminal activities. It represents a threat to those involved in the production of counterfeit goods, who may be exploited workers operating in unregulated, unsafe conditions. It represents a threat to consumers, who may be unaware

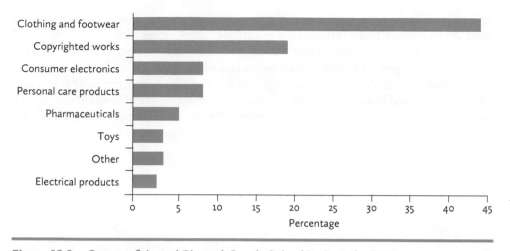

Figure 13.3 **Counterfeit and Pirated Goods Seized in Canada, 2012**

*Source:* RCMP. (2013). 2012 Intellectual Property (IP) Crime Statistics. Retrieved from http://www.rcmp-grc.gc.ca/fep-pelf/ipr-dpi/report-rapport-2012-eng.htm

that the designer goods they're buying at dramatically discounted prices are, in fact, not authentic and not produced to the named manufacturer's usual standards. There is also a safety risk: the RCMP (2013c) notes a steady increase in the seizure of dangerous counterfeit goods (see Figure 13.4). Driven by profit and flouting the quality controls and industry standards observed

---

**BOX 13.8**

**A CLOSER LOOK**
**Counterfeit Money**

In 2011, after considerable research and investment, the Bank of Canada introduced its new polymer bank notes to great fanfare. The new bills were designed not only to last longer but to thwart would-be counterfeiters: designed with the latest security features, they were supposed to be much more difficult than traditional paper bills to copy.

The new bills were indeed more difficult to copy—but not impossible. In May 2013, police in New Westminster, BC, reported the first cases of counterfeit $100 notes found in circulation. Just a few months earlier, the RCMP had successfully dismantled an operation that was mass-producing counterfeit $100s in BC's lower mainland. Over $1.2 million in nearly completed bills was seized during the bust (Luba, 2013).

The old (*left*) and new (*right*) Canadian $20 bill. The new bills incorporate several security features, including the polymer material on which they are printed, the see-through stripe, raised and metallic printing, and hidden numbers in the frosted maple leaf. Despite all of these features, counterfeits still exist.

by legitimate operators, manufacturers of counterfeit items do not have consumer safety in mind: cheap electrical goods that present a risk of fire or shock, untested automotive parts, and contaminated skin care products await the unwary consumer. A number of life-saving drugs have also been illegally produced, putting the patients who depend on them in jeopardy.

In response to the growing problem of IP crime in Canada, in 2011, the RCMP launched a pilot project dubbed Project O-Scorpion in Ontario. The objective was to devote greater resources to detect counterfeit goods entering the country. The success of the project (see Figure 13.5) shows what law enforcement agencies can accomplish when they are given adequate resources.

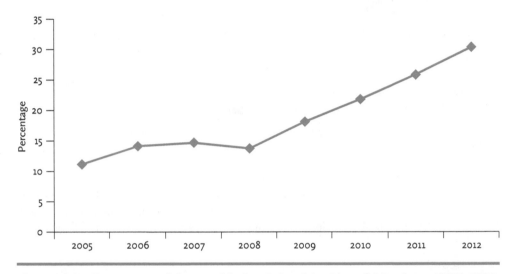

**Figure 13.4    Percentage of Counterfeit Goods Involving Harmful Products, 2005–2012**

Note: Some of the harmful products include toys, pharmaceuticals, perfume, integrated circuits, makeup, headphones, wheel bearings, cellular phones, and batteries.

*Source:* RCMP. (2013). 2012 Intellectual Property (IP) Crime Statistics. Retrieved from http://www.rcmp-grc.gc.ca/fep-pelf/ipr-dpi/report-rapport-2012-eng.htm

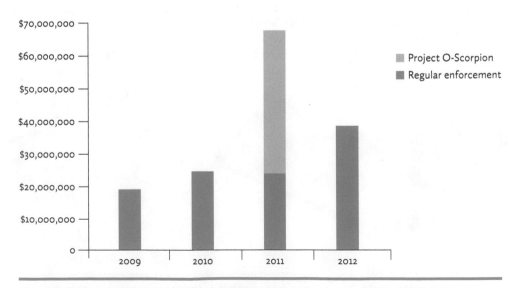

**Figure 13.5    Retail Value of Counterfeit Goods Seized in Canada, 2009–2012**

*Source:* RCMP. (2013). 2012 Intellectual Property (IP) Crime Statistics. Retrieved from http://www.rcmp-grc.gc.ca/fep-pelf/ipr-dpi/report-rapport-2012-eng.htm

## Money Laundering

As a result of the significant financial profits that many transnational syndicates generate, there is a need to engage in money laundering, which is the process of converting the proceeds of crime into a less suspicious form to conceal their illegal origins. As we saw in Chapter 11 (Box 11.9), money laundering, on a basic level, is what a neighbourhood burglar does in selling stolen goods for cash. For organized crime groups operating internationally, it typically involves transferring money obtained through illegal activities through a number of legitimate financial institutions or businesses (sometimes owned by a crime syndicate) in an effort to disguise how the money was obtained.

In 2013, the Canadian Security Intelligence Service (CSIS) estimated that the total amount of money laundered in Canada alone was somewhere between $5 billion and $17 billion. That is a drop in the bucket compared to the annual amount of money laundered globally, which the United Nations Office on Drugs and Crime (2016) pegs at a staggering $2 trillion, representing roughly 5 per cent of global GDP. Bear in mind that these are merely educated guesses. Nevertheless, as the national and global financial estimates have increased, it is apparent that the crime syndicates are evolving and becoming more adapt at concealing their profits, making them more powerful and more difficult to stop.

**money laundering**
The illegal act of converting money or goods obtained through crime into a less suspicious form in order to conceal their origins and provide a legitimate way to account for the revenue.

## Cybercrime

In 1974, the famous writer of science fiction Arthur C. Clarke predicted that in time everyone would own a personal computer. I was then an avid reader of science (or "speculative") fiction and thought the idea that everyone would own a computer was simply fantasy. Little did I know! When my university unveiled its first set of public-access computers at the newly created computer lab, we had very limited access to terminals (only my most privileged colleagues had computers in their own homes!). When one of us was fortunate enough to get time on one of the campus computers—normally to type up and print an essay we had written by hand beforehand—there was no need for a password or any other security device. As students, we were simply in awe of what was then new but still very limited technology that meant using keystrokes instead of correction fluid to correct our typos, and floppy disks rather than carbon paper to keep copies of all our (important) written assignments.

Fast-forward to today, and you may have to pause to count up how many computers you have—not just in your home but with you right now! Laptop, tablet, smartwatch, phone. . . . All of these once undreamt-of innovations are now indispensable parts of the way we stay connected to one another. They also make us vulnerable to criminals who have been quick to recognize the exploitive opportunities of Internet-based technologies.

As Clifford (2011) points out, we have so far managed to avoid what were once considered the core concerns for cybercrime—notably, hacking attacks against banks and financial networks. In 2012, the top three areas of cybercrime were fraud (54 per cent of all police-reported cybercrimes), online bullying/harassment (20 per cent), and sexual violations (16 per cent), including child pornography and luring a child via a computer (Mazowita & Vézina, 2014, p. 3). Some of the notable findings from a 2014 Statistics Canada report (Mazowita & Vézina, 2014) include the following:

- The majority (76 per cent) of people accused of cybercrimes in Canada in 2012 were men; men made up 94 per cent of those accused of sexual cybercrimes.
- The majority (69 per cent) of people identified by police as victims of violent cybercrimes in 2012 were women, including 84 per cent of victims of cybercrime involving a sexual violation.

- One-quarter (28 per cent) of those accused of computer-related intimidation/bullying incidents were under the age of 18.
- People under 18 made up 96 per cent of victims of sex-related cybercrime reported to police and 42 per cent of victims of cybercrime overall.

Among the developments in cybercrime that criminologists today are monitoring is the emergence of two "new" forms of computer-related crime: *cyberterrorism* and *cyberwarfare*. We will review these categories in connection with the Websense report on page 349. The growth of computer crime as an area of research led to the creation in 2007 of a journal dedicated solely to cybercrime, the multidisciplinary *International Journal of Cyber Criminology*. The journal's founding editor, Dr K. Jaishankar, is the pioneer of *space transition theory*, which proposes to explain the causation of crimes in the cyberspace (see Box 13.9).

As we saw in Chapter 10, theft is a crime that has been around since recorded history. Over time, advances in technology (for example, the introduction of telephones, then automobiles, then mass-marketing agencies) have created a host of new opportunities for criminal misconduct in the area of theft. Likewise, many cybercrimes are essentially traditional crimes

© AF archive / Alamy Stock Photo

*The Matrix* (1999) is one of the most iconic films depicting hacking. In this scene, Trinity literally plugs the character Neo—a computer hacker—into "the Matrix," a computer-simulated version of reality used to pacify and enslave humans. Can you imagine a time when humans wage war against the intelligent machines they have created?

| Table 13.2    Computers as Instruments and Targets of Crime | |
|---|---|
| **Cybercrime Categories** | |
| **Technology as Instrument[1]** | **Technology as Target[2]** |
| • mass-marketing fraud | • hacking for criminal purposes |
| • money laundering | • criminal botnet operations |
| • identity theft | • malware threats |
| • child exploitation | • distributed denial of service (DDS) |
| • intellectual property infringements | |
| • Internet-based drug trafficking | |

1 This category includes "criminal offences targeting computers and other information technologies, such as those involving the unauthorized use of computers or mischief in relation to data."

2 This category includes "criminal offences where the Internet and information technologies are instrumental in the commission of a crime, such as those involving fraud, identity theft, intellectual property infringements, money laundering, drug trafficking, human trafficking, organized crime activities, child sexual exploitation, or cyber bullying."

*Source:* Statistics Canada, Canadian Centre for Justice Statistics, Incident-based Uniform Crime Reporting Survey.

carried out using computers—"old wine in new bottles," to quote Susan Brenner's colourful phrase (2011, p. 17). The more common types of computer-mediated crime include fraud, theft of funds or information, embezzlement, forgery, and the creation and/or dissemination of (child) pornography—crimes that have long been carried out without computers (Brenner, 2011, pp. 19–20). This reflects a point emphasized repeatedly in the book so far: that crime is *evolutive*, changing over time. Cybercriminals, whether they are trying to scam online users with bogus goods or defraud them through creative strategies, are looking for maximal profit with minimal effort. But while its evolutive nature may make a crime such as cybertheft more lucrative for the perpetrator, it also makes it more difficult for law enforcement agencies to detect and prosecute.

Before examining different forms of computer crime, we'll look at some highlights of a report produced by a Canadian security company that began monitoring Internet security issues only three years ago.

## Insights from a Cybersecurity Firm

In 2010, Websense, a US-based cybersecurity company that was recently acquired by US arms maker Raytheon and rebranded Forcepoint, began producing an annual report on the threats posed by cybercrime. The company's 2013 annual report provided some information on cybercrime in Canada:

- "Foreign companies and governments are increasingly setting up virtual bases in Canada to drive corporate espionage attacks."
- Between 2012 and 2013, "malware hosting on Canadian websites increased 25%." In the first three months of 2013, "Canada claimed the tenth position for all countries hosting malware," with the United States and Russia ranking first and second on the list.

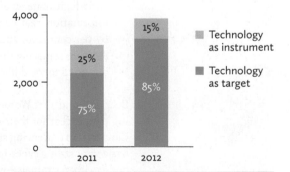

**Figure 13.6    Cybercrime Incidents Reported to the RCMP, 2011 and 2012**

*Source:* Statistics Canada, Canadian Centre for Justice Statistics, Incident-based Uniform Crime Reporting Survey.

BOX 13.9          WHAT DO YOU THINK?

## Space Transition Theory: A Breakthrough in Cybercrime Research?

The basic premise of space transition theory is that people's behaviour changes as they move from one space to another. In other words, cyberspace offers criminal opportunities to people who might not commit crimes in the physical world. Consider the following postulates of space transition theory, quoted verbatim from Dr K. Jaishankar (2007, p. 7):

1. Persons, with repressed criminal behaviour (in the physical space) have a propensity to commit crime in cyberspace, which, otherwise they would not commit in physical space, due to their status and position.
2. Identity flexibility, dissociative anonymity, and lack of deterrence factor in the cyberspace provides the offenders the choice to commit cyber crime.
3. Criminal behavior of offenders in cyberspace is likely to be imported to physical space which, in physical space may be exported to cyberspace as well.
4. Intermittent ventures of offenders in to the cyberspace and the dynamic spatio-temporal nature of cyberspace provide the chance to escape.

5. (a) Strangers are likely to unite together in cyberspace to commit crime in the physical space.
   (b) Associates of physical space are likely to unite to commit crime in cyberspace.
6. Persons from closed society are more likely to commit crimes in cyberspace than persons from open society.
7. The conflict of norms and values of physical space with the norms and values of cyberspace may lead to cyber crimes.

To summarize Jaishankar's ideas, people who are predisposed to criminal behaviour may take advantage of the anonymity and freedom of the Internet to commit crimes online that they would not or could not create in the physical world because of the damage to their reputation and social standing that such crimes could bring. The Internet also has a way of bringing together likeminded people who might have no chance of meeting in the physical world but, once they have met online, might conspire to engage in criminal activities.

What do you think of this theory? Consider applying the theory to one of the types of cybercrime discussed in this section.

- The number of Canadian command and control servers, which are used to control malware, increased by 83 per cent from 2012 to 2013, placing Canada among the top eight in the world for this type of cybercrime.
- Cases of phishing (sometimes also referred to as "carding" or "spoofing"), in which apparently legitimate emails are sent to random recipients to get people to surrender personal information that can then be used to commit crimes for financial gain, dropped by 67 per cent from 2012 to 2013. However, according to the report, Canadian cybercriminals were replacing their scattershot approach with more sophisticated targeting strategies designed to yield higher returns on their efforts.

Bear in mind that Websense, now Forcepoint, is a company that is in the business of making people fear for their cybersecurity. Nevertheless, their results are interesting. As for why Canada is experiencing such a growth in malware activity, the company points out that Canada has a very strong cyber-infrastructure but lacks an active malware-takedown protocol, thereby giving cybercriminals—whether based in Canada or not—more time to engage in their activities before being detected and shut down.

*Cyberwarfare* is a term used to describe government-sponsored acts of cybercrime undertaken against the government or infrastructure of another country. One of the biggest cases of cyberwarfare in recent years involved the Stuxnet virus, which was deployed in 2007 to attack a uranium enrichment facility in Iran (Finkle, 2013). The virus, which is widely believed to have

---

**BOX 13.10        REALITY CHECK**

### Internet Scams: Fool Me Once . . .

In August 2013, four Canadians and several American accomplices were charged with fraud involving a penny stock scam. The accused allegedly bought fledgling start-up companies and inflated their value artificially through fictitious e-mails, news releases, and social media messages so that they could sell off penny stocks issued by the companies. The fraudsters relied on call centres in Canada, Thailand, and Britain, and bilked investors in 35 countries out of more than $140 million over a relatively short period of time. They then cheated their victims a *second* time by posing as US Internal Revenue Service agents to help investors reclaim their losses in exchange for a small fee.

When interviewed, a Canadian legal expert pointed out that such scams are becoming increasingly sophisticated and hence more difficult to detect and prosecute. It took the co-operation of several police forces and banks from around the world to discover the breadth of this particular criminal operation ("4 Canadians charged," 2013).

What aspects of cybercrime make a scheme like the one described here possible to carry out? Consider some of the premises of space transition theory described in Box 13.9.

---

been developed jointly by the United States and Israel (Finkle, 2013), was designed to steal confidential information and damage equipment at the Iranian nuclear facility. Clifford (2011), in his review of the incident, suggests this might have been the very first incident of cyberwarfare.

## Different Forms of Cybercrime

### Theft and Illegal Use of Information

In the course of shopping, banking, selling, and dating online, we put an enormous amount of information about ourselves on the Internet. The transmission of this information, even through apparently secure channels, makes us vulnerable to the crime of identity theft, in which an individual's identity information—from user name and password to signature, fingerprint, or DNA profile—is taken or held without consent by another person for fraudulent purposes, such as purchasing goods or obtaining funds using the individual's banking details.

Identity theft is a fairly recent crime, prohibited by a law that has been in place only since January 2010, when Bill S-4 came into effect. Identity theft may give rise to identity fraud, which is the act of *using* stolen identity information—or impersonating someone by other means—in order to gain something, to avoid arrest, or to harm the reputation of the person whose identity is used. Cases of identity fraud significantly outnumber cases of identity theft in Canada (see Figure 13.7).

Traditional methods of identity theft could be quite unsophisticated: think, for example, of stealing someone's mail or going through someone's garbage to gather their personal information. By contrast, computer-mediated identity theft can be very sophisticated. It might involve an official-looking e-mail sent purportedly by your bank and advising you that your account has been compromised. In this scam, the recipient is instructed that the problem will be fixed once the recipient provides "the bank" with personal information via an e-mail address or phone number specified in the e-mail. Another scam involves an e-mail supposedly from the Canada Revenue Agency advising the recipient of a pending refund that will be deposited into the recipient's bank account once the appropriate banking information has been provided. These "phishing" scams don't rely on hacking; they depend on the fact that individuals

**identity theft**
The act of obtaining or possessing another person's name and personal identity information without consent in order to commit fraud or another offence.

**identity fraud**
The fraudulent impersonation of a person, living or dead, to gain some advantage, to avoid identification, or to harm the reputation of the person whose identity is used.

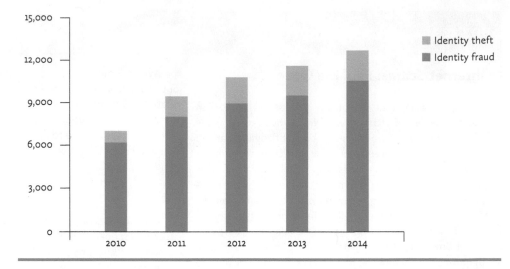

**Figure 13.7    Police-Reported Cases of Identity Fraud and Identity Theft in Canada, 2010–2014**

*Source:* Statistics Canada CANSIM Table 252-0051.

will willingly surrender personal information. According to the Canadian Anti-Fraud Centre, the number of Canadian victims of identity fraud has increased since 2012, even though the amount of money lost to identity fraud has decreased (see Figure 13.8).

Corporate espionage is another form of information theft, this time targeting large companies or even government networks in the theft of protected information. With so much corporate information now held online, this type of crime is typically carried out by hackers, operating either independently or on behalf of criminal groups or governments (see the discussion of cybercrime in Chapter 11 for information on the motives and methods of hackers).

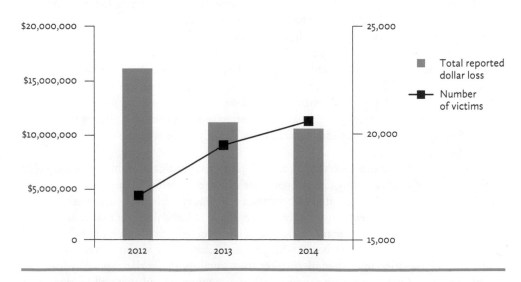

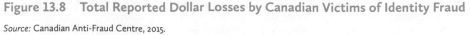

**Figure 13.8    Total Reported Dollar Losses by Canadian Victims of Identity Fraud**

*Source:* Canadian Anti-Fraud Centre, 2015.

**BOX 13.11**

### A CLOSER LOOK
### Phishing Trips

In the early 2010s, a common e-mail scam involved a message from a supposed friend in need of help. In the e-mail, the "friend"—who was typically named John or Emma: something common enough that the recipient would be likely to have a friend by that name—explains that he or she had come down with a serious illness or had been in an accident in some foreign country and desperately needed money to cover the unplanned medical costs or get back home. Don't worry, though: the money will be paid back as soon as your friend gets home. Terrible to say, but never trust such e-mails!

While preparing this chapter I received an e-mail from my department's help desk indicating that my account had been compromised by a third party. I needed to provide certain details about myself within 24 hours or my account would be shut down until the matter was resolved. It looked very official, but it was a phishing scam.

The list of phishing scams is almost endless. They can include account verification scams, bogus lottery winnings, e-mail chain letters, and job advertisements that offer high-paying jobs but require your social insurance number. Here is an abridged copy of an e-mail I received while preparing this chapter. It was from a "good friend." Does it sound familiar to you?

Dear John

My regrets for this sudden request, On Our trip to Philippines. My Family and I got mugged and all our belongings cash, mobile and credit cards were all stolen at "gun point" but fortunately for us we still have our passports with us . . . We need your help flying back home as I am trying to raise some money. I have made contact with my bank but the best they can do is to mail me a new card which will take 2–3 days to arrive here. I need you to lend me some money to sort myself out of this predicament, will pay back once we get this over with, kindly assist me . . . I will be back shortly online to read from you. Western Union Transfer is the fastest option to wire funds to me. Let me know if you need my details (Full names/location) to effect a transfer. You can reach me via email. I'm freaked out at the moment. . . .

Regards. . . .

--------------

How do you think you would respond if you received such an e-mail? Do you think you'd be fooled? How might we prevent people from becoming victims of such scams?

---

Software theft or piracy, a final form of online information theft, occurs when someone downloads and makes an illegal copy of computer software in order to sell it illegally, thereby undermining legitimate revenues for the developer of the product. In 2012, Dale Thompson of Toronto was found guilty of pirating software from Adobe, Microsoft, and Rosetta Stone, which he then reproduced and sold (under the name Appletree Solutions) on Kijiji and Craigslist. The judge awarded the plaintiffs maximum statutory damages under the Copyright Act, as well as punitive damages, in order to send a strong message about the illegality of profiting from the sale of counterfeit software ("Maximum statutory damages," 2012).

### Child Sexual Exploitation

Canada's Criminal Code includes a number of laws designed to protect children from sexual abuse and exploitation. These include laws against the production, distribution, and possession of child pornography, discussed in Chapter 12; laws against engaging children in prostitution; laws against sexual interference and sexual exploitation; and laws against luring children for the purpose of committing one of the aforementioned offences. While all of these crimes, with the exception of luring, can occur without the use of computer technology, the Internet makes children much more vulnerable to these offences. Figure 12.6 (page 317) showed the dramatic rise since 2000 in cases of child pornography, which can be attributed largely to the growth in online content featuring sexually explicit images and videos involving

**sexual interference**
The illegal act of touching, directly or indirectly, any part of the body of a person under the age of 16 for sexual purposes (with certain exceptions depending, for example, on the specific ages of the parties involved).

**sexual exploitation**
The illegal act of sexual touching with a young person when the offender is in a position of trust or authority or when the victim is in a position of dependency on the offender.

children. Figure 13.9 shows the increase in cases of child-luring over the Internet as a percentage of total sexual violations against children.

Child pornography is a big business, with an estimated annual revenue of $3 billion (Pulido, 2013). But as an RCMP report (2014) notes, citing child exploitation as a case in point, "cybercrime does not have to be financially motivated to have a devastating impact on victims." Children may be exploited in the production of explicit materials designed for personal use or for free exchange over person-to-person (P2P) networks. Children may be harmed—physically or emotionally—during a personal encounter set up by an act of online luring. The very serious and growing dangers of online child sexual exploitation have led the RCMP to devote considerable resources to combatting these crimes. In 2004, they set up the National Child Exploitation Coordination Centre (NCECC), which works closely with law enforcement partners across Canada and internationally. The centre was responsible for coordinating Project Salvo, which in 2009 produced 50 arrests on charges of sexual assault, sexual interference, and possessing, making, and distributing child pornography (Public Safety Canada, 2015a). According to an RCMP report (2014, p. 7), in 2013 the NCECC received over 9,000 requests for assistance from various partners concerning child sexual exploitation. The NCECC also partners with the Canadian Centre for Child Protection, which operates cybertip.ca, a tipline for reporting online sexual exploitation of children.

### Cyberbullying

**cyberbullying**
The use of communication technology to repeatedly harass, threaten, or intimidate others, usually anonymously.

Like online sexual exploitation, cyberbullying is an activity that disproportionately affects young people. It involves the use of e-mail, text messages, social networking sites, and other communication technology to threaten or harass others. It can involve an act as simple as sending around an embarrassing photo of someone, or a more concerted campaign of harassment by means of a website created solely to attack or make fun of others. In any form, cyberbullying can have devastating consequences for its victims, including depression, social anxiety, problems at school, acting out, and suicide (Centre for Youth Crime Prevention, 2015).

Cyberbullying was not written into the Criminal Code until December 2014, when the federal government passed Bill C-13, styled as the Protecting Canadians from Online Crime Act.

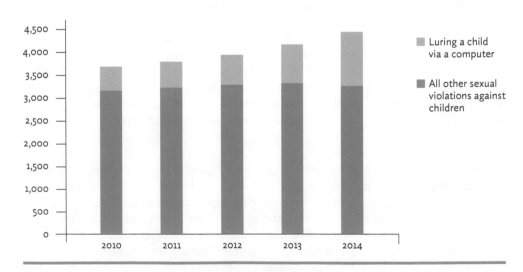

**Figure 13.9    Police-Reported Cases of Child Luring via a Computer and All Other Sexual Violations against Children, 2010–2014**

*Source:* Statistics Canada CANSIM Table 252-0051.

The new law made it illegal to distribute intimate pictures and videos without the consent of the person or people shown. It also provided courts with the ability to have offending images removed from the Internet, and gave police broader powers of surveillance to monitor and intercept private communications linked to suspected cases of cyberbullying. The bill passed in spite of opposition from critics who claimed the law was more about granting anti-terrorism forces lawful access to transmission data for security purposes (see e.g. Austin, Stewart, & Clement, 2014). Prior to the passage of Bill C-13, cyberbullying was prosecuted federally under one of two Criminal Code charges: criminal harassment (s. 264) and defamatory libel (s. 298) ("Cyberbullying laws," 2015). Some provinces, such as Nova Scotia, had already enacted their own anti-cyberbullying laws by the time federal Bill C-13 passed.

Two tragic and well-publicized cases of cyberbullying helped to raise awareness of the devastating consequences of online harassment in Canada. In October 2012, British Columbia teen Amanda Todd killed herself at the age of 15, after enduring two years of Facebook taunts from classmates and strangers after a topless photo of her was circulated online. A poignant YouTube video in which she described her misery went viral, but the cyberbullying continued even after Todd's death, with abusive comments posted on her Facebook memorial page. Less than six months later, a 17-year-old in Nova Scotia, Rehtaeh Parsons, died after attempting suicide. She had been harassed via Facebook posts and text messages for over a year and a half after photos of her being raped were shared online. Together, these cases gave force to the anti-cyberbullying laws enacted in 2014.

## Cyberterrorism and Cyberespionage

It all started when someone opened a scam e-mail and clicked on the link. It opened the door to the biggest cyberattack in history. In 2012, cyberterrorists used a deadly virus to attack the information network of Saudi Aramco, one of the world's largest oil companies, located in Saudi Arabia. Journalist Josie Pagliery (2015) describes what happened next:

> In a matter of hours, 35,000 computers were partially wiped or totally destroyed. Without a way to pay them, gasoline tank trucks seeking refills had to be turned away. Saudi Aramco's ability to supply 10% of the world's oil was suddenly at risk.
>
> And one of the most valuable companies on Earth was propelled back into 1970s technology, using typewriters and faxes.

What was the motive for the attack? We can only speculate. According to some reports (e.g. Perlroth, 2012), the affected computers were left with an image of a burning American flag, suggesting forces hostile to the United States were behind the hack. Other sources indicate that an extremist group opposed to Saudi policies and calling themselves the Cutting Sword of Justice claimed credit. Saudi officials accused people outside the country of being responsible (Mahdi, 2012); others suggested that an attack of this scale could only be perpetrated with help from insiders with high-level access (Finkle, 2012). And in a leaked NSA document, the United States blamed the attack on Iran, suggesting the country had learned from earlier attacks like the Stuxnet cyberattack (discussed earlier in this chapter) that had crippled an Iranian nuclear facility (Zetter, 2015). Regardless of who was behind the attack, the incident demonstrated how a major world energy supplier could be destabilized with the swiftness of keystrokes.

As with most emerging crimes, cyberterrorism and cyberespionage are fraught with definitional issues. As Taylor (2012) comments, the problem in defining cyberterrorism has to do in part with problems in defining traditional terrorism. Nevertheless, borrowing from the work of Conway (2007), we can say that cyberterrorism refers generally to Internet-based attacks that could result in violence against a group or organization or in severe economic

**cyberterrorism**
Politically motivated attacks against private, government, or corporate computer systems in order to cause widespread social, political, or economic instability.

**cyberespionage**

The illicit activity of hacking into the computer networks of a rival government or company in order to access confidential information.

loss. Cyberespionage, meanwhile, is the illicit use of computer technology to hack into the IT network of a rival government or company in order to access secret information.

So is cyberterrorism the new warfare? Is cyberespionage a greater threat to national security than traditional spy networks deployed for state-sponsored intelligence-gathering? It is too early to know if national military forces will one day be replaced with teams of hackers, but governments take the threat of cyberattacks seriously. In a 2010 document outlining Canada's cybersecurity strategy, Canada's then minister of public safety declared that "the most sophisticated cyber threats come from the intelligence and military services of foreign states . . . [whose] purpose is to gain political, economic, commercial or military advantage" (GoC, 2010, p. 5). He also warned that "a number of terrorist groups . . . have expressed their intention to launch cyber attacks against Western states," and that their capacity to do so was expected to increase (GoC, 2010, p. 5). Indeed, terrorist groups are showing increasing sophistication in the way they use the Internet not just to launch attacks but to disseminate propaganda, to network and recruit new members, and to gather information (Kirwin & Power, 2013).

The appeal to terrorists and spies of taking their campaigns to cyberspace is that it enables operatives to be more precise with their intended targets. They can carry out their missions more efficiently, with less chance of detection and less collateral damage than they would experience with conventional terrorists attacks such as suicide bombing. They engage in their attacks at any time and with minimal cost. In other words, cyberspace offers the same appeal to terrorists that it does to online bullies, cyberstalkers and pedophiles, and Internet scammers: it shrinks distances, making accessible targets more plentiful, and it provides anonymity.

Premised on a plot to assassinate North Korean leader Kim Jong-un, the movie *The Interview* (2014) is notorious for having sparked a retaliatory cyberattack on Sony Entertainment, allegedly by North Korea. Further threats caused Sony to limit the film's December 2014 release.

© Richard Levine/Alamy Live News

Furthermore, there appears to be no shortage of highly educated and skilled experts who are willing serve the terrorist cause as mercenaries for a reasonable cost.

At the same time, experts like James Lewis of the American Center for Strategic and International Studies suggest that the threat of cyberterrorism may be exaggerated. Lewis cites a number of reasons, including the following:

- Conventional terrorist attacks such as suicide bombings carried out against prominent public targets (e.g. hotels, embassies and other government buildings, etc.) have a powerful visible impact that gives them a strategic value that cyberattacks lack.
- While cyberterrorists can target utilities to interrupt essential services such as power and water, such disruptions are not uncommon in North American and other Western societies; when they have occurred, there have caused mass panic or civic chaos.

- As organizations become increasingly aware of and sensitive to their potential vulnerability, they have developed more sophisticated techniques to prevent/deter hackers from infiltrating their networks and doing harm (see Box 13.12).

> **BOX 13.12          WHAT DO YOU THINK?**
>
> ## Will Cases of Cyberterrorism Increase in Number and in Amount of Damage Caused?
>
> Cyberterrorism is a growing concern for high-profile businesses and national governments. But as we saw earlier this chapter, cases of conventional terrorism are also on the rise.
>
> > Which do you think presents the greater potential risk to society: cyberterrorism or conventional terrorism? Do you think that cases of cyberterrorism will increase relative to acts of conventional terrorism? Explain.

## Summary

Cybercrime, and now cyber criminology, has quickly moved from what Nhan and Bachmann (2010, p. 175) call a "niche area that is often marginalized by mainstream criminology to one of high importance." But as Jaishankar (2011) asks, will it evolve into a separate discipline? Although he suggests it probably shouldn't, he acknowledges it might well happen. One thing that does seem certain is that cyber-based crime is an emerging area of study that warrants specialized courses and focused research. As of 2016, the School of Criminology at Simon Fraser University is one of the few Canadian schools to offer a series of cybercrime courses. Part of the challenge for other criminology programs is a lack of faculty with the expertise to teach such classes. However, as the crime evolves and more researchers become engaged in researching the topic, this will likely change as well.

## Summary

- Transnational crime involves crimes that transcend or cross international borders. The crimes tend to be diverse and lucrative, but also complex, requiring a high degree of sophistication to carry out. For this reason, they often involve organized criminal groups. Some of the countries most affected by illegal enterprises are those that are characterized by unstable politics, civil unrest, and corruption. Typical transnational crimes include money laundering and personal identity theft. Combatting transnational crimes is challenging because it requires the co-operation of law enforcement agencies in different countries.
- Terrorism, while not new to criminologists or to history, is a crime that has developed into a significant global concern. With increasing globalization and competing ideologies, the risk and opportunities for terrorism to flourish appear to be increasing. Although Canada has been

relatively immune to terrorist attacks, it has joined the international community in trying to combat and prevent them from occurring, both on Canadian soil and abroad.

- Human trafficking and smuggling are age-old practices that have become major concerns because of the ease of moving people and goods across international borders. Trafficking provides lucrative opportunities for criminal entrepreneurs, and so it has evolved to address new markets, such as the market for human organs. Canada has had minimal success in prosecuting cases of trafficking and smuggling, owing to limited resources and a lack of public attention and education around the issue.

- Cybercrime is not only an emerging crime but a rapidly evolving one that is difficult to combat through conventional criminal justice practices. As cybercrime becomes increasing transnational, there is a growing need to develop new legislation and engage in greater international co-operation to fight it.

## Discussion Questions

1. Do you believe that acts of terrorism should be treated differently than more conventional forms of violent crime? For example, even if no one is killed in a terrorist act (such as the fire-bombing of a building resulting in no casualties), should the terrorist be held to a higher level of accountability than an arsonist?

2. Do you agree that one person's terrorist is another person's freedom fighter?

3. How serious do you think human trafficking is in Canada? Given the low conviction rates in Canada (and internationally), how else might we better address the problem?

4. Why are intellectual property crime and money laundering serious issues? Is it worth investing greater resources in combatting these two crimes?

5. With all the recent and rapidly expanding efforts to combat cybercrime, is there a risk of creating a Big Brother society, where privacy and individual rights are sacrificed in the interest of public safety? To what extent do you feel that advances in IT technology have, or have not, opened the door to more criminal opportunities? Conversely, how might we use the same technology to control computer-mediated crimes?

## Key Concepts

cyberbullying

cybercrime

cyberespionage

cyberterrorism

human trafficking

identity fraud

identity theft

money laundering

non-conventional crime

sexual exploitation

sexual interference

terrorism

transnational crime

## Weblinks

**Canada's Anti–Human Trafficking Newsletter**
Issued by Public Safety Canada, this bulletin provides information on different forms of human trafficking and regional Canadian initiatives to raise awareness. This is the website hosted by Public Safety Canada on human trafficking.
www.publicsafety.gc.ca/cnt/rsrcs/pblctns/hmn-trffckng-nwslttr-2013-03/index-eng.aspx

**ACT Alberta**
ACT Alberta is a non-governmental organization devoted to stopping human trafficking in the province. Their About Trafficking page will be of interest to anyone who believes that human trafficking is not really a problem in Canada.
www.actalberta.org

**Transparency International**
Operated by an international coalition, the website examines global levels of and releases an annual world ranking of countries based on their perceived levels of corruption.
www.transparency.org/research/cpi/overview

**Building Resilience Against Terrorism: Canada's Counter-Terrorism Strategy**
Produced in 2011 under the auspices of the former Conservative minister of public safety, this report evaluates the threat of terrorism in Canada and outlines some of the initiatives taken to fight it.
www.publicsafety.gc.ca/cnt/rsrcs/pblctns/rslnc-gnst-trrrsm/index-eng.aspx

**Bullying and Cyberbullying**
The RCMP's information page on bullying and cyberbullying provides definitions, legal implications, and tips on preventing and reporting bullying.
www.rcmp-grc.gc.ca/cycp-cpcj/bull-inti/index-eng.htm

**Cybertip.ca**
Operated by the Canadian Centre for Child Protection in connection with the RCMP's National Child Exploitation Coordination Centre, this tipline allows anyone to report suspected cases of online exploitation of children and offers information on such topics as Internet safety and identifying child sexual abuse.
www.cybertip.ca

# PART IV
## Trends in Criminological Research

# Chapter 14

## Future Directions in Criminology and Crime Prevention

Helen H. Richardson/Getty Images

It was only gradually . . . that I realized that what is
interesting is not necessarily useful.

J.Q. WILSON (2013, P. 45)

## Learning Outcomes

After reading this chapter, you should be able to

- Discuss the importance of developing an interdisciplinary and integrated approach to the study of criminology;
- Understand the dynamic nature of crime and criminality;
- Recognize some of the likely future trends in crime and crime research;
- Appreciate the need to merge criminology and criminal justice issues; and
- Discuss the importance of comparative criminology in bridging criminological issues.

## Introduction: Why Criminology Must Evolve

Criminologists have a personal stake in the issues they study, publish, and bring to the public's attention. Whether their studies focus on criminological theory, property crime, victimology, corporate crime, the emerging sphere of transnational crime, or any of the other elements that make up what we referred to in Chapter 1 as the *criminological enterprise*, they evolve with the ebb and flow of cultural, political, and social trends and with the growing body of scientific evidence. No matter how advanced our research and knowledge seem, we must always be careful about what we believe to be true about crime and about the approaches we promote to control or prevent crime.

In the quotation opening this chapter, James Q. Wilson, who served as Ronald Reagan Professor of Public Policy at the Pepperdine University School of Public Policy, is referring to the gap between what criminologists do and what people who practise criminal justice do. Although both are interested in the subject of crime control, they have not always worked in concert. Criminology lacks the stability of the natural sciences, and its research often follows fads that have short lifespans. For example, under the 1990s wave of post-positivism and postmodernism, many of the conventional concepts of the discipline were being challenged. A little under two decades ago, Milovanovic (1997, p. 5) suggested that the modernist conventional views of criminology (such as determinism, Newtonian ideas, and adherence to a structural-functionalist approach to knowledge) led him to conclude that the "search for

**postmodernism**

A theoretical framework derived from critical criminology that essentially rejects the self-evident reality of distinctions made by conventional scientific knowledge and/or common sense.

---

| BOX 14.1 | REALITY CHECK |
|---|---|

### Why It Is Important to Keep an Open Mind

*You can never plan the future by the past.* (Edmund Burke, 1729–1797)

The following list of amusingly inaccurate predictions and judgments illustrates the value of keeping an open mind to new approaches:

- "Computers in the future may weigh no more than 1.5 tons." (*Popular Mechanics*, 1949)

- "We don't like their sound, and guitar music is on the way out." (Decca Recording Company rejecting the Beatles, 1962)
- "Stocks have reached what looks like a permanently high plateau." (Irving Fisher, Yale University professor of economics, 1929)
- "Louis Pasteur's theory of germs is ridiculous fiction." (Pierre Pachet, professor of physiology at Toulouse, 1872)
- "There is no chance that the iPhone is going to get any significant market share, no chance." (Microsoft CEO Steve Ballmer, 2007)

over-encompassing theories of society and social development" is fundamentally flawed. He claimed the new postmodern paradigm "is neither fatalistic nor nihilistic" but an approach that views knowledge differently and in a way that may hold more promise than the ways in which we have traditionally studied crime (Milovanovic, 1997, p. 23).

Throughout this textbook, we have examined the subject of criminology and its major elements. We have seen that this field of inquiry is evolving into an interdisciplinary and integrated science. First introduced in the late 1970s by C.R. Jeffrey (1978), the idea of an interdisciplinary and/or integrated approach to criminology remains somewhat contentious, but nevertheless, the paradigm shift has rooted itself in most criminology departments. For example, today there is a growing number of textbooks that have embraced the integrative/interdisciplinary approach (see e.g. Barak, 2009; Fishbein, 2006; and Robinson & Beaver, 2009). Osgood (1998, p. 1) perhaps put it most bluntly when he stated: "It is best for criminology if many of us make a regular practice of academic thievery by keeping our eyes on sister disciplines to see what ideas would be useful to take for ourselves. . . . " However, as Henry (2012) pointed out, the path is not as straightforward as we might wish. For example, why and how is it that social learning and developmental theory, followed by social control, appear in integrated/interdisciplinary theories significantly more often than does any of the feminist perspectives or peacemaking theory (Henry, 2012, p. 72)?

Throughout this book you have been reminded that criminology must move beyond its traditional mono-disciplinary biases and that it must cross boundaries and build new bridges in order to overcome the challenges that face criminologists. Although the concept of crime has always been dynamic, the challenges that lie ahead are perhaps more exciting than ever. As crime continues to draw wide public attention, and as issues of accountability escalate, so will competing viewpoints of crime control. Policy-makers will need to work more closely with criminologists. Criminologists, in turn, will have to move beyond their cherished ideologies or favourite policies that have no, or at best limited, scientific foundation.

In this final chapter, we examine some of the issues with which criminologists will have to contend. Crime, being *relative* and *evolutive*, constantly presents new and changing challenges. If criminology is to help reduce crime and rectify inequalities, it must find a balance between responding to complex human behaviour issues and dealing with the more pragmatic policy-based criminal justice decisions.

## Criminology: A Frame of Reference

### Four Approaches to Crime Control

Repeatedly throughout this textbook, we have seen that the ultimate objective of criminology is crime control or the science of "controlology"—a term coined by Ditton (1979). The objective is to maximize the quality of life for the greatest number in society, following the utilitarian principle (see Chapter 5). However, those who espouse the integrated and interdisciplinary approach advocated throughout this text struggle with how best to address the issue of crime control and social order, or, as Detombe (2003) put is, how to "handle" crime as opposed to solving or controlling it.

Until recently, there have been three basic approaches to crime control: *conservative, liberal,* and *critical* (Conklin, 2013). Today, the *integrated and interdisciplinary* approach represents a fourth.

The conservative approach emphasizes the following objectives:

- controlling crime in order to preserve the status quo, legal order, and "family values";
- conventional crime, generally attributed to the lower and middle classes;

**conservative approach**
An approach to crime control that relies on the criminal justice system to deter and incapacitate criminals by incarcerating offenders; it originates in a belief that all humans possess the capacity for both good and evil.

- incarceration and the principle of "just deserts";
- expanding the size, reach, and authority of police forces; and
- maintaining social control, even if that means compromising individual freedoms.

The legal order that conservatives uphold is political rather than "humanistic" in intent. Its rise means that the law in general is "becoming an instrument of utility [i.e. production], removed from its proximity to the cultural institutions" (Christie, 1996, p. 182). Christie (1996) argues that as an instrument of social control, the law is becoming more political than scientific, and losing "essential qualities, particularly its roots in the core area of human experience" (p. 182). However, as we have seen throughout this textbook, while crime rates have declined significantly since the mid-1990s, research has repeatedly shown that reliance on punitive laws and legislation (such as the omnibus Bill C-10) to control the crime problem has not yielded particularly good results.

The liberal approach, in contrast, is more humanistic than political. It emphasizes this set of goals:

- addressing the social and economic problems that it sees as the underlying causes of crime;
- achieving social reform through vocational training, social assistance, job creation, and community involvement; and
- treating and rehabilitating offenders.

Although the liberal approach has received considerable support since the 1970s, it has been only marginally successful in controlling crime (Waller, 2008).

The critical approach emphasizes these aims:

- adopting an anti-establishment view of social order;
- viewing capitalist competition for wealth as an underlying motivator of crime;
- using unofficial sources (e.g. self-report and victimization surveys) that indicate that crime is not concentrated in lower socioeconomic groups but can be found across all social classes;
- examining the non-conventional crime committed by privileged groups (e.g. political crime, white-collar crime, and corruption);
- shifting the focus from the offender to the social system; and
- calling for the construction of a fundamentally different social system.

While Conklin (2013, p. 412) notes that critical, or "radical," criminologists offer few specific solutions to the crime problem, other critics have been much harsher. For example, as early as 1980, Klockar (cited in Fattah, 1997, p. 296) described critical criminology as lacking in empirical evidence and "strident" in its "moral and political imperialism." More recently, Madfis (2014), drawing on a meta-review of the critical criminology literature, concludes that despite various efforts to address past criticisms, critical criminology remains peripheral to the discipline.

Finally, the integrated and interdisciplinary approach:

- sees "handling" crime (Detombe, 2003) as its principal objective, as opposed to controlling it or solving the problems behind it;
- views criminal behaviour as human behaviour;
- stresses an interaction between the individual and the environment (i.e. nature versus nurture); and
- adopts a "soft deterministic" approach to the study of human behaviour that draws on both objective (i.e. quantitative) and subjective (i.e. qualitative) analysis.

**liberal approach**
An approach to crime control that focuses on alleviating social inequalities and providing legitimate opportunities for everyone; it originates in the belief that humans are naturally and fundamentally good.

**critical approach**
An approach to crime control that addresses both conventional and non-conventional crimes by attempting to eliminate structural inequalities that are the basis of capitalism.

**integrated and interdisciplinary approach**
An approach to crime control that attempts to combine two or more complementary theories as well as knowledge from at least two disciplinary perspectives in order to produce theories of behaviour that can better serve as the basis for intervention and prevention strategies.

The integrated and interdisciplinary attempt to reconcile differences among the other three approaches is a tall order. However, it represents our best chance of overcoming those divisions. At the same time, we will have to develop a model of social control/public order that respects people's freedom and dignity, and then persuade those who legislate criminal policy and administer justice to embrace it—another significant challenge.

## Criminology and Social Responsibility

It is easier to criticize existing theory and social policy than it is to offer constructive insights. Over the years, many criminologists have espoused policy recommendations that when implemented have failed to produce the expected results. When Robert Martinson (1974) assessed the then current corrections policies based on the liberal rehabilitation models of the 231 programs he surveyed, he famously concluded that "nothing works." The response to this conclusion was a renewed emphasis on the conservative model of justice, emphasizing retribution. This punitive approach, characteristic of the conservative model, continues to dominate the criminal justice system today, even though its successes have been limited. Other examples of policies inspired by criminological research that have failed to produce the expected outcomes include the "war on poverty" in the 1960s, the "war on drugs" in the 1970s, the shift to zero-tolerance policies around such behaviours as speeding and drinking and driving, and

Wilfred Hildonen/Cartoonstock

"Let's see . . . What kind of war should we have now?" The war on drugs, the war on poverty, the war on terror: when legislators adopt antagonistic language to frame crime-prevention efforts, which of the four approaches do you think they're adopting?

most recently the "war on terror." Collectively, these examples show that turning criminological findings into social policy is a risky venture at best.

Human behaviour is unquestionably the most complex of the phenomena that criminology must understand. If Charles H. Cooley was correct when he said that all human beings have a common ground (in that we all share the same basic human experiences), why has it been so difficult to explain, control, and regulate criminal behaviour? Universally, we value freedom and life. As long as we continue to do so, deviance and crime will remain fundamental concerns.

## Future Trends

### New Forms of Crime

Humans are characterized by an ability to adapt to new conditions, and recent decades have provided extraordinary examples of how we are adapting to the conditions and opportunities presented by the evolving digital landscape. As the global security futurist Marc Goodman noted in his 2012 TED Talk "A Vision of Crimes in the Future," these rapid changes in technology are creating a new series of criminal challenges. While conventional crimes such as homicide, theft, and fraud persist, these new forms of crime present criminology with additional challenges.

belekekin/Shutterstock.com

3-D printers have made it possible for anyone to print a working gun at home, and to do so without creating any record of the gun's existence. In 2014, a Japanese man named Yoshimoto Imura became the first person to be arrested for printing guns. How else might new technologies change crime and criminology in the future?

Canadian criminologist **Ezzat Fattah** (1997, p. 286) has called the invention of the automobile "the most important single factor responsible for the fundamental changes in the nature of crime in the 20th century." Yet he points out that very few criminologists study the role that the "car has played in transforming many types of crime and in producing new forms of criminality" (p. 286). Consider this example: in 2004 Alberta reported a noticeable increase in rural break-and-enters executed by the same methods used in major urban centres (Gannon & Taylor-Butts, 2006). Upon closer investigation, it was found that many of those break-and-enters had been committed by people who had driven to the targeted homes from the city (a twist on the concept of commuting to work!). This kind of evidence has led some environmental criminologists to take a closer look at how the availability of automobiles has affected both the choice of targets and the distance that offenders are willing to travel to commit their crimes, partly to reduce the risk of being recognized.

We could make similar studies of how crime patterns have changed as a result of other technological developments, including radios, credit cards, airplanes, computers, cellphones, and the Internet. In each case, criminals have found ways to capitalize on the new technology. Consider printing technology. In 2004, Canada saw a record high number of counterfeit banknotes passed into circulation, thanks in large part to improvements in colour printing technology and graphic design software that made it easier to produce convincing fake bills (RCMP, 2015). In 2006, the RCMP made counterfeit currency a target and deployed its integrated counterfeit enforcement teams (ICETs) to crack down on the spread of fake bills, through enforcement and education. At the same time, the Bank of Canada adopted new measures to make banknotes more difficult to reproduce, beginning with holograms and watermarks and culminating in 2011 with the introduction of the first polymer banknotes. As a result, the volume of counterfeit Canadian banknotes passed into circulation has fallen dramatically since 2004 (see Figure 14.1). Counterfeiters—many of them working for organized crime groups—continue to pass fake versions of old-issue paper bills that are still in circulation, but law enforcement agencies are finding that the polymer notes are stymieing criminals. The difficulty of sourcing the rare polymer substrate used for the real bills is forcing counterfeiters to print their fakes on paper, making them much easier to detect (Crawford, 2016). In this case, technology that once gave criminals the upper hand has evolved to where it is now enabling governments to stay ahead of the crooks.

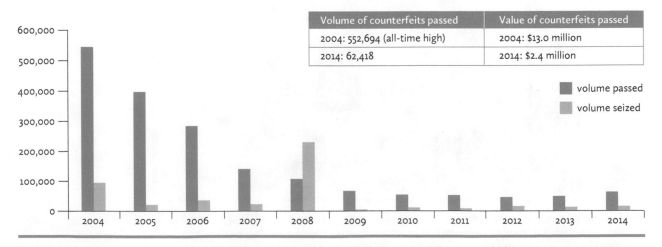

| Volume of counterfeits passed | Value of counterfeits passed |
| --- | --- |
| 2004: 552,694 (all-time high) | 2004: $13.0 million |
| 2014: 62,418 | 2014: $2.4 million |

■ volume passed
■ volume seized

**Figure 14.1    Volume of Counterfeit Canadian Banknotes Passed and Seized, 2004–2014**

*Source:* RCMP National Anti-Counterfeiting Bureau (NACB), 2015.

Areas that may pose increasing challenges for criminology and crime control include the following:

- computer and other high-tech crimes (see Figure 14.2);
- international sex trade;
- smuggling of migrants;
- international trade in human organs;
- transnational organized crime groups;
- transnational corporate crime;
- transnational environmental crime;
- transnational drug trafficking;
- international money laundering, gemstone scams, land sale scams, etc.; and
- international terrorism, both conventional and cyberterrorism and new forms of terrorist violence, used by groups ranging from businesses and governments to religious leaders and cyberterrorists.

As crimes such as these become more common, it will become even more important for criminologists to develop theoretical understandings that transcend cultural, gender, and political boundaries. This will put the spotlight on comparative criminology.

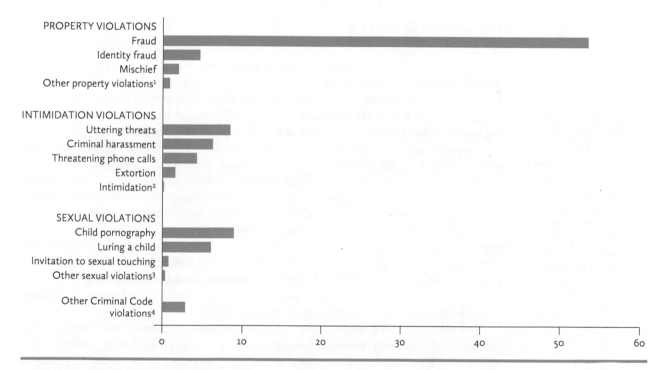

**Figure 14.2   Police-Reported Cybercrime, by Violation Type, 2012**

1 Other property violations include theft and trafficking in stolen goods.

2 Intimidation of an individual includes intimidation of a justice system participant or journalist and intimidation of a non-justice system participant

3 Other sexual violations include voyeurism, sexual exploitation, corrupting children, making sexually explicit material available to children, and bestiality—commit or compel person.

4 Other Criminal Code violations include offences such as corrupting morals, indecent acts, offences against the person and reputation, fail to comply with order, and breach of probation.

*Source:* Statistics Canada, Canadian Centre for Justice Statistics, Incident-based Uniform Crime Reporting Survey.

## BOX 14.2   FACTS AND FIGURES   THE EVOLVING NATURE OF CRIME

The following examples point to the evolving nature of crime.

- Although there are examples of computer hacking that date back to the early 1930s and 1940s (see, for example, the 2014 movie *The Imitation Game*, in which the British mathematician Alan Turning broke the code produced by the German Enigma machines), it wasn't until the 1980s that there was a dramatic proliferation of computer hacking. Given the profits to be earned and the low risk of detection, apprehension, and prosecution, hacking techniques and strategies will continue to evolve (see Chapter 13 for further discussion). In 2015, United Airlines offered a "bug bounty" to entice professional hackers to test its online security. Two hackers were awarded a million air miles each and a number of others received other lesser awards for bringing security flaws to the airline's attention (Bounties, 2015).

- A 2011 report prepared for the 41st Parliament identified cybercrime and human trafficking as "emerging" and evolving threats to public safety and human rights in Canada (Library of Parliament, 2011). Domestic as well as international human trafficking have evolved to become a concern for Canadian law enforcement agencies.

- In 2013, a six-year-old Chinese boy was kidnapped and had his eyes removed to be sold on the black market ("Organ trafficking," 2013). A 2013 report by the Global Financial Integrity organization estimated that the profit generated annually from organ trafficking was between $600 million and $1.2 billion ("Organ trafficking," 2013).

## Comparative Criminology

**comparative criminology**

The study of crime patterns and prevention methods in different cultural and national settings, undertaken in an attempt to develop theories and strategies that can be applied across cultural and political boundaries.

In addition to adopting an interdisciplinary perspective, criminologists must devote more attention to comparative research. The idea of comparative research is not new: the esteemed American sociologist **Thorsten Sellin** wrote about it in 1938 in his landmark book *Culture, Conflict and Crime*. Yet until fairly recently, there was limited support for comparative criminology, largely because of the challenges posed by differences in language, definitions, reporting and recording practices, and administration (see Pakes, 2015; Reichel, 2013).

Advances in technology and methodology have helped make international and comparative criminological research a major area of study since the late twentieth century. For example, the American Society of Criminology's Division of International Criminology has grown from 295 members in 2001 to over 400 members as of 2014, and there is now a journal—the *International Journal of Comparative Criminology*—devoted entirely to the topic. The percentage of American criminology programs offering a comparative course rose from 10 per cent in 1990 to 30 per cent in 2000 (Dammer & Cordner, 2000), and by 2015, virtually every major criminology or criminal justice program in the United States was offering one or more comparative courses. Although Canadian programs have lagged behind their counterparts in the United States and Europe, there are now a number of Canadian universities and colleges offering a course on comparative criminal justice.

The value of a comparative approach is evident when you survey the growing list of international criminology journals. A review of these journals reveals that different countries and regions specialize in different areas of research. For example, the *Canadian Journal of Criminology and Criminal Justice* contains research primarily on young offenders and issues such as policing and punishment. In the United States, the focus is more on social control theory and the general theory of crime. In the UK, there is a split between crime prevention and British left-realism theory. Journals published in China, such as the *Asian Journal of Criminology*, show a strong interest in pragmatic issues such as terrorism. Meanwhile, the *Australian and New Zealand Journal of Criminology* focuses on restorative justice and reintegrative practices.

| BOX 14.3 | **A Closer Look** |
| --- | --- |
| | **An International Focus on Criminology in Canada** |

The former Canadian Foundation for the Americas (FOCAL; 1990–2011) was an independent non-governmental organization dedicated to strengthening Canada's relations with countries in Latin America and the Caribbean through policy discussion and analysis. In response to the problems of civil war and social and political unrest in those regions, the foundation offered expertise in crime prevention and criminal justice.

Another example of international activity is the criminology program at the University of Montreal, which has taken part in many international and comparative research projects (especially in Europe). However, because most of its work has been done in French, it is not widely known in English-speaking Canada. The Human Justice program at the University of Regina and the School of Criminology at Simon Fraser University have also participated in international restorative justice projects. Finally, a number of criminology/criminal justice programs across the country now offer comparative criminology courses and/or accredited study tours. The Department of Justice Studies at Mount Royal University in Calgary has offered a comparative criminology study tour every other year since 1988.

Students of criminology are encouraged to consult criminological journals from other parts of the world to obtain an international perspective and draw comparisons.

As Canada becomes more multicultural, it is increasingly important to understand how cultural differences influence crime trends. For example, there has been some research showing a link between the fairly recent increase in drive-by shootings—virtually unknown in Canada until the 1980s—and the emergence of certain ethnic gangs (see Totten, 2012). Law enforcement agencies have been reluctant to release information liking certain crimes to specific ethnic groups lest it damage police relationships with those communities (Quan, 2012). However, high-profile cases like that of Kent Hehr might open the door to more research on the matter. Hehr, a Calgary MLA and former federal minister of veterans' affairs, is a survivor of a drive-by shooting in 1991, which left him a paraplegic. Criminologists might examine and compare the drive-by-shooting rates in other countries to explore whether there are conclusions to be drawn about the prevalence of this crime among certain ethnocultural groups. Many of the transnational crimes that we examined in Chapter 13 are likewise best dealt with from an international and comparative perspective (see Reichel, 2013; Reichel and Albanese, 2013).

Canadians are not the only ones who can benefit from a comparative approach. In 2013, the United States had the highest incarceration rate in the world: for every 100,000 people in the US, 716 were in prison. Compare that figure with Canada's rate of 118 per 100,000 (making it number 135 out of 223 countries), Germany's rate of 79, and Finland's rate of 58 (Walmsley, 2013). Such findings should encourage criminologists and criminal justice officials in the United States to examine the reasons behind these sharp differences. In Canada, the decrease from a high of 152 per 100,000 in 1995–6 has been accomplished largely through the use of alternative programs. But what accounts for the dramatically lower incarceration rates in Europe? The only way to find out is to engage in cross-national research.

Fairchild (1993, p. 3) identified three main reasons for criminologists to engage in cross-national and cross-cultural studies:

- to benefit from the experience of others;
- to broaden our understanding of different cultures and approaches to problems; and
- to help us deal with international crime problems such as terrorism and drug smuggling.

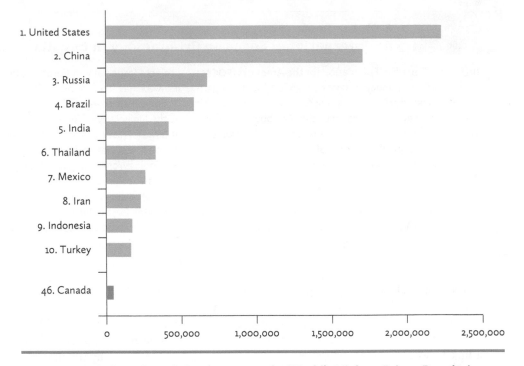

**Figure 14.3    Where Canada Ranks among the World's Highest Prison Populations, 2014**

*Source:* "The World Prison Brief (WPB)." Institute for Criminal Policy Research at Birkbeck, University of London.

Today, the last point could be expanded to include crimes such as human trafficking. However, in his informative account of INTERPOL, the international police association, Martha (2010) suggests that to date the professional community and institutions of higher learning have ignored international issues: global crime is a reality, but criminologists and criminal justice agencies have been slow to respond. (For more on INTERPOL, see Box 14.4.)

The United Nations Office on Drugs and Crime recently described corruption as a "complex social, political and economic phenomenon that affects all countries" (UNODC, 2014). In its counter-response, the agency has launched a Web-based anti-corruption portal known as TRACK (Tools and Resources for Anti-Corruption Knowledge). According to the UNODC website, "The TRACK portal brings together legal and non-legal knowledge on anti-corruption and asset recovery enabling Member States, the anti-corruption community and the general public

---

**BOX 14.4**    **A Closer Look**
**INTERPOL in Canada**

In 2016, 190 countries belonged to INTERPOL. The Canadian branch, established in 1949, is based in Ottawa and operated by the RCMP, which forwards information pertaining to international law enforcement to INTERPOL (McKenna, 1998). INTERPOL Ottawa played a key role in the 1996 capture of Albert Walker, who had defrauded his Canadian clients of millions of dollars while posing as a financial adviser in Paris, Ontario, before fleeing to England. In 2009, INTERPOL Ottawa made INTERPOL databases accessible to all police officers from 380 police and law enforcement agencies across the country—a significant step towards enhancing national safety and security.

to access this information in a central location." Other UN anti-corruption strategies include corruption surveys and public-awareness outreach campaigns. Sharing information is essential, and initiatives such as the TRACK portal can help to forge the international co-operation that is increasingly necessary in the age of transnational crime.

What the differences revealed by comparative research mean, by definition, is that its practitioners cannot aspire to produce any all-encompassing theory of crime or crime control; rather, they must focus on the kind of "middle-range" theorizing called for by Robert K. Merton: "Our task today is to develop *special* theories, applicable to limited ranges of data—theories, for example, of deviant behavior, or the flow of power from generation to generation, or the unseen ways in which personal influence is exercised" (cited in Wallace & Wolf, 1995, p. 56). As Sheptycki and Wardak (2012) have noted, comparative criminology has the potential to play a primary role in leading criminology out of the ideological approaches that have dominated in the past and into the interdisciplinary model. However, to do so it must "stand on two legs: one of positive science and the other the capacity for relativistic reflection." That is, what should determine the directions that comparative and transnational criminologists take should be informed from outside the discipline so as to avoid the persistence of the provincial perspectives that have, until recently, dominated the discipline.

## The Knowledge Explosion in Criminology

> *This is the bitterest pain among men, to have much knowledge but no power.* (Herodotus, c. 485-425 BCE)

In the early twentieth century, North American criminology was dominated by sociologists—in particular, the small group known as the Chicago School (see Chapter 8). It was only after the Second World War that the study of criminology began to incorporate ideas from other disciplines, including psychology, biology, economics, and political science, and today it encompasses many perspectives, whose proponents often seem more interested in competing than collaborating. Wolfgang and Feracuti (1967) introduced the term *integrated theory* to illustrate the importance of an interdisciplinary perspective in the future development of criminology. And, while the different perspectives, individually and when integrated or combined, do facilitate criminological research to some degree, the vast resources and high-tech information dissemination methods available today also complicate it, since they mean that there is always something else, if not simply a different perspective, to consider.

In recent years, a growing number of criminologists have commented on what they see as a general lack of soundness in criminological thought. Several have pointed out that "theories" based on untested assumptions are, in fact, myths (Cao, 2004). Charles Tittle (1997, p. 101) has cautioned that while theoretical integration is the most useful approach for criminologists interested in improving their theories, a number of limitations still need to be resolved:

(1) the necessity for compatible dependent variables,
(2) agreement on the purpose and nature of theory,
(3) difficulty in articulating interconnections of parts, and
(4) inadequacy of data for checking out problematic elements (Tittle, 1997, p. 101).

Nevertheless, the integrated and interdisciplinary approach offers our best prospect of reaching a more realistic understanding of crime. And, as Cao (2004) suggests, explanatory models will become more robust as theoretical and methodological strategies that bridge the current gaps are developed.

Criminologists must grapple with such issues when deciding what topics need to be researched, from which perspectives, and with what objectives in mind. Each type of research—aggregate data, experimental, longitudinal, survey—has its own strengths and weaknesses, not to mention methodological and ethical issues. One of the challenges for criminology is to recognize that criminality is the product of multiple interrelated variables. An integrated and interdisciplinary approach will assist in the development of theories that recognize this multi-causality, but it will also require the use of sophisticated statistical and multi-methods research techniques.

If the knowledge explosion in criminology has been a blessing, it has also been a curse by proving the truth behind the adage, "the more you learn, the more you realized how little you know." Criminologists must recognize the limits of their knowledge and be prepared to accept slow, perhaps painful growth in their understanding of criminal behaviour. As Einstadter and Henry (2006), among many others, have noted, "there are no simple explanations; there are no simple solutions. Complexity is the nature of social science."

## Controlling Crime: Punishment or Prevention?

A 1997 article on "innovative" incarceration practices in the states of Wisconsin and Maryland explained that inmates would soon be required to "wear stun belts which fire 50,000 volts through their bodies if they try to escape" (Gordon, 1997, p. A3). As of 2016, these belts were still in use, even though Amnesty International and Human Rights Watch argue that they constitute "cruel and unusual punishment."

The Canadian corrections system does not use such devices, but that doesn't mean Canadian legislators aren't looking for new ways to punish offenders. In March 2015, the Conservative federal government introduced Bill C-53 (the Life Means Life Act), which would have made life in prison without parole mandatory for certain heinous offences, such as murder. The bill died on the order paper when the federal election was called, but it generated discussion about whether Canada's sentencing laws are too lenient. In a report prepared for the Macdonald–Laurier Institute, a public policy think tank, UBC law professor Benjamin Perrin (2015) concluded that life without parole would be an appropriate sentence in some circumstances, as it would bring proportionality to murder sentences, spare victims having to attend repeated parole hearings, preserve public safety, and fortify the deterrent effect of a life sentence (pp. 2–3). Of course, longer prison sentences means more prisoners overall in Canada's penitentiaries. Less than a year before Perrin's paper was published, Canada's correctional investigator released a report (Sapers, 2014) indicating that Canada's prison population had already grown by 10 per cent over five years, contributing directly or indirectly to a number of other five-year increases, including:

- a 93 per cent increase in the incidence of "double-bunking" (where two inmates are placed in a cell designed for one);
- a 56 per cent increase in cases of inmate self-injury; and
- a 19 per cent increase in cases of bodily injury involving inmates.

What's more, over a 10-year period there had been 536 inmate deaths (Sapers, 2014). While two-thirds of them were attributed to natural causes, 16.5 per cent were suicides and 5.5 per cent were homicides. All of this raises questions about whether Canada's prison system can manage the increase in inmates that stiffer sentences would bring (see Winterdyk & Weinwrath, 2015, for further discussion of these and related issues; also see Box 14.5).

Is more punishment the best way to deliver greater justice? Consider the results of a 2014 report by the Fraser Institute, which showed that from 2002 to 2012, the cost of crime

---

**BOX 14.5    FACTS AND FIGURES** MORE PUNISHMENT DOES NOT MEAN MORE JUSTICE

---

In 1998, Canadian criminologist Ezzat Fattah wrote an article refuting the idea that punishment is an appropriate justice model. Although the article is now nearly 20 years old, Fattah's arguments still resonate:

1. Punishment is an ineffective deterrent: although the United States sends more people per capita to prison than any other Western country, numerous studies have shown that it has no direct relationship with the increase or decrease in crime rates.
2. Punishment breeds anger, hostility, resentment, and antagonism; violence breeds violence.
3. Punishment is costly: the financial costs of the prison system have escalated year after year.
4. Punishment degrades, humiliates, and stigmatizes offenders.

5. Punishment may have serious consequences for offenders' families.
6. Punishment sacrifices the interests of offenders and victims to provide catharsis for the public.
7. Punishment focuses on the past rather than the future.
8. Punishment perpetuates rather than settles conflicts, generating further animosity and antagonism among the parties involved.
9. A justice system based on punishment victimizes victims by diverting resources that would be better used to compensate them and help them heal.

How would you counter these arguments to make the case that greater punishment is an appropriate justice model?

---

in Canada rose from $42.4 billion to over $85 billion even as the crime rate fell by roughly 27 per cent (Easton, Furness, & Brantingham, 2014, p. iii). The cost of crime includes victim losses, which make up over half the $85 billion total; the remainder is the cost of fighting and punishing crime. Of that amount, the greatest increases over the 10-year period have been in policing (44 per cent) and corrections (33 per cent) (Easton et al., 2014, p. iii).

Statistics like these underline the need for governments to find more cost-effective ways to control crime. They also suggest that a shift in emphasis from punishing offenders to preventing crime might be in order. As we saw in Chapter 1, only a small fraction of federal spending on criminal justice goes towards crime prevention—an area that, as Mackrael comments, "could improve public safety and reduce the number of victims" (Mackrael, 2013).

A comprehensive study conducted for the American Office of Juvenile Justice and Delinquency Prevention in the 1990s found that the "only way to substantially reduce serious and violent offending is through prevention and early intervention with youth who are on paths toward becoming serious violent chronic offenders" (Howell, 1995, p. 6). The report pointed out that the risk factors for violent crime lie in many different conditions, involving family, school, peer, and neighbourhood characteristics, and that these factors interact in ways that are not necessarily linear. However, it also noted that family, school, and peer groups can serve as protective factors. While they may have a minimal impact on an individual basis, collectively they can help to prevent high-risk youth from becoming chronic offenders.

As summarized by Kelly, Loeber, Keenan, and DeLamatre (1997), the study identified three "developmental pathways" that can lead to serious, violent, and chronic offending (see Figure 14.4). The first is the *authority conflict pathway*, where stubborn behaviour progresses to authority avoidance (e.g. staying out late, running away from home). The second, the *covert pathway*, develops when young people become secretive and then progress to overt behaviour such as property damage, which may in turn escalate to more serious acts (e.g. break-and-enter, fraud, and theft). Finally, the *overt pathway* begins with minor aggression and progresses to more serious violence (e.g. assault and sexual assault). According to

**BOX 14.6**    **FACTS AND FIGURES**  WHAT WORKS AND WHAT DOESN'T WHEN IT COMES TO CRIME PREVENTION

In the late 1990s, the US National Institute of Justice commissioned a team of criminologists, led by Lawrence W. Sherman, to evaluate the effectiveness of various crime control programs. They examined five types: community programs, family-based programs, school-based programs, policing, and criminal justice system programs. A summary of their findings is presented here.

## COMMUNITY PROGRAMS
What works:
- No community program had enough positive evaluations to be described as "working."

What's promising:
- Gang violence prevention.
- Community-based mentoring.
- After-school recreation.

What doesn't work:
- Gun buy-back programs.
- Community mobilization (e.g. lobbying against renewal of tavern liquor licences).

## FAMILY-BASED PROGRAMS
What works:
- Home visits for infants and preschoolers.
- Parent training or family therapy for high-risk adolescents and children.

What's promising:
- Battered women's shelters.
- Orders of protection for battered women.

What doesn't work:
- Home visits by police after domestic violence incidents, as these fail to reduce repeat violence.

## SCHOOL-BASED PROGRAMS
What works:
- For youth, programs aimed at building capacity to initiate and sustain innovation.
- Clarifying norms of behaviour and ensuring they are consistently enforced in schools.
- For substance abusers, training or coaching in thinking skills using behaviour modification or rewards and punishments.

What's promising:
- Use of small groups within a school setting that provide the opportunity for supportive interaction and greater flexibility to students' needs.
- Behaviour modification programs.

What doesn't work:
- Counselling and peer counselling.
- Alternative activities such as recreation and community services for substance abusers.
- Instructional programs focusing on information dissemination, fear arousal, and moral appeal.

## POLICING
What works:
- Increased police presence at "hot spots" for crime.
- Proactive arrest, drug testing, drunk driving programs.

What's promising:
- Community policing with community participation.
- Zero tolerance of disorder, in certain circumstances.
- Problem-oriented policing, generally.

What doesn't work:
- Neighbourhood Block Watch.
- Arrest of unemployed suspects for domestic assault.
- Community policing with no clear focus on crime-risk factors.

iStock.com/jeffclow

Keeping kids occupied with after-school activities such as sports (skateboarding, basketball, hockey, etc.), access to computers, and art projects is one of the more effective ways to prevent crime at the community level.

## CRIMINAL JUSTICE SYSTEM PROGRAMS

What works:

- Rehabilitation programs with particular characteristics.
- Incarceration of repeat offenders.

What's promising:

- Day fines.
- Juvenile after-school programs.
- Drug courts combining rehabilitation and criminal justice control.

What doesn't work:

- Rehab programs that use vague, non-directive, unstructured counselling.

- Programs that rely on shock intervention strategies.
- Programs with vague behavioural targets directed at low-risk offenders.

## CONCLUSIONS

- The only way to achieve substantial reductions in serious crime is to concentrate prevention efforts "in areas of concentrated poverty, . . . where homicide rates are 20 times the national average."
- Funding agencies must be willing to provide high-quality advice as to which programs work and how they are best implemented.

For details, see www.ncjrs.org/works.

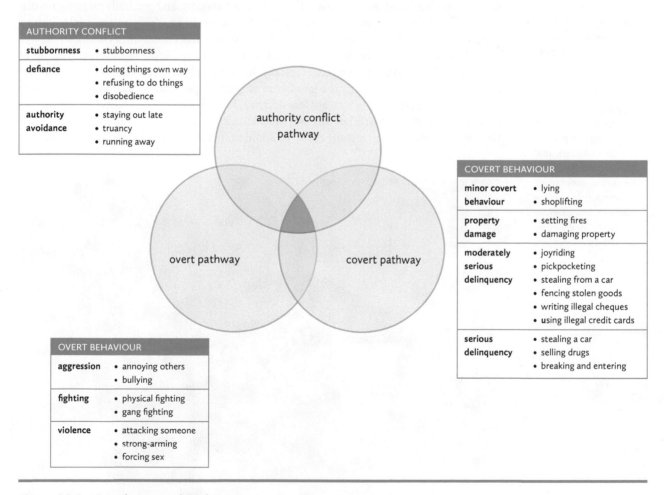

| AUTHORITY CONFLICT | |
| --- | --- |
| stubbornness | • stubbornness |
| defiance | • doing things own way<br>• refusing to do things<br>• disobedience |
| authority avoidance | • staying out late<br>• truancy<br>• running away |

| COVERT BEHAVIOUR | |
| --- | --- |
| minor covert behaviour | • lying<br>• shoplifting |
| property damage | • setting fires<br>• damaging property |
| moderately serious delinquency | • joyriding<br>• pickpocketing<br>• stealing from a car<br>• fencing stolen goods<br>• writing illegal cheques<br>• using illegal credit cards |
| serious delinquency | • stealing a car<br>• selling drugs<br>• breaking and entering |

| OVERT BEHAVIOUR | |
| --- | --- |
| aggression | • annoying others<br>• bullying |
| fighting | • physical fighting<br>• gang fighting |
| violence | • attacking someone<br>• strong-arming<br>• forcing sex |

**Figure 14.4  Developmental Pathways**

*Source:* Kelley, Loeber, Keenan, & DeLamatre, 1997, p. 14, Fig. 10.

Howell (1995), approximately 75 per cent of high-risk offenders follow one or more of these pathways. The study also lent support to other studies reporting that only a small proportion of young offenders—between 6 and 14 per cent, depending on the source—is responsible for approximately 70 per cent of serious and violent youth crime.

One of the prevention strategies suggested by this study was to encourage healthy beliefs and behaviours through programs such as the 1980s "Just Say NO to Drugs" campaign, in which young people were encouraged to experience a sense of involvement. However, that campaign ignored the larger social and psychological factors that lead to drug use, and today it is not generally considered effective (see e.g. Loeber & Burke, 2011).

Research from both sides of the Atlantic suggests that conventional strategies to control crime by, for example, hiring more police and imposing longer sentences are not fruitful (McLean & Applegate Pease, 2013). One alternative strategy that has been more effective in some places is to reduce the opportunities for crime (see Box 14.7).

Opportunity reduction can take three forms. Primary prevention involves addressing the environmental conditions that are thought to be directly related to crime risk and includes activities such as maintaining streets, fixing broken windows, and generally cleaning up disorganized communities. Initiatives include the Neighbourhood Watch program (also known variously as Block Watch, Apartment Watch, Home Watch, and Community Watch), which was started in the late 1960s in the United States in an effort to promote greater involvement of citizens in the prevention of crime. Typically, having local residents take responsibility for monitoring the crime problem is a good form of primary prevention, though there are risks. For instance, it may serve to increase fear of crime, leading some people to isolate themselves behind barred doors, fearful of any but their immediate friends and family members (see Bennett, Holloway, & Farrington, 2008). In addition, the program may lead to acts of citizen

**opportunity reduction**
Strategies designed to prevent crime by minimizing the opportunities for criminal activity to occur.

**primary prevention**
An opportunity reduction strategy that focuses on addressing the environmental conditions that promote crime by, for example, maintaining streets, fixing broken windows, and generally cleaning up disorganized communities.

© Ted Foxx / Alamy Stock Photo

The "Just Say NO to Drugs" campaign tried to engage youth as active participants in preventing drug use. Does the message resonate with you?

vigilantism, like the fatal shooting in Florida of Trayvon Martin, an unarmed teenager, by a local neighborhood watch coordinator in 2012. On this side of the border, former prime minister Stephen Harper came under criticism for supporting the idea that Canadians have a right to own a gun to ensure "a certain level of security," leading critics to warn that self-protection opens the door to vigilante justice carried out by untrained civilians (Perkel, 2015). In this way, as Fattah (1997, p. 294) observed, such an approach may actually "undermine the social democracy it wishes to protect."

While primary prevention focuses on environmental factors that give rise to crime, secondary prevention focuses on potential offenders and potential targets of crime, and consists of programs designed to cut off the pathways to crime among young people. For example, because of the known relationship between drug use and crime, secondary prevention programs have been developed to educate youth about the hazards of drugs. Other secondary prevention practices include patrolling crime "hot spots," conducting surveillance (natural and formal), and applying "target-hardening" strategies (e.g. installing deadbolts and house alarms). While these ideas are appealing, Lab (2013) observes that future criminologists will need to come to terms with *crime displacement*, which occurs when target-hardening simply causes offenders to move to a different location. As well, the idea of identifying potential offenders recalls the discussion of labelling in Chapter 8: what risks do you think over-predicting criminal behaviour might pose?

The final form of opportunity reduction is tertiary prevention. This strategy focuses on reducing rates of recidivism by preventing individuals who have already committed a crime from re-offending. In the United States, the chief strategy of tertiary prevention is incarceration, but in Canada it includes restorative justice initiatives, which we will discuss later in the chapter. While tertiary prevention does not prevent crime from occurring, it does reduce the risk of victimization by repeat offenders.

Another approach that has captured the attention of some Canadian scholars is social development, a primary prevention strategy that uses social or community-based programs to make people more aware of their risk of being victimized. It was one of the key approaches to

**secondary prevention**

An opportunity reduction strategy that focuses on identifying potential offenders and targets (people, places, situations, times, etc.) and intervening before a crime is committed.

**tertiary prevention**

An opportunity reduction strategy that focuses on preventing individuals who have already violated the law from re-offending.

**social development approach**

A primary prevention strategy in which community-based public education programs are used to inform people of the risks to their safety to encourage them to take appropriate steps to avoid becoming victims of crime.

---

**BOX 14.7**

**A CLOSER LOOK**
**Opportunity Reduction**

There are many ways of reducing the opportunities for crime:

- In 2013, REACH Edmonton, in partnership with YOUCAN, the Native Counselling Services of Alberta, the Edmonton Police Service, the Edmonton John Howard Society, and the Africa Centre, introduced their "WrapEd" program, designed to provide youth outreach and engagement, advocacy, and trauma counselling to young people aged 12–17 in communities where the risk of becoming involved in gangs is greatest (Public Safety Canada, 2015b).
- In the Netherlands, theft of motorized bicycles dropped by one-third after the introduction of a law requiring anyone driving such a vehicle to wear a helmet.
- After closed-circuit television cameras were installed

in French supermarkets, losses due to theft decreased by 33 per cent (Pease & Litton, 1984).
- The Australian Institute of Criminology's Research and Public Policy Service provides a list of opportunity reduction initiatives. For example, the Julalikari Night Patrol was set-up in the 1980s to break the cycle of violence associated with excessive alcohol consumption in a remote Aboriginal community. Volunteers on patrol are trained to mediate disputes before they escalate to violence, and admonish potential offenders in a culturally appropriate context (Grabosky & James, 1995).
- The Home Office in England has also promoted a wide range of opportunity reduction initiatives, including public education campaigns on domestic violence, convenience store robberies, and antisocial behaviour in local housing developments.

CTV News Toronto

Carding is the controversial police practice of stopping, questioning, and documenting people when no offence has been committed as a way of gathering intelligence in crime-prone neighbourhoods. Supporters say it is an important secondary prevention strategy that allows police to anticipate trouble in neighbourhoods with high crime rates; opponents call it a form of racial harassment that disproportionately targets young black men. What do you think?

**TERTIARY**
Intervene to
prevent those
who have committed
crimes from re-offending.

**SECONDARY**
Identify potential
offenders and intervene
before a crime is committed.

**PRIMARY**
Intervene to correct conditions
that could encourage crime.

Figure 14.5   Primary, Secondary, and Tertiary Prevention Strategies

---

**BOX 14.8**

**A CLOSER LOOK**
## Community Collaboration in Saskatchewan

In response to growing crime and social order problems in the province, the Saskatchewan Crime Prevention Police Practitioners (SCPPP)—a sub-committee of the province's chiefs of police—was formed in 2000. Drawing on the "broken window" theory developed by J.Q. Wilson and G. Kelling (see Kelling & Coles, 1996), the SCPPP seeks to address antisocial behaviour through proactive initiatives that include community building and that invite the co-operation of an assortment of human service providers.

In 2011, the SCPPP helped to develop the Community Mobilization Prince Albert (CMPA) model as a way to stop crime before it happens. A key aspect of the CMPA model is the "Hub," a committee of around 20 people representing a cross-section of CMPA members—police, health workers, social workers, corrections officers, and educators—who meet twice a week to discuss specific cases involving families and individuals with "acutely elevated risk factors" (BPRC, 2016) and devise immediate strategies. The second main component of the CMPA model is the COR, or "Centre of Responsibility," whose members use information gathered by the Hub to develop long-term community goals and initiatives.

Since it was pioneered in 2011, the CMPA model has been adopted in other jurisdictions in Saskatchewan and elsewhere. In 2012, it was implemented in Toronto as a means of fighting the city's then growing problem with violent crime (Paperny, 2012).

---

crime prevention identified in 2002 by the United Nations in its Guidelines for the Prevention of Crime. However, in a survey of 57 countries, the International Centre for the Prevention of Crime (or ICPC, based in Montreal) found that while more and more countries are embracing tertiary crime prevention methods, most jurisdictions still have not made crime prevention through primary and secondary strategies a major priority (Sagant & Shaw 2010; Waller, 2014).

Traditional efforts to identify and correct criminogenic social conditions have not proven very effective. However, the chances of success do seem to improve when police are more closely integrated into the community, and when the community participates in defining and solving problems (see Box 14.8).

There have been encouraging signs of willingness to invest in crime prevention shown by governments at both the federal and provincial levels. In 2011 the federal government budgeted approximately $112 million over a three-year period for the National Crime Prevention Strategy (Public Safety Canada, 2011). Two years earlier, the province of Alberta had earmarked $90 million over three years for its Safe Communities Initiative Fund (SCIF); the fund has, unfortunately, been discontinued following a major shift in provincial politics in 2014. Saskatchewan and Ontario are other provinces that have made pledges to invest in crime prevention programs and initiatives. The apparent willingness to invest in crime prevention is a welcome change in direction from some of the "tough on crime" measures introduced by the former Conservative government of Canada, including a $400 million commitment to hiring new police officers and increased penalties for offenders through mandatory minimum sentences.

## Politics and Criminal Law

*If we desire respect for the law, we must first make the law respectable.* (US Supreme Court associate justice Louis B. Brandeis, 1856–1941)

In 1973, Norval Morris suggested that criminal law in the future would be mainly administrative in nature, focusing on compensation and restitution rather than punishment. If that were the case, the law would no longer function primarily (as critical criminologists charge) to protect the interests of the elite, but would uphold values and norms of a more universal nature. More than forty years later, however, that vision still has not come true, at least in North America. In Canada we now have more than 90,000 laws covering substantive offences, while the United States has more than 250,000 such laws—even though it has been pointed out that increasing the number of criminal laws has served only to artificially inflate crime statistics (see Goff, 2014).

Many members of the criminal justice system are well aware that the current laws are ineffective. That system plays a crucial role in maintaining social order, but it does not make the laws that it enforces. Laws are made by governments, governments have political agendas, and, as Roberts, Stalans, Indermaur, and Hough (2003) point out, political agendas tend to be driven by public attitudes.

Even though official crime rates have declined since the mid-1990s, many members of the public still perceive crime to be omnipresent, largely because of media coverage. In order to stay in business, the news media need to offer stories that will pique the public's interest. Thus, along with features about sex and celebrities, they often focus on violent high-profile offenders and "crime waves" that tend to heighten people's sense of vulnerability even when the actual risk to them is very small. Even if all the information the media present is accurate, their coverage is not likely to be comprehensive, if only because most journalists are not experts in all the areas they cover, and both the time and the money required for research are limited. As a consequence, they may not be aware of all the relevant facts or angles, may misinterpret some of the information they find, and in some cases may be misled by sources. Thus, as Kappeler, Blumberg, and Potter (2004, p. 358) observe, media portrayals of crime and criminal justice tend to be more myth than fact; yet these myths "become mental filters through which social issues are sifted," feeding public misconceptions.

Many people, for example, continue to support law enforcement officials' requests for more police officers (and more high-tech equipment) to combat crime, even though research such as the now-iconic Kansas City Patrol Study of the 1970s has consistently shown that increasing police presence has no effect on crime rates (see Weisburd & Eck, 2004). In the same way, many people continue to believe that more laws and more prisons will make them safer, despite the evidence to the contrary. Recidivism data strongly indicate that imprisonment of offenders is not an effective deterrent; all imprisonment does is temporarily remove those individuals from society. Yet new institutions are continually being built to house more inmates for longer periods of time. For example, in 2011, Canada's federal government engaged in its largest prison expansion since the 1930s by funding over 570 new prison beds across the country, with a cost of around $32 million (Carlson, 2011). As for the judicial system, the offenders most likely to be punished are members of minority groups and the lower and middle classes who have committed minor crimes (Owusu-Bempah & Wortley, 2013), while white-collar/non-conventional offenders seldom face prosecution, let alone receive criminal sentences, even though their crimes are often more costly to society.

Public misconceptions also have the effect of preventing the adoption of new ideas. However well founded the criminological arguments for a different approach may be, politicians know that a tough-on-crime stance will attract a large segment of voters; the result is continued adherence to antiquated ideas of justice.

## Restorative Justice: The Way Ahead?

Throughout history, most societies have based their responses to crime on the ancient principle of retaliation: "an eye for an eye and a tooth for a tooth." Since this negative model has done little to control crime, perhaps it is time to try a more positive alternative.

As we saw in Chapter 3, one of the more promising ideas to gain momentum in the 1990s was the communitarian concept of restorative justice (Johnstone, 2011). Although it is still controversial (for a non-criminal example, see Box 14.9), Correctional Service Canada is actively promoting it through the Centre for Restorative Justice at Simon Fraser University, and the third week in November is now celebrated as "Restorative Justice Week" around the world.

The principles underlying the restorative justice approach include the following:

- As a communitarian philosophy, restorative justice emphasizes social rather than moral responsibility. Offenders are obliged to make some form of restitution—for example, to apologize or to provide financial compensation—to victims, and by extension to the community.
- Public shaming, which forces the offender to face his or her accuser and the accuser's supporters in a powerfully emotional setting, reduces the rates of re-offending, thereby helping the offender make a more successful return to the community (McAlinden, 2005).
- Whereas the punishment model sees crime as an abstract injury to the state that requires retribution, the restoration model sees it not as an abstraction but as an actual injury to a person and a community that must be repaired. Instead of revenge and retribution, it calls for emotional, physical, social, and spiritual restitution.
- The process of restitution should respect all parties involved—victim, offender, and agents of justice.

Even though the ideas underlying the restorative justice movement are sometimes taken as being new and innovative, Braithwaite (1998, p. 323) asserted that "restorative justice has been the dominant model of criminal justice throughout most of human history for all the world's people." Gavrielides (2011) and Mantle, Fox, and Dhami (2005) have supported this assertion with historical examples. In North America, the Mennonites were among the first to formally put restorative principles into practice. However, the Aboriginal people of Canada had practised restorative justice long before the arrival of Europeans, relying on informal social processes to reintegrate offenders into the community and gradually re-establish trust (see Gavrielides, 2015). Disputes were resolved through a process that emphasized healing for victims and offenders alike. The colonial state eradicated those cultural traditions, and in the course of the twentieth century Aboriginal people came to be significantly overrepresented not only in Canada's child welfare, juvenile justice, unemployment, and drug/alcohol treatment systems, but in its criminal justice system (Carrière, 2003). By 2013, when Aboriginal people accounted for roughly 4 per cent of the total population, they made up nearly one-quarter (23 per cent) of the federal inmate population, and "the incarceration rate for Aboriginal adults in Canada [was] estimated to be 10 times higher than the incarceration rate of non-Aboriginal adults" (Correctional Investigator Canada, 2013).

---

**BOX 14.9    WHAT DO YOU THINK?**

## The Dalhousie Dentistry School Controversy

In December 2014, the dentistry school at Dalhousie University in Halifax attracted national attention when it was discovered that 13 male students had made sexually violent and abusive comments about their female classmates on Facebook. When the university's president announced that he would take a restorative justice approach to the situation, many people found this response inadequate and called for the perpetrators to be expelled (Walsh, 2014).

Why do you think some people objected to the use of restorative justice in this situation? What are the advantages and disadvantages of this approach versus suspension or expulsion of the wrongdoers?

**restorative justice**
A direct and indirect mediation model that emphasizes restitution and community participation, aimed at rehabilitating offenders and reintegrating them back into their communities.

© Correctional Service Canada, 2016. Reproduced with the permission of the Minister of Public Woks and Government Services Canada, 2016.

The Okimaw Ohci Healing Lodge in Saskatchewan is one example of how traditional Aboriginal beliefs can be integrated into corrections. A women-only multi-level facility, it offers healing through Aboriginal teachings and ceremonies, contact with elders, and culturally relevant programs. The objective is to improve the women's prospects for reintegration into their families after release.

The current restorative justice principles in sentencing offenders can be traced to a 1999 ruling by the Supreme Court in a case known as "Gladue." In it, the court called on judges sentencing Aboriginal offenders to take into account the unique circumstances of Aboriginal people (including systemic discrimination) and to consider all available sanctions other than incarceration. The restorative justice approach today is reflected in a practice known as *circle sentencing*, in which an offender, having accepted responsibility for his or her act, meets with the victim(s), community elders, and representatives of the justice system to present his or her views of the offence, its consequences, and what will be required to make amends. Institutions such as the Tsuu T'ina Peacemaker Court in Alberta (Parker, 2004) and the Saskatchewan Cree Court follow the same basic model.

Associated in Canada primarily with Indigenous people (Goldbach, 2011), restorative justice is practised in many other communities and countries around the world under a variety of names: victim–offender reconciliation (VOR), victim–offender mediation (VOM), community justice circles (CJCs), reparative probation (RP), reintegrative shaming, and transformative justice. For more information, see Restorative Justice Online.

From a pragmatic perspective, however, wider implementation of restorative principles will not be easy. The Canadian Criminal Justice Association (CCJA), along with various provincial associations, is working to bridge the gap between theory and practice, but it remains to be seen whether there is enough broad public support to advance the political agenda (see the link for the CCJA in the Weblinks section below).

Nevertheless, if one thing is certain, it is that crime and criminology are constantly evolving, in Canada and around the world. We must have the courage to look beyond the status quo and continue to push the boundaries of both our understanding and our responses. Restorative justice initiatives offer a significant opportunity to integrate theoretical ideas with practice and to bridge the discontinuities between criminological theory and public policy.

## Summary

- Criminology must embrace an integrated, interdisciplinary approach to the study of human behaviour and criminological issues if it is to move forward as a discipline and to help create sound policy that effectively addresses crime in our society.
- In an increasingly globalized environment, criminologists need to embrace an international perspective that will allow them to make cross-national and cross-cultural comparisons.
- As Beccaria argued over 300 years ago, it is better to prevent crime than to punish it. Restorative justice may represent a way of accomplishing this task.
- Criminologists should feel morally and ethically bound to develop new approaches to understanding human behaviour while building and control models that universally respect human freedom and dignity.

## Discussion Questions

1. How do the four basic approaches to crime control reflect the relative and evolutive nature of crime? Which of them do you think is best suited to address criminological concerns?
2. What are the barriers to conducting comparative research? What are the advantages for criminology in trying to overcome them?
3. Why has the knowledge explosion in criminology been both a blessing and a curse? How can we begin to synthesize all this knowledge?
4. Based on your readings, and regardless of current trends, what do *you* think is the most effective strategy for crime control? With which perspective does it align?
5. Using the concept of restorative justice, what could we do at a local and national level to implement new policies of social control?

## Key Concepts

comparative criminology
conservative approach
critical approach
integrated and interdisciplinary approach
liberal approach
opportunity reduction

postmodernism
primary prevention
restorative justice
secondary prevention
social development approach
tertiary prevention

## Key Names

Ezzat Fattah (b. 1929)
Thorsten Sellin (1896–1994)

## Weblinks

**Real Justice: Restorative Responses to Crime and Wrongdoing**
The International Institute for Restorative Practices offers information on restorative justice and provides an extensive online library of articles on the topic.
www.realjustice.org

**About Restorative Justice**
The Correctional Service of Canada's website for restorative justice provides information and links to numerous other related sites.
www.csc-scc.gc.ca/restorative-justice/003005-0007-eng.shtml

**International Centre for the Prevention of Crime**
Based in Montreal, the ICPC offers extensive online resources on crime prevention.
www.crime-prevention-intl.org

**Community Safety and Crime Prevention**
Administered by the British Columbia Ministry of Justice, this page offers information on preventing child exploitation and crime related to gangs, as well as links to other government and non-government websites, including the National Crime Prevention Centre.
www.pssg.gov.bc.ca/crimeprevention

**Welcome to the Australian Institute of Criminology**
The website of the Australian Institute of Criminology includes links to sites addressing various criminological issues as well as crime prevention initiatives.
www.aic.gov.au

**Centre for Restorative Justice**
The website for Simon Fraser University's Restorative Justice Centre includes a current timeline of related events going on throughout Canada, as well as information on its world-renowned academic program.
www.sfu.ca/crj.html

# Glossary

**abduction**, also referred to as kidnapping, is the illegal apprehension of another person, typically for financial, personal, or political gain or for retribution. Legally, an abduction involves taking a person under the age of 16 and detaining him or her more than 6 metres from his or her residence for more than one hour, without authorization.

**Aboriginal crime groups** are organized crime groups started or operated in Canada by individuals within the First Nations, Métis, or Inuit community. These groups have been involved in crimes ranging from smuggling of cigarettes to running illegal gambling establishments.

**anomie** is a sociological term, coined by Émile Durkheim, that refers to a state of normlessness or breakdown in society. Anomie is usually attributed to decreased homogeneity, which provides a social environment conducive to crimes and criminality.

**arson** involves the destruction of one's own or another's property through the use of fire or an explosion. Arson involving one's own property may be committed for fraudulent purposes or by negligence. Once considered a form of vandalism, it is now defined as a separate offence.

**atavism** refers to a hereditary biological condition that supposedly renders a person incapable of living within the social norms of a society. The notion was first advanced by Cesare Lombroso, who believed that *atavistic* people were throwbacks to a more primitive time and were insufficiently evolved to live in a modern setting. A positivist, Lombroso believed atavistic people could be identified by certain distinguishing physical characteristics, including an asymmetrical face, an excessively large jaw, eye defects, a large nose, large ears, a receding forehead, long arms, and swollen lips.

**attention deficit hyperactivity disorder** (or ADHD) is a psychological and/or biological disorder that is characterized by restlessness and an inability to concentrate for periods of time. Many inmates are thought to suffer from some degree of ADHD.

**avoidance learning**, also known as **aversion therapy**, is a form of behavioural learning in which the individual learns to avoid an undesirable behaviour as a result of associating the fear of punishment with that behaviour.

**Badgley Report**, known fully as the Report of the Committee on Sexual Offences Against Children and Youths, was the first major Canadian study on the abuse of children and young people, released in 1984. It was released a year before the **Fraser Report** on pornography and prostitution.

**behavioural learning theory** is the psychological theory asserting that all behaviour is learned through some type of stimulus (negative or positive). It assumes that behaviour consists of determinable relationships, and that changes in behaviour are brought about through experience or practice.

**behaviour modification** is a psychological theory and treatment that emphasizes changing behaviour rather than personality. The process relies on a series of either rewards or undesirable punishments.

**biological determinism** is the idea that individual physical and mental characteristics are governed solely by heredity.

**biosocial factors** linked to criminal behaviour are factors arising from biological and social characteristics that predispose individuals to certain criminal acts.

**black market** is another term for **illicit market**.

**break-and-enter** (or **breaking and entering**) is a form of property crime that involves the illegal entry into a building or dwelling without permission and with the intention of committing a theft or an act of violence.

**Canadian Centre for Justice Statistics** (or the CCJS) is the agency responsible for collecting and compiling crime data on a wide range of criminological and criminal justice topics. Its findings are published in the *Juristat* bulletins.

**Canadian Urban Victimization Survey** (or the CUVS) was conducted during the 1980s and was the first major attempt to survey Canadians who had been victims of crime. The data generally show that certain crimes are far less reported than others.

**cartel** is an association of manufacturers or suppliers who have entered into an informal agreement to fix prices, to limit supply, and to minimize competition by various means, some of which may be illegal and may involve violence. Although cartels are prohibited by anti-trust laws in most countries, they continue to exist nationally and internationally.

**causality** (or **causation**) is the idea that one event is the result of one or more other events. Criminologists strive to identify causal relationships in the hope that if causes can be identified, action can be taken to prevent undesirable effects.

**classical conditioning**, sometimes known as **Pavlovian conditioning**, is a process of behaviour modification that encourages a subject to respond in a desired manner to a neutral stimulus by repeatedly presenting the stimulus along with an unconditioned stimulus that elicits the desired response. For example, a dog who is rewarded with a treat for sitting on command learns to sit when told to do so, even when the treat is no longer given; in this scenario, the neutral stimulus is the command, and the unconditioned stimulus is the treat.

**classical school of criminology** traces its origins to the work of Cesare Beccaria in 1764. It was premised on the idea that criminals were rational and capable of free will, and that the severity, swiftness, and certainty of punishment would therefore serve as an effective deterrent to crime.

**clearance rate** is the percentage of reported crimes that are solved over a fixed period of time. The rate varies considerably depending on the type of offence and is generally considered a reasonable indicator of the effectiveness of crime prevention strategies.

**cognition** is a term used in social psychology that refers to the processes we use to organize our thoughts and make sense of our environment. It comprises attention, perception, memory, and language.

**comparative criminology** is the cross-cultural and cross-national study of crime patterns and prevention strategies. Researchers look at what has been done and what has been learned elsewhere in an attempt to develop theories and strategies that cut across cultural and political boundaries.

**computer crime** is another term for **cybercrime**.

**concentric-circle theory** is an early model of human ecological theory, based on the premise that cities develop from the inner city to the suburbs in a predictable series of concentric rings, each encompassing a particular set of social and environmental characteristics. Applied to crime, the theory maintains that crime rates are highest in Zone 2 and decline in each successive ring.

**conflict crimes** are activities and behaviours that are not universally considered crimes, although they are legally defined as such. Examples include using marijuana for recreational purposes, procuring the services of a prostitute, and appearing topless in public (in some provinces). The opposite of conflict crimes is **consensus crimes**.

**conflict perspective** is a criminological approach that views laws as representing the interests of specific groups in society. It is often contrasted with the **consensus perspective**.

**conflict theory** is a theory asserting that crime is the product of social and/or economic disparities in society. It views people as social creatures who may resort to criminal activity when subjected to division and competition.

**consensual crimes** are unlawful activities involving people who have all given their consent as willing participants.

**consensus crimes** are activities and behaviours that are widely considered to be very harmful; as a result, there is strong support to sanction and control them. The opposite of consensus crimes is **conflict crimes**.

**consensus perspective** is a criminological approach that views laws as representing the interests of society generally. It is often contrasted with the **conflict perspective**.

**conservative approach** to crime control proposes to rely on the criminal justice system to deter and incapacitate criminals as a means of controlling crime; it originates in a belief that all humans possess the capacity for both good and evil. It is often compared with the **critical approach**, the **integrated and interdisciplinary approach**, and the **liberal approach**.

**conventional crimes** are the illegal activities that most commonly come to mind when we think of crime. They typically include violent crimes such as murder, robbery, and assault, as well as property crimes such as break-and-enter, motor-vehicle theft, and arson. Conventional crimes are often contrasted with **non-conventional crimes**.

**corporate crime** is illegal activity conducted by employees or officers of a business to benefit the financial performance or reputation of the company. It is slightly different to **white-collar crime**, which may directly benefit individuals within the company.

**correctional statistics** are data on people being held in federal and provincial corrections facilities. The data include such information as age, sex, offence, and prior convictions.

**correlation** (or **direct correlation**) is a statistical term used to refer to the observed association between two or more variables. A correlation occurs when two or more variables appear to change together, and may be either *positive* or *negative*. The higher a correlation between the variables, the greater the likelihood that they are associated in some way. For example, many prostitutes have a history of sexual abuse: in other words, there is a correlation between prostitution and sexual abuse. Note that a correlation does not imply **causality** or a causal relationship between the variables. For more information, see **negative correlation** and **positive correlation**.

**crime** is a socially constructed concept used to categorize certain behaviours as requiring formal control and warranting some form of social intervention.

**crime data** is a term referring to the information collected by criminal justice agencies and independent researchers to measure the frequency and severity of criminal events.

**crime funnel** is a metaphor used to describe the fact that the number of crimes processed decreases at successive levels of the justice system. The wide top of the funnel represents all the crime that has occurred; the number of cases that are officially processed by law enforcement, the courts, and corrections gets increasingly smaller, following the shape of the funnel as it becomes narrower. The difference between the absolute number of crimes and those that are officially processed is sometimes referred to as the **dark figure of crime**.

**crime prevention through environmental design** (or CPTED) is an integrated social ecological model that focuses on proactive strategies for preventing crime through changes to the physical environment—for example, installing bicycle racks in greater numbers and in well-lit areas as a way to decrease bike theft.

**crime rate** refers to the number of offences in a category recorded in a fixed ratio, such as per 100,000 people. The Uniform Crime Reports provide crime rates for most crimes.

**criminal harassment**, also known as **stalking**, is a criminal offence in which the offender intentionally and repeatedly follows a person with the intention of causing emotional and/or physical discomfort.

**criminalistics** is the science of crime detection and investigation, which today includes many areas of specialization, ranging from weapons to DNA analysis.

**criminal personality** is a personality type that, according to some theorists, is a characteristic shared by many offenders. Typified by such traits as antisocial behaviour, social immaturity, and nervous systems that do not condition well, it is thought to be correctable by those who subscribe to its existence.

criminologist is a behavioural scientist who specializes in identifying, classifying, and describing criminal behaviour.

criminology is an integrated, interdisciplinary science that studies human behaviour, crime causation, crime prevention, and the punishment and rehabilitation of offenders.

critical approach to crime control addresses both conventional and non-conventional crimes by attempting to eliminate structural inequalities brought on through capitalism. It is frequently discussed and compared with the **conservative approach**, the **integrated and interdisciplinary approach**, and the **liberal approach**.

culpable homicide is the term for those forms of **homicide** that are considered criminal offences. It is contrasted with **non-culpable homicide**.

cultural transmission theory, also known as cultural deviance theory, is a sociological theory that views crime as a socially learned behaviour that is transmitted through successive generations, especially in disorganized urban settings. It is sometimes discussed together with **social disorganization theory**.

cyberbullying is the use of e-mail, text messages, social networking sites, and other communication technology to repeatedly harass or intimidate others.

cybercrime, sometimes called computer crime, is any illegal activity that involves the use of computer technology or the Internet as the means of committing the crime. It includes illegal damage and destruction of data, theft of software via unlawful copying, and use of computers to gain illegal access to information or to steal money.

cyberespionage is the illicit activity of hacking into the computer networks of a rival government or company in order to gain access to confidential information.

cyberterrorism consists of politically motivated attacks against private, government, or corporate computer systems in order to cause widespread social, political, or economic instability.

dark figure of crime is a term coined by British criminologists Richard Hood and Richard Sparks in 1970 to refer to crime that goes undetected or unreported by official sources.

date rape is a form of sexual assault that involves unlawfully coercing sexual interactions with someone against his or her will within the context of a dating relationship.

decriminalization is the process of reducing or removing criminal penalties attached to an act without actually making it legal.

demonic possession is the idea that deviant or criminal behaviour is caused by some supernatural spirit or power acting beyond the individual's control.

determinism is a philosophical doctrine that maintains that our decisions and actions are decided by external causes that act on our character. It denies the existence of free will and, according to some, moral responsibility for criminal behaviour.

deterministic means having to do with **determinism**.

deterrence theory is the belief that the threat of punishment can prevent people from committing a crime. It is based on the doctrine of free will, the idea that people consciously weigh the probabilities of pleasure against the risks of future pain.

Proponents of the theory thus believe that people choose to obey laws after calculating the consequences and gains of their action.

deviance is a sociological term that refers to behaviour that violates a social norm but that is not necessarily prohibited by law. For example, it is impolite to stick one's tongue out at someone, but it is not a crime to do so.

diathesis–stress model is an approach to understanding and treating substance abusers that views compulsive behaviour as a product of the interaction between an individual's predisposition to the behaviour and stress from life experiences.

differential association theory is a sociological theory positing that criminal behaviour is socially learned through frequent exposure to negative influences.

differential reinforcement theory is a sociological theory developed by C.R. Jeffery in the 1960s. It views crime as a learned behaviour reinforced by its consequences. Although sharing a number of parallels with **differential association** theory, it has received far less attention.

direct correlation is another term for **correlation**.

discretion is a criminal justice system term denoting the process by which an authority exercises his or her judgement rather than following specific rules and facts. In the case of judges, discretion may be exercised only within certain bounds: for example, for the crime of identity theft (s. 402.2 of the Canadian Criminal Code), the court has the discretion to administer an imprisonment term of not more than five years.

ecological school of criminology involves the study of how elements of the physical environment (from buildings to climate and social settings) interact to create a criminal environment.

ego, in Freudian psychodynamic theory, is our rational state, responsible for making daily decisions. It mediates between the id and superego and is the conscious aspect of our personality. The term is often discussed together with **id** and **superego**.

Elizabeth Fry Society was created by Elizabeth Fry (née Gurney) in the mid-1800s in response to the perceived need to promote prison reform for women prisoners. Elizabeth Fry Societies can be found across Canada.

empiricism is the principle that knowledge is acquired only through experience. When applied to criminology, it is guiding principle of researchers who rely on an experimental approach to the study of crime and criminality. The concept is often compared with **rationalism**.

epigenetics is a term used to describe external (i.e. environmental) modifications to DNA that can effectively turn the gene "on" or "off." These modifications do not alter the DNA sequence but rather affect how cells "read" genes.

etiology of crime refers to the study of its origins or causes.

evolutive is a term coined by Maurice Parmelee in 1918 to capture the idea that the nature and characteristics of crime can change over time. For example, pickpocketing was once a common way for thieves to steal money and credit cards from individuals; today, money and credit card information are more likely to be stolen using computers, reflecting the evolutive nature of theft.

**false positive** (or **false alarm**) is a research methodology concept that refers to in incorrect test result, showing the presence of a condition that does not exist and leading to risk of making a prediction about an event/individual that may not be true.

**feminist perspective** is a general term encompassing a variety of sociological approaches to the study of crime that focus on the female offender and the female victim. The feminist perspective emphasizes the patriarchal bias in society and calls for greater equality between men and women within the criminal justice system and within the study of criminology generally.

**Fraser Report** is the 1985 report of the Special Committee on Pornography and Prostitution (SCPP), frequently called the Fraser Committee, whose mandate was to review the status of prostitution and pornography and their related regulatory laws. Specifically, the committee was tasked with examining prostitution with reference to loitering and street solicitation, as well as the operation of bawdy houses. It was released a year after the **Badgley Report** on sexual offences against children and youths.

**fraud** is the unlawful use of cheating or deception for personal financial gain.

**General Social Survey** (or the GSS) is a series of annual surveys initiated by Statistics Canada in 1985 to gather data on social trends and to provide information on specific policy issues of current or emerging interest. In general, the GSS focuses on a different topic each year, and each topic is repeated every five years.

**general theory of crime** is a sociological perspective asserting that criminal behaviour is a product of defective socialization processes that make it difficult for a potential offender to exercise self-control. It is a modification of the **social control theory** and shares much in common with **power–control theory**.

**hate crime** is a crime in which the perpetrator's conduct is motivated by bias or prejudice toward the actual or perceived race, colour, religion, national origin, gender, disability, or sexual orientation of another group or individual.

**homicide** is the act of deliberately and in most cases unlawfully causing the death of another person. **Culpable homicide** includes first- and second-degree murder, manslaughter, and infanticide. **Non-culpable homicide** includes deaths caused in self-defence and is not a criminal offence.

**honour killing** is homicide committed against a relative (usually female) who has supposedly brought dishonour upon the family. Honour killing is associated especially with cultures that consider family honour to be compromised by sexual misdemeanours and relationships with people from outside the culture.

**human trafficking** is the trade in human beings, carried out through force or deception, for the purpose of sexual exploitation or forced labour.

**hypothesis** is an idea about a situation or a relationship between variables that a researcher sets out to prove or disprove. The hypothesis thus serves as the starting point for inquiry and research.

**id**, in Freudian psychodynamic theory, refers to the primitive, instinctual urges of our behaviour that address our primal needs for gratification (e.g. food, drink, and procreation). The term is often discussed together with **ego** and **superego**.

**id**, **ego**, and **superego** are three aspects of personality, according to Freud's psychoanalytic approach. The id refers to the primitive, instinctual urges that address the primal need for gratification; the ego is the rational aspect that mediates between the id and superego and is the conscious aspect of personality; the superego represents the moral and ethical dimension of personality.

**identity fraud** is the illegal use of the personal information of another person (living or dead) for fraudulent purposes, such as accessing the other person's bank account, harming the reputation of the person, or avoiding detection or arrest.

**identity theft** is the act of obtaining or possessing another person's name and personal identity information without consent in order to commit an indictable offence that involves fraud or deceit. The Criminal Code (s. 402.1) defines identity information as any information "that is commonly used ... to identify an individual, including a fingerprint, voice print, retina image, iris image, DNA profile, name, address, date of birth, written signature, electronic signature, digital signature, user name, credit card number, debit card number, financial institution account number, passport number, Social Insurance Number, health insurance number, driver's licence number, or password."

**illicit market**, also called the **black market**, is the free market for illegal goods and services, including prostitution, illegal drugs, contraband computer software, off-market cigarettes, and so on. The illicit market may be made up of otherwise law-abiding citizens in countries where certain consumer goods are impossible or very expensive to obtain legally. The illicit market is serviced primarily by organized crime groups.

**indictable offences** are offences that are considered more serious than **summary offences** and usually carry a more serious penalty. They include such crimes as murder, robbery, and assault. Sentences for indictable offences are usually served in federal institutions.

**integrated and interdisciplinary approach** to criminology attempts to combine two or more theories that are considered complementary (e.g. strain theory and differential association theory) as well as knowledge from at least two disciplinary perspectives (e.g. biology, economics, law, psychology, and sociology) in order to produce theories of behaviour that can better serve as the basis for intervention and prevention strategies.

*Juristat*, a regular publication of the Canadian Centre for Justice Statistics, is considered the most authoritative source of criminal justice statistics in Canada. Its issues address a broad range of criminal justice topics using data from Statistics Canada.

**just deserts** is a punishment model asserting that an individual who commits an offence deserves to be punished for it. The more formal term for the concept is **retribution**.

**kidnapping** is an informal term for **abduction**.

**labelling theory** is a sociological explanation of crime, associated with Howard Becker, that proposes that negative labelling, either direct or indirect, can predispose people to feel like outcasts, increasing the likelihood that they will engage in deviant or criminal behaviour.

**left-realism** is a theoretical approach that emerged in the mid-1980s in response to law-and-order movements. It seeks to understand the implications of crime control policies rather than the causes of crime and emphasizes the importance of crime prevention strategies.

**liberal approach** to crime control proposes to control crime by alleviating social inequalities and providing legitimate opportunities for everyone, originating in the belief that humans are naturally and fundamentally good. It is often discussed and compared with the **conservative approach**, the **critical approach**, and the **integrated and interdisciplinary approach**.

**life course theory** is an integrated theory that involves the study of changes in the offending pattern of an individual over the course of his or her life. Researchers attempt to identify differentiating factors that predispose individuals to criminal activity.

**lifestyle theory** asserts that some people experience a greater risk of being victims of crime because of their lifestyle habits and their patterns of behaviour (e.g. frequenting certain public places known to be home to a criminal element).

**low arousal** is a condition in which an individual experiences lower than normal emotional arousal to external stimuli, often leading to restlessness, impulsivity, and sensation-seeking. Low arousal, which may result from a poorly functioning automatic nervous system, has been linked to antisocial personality disorder and **attention deficit hyperactivity disorder**.

**money laundering** is the illegal act of converting money or goods obtained through crime into a less suspicious form in order to conceal their origins and provide a legitimate way to account for the revenue.

**moral development theory** is a psychological theory that asserts that morality develops in stages according to how we are able to meet certain needs at different periods of life. Criminals are thought to exhibit a lower level of moral development.

**moral entrepreneurs** are people who use their power and influence to shape the legal process to their advantage, typically by arousing concern over issues they have identified as social problems that must be addressed.

**moral insanity** is a theory of mental illness proposed in 1835 by Isaac Ray, who argued that an offender's ability to reason could be temporarily suspended. Widespread acceptance of this idea made it possible for physicians to offer medical testimony in court cases. Since 1954 the concept has been entrenched in the Durham Rule, which states that an offender can be considered not criminally responsible of a crime judged to have been the product of a mental illness.

**moral panic** is a sociological term that refers to widespread and often exaggerated public concern over crimes associated with morality, such as prostitution, pornography, and gambling.

**motor-vehicle crime** is a term that covers the broader range of offences involving a car or truck etc., including not just theft *of* a vehicle but theft *from* a vehicle and criminal damage to a vehicle.

**negative correlation** is a direct correlation in which an increase in one variable is associated with a decrease in another variable. It is the opposite of **positive correlation**. See the definition of **correlation**.

**neoclassical school of criminology** promotes the view that different situations or circumstances can make it impossible to exercise free will. These circumstances, if they can be identified, can be used to exempt the accused from conviction.

**neopositivist school** is an approach to criminal justice popular between the 1930s and 1960s, which focused on the development of rational penal policy, emphasizing the systematic resocialization of offenders through treatment and rehabilitation. It succeeded the positivist movement associated with the school of social defence.

**net widening** is a term coined in the 1970s by critical criminologists to explain how the criminal justice system would use alternatives to conventional crime control to divert prospective offenders from the criminal justice system. More generally, it refers to using greater social control mechanisms to expand the state's control over behaviour.

**neurocriminology** is the study of the interaction between social and biological factors as they relate to crime.

**neutralization** is the theory that criminals, in order to commit an offence, must first suppress, or "neutralize," their internal moral obligation to abide by the law. According to the theory, there are certain neutralization techniques that enable criminals to temporarily overcome their natural hesitation to commit an offence. The theory is based on ideas developed in the 1960s by David Matza and Gresham Sykes, who postulated that young offenders follow conventional values most of the time while occasionally "drifting" into periods of illegal behaviour by neutralizing the legal and moral values of the act. The theory has since been used to explain other types of criminal behaviour, including corporate crime.

**non-conventional crimes** are those illegal acts that most people tend not to associate with crime and that are often not pursued by the criminal justice system. They include organized crime, political crime, and cybercrime. The term is frequently contrasted with **conventional crimes**.

**non-culpable homicide** refers to deaths caused in self-defence, which are not considered a criminal offence. It is the opposite of **culpable homicide**, which is described at the definition for **homicide**.

operationalization involves defining criminological concepts or events so that they can be observed and measured in a scientific manner.

opportunity reduction refers to strategies designed to prevent crime by minimizing the opportunities for criminal activity to occur. The main strategies for opportunity reduction are classified as **primary prevention, secondary prevention**, and **tertiary prevention** strategies (*see* **prevention**).

organized crime is illegal activity conducted by individuals or groups acting in consort. Crimes commonly committed by organized crime groups include extortion, fraud, theft, smuggling, and the sale of illicit products.

paradigm shift is a sociological term that refers to the process that takes place when a prevailing model or theoretical orientation changes in a fundamental way.

paraphilia is a condition characterized by abnormal sexual desires, typically involving activities, situations, or objects that most people do not consider sexually arousing.

Pavlovian conditioning is another term for **classical conditioning**.

peacemaking theory is a humanistic approach to crime control that emphasizes reconciliation through mediation and dispute settlement, rather than punishment and retribution.

pedophilia is a psychological disorder in which an adult (or older adolescent) is sexually aroused primarily by underage (usually prepubescent) children.

penology is the study of how crime is punished.

plea bargain is an arrangement between the defence and the prosecution in which the accused agrees to plead guilty in in return for some benefit, such as a lesser sentence.

political economy perspective is a social framework with roots in feminist theory. Used to explain prostitution, it emphasizes the social inequalities that force some women to turn to prostitution out of economic necessity.

pornography is the explicit description or representation of sexual activity. In some circumstances, such as when it involves the exploitation of children, it is a type of public order offence prohibited by law.

positive correlation is a direct correlation in which an increase in one variable is associated with an increase in another variable. It is the opposite of **negative correlation** (*see* **correlation**).

positivist school of criminology is a school of thought asserting that the study of crime should emphasize the individual. Its adherents rely on the scientific method to measure behaviour quantitatively and focus on treatment and rehabilitation over punishment as a means of correcting behaviour.

postmodernism is a theoretical framework derived from critical criminology that essentially rejects the self-evident reality of distinctions made by conventional scientific knowledge and/or common sense.

power–control theory is a sociological perspective that focuses on how power dynamics, patriarchy, and gender role socialization within the family contribute to delinquency and crime. It is a modification of **social control theory** and has much in common with the **general theory of crime**.

prevention of crime is an **opportunity reduction** strategy that focuses on proactive ways to forestall crimes before they occur. There are three major types of prevention. Primary prevention involves addressing the conditions in the environment and includes such things as maintaining streets, fixing broken windows, and generally cleaning up disorganized communities. Secondary prevention involves identifying targets (in terms of people, places, situations, time, etc.) and trying to prevent the target from being victimized. Tertiary prevention is a type of prevention used for individuals who have already violated the law or situations where crimes have already occurred; the focus is on reducing the recidivism rate.

primary deviance is a sociological term for deviant acts or behaviour that contravene societal norms but that have not been socially labelled as deviant. It is frequently compared with **secondary deviance**.

primary prevention is an opportunity reduction strategy described in the definition for **prevention**.

procuring is the act of arranging for, recruiting, or forcing a person to act as a prostitute, providing sexual services to another in exchange for money. It is illegal under section 268.3 of the Criminal Code.

property crime constitutes a broad range of offences involving property, including breaking and entering, fraud, theft, and motor vehicle theft.

prostitution is the practice or occupation of engaging in sexual services in exchange for money.

protection racket is a criminal arrangement in which a business is provided with protection in exchange for a regular fee, typically paid to an individual or group that has threatened violence or other retribution if the payment is not paid. The protection racket is a scheme typical of organized crime groups, especially the Mafia.

psychoanalysis is a treatment developed by Sigmund Freud to resolve internal conflict and tension resulting from certain childhood experiences.

psychodynamic theory was developed by Sigmund Freud as a way to understand how the conscious and unconscious mind shape human personality and motivation. Applied to crime, it views criminal behaviour as the expression of internal conflict stemming from unresolved, often unconscious experiences during childhood. These conflicts can be resolved through **psychoanalysis**.

psychopathy is a personality disorder characterized by a lack of empathy and remorse, an inability to learn from experience, low arousal levels, and antisocial behavior. A growing body of literature suggests that many chronic criminal offenders suffer from some degree of psychopathy.

public-order crimes are activities that are considered immoral or harmful, even though they are typically engaged in consensually by willing participants. Because they involve a degree of compliance on the victim's part, they are frequently described as "victimless." They include gambling, prostitution, pornography, substance abuse, and vandalism.

**qualitative research** is research designed to study characteristics that cannot be measured or counted. It is associated with the *Versteben* approach of sociologist Max Weber and is typically contrasted with **quantitative research**.

**quantitative research** is research designed to amass statistics or data by examining characteristics that can be readily measured or counted. It is typically contrasted with **qualitative research**.

**random error** is an error that occurs during data collection as a result of some unforeseen intervening variable; a random error is not predictable. It is often compared with **systematic error**.

**rationalism** is the principle that some kinds of knowledge are innate while others can be acquired through reasoning; in other words, it is a belief in the ability of individuals to determine the reality of a situation through common sense. The concept is often compared with **empiricism**.

**recidivism** is a term that describes the behaviour of a convicted criminal who reoffends, especially repeatedly.

**reintegrative shaming** is a correctional philosophy, introduced by John Braithwaite, that advocates the use of public shaming and/or public acceptance of one's wrongdoing as a way of having offenders re-enter general society.

**relative**, as applied to crime, describes the idea that the meaning and nature of crime can vary over time and from place to place.

**reliability** in research methodology refers to the likelihood that a relationship between two or more variables observed in one study can or will be observed consistently in other studies attempting to replicate and confirm the original study's findings.

**restorative justice** is a direct and indirect mediation model that emphasizes restitution and community participation with the aim of restoring a sense of community and rehabilitating offenders so that they can be reintegrated back into their communities.

**retribution** is punishment considered morally right and fully deserved. It is informally referred to as **just deserts**.

**routine activity theory (RAT)** is a sociological explanation of crime introduced by Lawrence Cohen and Marcus Felson in 1979. They argued that crime is a predictable function of normal activities of daily living, and that victimization is greater when three elements converge: the presence of a motivated offender or offenders; the availability of a suitable target or targets; and the absence of capable guardians.

**sampling** is the process of selecting a group of research subjects that is representative of the entire population under investigation. Effective sampling will produce results that can be generalized to the broader population.

**secondary deviance** is a sociological term for deviant acts or behaviour that results from labelling. It is often compared with **primary deviance**.

**secondary prevention** is an opportunity reduction strategy described in the definition for **prevention**.

**self-report studies** involve asking individuals to voluntarily disclose whether they have ever committed an offence. These studies represent an unofficial source of crime data but a very useful one in some contexts, such as youth crime, a great deal of which goes undetected.

**sexual exploitation** is the illegal act of sexual touching or invitation to sexual touching with a young person when the offender is in a position of trust or authority or when the victim is in a position of dependency on the offender.

**sexual interference** is the illegal act of touching, directly or indirectly, any part of the body of a person under the age of 16 for sexual purposes. There are some exceptions depending, for instance, on the specific ages of the parties involved and whether or not the activity is consensual.

**social control theory** is a social-process theory asserting that criminal behaviour stems from a breakdown in self-control sparked by exposure to criminal opportunities.

**social development approach** is a primary prevention strategy in which community-based public education programs are used to inform people of the risks to their safety and to encourage them to take appropriate steps to avoid becoming victims of crime.

**social disorganization theory** is a sociological theory that defines deviance and crime as consequences of a breakdown of social control bonds in areas characterized by social and economic instability. It is sometimes discussed together with **cultural transmission theory**.

**social structure** is a sociological concept used to describe consistent and stable patterns of social interaction.

**soliciting** is the illegal activity of communicating with another person in a public place for the purpose of offering or providing sexual services as a prostitute.

**somatotyping** is a technique used for categorizing the behaviours or temperaments of individuals based on specific body types or physique.

**stalking** is another term for **criminal harassment**.

**strain theory** is a sociological theory, associated with Robert K. Merton, that interprets emotional turmoil and conflict as results of being unable to achieve desired goals through legitimate means.

**summary offences** are considered less serious than **indictable offences**. Penalties are restricted a maximum $5,000 fine and a maximum six months prison sentence, which is typically served in a provincial (as opposed to federal) institution.

**superego**, in Freudian psychodynamic theory, represents the moral and ethical dimension of our personality. It is the part of our unconscious personality that acts as our conscience. The term is often discussed together with **ego** and **id**.

**symbolic interactionism** is a sociological approach to studying behaviour, associated with Charles Horton Cooley, that focuses on the symbolic value of words and gestures in everyday social interactions.

**systematic error** is an error in data collection that the researcher has been able to anticipate and account for. When collecting data, the observer is aware of the approximate error in the reliability of the observation. It is often contrasted with **random error**.

**terrorism** involves the use of propaganda, violence, or dangerous acts against an organization, an agency, or a state for the purpose of obtaining concessions for a deeply held personal or political cause.

**tertiary prevention** is an opportunity reduction strategy described in the definition for **prevention**.

**theft** is a type of property crime that involves the unlawful taking of property or services that belong to another person, a business, or an organization, typically without the intention to return it.

**token economy** is a reinforcement strategy used by behavioural therapists in which participants are given certain symbolic rewards (poker chips, gold stars, or other "tokens") for desired behaviour.

**transnational crime** involves criminal acts or transactions that violate the laws of more than one country. Examples include international drug trafficking, human smuggling, terrorism, money laundering, and various organized crime activities that cross national boundaries.

**triangulation** is a research methods technique that involves using more than one source of data to assess the validity of what is being observed.

**Trojan horse** is a computer program designed to damage a local computer system when the software is activated by the user in the course of performing some other, non-threatening task. The term is borrowed from the legendary Greek battle in which the attacking Greek army was able to enter the heavily fortified city of Troy by hiding within a large wooden horse left as a gift outside the city walls.

**Uniform Crime Reporting** (or UCR) is the system that compiles the records of all crimes substantiated by police in Canada. UCR data include the number of criminal incidents, the clearance status of those incidents, and persons-charged information. Together, UCR data represent a continuous historical record of crime statistics dating back to 1962.

**unofficial (crime) data** is a term pertaining to crime data that are not collected by official criminal justice agencies, including self-report data, victimization data, and field observation data. The research is usually conducted by academics and/or research organizations with no specific regularity and essentially serves interests of the host rather than the general public. This type of data is usually used to elucidate existing official data and verify the validity of official sources.

**utilitarianism** is an ethical doctrine associated with Jeremy Bentham and J.S. Mill and the classical school of criminology. Based on the notion that actions are right if they benefit the majority, it states that laws should be designed to deliver the greatest good or benefit to the greatest number of people.

**vagrancy** is the crime of being intentionally unemployed and therefore having no lawful means of supporting oneself or one's family.

**validity**, in research methodology, pertains to the likelihood that relationships being observed and measured are in fact real.

*Verstehen* is a term used by German sociologist Max Weber to refer to social scientists' efforts to understand both the intent and the context of human action. It is associated with qualitative research.

**victim impact statement** (or VIS) is a statement written by the victim of a crime describing the loss or harm the victim has suffered as a result of the offender's behaviour. It is admissible in court and may be read by the victim (or by another person on the victim's behalf) during the sentencing phase of a trial.

**victimization surveys** are conducted by collecting data from individuals who have been victims of crimes, or in some cases from individuals who know someone who has been a victim of crime. Victimization surveys are a source of **unofficial crime data**.

**victimless crime** is illegal activity in which no identifiable person or group is harmed. The term has been applied both to **public-order** or **consensual crimes** such as prostitution and gambling, in which the parties involved are willing participants, and to **corporate crimes**, where the victim is a faceless corporate entity.

**victimology** is a sub-field of criminology that focuses on the relationship between victims and perpetrators of crimes, against the backdrop of social institutions such as the criminal justice system. The term was coined by American psychiatrist Fredric Wertham in 1948.

**victim precipitation theory** states that some people, through their actions (or lack of actions), present themselves as potential targets for victimization. In other words, the victim is a direct, positive precipitator of the crime.

**Violence Against Women Survey** (or the VAWS) was a 1993 survey of over 12,000 Canadian women aged 18 and older, which examined the safety of women both inside and outside the home, focusing on issues such as sexual harassment, sexual violence, physical violence, and perceptions of fear.

**violent crime** is a general category of crime that includes offences such as homicide, attempted murder, robbery, assault, and sexual assault. Violent crimes are those that involve the physical violation of a person, and most are **indictable offences**.

**white-collar crime** refers to business-related crime committed by employees and officers of a company who take advantage of their professional status for personal and/or corporate gain. White-collar crimes include theft, fraud, insider trading, and embezzlement. It is slightly different to **corporate crime**, which benefits the company but does not directly benefit individuals.

**XYY chromosome theory** is a theory asserting that there is a relationship between the extra Y chromosome found in some males and a propensity toward criminal or antisocial behaviour.

# References

Abadinsky, H. (2012). *Organized crime* (10th edn). Boston, MA: Cengage Learning.

Adams, D. (2007). *Why do they kill? Men who murder their intimate partners*. Nashville, TN: Vanderbilt University Press.

Adams, J. (1976). *Learning and memory: An introduction*. New York: Dorsey Press.

Adams, R. (1973). "Differential association and learning principles revisited." *Social Problems, 20*, 458–70.

Adams, S. (1998, January 28). "Diet found to play role in attention deficit disorder." *Calgary Herald*, p. B4.

Adlaf, E.M., Begin, P., & Sawka, E. (Eds) (2005). *Canadian Addiction Survey (CAS): A national survey of Canadians' use of alcohol and other drugs: Prevalence of use and related harms: Detailed report*. Ottawa, ON: Canadian Centre on Substance Abuse.

Adler, F. (1975). *Sisters in crime: The rise of the new female criminal*. New York: McGraw-Hill.

Adomanis, M. (2013, October 18). "Russians are finally drinking less (really)." Forbes. (Online).

Afifi, T.O., Cox, B.J., Martens, P.J., Sareen, J., & Enns, M.W. (2010, March/April). "The relationship between problem gambling and mental and physical health correlates among a nationally representative sample of Canadian women." *Canadian Journal of Public Health, 101*(2), 171–5.

Agiesta, J. (2015, June 30). "Poll: Majorities back Supreme Court rulings on marriage, Obamacare." CNN. (Online).

Aichhorn, A. (1935). *Wayward youth*. New York: Viking Press.

Akers, R., & Jennings, W.G. (2009). "Social Learning Theory." In M. Miller (Ed.), *21st century criminology: A reference book*. Thousand Oaks, CA: Sage.

Akers, R.L. (1973). *Deviant behavior: A social learning approach*. Belmont, CA: Wadsworth.

Akers, R.L., & Sellers, C.S. (2013). *Criminological theories: Introduction, evaluation, and application* (6th edn). New York: Oxford University Press.

Akman, D.D., & Normandeau, A. (1967). "The measurement of crime and delinquency in Canada." *Criminal Law Quarterly, 9*, 323–8.

Albanese, J.S. (1996). "Looking for a new approach to an old problem: The future of obscenity and pornography." In R. Muraskin & A.R. Roberts (Eds), *Visions for change: Crime and justice in the twenty-first century* (pp. 60–72). Upper Saddle River, NJ: Prentice-Hall.

——. (2014). *Organized crime in our times* (6th edn). London and New York: Routledge.

Alberta Solicitor General and Criminal Intelligence Service Alberta. (2002, June). "Organized serious crime initiatives. Business Plan 2002–2005." Edmonton, AB: Criminal Intelligence Service Alberta.

Aldred, K. (2004). "Street-gang savvy." *Gazette, 66*(2), 17–19.

Allen, M. (2014). "Police-reported hate crime in Canada, 2012." *Juristat*. Statistics Canada cat. no. 85-002-X. Ottawa, ON: Minister of Industry.

Allen, M., & Boyce, J. (2013). "Police-reported hate crime in Canada, 2011." *Juristat*. Statistics Canada cat. no. 85-002-X. Ottawa, ON: Minister of Industry.

Alter, Susan. (1996). *Violence on television*. Ottawa, ON: Library of Parliament.

American Academy of Child and Adolescent Psychiatry. (2011). "Facts for families: TV violence and children." (Online).

Amir, M. (1971). *Patterns in forcible rape*. Chicago, IL: University of Chicago Press.

Ancel, M. (1994). "Social defence." In J.E. Jacoby (Ed.), *Classics of criminology* (Chapter 41). Prospect Heights, IL: Waveland Press.

——. (2001). *Social Defense* (reprinted edn). London: Routledge.

Anderson, C.A., & Bushman, B.J. (2001)." Effects of violent video games on aggressive behavior, aggressive cognition, aggressive affect, physiological arousal, and prosocial behavior: A meta-analytic review of the scientific literature." *Psychological Science 12*(5), 353–9. doi: 10.1111/1467-92800.00366

——, & ——. (2002). "Human aggression." *Annual Review of Psychology, 53*, 27–51.

Anderson, C.A., & Dill, K.E. (2000). "Video games and aggressive thoughts, feelings, and behavior in the laboratory and in life." *Journal of Personality and Social Psychology, 78*, 772–90.

Anderson, G.S. (2007). *Biological influences on criminal behavior*. Boca Raton, FL: CRC Press.

Andrews, D.A., & Bonta, J. (2010). *The psychology of criminal conduct* (5th edn). Providence, NJ: LexisNexis Group.

Andrews, D.A., Bonta, J., & Hoge, R.D. (1990). "Classification for effective rehabilitation: Rediscovering psychology." *Criminal Justice and Behavior, 17*, 19–52.

"Another three victims' families sue Pickton, police bringing total to nine." (2013, August 20). *Maclean's*. (Online).

"A profile of robbery offenders in Canada." (1995). Research Brief B-10. Ottawa, ON: Correctional Service Canada.

Argo, J.J., & Main, K.J. (2004). "Meta-analyses of the effectiveness of warning labels." *Journal of Public Policy & Marketing, 23*(2), 193–208.

Aromaa, K. (1974). "Our violence." *Scandinavian Studies in Criminology, 5*, 35–46.

"Arrest in Kanesatake arson case." (2004, June 10). CBC News. (Online).

Arrigo, B.A. (2007). "The role of escalating paraphilic fantasies and behaviours in sexual, sadistic, and serial violence: A review of theoretical models." Ottawa, ON: Correctional Service Canada.

Artz, S., Stoneman, A., & Reitsma-Street, M. (2012). "Canadian girls and crime." In J. Winterdyk & R. Smandych (Eds), *Youth at risk and youth justice: A Canadian overview* (2nd edn). Toronto, ON: Oxford University Press.

Association of Workers' Compensation Boards of Canada (AWCBC). (2013). "National work injury/disease statistics program, Table 22: Number of fatalities, by jurisdiction, 1993–2013."

Aubrey, M. (2013, July 5). "Rwandan refugee Jacques Mungwarere not guilty of crimes against humanity." *Ottawa Sun*. (Online).

Austin, L.M., Stewart, H., & Clement, A. (2014, November 22). "Bill C-13 has little to do with cyberbullying." *The Star* (Toronto). (Online).

Babbie, E. (2004). "Laud Humphreys and research ethics." *International Journal of Sociology and Social Policy, 24*(3), 12–19.

Bailey, M. (1991). "Servant girls and masters: The Tort seduction and the support of bastards." *Canadian Journal of Family Law, 10*(1), 153–66.

Bajovic, M. (2013). "Violent video gaming and moral reasoning in adolescents: Is there an association?" *Educational Media International, 50*(3), 177–91. doi:10.1080/09523987.2013.836367

Ballard, J.D. (1998). "The Oklahoma City bombing case, the media and public policy on domestic terrorism." Paper presented at the Academy of Criminal Justice Science 35th Annual Meeting, 10–14 March, Albuquerque, NM.

Bandura, A. (1965). "Vicarious processes: A case of no-trial learning." In L. Berkowitz (Ed.), *Advances in experimental social psychology* (Vol. 2) (Chapter 1). New York: Academic Press.

——. (1979). "The social learning perspective mechanisms of aggression." In H. Toch (Ed.), *Psychology of crime and criminal justice*. New York: Holt, Rinehart and Winston.

Bandura, A., & Walters, R.H. (1959). *Adolescent aggression*. New York: Ronald Press.

Banerjee, S. (2014, July 25). RCMP apologize for code name for anti-Mafia bust. *The Star* (Toronto). (Online)

Barak, G. (1998). *Integrating criminologies*. Boston, MA: Allyn and Bacon.

——. (2009). *Criminology: An integrated approach*. Lanham, MD: Rowman and Littlefield Publishers.

Barbara, J.S. (1995). *Media violence and real life aggression and militarism*. (Online).

Barbaret, R. (2004). "Mainstreaming comparative methodology in criminal justice/criminology research methods courses." *International Journal of Comparative Criminology, 4*(2).

Barkan, S.E. (2011). *Criminology: A sociological understanding* (5th edn). Englewood Cliffs, NJ: Prentice-Hall.

Barry, J.V. (1973). "Alexander Maconochie." In H. Mannheim (Ed.), *Pioneers in criminology* (2nd edn). Montclair, NJ: Patterson Smith.

Bartol, C., & Bartol, A. (2010). *Criminal behavior: A psychological approach* (9th edn). Upper Saddle River, NJ: Prentice-Hall.

——. (2012). *Criminal behavior: A psychological approach* (10th edn). Oxford: Oxford University Press.

Bates, B.J., & Donnerstein, E.I. (1990). "Public opinion and the two pornography commissions: Comparing the incomparable." *Southwestern Mass Communication Journal 6*(1), 1–14.

Baudes-Rotger, M., & Gallardo-Pujol, D. (2014). "The role of the *monoamine oxidase* A gene in moderating the response to adversity and associated antisocial behavior: A review." *Psychology and Research Behaviour Management, 7*, 185–200.

Beare, M. (1996). "Organized crime and money laundering." In R.D. Silverman, J.T. Teevan, & V.F. Sacco (Eds), *Crime in Canadian society* (5th edn). Toronto, ON: Harcourt Brace.

Beauchamp, D.L. (2004). "Sexual orientation and victimization." Canadian Centre for Justice Statistics profile series. Statistics Canada cat. no. 85F0033M. Ottawa, ON: Minister of Industry.

Beaudin, M. (2012, December 27). "Police receive tips relating to deacon facing child-porn charges." *Montreal Gazette*. (Online).

Beaver, K.M. (2012). *Biosocial criminology: A primer* (2nd edn). Dubuque, IA: Kendall Hunt Publishing Company.

Beaver, K.M., & Walsh, A. (Eds). (2011). *Biosocial theories of crime*. Surrey, UK: Ashgate.

Beaver, K.M., & Wright, J.P. (2011). "The Association between county-level IQ and county-level crime rates." *Intelligence, 39*, 193–7.

Beccaria, C. (1963). *On crimes and punishment*. (H. Paolucci, Trans.). Indianapolis, IN: Bobbs-Merrill.

Becker, H.S. (1963). *Outsiders: Studies in the sociology of deviance*. New York: The Free Press.

Bennett, T., Holloway, K., & Farrington, D. (2008). *The effectiveness of neighborhood watch*. Oslo, Norway: Campbell Systemic Reviews.

Benson, M.L. (1990). Emotions and adjudication: Status degradation ceremonies among white collar criminals. *Justice Quarterly, 7*, 515–28.

Bentham, J. (1776). "Preface." In *A fragment on government*. London: T. Payne.

Berger, R., Searles, P., & Cottle, C. E. (1991). *Feminism and pornography*. Westport, CT: Praeger Publications.

Berkowitz, L. (1962). *Aggression: A social-psychological analysis*. New York: McGraw-Hill.

Berman, J., & Siegel, M.-H. (1992). *Behind the 8–ball: A guide for families of gamblers*. NY: Simon and Schuster.

Bernard, T.J., Snipes, J.B., & Gerould, A.L. (2010). *Vold's theoretical criminology* (6th edn). New York: Oxford University Press.

Bernie, P. (1991). "Inventing criminology: The 'science of man' in Cesare Beccaria's Dei Delitti E Delle Pene (1764)." *Criminology, 29*(4), 777–820.

Besserer, S. (2002). "Criminal victimization: An international perspective." *Juristat, 22*(4). Statistics Canada cat. no. 85-002-XPE. Ottawa, ON: Minister of Industry.

Besserer, S., & Trainor, C. (2000). "Criminal victimization in Canada, 1999." *Juristat, 20*(10). Statistics Canada cat. no. 85-002-XIE. Ottawa, ON: Minister of Industry.

Binder, A. (1979). "The juvenile justice system. Where pretense and reality clash." *American Behavioral Scientist 22*, 621–51.

Bischof, L. (1964). *Interpreting personality theories*. NY: Harper and Row.

"Bitcoin ransom demanded by hackers of Calgary wine store." (2015, December 10). CBC News (Online).

Bittle, S. (1999). "Youth Involvement in prostitution: A focus on intrafamilial violence—A literature review." Ottawa, ON: Department of Justice. (Online).

———. (2002). *Youth involvement in prostitution: A literature review and annotated bibliography.* Department of Justice Canada. (Online).

Blackwell, J.E. (1988). "Sin, sickness, or social problem? The concept of drug dependence." In J. Blackwell & P. Erickson (Eds). *Illicit drugs in Canada.* Scarborough, ON: Nelson.

Blackwell, T. (2011, December 7). "'Prozac defence' stands in Manitoba teen's murder case." *National Post.* (Online).

Blair, R.J.R. (2003). "Neurobiological basis of psychopathy." *The British Journal of Psychiatry, 182,* 5–7.

Boesveld, S. (2012, January 30). "Shafia trial: Six perspectives on 'honour' killings in Canada." *National Post.* (Online).

Boggs, S. (1965). "Urban crime patterns." *American Sociological Review, 30,* 899–908.

Bogomolov, A., Lepri, B., Staiano, J., Oliver, N., Pianesi, F., & Pentland, A. (2014). "Once upon a crime: Towards crime prediction from demographics and mobile data." Retrieved from http://arxiv.org/pdf/1409.2983.pdf

Bolan, K. (2014a, February 24). "Biker expert says Hells Angels selling their assets." *The Vancouver Sun.* (Online).

———. (2014b, December 10). "Cartel connection: How Mexico's drug gangs set up shop in Vancouver." *The Vancouver Sun.* (Online).

Bond, A.J., Wingrove, J., & Critchlow, D.G. (2001). "Tryptophan depletion increases aggression in women during the premenstrual phase." *Psychopharmacology, 156,* 477–80.

Bonger, W.A. (1905). *Criminalité et conditions economiques.* Amsterdam, Netherlands: G.P. Tierie.

Bonta, J., LaPrairie, C., & Wallace-Capretta, S. (1997). "Risk prediction and re-offending: Aboriginal and non-aboriginal offenders." *Canadian Journal of Criminology, 32*(2), 127–44.

Boritch, H. (1997). *Fallen women: Female crime and criminal justice in Canada.* Scarborough, ON: Nelson

Bounties, B. (2015, July 17-19). "Two hackers get million air miles for finidng security holes." *Calgary Metro,* p. 22.

Bourgois, P., & Bruneau, J. (2000). "Needle exchange, HIV infection, and the politics of science: Confronting Canada's cocaine injection epidemic with participant observation." *Medical Anthropology, 18*(4), 325–50.

Box, S. (1983). *Power, crime, and mystification.* London: Tavistock.

"Boy, 2, pepper sprayed in road-rage attack." (2014, April 30). CBC News. (Online).

Boyce, J. (2015). "Police-reported crime statistics in Canada, 2014." *Juristat.* Statistics Canada cat. no. 85-002-X. Ottawa, ON: Canadian Centre for Justice Statistics.

Boyce, J., Cotter, A., & Perreault, S. (2014). "Police-reported crime statistics in Canada, 2013." *Juristat.* Statistics Canada cat. no. 85-002-X. Ottawa, ON: Minister of Industry.

Boyd, N. (1988). *The last dance: Murder in Canada.* Scarborough, ON: Prentice-Hall.

———. (1991). *High society: Legal and illegal drugs in Canada.* Toronto, ON: Key Porter Books.

Braithewaite, J. (1981). "The myth of social class and criminality reconsidered." *American Sociological Review, 46*(1), 36–57.

———. (1989). *Crime, shame and reintegration.* Cambridge, UK: Cambridge University Press.

———. (1998). "Restorative justice." In M. Tonry (Ed.), *The handbook of crime and punishment* (pp. 323–44). Oxford, UK: Oxford University Press.

Brannigan, A., Knafla, L., & Levy, C. (1989). *Street prostitution: Assessing the impact of the law, Calgary, Regina, and Winnipeg.* Ottawa, ON: Department of Justice.

Brantingham, P.J., & Brantingham, P.L. (1984). *Patterns in crime.* New York: Macmillan.

Braswell, M., Fuller, J., & Lozoff, B. (2001). *Corrections: Peacemaking, restorative justice: Transforming individuals and institutions.* Cincinnati, OH: Anderson.

Brean, J. (2013, November 8). "Why has Rob Ford's use of crack sparked such an intense moral panic?" *National Post.* (Online).

Brennan, B. (1999, March 22). "Fraud squad: Calgary seniors tell their peers how to protect themselves against scams, cons." *Calgary Herald,* p. B6.

Brennan, R.J. (2012, February 8). "Majority of Canadians support return of death penalty, poll finds." *The Star* (Online).

Brennan, S. (2011a). "Canadians' perceptions of personal safety and crime, 2009." *Juristat.* Statistics Canada cat. no. 85-002-X. Ottawa, ON: Minister of Industry.

———. (2011b). "Defining cyber crime: A review of federal and state law." In R.D. Clifford (Ed.), *Cybercrime: The investigation, prosecution and defence of a computer-related crime* (3rd edn) (Chapter 2). Durham, NC: Carolina Academic Press.

———. (2012, March 8). "Victimization of older Canadians." *Juristat.* Statistics Canada cat. no. 85-002-X. Ottawa, ON: Minister of Industry.

Brennan, S., & Dauvergne, M. (2011). "Police report crime statistics in Canada, 2010." *Juristat.* Statistics Canada cat. no. 85-002-X. Ottawa, ON: Minister of Industry.

Brennan, S. & Taylor-Butts, A. (2008). *Sexual assault in Canada, 2004 and 2007.* (Canadian Centre for Justice Statistics Profile Series, no. 19.) Statistics Canada cat. no. 85F0033M. (accessed June 5, 2012).

Brenner, R. (2010, November 16). "Sins of commission: The 40th anniversary of the Illustrated Presidential Report of the Commission on Obscenity and Pornography." *The Huffington Post.* (Online).

Brillon, Y. (1987). *Victimization and fear of crime among the elderly.* Toronto, ON: Butterworths.

Brinzeau, S. (2014). "Beaten, raped, tortured and starved: The shocking fate of Eastern European sex trafficking victims revealed." Mail Online. (Online).

Brochu, S., Cousineau, M., Gillet, M., Cournoyer, L.-G., Permanen, K., & Motiuk, L. (2002). "Drugs, alcohol and criminal behaviour: A profile of inmates in Canadian institutions." *Forum, 20–4.*

Bronskill, J. (2012, September 11) "Cybercrime in Canada: Ottawa fears we're becoming a host nation." *The Huffington Post.* (Online).

——. (2014, May 18). "RCMP study found 322 incidents of corruption in Mountie ranks and 12 cases involved organized crime." *National Post.* (Online).

Browne, T. (2014, October 30). "Why don't Canadian universities want to talk about sexual assault?" *Maclean's.* (Online).

Brunner, H.G., Nelen, M., Breakefield, X.O., Ropers, H.H., & van Oost, B.A. (1993). "Abnormal behavior associated with a point mutation in the structural gene for monoamine oxidase A." *Science, 262,* 578–80.

Brutus, S., Aguinis, H., & Wassmer, H. (2012). "Self-report limitations and future directions in scholarly reports: Analysis and recommendations." *Journal of Management, 39*(1), 47–75.

Bryden, J. (2014, June 1). "Michael Sona, Lone Person charged in robocalls scandal, sees trial begin Monday." *The Huffington Post.* (Online).

Buckle, A., & Farrington, D.P. (1984). "An Observational Study of Shoplifting." *British Journal of Criminology, 24,* 63–73.

Building Partnerships to Reduce Crime (BPRC). (2016). "The Hub & COR model." Regina, SK: Government of Saskatchewan.

Bullough, V.L., & Bullough, B. (1987). *Women and prostitution: A social history.* Buffalo, NY: Prometheus.

Bureau du coroner du Québec. (2004, February). *Relevé des suicides de joueurs compulsifs.*

Burgess, A.W. (2010). *Victimology: Theories and applications.* Mississauga, ON: Jones and Bartlett Pub.

Burgess, R., & Akers, R. (1966). "A differential association-reinforcement theory of criminal behavior." *Social Problems, 14,* 128–47.

Burnside, L., & Fuch, D. (2013). "Bound by the clock: FASC transitioning to adulthood from child welfare care." *First Peoples Child and Family Review: An Interdisciplinary Journal, 8*(1), 40–61.

Bursik, R.J. (1995). "The Distribution and Dynamics of Property Crime." In J.F. Sheley (Ed.), *Criminology: A contemporary handbook* (pp. 211–57). Philadelphia, PA: Temple University Press.

Bursik, R.J., Jr. (1988). "Social disorganization and theories of crime and delinquency: Problems and prospects." *Criminology, 26,* 519–51.

Butt, D. (2015, January 19). "Canada's law on hate speech is the embodiment of compromise." *The Globe and Mail.* (Online).

Cadoret, R.J. (1995). "Adoption Studies." *Alcohol Health and Research World, 19*(3), 195–201.

Caine, A. (2012). *Charlie and the angels.* Toronto, ON: Random House.

Cale, J., Leclerc, B., & Smallbone, S. (2014). "The sexual lives of sexual offenders: The link between childhood sexual victimization and non-criminal sexual lifestyles between types of offenders." *Psychology, Crime and Law, 20,* 37–60.

Cale, J., Plecas, D., Cohen, I., & Fortier, S. (2010). "An exploratory analysis of factors associated with repeat homicide in Canada." *Homicide Studies, 14,* 159–80.

Calgary Police Services. (2015). "Centralized Intelligence and Analysis Section." Calgary, AB.

Cameron, M. O. (1964). *The booster and the snitch.* New York: Free Press.

Canada. (2015, July 23). "Canadian Victims Bill of Rights." S.C. 2015, c. 13, s. 2. Ottawa, ON: Minister of Justice.

Canada, Department of Justice. (2014). "Technical paper: Bill C-36, *Protection of Communities and Exploited Persons Act.*" (Online).

"Canada's crime rate: Two decades of decline." (2014). *The Daily*: Canadian Megatrends. Ottawa, ON: Statistics Canada.

"Canada's most dangerous cities: Breaking and entering." (2011, December 15). *Maclean's* (Online).

"Canada/US Organized Crime Threat Assessment." (2006). US Department of Justice; Federal Bureau of Investigation; Royal Canadian Mounted Police. (Online).

"Canadian Alcohol and Drug Use Monitoring Survey (CADMUS)." (2013). Ottawa, ON: Health Canada. Retrieved from www.hc-sc .gc.ca/hc-ps/drugs-drogues/stat/_2011/summary-sommaire-eng .php#a7

Canadian Anti-Fraud Centre. (2015, May 26). "Annual statistical report 2014: Mass marketing fraud & ID theft activities." (Online).

Canadian Cancer Society. (2004). *Canadian Cancer Statistics 2004.* Retrieved from www.cancer.ca/vgn/images/portal/ cit_86751114/14/33/195986411niw_stats2004_en.pdf.

Canadian Centre for Occupational Health and Safety (CCOHS). (2015). "National Day of Mourning—April 28." Retrieved from http://www.ccohs.ca/events/mourning/

Canadian Centre on Substance Abuse (CCSA). (2014, Autumn). "Canadian drug summary: Cocaine." Ottawa, ON: CCSA.

Canadian Federation of Students—Ontario (CFS). (2013, Apr.). "Fact sheet: Sexual violence on campuses." Retrieved from http://cfsontario.ca/downloads/CFS_factsheet_antiviolence .pdf

Canadian Gaming Association. (2006, March 16). "Study on VLT gaming in Canada." Retrieved from www.canadiangaming.ca/ news-a-articles/41-canadian-gaming-association-study-on-vlt -gaming-in-canada.html

Canadian Partnership for Responsible Gambling (CPRG). (2015). *2013–2014 Digest.* Retrieved from http://www.cprg.ca/ Digests/ViewMainCards?yearId=70758843-d483-e511-8104 -1abbb38a3094

Canadian Press. (2014, May 18). "RCMP tracks its own corruption, implements strategy to reduce it." CBC News (Online).

Canadian Radio-television and Telecommunications Commission (CRTC). (1996). "Public Notice CRTC 1996-36: Policy on Violence in Television Programming." (Online).

Canadian Security Intelligence Service (CSIS). (1999). "Transnational criminal activity." Retrieved from http://fas.org/irp/ threat/back10e.htm

——. (2014). *Public report 2011–2013.* (Online)

Canadian Tribal gaming. (2014). Retrieved from www.casinocity .com/canada/tribal-gaming

Cao, L. (2004). *Major criminological theories.* Belmont, CA: Wadsworth.

Caputo, T., & Vallee, M. (2010). "A report prepared for the review of the roots of youth violence." Toronto, ON: Ministry of Children and Youth Services.

Carlson, K.B. (2011, September 24). "The largest expansion of prison building 'since the 1930s.'" *The National Post.* (Online).

Caron, A.H. et al. (2010). "A national study on children's television programming in Canada." Centre for Youth and Media Studies, Montreal.

Carrière, D. (2003). "Adult correctional services in Canada, 2001/02." *Juristat, 23*(11). Statistics Canada cat. no. 85-002-X. Ottawa, ON: Minster of Industry.

Carrigan, D.O. (1991). *Crime and punishment in Canada: A history.* Toronto, ON: McClelland & Stewart.

Carrington, P.J., & Moyer, S. (1998). *A statistical profile of female young offenders.* (Technical Report No. TR-1998-4e). Ottawa, ON: Department of Justice Canada.

Carson, T. (2013, October 10). "Canadian environmental activist pleads guilty to arson attacks in U.S. West." *Reuters Canada.* (Online).

Carter, P. (1995, September). "Violence: From the grave to the cradle." *Financial Post Magazine,* 23–48.

Carville, O. (2015, December 14). "The game: Living hell in hotel chains." *The Star* (Toronto). (Online).

Cates, J.A., & Markley, J. (1992). "Demographic, clinical, and personality variables associated with male prostitution by choice." *Adolescence, 27,* 695–714.

Cavender, G. (2004). "Media and crime policy: a reconsideration of David Garland's *The Culture of Control.*" *Punishment and Society* 6(3), 335–48.

Cawte, J., & Florence, M. (1989). "A manganic milieu in North Australia: Ecological manganese: Ecology, diagnosis, individual susceptibility, synergism, therapy prevention, advice for the community." *International Journal of Biosocial Medicine and Research, 11,* 43–56.

CCJS, 1998, 18(2).

CCJS, 2000, 20(10). "Adult correctional services in Canada 2000/01."

CCJS, 2002, 22(11). "Justice spending in Canada, 2000/01."

CCJS, 2003, 23(1). "Motor vehicle theft in Canada—2001."

CCJS, 2003, 23(11). "Adult correctional services in Canada, 2001/02."

CCJS, 2003, 23(5). "Crime statistics in Canada, 2002."

CCJS, 2003, 23(5). "Crime statistics in Canada, 2002."

CCJS, 2003, 23(6). "Sexual offences in Canada."

CCJS, 2003, 23(8). "Homicide in Canada, 2002."

CCJS, 2003, 23(8). "Homicide in Canada, 2002."

CCJS, 2004, 24(1). "Trends in drug offences and the role of alcohol and drugs in crime."

CCJS, 2004, 24(4). "Hate crime in Canada."

CCJS, 2004, 24(6). "Crime statistics in Canada, 2003."

CCJS, 2004, 24(8). "Homicide in Canada, 2003."

Cedilot, A., & Noel, A. (2012). *Mafia inc: The long, bloody reign of Canada's Sicilian clan.* Toronto, ON: Vintage Books.

Centre for Youth Crime Prevention. (2015). "Bullying and cyberbullying." Ottawa, ON: RCMP.

Chai, C. (2014, July 3). "Update: Saint John police officer sexually abused over 260 children, investigators suspect." Global News. (Online).

Challem, J. (2001). "Mean streets or mean minerals?" *The Nutrition Reporter.*

Chambliss, W. (1988). *On the take* (2nd edn). Bloomington, ID: Indiana University Press.

"Charbonneau commission finds corruption widespread in Quebec's construction sector." (2015, November 24). CBC News. (Online).

Cheraskin, E. (2005). *Diet and supplementation: A key to optimal health.* Washington, DC: International Academy of Science.

Chermak, S.M. (1995). *Victims in the news: Crime and the American news media.* Boulder, CO: Westview Press.

Cho, H., Reimer, T., & McComas, C.A. (2015). *SAGE handbook of risk communication.* Thousand Oaks, CA: Sage.

Christie, N. (1996). *Crime control as industry* (2nd edn). London: Routledge.

———. (1997). "Four blocks against insight: Notes on the oversocialization of criminologists." *Theoretical criminology, 1*(1), 11–23.

Chui, T., & Flanders, J. (2013). "Immigration and ethnocultural diversity in Canada: National household survey, 2011." Statistics Canada cat. no. 99-010-X2011001. Ottawa, ON: Minister of Industry.

Clarke, R.V., & Felson, M. (1993). "Introduction: Criminology, routine activity, and rational choice." In R.V. Clarke and M. Felson (Eds), *Routine activity and rational choice* (pp. 1–14). New Brunswick, NJ: Transaction.

Clark-Flory, T. (2015, June 22). "FBI anti-LGBT hate crime statistics point to reporting problem." *Vocativ.*

Clermont, Y. (1996). "Robbery." In L.W. Kennedy & V.F. Sacco (Eds), *Crime Counts: A Criminal Event Analysis.* Scarborough, ON: Nelson.

Clifford, R.D. (Ed.). (2011). *Cybercrime: The investigation, prosecution and defence of a computer-related crime* (3rd edn). Durham, NC: Carolina Academic Press.

Clinard, M., & Yeager, P. (2011). *Corporate crime.* New York: Transaction Publications.

Clinard, R., & Quinney, R. (1973). *Criminal behavior systems: A typology.* New York: Holt, Rinehart and Winston.

Cloward, R.A., & Ohlin, L.E. (1960). *Delinquency and opportunity: A theory of delinquent gangs.* New York, NK: Free Press.

Cohen, L.E., & Felson, M. (1979). "Social Change and Crime Rate Trends: A routine activities approach." *American Sociological Review, 44,* 588–607.

Cohen, S. (2001). *State of denial: Knowing about atrocities and suffering.* London: Polity Press.

Coldren, J.D. (1995, July/August). "Change at the speed of light: Doing justice in the information age." *CJ International,* 8–12.

Collacott, M. (2006). *Canada's inadequate response to terrorism: The need for policy reform.* Vancouver, BC: Fraser Institute.

Competition Bureau. (2015a, June 23). "Montreal-based deceptive telemarketers sentenced." Ottawa, ON: Government of Canada.

———. (2015b, September 10). "Price-fixing charges stayed in chocolate case." Ottawa, ON: Government of Canada.

———. (2015c). "Common scams." Ottawa, ON: Government of Canada. (Online).

Conklin, J.E. (2013). *Criminology* (11th edn). Englewood Cliffs, NJ: Prentice-Hall.

Connolly, A. (2015, June 9). "Muslims only religious group to see increase in hate crimes: StatsCan." *iPolitics.*

Conway, M. (2007). "Cyberterrorism: hype and reality." In L. Armistead (Ed.), *Information warfare: Separating hype form reality* (pp. 73–93). Lincoln, NE: Potomac Books, Inc.

Cooper, B. (1996). "The fall of the Wall and the East German police." In M. Pagon (Ed.), *Policing in central and eastern Europe: Comparing firsthand knowledge with experience from the West.* Slovenia: College of Police and Security Studies.

Cornish, D.B., & Clarke, R.V. (Eds). (1986). *The reasoning criminal: Rational choice perspectives on offending.* New York: Springer-Verlag.

Corporate Knights. (2015a). "Best 50: Our annual report on the best 50 corporate citizens in Canada." *Corporate Knights: The Magazine for Clean Capitalism.*

———. (2015b). "Global 100: An index of the global 100 most sustainable corporations in the world." *Corporate Knights: The Magazine for Clean Capitalism.*

Corrado, R., Cohen, I., & Cale, J. (2004). "Aboriginal resource access in response to criminal victimization in an urban context." In J.P. White, P. Maxim & D. Beavon (Eds), *Aboriginal Policy Research Volume II Setting the Agenda for Change.* Toronto, ON: Thompson Education Publishing.

Correctional Investigator Canada. (2012). *Annual report of the Office of the Correctional Investigator, 2011–2012.* Ottawa, ON: Office of the Correctional Investigator.

———. (2013). "Aboriginal offenders: A Critical Situation." Retrieved from www.oci-bec.gc.ca/cnt/rpt/oth-aut/oth-aut20121022info-eng.aspx

———. (2014). *Annual report of the Office of the Correctional Investigator, 2013–2014.* Ottawa, ON: Office of the Correctional Investigator.

Cotter, A. (2014, December 1). "Homicide in Canada, 2013." *Juristat.* Statistics Canada cat. no. 85-002-X. Ottawa, ON: Minister of Industry.

Council of Europe. (2002, July 22). *Crime analysis: Organized crime—best practice survey no. 4.* Strasbourg, France: COE.

Cowles, E.L., & Castellano, T.C. (1995). "'Boot camps,' drug treatment and aftercare intervention: An evaluation review." Rockville, MD: National Institute of Justice.

Cowper, D.G. (2012, August 27). "A criminal justice system for the 21st century: Final Report to the Minister of Justice and Attorney General, Honourable Shirley Bond." Vancouver, BC: Ministry of Justice.

Coyle, J. (1998, May 9). "Road rage is driving us around the bend." *Toronto Star.* (Online).

Crawford, A. (2016, January 13). "Counterfeiters perplexed by Canada's plastic money. RCMP seizures show even the best attempts to simulate new bills' security features are easy to spot." CBC News (Online).

Criminal Code (An Act Respecting the Criminal Law). R.S.C. 1985, c. C-46.

Criminal Intelligence Service Canada (CISC). (2004). *Traditional organized crime.* Ottawa, ON: CISC.

———. (2014). "Organized crime in Canada: Backgrounder." Ottawa, ON: CISC.

Cromwell, P.F., Olson, J.N., & Avary, D.W. (1991). *Breaking and entering: An ethnographic analysis of burglary.* Newbury Park, CA: Sage.

Crowell, N.A., & Burgess, A.W. (Eds). (1996). *Understanding violence against women.* Washington, DC: National Academy Press.

CRS Report for Congress, International Drug Control Policy. (2008, June 23). Order Code RL34543

Cullen, F.F., Wright, J.P., & Blevins, K.R. (Eds). (2011). *Taking stock: The status of criminological theory.* New Brunswick, NJ: Transaction Pub.

Cullen, F.T., & Wilcox, P. (Eds). (2010). *Encyclopedia of criminological theory.* Thousand Oaks, CA: Sage.

CWF. (2013, July 9). "One in five Canadians think a woman encourages sexual assault when she is drunk." Canadian Women's Foundation. (Online).

"Cyberbullying laws in Canada." (2015, December 22). NoBullying.com. Retrieved from http://nobullying.com/cyberbullying-laws-canada

Dalton, K. (1961). "Menstruation and crime." *British Medical Journal, 2,* 1752–3.

Daly, K. (1989). "Neither conflict nor labeling nor paternalism will suffice." *Crime and Delinquency, 35,* 136–68.

Daly, K., & Chesney-Lind, M. (1988). "Feminism and criminology." *Justice Quarterly, 5,* 497–533.

Dammer, H., & Cordner, F. (2000). "A national survey of comparative criminal justice courses in universities in the United States." *Journal of Criminal Justice Education, 11*(2), 211–36.

Dandurand, Y. (2009). "Addressing inefficiencies in the criminal justice process: A preliminary review." Vancouver, BC: International Centre for Criminal Law Reform and Criminal Justice Policy.

"Data on hate-motivated violence." (1995, August). Retrieved from http://canada.justice.gc.ca/orientations/reforme/naine/hate_en_7.html

Dauvergne, M. (2008). "Motor vehicle theft in Canada, 2007." *Juristat, 28*(10). Statistics Canada cat. no. 85-002-X.

———. (2010). "Police-reported robbery in Canada, 2008." *Juristat.* Statistics Canada cat. no. 85-002-X. Ottawa, ON: Minister of Industry.

Davis, J. (2011, July 18). "Prison costs soar 86% in past five years: Report." *Postmedia News.* (Online).

Davis, S., & Shaffer, M. (1994). *Prostitution in Canada: The invisible menace or the menace of invisibility?* (Online).

Deady, C.W. (2014, March). "Incarceration and recidivism: Lessons from abroad." Newport, RI: Slave Regina University. (Online).

Deegan, M.J. (2014). *Annie Marion McLean and the Chicago Schools of Sociology*. New Brunswick, NJ: Transaction Pub.

DeKeseredy, W.S. (2011). *Contemporary critical criminology*. London: Routledge.

DeKeseredy, W.S., & Perry, B. (Eds). (2006). *Advancing critical criminology theory and application*. Landham, MD: Lexington Books.

DeKeseredy, W.S., & Hinch, R. (1991). *Woman abuse: Sociological perspectives*. Toronto, ON: Thompson.

DeKeseredy, W.S., & Kelly, K. (1993). "The incidence and prevalence of woman abuse in Canadian university and college dating relationships." *Canadian Journal of Sociology, 18*(2), 137–59.

DeKeseredy, W.S., & Schwartz, M.D. (1996). *Contemporary criminology*. Belmont, CA: Wadsworth.

DeLisi, M., & Beaver. K.M. (Eds). (2014). *Criminological theory: A life-course approach* (2nd edn). Burlington, MA: Jones & Bartlett Learning.

Desroches, F.J. (2005). *Force and fear: Robbery in Canada*. Toronto, ON: Canadian Scholars' Press.

Detombe, D.J. (2003). "Defining complex interdisciplinary societal problems." Retrieved from www.complexitycourse.org/detombecompramh1thesis.htm

Deveau, S. (2013, August 1). "Canadian auto sales reach record in July as global demand strengthens." *Financial Post*. (Online).

DeVoe, J. et al. (2002). Indicators of school crime and safety. Washington, DC: National Center for Education Statistics.

DeWalt, K.M., & DeWalt, B.R. (2011). *Participant observation* (pp. 165–8). Walnut Creek, CA: AltaMira Press

Dhillon, S. (2013, September 3). "Alleged triad leader appeals deportation order." *The Globe and Mail*. (Online).

Dilalla, L.F., & Gheyara, S. (2011). "The genetics of criminality and delinquency." In K.M. Beaver & A. Walsh (Eds), *Biosocial theories of crime* (Chapter 4). Surrey, UK: Ashgate.

Dilger, J. (2012). "The law of honor: Operating within Sicilian Cosa Nostra." (Online).

DiLorenzo, T.J. (2012). *Organized crime: The unvarnished truth about government*. MISES Institute, Auburn, AL, USA.

Ditton, J. (1979). *Controlology: Beyond criminology*. London: MacMillan.

Ditton, J., Bannister, J., Gilchrist, E., & Farrell, S. (1999). "Afraid or angry? Recalibrating the 'fear of crime.'" *International Review of Victimology, 6*, 83–99.

Doerner, W.G., & Lab, S.P. (2015). *Victiminology* (7th edn). Waltham, MA: Anderson Pub.

Dolha, L. (2003). "Aboriginal gangs in Prairie Provinces in 'crisis proportions.'" *First Nations Drum* (Fall), 1–3.

Dollard, J., Doob, L.W., Miller, N.E., Mowrer, O.H., & Sears, R.R. (1939). *Frustration and aggression*. New Haven, CT: Yale University Press.

Domjan, M. (2014). *The principles of learning and behavior* (7th edn). Stanford, CT: Cengage Learning.

Doob, A.N. (2014, January). "Research on public confidence in the criminal justice system: A compendium of research findings from *Criminological highlights*." Vancouver, BC: The International Centre for Criminal Law Reform and Criminal Justice Policy.

Doob, A.N., Webster, C.M., & Gartner, R. (2014). "Issues related to harsh sentences and mandatory minimum sentence: General deterrence and incapacitation." Toronto, ON: Centre for Criminology and Social Studies, University of Toronto.

Douglas, J.E., & Olshaker, M. (2000). *Anatomy of motive*. New York: Pocket Books.

Doyle, A., & Moore, D. (Eds). (2011). *Critical criminology in Canada: New voices, new directions*. Vancouver, BC: University of British Columbia Press.

Draeger, C. (1997). "Law and the Feminist Debate about Pornography and Censorship on the Internet." Retrieved from www.ucalgary.ca/~dabrent/380/webproj/ChelseaD.html

Drew, E. (2014, December 12). "Vishing—The latest emerging crime trend." Retrieved from www.perkins-slade.com/insurance-blog/2014/12/12/vishing-the-latest-emerging-crime-trend

Drug Enforcement Branch. (2011). Retrieved from www.rcmp-grc.gc.ca/de-pd/index-eng.htm

Dugger, A. (1996). "Victim impact evidence in capital sentencing: A history of incompatibility." *American Journal of Criminal Law, 23*, 375–404.

Duguid, S. (1979). History and moral education in correctional education. *Canadian Journal of Education, 4*, 81–92.

Duhaime, L. (1996). "Canadian law: A history." Retrieved from www.duhaime.org/canadian_history/default.aspx

Dunn, C.S. (1976). *Patterns of robbery characteristics and their occurrence among social areas*. Washington, DC: US Department of Justice.

Durant, W. (1953). *The Renaissance*. New York: Simon & Schuster.

Durkan, S. (1997, February 14). "Most hooker killers go free." *The Star* (Toronto). (Online).

Durkheim, E. (1895). *Rules of sociological method* (S.A. Soloway & J. H. Mueller, Trans.). New York: Free Press. (Reprinted 1965).

Easton, S., Furness, H., & Brantingham, P. (2014, October). *Cost of crime in Canada: 2014 report*. Vancouver, BC: Fraser Institute.

Edmiston, J. (2012, August 4). "Canada's inexplicable anxiety over violent crime." *National Post*. (Online).

Edwards, P. (2015, November 24). "Corruption in Quebec construction industry 'far more widespread' than originally believed, report says." *The Star* (Toronto). (Online).

Einstadter, W.J., & Henry, S. (2006). *Criminological theory: An analysis of its underlying assumptions* (2nd edn). Lanham, MD: Rowman and Littlefield Pub.

Eisner, M. (2003). *Long-term historical trends in violent crime*. Chicago, IL: University of Chicago Press.

Elias, R. (1986). *The politics of victimization: Victims, victimology and human rights*. New York: Oxford University Press.

——. (1993). *Victim still: The political manipulation of crime victims*. Newbury Park, CA: Sage.

Elmer, M.C. (1982). Century-old ecological studies in France. In G.A. Theodorson (Ed.), *Urban patterns: Studies in human ecology*. Philadelphia, PA: Pennsylvania State University Press.

Erickson, R. (2003). *Teenage robbers: How and why they rob*. San Diego: Athena Research.

Ericson, R.V., Baranek, P.M., & Chan, J.B.L. (1987). *Visualizing deviance: A study of news organizations.* Toronto, ON: University of Toronto Press.

——. (1991). *Representing order: Crime, law, and justice in the news media.* Toronto: University of Toronto Press.

Evans, J., & Himelfarb, A. (1992). "Counting crime." In R. Linden (Ed.), *Criminology: A Canadian perspective* (2nd edn). Toronto, ON: Harcourt Brace.

Evans, J., and Leger, P. (1980). "Canadian victimization surveys." *Canadian Journal of Criminology*, 21(2), 166–83.

Eysenck, H. (1964). *Crime and personality.* London: Routledge and Kegan Paul.

——. (1985). *Decline and fall of the Freudian empire.* Washington, DC: Scott-Townsend Publishers.

Fairchild, E. (1993). *Comparative criminal justice.* Belmont, CA: Wadsworth.

Fairclough, I. (2015, June 24). "Ex-paramedic James Duncan Keats guilty of sexual assault." *The Chronicle Herald* (Halifax). (Online).

Faith, K. (2002). "La resistance a la penalite: un imperative feministe." *Criminologie, 35,* 113–34.

"Fake police site 'fines' surfers for phony cyber crimes: Virus locks computer while pop-up site demands $100 payment." (2013, January 3). CBC News. (Online).

"FanDuel & DraftKings deemed 'gambling' and banned by NY attorney general." (2015, November 11). CBC News (Online).

Farrington, D.P. (Ed.). (1994). *Psychological explanations of crime.* Aldershot, UK: Dartmouth.

Fattah, E. (1972). "White paper on capital punishment." Ottawa: Information Canada.

——. (1997). *Criminology: Past, present and future.* New York: St. Martin.

——. (1991). *Understanding criminal victimization.* Scarborough, ON: Prentice-Hall.

——. (1995). "Restorative and retributive justice models: A comparison." In H-H. Kuhne (Ed.), *Festschrift fur Koichi Miyazawa.* Baden-Baden, Germany: Nomos Verlagsgesllschaft.

——. (1998). "Some reflections on the paradigm of restorative justice and its viability for juvenile justice." In L. Walgrave (Ed.), *Restorative justice for juveniles: Potentialities, risks and problems for research* (pp. 389–401). Leuven, Belgium: Leuven University Press.

——. (2000). "Victimology: past, present and future." *Criminologie,* 30(1),17–46.

Fattah, E.A., & Sacco, V.F. (1989). *Crime and victimization of the elderly.* New York: Springer-Verlag.

Federal Bureau of Investigation (FBI). (2015, August) "ISIL and antiquities trafficking: FBI warns dealers, collectors about terrorist loot." Washington, DC: Department of Justice.

Federal Bureau of Investigation (FBI), Criminal Justice Information Services Division. (2014). "Crime in the United States, 2013." Washington, DC: US Department of Justice.

Federal Communications Commission [US]. (2007, April 25). "In the Matter of Violent Television Programming and Its Impact on Children." (MB Docket No. 04-261.) Washington, DC: FCC.

Fedorowycz, O. (2004). "Breaking and entering in Canada–2002." *Juristat, 24( 5).* Statistics Canada Catalogue no. 85-002-XIE. Ottawa, ON: Minister of Industry.

Ferguson, C.J., & Hartley, R.D. (2009). "The pleasure is momentary . . . the expense damnable? The influence of pornography on rape and sexual assault." *Aggression and Violent Behavior 14,* 323–9.

Fergusson, D.M., Horwood, L.J., & Lynskey, M.T. (1997). "Childhood sexual abuse, adolescent sexual behaviours and sexual revictimization." *Child Abuse and Neglect, 1,* 789–803.

Ferrell, J. (1994). "Confronting the agenda of authority: Critical criminology, anarchism and urban graffiti." In G. Barak (Ed.), *Varieties of criminology* (pp. 161–178). New York: Praeger.

——. (1995). "Culture, crime and cultural criminology." *Journal of Criminal Justice and Popular Culture, 3,* 25–42.

Ferrell, J., & Hayward, K. (2011). *Cultural criminology: Theories of crime.* London: Ashgate.

Feshbach, S. (1964). The function of aggression and the regulation of aggressive drive. *Psychological Review, 71,* 257–72.

Feyerabend, P.K. (1986). *Against method.* London: New Left Books.

Financial Action Task Force (FATF). (2015, February). *FATF report: Financing of the terrorist organization Islamic State in Iraq and the Levant (ISIL).* Paris, France: FATF/OECD.

Financial Transactions and Reports Analysis Centre of Canada (FINTRAC). (2013). "Money laundering trends and typologies in the Canadian securities sector." *FINTRAC typologies and trends report.* Ottawa, ON: Her Majesty the Queen in Right of Canada.

Finckenauer, J.O., & Waring, E. (2001, April). "Challenging the Russian Mafia. Mystique." *National Institute Journal,* 2–7.

Fine, S. (2013, December 20). "Supreme Court strikes down Canada's prostitution laws." *The Globe and Mail.* (Online).

Finkle, J. (2012, September 7). "Exclusive: Insiders suspected in Saudi cyber attack." *Reuters* (Online).

——. (2013, February 27). "Weaponized computer virus Stuxnet hit Iran as early as 2007." *The Globe and Mail.* (Online).

Fishbein, D.H. (2006). "Integrating findings from neurobiology into criminological thought: issues, solutions, and implications." In S. Henry & M.M. Lanier (Eds), *The essential criminology reader* (pp. 43-68). Boulder, CO: Westview Press.

Fishbein, D.H., & Pease, S.E. (1996). *The dynamics of drug abuse.* Needham Heights, MA: Allyn and Bacon.

Fisher, B.S., & Lab, S.P. (2010). *Encyclopedia of victimology and crime prevention.* London: Sage.

Fiske, A.P., & Rai, T.S. (2015). *Virtuous violence: Hurting and killing to create, sustain, end, and honor social relationships.* Cambridge, UK: Cambridge University Press.

Food and Agriculture Organization of the United Nations. (2014). Food insecurity in the world: Strengthening the enabling environment for food security and nutrition. Rome: FAO.

Food Banks Canada. (2014). HungerCount 2014. Toronto, ON: Food Banks Canada.

"Food truck for homeless burned down in Gatineau." (2013, June 9). CBC News. (Online).

"Former govt employee gets 15 months in jail for fraud." (2008, July 5). *Moose Jaw Times Herald.* (Online).

Fortune, E.P., Vega, M., & Silverman, I. (1980). "A study of female robbers in southern correctional institutions." *Journal of Criminal Justice, 8,* 317–25.

"4 Canadians charged in $140 M international penny stock fraud." (2013, August 13). CBC News. (Online).

Fox, R.G. (1969). "XYY chromosome and crime." *Australian and New Zealand Journal of Criminology, 2*(1), 5–19.

Francis, A.J. (2012, December 2). "*DSM 5* is guide not Bible—Ignore its ten worst changes: APA approval of *DSM-5* is a sad day for psychiatry." *Psychology Today.* (Online).

Fraser Forum (1996, September). "Critical Issues Bulletins—1996." *The crime bill: Who pays and how much?* Vancouver, B.C. (Online).

Freedman, L. (2004). *Deterrence.* Cambridge, UK: Polity.

French, C. (2013, January 15). "Analysis: Nortel case spotlights Canada corporate crime record." *Reuters Canada.* (Online).

Freidriches, D.O. (1991). "Introduction: Peacemaking criminology in a world filled with conflict." In B.D. MacLean & D. Milovanovic (Eds), *New directions in critical criminology.* Vancouver, BC: Collective Press.

——. (2010). *Trusted criminal: White collar crime in contemporary society* (4th edn). Belmont, CA: Wadsworth.

Gabor, T. (2003, March 31). "Assessing the effectiveness of organized crime control strategies: A review of the literature." Ottawa, ON: Department of Justice Canada, Research and Statistics Division.

Gambetta, D. (2009). *Codes of the underworld.* Princeton, NJ: Princeton University Press.

Gannon, M., & Mihorean, K. (2005). "Criminal victimization in Canada, 2004." *Juristat, 25*(7). Statistics Canada cat no. 85-002-XIE. Ottawa, ON: Minister of Industry.

Gannon, M., & Taylor-Butts, A. (2006). "Canadians' use of crime prevention measures, 2004". (Statistics Canada Catalogue no. 85F0033MWE. Ottawa, ON: Minister of Industry.

Gannon, T.A., & Pina, A. (2010). "Firesetting: Psychopathy, theory and treatment." *Aggression and Violent Behavior, 15,* 224–38.

Gardner, H. (1983). *Frames of mind.* New York: Basic Book Inc.

Garland, D. (2001). *The culture of control.* Chicago, IL: The University of Chicago Press.

Gaughan, J.E. (2009). *Murder was not a crime: Homicide and power in the Roman Repulic.* Austin, TX: University of Texas Press.

Gavrielides, T. (2011, November). "Restorative practices: From the early societies to the 1970s." *Internet Journal of Criminology.*

——. (Ed.). (2012). *Rights and restoration within youth justice.* Whitby, ON: deSitter Pub.

——. (2015). *The psychology of restorative justice: Managing the power within.* Dorchester, UK: Ashgate.

Gaynor, J., & Stern, D. (1993). "Child and juvenile firesetters: Examining their psychological profiles." *Firehouse, 18,* 24–6.

Gebotys, R.J., Roberts, J.V., & DasGupta, B. (1988). "News media use and public perceptions of crime seriousness." *Canadian Journal of Criminology, 30*(1), 3–16.

Geis, G. (1973). "Jeremy Bentham." In H. Mannheim (Ed.), *Pioneers in criminology* (2nd edn). Montclair, NJ: Patterson Smith.

——. (1989). "Prostitution in Portugal." In N. Davis (Ed.), *International handbook of prostitution.* Westport, CT: Greenwood.

Geiss, R., & Petrig, A. (2011). *Piracy and Armed Robbery at Sea.* Oxford: Oxford University Press.

Gendreau, P., & Ross, R.R. (1987). "Revivification of rehabilitation: Evidence from the 1980s." *Justice Quarterly, 4,* 349–407.

George, T.P. (2007). "Alcohol use and misuse." *Canadian Medical Association Journal 176*(5).

Gerson, J. (2013, March 20). "Privately run shelter for male victims of domestic abuse forced to close its doors due to lack of funding." *National Post.* (Online).

Gesch, B. (2013). Adolescents: Does good nutrition = good behavior? *Nutrition and Health, 22*(1): 55–65.

Gesch, B., Hammon, S.M., Hampson, S.E., Eves, A., & Crowder, M.J. (2002). "Influence of supplementary vitamins, minerals, and essential fatty acids on the antisocial behaviour of young adult prisoners: Randomised, placebo-controlled trial." *British Journal of Psychiatry, 181*(1), 22–8.

Ghosh, P. (2002, February 18). "Behaviour research is 'overstated.'" BBC News (Online).

Gibbons, D. (1979). *The criminological enterprise: Theories and perspectives.* Englewood Cliffs, CA: Prentice-Hall.

——. (1994). *Talking about crime and criminals: Problems and issues in theory development in criminology.* Englewood Cliffs, NJ: Prentice-Hall.

Gibbs, J. (1975). "Crime, punishment, and deterrence." *Southwestern Social Science Quarterly, 48,* 515–30.

Gibbs, J.C. (2014). *Beyond the theories of Kohlberg, Hoffman, and Haidt: Moral development and reality* (3rd edn). New York: Oxford University Press.

Gibbs, J.P. (2006). "The state of criminological theory." *Criminology, 25*(4), 821–40.

Gibbs, W.W. (1995, March). "Seeking the criminal element." *Scientific American,* 100–107.

Giesbrecht, N., & Greenfield, T.K. (1999). "Public opinions on alcohol policy issues: A comparison of American and Canadian surveys." *Addiction, 94*(4), 521–31.

Gilligan, C. (1982). *In a different voice: Psychological theory and women's development.* Cambridge, MA: Harvard University Press.

Gillis, W. (2013, September 29). "B.C. terror plot: How seriously should we be taking terrorism in Canada?" *The Star* (Toronto). (Online).

Gilman, L. (2012). *The theory of multiple intelligences.* Indiana University.

Gobeil, R., & Barrett, M.R. (2007). *Rates of recidivism for women offenders.* Ottawa, ON: CSC. Retrieved from www.statcan.gc.ca/daily-quotidien/130725/dq130725b-eng.htm

Goff, C. (2014). *Criminal justice in Canada* (6th edn). Toronto, ON: Nelson.

Goff, C., & Reasons, C.E. (1978). *Corporate crime in Canada: A critical analysis of Anti-Combines legislation.* Scarborough, ON: Prentice-Hall.

Goffin, P. (2013, March 25). "Helping or harming? Ontario gambling expansion and First Nations." Retrieved from http://rabble.ca/news/2013/03/helping-or-harming-ontario-gambling-expansion-and-first-nations

Goggin, C., Smith, L., & Gendreau, P. (2013). "The efficacy of treatment programs in corrections." In J. Winterdyk & M. Weinrath (Eds), *Adult corrections in Canada* (Chapter 11). Whitby, ON: deSitter Pub.

Goldbach, T.S. (2011). "Sentencing circles, clashing worldviews, and the case of Christopher Pauchay." *Journal for the Centre of Studies in Religion and Society Graduate Student Association, 10*(1), 53–76.

Gomme, I.M. (1993). *The shadow line: Deviance and crime in Canada.* Toronto, ON: Harcourt Brace Jovanovich.

Goodwin, T. (1995, Winter Solstice). "Crime in Russia: Bitter fruit of capitalism and democracy." *Synapse.* (Online).

Gordon, H. (1997, March, 12). State has stunning plan for jailbreakers. *Calgary Herald,* p. A3.

Gordon, R., & Coneybeer, I. (1995). "Corporate crime." In M.A. Jackson & C.T. Griffiths (Eds), *Canadian criminology: Perspectives on crime and criminality* (2nd edn). Toronto, ON: Harcourt Brace.

Gordon, R.A. (1987). "SES versus IQ in the race-IQ delinquency model." *International Journal of Sociology and Social Policy, 7,* 29–56.

Gottfredson, M. R., & Hirschi, T. (1990). *A general theory of crime.* Stanford, CA: Stanford University Press.

Gottschalk, L.A., Rebello, T., Buchsbaum, M.S., Tucker, H.G., & Hodges, E.L. (1991). "Abnormalities in hair trace elements as indicators of aberrant behavior." *Comprehensive Psychiatry, 32*(3), 229–37.

Government of Canada (GoC). (2010). *Canada's cyber security strategy: For a stronger and more prosperous Canada.* Ottawa, ON: Minister of Public Safety.

Grabosky, P., & James, N. (Eds). (1995). Julalikari Night Patrol. (Online).

"Graham James, former hockey coach, gets another 2 years for sexual assault." (2015, June 19). CBC News. (Online).

Grant, M. (2014, April 30). "Mennonite ties to Mexican drug cartels years in the making." CBC News (Online).

Grant, M., & Bakx, K. (2013, August 27). "Nick Chan and the decline of Calgary's notorious FOB gang." CBC News. (Online).

Grassberger, R. (1973). "Hans Gross." In H. Mannheim (Ed.), *Pioneers in criminology* (2nd edn). Montclair, NJ: Patterson Smith.

Graveland, B. (2015, September 1). "Ronald Smith, Canadian on death row, challenges execution methods." *The Huffington Post.* (Online).

Gray, J. (2014, April 20). "Rubin (Hurricane) Carter dead at 76." *The Globe and Mail.* (Online).

Green, J. (2013, February 28). "Former political adviser Tom Flanagan says viewing child porn shouldn't be a crime." *The Star* (Toronto). (Online).

Green, R. (2013). "Explaining the Youth Criminal Justice Act." In J. Winterdyk & R. Smandych (Eds), *Youth at risk and youth justice: A Canadian overview.* Don Mills, ON: Oxford University Press.

Greenberg, P. (1996). "Break and enter." In L.W. Kennedy & V.F. Sacco (Eds), *Crime counts: A criminal event analysis* (Chapter 9). Scarborough, ON: Nelson.

Gregory, J., & Lees, S. (2012). *Policing sexual assault.* London: Taylor and Francis.

Grekul, J., Krahn, H., & Odynak, D. (2004). "Sterilizing the 'feeble-minded': Eugenics in Alberta, Canada, 1929–1972." *Journal of Historical Sociology, 17*(4), 358–84.

Grekul, J., & LaBoucane-Benson, P. (2006). *An investigation into the formation and recruitment process of Aboriginal gangs in western Canada.* Ottawa, ON: Public Safety Canada.

Grenier, E. (2013, August 29). "Majority of Canadians want to loosen marijuana laws: poll." *The Globe and Mail.* (Online).

Griffin, J.H. (1961). *Black like me.* Boston, MA: Houghton Mifflin.

Griffiths, C.T. (2015). *Canadian police work.* Toronto, ON: Nelson.

Griffiths, C.T., & Verdun-Jones, S. (1994). *Canadian criminal justice* (2nd edn). Toronto, ON: Harcourt Brace.

Grillo, I. (2012). *El Narco: The bloody rise of Mexican drug cartels.* London: Bloomsbury.

Groot, N. (2014). "Enforcing criminal restitution orders and the Canadian Victims Bill of Rights." Retrieved from www.investigationcounsel.com/enforcing-criminal-restitution-orders-and-the-canadian-victims-bill-of-rights

Gropper, B.A. (1985). "Probing the link between drugs and crime." Washington, DC: National Institute of Justice.

Grossman, D., & DeGaetano, G. (1999). *Stop teaching our kids to kill: A call to action against TV, movie and video game violence.* New York: Crown.

Gulf War and Health. (2006). Health effects of serving in the Gulf War (Vol. 4). Washington, DC: The National Academies Press.

Gupta, R.C. (2010). *Collapse of the Soviet Union.* Meerut, India: Krishna Prakashan Media Ltd.

Gurr, T.R. (1981). "Historical trends in violent crimes: A historical review of the evidence." *Crime and Justice, 3,* 295–353.

"Hacker charged with cracking major US codes." (1998, June 4). CBC News (Online).

Hackler, J. (2006). *Canadian criminology: Strategies and perspectives* (4th edn). Toronto, ON: Pearson Education.

———. (2007). Criminology (4th edn). Toronto, ON: Prentice-Hall.

Haden, M. (2008). *Economic facts and figures relating to illegal drugs.* Victoria, BC. Retrieved from http://harmreductionvictoria.ca/?q=node/57

Hagan, F.E. (2013). *Introduction to criminology: Theories, methods, and criminal behavior* (8th edn). Thousand Oaks, CA: Sage.

Hagan, J. (1991). *The disreputable pleasures: Crime and deviance in Canada* (3rd edn). Toronto, ON: McGraw-Hill.

———. (1994). *Crime and disrepute.* Thousand Oaks, CA: Pine Forge Press.

Hall, N., & G. Richards. (2004, August 21). "Criminal gangs still endanger Canadians." *National Post,* p. A5.

Halleck, S.L. (1967). *Psychiatry and the dilemmas of crime.* New York: Harper and Row.

Halley, J., Kotiswaran, R, Shamire, H., & Thomas, C. (2005). "From the international to the local in feminist legal responses to rape, prostitution/sex work, & sex trafficking: Four studies in contemporary governance feminism." *Harvard Journal of Law and Gender, 29,* 334–423.

Hamm, M.S. (1998). *Ethnography at the edge: Crime, deviance, and field research.* Paper presented at the Academy of Criminal Justice 35th Annual Meeting, March 10–14, Albuquerque, NM.

Hanson, K.R., & Morton-Bourgon, K.E. (2005). "The characteristics of persistent sexual offenders: A meta-analysis of recidivism studies." *Journal of Consulting and Clinical Psychology, 73*(6), 1153–63.

Harmon, H. (2015, November 2). "First Nations casinos." *Gaming Post* (Online).

Harris, J.R. (1998). *The nature assumption.* New York: Free Press.

Harris, N. (2006). "Reintegrative shaming, shame and criminal justice." *Journal of Social Issues, 62*(2), 327–46.

Hasham, A. (2014, February 25). "Dr George Doodnaught sentenced to 10 years in prison for sex assaults on women during surgery." *The Star* (Toronto). (Online).

Haskell, R., & Burtch, B. (2010). *Get that freak: Homophobia and transphobia in high schools.* Halifax, ON: Fernwood.

Hatch, A. (1995). "Historical legacies of crime and criminal justice in Canada." In M.A. Jackson & C.T. Griffiths (Eds), *Canadian criminology* (3rd edn) (Chapter 7). Toronto, ON: Harcourt-Brace.

Health Canada. (2013). "Drug and Alcohol Use Statistics." Retrieved from www.hc-sc.gc.ca/hc-ps/drugs-drogues/stat/index-eng.php

Health Officers Council of British Columbia (HOC). (2005, October). "A public health approach to drug control in Canada." Victoria, BC: HOC.

Helfand, N.S., & Osborne, D.L. (2003). "A report by the Federal research division, Library of Congress under an Interagency Agreement with the United States government." Washington, DC: Library of Congress.

Hirtenlehner, H., Blackwell, B.S., Leitgoeb, H., & Bacher, J. (2014). "Explaining the gender gap in juvenile shoplifting: A power-control theoretical analysis." *Deviant Behavior, 35*(1), 41–65.

Helworth, M. (1975). *Blackmail: Publicity and secrecy in everyday life.* London: Routledge and Kegan.

Hendrick, Dianne. (1996). "Canadian crime statistics, 1995." *Juristat, 16*(10). Ottawa, ON: Canadian Centre for Justice Statistics.

Henry, S. (2012). "Expanding our thinking on theorizing criminology and criminal justice?" *Journal of Theoretical and Philosophical Criminology, 4*(1), 62–89.

Herrnstein, R.J. (1989). *Biology and crime.* National Institute of Justice. Rockville, MD: US Department of Justice.

Hesterman, J.L. (2004). *Transnational crime and the criminal–terrorist nexus: Synergies and corporate trends.* Maxwell Air Force Base, AB: Air University Press.

Hickey, E.H. (1991). "Female serial murderesses: Constructing differentiating typologies." *Contemporary Journal of Criminal Justice, 7*(4), 245–56.

———. (1991). *Serial murderers and their victims.* Belmont, CA: Wadsworth.

Hill, L. (2007). *The book of negroes.*

Hillman, J. (1996). *The soul's code.* New York: Random House.

Hinch, R. (1994). *Introduction: Theoretical diversity.* In R. Hinch (Ed.), *Readings in critical criminology.* Scarborough, ON: Prentice-Hall.

———. (2003). *Debates in Canadian criminology.* Toronto, ON: Pearson Pub.

Hincks, C., & Winterdyk, J. (2015). "Youth justice in Alberta: Developments and issues under the YCJAS." In M. Alain, S. Reid, & R. Corrado (Eds), *Implementing and working with the YCJAS across Canada.* Toronto, ON: University of Toronto Press.

Hindelang, M.J., Gottfredson, M.R., & Garofalo, J. (1978). *Victims of personal crime: An empirical foundation for a theory of personal victimization.* Cambridge, MA: Ballinger.

Hirschi, T., & Gottfredson, M. (1987). "Causes of white-collar crime." *Criminology, 25*(4), 949–74.

———. (1989). "The significance of white-collar crime and a general theory of crime." *Criminology, 27*(2), 359–72.

Hoff, B.H. (2001). "Family violence in Canada: A statistical profile—2000." Retrieved from www.batteredmen.com/batrcan.htm

Hoge, R.D., Andrews, D.A., & Leschied, A.W. (1996). "An Investigation of Risk and Protective Factors in a Sample of Youthful Offenders." *Journal of Child Psychology and Psychiatry, 37*(4), 419–24.

Holmes, R.M. (1983). *The sex offender and the criminal justice system.* Springfield, IL: Charles C. Thomas Pub.

———. (1991). *Sex crimes.* Newbury Park, CA: Sage.

Honeyman, J.C., & Ogloff, J.R.P. (1996). "Capital punishment: Arguments for life and death." *Canadian Journal of Behavioural Science, 28*(1) 27–35.

Howell, J.C. (Ed.). (1995). *Guide to implementing the comprehensive strategy for serious, violent, and chronic juvenile offenders.* Washington, DC: US Department of Justice. Office of Juvenile Justice and Delinquency Prevention.

Hudson, A. (2013, June 27). "RCMP issue warning in wake of rural break-ins." Retrieved from www.sprucegroveexaminer.com/2013/06/27/rcmp-issues-warning-in-wake-of-rural-break-ins-in-parkland-county

Huesmann, L.R., Moise-Titus, J., Podolski, C., & Eron, L.D. (2003). "Longitudinal relations between children's exposure to TV violence and their aggressive and violent behavior in young adulthood: 1977–1992." *Developmental Psychology, 39,* 201–21.

Huff, D. (1954). *How to lie with statistics.* New York: W.W. Norton.

"Human rights complaint against Maclean's dismissed." (2008, June 28). *The Globe and Mail.* (Online).

Human Rights Watch (2013). "Those who take us away." Retrieved from www.hrw.org/node/113506/section/8

Humphreys, A. (2015). "Hells Angels under pressure." *National Post.* (Online).

Hunter, J. (2015, August 10). "2015: An epidemic of suicide bombs." *AOAV: Action on Armed Violence* (Online).

Hutchins, H. (2015, March 30). "Police resources in Canada, 2014." *Juristat.* Statistics Canada cat. no. 85-002-X. Ottawa, ON: Minister of Industry.

Hutchinson, B. (2013, November 22). "Mumtaz Ladha, BC woman accused of enslaving young African woman, found not guilty of human trafficking." *National Post.* (Online).

idAlerts. (2013). "Identity theft statistics." Retrieved from http://www.idalerts.ca/identity-theft-statistics

"Identity theft, fraud so easy 'it's absurd.'" (2004, April 16). Retrieved from http://operationalrisk.blogspot.co.uk/2004/04/identity-theft-fraud-so-easy-its.html

"Inflatable SpongeBobs disappear from Bruger King." (2004, December 4). Retrieved from www.mytelus.com

Interpol. (1988). First National Symposium on Organized Crime, May, St Cloud, France.

"Ismail Taher, Edmonton-area doctor, guilty of sexual assault." (2015, April 22). CBC News. (Online).

Ito, M. (2014, August 30). "Dealing with addiction: Japan's drinking problem." The Japan Times. (Online).

Jackson, S.L. (2012). Research methods and statistics: A critical thinking approach (4th edn). Belmont, CA: Wadsworth.

Jackson, J., & Gray, E. (2010). "Functional fear and public insecurities about crime." British Journal of Criminology, 50(1), 1–21.

Jacobs, J. (1961). The death and life of great American cities. New York: Random House.

Jacobs, D.F., Marston, A.R., Singer, R.D., Widaman, K., Little, T., & Veizades, J. (1989). "Children of problem gamblers." Journal of Gambling Behavior, 5(4), 261–8.

Jacoby, J.E. (1994). Classics of criminology (2nd edn). Prospect Heights, IL: Waveland.

Jaishankar, K. (2007). "Establishing a theory of cyber crimes." International Journal of Cyber Criminology, 1(2), 7–9.

Jaishankar, K. (Ed.). (2011). Cyber criminology: Exploring Internet crimes and criminal behavior. Boca Raton, FL: CRC Press.

Jeffery, C.R. (1973). "The historical development of criminology." In H. Mannheim (Ed.), Pioneers in criminology (2nd edn) (Chapter 25). Montclair, NJ: Patterson Smith.

——. (1978). "Criminology as an interdisciplinary science." Criminology, 16(2), 149–70.

——. (1990). Criminology: An interdisciplinary approach. Englewood Cliffs, NJ: Prentice-Hall.

Johnson, H. (1996a). "Sexual assault." In L. Kennedy & V. F. Sacco (Eds), Crime counts (Chapter 8). Scarborough, ON: Nelson.

——. (1996b). "Violence against women: A special topic survey." In R.A. Silverman, J.J. Teevan & V.F. Sacco (Eds), Crime in Canadian society (5th edn) (pp. 210–21). Toronto, ON: Harcourt Brace.

——. (2012). "Limits of a criminal justice response: Trends in police and court processing of sexual assault." In E. Sheehy (Ed.), Sexual assault in Canada: Law, legal practice and women's activism (pp. 613–34). Ottawa, ON: University of Ottawa Press.

Johnson, D.J., Sidebottom, A., & Thorpe, A. (2008). "Bicycle theft." Center for Problem-Oriented Policing. (Online).

Johnson, S.C. (2013). "The new theory that could explain crime and violence in America." Retrieved from https://medium.com/matter-archive/the-new-theory-that-could-explain-crime-and-violence-in-america-945462826399

Johnson, T.A. (2009). The war on terrorism: A collision of values, strategies, and societies. Boca Raton, FL: CRC Press.

Jones, G. (2012). Organizational theory, design, and change (7th edn.). Pearson International.

Joyce, J.A. (2006). "'Social Defense' and the United Nations." Criminology, 5(1), 23–34.

Kaplan, A. (2012). "Violence in the media: What effects on behavior." Psychiatric Times. (Online).

Kappeler, V.E., Blumberg, M., & Potter, G.W. (2004). The mythology of crime and justice (4th edn). Prospect Heights, IL: Waveland Press.

Karmen, A. (1979). "Victim facilitation: The case of automobile theft." Victimology, 4(4), 361–70.

——. (1996). Crime victim (2nd edn). Pacific Grove, CA: Brooks/Cole.

——. (2013). Crime and victims: An introduction to victimology (8th edn). Belmont, CA: Wadsworth.

Katz, J. (1988). Seduction of crime: Moral and sensual attraction of doing evil. New York: Basic Books.

Katz, J., & Chambliss, W.J. (1995). "Biology and crime." In J.F. Shelly (Ed.), Criminology: A contemporary handbook. Belmont, CA: Wadsworth.

Kaufmann, B. (2013, March 19). "Alberta more than doubles top prices on VLTs, tries to cut down on problem gambling." Edmonton Sun. (Online).

Kaye, J. (2013). Human insecurity and anti-trafficking policy: Representations of trafficked persons in Canada (Doctoral dissertation). Department of Sociology, University of Saskatoon, Saskatoon.

Kaye, J., Winterdyk, J., & Quartman, L. (2014, January). "Beyond Criminal Justice: A Case Study of Responding to Human Trafficking in Canada." Canadian Journal of Criminology and Criminal Justice, 56(1), 23–48.

Keane, C. (1996). "Corporate crime." In R.A. Silverman, J.J. Teevan & V.F. Sacco (Eds), Crime in Canadian society (5th edn). Toronto, ON: Harcourt Brace.

Kearney, C. (2012, November 16). "Vitamin C deficiency in pregnant women can cause fetal brain damage." Retrieved from www.medicalnewstoday.com/articles/252946.php

Kelley, B.T., Loeber, R., Keenan, K., & DeLamatre, M. (1997, December). "Developmental pathways in boys' disruptive and delinquent behavior." Juvenile Justice Bulletin. Washington, DC: US Department of Justice.

Kennedy, L.W., & Forde, D.R. (1995). Pathways to aggression: Towards a theory of "Routine Conflict." Conflict Series Paper No. 1, Centre for Criminological Research, University of Alberta, Edmonton.

Kidder, L.H., & Judd, C.M. (1986). Research methods in social relations (5th edn). New York: Holt, Rinehart and Winston.

Kilpatrick, D., & Acierno, R. (2003). "Mental health needs of crime victims: Epidemiology and outcomes." Journal of Traumatic Stress, 16(2), 119–32.

Kim, S.W., Grant, J.E., Eckert, E.D., Faris, P.L., & Hartman, B.K. (2006, May). "Pathological gambling and mood disorders: Clinical associations and treatment implications." Journal of Affective Disorders, 92(1), 109–16.

King, R. (2011, November 7). "The secret to stopping break-ins." Retrieved from www.moneysense.ca/property/the-secret-to-stopping-break-ins

Kirwin, G., & Power, A. (2013). *Cybercrime: The psychology of online offenders*. New York: Cambridge University Press.

Klemke, L W. (1978). "Does apprehension for shoplifting amplify or terminate shoplifting activity." *Law and Society Review, 12*, 390–403.

——. (1992). *The sociology of shoplifting: Boosters and snitches today*. New York: Praeger.

Knobe, D., Trocme, N., MacLaurin, B., & Fallon, B. (2009). "Reliability of the Canadian Incidence Study data collection instrument." *The Canadian Journal of Program Evaluation, 23*(1), 87–112.

Koenig, D.J. (2003). "Organized crime: A Canadian perspective." In J.S. Albanese, D.K. Das, & A. Verma (Eds), *Organized crime: International perspectives* (pp. 46–77). Upper Saddle River, NJ: Prentice-Hall.

Kohlberg, L. (1969). "Stage and sequence: The cognitive developmental approach of socialization." In D.A. Goslin (Ed.), *Handbook of socialization theory and research*. Chicago, IL: Rand McNally.

Kohlberg, L., Kauffman, K., Scharf, P., & Hickey, J. (1973). *The just community approach in corrections: A manual*. Niantic, CT: Department of Corrections.

Kowalski, M. (2002, June). "Home invasions." *Bulletin: Canadian Centre for Justice Statistics*. Cat. no. 85F0027XIE. Ottawa, ON: Minister of Industry.

Kramer, R.C. (1984). "Corporate criminality: The development of an idea." In E. Hochstedler (Ed.), *Corporations as criminals*. Beverly Hills, CA: Sage.

Krason, S.M. (2014). "On our dysfunctional criminal justice system." *Catholic Social Science Review, 19*, 265–8.

Kreiter, T. (2012, March 29). "The state of fraud in Canada." Ottawa, ON: RCMP Commercial Crime Branch.

Kuhn, T. (1970). *The structure of scientific revolution* (2nd edn). Chicago, IL: University of Chicago Press.

Lab, S.P. (2013). *Crime prevention: Approaches, practices, and evaluations* (8th edn). New York: Routledge.

Lamberti, R. (2014, April 26). "Striking fear in the heart of Ontario's mob." *Toronto Sun*. (Online).

Landau, T.C. (2006). *Challenging notions: Critical victimology in Canada*. Toronto, ON: Canadian Scholars' Press Inc.

Landler, M. (2013, April 16). "Obama calls blasts an 'act of terrorism.'" *The New York Times* (Online).

Langton, J. (2010). *Showdown: How the Outlaws, Hells Angels and cops fought for control of the streets*. Mississauga, ON: John Wiley and Sons.

Lau, R. (2013, July 9). "Victim blaming still exists in sexual assault cases: poll." Global News. (Online).

Lautt, M. (1984). *A report on prostitution in the prairie provinces*. Working Papers on Pornography and Prostitution Report No. 9. Ottawa, ON: Department of Justice.

Lavigna, Y. (1996). *Into the abyss*. Toronto, ON: HarperCollins.

Lavond, D.G.L., & Steinmetz, J.E. (2003). *Handbook on classical conditioning*. Netherlands: Kluwer Academic Pub.

Lee, M. (2007). *Inventing fear of crime: Criminology and the politics of anxiety*. Cullompton, UK: Willan Pub.

Lemay, J.J. (1994, November). "Hells Angels forever!" *Royal Canadian Mounted Police Gazette, 56*, 3–4.

Lemert, E.M. (1951). *Social pathology*. New York: McGraw-Hill.

——. (1953). "An isolation and closure theory of naïve check forgery." *Journal of Criminal Law and Police Science, 44*, 297–8.

Leonard, E.B. (1982). *Women, crime and society: A critique of criminological theory*. New York: Longman.

Letkemann, P. (1973). *Crime as work*. Englewood Cliffs, NJ: Prentice-Hall.

Levy, C. (1997, May 22–24). Presentation given at the annual Alberta Criminal Justice Association meetings. Red Deer, AB.

Levy, S. (2010). *Hackers: heroes of the computer revolution*. Sebastopol, CA: O'Reilly Media, Inc.

Library of Parliament (2011). "Current and emerging issues." Retrieved from www.parl.gc.ca/Content/LOP/ResearchPublications/CurrentEmergingIssues-e.pdf

Lichtenwald, T.G. (2003, November/December). "Drug Smuggling Behavior: A Developmental Smuggling Model (Part 1)." *Forensic Examiner, 12*, 15–22.

Lichtenwald, T.G., Perri, F.S., & MacKenzie, P. (2009, Summer). "Smuggling Multi-Consignment Contraband: Isolated Incidents or a New Trend?" *Inside Homeland Security*.

Light, R.C., Nee, C., & Ingham, H. (1993). *Car theft: The offender's perspective*. Home Office Research Study No.130. London Home Office.

Limer, E. (2014, December 18). "How to explain the Sony hack to your relatives." Retrieved from http://gizmodo.com/how-to-explain-the-sony-hack-to-your-relatives-1674119822

Lippert, R. (1990). "The construction of Satanism as a social problem in Canada." *The Canadian Journal of Sociology, XV*(4), 417–40.

Livingston, J. (1992). *Crime and criminology*. Englewood Cliffs, NJ: Prentice-Hall.

Livesey, B. (2013). *Thieves of Bay Street: How banks, brokerages and the wealthy steal billions from Canadians*. Toronto, ON: Vintage Books.

Ljunggren, D. (2014, Oct. 31). "Canada's security services struggle with extremist threat, resources gap." Reuters Canada (Online).

Loeber, R., & Burke, J.D. (2011). "Developmental pathways in juvenile externalizing and internalizing problems." *Journal of Research on Adolescence, 21*(1), 34–46.

London, R. (2011). *Crime, punishment, and restorative justice: From the margins to the mainstream*. London: Lynne Rienner Pub.

Longmire, D.R. (1983). Ethical dilemmas in the research setting. *Criminology, 21*, 333–48.

Loree, D. (2004). "What is organized crime?" *Gazette, 66*(2),10–11.

Lowman, J. (1995). "Prostitution in Canada." In M.A. Jackson & C.T. Griffiths (Eds), *Canadian criminology* (3rd edn) (Chapter 10). Toronto, ON: Harcourt Brace.

——. (1997, Fall). "Sterling Prize Winner Challenges Prostitution Law." *SFU Alumni Journal*, 8.

Lowman, J., & Louie, C. (2012). "Public Opinion on Prostitution Law Reform in Canada." *Canadian Journal of Criminology and Criminal Justice, 54*(2), 245–60.

Luba, F. (2013, May 16). "B.C. police find counterfeit versions of new polymer $100 bills." *Postmedia News*. (Online).

Lucas, A., Morley, R., Cole, T.J., Lister, G., & Leeson-Payne, C. (1992). "Breast milk and subsequent intelligence quotionent in children born preterm." *Lancet, 339*(8788), 261–4.

Luis, S., & Puri, B. (2014, January 30). "3 children held hostage in Surrey, B.C. home invasion." CBC News. (Online).

Lungen, P. (2010, September 15). "Calgary man convicted of hate crime, mischief." *The Canadian Jewish News*. (Online).

Lynch, M.J., & Groves, W.B. (1989). *A primer in radical criminology* (2nd edn). Albany, NY: Harrow and Heston.

McAlinden, A-M. (2005). "The use of 'shame' with sex offenders." *British Journal of Criminology, 45*, 373–94.

McCaghy, C.H., Giordano, P.C., & Henson, T.K. (1977). "Auto theft: Offender and offense characteristics." *Criminology, 15*(3), 367–85.

McCarthy, B. (1995). "Getting into street crime: The structure and process of criminal embeddedness." *Social Science Research, 24*, 63–95.

McCarthy, M.P. (2011). *An economic history of organized crime: A national and transnational approach.* New York: Routledge.

McCartney, S. (2010, July 22). "The golden age of flight." *The Wall Street Journal*. (Online).

MacCharles, T. (2012, October 23). "Mental health problems treated as security issue in federal prisons, report says." *The Star* (Toronto). (Online).

McCord, W., & McCord, J. (1959). *Origins of crime*. New York: Columbia University.

McCormick, C. (2013). "Youth deviance and the media: Mapping knowledge and the limits of certainty." In J. Winterdyk & R. Smandych (Eds), *Youth at risk and youth justice: A Canadian overview* (Chapter 5). Don Mills, ON: Oxford University Press.

Macdougall, J. (2013). "There's no such thing as a free puffy jacket: The price we all pay for shoplifters." *National Post*. (Online).

McFarland, J. (2011, September 22). "Four Montreal telemarketing companies charged with fraud." *The Globe and Mail*. (Online).

——. (2014, April 6). "Livent creditors win key ruling, awarded $85-million." *The Globe and Mail*. (Online).

Machold, C. (2014, May 12). "1 in 25 Canadian school kids say they binge drink." CBC News. (Online).

McInnes-Rae, R., & Gollom, M. (2014, March 3). "How 'synthetic' identity fraud costs Canada $1B a year." CBC News (Online).

McIntosh, A. (1998, June 11). RCMP's sting aided drug lords. *Calgary Herald*, pp. A1–2.

MacIntyre, S. (1994). *The youngest profession: The oldest oppression* (Unpublished doctoral dissertation). Department of Law, University of Sheffield, Sheffield, England.

——. (2002, August). "Strolling away." RR2002-4e. Ottawa, ON: Department of Justice.

——. (2012, November). "Buyer beware: A study into the demand side of the sexual exploitation industry." Calgary, AB: The Hindsight Group.

——. (2013). "Under the radar: The sexual exploitation of young men in Western Canada." In J. Winterdyk & R. Smandych (Eds), *Youth at risk and youth justice: A Canadian overview* (Chapter 12). Don Mills, ON: Oxford University Press.

MacIntyre, S., & Miller, A. (2016). "Under the radar: The sexual exploitation of young men in western Canada." In J. Winterdyk & R. Smandych (Eds). *Youth at risk and youth justice* (2nd edn) (Chapter 14). Don Mills, ON: Oxford University Press.

McKenna, B. (2014, February 24). "White collar crime hits more than a third of Canadian organizations." *The Globe and Mail*. (Online).

McKenna, P.F. (1998). *Foundations of policing in Canada*. Don Mills, ON: Pearson.

Mckenna, M. (2013, April 24). "A comprehensive timeline of Canadian terrorism." *VICE* (Online).

McKibbin, W.F., Shackelford, T.K., Goetz, A.T., & Starratt, V.G. (2008). "Why do men rape? An evolutionary psychological perspective." *Review of General Psychology, 12*, 86–97.

Mackreal, K. (2013, March 20). "Justice spending rising sharply as crime rates fall, budget watchdog warns." *The Globe and Mail*. (Online).

MacLaurin , B., & Worthington, C. (2013). "Street involved youth." In J. Winterdyk & R. Smandych (Eds), *Youth at risk and youth justice: A Canadian overview* (Chapter 12). Don Mills, ON: Oxford University Press.

MacLean, B.D. (1986). *The political economy of crime* (Chapter 7). Scarborough, ON: Prentice-Hall.

——. (1992). "Critical criminology and the emergence of critical justice studies in Canada." *Humanity and Society, 16*, 414–26.

McLean, W., & M. Applegate Pease (2013). *Economics and contemporary issues* (9th edn). Mason, OH: South-Western.

McMahon, T. (2013, June 3). "Doubling down on casinos." *Maclean's* (Online).

Maconochesi, E. (1973). "Cesare Beccaria." In H. Mannheim (Ed.), *Pioneers in Criminology* (2nd edn) (Chapter 2). Monctlair, NJ: Patterson Smith.

McPhie, P. (1996). "Fraud." In L.W. Kennedy & V.F. Sacco (Eds), *Crime counts: A criminal event analysis*. Scarborough, ON: Nelson.

Madfis, E. (2014). "Postmodern criminology." In M. Michell (Ed.), *The Encyclopedia of theoretical criminology* (pp. 1–4). Hoboken, NJ: Blackwell Pub. Ltd.

Mahdi, W. (2012, December 9). "Saudi Arabia says Aramco cyberattack came from foreign states." *Bloomberg Business* (Online).

Mahony, T., & Turner, J. (2012, June 7). "Police-reported clearance rates in Canada, 2010." *Juristat*. Statistics Canada cat. no. 85-002-X. Ottawa, ON: Minister of Industry.

Mailhot, J. (2015, April 14). "Peine d'emprisonnement de 2 ans pour Daniel Vallières." *Le Courrier Sud*. (Online).

Makin, K. (2010, January 21). "Canadians' views on crime are hardening, poll finds." *The Globe and Mail*. (Online).

——. (2013). "No new trial for woman who hired hit man against abusive husband: Supreme Court." *The Globe and Mail*. (Online).

Malamuth, N. M., Addison A., & Koss, M. (2000). "Pornography and sexual aggression: Are there reliable effects and can we understand them?" *Annual Review of Sex Research, 11*, 26–91.

Maletzky, B.M. (1991). *Treating the sexual offender*. Newbury, CA: Sage.

Malinowski, S. (1997, October). "Emerging gangs: An international trend?" *Crime and Justice International, 13*(9), 4–5.

Mannheim, H. (Ed.). (1973). *Pioneers in criminology* (2nd edn). Montclair, NJ: Patterson Smith.

Manski, C.F., & Nagin, D.S. (2011). "Bounding disagreements about treatment effects with an application to criminology." In J. MacDonald (Ed.), *Measuring Crime and Criminality: Advances in Criminological Theory* (Vol. 17) (pp. 161–200). New Brunswick, NJ: Transaction Publishers.

Mantle, G., Fox, D., & Dhami, M.K. (2005). "Restorative justice and three individual theories." *Internet Journal of Criminology*.

Marks, H. (2009). "Risk factors for drug addiction and alcoholism." Everyday Health. (Online).

Marlowe, M., Bliss, L., & Schneider, H.G. (1994). "Hair trace element content of violence prone male children." *Journal of Advancement in Medicine, 7*(1), 5–18.

Marsh, I., & Melville, G. (2009). *Crime, justice and the media*. New York: Routhledge.

Marshall, K. (2009, July). "Perspectives on labour and income: Gambling." Statistics Canada cat. no. 75-001-X.

Martha, R.S.J. (2010). *The legal foundations of Interpol*. Portland, OR: Hart Pub.

Martin, K. (2015, May 28). "Calgary teacher sentenced to 5 years for 'monstrous' relationship with student." *Calgary Sun*. (Online).

Martin, P. (2011, October 18). "Hamas frees Israeli soldier Gilad Shalit in prisoner swap." *The Globe and Mail*. (Online).

Martin, R., Mutchnick, R.J., & Austin, W.T. (1990). *Criminological thought: Pioneers past and present*. New York: Macmillan.

Martinson, R. (1974). "What works? Questions and answers about prison reform." *Public Interest, 35*, 22–54.

Masters, R., Hone, B., & Doshi, A. (2005). "Environmental pollution, neurotoxicity, and criminal violence." In J. Rose (Ed.), *Environmental toxicology: Current developments*. Amsterdam: Taylor and Francis.

Matsueda, R. (1992). "Reflected appraisals: Parental labelling, and delinquency: Specifying a symbolic interactionist theory." *American Sociological Review, 97*, 1577–611.

Matthews, R. (1992). "Developing a realist approach to penal reform." In J. Lowman & B.D. MacLean (Eds), *Realist criminology: Crime control and policing in the 1990s* (Chapter 3). Toronto: University of Toronto Press.

——. (2010). "Realist criminology revisited." In E. McLaughlin & T. Newburn (Eds), *The Sage handbook of criminological theory*. London: Sage.

Matza, D. (1964). *Delinquency and drift*. New York: Wiley.

May, P.A., & Gossage, J.P. (2011). "Maternal risk factors for fetal alcohol spectrum disorders: Not as simple as it might seem." *The Journal of the National Institute on Alcohol Abuse and Alcoholism, 34*(1), 15–26.

May, R. (1969). *Love and will*. New York: Norton.

"Maximum statutory damages, punitive damages, and solicitor–client costs awarded against unapologetic software bootlegger." (2012, November 6). *Lexology*. (Online).

Mazerolle, P., & J. Maahs. (2000). "General strain and delinquency: An alternative examination of conditioning influences." *Justice Quarterly, 17*, 753–78.

Mazowita, B., & Burczycka, M. (2014). "Shelters for abused women in Canada, 2012." *Juristat*. Statistics Canada cat. no. 85-002-X. Ottawa, ON: Minister of Industry.

Mazowita, B., & Vézina, M. (2014, September 25). "Police-reported cybercrime in Canada, 2012." *Juristat*. Statistics Canada cat. no. 85-002-X. Ottawa, ON: Minister of Industry.

Mednick, S., & Christiansen, K.O. (1977). *Biosocial bases of criminal behavior*. New York: Gardner Press.

Mehta, Diana. (2015, October 14). "Shafia family members convicted in 'honour killings' case seek new trials." *The Globe and Mail*. (Online).

Mendelsohn, B. (1937, August–October). "Methods to be used by Counsel for the defence in the researches into the personality of the criminal." *Revue de Droit Penal et de Criminologie*.

——. (1956). "Une nouvelle branche de la science bio-psycho-sociale: Victimologie. " *Revue Internationale de Criminologie et de Police Technique*, 10–31.

"Mennonite drug pipeline expanding." (1997). *The Star* (Toronto). (Online).

"Mennonite ties to Mexican drug cartels concern authorities." (2014, July 8). *The Huffington Post*. (Online).

Menzies, R. (1992). "Beyond realist criminology." In J. Lowman & B.D. MacLean (Eds), *Realist criminology*. Toronto, ON: University of Toronto.

Mertl, S. (2012, July 26). "Online dating scams top source of fraud against Canadians." Retrieved from http://ca.news.yahoo.com/blogs/dailybrew/online-dating-scams-top-source-fraud-against-canadians-190127562.html

Merton, R.K. (1938). "Social structure and anomie." *American Sociological Review, 3*, 672–82.

——. (1968). *Social theory and social structure*. New York: The Free Press.

Milivojevic, S., & Pickering, S. (2013). "Trafficking in people twenty years on: moral panic, immobilised bodies and the global trafficking complex," *Current Issues in Criminal Justice, 25*(2), 585–604

Miller, H.V. (Ed.). (2011). *Restorative justice from theory to practice*. Bingley, UK: Emerald Group Pub. Ltd.

Miller, M. (Ed.). (2009). *21st century criminology: A reference book*. Thousand Oaks, CA: Sage.

Miller, T.R., Cohen, M.A., & Wiersema, B. (1998). *Victim costs and consequences: A new look*. Washington, DC: National Institute of Justice.

Mills, C.W. (1959). *The sociological imagination*. London: Oxford University Press.

Milovanovic, D. (Ed.). (1997). *Chaos, criminology, and social justice: The new orderly (dis)order*. Westport, CT: Praeger.

Mischel, W. (1995). *Personality and assessment*. London: Wiley.

Mitchell, B. (1996, September 26). "Police smash ring sending stolen cars to Vietnam." *The Star* (Toronto). (Online).

Monahan, J. (1981). *Predicting violent behaviour*. Beverly Hills, CA: Sage.

Morrison, P. (1996). "Motor-vehicle crimes." In L.W. Kennedy & V.F. Sacco (Eds), *Crime counts*. Toronto, ON: Nelson.

Moskowitz, C. (2011, March 4). "Criminal minds are different from yours, brain scans reveal." Retrieved from www.livescience.com/13083-criminals-brain-neuroscience-ethics.html

Mueller, J. (2006). *Overblown: How politicians and the terrorism industry inflate national security threats, and why we believe them*. New York: Free Press.

Muhammad, A.A. (2010, June). "Preliminary examination of so-called 'Honour based' killings." Ottawa: Department of Justice: Family, Children and Youth Section.

Muncie, J. (2009). *Youth and crime* (Chapter 3). London: Sage.

Murphy, C. (1995). "Traditional sociological approaches." In M.A. Jackson & C.T. Griffiths (Eds), *Canadian criminology* (3rd edn) (Chapter 6). Toronto, ON: Harcourt Brace.

Murphy, C., & Stenning, P. (1999). "Introduction." *Canadian Journal of Criminology and Criminal Justice, 41,* 127–30.

Myers, S. (2004, July 30). Vandals deface Lougheed mansion. *Calgary Herald,* p. B1.

Nagin, D.S., Farrington, D.P., & Moffitt, T.E. (1995). Life-course trajectories of different types of offenders. *Criminology, 33,*111–39.

Nanji, S. (2012, July 20). "Piracy concerns sailing into Canadian waters." *OHS Canada.* Retrieved from www.ohscanada.com/news/piracy-concerns-sailing-into-canadian-waters/1001579309

"National Action Plan to Combat Human Trafficking." (2014). Retrieved from www.publicsafety.gc.ca/cnt/rsrcs/pblctns/ntnl-ctn-pln-cmbt/index-eng.aspx

National Crime Prevention Centre (NCPC). (1998). "Safer communities: A parliamentarian's crime prevention handbook." Ottawa, ON: Department of Justice Canada.

——. (2012). "A statistical snapshot of youth at risk and youth offending in Canada." Ottawa, ON: Public Safety Canada.

"National Day of mourning: April 28." (2014). CCOHS. Retrieved from www.ccohs.ca/events/mourning

Nault, F. (2014, November). "Measuring gender-based violence in Canada." Presentation. Ottawa, ON: Statistics Canada. Retrieved from http://unstats.un.org/unsd/gender/Mexico_Nov2014/Session%203%20Canada%20ppt.pdf

Naumetz, T. (1999, January, 14). "Control of death penalty could shift to regions." *Calgary Herald,* p. A6.

Nelson, R.J. (Ed.). (2006). *Biology of aggression.* Oxford: Oxford University Press.

Nettler, G. (1982). *Killing one another.* Cincinnati, OH: Anderson.

——. (1984). *Explaining crime.* New York: McGraw-Hill.

——. (1987). *Explaining crime* (2nd edn). Toronto, ON: McGraw-Hill.

Neuman, W.L. (1997). *Social research methods: Qualitative and quantitative approaches* (3rd edn). Boston, MA: Allyn and Bacon.

Neumayer, E. (2005). "Inequality and violent crime: Education from data on robbery and violent theft." *Journal of Peace Research, 42*(1), 101–12.

Neuner, F., Pfeiffer, A., Schauer-Kaiser, E., Odenwald, M. et al. (2012). "Haunted by ghosts: Prevelence, predictors and outcomes of spirit possession experiences among former child soldier and war-affected civilians in Northern Nigeria." *Social Science and Medicine, 76*(3), 548–64.

Newark, S. (2013, February). "Police-reported crime statistics in Canada: Still more questions than answers" (Report prepared for the Macdonald-Laurier Institute). Ottawa, ON: Macdonald-Laurier Institute.

Newman, G., & Marongiu, P. (1990). "Penological reform and the myth of Becarria." *Criminology, 28,* 325–46.

Newman, O. (1972). *Defensible space.* New York: Macmillan.

——. (1996). *Creating defensible space.* Washington, DC: US Department of Housing and Urban Development.

New York City Alliance Against Sexual Assault. (2012). "Factsheets: Teen dating violence." Retrieved from http://www.svfreenyc.org/survivors_factsheet_48.html

Nhan, J., & Bachmann, M. (2010). "Developments in cyber criminology." In M. Maguire & D. Okada (Eds), *Critical issues in crime and justice: Thought, policy, and practice* (pp. 164–83). Thousand Oaks, CA: Sage.

Nickerson, C. (2004, January 1). "Crime gangs get free roam on Canada Indian reserves." Retrieved from Mytwobeadsworth.com/CAgangs2104.html

Nissen, L. (2011). "Beyond 'scared straight'—Moving to programs that actually work." Retrieved from www.reclaimingfutures.org/blog/juvenile-justice-reform-moving-beyond-scared-straight-to-what-works

Normandeau, A. (1968). *Trends and patterns in crimes of robbery (with special reference to Philadelphia, Pennsylvania, 1960–1966)* (Doctoral dissertation). University of Pennsylvania, Philadelphia, PA.

——. (1970). "Pioneers in criminology: Charles Lucas—opponent of capital punishment. *Journal of Criminal Law and Criminology, 61*(2), 218–28.

——. (2012). "52 ans de 'criminologie et justice pénale' à Montréal." *Justice Report / Actualités Justice, 27*(4), 6–10.

"Nunavut Mountie acquitted on sexual assault charge." (2013, August 23). CBC News. (Online).

Nurco, D.N., Cisin, I.H., & Ball, J.C. (1985). "Crime as a source of income for narcotic addicts." *Journal of Substance Abuse Treatment, 2,* 113–15.

O'Brien, J. (2014, May 22). "Three Southwestern Ontario drug rings busted." *The London Free Press.* (Online).

O'Connell, M., & Whelan, A. (1996). "The public perception of crime prevalence, newspaper readership, and 'mean world' attitudes. *Legal and Criminological Psychology, 1*(2), 179–95.

O'Leary, M. (2011). "Modelling criminal distance decay." *A Journal of Policy Development and Research, 13*(3), 161–198.

Office of Audit and Evaluation. (2013, June 13). "2011-612 Evaluation of the Forensic Accounting Management Group." Ottawa, ON: Public Works and Government Services Canada.

Office of the Parliamentary Budget Officer (2013, March). "Expenditure Analysis of Criminal Justice in Canada." Retrieved from www.pbo-dpb.gc.ca/files/files/crime%20cost%20presentation%20EN%20PDF.pdf

O'Grady, B. (2014, April 29). "Street youth and their increased risk of criminal victimization." Retrieved from http://www.homelesshub.ca/blog/street-youth-and-their-increased-risk-criminal-victimization

Ogrodnick, L. (2007). *Seniors as victims of crime 2004 and 2005.* Ottawa, ON: Canadian Centre for Justice Statistics.

——. (2008). *Family violence in Canada: A statistical profile.* Ottawa, ON: Statistics Canada.

Oliveira, M. (2013, February 18). "Poll: More Canadians watching programs online." *Canadian Press* (Online).

Onal, A. (2008). *Honor killing: Stories of men who killed*. London: SAQI.

"One in five Canadians think a woman encourages sexual assault when she is drunk." (2013). Canadian Women's Foundation. Retrieved from http://canadianwomen.org/sexualassault

Onyanga-Omara, J. (2016, January 23). "Modern day slavery a multi-billion dollar business." *USA Today*. (Online).

"Organ trafficking: did dark trade steal little boy's eyes?" (2013, August 26). Retrieved from www.theweek.co.uk/world-news/54855/organ-trafficking-did-dark-trade-steal-little-boys-eyes

Organized Crime Research Unit. (2014). "Organized crime research brief no. 8: Integrated anti-OC units." Ottawa, ON: Public Safety Canada.

"Organized crime sing, Operation J-Tornado, lands first conviction." (2014, October 17). CBC News (Online).

Osgood, D.W. (1998, July/August). "Interdisciplinary integration: Building criminology by stealing from our friends." *The Criminologist, 23,* 1–4.

Osgood, D.W., & Chambers, J.M. (2000). "Social disorganization outside the metropolis: An analysis of rural youth violence." *Criminology, 38,* 81–115.

Overholser, W. (1973). "Isaac Ray." In H. Mannheim (Ed.), *Pioneers in criminology* (2nd edn) (Chapter 11). Montclair, NJ: Patterson Smith.

Owen, T. (2014). *Criminological theory: A genetic-social approach*. London: Palgrave.

Owusu-Bempah, A., & Wortley, S. (2013). "Race, crime and criminal justice in Canada." *Oxford handbooks online*.

Pace, D.F. (1991). *Concepts of vice, narcotics, and organized crime* (3rd edn). Engelwood Cliffs, NJ: Prentice-Hall.

Pagliery, J. (2015, August 5). "The inside story of the biggest hack in history." *CNN Money*. (Online).

Pakes, F. (2015). *Comparative criminal justice* (3rd edn). New York: Taylor & Francis.

Palys, T., & Atchison, C. (2013). *Research decisions: Quantitative, qualitative, and mixed-method approaches*. Scarborough, ON: Nelson.

Paperny, A.M. (2012, July 19). "Toronto tries Saskatchewan's method for stopping crime before it starts." *The Globe and Mail*. (Online).

Paulin, J., Searle, W., & Knaggs, T. (2003). "Attitudes to crime and punishment: A New Zealand Study." Wellington, NZ: Ministry of Justice.

Payne, B.K. (2011). *Crime and elder abuse: An integrated perspective* (3rd edn). Springfield, IL: Charles C. Thomas Pub.

Payton, L. (2014, November 19). "Michael Sona sentenced to 9 months in jail for 'callous' robocalls." CBC News. (Online).

Pazzano, S. (2015, May 6). "Priest exploited position to sexually assault women." *Toronto Sun*. (Online).

Pease, K., & Litton, R. (1984). "Crime prevention: Practice and motivation." In D.J. Muller, D.E. Blackman, & A.J. Chapman (Eds), *Psychology and law*. New York: John Wiley and Sons.

Pelham, V. (2011, June 27). "Fight against human trafficking loses ground in 11 nations." Bloomberg. (Online).

Pepinsky, H. (1991). "Peacemaking in criminology." In B.D. MacLean & D. Milovanovic (Eds), *New directions in critical criminology*. Vancouver, BC: Collective Press.

——. (2000). *A criminologist's quest for peace*. Bloomington, IN: University of Indiana Press.

Pepinsky, H., & Jesilow, P. (1984). *Myths that cause crime* (2nd edn). Cabin John, MY: Seven Locks.

Perkel, C. (2015, March 15). "PM dismisses critics of his gun remarks: says vigilante idea 'absurd.'" *The Canadian Press* (Online).

Perlroth, N. (2012, October 23). "In cyberattack on Saudi firm, US sees Iran firing back." *The New York Times* (Online).

Perreault, S. (2013a). "Police-report crime statistics, 2012." *Juristat*. Statistics Canada cat. no. 85-002-X. Ottawa, ON: Minister of Industry.

——. (2013b). "Violent victimization of Aboriginal people in Canadian provinces, 2009." *Juristat*. Statistics Canada cat. no. 85-002-X. Ottawa, ON: Minister of Industry.

——. (2014). "Correctional services key indicators, 2012/2013." *Juristat*. Statistics Canada cat. no. 85-002-X. Ottawa, ON: Minister of Industry.

Perreault, S., & Brennan, S. (2010). Criminal victimization in Canada, 2009. *Juristat, 30*(2). Statistics Canada cat. no. 85-002-X. Ottawa, ON: Minister of Industry.

Perrin, B. (2015). "Punishing the most heinous crimes: Analysis and recommendations related to Bill C-53 (Life Means Life Act)." Ottawa, ON: Macdonald–Laurier Institute.

Peterson, S.B. (2009). "Made in America: The Global Youth Justice movement." *Reclaiming Children and Youth, 18*(2), 48–52.

Pettiway, L.E. (1988). "Urban spatial structure and arson incidence: Differences between ghetto and nonghetto environments." *Justice Quarterly, 5,* 113–30.

Pew Research Center. (2011, June 21). "US image in Pakistan falls no further following bin Laden killing. Support for campaign against extremists wanes." Washington, DC: Pew Research Center. (Online).

Pfohl, S. (1994). *Images of deviance and social control: A sociological history*. New York: McGraw-Hill.

Pfuhl, E.H., & Henry, S. (1993). *The deviance process* (3rd edn). New York: Aldine.

Philpott, W.H. (1978). "Ecological aspects of antisocial behavior." In L.J. Hippchen (Ed.), *Ecological-biochemical approaches to treatment of delinquents and criminals*. New York: Van Nostrand Reinhold.

Pilieci, V. (2014, June 4). "Canadians are bucking the global computer virus trend, Microsoft conference told." *Ottawa Citizen*. (Online).

Pillmann, F., Rohde, A., Ullrich, S., Draba, S., Sannemüller, U., & A. Marneros. (1999). "Violence, criminal behavior, and the EEG: Significance of left hemispheric focal abnormalities." *Journal of Neuropsychiatry and Clinical Neurosciences, 11,* 454–7.

Pitts, G. (2013, January 18). "Lunch with the irreplaceable Canadian billionaire Jimmy Pattison." *The Globe and Mail*. (Online).

"Police-reported sexual offences against children and youth in Canada, 2012." (2014, May 28). *The Daily*, Statistics Canada. Retrieved from www.statcan.gc.ca/daily-quotidien/140528/dq140528a-eng.htm

Policy Centre for Victim Issues. (2004). "Multi-site survey of victims of crime and criminal justice professionals across Canada." Ottawa, ON: Department of Justice Canada.

Pona, N. (2012, May 5). "Speed limits on Canadian roads: Officials looking at whether they need to be changed." Retrieved from http://o.canada.com/news/speed-limits-safety-canadian-roads

Porteous, S.D. (1998). *Organized crime impact study*. Ottawa, ON: Solicitor General Canada.

Poterfield, A.L. (1943). "Delinquency and its outcome in court and college." *American Journal of Sociology, 49*, 199–208.

Potter, G. (1994). *Criminal organizations: Vice, racketeering, and politics in an American city*. Prospect Heights, IL: Waveland.

Pramuk, J. (2015, December 24). "Illinois: Daily fantasy sports is illegal gambling." CNBC. (Online).

Pressman, A. (1997, May 8). "USA: Big countries differ on regulating electronic money." *Reuters*. (Online).

"Preventing Auto Theft." (2013). Retrieved from www.winnipeg.ca/police/TakeAction/auto_theft.stm

PricewaterhouseCoopers. (2015). "PwC's 2014 global economic crime survey: Canadian supplement." Retrieved from http://www.pwc.com/ca/en/risk/forensic-services/publications/pwc-economic-crime-survey-canadian-supplement-2014-02-en.pdf

Prime Minister of Canada Stephen Harper. (2013, February 8). "Not criminally responsible reform act." Retrieved from www.pm.gc.ca/eng/news/2013/02/08/not-criminally-responsible-reform-act

"Protest by arson?" (1997, February 24). *Calgary Herald*. (Online).

Prowse, C. (1994). "Vietnamese criminal organizations: Reconceptualizing Vietnam 'gangs.'" *RCMP Gazette, 56*(7), 2–8.

Public Safety and Emergency Preparedness Canada. (2003). "Facts about Organized Crime in Canada." Ottawa, ON: Public Safety Canada.

Public Safety Canada. (2008). "Bullying prevention—Building the evidence." National Crime Prevention Centre cat. no. PS4-42/20-2008.

——. (2011). "*Report on plans and priorities 2011–12*." Ottawa, ON: Public Safety Canada.

——. (2014a). "2012 Corrections and Conditional Release Statistical Overview." Ottawa, ON: Public Safety Canada.

——. (2014b). "Risk and protective factors." Ottawa, ON: Public Safety Canada.

——. (2015a). "Child sexual exploitation on the Internet." Ottawa, ON: Public Safety Canada.

——. (2015b). "Crime prevention projects 2013-2014." Ottawa, ON: Public Safety Canada.

Pulido, M.L. (2013, October 17). "Child pornography: Basic facts about a horrific crime." *The Huffington Post*. (Online).

Purdy, A. (June 17, 1997). "Four charged in hate crime." *Calgary Herald*, p. B4.

Putman, C., & Kirkpatrick, J.T. (2005, May). "Juvenile firesetting: A research overview." Washington, DC: OJJDP, US Department of Justice.

Puzic, S. (2013, September 24). "Kenya terrorist attack raises concerns about Canadian, western al-Shabaab recruits." CTV News. (Online).

Quan, D. (2012). "Police routinely suppress racial data in Canada, study says." *National Post*. (Online).

Quay, H.C. (Ed.). (1987). *Handbook of juvenile delinquency*. New York: John Wiley.

Quinney, R. (1970). *The social reality of crime*. Boston, MA: Little, Brown.

——. (1977). *Class state and crime*. New York: David McKay.

Price, M. (1996). "Victim–offender mediation: The state of the art. *VOMA Quarterly, 7*(3). (Online).

Radzinowicz, L. (1999). *Adventures in criminology*. London: Routledge.

Raine, A. (Ed.). (1993). *The psychopathology of crime: Criminal behavior as a clinical disorder*. New York: Academic Press.

Raine, A., Brennan, P., & Farrington, D. (1997a). "Biosocial bases of violence: Conceptual and theoretical issues." In A. Raine, P. Brennan, & D. Farrington (Eds), *Biosocial bases of violence*. New York: Plenum.

Raine, A., Buchsbaum, M., & LaCasse, L. (1997b). "Brain abnormalities in murderers indicated by positron emission tomography." *Biological Psychiatry, 42*, 495–508.

Rao, S.V. (Ed.). (1988). *Perspectives in criminology*. Sahibabad, India: New Printindia.

Rauhut, N. Ch. (2004). *Ultimate questions: Thinking about philosophy*. (Pengiun Academic Series). Upper Saddle River, NJ: Pearson Education.

Reasons, C.E., Ross, L., & Paterson, C. (1981). *Assault on the worker: Occupational health and safety in Canada*. Toronto, ON: Butterworths.

Reckless, W.C. (1970). American criminology. *Criminology, 8*(1), 4–20.

Redl, F., & Wineman, D. (1951). *Children who hate*. Glencoe, IL: Free Press.

Rehm, J., Baliunas, D., Brochu, S., Fischer, B., Gnam, W, Patra, J., Popova, S., Sarnocinska-Hart, A., & Taylor, B. in collaboration with Adlaf, E., Recel, M., & Single, E. 2006. "The Costs of Substance Abuse in Canada, 2002: Highlights." Ottawa, ON: Canadian Centre on Substance Abuse.

Reichel, P. (2013). *Comparative criminal justice systems: A topical approach* (6th edn). Boston, MA: Pearson.

Reichel, R., & Albanese, J. (Eds). (2013). *Transnational crime and justice* (2nd edn). Thousand Oaks, CA: Sage.

Reid, J.L., Hammond, D., Burkhalter, R., & Ahmed, R. (2012). *Tobacco use in Canada: Patterns and trends, 2012 Edition*. Waterloo, ON: Propel Centre for Population Health Impact, University of Waterloo. (Online).

Reid, J.L., Hammond, D., Rynard, V.L., & Burkhalter, R. (2015). *Tobacco use in Canada: Patterns and trends, 2015 Edition*. Waterloo, ON: Propel Centre for Population Health Impact, University of Waterloo.

Reiss, A.J. (1961). "The social integration of peers and queers." *Social Problems, 9*, 102–20.

Remar, S. (1991, August). "Dial '900' for trouble." *Reader's Digest, 139*, 39–43.

Rengert, G., & Wasilchick, J. (1985). *Suburban burglary: A time and place for everything.* Springfield, IL: Charles C. Thomas Pub.

Repetto, T. (1974). *Residential crime.* Cambridge, MA: Ballinger.

*Report of the Commission on Obscenity and Pornography.* (1970). Washington, DC: US Government Printing Office.

Resnik, D.B., & Vorhaus, D.B. (2006). "Genetic modification and genetic determinism." *Philosophy, Ethics and Humanities in Medicine, 1,* 1–11.

Rhodes, J. (2008). "Ex-offenders, social ties and the route to employment." *Internet Journal of Criminology,* 1–20. (Online).

Rhodes, R. (2000). *Why they kill: The discoveries of a maverick criminologist.* New York: Vintage Books.

Rhodes, W.M., & Conly, C. (1981). "Crime and mobility: An empirical study." In P.J. Brantingham & P. Brantingham (Eds), *Environmental criminology* (pp. 161–78). Beverly Hills, CA: Sage.

Richards, J. (2009, December 7). "Male Criminal Defendants Outnumber Female by More than 3 to 1." LegalMatch. (Online).

Rieger, S. (2015, December 14). "Alberta fentanyl deaths reach crisis levels." *The Huffington Post.* (Online).

Ro, S. (2014, October 3). "BRE-X: Inside the $6 billion gold fraud that shocked the mining industry." *Business Insider* (UK). (Online).

Roberts, J. (1995). "Disproportionate harm: Hate crime in Canada." Ottawa, ON: Department of Justice.

Roberts, J., & Hough, M. (Eds.). (2005). *Understanding public attitudes towards criminal justice.* New York: Open University Press.

Roberts, J., Stalans, L.J., Indermaur, D., & Hough, M. (2003). *Penal populism and public opinion: Lessons from five countries.* New York: Oxford University Press.

Roberts, J.V., & Edgar, A. (2006). *Victim impact statements at sentencing: Judicial experiences and perceptions.* Ottawa, ON: Policy Centre for Victim Issues, Department of Justice Canada.

Robinson, M.B., & Beaver, K. (2009). *Why crime? An interdisciplinary approach to explaining criminal behavior.* Durham, NC: Carolina Academic Press.

Roeder, O., Eisen, L-B., & Bowling, J. (2015). *What caused crime to decline?* New York: The Brennan Centre for Justice, New York University School of Law.

Roesch, R., & Winterdyk, J.A. (1985). *The Vancouver convenience store robbery prevention program: Final report* (No. 1985–42). Ottawa, ON: Ministry of the Solicitor General of Canada.

Rosenzweig, J. (2013). "Disappearing justice: Public opinion, secret arrest and criminal procedure reform in China," *China Journal, 70,* 73–97.

Rosoff, S.M., Pontell, H.N., & Tillman, R.H. (2004). *Profit without honor: White-collar crime and the looting of America* (3rd edn). Upper Saddle River, NJ: Prentice-Hall.

Ross, J. (2013, September 28). *Tryptophan depletion: The path to depression, low self-esteem, obsession, and eating disorders.* Retrieved from www.dietcure.com/the-diet-cure-blog/tag/Tryptophan_Depletion

Ross, J.I. (Ed.). (1995). *Violence in Canada: Sociological perspectives.* Don Mills, ON: Oxford University Press.

Ross, S. (2013, December 28). "Rehtaeh Parsons case: Not a routine procedure." *The Chronicle Herald* (Halifax). (Online).

Rossmo, D.K. (1995). "Place, space, and police investigations: Hunting serial violent criminals." In J.E. Eck & D. Weisburd (Eds), *Crime and place.* Washington, DC: Criminal Justice Press.

——. (2000). *Geographic profiling.* Boca Raton, FL: CRC Press.

——. (2009). *Criminal investigation failures.* Boca Raton, FL: CRC Press.

——. (2013). "Geographic profiling." In G. Bruinsma & D.L. Weisburd (Eds), *Encyclopedia of criminology and criminal justice* (pp. 1934–42). New York: Springer.

Rowe, D. (2002). *Biology and crime.* Los Angeles, CA: Roxbury.

Rowe, D.C., & Farrington, D.P. (1997). "The familial transmission of criminal convictions." *Criminology, 35*(1), 177–201.

Royal Canadian Mounted Police (RCMP). (2013a). "Money laundering." (Online).

——. (2013b). "Illicit tobacco." (Online).

——. (2013c). "2012 Intellectual property crime statistics." (Online).

——. (2013d). "Violent Crime Linkage Analysis System (ViCLAS)." (Online).

——. (2014). "Cybercrime: An overview of incidents and issues in Canada." Cat. no. PS64-116/2014E-PDF. Ottawa, ON: RCMP.

——. (2015). "Counterfeit currency." (Online).

Rushton, J.P., & Harris, J.A. (1994). *Genetic and environmental components to self-report violence in male and female twins.* Paper presented at the American Society of Criminology annual meetings, November, Miami, FL.

Russell, A. (2013, July 18). "What does 'corrupting morals' mean?" Global News (Calgary). (Online).

Russell, H.C., & Taylor, N.E. (2014). *New directions in community safety.* Ottawa, ON: Report prepared for the Ontario Chiefs of Police. (Online).

Rutsey, B. (2009, May). "Four years and counting." *Canadian Gaming Business: The State of Gaming in Canada, 4*(3), 6.

Sacco, P., Cunningham-Williams, R.M., Ostmann, E., & Spitznagel Jr, E.L. (2008). "The association between gambling pathology and personality disorders." *Journal of Psychiatric Research, 42*(13), 1122–30.

Sacco, V.F. (1982). "The effects of mass media on perceptions of crime." *Pacific Sociological Review, 25*(4), 475–93.

Sacco, V.F., & Kennedy, L.W. (1998). *The criminal event* (2nd edn). Scarborough, ON: Nelson.

Saferstein, R. (1998). *Criminalistics: An introduction to forensic science* (6th edn). Upper Saddle River, NJ: Prentice-Hall.

Sagan, A. (2015, August 10). "Fentanyl deaths are a Canada-wide 'disaster.'" CBC News (Online).

Sagant, V., & Shaw, M. (2010). *International report on crime prevention and community safety: Trends and perspectives, 2010.* Montreal: ICPC.

Salmon, A. (2011). "Aboriginal mothering, FASD prevention and contestation of neoliberal citizenship." *Critical Public Health, 21*(2), 165–78.

Saltman, J. (2008, January 20). "Former BC judge Ramsay, who preyed on young girls, dies in jail." *The Province* (Vancouver). (Online).

Sanders, T., & Roberts, J.V. (2004). Exploring public attitudes to conditional sentencing. In J. Winterdyk, L. Coates, & S. Brodie

(Eds), *Quantitative and qualitative research methods*. Toronto, ON: Pearson.

Sanguins, H. (2014). "The Canadian 'get tough' discourse needs a hard look too. *International Journal of Humanities and Social Science, 4*(3), 54–9.

Sapers, H. (2014, June 27). *Annual report of the Office of the Correctional Investigator 2013–2014*. Ottawa, ON: Ministry of Public Safety.

Saul, A.W. (2004, September 3). Alexander Schauss. Retrieved from http://www.doctoryourself.com/schauss.html

Savoie, J. (2007). "Youth self-report delinquency, Toronto, 2006." *Juristat, 27*(6). Statistics Canada cat. no. 85-002-X. Ottawa, ON: Minister of Industry.

Scaramella, G., Brensinger, M., & Miller, P. (1997, October). "Outlaw motorcycle gangs: Tattoo-laden misfits or sophisticated criminals?" *Crime and Justice International, 13*(9), 10–13.

Schafer, S. (1968). *The victim and his criminal*. New York: Random House.

——. (1976). *Introduction to criminology*. Reston, VA: Reston.

Schauss, A. (1988). *Diet, crime and delinquency*. Berkeley, CA: Parker House.

Schissel, B., & Brookes, C. (2008). *Marginality and condemnation: An introduction to criminology* (2nd edn). Halifax, NS: Fernwood.

Schlaadt, R.G. (1992). *Alcohol use and abuse*. Guilford, CT: Duskin.

Schmalleger, F. (2014). *Criminal justice: A brief introduction* (10th edn). Upper Saddle River, NJ: Pearson.

Schoenthaler, S., Amos, S., Eysenck, H., Hudes, M., & Korda, D. (1995). *A controlled trial of the effect of vitamin–mineral supplementation on the incidence of serious institutional rule violations*. Unpublished manuscript—courtesy of H. Eysenck.

Schroeder, A. (1997). *Cheats, charlatans, and chicanery*. Toronto, ON: McLelland and Stewart.

Schulenberg, J.L. (2014)." Systematic social observation of police decision-making: the process, logistics, and challenges in a Canadian context". *Qualitative and Quantitative Journal, 48*(1), 297–315.

Schulsinger, F. (1972). "Psychopathy, heredity, and environment." *International Journal. of Mental Health, 1*, 190–206.

Schulz, S. (2006). *Beyond self-control: analysis and critique of Gottfredson and Hirschi's General theory of crime 1990*. Hamburg: Duncker and Humblot.

Schur, E. (1972). *Labelling deviant behavior*. New York: Harper and Row.

Schwarz, D. (2003). "Shame, stigma, and crime: Evaluating the efficacy of shaming sanctions in criminal law." *Harvard Law Review, 116*(7), 2186–207.

Schwartz, J., & Steffensmeier, D.J. (2014). "The nature of female offending: Patterns and explanations." In F.T. Cullen & P. Wilcox (Eds), *Encyclopedia of criminological theory* (Chapter 2). Thousand Oaks, CA: Sage.

Schwartz, M.D., & Friedrichs, D.O. (1994). "Postmodern thought and criminological discontent: New metaphors for understanding violence." *Criminology, 32*, 221–46.

Schwendinger, H., & Schwendinger, J. (1991). "Feminism,

criminology and complex variations." In B.D. MacLean & D. Milovanovic (Eds), *New directions in critical criminology* (Chapter 7). Vancouver, BC: The Collective Press.

Scott, H. (2011). *Victimology: Canadians in context*. Don Mills, ON: Oxford University Press.

Scott, J.E., & Schwalm, L.A. (1987). "Pornography and rape: An examination of adult theater rates and rape rates by State." In J.E. Scott & T. Hirschi (Eds), *Controversial issues in crime and justice*. Newbury Park, CA: Sage.

Scott, P. (1973). "Henry Maudsley." In H. Mannheim (Ed.), *Pioneers in criminology* (2nd edn) (Chapter 12). Montclair, NJ: Patterson Smith.

Sellin, T. (1931). "The basis of a crime index." *Journal of Criminal law and Criminology, 22*, 335–6.

——. (1938). *Culture, conflict and crime*. Social Science Research Council, Bulletin 41. New York: Social Science Research Council.

——. (1973). "Enrico Ferri 1856–1929." In H. Mannheim (Ed.), *Pioneers in criminology* (2nd edn). Montclair, NJ: Patterson Smith.

Seto, M.C., Maric, A., & Barbaree, H.E. (2001). "The role of pornography in the etiology of sexual aggression." *Aggression and Violent Behavior, 6*, 35–53.

Sexual Assault Centre. (2013). "Sexual assault statistics." Retrieved from http://sacha.ca/fact-sheets/statistics

Shah, S., & Roth, L.H. (1974). Biological and psychophysiological factors in criminality." In D. Glaser (Ed.), *Handbook of criminology* (pp. 101–73). Chicago, IL.: Rand McNally.

Shannon, K., Kerr, T., Strathdee, S.A., Shoveller, J., Montaner, J.S., & Tyndall, M.W. (2009). "Prevalence and structural correlates of gender based violence among a prospective cohort of female sex workers." *British Medical Journal, 339*. doi: http://dx.doi.org/10.1136/bmj.b2939

Shaw, C., & McKay, H. (1942). *Juvenile delinquency and urban areas: A study of rates of delinquency in relation to differential characteristics of local communities in American cities*. Chicago, IL: University of Chicago Press.

Shelley, L. (2010). *Human trafficking: A global perspective*. Cambridge: University Press.

Sheptycki, J., & Wardak, A., *Transnational and comparative criminology*. London: Glass House Press.

Siegel, L. (2010). *Criminology: The core* (4th edn). Belmont, CA: Wadsworth.

Siegel, L.J., Brown, G.P., & Hoffman, R. (1995). *Criminology: Theories, patterns, and typologies* (5th edn). Minneapolis/St Paul, MN: Wadsworth.

——. (2013). *Crim* (2nd Canadian edn). Scarborough, ON: Nelson.

Silverman, R.A., & Kennedy, L. (1992). *Deadly deeds: Murder in Canada*. Scarborough, ON: Nelson.

Simon, R. (1975). *Women and crime*. Lexington, MA: D.C. Heath.

Simonds, M. (1996, March/April). "Code of arms." *Canadian Geographic*, 45–56.

Simpson, S. (1989). "Feminist theory, crime and justice." *Criminology, 27*, 497–538.

Sims, B., & Johnston, E. (2004, September). "Examining Public Opinion about Crime and Justice: A Statewide Study." *Criminal Justice Policy Review 15*(3), 270–93.

Singapore Police Force. (2014). "News release: Annual crime brief 2014." Retrieved from www.police.gov.sg/stats/crimebrief2005.html

Single, E., Robson, L., Relm, J., & Xie, X. (1996). *The cost of substance abuse in Canada*. Toronto, ON: Canadian Centre for Substance Abuse.

Sinha, M. (2012). "Family violence in Canada: A statistical profile, 2010." *Juristat, 32*(1). Statistics Canada cat. no. 85-002-X. Ottawa, ON: Minister of Industry.

——. (2013). "Measuring violence against women: Statistical trends." *Juristat, 33*(1). Statistics Canada cat. no. 85-002-X. Ottawa, ON: Minister of Industry.

Smith, G.J., & Wynne, H.J. (2004). *VLT gambling in Alberta: A preliminary analysis*. Edmonton, AB: Alberta Gambling Research Institute.

Smith, K.A., Fairburn, C. G., & Cowen, P.J. (1997). "Relapse of depression after rapid depletion of tryptophan." *Lancet, 349,* 915–19.

Smyth, J. (2015, June 8). "Canada's top 50 socially responsible corporations: 2015." *Maclean's*. (Online).

Smythe, P. (1996). "Terrorism in Canada: Recent trends and future prospects." *RCMP Gazette, 58*(10), 18–22.

Snider, L. (1993). *Bad business: Corporate crime in Canada*. Toronto, ON: Nelson.

——. (2002). "Corporate crime: Business as usual?" In B. Schissel & C. Brooks (Eds), *Critical criminology in Canada: Breaking the links between marginality and condemnation*. Toronto, ON: Fernwood Press.

——. (2015). *About Canada: Corporate crime*. Halifax, NS: Fernwood.

Sodaro, J. (2012, June 14). "Neighborhood watch groups in the cross hairs: After the Trayvon Martin killing, neighborhood watch groups have come under renewed scrutiny." *Salon* (Online).

Somers, L.E. (1984). *Economic crimes*. New York: Clark Boardman.

Speckart, G.R., & Anglin, M.D. (1986). "Narcotics and crime: A causal modeling approach." *Journal of Quantitative Criminology, 2*(1), 3–28.

Sprott, J., and Doob, A. (2008). "Youth crime rates and youth justice system." *Canadian Journal of Criminology and Criminal Justice, 50*(5), 621–39.

Stahura, J.N., & Hollinger, R.C. (1988). "A routine activities approach to suburban arson rates." *Sociological Spectrum, 8,* 349–69.

Standing, G. (2013). *The precariat: The new dangerous class*. New York: Bloomsbury.

Stansfield, R.T. (1996). *Issues in policing: A Canadian perspective*. Toronto, ON: Thompson Educational Pub.

Statistics Canada. (2010a, September 28). "General social survey: Victimization." *The Daily*. Retrieved from www.statcan.gc.ca/daily-quotidien/100928/dq100928a-eng.htm

——. (2013a). "Police Resources in Canada, 2012." Statistics Canada cat. no. 85-225-X.

——. (2013b). "Childhood conditions." Ottawa, ON: Statistics Canada. Retrieved from www.statcan.gc.ca/pub/82-619-m/2012004/sections/sectionc-eng.htm

——. (2014a). "CANSIM Table 252-0051: Incident-based crime statistics, by detailed violations."

——. (2014b, December 1). "Homicide in Canada, 2013." *The Daily*. Retrieved from www.statcan.gc.ca/daily-quotidien/141201/dq141201a-eng.htm

Stoff, D.M., & Cairns, R.B. (Eds). (1996). *Aggression and violence: Genetic, neurobiological, and biosocial perspectives*. Mahwah, NJ: Lawrence Erlbaum Assoc.

Stone, T. (1998, May). "Slavic women in demand in sex slave markets throughout world." *Crime and Justice International*, 7–8.

Story, R., & Yalkin, T.R. (2013, March 20). "Expenditure analysis of criminal justice in Canada." Ottawa, ON: Office of the Parliamentary Budget Office. Retrieved from www.pbo-dpb.gc.ca/files/files/Crime_Cost_EN.pdf

Strasburg, P.A. (1978). *Violent Delinquents*. New York: Monarch Books.

Streshinsky, S.G. (2014, September 8). "The grandparent scam." *Pacific Standard magazine*. (Online).

Su, Y.-Y., & Yang, S.-M. (2014). "TSAA WP 14-04: Eco-terrorism and corresponding legislative efforts to intervene and prevent future attacks." Vancouver, BC: TSAS—Department of Geography, University of British Columbia.

Sulloway, F.J. (1979). *Freud: Biologist of the mind*. New York: Basic Books.

Surette, R. (2015). *Media, crime and criminal justice: Images, realities and policies* (5th edn). Stamford, CT: Cengage Pub.

Sutherland, E.H. (1939). *Principles of criminology* (3rd edn). Chicago and Philadelphia: J.B. Lippincott.

——. (1947). *Principles of Criminology* (4th edn). Philadelphia, PA: J.B. Lippincott.

Sutherland, E.H., & Cressey, D. (1955). *Principles of criminology* (5th edn). Philadelphia, PA: J.B. Lippincott.

——, & ——. (1960). *Principles of criminology* (6th edn). Philadelphia, PA: J.B. Lippincott.

Swaffer, T., & Hollin, C.R. (1995). "Adolescent firesetting: Why do they say they do it?" *Journal of Adolescence, 18,* 619–23.

Sykes, G., & Matza, D. (1957). "Techniques of neutralization: A theory of delinquency." *American Sociological Review, 22,* 664–70.

Tait, C.L. (2003). "Fetal alcohol syndrome among Aboriginal people in Canada: Review and analysis of intergenerational links to residential schools." Prepared for the Aboriginal Healing Centre, Montreal.

Tanner, J., & Wortley, S. (2002). *Toronto youth crime and victimization survey: Overview report*. University of Toronto.

Taylor, M. (2012). Terrorism. In G. Davies & A. Beech (Eds), *Forensic psychology: Crime, justice, law, interventions* (2nd edn) (pp. 207–25). Chichester, UK: BPS Blackwell.

Tefs, W. (2011). *Bandit: A portrait of Ken Leishman*. Winnipeg, MB.: Turnstone Press.

Theodorson, G.A. (Ed.). (1982). *Urban patterns: Studies in human ecology*. Philadelphia, PA: The Pennsylvania State University Press.

Thomas, W. (2013, July 19). "Nostalgic terrorism—in Canada we once hijacked buses." Retrieved from www.wellandtribune .ca/2013/07/18/nostalgic-terrorism--in-canada-we-once-hijacked -buses

Thornberry, T.P., & Farnsworth, M. (1982). "Social correlates of criminal involvement: Further evidence on the relationship between social status and criminal behavior." *American Sociological Review, 47*, 505–18.

Thornberry, T.P., & Krohn, M.D. (2000). "The self-report method of measuring crime and delinquency" *Criminal Justice, 4*, 33–84.

"Three Gatineau teens arrested for burning down soup kitchen's food truck." (2014, July 10). *Metro News* (Ottawa). (Online).

Tiegreen, S., & Newman, E. (2009, February 18). "Violence: Comparing reporting and reality." New York: Columbia Journalism School. (Online).

Tittle, C.R. (1997). *Control balance: Toward a general theory of deviance.* Boulder, CO: Westview.

"Tobacco smuggling between Canada–US results in 25 arrests." (2014, April 20). CBC News (Online).

Todres, J. (2015, February 3). "Why preventing human trafficking sounds a lot like human rights advocacy." Human Rights at Home Blog. (Online).

Tombs, S. (2007). "'Violence', safety crimes and criminology." *British Journal of Criminology, 47*(4), 531–50.

"Top 10 corporate criminals list." (2014). Global Exchange. (Online).

Totten, M. (2012). *Nasty, brutish, and short: The lives of gang members in Canada.* Toronto, ON: Lorimer Press.

——. (2014). *Gang life.* Toronto, ON: Lorimer Press.

Totten, M., & Kelly, K. (2002). *When children kill: A social-psychological study of youth homicide.* Peterborough, ON: Broadview Press.

Transparency International. (2014). "Corruption perceptions index 2014." Retrieved from www.transparency.org/pressreleases _archive/2003/2003.10.07.cpi.en.html

Trembley, P. (1986). "Designing crime: The short life expectancy and the workings of a recent wave of credit card bank frauds." *British Journal of Criminology, 26*, 673–90.

Trembley, P., Clermont, Y., & Cusson, M. (1996). "Jockeys and joyriders." In R.A. Silverman, J.J. Teevan, & V.F. Sacco (Eds), *Crime in Canadian society* (5th edn) (Chapter 20). Toronto, ON: Harcourt Brace.

Trocme, N., Fallon, B., Maclaurin, B. et al. (2010). "Canadian incidence study of reported child abuse and neglect: Major findings." Ottawa, ON: Public Health Agency of Canada.

Turk, A. (1995). "Transformation versus revolutionism and reformism: Policy implications of conflict theory." In H.D. Barlow (Ed.), *Crime and public policy: Putting theory to work* (pp. 15–28). Boulder, CO: Westview (pp. 15–28).

TV Basics: 2013–2014. (2014). Ottawa, ON: Television Bureau of Canada. Retrieved from www.tvb.ca/page_files/pdf/InfoCentre/ TVBasics.pdf

UNdata. (2015). "UNODC homicide statistics 2012: Intentional homicide, number and rate per 100,000 population." Retrieved from https://data.un.org/Data.aspx?d=UNODC&f=tableCode%3A1

"Understand how your car measures up." (2013). Insurance Bureau of Canada. Retrieved from www.ibc.ca/en/car_insurance/ buying_a_new_car/hcmu.asp

United Nations Office on Drugs and Crime (UNODC). (2013). *Global study on homicide 2013: Trends, contexts, data.* Vienna: UNODC.

——. (2014). *Global report on trafficking in persons, 2014.* Vienna, Austria: UNODC.

——. (2016). *Money-laundering and globalization.* Retrieved from http://www.unodc.org/unodc/en/money-laundering/globalization .html

van Bokhoven. I., van Goozen. S.H.M., van Engeland. H., Schaal, B., Arsenault, L., Séguin, J.R.,... Tremblay, R.E. (2006). "Salivary testosterone and aggression, delinquency, and social dominance in a population-based longitudinal study of adolescent males." *Hormones and Behavior Journal, 50*(1), 118–25.

van Brunschot, E.G., & Brannigan, A. (1997). "Youthful prostitution and child sexual trauma." *International Journal of Law and Psychiatry, 20*(3), 337–54.

Vancouver Board of Trade. (2003). "Report on property crime in Vancouver." Retrieved from www.vancouver.boardoftrade.com/ crime_report.html

Vancouver Board of Trade Information. (1997, June). *Report on property crime in Vancouver—June 1997.* (Online).

van Dijk, J.J.M. (1997). "Towards a research-based crime reduction policy: Crime prevention as a cost-effective policy option." *European Journal on Criminal Policy and Research, 5*(3), 13–27.

——. (1999). "Introducing victimology." In J.J.M. van Dijk, R.G.H. van Kaam, & J. Wemmers (Eds), *Caring for crime victims: Selected proceedings of the Ninth International Symposium on Victimology*, Amsterdam, 25–29 August 1997. Monsey, NY: Criminal Justice Press.

——. (2005). "Introducing victimology." World Society of Victimology. Retrieved from http://rechten.uvt.nl/victimology/ other/vandijk.pdf

van Duyne, P.C., & Spencer, J. (2011). "The traded human body: The ultimate commercial option?" In P.C. Petrus & J. Spencer (Eds). *Flesh and money: trafficking in human beings* (pp. 5–18). Nijmegan, The Netherlands: Wolf Legal Pub.

van Gundy, A. (2014). *Feminist theory, crime, and social justice.* New York: Anderson Press.

van Kesteren, J.N., Mayhew, P., & Nieuwbeerta, P. (2000). "Criminal victimisation in seventeen industrialised countries: Key findings from the 2000 International Crime Victims Survey." The Hague: Onderzoek en beleid, 187. Ministry of Justice, WODC.

van Kesteren, J., van, Dijk, J., & Mayhew, P. (2014). The International Crime Victimization Survey: A retrospective. *International Review of Victimology, 20*(1), 49–69.

van Koningsveld, J. (1998, December 3). "*Money laundering and FIOD.*" Summary of paper presented at the FATF meeting, November 1998, in London.

Veltri, C.A. (n.d.). "A Mission milestone: Billy Miner." Mission Museum. Retrieved from www.missionmuseum.com/milestone -billy-miner.php

Verdun-Jones, S. (2012). "Plea bargaining." In J.V. Roberts & M.G. Grossman (Eds), *Criminal justice in Canada* (4th edn). Toronto, ON: Nelson.

Vest, J., Cohen, W., & Tharp, M. (1997, June). "Road rage." *U.S. News and World Report*. (Online).

Violence Research Foundation. (VRF). (1994). Material forwarded by R. Hodges, President of the VRF, Tustin, CA.

Vito, G.F., & Holmes, R.M. (1994). *Criminology: Theory, research, and policy*. Belmont, CA: Wadsworth.

Vito, G.F., Maahs, J.R., & Holmes, R.M. (2007). *Criminology: Theory, research, and policy* (2nd edn). Sudbury, MA: Jones and Bartlett Pub.

Vold, G.B., & Bernard, T.J. (1981). *Theoretical criminology* (2nd edn). New York: Oxford University Press.

Vold, G.B., Bernard, T.J., & Snipes, J.B. (1998). *Theoretical criminology* (4th edn). New York: Oxford University Press.

von Hentig, H. (1940). "Remarks on the interaction of perpetrator and victims." *Journal of Criminal Law, Criminology and Police Science, 31*(3), 303–9.

———. (1948). *The criminal and his victim: Studies in the sociobiology of crime*. New Haven, CT: Yale University Press.

———. (1973). "Gustuv Aschaffenburg." In H. Mannheim (Ed.), *Pioneers in criminology* (2nd edn) (Chapter 2). Montclair, NJ: Patterson Smith.

Vozzola, E. (2014). *Moral development: Theory and application*. New York: Routledge.

Walklate, S. (2000). "Researching victims." In R.D. King & E. Wincup (Eds), *Doing research on crime and justice* (2nd edn). New York: Oxford University Press.

———. (2006). *Imagining the victim of crime*. Berkshire, UK: McGraw-Hill.

Wallace, M., Turner, J., Matarazzo, A., & Babyak, C. (2009). "Measuring crime in Canada: Introducing the Crime Severity Index and improvements to the Uniform Crime Reporting Survey." Statistics Canada cat. no. 85-004-X. Ottawa, ON: Minister of Industry.

Wallace, R.A., & Wolf, A. (1995). *Contemporary sociological theory: Continuing the classical tradition* (4th edn). Englewood Cliffs, NJ: Prentice-Hall.

Wallace, W.L. *Sociological theory: An introduction*. New York: de Gruyter.

Waller, I. (2008). *Less law, more order: The truth of reducing crime*. West PortCT: Praeger Pub.

———. (2010). *Rights for victims of crime: Rebalancing justice*. Plymouth, UK: Roweman and Littlefield Pub.

———. (2014). *Smarter crime control*. Lanham, MD: Rowman and Littlefield.

Walmsley, R. (2013). *World prison population list* (10th edn). London: International Centre for Prison Studies. (Online).

Walsh, A. (2002). *Biosocial criminology*. Cincinnati, OH: Anderson.

———. (2009). *Biology and criminology: The biosocial synthesis*. New York: Routledge.

Walsh, A., & Ellis, L. (2007). *Criminology: An interdisciplinary approach*. Thousand Oaks, CA: Sage.

Walsh, A., & Hemmens, C. (2013). *Introduction to criminology: A text/reader* (3rd edn). Thousand Oaks, CA: Sage.

Walsh, D. (2007). "Video game report cards." National Institute on Media and the Family. Minneapolis, MN.

Walsh, M. (2014, December 19). "Hundreds rally against Dalhousie." Global News. (Online).

Walsh, W.J., Isaacson, H.R., Rehman, F., & Hall, A. (1997). "Elevated blood copper/zinc ratios in assaultive young males." *Physiology & Behavior, 62*(2), 327–9.

Wander, A. (2010, October 24). "How suicide bombings shattered Iraq." *Al Jazeera* (Online).

Warnica, R. (2015, May 7). "Barely illegal. New prostitution laws may drive sex work underground—but can it stop it?" *National Post*. (Online).

Warren, M.Q., & Hindelang, M.J. (1986). "Current explanations of offender behaviour." In H. Toch (Ed.), *Psychology of crime and criminal justice* (pp. 116–82). Prospect Heights, IL: Waveland Press.

Wasserman, D., & Wachtbriot, R. (Eds). (2001). *Genetic and criminal behavior*. Cambridge, UK: Cambirdge University Press.

Webb, G.R. (2004, November 17). "Rollovers, recalls, and rhetoric: Corporate framing of the Ford/Firestone controversy." Paper presented at the American Society of Criminology, Nashville, TN.

Webb, N., Sakheim, G., Towns-Miranda, L., & Wagner, C. (1990). "Collaborative treatment of juvenile firestarters: Assessment and outreach." *American Journal of Orthopsychiatry, 60*, 305–10.

Webber, C. (2010). *Psychology and crime*. Thousand Oaks, CA: Sage.

Weekes, J., Thomas, G., & Graves, G. (2004). Substance abuse in corrections. Report prepared for CCSA. Retrieved from www .ccsa.ca/Resource%20Library/ccsa-011058-2004.pdf

Weichman, D. (1994). Caning and corporal punishment: Viewpoint. *CJ International, 10*(5), 13–20.

Weinwrath, M., & Gartrell, J. (1996). Victimization and fear of crime. *Violence and victims, 11*(3), 187–97.

Weisburd, D., Chayet, E.F., & Waring, E.J. (1990). "White-collar crime and criminal careers: Some preliminary findings." *Crime and Delinquency, 36*, 342–55.

Weisburd, D., & Eck, J.E. (2004). "What can police do to reduce crime, disorder, and fear?" *The Annals of the American academy, 593*, 42–61.

Weitzer, R. (2015). *Legalizing prostitution: From illicit vice to lawful business*. New York: New York University Press.

Wellford, C.F. (1997a, December). "Two goals of criminal justice." *Crime and Justice International, 13*(11), 4.

———. (1997b). "1996 Presidential Address: Controlling crime and achieving justice." *Criminology, 35*(1), 1–12.

Welsh, M., & Donovan, K. (1998, June 27). "Four giant casinos on the way." *The Star* (Toronto). (Online).

Wemmers, J.-A. (2002). "Declaration of basic principles of restorative justice." *The Victimologist, 1*, 5–7.

White, J.R. (2013). *Terrorism and homeland security* (8th edn). Belmont, CA: Wadsworth.

Whitelaw, B., Parent, R., & Griffiths, C.T. (2008). *Community-based strategic policing in Canada*. Toronto, ON: Nelson.

Wilkins, L. (1965). "New thinking in cirminal statistics." *Journal of Criminal Law and Criminology, 56*(3), 277–84.

Williams, F.P. III, & McShane, M.D. (2013). *Criminological theory* (6th edn). Upper Saddle River, NJ: Prentice-Hall.

Williams, K.R., & Hawkins, R. (1986). "The meaning of arrest for wife assault." *Criminology, 27*, 163–81.

Williams, R.J., & Kalita, D.K. (1977). *A physician's handbook on orthomolecular medicine*. New York: Pergamon Press.

Williams, R. J., & Simpson, R. I. (2008). *Promising practices in the prevention of problem gambling.* Report prepared for the Ontario Problem Gambling Research Centre. Guelph, ON: Ontario Problem Gambling Research Centre.

Williams, R.J., West, B., & Simpson, R.I. (2007). *Prevention of problem gambling: A comprehensive review of the evidence.* Report prepared for the Ontario Problem Gambling Research Centre. Guelph, ON: Ontario Problem Gambling Research Centre.

Willis, K. (2006). "Armed robbery: Who commits it and why?" *Trends and Issues in Crime and Criminal Justice, 348.*

Wilson, E.O. (1975). *Sociobiology: The new synthesis.* Cambridge, MA: The Belknap Press of Harvard University Press.

———. (2000). *Sociobiology: The new synthesis, 25th anniversary edition.* Cambridge, MA: Harvard University Press.

Wilson, J.Q. (1975). *Thinking about crime.* New York: Vantage.

———. (2013). *Thinking about crime* (revised edn). New York: Basic Books.

Wilson, J.Q., & Herrnstein, R. (1985). *Crime and human nature.* New York: Simon and Schuster.

Winner, C. (2014). "WSU study shows environmental toxins can cause inherited diseases." Retrieved from http://researchnews.wsu.edu/environment/139.html

Winterdyk, J. (Ed.). (2001). *Issues and perspectives on young offenders in Canada* (2nd edn). Toronto, ON: Harcourt Brace.

Winterdyk, J. (2016). "Trends and patterns . . ." In J. Winterdyk and R.C. Smandych (Eds), *Youth at risk and youth justice* (2nd edn) (Chapter 2). Don Mills, ON: Oxford University Press.

Winterdyk, J., & Cao, L. (Eds). (2004). *Lessons from Intenational/Comparative Criminology/Criminal Justice.* Toronto, ON: deSitter Pub.

Winterdyk, J., & Kaye, J. (2014, January). "Human trafficking." In J. Albanese (Ed.), *The encyclopedia of criminology and criminal justice, 1.* New York: Blackwell Pub.

Winterdyk, J., Perrin, B., & Reichel, P. (Eds). (2012). *Human trafficking: Exploring the international nature, concerns and complexities.* Boca Raton, FL: CRC Press.

Winterdyk, J., & Weinwrath, M. (Eds). (2013). *Adult corrections.* Whitby, ON: deSitter Pub.

———, & ———. (2015). *Adult corrections in Canada.* Whitby, ON: deSitter Pub.

Wolf, D. (1991). *The rebels: A brotherhood of outlaw bikers.* Toronto, ON: University of Toronto Press.

Wolff, R.P. (1971). *Philosophy: A modern encounter.* Englewood Cliffs, NJ: Prentice-Hall.

Wolfgang, M.E. (1958). *Patterns in criminal homicide.* Philadelphia, PA: University of Pennsylvania Press.

Wolfgang, M.E., & Ferracuti, F. (1967). *The subculture of violence: Toward an integrated theory of criminology.* London: Tavistock.

Woo, A. (2013, August 13). "Former B.C. nanny can't trust anyone anymore, court told in human-trafficking case." *The Globe and Mail.* (Online).

———. (2014, May 31). "B.C. teachers, government use funding statistic to tell different stories." *The Globe and Mail.* (Online).

Woods, M. (2014, August 29). "Former Quebec teacher gets 20 months in jail for two-year sexual relationship with student." *National Post.* (Online).

Working Paper 36—*Damage to property: Arson.* (1984). Ottawa, ON: Law Reform Commission of Canada.

Wortley, R., & Mazerolle, L. (2008). *Environmental criminology and crime analysis.* Cullompton, UK: Willan Pub.

Worton, D.A. (1998). *The Dominion Bureau of Statistics. A history of Canada's Central Statistical Office and its antecedents, 1841–1972.* Ottawa, ON: Canadian Public Administration Series #22.

Wright, B., & Fox, V. (1978). *Criminal justice and the social sciences.* Philadelphia, PA: W.B. Saunders.

Wright, D. (1997). *Acknowledging the continuum from childhood abuse to male prostitution.* Retrieved from www.netizen.org/narc/ bcifv/backiss2/spring95/nf_continuum.html

Wright, R., & Decker, S. (1994). *Burglars on the job: Streetlife and residential break-ins.* Boston, MA: Northeastern University Press.

———, & ———. (1997). *Armed robbers in action: Stickups and street culture.* Boston, MA: Northeastern University Press.

Young, J. (1986). "The failure of criminology: The need for a radical realism." In R. Matthews & J. Young (Eds), *Confronting crime.* London: Sage.

———. (2002). "Critical criminology in the twenty-first century: Critique, irony, and the always unfinished." In K. Carrington & R. Hogg (Eds), *Critical criminology: Issues, debates, challenges.* Cullompton, UK: Willan Pub.

Zavan, M. (2014, May 14). "Train fight blamed on demonic possession." *9News World.* (Online).

Zawitz, M.W. (Ed.). (1992). *Drugs, crime, and the justice system: A national report from the Bureau of Justice Statistics.* Washington, DC: Department of Justice, Bureau of Justice Statistics.

Zetter, K. (2015, February 10). "The NSA acknowledges what we all feared: Iran learns from US cyberattacks." *Wired* (Online).

Zimring, F.E., & Hawkins, G. (1975). *Deterrence: The legal threat to crime control.* Chicago, IL: University of Chicago Press.

Zukov, I., Ptacek, R., & Fisher, S. (2008). "EEG abnormalities in different types of criminal behavior." *Activitas Nervosa Superior, 50,* 100–13. (Online).

# Index